Robert A. Cord · Richard G. Anderson ·
William A. Barnett
Editors

Paul Samuelson

Master of Modern Economics

palgrave
macmillan

Editors
Robert A. Cord
London, UK

William A. Barnett
Department of Economics
University of Kansas
Lawrence, KS, USA

Richard G. Anderson
Center for Economics and the Environment
Lindenwood University
St. Charles, MO, USA

ISSN 2662-6632 ISSN 2662-6640 (electronic)
Remaking Economics: Eminent Post-War Economists
ISBN 978-1-137-56811-3 ISBN 978-1-137-56812-0 (eBook)
https://doi.org/10.1057/978-1-137-56812-0

Cover credit: Bachrach/Getty Images
Cover design by eStudio Calamar

This Palgrave Macmillan imprint is published by the registered company Springer Nature Limited
The registered company address is: The Campus, 4 Crinan Street, London, N1 9XW, United Kingdom

For my mother
—Robert A. Cord

For my teachers, PAS, RMS, CPK, FMF, RFE, PAD, SF, and FM
—Richard G. Anderson

For my wife, Melinda Barnett
—William A. Barnett

Introduction from the Series Editor

Economics has witnessed a dramatic transformation since the Second World War, both in terms of its depth and range. This series of volumes, entitled *Remaking Economics: Eminent Post-War Economists*, will examine the nature of this transformation through the work of those economists who have been responsible for the changes that have taken place. In some cases, relatively little has been written about these transformative figures in terms of single edited volumes dedicated to examining their work and influence. The series hopes to fill this gap with volumes edited by important economists in their own right, with contributions in each volume not only from some of the most prestigious scholars currently working in economics but also from promising younger economists. By addressing key themes and retaining a focus on originality, each volume will give the reader new and valuable insights. The series will also strengthen economists' knowledge of the history of their subject and hopefully inspire future research.

Robert A. Cord
Managing Editor

A Note on *The Collected Scientific Papers of Paul A. Samuelson*

The Collected Scientific Papers of Paul A. Samuelson collects together nearly 600 of Samuelson's articles, comments, lectures, reviews and other miscellany in seven substantial volumes. Many of Samuelson's writings that are only cited in the original in the current volume can be found reprinted in *The Collected Scientific Papers*:

The Collected Scientific Papers of Paul A. Samuelson, Volume I, edited by Joseph E. Stiglitz, 1966. Cambridge, MA and London, England, The MIT Press.

The Collected Scientific Papers of Paul A. Samuelson, Volume II, edited by Joseph E. Stiglitz, 1966. Cambridge, MA and London, England, The MIT Press.

The Collected Scientific Papers of Paul A. Samuelson, Volume III, edited by Robert C. Merton, 1972. Cambridge, MA and London, England, The MIT Press.

The Collected Scientific Papers of Paul A. Samuelson, Volume IV, edited by Hiroaki Nagatani and Kate Crowley, 1977. Cambridge, MA and London, England, The MIT Press.

The Collected Scientific Papers of Paul A. Samuelson, Volume V, edited by Kate Crowley, 1986. Cambridge, MA and London, England, The MIT Press.

The Collected Scientific Papers of Paul A. Samuelson, Volume VI, edited by Janice Murray, 2011. Cambridge, MA and London, England, The MIT Press.

The Collected Scientific Papers of Paul A. Samuelson, Volume VII, edited by Janice Murray, 2011. Cambridge, MA and London, England, The MIT Press.

Contents

Editors and Contributors

About the Editors

Robert A. Cord is currently working as an independent researcher in economics. His specialist area of interest is the history of economic thought and, within this, the history of macroeconomics. His published books include *Reinterpreting the Keynesian Revolution* (2012), *Milton Friedman: Contributions to Economics and Public Policy* (co-edited with J. Daniel Hammond; 2016), *The Palgrave Companion to Cambridge Economics* (editor; 2017) and *The Palgrave Companion to LSE Economics* (editor; 2018), and his articles have appeared in the *Cambridge Journal of Economics* and the *History of Political Economy*. Cord is also the Managing Editor of the Palgrave series *Remaking Economics: Eminent Post-War Economists*, which includes volumes on *James Buchanan* and *Paul Samuelson*. He holds a Ph.D. from Cambridge University.

Richard G. Anderson is Visiting Professor of Economics at the University of Missouri-Kansas City, Senior Research Fellow at the Robert W. Plaster School of Business and Entrepreneurship,

Lindenwood University, St. Charles, Missouri, and, prior to 2013, vice president and economist at the Federal Reserve Bank of St. Louis (retired). He holds degrees in economics from the University of Minnesota and MIT.

William A. Barnett is Oswald Distinguished Professor of Macroeconomics at the University of Kansas, Director of the Center for Financial Stability in New York City, and Director of the Institute for Nonlinear Dynamical Inference in Moscow. He is Editor of the journal, *Macroeconomic Dynamics*, and the monograph series, *International Symposia in Economic Theory and Econometrics*. With Paul Samuelson, he coedited the book, *Inside the Economist's Mind*, translated into seven languages. He is author of the book, *Getting It Wrong*, which won the American Publishers Award for Professional and Scholarly Excellence. He was Founder and First-President of the Society for Economic Measurement.

Contributors

Mauro Boianovsky is Full Professor of Economics at Universidade de Brasilia, where he teaches history of economic thought and growth economics. He has published a number of articles in international journals and chapters in collected volumes, as well as edited and co-authored books. His main areas of interest are in the histories of macro-economics, development economics and growth economics. He served as President of the History of Economics Society (2016–2017).

Michael J. Boskin is the Tully M. Friedman Professor of Economics and Wohlford Family Senior Fellow, Hoover Institution, Stanford University, and Research Associate, NBER. He has also taught at Harvard and Yale. Boskin is the author of more than one hundred and fifty articles and books on a wide range of issues including economic growth, taxation, and budget policy. His op-eds appear regularly in *The Wall Street Journal* and other leading newspapers. Boskin was Chairman of the President's Council of Economic Advisers (CEA) from 1989 to 1993, where he helped design and implement fiscal, trade and regulatory policy. In 1995–1996 he chaired the highly influential Commission on the Consumer Price Index. Boskin received his B.A. with highest honors and the Chancellor's award as outstanding undergraduate from the University of California, Berkeley, where he also received his M.A. and his Ph.D., all in economics.

Juan Carvajalino is an assistant professor at University Paris VIII, Vincennes-Saint-Denis. He is interested in the recent history and philosophy of economics, with an emphasis on the technical, mathematical and statistical turn that the discipline took in the 1930s and 1940s. Following an interdisciplinary approach, he endeavours to interweave the histories and philosophies of economics, mathematics, and the social and natural sciences.

Gregory C. Chow is Professor of Economics and Class of 1913 Professor of Political Economy Emeritus at Princeton University. His contributions cover econometrics (including the Chow test), applied economics, dynamic economics and the Chinese economy. Author of 15 books and over 200 journal articles, he has been awarded an honorary doctor's degree from Zhongshan University, an LDD from Lingnan University and a Doctor of Business Administration from the Hong Kong University of Science and Technology, and has been a senior government adviser in China and Taiwan. He is a columnist for various major newspapers.

Thomas Demuynck is Chargé de Cours at the Université Libre de Bruxelles at the Solvay Brussels School of Economics and Management (SBS-EM). He is also a member of the European Center for Advanced Research in Economics and Statistics (ECARES), a member of the Group for the Advancement of Revealed Preference (GARP) and a co-PI for the EOS funded research project: "Individual Welfare Analysis based on Behavioral Economics" (IWABE). His main research involves applying revealed preference theory to various models of individual and joint decision making.

Joseph Farrell was educated at Oxford University, where he received his D.Phil. in 1981. He joined UC Berkeley in 1989 as an associate professor and became a full professor in 1991. Farrell was elected a Fellow of the Econometric Society in 2002. He was Director of the FTC Bureau of Economics, Deputy Assistant Attorney General for Economics with the US Department of Justice, Chief Economist at the Federal Communications Commission, assistant professor at MIT, a principal member of the technical staff at GTE Laboratories, and National Fellow at the Hoover Institution. Farrell served on the Computer Science and Telecommunications Board at the National Academies of Science, was Editor of the *Journal of Industrial Economics*, president of the Industrial Organization Society, and Chair of Berkeley's Competition Policy Center. He received the Industrial Organization Society's public service award in 2016.

Harvey Gram is Professor Emeritus, Department of Economics, Queens College, City University of New York. He was co-author (with Vivian Walsh) of Classical and Neoclassical Theories of General Equilibrium (Oxford University Press, 1980), and has authored articles on the role of perfect foresight in mainstream reactions to the Cambridge critique of capital theory. Other work concerns the economics of international debts and deficits and the role of capital theoretic problems in two-sector growth models, general equilibrium theory, and the pure theory of international trade. Book reviews, dictionary entries, and several articles on Joan Robinson have also been published. Gram is an Associate Editor of the *Cambridge Journal of Economics*.

J. Daniel Hammond is Hultquist Family Professor, Emeritus, and Scholar in Residence, Eudaimonia, Wake Forest University. He is a graduate of Wake Forest (B.A.) and the University of Virginia (Ph.D.). He served as President of the History of Economics Society in 2001–2002 and currently serves on the Editorial Board of *History of Economic Ideas*. Having written extensively about Chicago School economics, recent work includes "Milton Friedman and George J. Stigler: Early Interactions and Connections," in *Milton Friedman: Contributions to Economics and Public Policy* (Robert A. Cord and J. D. Hammond, eds., Oxford University Press, 2016) and "Between Old and New: George Stigler's Chicago Price Theory," in *Understanding the Enigmatic George Stigler: Extending Price Theory in Economics and Beyond* (Craig Freedman, ed., Palgrave Macmillan, forthcoming).

Geoff Harcourt is Emeritus Reader in the History of Economic Theory, Cambridge, 1998; Emeritus Fellow, Jesus College, Cambridge, 1998; Professor Emeritus, Adelaide, 1988; and currently Honorary Professor, School of Economics, UNSW Sydney, 2010–2019. He has published 33 books and over 400 articles, chapters in books, and reviews. His research interests include post-Keynesian theory, applications and policy, intellectual biography and history of economic theory. Harcourt's books include *Some Cambridge Controversies in the Theory of Capital* (Cambridge University Press, 1972), *The Structure of Post-Keynesian Economics* (Cambridge University Press, 2006), (with Prue Kerr) *Joan Robinson* (Palgrave Macmillan, 2009), (edited with Peter Kriesler) *The Oxford Handbook of Post-Keynesian Economics* (two volumes, Oxford University Press, 2013) and (with Joseph Halevi, Peter Kriesler and John Nevile) *Post-Keynesian Essays from Down Under* (four volumes, Palgrave Macmillan, 2015). He is, or has been, co-editor of many journals, including *Australian Economic Papers* and the *Cambridge Journal of Economics*.

Arnold Heertje is a Dutch Emeritus Professor of the Faculty of Economics at the University of Amsterdam. He studied economics at Amsterdam and took his doctoral degree (cum laude) with Professors Piet de Wolff and Pieter Hennipman as his "promotors." Heertje is known for his theory of oligopoly, which appeared in 1960, and for his classic book on the economic analysis of technical change, published in 1973.

Per Hjertstrand is Research Fellow and Associate Professor at the Research Institute of Industrial Economics (IFN) in Stockholm. His broad research interests are in demand analysis and production economics, and more specifically, in revealed preference theory and nonparametric econometrics. In recent years, he has been teaching econometrics and mathematics at Lund University, Hanken School of Economics and the Stockholm School of Economics. He is Associate Editor of the journal *Macroeconomic Dynamics*.

Herrade Igersheim is a permanent CNRS researcher and teaches at the University of Strasbourg. Her research domains are history of economic thought, welfare economics and experimental economics applied to voting. Igersheim earned her Ph.D. in economics at the University of Strasbourg in 2004. She then pursued her research at Barcelona, Aix-Marseille and back at Strasbourg. She was a research fellow at Duke University (NC) in 2015/2016, received the "Young Researcher Award" of the European Society for the History of Economic Thought (ESHET) in 2016 and the award "Espoirs de l'Université de Strasbourg" in 2017. She has led or co-led several projects founded by the French National Research Agency, France Stratégie and the Foundation of the University of Strasbourg. Since 2018, she has also been Deputy Director of her research lab, the Bureau d'Economie Théorique et Appliquée (BETA).

Ronald Lee is an economic demographer (Berkeley M.A., Harvard Ph.D.) who taught in the departments of Demography and Economics at Berkeley from 1979 to 2014, and now does research on macroeconomic consequences of population ageing. From 2010 to 2015 he co-chaired a National Academy of Sciences Committee on the Long-Run Macroeconomic Effects of the Aging US Population. He also continues to work on modeling and forecasting demographic variables, including mortality, and on evolutionary biodemography and life history theory. He is the Founding Director of the Center for Economics and Demography of Aging (CEDA) and of National Transfer Accounts (NTA). He is an elected member of the National Academy of Sciences and four other honorary societies.

Ronald MacDonald is currently Research Professor in Macroeconomics and International Finance, and previously held the Adam Smith Chair of Political Economy, both at the University of Glasgow. His peer reviewed papers have been published in leading journals, and he has over 16,000 citations of his work on Google Scholar. MacDonald has acted as an adviser and consultant to a large number of governments and public agencies, such as the European Commission, General Secretariat for Development Planning, Qatar, the European Central Bank, the Monetary Authority of Singapore, the Reserve Bank of New Zealand, the UK National Audit Office, the IMF and the World Bank. He is also a Research Fellow of the CESifo Research Network, University of Munich, an International Fellow of the Kiel Institute of Economic Policy, and he consistently ranks in the top 1% of the IDEAS/RePEc world ranking of economists. He was awarded an OBE in the 2015 Queen's Birthday Honours list for services to Economic Policy.

Alex Millmow is an associate professor in economics at the School of Business, Federation University Australia. His research interests include the economics of Joan Robinson, the making of the Australian economics profession and the role of economic ideas in steering public policy. In 2004, he completed his doctorate at the Australian National University on *The Power of Economic Ideas: The Rise of Macroeconomic Management in Australia*, which was subsequently published. He is currently the President of the History of Economic Thought Society of Australia (HETSA). In 2017, he published *A History of Australasian Economic Thought*. He is now finalising a biography of the Anglo-Australian economist Colin Clark.

Ivan Moscati is Professor of Economics at the University of Insubria, Varese, and teaches History of Economics at Bocconi University, Milan, and USI, Lugano. His research focuses on the history and methodology of microeconomics, with special attention to choice and utility theory. His articles have been published in a range of journals on economics, history of economic thought, and economic methodology. Recent articles of Moscati have been awarded the Best Article Award of the *History of Economics Society* and the Best Article Award of the *European Society for the History of Economic Thought*. He recently published a book on *Measuring Utility* for Oxford University Press.

Lall B. Ramrattan holds a Ph.D. from the New School for Social Research, New York. He is an instructor at the University of California, Berkeley Extension and Holy Names University, Oakland, California. He has published articles in several major journals and has served as an Associate Editor of *The American Economist*.

Jeremy J. Siegel is the Russell E. Palmer Professor of Finance at The Wharton School of the University of Pennsylvania, where he has taught since 1976. He received his Ph.D. in economics from MIT in 1971. Siegel is the author of numerous professional articles and two books. His bestselling book, *Stocks for the Long Run*, now in its fifth edition, was named by the Washington Post and Business Week as one of the ten-best investment books of all time. Siegel has received many awards and citations for his research and excellence in teaching, including the Distinguished Leadership Award by the Securities Industry Association and the prestigious Nicholas Molodovsky Award by the Chartered Financial Analysts Institute. He also serves as the Academic Director of the Securities Industry Institute and the Senior Investment Strategy Advisor of WisdomTree Investments, Inc.

Michael Szenberg is Distinguished Professor of Economics and Chair, Business and Economics Department, Touro College and University System. He is Distinguished Professor Emeritus, Lubin School of Business, Pace University. Szenberg is recipient of many awards, including the 2013 John R. Commons Award, 2013 Homer and Charles Pace Award, 1983 Kenan Award for excellence in teaching, and the 1971 Irving Fisher Monograph Award. He also served as the Editor, Emeritus, of *The American Economist (1973–2011).* Szenberg is the author or coauthor with Lall B. Ramrattan of more than eighteen books and many journal articles and encyclopedia entries.

K. Vela Vellupillai is a retired, Emeritus Professor, living in Stockholm, Sweden. He was educated at the Universities of Kyoto, Lund and Cambridge and was deeply influenced and inspired, by his mathematics teacher at Kyoto, Ryoichiro Kawai, and the supervision in macroeconomic dynamics he received from Björn Thalberg at Lund and Richard Goodwin at Cambridge. Both Thalberg and Goodwin introduced him to Paul Samuelson's pioneering works in macroeconomic dynamics. During many hours of personal conversations, Goodwin, who knew and admired Samuelson, did his best to convey his respect for this universal economist.

D. Wade Hands is a Distinguished Professor of Economics at the University of Puget Sound. He is author of *Reflection Without Rules: Economic Methodology and Contemporary Science Theory* (2001), editor (with John Davis) of *The Elgar Companion to Recent Economic Methodology* (2011) and (with Philip Mirowski) *Agreement on Demand: Consumer Theory in the Twentieth Century* (2006). He is a past president of the History of Economics Society and is currently Co-editor (with John Davis) of *The Journal of Economic Methodology*. His research crosses the fields of economic methodology, the philosophy of economics, and the history of modern economic thought.

Donald A. Walker specializes in microeconomic theory and the history of neoclassical economic thought. He was president of the History of Economics Society (1987–1988), named Distinguished Fellow of that Society (2006), Editor of the *Journal of the History of Economic Thought* (1990–1998), and founder and first president of the International Walras Association (1997–2000). Among many other publications, he is the author of *Walras's Market Models* (Cambridge, 1996), *Advances in General Equilibrium Theory* (Elgar, 1997), *Walrasian Economics* (Cambridge, 2006), and editor of *Equilibrium* (3 vols., Elgar, 2000), and *The Legacy of Léon Walras* (2 vols., Elgar, 2001), and editor and translator (with Jan van Daal) of *Léon Walras's Studies in Social Economics* (Routledge, 2010) and *Elements of Theoretical Economics* (Cambridge, 2014).

List of Figures

Chapter 21

1 Introduction

Richard G. Anderson

1 Samuelson the Scientist

Paul A. Samuelson (1915–2009) was a scientist. In his author's preface to volume 5 of his *Collected Papers*, he alibies his lack of progress on a commissioned study of the growth, during his lifetime, of economic science with the argument: "How can I write *about* science while busily engaged in *doing* science?" (Samuelson 1986: xi; italics in original).

R. G. Anderson (✉)
University of Missouri-Kansas City, Kansas City, MO, USA
e-mail: rganderson@alum.mit.edu

R. A. Cord et al. (eds.), *Paul Samuelson*, Remaking Economics: Eminent Post-War Economists, https://doi.org/10.1057/978-1-137-56812-0_1

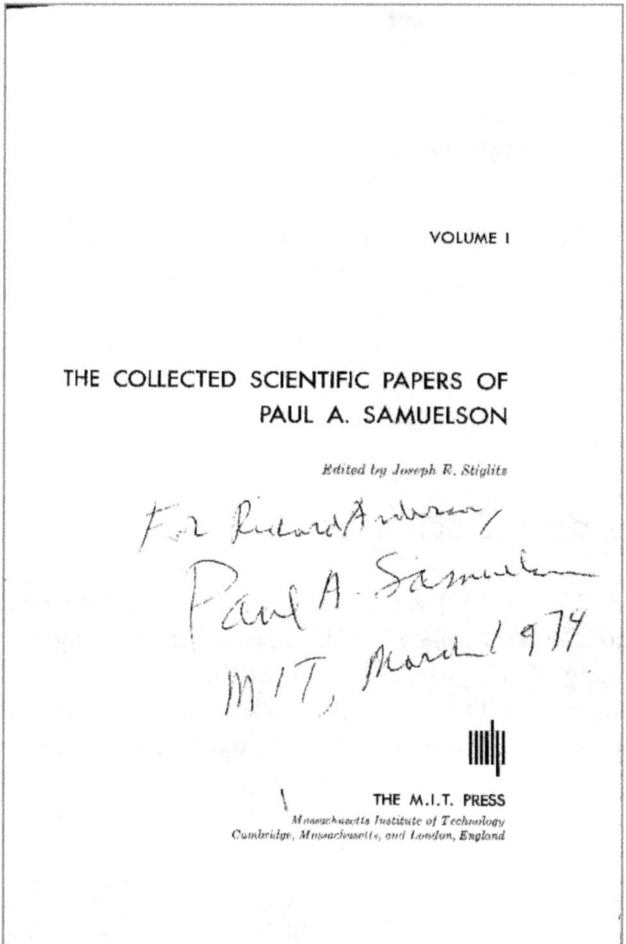
VOLUME I

THE COLLECTED SCIENTIFIC PAPERS OF
PAUL A. SAMUELSON

Edited by Joseph E. Stiglitz

THE M.I.T. PRESS
Massachusetts Institute of Technology
Cambridge, Massachusetts, and London, England

Samuelson's dedication of a copy of volume 1 of his *Collected Scientific Papers* to the author, on the occasion of taking Samuelson's second-year welfare economics class.

Scientists build models that suggest hypotheses (or assertions) that can be judged against data. No idle observer, Samuelson did not speculate about economic behavior by examining charts of data. Nor was he an iconoclast who rejected all evidence contrary to a preconceived stance.

Rather, his models built on the foundation of economic analysis: that economic agents seek to maximize an (often dynamic) objective function subject to (often intertemporal) constraints. Samuelson's *Collected Scientific Papers* comprise seven substantial volumes from The MIT Press. Beyond scientific papers, the volumes include essays written for the popular press that some might regard as non-scientific. In the author's preface to volume 5, Samuelson thanks Kate Crowley for saving "from my rejection various popularizations, arguing persuasively that historians of our times will need to know how scholars reacted from year to year to the important problems of the age" (ibid.). Janice Murray, his longtime assistant at MIT, has done the same in volumes 6 and 7.

Samuelson's efforts touched all subject areas within economics and finance: pure theory (demand theory for households and firms, welfare economics, growth theory, game theory); history of economic thought, including biographical and autobiographical writings; international economics; stochastic process theory, particularly with respect to finance and investing; mathematical biology; and essays on current economic policy. His science was both deep and broad, mathematically precise and yet focused on real-world economic problems.

Although it has been suggested that Samuelson's work in economics reflected little more than an application of physical-science mathematics (a cross-fertilization that has built some distinguished careers), Samuelson himself argued firmly that this was not true: his interest in economics was all-consuming from his first days at Chicago. Samuelson found economics in 1932 "poised to become mathematical" (Samuelson 1991 [2011]: 937). He added: "The generation of my teachers found mathematics a sore cross to bear. In their presidential addresses, they inveighed against it as pretentious and sterile, seeking comfort by quoting the views of Marshall, Pigou and Keynes on the triviality of mathematical economics. But that wolf at their door just would not go away. Funeral by funeral they lost their battle" (ibid.: 939).

Samuelson noted several times in his papers a debt to Edwin Bidwell Wilson, an extraordinary mathematician, the only graduate student of Yale's William Gibbs (the founder of the field of chemical thermodynamics), a professor at MIT from 1907 to 1922, and at Harvard's School of Public Health during Samuelson's time at Harvard. Samuelson stated that: "I was perhaps his only disciple: in 1935–1936, Abram Bergson, Sidney Alexander, Joseph Schumpeter and I were the only students in his mathematical economics seminar" (Samuelson 1998: 1376). He added that Wilson "had great contempt for social scientists who aped the more exact sciences in a parrot-like way. I was vaccinated early to understand that economics and physics could share the same formal mathematical theorems…while still not resting on the same empirical foundations and certainties" (ibid.). Wilson, later in 1940, strongly encouraged Samuelson to accept MIT's offer as an assistant professor rather than remain at Harvard as an instructor. Yet, Samuelson was eclectic: He noted that for intellectual recreation, he often sought to solve problems in thermodynamics, and he kept his eyes open for practical mathematical tools that might be applied in economic theory. Beyond these, he preferred tennis and reading mystery novels as recreation, not mathematical puzzles.

2 Samuelson the Autobiographer

Samuelson remarked that he did not "shirk" in his writings from talking about his professional development. His personal reflections are "peppered" through many of his papers, in addition to several autobiographical papers: 1968's Presidential Address before the World Congress of the International Economic Association, "The Way of an Economist"; 1972's "Economics in a Golden Age: A Personal Memoir"; 1983's "My Lifetime Philosophy"; and 1986's "Economics in My Time." Kate Crowley, in volume 5 of the *Collected Scientific Papers*, devotes part VII to Samuelson's autobiographical writings. Janice Murray, in volume 7, devotes part X—some 250 pages—to similar writings. In these, we learn that Samuelson was born in Gary, Indiana; that between the age of 17 months and 5 1/2 years, he was sent to live half-time with relatives on a farm near Valparaiso, Indiana, that lacked both electricity and indoor plumbing; that his father was a Polish Jewish pharmacist who prospered during the First World War; that his family moved to Miami Beach during the mid-1920s Florida land boom and bust, making a small fortune in real estate "by starting with a large one"; that when the family returned to Chicago he attended Hyde Park High School; and that he was a strong student, graduating at age 16. We also learn how he met and romanced his wife, and we view the multiple intersecting forces (Wilson's push, Harold Freeman's pull, and subtle anti-Semitism at Harvard and elsewhere in academia) that affected his 1940 decision to accept a position at MIT. Samuelson withholds few details.

We also learn of the Great Depression's lifelong impact on his macroeconomics—he noted that as an undergraduate, he spent four pleasant summers on Chicago's Lake Michigan beaches because there were no jobs to be found (he notes that he seldom used his time applying for jobs since the failure of hundreds of his classmates to obtain jobs revealed their scarcity). From this experience, short-term inflexible wages and prices became a part of his analysis, leading to an ingrained belief in activist government business cycle macroeconomic policy, both fiscal and monetary. Samuelson noted that at first, he rejected Keynes's *General Theory* as ad hoc and inconsistent with economic theory—but on subsequent readings, he came to accept much of Keynes's analysis. Throughout his career, he remained a self-described Keynesian.

Samuelson noted several times in his autobiographical writings that he came to economics at 8 a.m. 2 January 1932 when, at the age of 16 and not yet officially graduated from Hyde Park High School, he became a commuter student at the University of Chicago. He states that no great thought went into selecting Chicago: It was close by and, in those days, most students went to nearby schools. By chance, Chicago, he argues, had the nation's best economics department and was the ideal place to learn classical economics. At the end of his undergraduate studies in 1935, he received a Social Science Research Council scholarship that required he undertake graduate studies at a different school. He chose Harvard. Superbly confident, he did not apply to do graduate study but simply showed up and presented himself. Samuelson noted that he developed at Chicago strong backgrounds in both economics and the physical sciences; at Harvard, he found his economics background superior to almost all classmates, allowing him to attack advanced courses sooner than his contemporaries.

Samuelson emphasized in a 1972 memoir that professional success is complicated. His success depended on having had great teachers, great colleagues, great collaborators, great students, great initial talent including analytical ability, good luck—plus a great deal of hard work (Samuelson 1972: 155). MIT graduate students, including this author, recall many an evening, holiday, and weekend when Samuelson's was the sole occupied faculty office in the third-floor economics corridor of building E52 (doesn't he ever *not* work?).

Samuelson's memoirs reward the careful reader with insights. Limited space precludes my saying more.

3 Samuelson and This Volume

Samuelson said that he had his fingers in every part of the economics pie, and the papers in this volume reflect his broad interests. If Samuelson had a methodology, it was that economics was about optimization subject to constraints; if Samuelson had an ideology, it was that markets should be allowed to solve most economic problems subject to an ethically acceptable set of initial conditions (including income and wealth distribution) and an absence of externalities and monopoly power (Samuelson 1991). In the event, the methodology, as exercised in mathematical models, was easier than the ideology, often exercised in his nontechnical writings. His *Collected Scientific Papers* contain both, especially the posthumous volumes 6 and 7.

There seems little value here in a detailed summary of this volume's 21 papers because readers of this introduction likely have those papers in hand. Hence, only a brief survey follows.

With a broad brush, the economics pie and Samuelson's contributions might be sliced into three pieces: methodology, especially the role of mathematical models that necessarily omit features of the actual world to illustrate specific important relationships; microeconomics and finance, including the pure theory of consumer choice, Samuelson's first area of applying mathematics to economics; and macroeconomics, including international trade and development.

Ours is not the first volume seeking to appraise the Samuelson revolution in economic science. Superb collections are Brown and Solow (1983), a Festschrift by MIT friends and colleagues on the occasion of Samuelson's

65th birthday, and Szenberg et al. (2006), a Festschrift on the occasion of his 90th birthday. In a 2012 survey article, Princeton's Avinash Dixit summarized the challenge for those who follow:

> These chapters [in these two volumes] provide excellent and thorough statements of Samuelson's research and its impact. That makes my job simultaneously easy and difficult. I need not give much detailed exposition or explanation of his work, but even brief sketches may be too repetitive. (Dixit 2012: 2)

Dixit added:

> Many principles of economics were hidden in obscure verbiage of previous generations; he reformulated and extended them with crystal clarity in the language of mathematics. The citation for his Nobel Prize reads, 'for the scientific work through which he has developed static and dynamic economic theory and actively contributed to raising the level of analysis in economic science.' He left his mark on most fields of economics. He launched new fields and revolutionized stagnant fields. And he spanned this amazing breadth without the least sacrifice of depth in any of his endeavors.
>
> In every one of the eight decades since the 1930s, he made fundamental contributions that enlightened, corrected, and challenged the rest of us. His collected works in seven massive volumes comprise 597 items. He firmly believed that it was a scientist's duty to communicate his knowledge to the profession; that it was 'a sin not to publish'... He molded several generations of graduate students at MIT and researchers throughout the profession. His introductory textbook guided the thinking of millions throughout the world; it was instrumental in spreading the Keynesian revolution; and it was a model that all subsequent textbooks followed. His advice to presidents and his popular writings helped shape policy. More than anyone else in the latter half of the twentieth century, Samuelson changed the way economists think and write. (ibid.)

Thus, the challenge for this volume is laid.

Part I of this volume consists of seven papers that explore the roles of mathematics, ideology, and methodology in Samuelson's work. The

Oxford English Dictionary offers four definitions for ideology, one of which is "a systematic scheme of ideas, usually relating to politics, economics, or society and forming the basis of action or policy; a set of beliefs governing conduct." In microeconomics, Samuelson was consistent in his writing: To every feasible extent, markets should be allowed to allocate resources *conditional on an ethical distribution of resources* and absent externalities and monopoly power—that is, he preferred "mixed market economies" in the spirit of Keynes to a "laissez-faire Whig utopia" in the spirit of Hayek. In macroeconomics, he accepted as a fact short-run inflexibility of wages and prices while embracing for the long-run a flexible-price neoclassical model (see, e.g., Fischer 2010). Three authors (Daniel Hammond, Wade Hands, and Juan Carvajalino) examine Samuelson's overall philosophy that economic models should address economic behavior and hypotheses within the mathematical framework of optimization subject to constraint. Gregory Chow offers a highly personal account of Samuelson as a teacher. Donald Walker contributes two distinctive (and perhaps unique) papers based entirely on written correspondence with Samuelson. Alex Millmow provides a perspective on how Samuelson's work traveled the 10,000 miles from Cambridge, Massachusetts to Australia.

Part II includes six papers exploring Samuelson's contribution to microeconomics and finance. Thomas Demuynck and Per Hjertstrand review recent advances in one of Samuelson's earliest areas of published work, consumer choice. Joseph Farrell looks at the economics of pass-through and the envelope theorem, while Ivan Moscati reviews Samuelson's contribution to utility theory during his years at Harvard. Herrade Igersheim reviews Samuelson's extensions to Bergson's social welfare function; in his writing, Samuelson consistently acknowledged Bergson's seminal contribution as the foundation of his own work. Jeremy J. Siegel and Ronald MacDonald address Samuelson's contribution to finance. As Samuelson himself noted, mathematical finance as we know it today developed entirely within his professional career; his student Robert Merton has noted that most of Samuelson's contributions came after age 50 (Samuelson was Merton's Ph.D. supervisor. Merton's Ph.D. is dated 1970, when Samuelson was 55 years old).

Part III is heavy lifting. It includes eight papers addressing macroeconomics, international trade, Samuelson's relations with Joan Robinson, his work as an economic adviser, population modeling, public economics, capital theory, technical change, and development. In this section, perhaps more than earlier, we see that Samuelson indeed had his fingers in every slice of the economics pie. Vela Velupillai reviews Samuelson's contributions to macroeconomics. Harvey Gram and Geoff Harcourt address the modeling controversies between Samuelson and Joan Robinson. Robert Cord uses evidence from Samuelson's private papers to explore some of his government experience and his views on monetary policy: Samuelson was quite proud to say that he had never spent more than a week in Washington, D.C., rejecting invitations in the early 1960s to join there James Tobin and Robert Solow. Lall Ramratten and Michael Szenberg engage the enormous task of Samuelson and international trade. Ronald Lee reviews population theory and Samuelson's hugely influential overlapping generations model. Michael Boskin shoulders the almost as wide task of surveying Samuelson's contribution to public economics. Arnold Heertje reviews Samuelson's writings on technical change. Finally, Mauro Boianovsky discusses Samuelson's modeling of the process of economic development.

References

Brown, E.C. and R.M. Solow (eds.) (1983) *Paul Samuelson and Modern Economic Theory.* New York, McGraw-Hill.

Dixit, A. (2012) "Paul Samuelson's Legacy," *Annual Review of Economics*, 4: 1–31.

Fischer, S. (2010) "Paul Samuelson," Presented at the American Economic Association Meeting, Atlanta, 4 January 2010. Available at http://economics.mit.edu/files/5230.

Samuelson, P.A. (1972) "Economics in a Golden Age: A Personal Memoir," in G. Holton (ed.) *The Twentieth-Century Sciences: Studies in the Biography of Ideas.* New York, W.W. Norton: 155–170. Reprinted in H. Nagatani and K. Crowley (eds.) (1986) *The Collected Scientific Papers of Paul A. Samuelson, Volume 4.* Cambridge, The MIT Press: 881–896.

Samuelson, P.A. (1983) *Introduction to the Enlarged Edition of Foundations of Economic Analysis*, Cambridge, MA, Harvard University Press: xv–xxvi. Reprinted in K. Crowley (ed.) (1986) *The Collected Scientific Papers of Paul A. Samuelson, Volume 5.* Cambridge, The MIT Press: 846–857.

Samuelson, P.A. (1986) "Preface," in K. Crowley (ed.) *The Collected Scientific Papers of Paul A. Samuelson, Volume V.* Cambridge and London, UK, The MIT Press: xi.

Samuelson, P.A. (1991) "My Life Philosophy: Policy Credos and Working Ways," in M. Szenberg (ed.). *Eminent Economists: Their Life Philosophies.* New York, Cambridge University Press: 236–247. Reprinted in J. Murray (ed.) (2011) *The Collected Scientific Papers of Paul A. Samuelson, Volume 7.* Cambridge, The MIT Press: 887–898.

Samuelson, P.A. (1991) [2011] "Economics in Our Time," Speech Delivered on the Occasion of the 90th Anniversary of the Nobel Prize, Stockholm, Sweden, 6 December 1991. Reprinted in J. Murray (ed.) (2011) *The Collected Scientific Papers of Paul A. Samuelson, Volume 7.* Cambridge, The MIT Press: 935–949.

Samuelson, P.A. (1998) "How *Foundations* Came To Be," *Journal of Economic Literature,* 36(3): 1375–1386. Reprinted in J. Murray (ed.) (2011) *The Collected Scientific Papers of Paul A. Samuelson, Volume 7.* Cambridge, MA, The MIT Press: 1039–1058.

Szenberg, M., L. Ramrattan and A.A. Gottesman (eds.) (2006) *Samuelsonian Economics and the Twenty-First Century.* Oxford, Oxford University Press.

Part I

Samuelson's Contribution to Economics: Methodology and Mathematics

2

Paul Samuelson's Ideology and Scientific Economics

J. Daniel Hammond

1 Introduction

Paul Samuelson has been called "the founder of modern economics."[1] The research program that Samuelson established in the 1940s transformed neoclassical economics into a mathematical scientific discipline. To use Alfred Marshall's phrase, mathematics became the "engine of analysis" that economists use to derive empirical propositions.[2] As pure scientist, the economist's role is to discover facts and relations among facts of markets, prices, incomes, taxes, and regulations. As applied scientist, the economist's role is that of an engineer or technician; tell an economist what the policy goals are and he or she can provide assistance. Lionel Robbins famously defined economics as "the science which studies human behavior

[1] This is the title of volume one of Backhouse's biography of Samuelson (2017).

[2] Samuelson's term for this was "meaningful theorems."

J. Daniel Hammond (✉)
Eudaimonia Institute, Wake Forest University, Winston-Salem, NC, USA
e-mail: hammond@wfu.edu

R. A. Cord et al. (eds.), *Paul Samuelson*, Remaking Economics: Eminent Post-War Economists, https://doi.org/10.1057/978-1-137-56812-0_2

as a relationship between ends and scarce means which have alternative uses" (Robbins 1932: 15). Among the implications of this definition is that economists evaluate the means to ends, not the ends themselves. "Economics, then, is in no way to be conceived as we may conceive Ethics or Aesthetics as being concerned with ends as such" (ibid.: 31).[3] Samuelson affirmed this boundary around economics in the first edition of his textbook, *Economics*: "Ethical questions each citizen must decide for himself, and an expert is entitled to only one vote along with everyone else" (Samuelson 1948: 5).

Ethics and aesthetics are important aspects of individual and collective choices of ends, perhaps more important than choice of means. Choice of ends is primary; choice of means is secondary. But if economists adhere strictly to their role as scientists, they have no advice to offer on the choice of ends. They have no scientific authority to advise on matters of justice, equity, or freedom. The physical sciences—physics, chemistry, and biology—have a degree of natural protection from intrusion on science by scientists' goals and value judgments. No one would question whether a chemical reaction is fair, if the law of gravity is just, or if the human heart distributes oxygenated blood equitably to all parts of the body. But because economists study the consequences of human actions and like their subjects, economists have moral sentiments, to use Adam Smith's phrase, it is natural for economists to question the fairness, equity, and justice of market exchanges, the distribution of income resulting from these exchanges, or the distribution of the burden of taxes.

Though keeping scientific economics separate from ethics is generally regarded as important, it is not a simple thing to do. This is where questions of "ideology" most often enter debate among economists. By ideology, economists commonly mean the normative values, i.e., judgments about ends, which might influence or distort scientific analysis of the implications of scarcity. The meaning of ideology, however, is often left vague. This is because making demarcations between means and ends, facts and values, can be difficult, and economists are more interested in doing economics than philosophy of science. Nonetheless, beneath claims

---

[3]See Backhouse and Medema (2009).

about ideology in economics there are, often unarticulated, ideas on the nature of reality and our access to it.[4]

Samuelson's teacher, Joseph Schumpeter, took up the question of economic science and ideology in his 1948 Presidential Address to the American Economic Association. This was the same year that Samuelson's path-breaking textbook, *Economics*, was published.[5] Schumpeter developed a definition of ideology and applied it to Adam Smith, Karl Marx, and John Maynard Keynes. With their relationship as teacher and student in the background, along with their different perspectives on Keynes's economics, we will apply Schumpeter's insights about ideology to Samuelson. This will help us understand the innovations that Samuelson brought to economics and the relationship between ideology and economic science.

2 Schumpeter on Science and Ideology

As others have, Schumpeter made a distinction between ideology and science. He defined scientific economics as facts and the methods and theory economists use to analyze facts. He saw scientific economics as instrumental; it is a set of tools. The scientific enterprise is applying technique to facts in order to gain knowledge. Where Schumpeter's definition of ideology departs from the common science/ideology divide is that for him ideology is not so much outside science as preceding science. Also, where economists often follow Friedman (1953) in presuming that economics can be ideology-free, Schumpeter thought ideology was unavoidable. His definition of ideology is a scientist's prescientific vision of the nature and boundaries of the problem to which scientific methods, i.e., model building, are applied. "There exist in our minds preconceptions about the economic process" (Schumpeter 1949: 347). These preconceptions are separate from any values and interests the economist holds and may desire to promote. For Schumpeter, ideology is more deep-seated than values and interests. He believed that an honest and self-aware scientist could do

[4]Twentieth-century economics was deeply influenced by various forms of philosophical positivism, which in its heyday was expected to "hand the dark forces of metaphysics and superstition their final defeat" (Hands 1998: 374).

[5]See Backhouse (2017: Chapter 7) on Samuelson's relationship with Schumpeter.

analysis independently of his values and interests, i.e., could separate facts from values. With vigilance and effort, an economist could discover and report facts and relations between facts that he might wish to be otherwise. However, no economist could begin scientific analysis other than from a vision of the problem to be analyzed. This vision is the economist's ideology. Although the vision is prescientific, it is not necessarily preanalytic. For the vision includes supposed facts. So, in Schumpeter's view ideology is not a foreign germ that infects scientific economics. Rather ideology is the germ from which scientific economics develops. It is problematic only when it becomes the master of the analysis. The germ does not develop into science. Though elaborated, the preconception remains the germ that it was at the start.

Schumpeter's definition of ideology is somewhat akin to Marx's, and to the contemporary postmodern definition.[6] By Marxist and post-modern accounts, "class," including economic class, race, sex, etc., is wholly determinative of the way one sees the world. So science is wholly in the service of interests, and interests are themselves determined by "social location." But for Schumpeter, a scientist's social location—recent history, culture, class, biography, etc.—influences but is not determinative of the vision from which scientific work begins:

> [T]he original vision *is* ideology by nature and may contain any amount of delusions traceable to a man's social location, to the manner in which he wants to see himself or his class or group and the opponents of his own class or group. This should be extended even to peculiarities of his outlook that are related to his personal tastes and conditions and have no group connotation – there is even an ideology of the mathematical mind as well as an ideology of the mind that is allergic to mathematics. (ibid.: 351; italics in original)

To Schumpeter, a successful scientist does not so much work apart from ideology as proceed beyond his or her ideology. This is done by working scientifically with facts and techniques that are logically and effectively (through public scrutiny) independent of ideology. Science also has feedback effects on ideology, as scientists' visions are adapted to the knowledge

[6] See Minogue (2008).

produced by science. Thus, today's science helps shape the prescientific vision of tomorrow's scientists. On the other hand, if the scientific apparatus is put in service of the ideology, scientific progress is impeded. In the extreme case, we arrive at the Marxist outcome, with ideology determinative of science. Or we arrive at a postmodern world where there is no universal scientific knowledge; there are only diverse perspectives that add up to nothing permanent or coherent.

With his distinctions between values and interests, ideology, and scientific analysis, Schumpeter looked for evidence of ideology in the writings of three economists—Smith, Marx, and Keynes. Smith's social location was that of an eighteenth-century Scottish academic—"*homo academicus* who became a civil servant" (ibid.: 353). He was of neither the business class nor the political class. Smith was not bourgeois in outlook except for the virtue of parsimony, "eulogy of which evidently came from the bottom of his Scottish soul" (ibid.). In Schumpeter's judgment, these and other elements of Smith's ideological vision did little harm to his scientific analysis:

> There is some semiphilosophical foliage of an ideological nature but it can be removed without injury to his scientific argument. The analysis that supports his qualified free-trade conclusions is not – as it was with some contemporaneous philosophers, such as Morellet – based upon the proposition that by nature a man is free to buy or to sell where he pleases. The statement that the (whole) produce is the natural compensation of labor occurs, but no analytic use is made of it – everywhere the ideology spends itself in phraseology and for the rest receded before scientific research. (ibid.: 353–354)

Central to Karl Marx's ideology was the idea of "haves" exploiting "have-nots," though Marx did not originate this vision. It developed in eighteenth-century Paris. Schumpeter noted, as have other critics, that Marx saw ideology in everyone's analysis except his own. He claimed that Marx's ideology shows through in both his premises and his analysis. His was the ideology of a

> bourgeois radical who had broken away from bourgeois radicalism. He was formed by German philosophy and did not feel himself to be a professional

> economist until the end of the 1840s. But by that time, that is to say, *before* his serious analytic work had begun, his vision of the capitalist process had become set and his scientific work was to implement, not to correct it. (ibid.: 354; italics in original)

Schumpeter judged that Marx's ideology dominated his analysis, but did not thoroughly vitiate it. His scientific contributions included, for example, the concept of "surplus value." But it was Marx's ideology that appealed to his followers, and made them into disciples: "And so we behold in this case the victory of ideology over analysis: all the consequences of a vision that turns into a social creed and thereby renders analysis sterile" (ibid.: 355).

Keynes was the third economist that Schumpeter put to the ideology test. This case is the most pertinent for us because of Samuelson's role in developing and propagating Keynesian economic doctrine. Schumpeter identified the stagnation thesis as Keynes's ideological vision. This is the idea that economic stagnation results from a mismatch of continued saving and declining investment opportunities. As with Marx's vision of exploitation, Keynes's vision of stagnation was not original. Moreover, for Keynes it did not appear first in *The General Theory*. Schumpeter traces it from *The Economic Consequences of the Peace* (Keynes 1919 [1971]), through *A Tract on Monetary Reform* (Keynes 1923 [1971]) and *A Treatise on Money* (Keynes 1930 [1973]). Stagnation remained, however, a side issue for Keynes until the 1930s:

> In those pages of the *Economic Consequences of the Peace* we find nothing of the theoretical apparatus of the *General Theory*. But we find the whole of the vision of things social and economic of which that apparatus is the technical complement. The *General Theory* is the final result of a long struggle *to make that vision of our age analytically operative.* (Schumpeter 1946: 501; italics in original)

The experience of the Great Depression brought stagnation to the fore for Keynes and created a public for an economic theory built from his vision:

> Again it was the ideology – the vision of decaying capitalism that located (*saw*) the cause of the decay in one out of a large number of features of

> latter-day society – which appealed and won the day, and not the analytic implementation by the book of 1936 which, by itself and without the protection it found in the wide appeal of the ideology, would have suffered much more from the criticisms that were directed against it almost at once. (Schumpeter 1949: 356; italics in original)

Schumpeter's point was not to belittle Keynes's brilliance as a theorist. This very brilliance provided *The General Theory* with an "armour that prevented many of his followers from seeing the ideological element at all" (ibid.).

Schumpeter speculated on the sources of Keynes's ideology in his social location. In a broad sense, Keynes's social location was outside "the bourgeois scheme of life" (ibid.: 357). As we have seen, Schumpeter thought Smith began the move away from a bourgeois vision:

> If we analyze his [Smith's] argument closely – I am speaking, of course, only of the ideological elements of his system – it amounts to all-around vituperation directed against "slothful" landlords and grasping merchants or "masters" plus the famous eulogy of parsimony. And this remains the keynote of most non-Marxist economic ideology until Keynes. Marshall and Pigou were in this boat. They, especially the latter, took it for granted that inequality, or the existing degree of inequality, was "undesirable." But they stopped short of attack upon the pillar. (Schumpeter 1946: 516)

Schumpeter believed that many economists who entered teaching or research in the 1920s and 1930s had renounced allegiance to bourgeois values:

> Many of them sneered at the profit motive and at the element of personal performance in the capitalist process. But so far as they did not embrace straight socialism, they still had to pay respect to saving – under penalty of losing caste in their own eyes and ranging themselves with what Keynes so tellingly called the economist's "underworld." But Keynes broke their fetters: here, at last, was theoretical doctrine that not only obliterated the personal element and was, if not mechanistic itself, at least mechanizable, but also smashed the pillar into dust; a doctrine that may not actually say but can easily be made to say both that "who tries to save destroys real capital" and that, via saving, the "unequal distribution of income is the

> ultimate cause of unemployment." *This* is what the Keynesian Revolution amounts to. (ibid.: 516–517; italics in original)

Schumpeter thought that Keynes acquired a large school of disciples because his vision appealed both to the untutored who experienced the Great Depression and to trained economists. For economists, it provided a theoretical doctrine that was amenable to mathematical and statistical expression:

> Some of them felt—still feel for all I know – that all other work in "theory" should be scrapped. All of them paid homage to the man who had given them a well-defined model to handle, to criticize, and to improve – to the man whose work symbolizes at least, even though it may not embody, what they wanted to see done. (ibid.: 517)

3 Samuelson's Ideology

> To have been born as an economist before 1936 was a boon – yes. But not to have been born too long before! (Samuelson 1946: 187)

The thesis to be developed in this section is that, using Schumpeter's definition of ideology, Samuelson's ideology had two primary and complementary components—the Keynesian vision of economic stagnation and the mathematical approach to economics.[7] Recall that Schumpeter's definition of ideology is the scientist's prescientific vision. According to his retrospective account, written when he was thirty-one, Samuelson was at just the right stage of his life and career in 1936 (a first-year graduate student) to be infected with *The General Theory* (Keynes 1936 [1973]), which spread as "a disease first attacking and decimating an isolated tribe of South Sea islanders" (Samuelson 1946: 187). Yet Samuelson recalled

[7] Our attention will be to the early years of Samuelson's career, which is consistent with his teacher Schumpeter's view that the third decade of life is the "sacred decade" when a scholar "creates what is subsequently worked out" (Schumpeter quoted in Allen 1991: 51).

that he, like everyone else in Cambridge, MA (Harvard graduate students and faculty), could not at first make sense of Keynes's book—"I did not at all understand what it was about" (ibid.: 188). Understanding had to wait for the mathematical Keynesian models of Meade (1937), Lange (1938), Hicks (1937), and Harrod (1936, 1939).

That Samuelson was attracted to Keynes's vision of stagnation rather than to his scientific economics is suggested by several pieces of evidence. First, there is the language he used to describe the effect of Keynes's ideas on himself and others (ibid.). The ideas spread with the "virulence of a disease"; economists "began to run the fever"; they "took up the new Gospel"; they "joined the swim"; "the Keynesian taint is unmistakably there upon every one of us"; Keynes offered an alternative to "the classical philosophy." Second, there is the unorthodox manner in which Samuelson showed admiration for Keynes's book:

> Herein [the new system] lies the secret of the *General Theory*. It is a badly written book, poorly organized; any layman who, beguiled by the author's previous reputation, bought the book was cheated out of his 5 shillings. It is not well suited for classroom use. It is arrogant, bad-tempered, polemical, and not overly-generous in its acknowledgments. It abounds in mares' nests and confusions; involuntary unemployment, wage units, the equality of savings and investment, the timing of the multiplier, interactions of the marginal efficiency upon the rate of interest, forced savings, own rates of interest, and many others. In it the Keynesian system stands out indistinctly, as if the author was hardly aware of its existence or cognizant of its properties; and certainly he is at his worst when expounding its relations to its predecessors. Flashes of insight and intuition intersperse tedious algebra. An awkward definition suddenly gives way to an unforgettable cadenza. When it finally is mastered, we find its analysis to be obvious and at the same time new. In short, it is a work of genius. (ibid.: 190)

Samuelson speculated that future historians of economics would see that "the very obscurity and polemical character of the *General Theory* ultimately served to maximize its long-run influence" (ibid.). He thought Keynes's book would stand alongside those of Smith, Cournot, and Walras as "theoretical classics." Of these four, only Smith's was "easy reading or accessible to the intelligent layman" (ibid.). But notice that the difficulty an educated layman had in understanding *The General Theory* was different from the difficulty in understanding Cournot and Walras, and for that matter Samuelson's *Foundations of Economic Analysis*. Cournot, Walras, and Samuelson are difficult to read because of their mathematical technicality. *The General Theory* was difficult to read because "it is a badly written book." This raises the question of what Samuelson meant by "mastering" Keynes's book. He might have meant mastering *The General Theory* as one masters linear algebra; you master linear algebra by studying it until you learn the rules for working with systems of equations. But he might also have meant making *The General Theory* into a coherent theory. This would be to master Keynes's book in the way that a potter masters a lump of clay, forming it into a pot. Samuelson compared *The General Theory* to James Joyce's *Finnegans Wake* suggesting that readers of both are in need of a "skeleton key."

This brings us to the second part of Samuelson's ideology—his vision of economics as mathematics applied to economic problems. Recall that Schumpeter suggested, "there is even an ideology of the mathematical mind as well as an ideology of the mind that is allergic to mathematics" (Schumpeter 1949: 351). A skeleton key is not the key to a single lock; it is a key to *any* lock. For Samuelson, mathematics was the skeleton key to open not only *The General Theory*, but also all of economics. He introduced his PhD thesis with the claim that "the existence of analogies between central features of various theories implies the existence of a general theory which underlies the particular theories and unifies them with respect to those central features."[8] That Samuelson provided economists with a skeleton key, or *general theory*, for seemingly diverse economic questions has been widely acknowledged. This was the model of constrained optimization, developed to derive "meaningful," i.e., empirically testable, theorems. So for instance, Avinash Dixit wrote:

> Alexander Pope's epitaph for Isaac Newton was: "Nature and Nature's laws lay hid in night: 'God said, Let Newton be!' and all was light." The same could be said of Paul Samuelson. Many principles of economics were hidden

[8] Samuelson (1940a) quoted in Backhouse (2017: 274).

> in obscure verbiage of previous generations; he reformulated and extended them with crystal clarity in the language of mathematics. (Dixit 2012: 2)

We need not get into the question of whether the Keynesian models developed by Meade, Lange, Hicks, and Harrod are in a fundamental sense "the economics of Keynes."[9] It suffices that soon after Samuelson encountered Keynes's book, that "resembles the random notes over a period of years of a gifted man who in his youth gained the whip hand over his publishers" (Samuelson 1946: 191), the makings of a mathematical key was provided in their models. This placed Keynes's "system" squarely in Samuelson's sandbox of mathematics. Some economists considered Keynes's foremost contribution in *The General Theory* to be demand for money as liquidity preference. Others gave credit to Keynes for his treatment of uncertainty and speculation. Samuelson thought the primary contribution of *The General Theory* was that it

> provides a relatively realistic, complete system for analyzing the level of effective demand and its fluctuations. More narrowly, I conceive the heart of its contribution to be in that subset of equations which relate to the propensity to consume and to saving in relation to offsets-to-saving. In addition to linking saving explicitly to income, there is an equally important denial of the implicit "classical" axiom that motivated investment is *indefinitely expansible or contractable*, so that whatever people *try* to save will always be fully invested. … But it is vital for business-cycle analysis that we do assume definite amounts of investment which are highly variable over time in response to a myriad of exogenous and endogenous factors, *and which are not automatically equilibrated to full-employment saving levels by any internal efficacious economic process.* (ibid.: 192; italics in original)

In this passage, we have both elements of Samuelson's ideology—the vision of underemployment equilibrium he received from Keynes and the vision of sustained underemployment as a mathematical problem that he might solve. He reread *The General Theory* through its interpretation in mathematical models of Meade, Lange, Hicks, and Harrod. "Now for the first time, it [the classical synthesis] was confronted by a competing

[9]See Leijonhufvud (1968).

system – a well-reasoned body of thought containing among other things as many equations as unknowns" (ibid.: 189–190). Keynes provided "a complete system," the heart of which was in "a subset of equations." In using his "complete system," it was important "to assume definite amounts of investment which are highly variable over time in response to a myriad of exogenous and endogenous factors" (ibid.: 192).

Like Schumpeter, Samuelson looked to Keynes's writings prior to *The General Theory* for intuitions that were to become the book's core message—for "milestones on the road to Damascus." He credited Keynes for not allowing theoretical misadventures in his *Treatise* (its fundamental equations were a "detour and blind alley" [ibid.: 198]) to deflect his vision. The Great Depression provided both confirmation of his intuition and an immediate challenge for him to develop the intuition into a system. "Before it was over, he had emerged with the prize in hand, the system of thought for which he will be remembered" (ibid.: 199). What was Keynes's system? With the

> vitally important consumption function: giving the propensity to consume in terms of income; or looked at from the opposite side, specifying the propensity to save. With investment given, as a constant or in the schedule sense, we are in a position to set up the simplest determinate system of underemployment equilibrium. …
>
> Immediately everything falls into place: the recognition that the *attempt* to save may lower income and actual *realized* saving; the fact that a net autonomous increase in investment, foreign balance, government expenditure, consumption will result in increased income *greater* than itself, etc., etc. (ibid.; italics in original)

This was the Keynesian system and Samuelson's vision, i.e., the Keynesian portion of Samuelson's ideology. It signaled the dawn of a new era, for Keynes had denied the "classical axiom" and his interpreters had mathematized business cycle analysis.

We see the Keynesian vision of underemployment equilibrium adopted by Samuelson in his textbook (1948). He told instructors and students that the problem of underemployment must be solved for classical economics to have relevance. In effect, the classical economists (those before Keynes) had developed a science for a non-existent economic system: "If modern economics does its task well so that widespread unemployment is substantially banished from democratic societies, then its importance will wither away and the traditional economics (whose concern is *wise* allocation of fully employed resources) will really come into its own – almost for the first time" (Samuelson 1948: 10; italics in original).[10]

Samuelson began his scientific work on Keynesian economics while he was a member of the Harvard Society of Fellows. He did so at the instigation of Alvin Hansen.[11] Beginning with the Keynesian vision and a set of unresolved questions, he used mathematics to analyze business cycles and underemployment with the "Keynesian savings-investment-income cross" which he noted was "not formally different from the 'Marshallian supply-demand-price cross'" (Samuelson 1946: 199). An analysis of interactions between the multiplier and accelerator (Samuelson 1939a) was followed in quick succession by a "synthesis" of the multiplier and accelerator (Samuelson 1939b), and an evaluation of the theory of pump priming (Samuelson 1940b). Samuelson seems to have shared Schumpeter's concern that analysis put wholly in the service of ideology (pre-scientific vision) would stall scientific progress. The multiplier doctrine was, he averred, widely accepted as insightful. "Nevertheless, there would seem to be some ground for the fear that this extremely simplified mechanism is in danger of hardening into a dogma, hindering progress and obscuring important subsidiary relations and processes" (Samuelson 1939a: 75). In the two articles on the multiplier and accelerator, Samuelson began with the numerical analysis of Hansen, then switched to algebraic analysis of difference equations under several different assumptions about the marginal propensity to consume (MPC) and the accelerator (the "relation"). Samuelson used these model sequences to summarize the dynamic path of national income that could result from a given level of government expenditure, clearing up questions and ambiguities in other economists' work on the multiplier and accelerator. For example, when an increase in consumption spending leads directly to an increase in income, and also to an increase in investment via

---

[10]He suggested that "the economic world as we have known it for the last century and a half is not a stable system in full-employment equilibrium." It "occasionally" runs inflationary fever and "often, and for long periods, it is in the frozen torpor of unemployment and slump" (Samuelson 1948: 165).

[11]See Backhouse (2017: Chapter 13) on Samuelson's relationship with Hansen.

the accelerator, which in its turn leads to a further increase in consumption and income, does this process necessarily come to an end? If so, why does it end? Suggestions in the literature included the process ending because of a full-employment ceiling, or bottlenecks in key industries, or dynamic changes in the MPC. Among Keynesian economists, Samuelson took on the role of "mathematical economist settling disputes" (Backhouse 2017: 266).

The advantage of using mathematical models was the ability to arrive at clear answers to these and other questions: "Given our consumption function, the level of spontaneous investment, the strength of the 'relation,' and the value of consumption in two initial periods, the behavior of all future consumption and national income is easily determined" (Samuelson 1939b: 792). Among the conclusions he drew in these articles were that the multiplier and accelerator together could produce cumulative movements in national income; that cumulative movements can be either disequilibrating or equilibrating; and that there may be overshooting of equilibrium. Samuelson also concluded that from the long-run perspective, Keynes was justified in ignoring the accelerator principle.

In his "reexamination" of the theory of pump priming by fiscal policy, Samuelson again sought to "indicate [and clear up] certain difficulties and possible sources of confusion encountered in the analysis of this [multiplier effects of fiscal policy] process" (Samuelson 1940b: 492). The first step was to identify the key features of the private economy, the structure upon which fiscal actions operate. This list of features is Samuelson's own Keynesian vision of the "Nature of the Private Economy." He listed four: (1) the private economy is "not perfect and frictionless"; (2) it has the potential and perhaps "definite tendency toward cumulative movements of a disequilibrating kind"; (3) the average propensity to consume is less than one so that "in the absence of substantial amounts of net investment, there will necessarily be a large degree of unemployment and a low level of business activity"; (4) even if the capital market was perfect, "*there is no tendency for the rate of interest to equilibrate the demand and supply of employment.* … This means that in any community there exists a possibility of insufficient net investment, and perhaps in a wealthy community a likelihood of such an insufficiency" (ibid.: 492–493; italics in original).

These appear not to be simplifying assumptions for the purpose of theorizing, such as the assumption of maximization or of linear demand functions. They are rather Samuelson's vision of the nature of the private economy. His support for these features was "that in the recent business cycle literature they are regarded as fundamental" (ibid.: 492). A fifth assumption is more along the lines of simplification. This is that tax rates are fixed and that "there are no technical difficulties to prevent the government from financing deficits of the magnitudes discussed" (ibid.: 494). An additional feature of the public economy in relation to the private economy was that "the government is in a position to determine its own level of expenditure at each instant of time, to influence more or less strongly the subsequent behavior of all parts of the private economy, and to affect its own future tax revenues" (ibid.). Samuelson's only concern about the efficiency of public expenditure was with regard to its timing in relation to the business cycle. The allocation of government spending to different activities was not of concern. As he was to claim in his textbook, the core problem of pre-Keynesian "classical" economics of Marshall and Pigou—allocative efficiency—is not relevant until the economy is at full employment.

4 Personal Elements in Samuelson's Ideology

There may have been a personal element in Samuelson's attraction to Keynes apart from coming of age during the Great Depression and the Keynesian "system" being amenable to mathematical modeling.[12] The way Samuelson and others saw Keynes was similar to the way Samuelson saw himself. In Samuelson's view, Keynes was independent and heretical. He broke away from the classical orthodoxy that he learned from Marshall ("the stultifying backwash of Marshall's influence upon economic theory" [Samuelson 1946: 196]), founding a new system and movement: "With respect to the level of total purchasing power and employment, Keynes denies that there is an *Invisible Hand* channeling the self-centered action

[12] See Samuelson (1985).

of each individual to the social optimum. This is the sum and substance of his heresy" (ibid.: 192). Samuelson saw Keynes as Keynes saw himself—as a reforming heretic rather than as an apostate. Keynes was reforming economics in order to reform capitalism and thereby save it. According to Samuelson, "Such a philosophy [as Keynes's] is profoundly capitalistic in its nature. Its policies are offered 'as the only practical means of avoiding the destruction of existing economic forms in their entirety and as the condition of the successful functioning of individual initiative'" (ibid.). Far from a radical, Keynes was an "urbane and cosmopolitan provincial English liberal" (ibid.: 193). He stood apart from social and political conservatism and classical economics on the one hand, and from communism, socialism, and Marxist economics and revolution, on the other.

Samuelson claimed that he, like Keynes, had broken away from the orthodoxy of his youth—he might have said the "stultifying backwash of Marshall's influence"—in his undergraduate education at the University of Chicago. Roger Backhouse recounts Samuelson's experiences and his depictions of his education at Chicago:

> He praised the education he had received [at Chicago] – both the Hutchins curriculum…and his training in economic theory, the rigor of the latter equipping him much better than his contemporaries for what they were to encounter in Harvard's graduate program. He also formed long-lasting friendships with many of his teachers and other faculty members, notably Aaron Director, Paul Douglas, Frank Knight, Henry Simons, Lloyd Mints, and Jacob Viner … But he became very critical of what they taught him about monetary economics and the business cycle … He referred to 'the schoolmen,' describing the department as 'dogmatically conservative,' and he claimed several times that he was taught nothing more than the simple quantity theory of money, in which the price level was proportional to the money supply. (Backhouse 2017: 78)

Whereas Keynes was the "urbane and cosmopolitan English liberal," Samuelson developed the persona of the urbane and cosmopolitan American liberal. Along with the formal mathematics of economic theory, we find in his writings allusions, many no doubt obscure to his economist readers, to history, religion, and literature. Samuelson also took care to position himself between the political and intellectual poles of conservativism and socialism—squarely in the "middle of the road," the best position from which to observe and understand our "mixed free-enterprise economic system" (Samuelson 1948: 34).[13] Even as a Keynesian, he set himself apart from "that narrow band of zealots associated with some of the policy programs that Keynes himself espoused during the great depression" (ibid.: 254). Explaining the roles of saving and investment in income determination to students who used his textbook he wrote:

> Some monetary cranks think that this saving necessarily means unemployment and depression. Such a view is simply incorrect. If there happen to be profitable investment opportunities, business firms will be paying out wages, interest, and other costs for new capital equipment. … The saving will do no harm to national income so long as it is not greater than what business can profitably invest. …
>
> Monetary cranks who think that saving is always disastrous are plain wrong. But there is also a second school of monetary cranks: they go to the opposite extreme and insist that saving and investment can never cause income to be too high or too low. … It is only in the last few decades that economists have learned how to separate out the truth and falsity of both extreme viewpoints. (ibid.: 263–264)

Another personality trait of Keynes that was attractive to Samuelson was Keynes's self-confidence. In his memorial of Keynes, Samuelson wrote that "one must note that even when most wrong, he is often most confident and sure of himself" (Samuelson 1946: 195). He thought of Keynes as something of a pamphleteer who should be judged on his absolute hits without regard to his misses. Keynes's misses, according to Samuelson, included basic mistakes in his critique of the Treaty of Versailles, in debate with Sir William Beveridge on the terms of trade between agriculture and industry, and in an exchange with Bertil Ohlin on reparations. Keynes's

[13] See Backhouse (2017: Chapter 27) and Giraud (2014) on Samuelson positioning his textbook in the "middle-of-the-road." Samuelson also put the American economy in the middle, not a capitalist but a "mixed economy." Economics journalist Leonard Silk wrote of Samuelson in his book *The Economists*: "Within the American economics establishment, I consider Paul Samuelson to be the vital center, with intellectual and moral views which themselves extend over a wide spectrum and are difficult to categorize. Nevertheless, clearly to his right is Milton Friedman, to his left is John Kenneth Galbraith and Wassily Leontief" (Silk 1976: xi).

"strength and weakness lay in his intuition, audaciousness, and changeability" (ibid.).

Samuelson was similarly audacious. Backhouse notes that in early recollections of his education, Samuelson boasted under the cloak of modesty. For example, in a March 1935 diary entry he wrote: "In the field of economics I have made many discoveries quite independently (I think), only to find that somebody else had already arrived at similar results. … Many of the deeper problems of abstraction and equilibrium have occurred to me independently."[14]

Backhouse's assessment is that:

> The diary entry exhibits a pattern found in many of his later self-appraisals. Ostensibly it is modest, for he is arguing that he found nothing new, and that simultaneous discovery is universal. However, given that he is comparing his discoveries as a teenage undergraduate with the discovery of calculus by both Leibniz and Newton, he is anything but modest. A similar point could be made about the remark: 'It was as if, like a bird dog bred to point at hunt, my DNA was born to manipulate demand and supply curves.' He is modest in denying any merit in being a good economist, but he nonetheless sets himself apart from his fellow students whose DNA was less favorable. (Backhouse 2017: 97)

5 Conclusion

By virtue of his brilliance and boldness, Paul Samuelson gave shape to the mainstream of economics in the middle third of the twentieth century. Like John Maynard Keynes, Samuelson was an iconoclastic reformer, on a mission to break up traditional economic doctrine. The point was not to replace it with something wholly different, but to make economics fit for the modern economy. Keynes and Samuelson were reformers, not revolutionaries. Samuelson was also like Keynes in that he inspired a generation of disciples. Keynes's disciples, including Samuelson, turned his vision of underemployment equilibrium into a scientific program. Samuelson, his

[14]Quoted in Backhouse (2017: 96–97).

students at MIT, and others who came under his influence turned his vision of mathematical modeling as the means of scientific unification into a scientific program.[15] With the passing of Marshall, Pigou, Keynes, and other Cambridge University luminaries, a new era opened. The base of the neoclassical mainstream economics shifted from Cambridge, UK, to Cambridge, MA.

Samuelson acquired his vision – his "ideology" in Schumpeter's terms – as a young Harvard graduate student and MIT professor in the 1930s and 1940s. This vision was a marriage between Keynes's stagnation thesis and mathematical modelling. The scientific program he developed from this vision had a structure in common with other parts of the new mainstream, which followed the course set by Samuelson. Consumption theory, welfare economics, capital theory, international trade, finance, and macroeconomics – these were rebuilt or built anew with the mathematics of constrained optimization. The proximate goal of the theorist in all fields of economics was to derive "meaningful theorems." The Samuelsonian scientific program was extremely productive in identifying and solving analytical problems. The pace with which Samuelson and his followers pushed out the frontier of scientific knowledge was nothing short of breathtaking in comparison with pre-Samuelson research programs. Samuelson reflected, "as a theorist I have great advantages. All I need is a pencil (now a ball pen) and an empty pad of paper" (Samuelson 1983a: 10).

Yet the accumulation of theorems by economists working in the Samuelsonian program has not been an unmitigated success. Unification of economic fields was achieved by abstraction from decisions made by flesh-and-blood men and women in the institutional settings of business, government, and households. Samuelson envisioned meaningful theorems giving rise to testable hypotheses, allowing the application of scientific knowledge of the real world to matters of economic policy. However, in the 1950s and 1960s theorem derivation ran ahead of discovery of empirical regularities and the forecasting ability necessary to scientifically manage the economy. Samuelson himself suggested that it was appropriate to have lower standards for the empirical side of economics than for the theoretical

[15] See Brown and Solow (1983) and Dixit (2012).

side. In a discussion of the problem posed by time lags for countercyclical policy, he suggested a forecasting standard of the "prudent informed man":

> I would say that the problem of lags should predispose us even more toward the following view: instead of adapting policy passively to the recent past, the authorities should try to form a judgment of what a prudent informed man thinks the rough probabilities are for a couple of quarters ahead and should take action accordingly, being perfectly prepared to change their tack as new evidence becomes available to modify these prudent probabilities. (Samuelson 1960: 264)

The Samuelsonian program also highlights a larger but less acknowledged limitation of contemporary economics. This is a direct effect of economists' conception of scientific purpose and method. Since Adam Smith's time, economic analysis has become increasingly disconnected from ethical and moral analysis. In as much, economists have purchased rigor at the expense of relevance. The practice of economists as scientists and as participants in policy development is squarely within modern Rationalism as described by political theorist Michael Oakeshott:

> The conduct of affairs, for the Rationalist, is a matter of solving problems, and in this no man can hope to be successful whose reason has become inflexible by surrender to habit or is clouded by the fumes of tradition. In this activity the character which the Rationalist claims for himself is the character of the engineer, whose mind (it is supposed) is controlled throughout by the appropriate technique and whose first step is to dismiss from his attention everything not directly related to specific intentions. This assimilation of politics to engineering is, indeed, what may be called the myth of rationalist politics. (Oakeshott 1991: 9)

Rationalism in economics did not originate with the Samuelsonian research program. Its origins were much earlier. Recall that Schumpeter regarded Smith as a modern man breaking the fetters of tradition except for his Scottish regard for the virtue of parsimony. In the twentieth century, Keynes and, after him, Samuelson helped break the fetters of tradition by undermining traditional economic virtues. That neither Keynes nor

Samuelson viewed himself as a radical may be because the Rationalist revolution was so long an affair. They were in a long line of radicals who sought to remake society through exclusive use of their reason. Keynes's contemporary and critic Wilhelm Röpke asked what would become his [Keynes's] legacy:

> Is he the Copernicus of economics, as so many claim, the man who banished the ghosts of economics grown rigid in the chains of tradition, who opened the door to prosperity and stability? Or did he destroy more than he created and has he summoned into being spirits that today he possibly would be gladly rid of? (Röpke 1963: 223)

Röpke regarded Keynes as "the best economist of our times" (ibid.: 221). Nevertheless, Röpke thought his legacy was less in economics than in social philosophy and politics. This was because Keynes accelerated the move away from traditional virtues upon which sound economics and healthy society are based—"so that Keynes, in tragic opposition to his own intention, must be numbered among the grave-diggers of that very order of liberal democracy to which his innermost allegiance belonged" (ibid.: 222). The economic virtues included competition, free markets, wage flexibility, saving, and balanced budgets. However, such economic standards were but a facet of broader social and political standards:

> He not only demolished that which was decayed, but by his preaching of economic pragmatism and his attack on deeply rooted principles in the moral-political sphere, he became one of the principle agents in that general decay of standards, or norms, and of principles which constitutes the real core of the social crisis of our time. (ibid.: 223)

Röpke compared Keynes to Smith, who saw economics "as an organic part of the larger whole of the intellectual, moral, and historical life of society." To Keynes, economics "was part of a mathematical-mechanical universe." The eighteenth-century deistic moralist was followed by the twentieth-century exponent of positivist scientism. The invisible hand—"a living order with an immanent logic of its own which the human mind could comprehend and even destroy but could not duplicate" was replaced by "mechanical *quanta* subject to precise measurement and direction by an omnicompetent technical human intelligence." The teachings of Smith were "a promising beginning." Those of Keynes were "the end product of a process of disintegration in which the crisis of an exclusively rationalistic society finds its ultimate expression."[16]

With the unification of economics achieved through mathematization, Samuelson contributed to the narrowing of economics that Röpke saw happening from Smith to Keynes. Today, there is an even sharper contrast between the serious and rigorous intellectual work economists do on "positive" things mathematical and empirical, and their blind eye or armchair exhortations on "normative" things such as of justice and equity. Samuelson's writings witness his acknowledgment that a society's health depends on more than bread alone. We see this in titles he gave to his publications, such as *Economics from the Heart: A Samuelson Sampler* (Samuelson 1983b); in what he wrote about economists, public policy, and politics; and in what he wrote about himself. He identified himself as a Democratic economist, not because Democrats had a better grasp of economics than Republicans, but because in his opinion Democrats were the party of altruism, of the underdog, and Republicans the party of the rich. In a *New York Times* piece criticizing presidential candidate Barry Goldwater's economic platform, Samuelson accused "economic libertarians" of being excessively dependent on logical analysis:

> We economists spend most of our time pointing out the efficiencies of competitive markets. But it is not a question of fuzzy or illogical thinking to seek a golden mean in these matters. One must render to logic only what lies within the province of logic, rendering unto experience and value judgments that which is in their sphere. (Samuelson 1964: 28)

In "My Life Philosophy" (Samuelson 1983a: 6), he recounted a letter he received from an economist

> who has been preoccupied over the years solely with *Pareto optimality* … [This economist] wrote me long ago that I would be surprised to know how liberal he is. Indeed I would be. Reflecting on his writings, I wondered how he knew he had a heart: it had been so long since he had used it.

[16]Quotations are from Röpke (1963: 224).

Samuelson identified his long-held ideology, meaning by ideology his overriding moral stance:

> Although positivistic analysis of what the actual world is like commands and constrains my every move as an economist, there is never far from my consciousness a concern for the ethics of the outcome. Mine is a simple ideology that favors the underdog and (other things equal) abhors inequality.
>
> I take no credit for this moral stance. My parents were 'liberals' (in the American sense of the word, not in the 'Manchester School' sense), and I was conditioned in that general *Weltanschauung*. It is an easy faith to adhere to. When my income came to rise above the median, no guilt attached to that. Nor was there a compulsion to give away all my extra coats to shirtsleeved strangers: my parents would have thought me daft to do so. Some personal obligation for distributive justice liberals do expect of themselves; but what is far more important than acts of private charity is to weight the counterclaims of efficiency and equity, whenever public policy is concerned, in the direction of equity. (ibid.: 5)

Samuelson claimed that his "value-judgment ideology" was set from the age of 25, the age he was in 1940 when he left Harvard to join the MIT faculty. He did not identify any of his teachers at the University of Chicago or Harvard, or any of his studies, as influencing his moral philosophy. From his account, Samuelson seems not to have examined his moral stance. We would be hard-pressed to find a sharper contrast between the relative weights assigned by an economist to efficiency and to ethics in considerations of policy, and the weights revealed by the economist's intellectual inquiries into the two areas.

Whether because of or in spite of economic science, the material standard of living for Europeans and Americans today is beyond anything envisioned by Keynes and the early Keynesians. Yet gains in self-reported happiness have not kept pace with gains in income. Nor have gains in social, political, and cultural cohesiveness. From across the political spectrum, many would argue that on these non-material facets of well-being Europeans and Americans have lost rather than gained ground. Having traveled for so long and so far down the Rationalistic path of "scientific" economics, have economists undermined their relevance to the most pressing issues of our time?

Acknowledgements I express my gratitude to Roger E. Backhouse, Bruce J. Caldwell, John T. Dalton, Steven G. Medema, and Claire H. Hammond for helpful comments, and to Bob Cord for skillful editing.

References

Allen, R.L. (1991) *Opening Doors: The Life and Work of Joseph Schumpeter, Volume One: Europe*. New Brunswick, NJ and London, Transaction Publishers.

Backhouse, R.E. (2017) *Founder of Modern Economics: Paul A. Samuelson, Volume 1: Becoming Samuelson, 1915–1948*. New York, Oxford University Press.

Backhouse, R.E. and S.G. Medema (2009) "Defining Economics: The Long Road to Acceptance of the Robbins Definition," *Economica*, 76: 805–820.

Brown, E.C. and R.M. Solow (eds.) (1983) *Paul Samuelson and Modern Economic Theory*. New York, McGraw Hill.

Dixit, A. (2012) "Paul Samuelson's Legacy," *Annual Review of Economics*, 4: 1–31.

Friedman, M. (1953) "The Methodology of Positive Economics," in M. Friedman (ed.) *Essays in Positive Economics*. Chicago, University of Chicago Press: 3–43.

Giraud, Y. (2014) "Negotiating the 'Middle-of-the-Road' Position: Paul Samuelson, MIT, and the Politics of Textbook Writing, 1945–55," in E.R. Weintraub (ed.) *MIT and the Transformation of American Economics*, Annual Supplement to Volume 46, *History of Political Economy*. Durham, NC, Duke University Press: 134–152.

Hands, D.W. (1998) "Positivism," in J.B. Davis, D.W. Hands and U. Mäki (eds.) *The Handbook of Economic Methodology*. Cheltenham, UK and Northampton, MA, USA, Edward Elgar: 374–378.

Harrod, R.F. (1936) *The Trade Cycle*. Oxford, Oxford University Press.

Harrod, R.F. (1939) "An Essay in Dynamic Theory," *Economic Journal*, 49: 14–33.

Hicks, J.R. (1937) "Mr. Keynes and the Classics; A Suggested Interpretation," *Econometrica*, 5: 147–159.

Keynes, J.M. (1919) [1971]. *The Economic Consequences of the Peace, Volume II, The Collected Writings of John Maynard Keynes*. London, Macmillan.

Keynes, J.M. (1923) [1971]. *A Tract on Monetary Reform, Volume IV, The Collected Writings of John Maynard Keynes*. London, Macmillan.

Keynes, J.M. (1930) [1973]. *A Treatise on Money, Volumes V and VI, The Collected Writings of John Maynard Keynes.* London, Macmillan.

Keynes, J.M. (1936) [1973]. *The General Theory of Employment, Interest and Money, Volume VII, The Collected Writings of John Maynard Keynes.* London, Macmillan.

Lange, O. (1938) "The Rate of Interest and the Optimum Propensity to Consume," *Economica,* New Series, 5: 12–32.

Leijonhufvud, A. (1968) *On Keynesian Economics and the Economics of Keynes: A Study in Monetary Theory.* New York, Oxford University Press.

Meade, J.E. (1937) "A Simplified Model of Mr. Keynes' System," *Review of Economic Studies,* 4: 98–107.

Minogue, K. (2008) *Alien Powers: A Pure Theory of Ideology.* Wilmington, DE, ISI Books.

Oakeshott, M. (1991) "Rationalism in Politics," in M. Oakeshott (ed.) *Rationalism in Politics and Other Essays.* Indianapolis, IN, Liberty Press: 6–42.

Robbins, L. (1932) *An Essay on the Nature and Significance of Economic Science.* London, Macmillan.

Röpke, W. (1963) *Economics of the Free Society.* Chicago, Henry Regnery Company.

Samuelson, P.A. (1939a) "Interactions Between the Multiplier Analysis and the Principle of Acceleration," *Review of Economics and Statistics,* 21: 75–78.

Samuelson, P.A. (1939b) "A Synthesis of the Principle of Acceleration and the Multiplier," *Journal of Political Economy,* 47: 786–797.

Samuelson, P.A. (1940a) *Foundations of Economic Analysis: The Observational Significance of Economic Theory.* PhD thesis, Harvard University.

Samuelson, P.A. (1940b) "The Theory of Pump-Priming Reexamined," *American Economic Review,* 30: 492–506.

Samuelson, P.A. (1946) "Lord Keynes and the General Theory," *Econometrica,* 14: 187–200.

Samuelson, P.A. (1948) *Economics: An Introductory Analysis.* New York, McGraw-Hill.

Samuelson, P.A. (1960) "Reflections on Monetary Policy," *Review of Economics and Statistics,* 42: 263–269.

Samuelson, P.A. (1964) "The Case Against Goldwater's Economics," *The New York Times Magazine,* 25 October: SM28 and SM131–SM134.

Samuelson, P.A. (1983a) "My Life Philosophy," *The American Economist,* 27: 5–12.

Samuelson, P.A. (1983b) *Economics from the Heart: A Samuelson Sampler.* San Diego, Harcourt Brace Jovanovich.

Samuelson, P.A. (1985) "Succumbing to Keynesianism," *Challenge*, 27: 4–11.

Schumpeter, J.A. (1946) "John Maynard Keynes, 1883–1946," *American Economic Review*, 36: 495–518.

Schumpeter, J.A. (1949) "Science and Ideology," *American Economic Review*, 39: 346–359.

Silk, L. (1976) *The Economists.* New York, Basic Books.

3

Re-examining Samuelson's Operationalist Methodology

D. Wade Hands

> Today logical positivism is in a bear market. Quine, Kuhn, and other one-syllable local sages...are supposed to have killed it off. But experience has not enabled me to change my...methodologies. And the scientific guys who win the prizes still judge matters...the way I do. (Samuelson to Stephen Stigler, 5 June 1995)[1]

> I rather shy away from discussions of Methodology with a capital M. To paraphrase Shaw: those who can do science and those who can't prattle about its methodology. (Samuelson 1991: 240)

[1] Box 71, Paul A. Samuelson Papers, Economists' Papers Archive, David M. Rubenstein Rare Book & Manuscript Library, Duke University (all archival references in this chapter refer to the Economists' Papers Archive at Duke).

D. Wade Hands (✉)
University of Puget Sound, Tacoma, WA, USA
e-mail: hands@pugetsound.edu

R. A. Cord et al. (eds.), *Paul Samuelson*, Remaking Economics: Eminent Post-War Economists, https://doi.org/10.1057/978-1-137-56812-0_3

1 Introduction

Paul Samuelson's ideas about economic methodology have always been identified with Percy Bridgman's (1927) *operationalist* account of the meaning of scientific concepts. Samuelson was exposed to operationalist ideas as an undergraduate at the University of Chicago, and he began thinking about methodological issues in operationalist terms very early; one of his earliest publications began by questioning whether utility analysis had become "*meaningless* in the operational sense of modern science?" (Samuelson 1938a: 344; italics in original). The operationalist theme runs throughout *Foundations* (1947) and also his earlier thesis: *Foundations of Analytical Economics: The Observational Significance of Economic Theory* (Samuelson 1940). In the opening paragraphs of *Foundations,* Samuelson argues that previous economists have not paid sufficient attention to "the derivation of *operationally meaningful* theorems" (Samuelson 1947: 3–4; italics in original).

Not only did Samuelson endorse operationalism as the proper approach to economic methodology, his *Foundations* provided the technical tools for economic analysis along operationalist lines; he also identified the revealed preference theory he introduced in 1938 as the best example of economic theorizing exemplifying the operationalist methodology. As he put it later in life:

> Since the emphasis of my *Foundations of Economic Analysis* on "operationally meaningful theorems" has been brought up, it gives me the opportunity to use my strength ... The doctrines of revealed preference provide the most literal example of a theory that has been stripped down to its bare implications for empirical realism: Occam's Razor has cut away every zipper, collar, shift, and fig leaf. (Samuelson 1964: 738)

Although Samuelson's operationalism received less attention than Milton Friedman's 1953 essay (Friedman 1953), it is fair to say that the ideas of Friedman and Samuelson were two of the most popular subjects for methodological debate by economists during the second half of the twentieth century,[2] at least until they were crowded out by the ideas of philosophers and historians of science like Karl Popper, Thomas Kuhn, and Imre Lakatos during the 1970s and 1980s. All of these developments are now relatively non-controversial and discussed in detail in various surveys of economic methodology (e.g., Blaug 1992; Boumans and Davis 2015; Caldwell 1994; Hands 2001).

The goal of this paper is to *re-examine* Samuelson's operationalist methodology in light of (i) recent historical work on Samuelson (facilitated by the extensive Samuelson Papers at Duke University) and (ii) the economic theory most emblematic of that methodology (revealed preference theory). In both cases, the paper will provide a thicker and more detailed history of what Samuelson wrote about operationalist methodology in *Foundations* and his cluster of papers on the subject during the 1960s.

2 Samuelson, Bridgman, Operationalism, Positivism, and All That

Bridgman's operationalism was part of the positivist tradition in the philosophy of science, but it represented only one particular interpretation of a fairly narrow aspect of the broader positivist tradition. Most operationalists were influenced by positivist ideas, but only a small fraction of positivists would call themselves operationalists.[3] Although there are many different versions of positivist philosophy of science, one early theme was a sharp demarcation between that which is *meaningful* and that which is *meaningless.* In later accounts, the criterion of meaningfulness was softened to cognitively meaningful or cognitively significant, and eventually

[2]This literature includes Archibald (1963), Cohen (1995), Garb (1965), Gordon (1955a, b), Lerner (1965), Machlup (1964, 1966), Massey (1965), Nagel (1963), Samuelson (1955, 1963, 1964, 1965), Simon (1963), and Wong (1973, 2006).

[3]I say "most" and not "all" because there were some American pragmatists—John Dewey in particular—who were sympathetic to operationalist ideas but interpreted them differently than most operationalists and did not self-identify with the positivist tradition. See Hands (2004) for a discussion of these issues.

just scientific, but the notion that some forms of discourse have the epistemic/cognitive right stuff and that others do not is a defining feature of the positivist conception of science.[4] Logic and mathematics were meaningful (when validly derived). However, they were purely analytic and true in all possible worlds; only *science* provided meaningful synthetic knowledge about the empirical world. Given the positivist commitment to empiricism, science started from statements in some phenomenal observation (protocol) language—the empirical basis—and statements involving scientific theories and laws were meaningful only when they were built up from, or rigidly linked to, this empirical basis. Although it was assumed that the empirical basis was purely observational, it was clear that scientific theories and laws involved *theoretical terms*—electron, force, gene, utility, preferences, etc.—that were not purely observational. Thus, cognitively meaningful science required *correspondence rules* (or rules of interpretation) that connected the various theoretical terms and concepts with the empirical basis. Given such correspondence rules, scientific propositions involving theoretical terms would be linked to observation statements and thus could be potentially testable by empirical evidence. As the philosopher Gerald Massy put it in his comment on Samuelson (1964): correspondence rules "legislate the official rates for converting theoretical paper money into factual coin" (Massey 1965: 1159). Such correspondence rules are part of the necessary background for the *verifiability criterion of meaningfulness*; for a proposition to be scientifically meaningful, it must be "in principle verifiable," that is "observational evidence can be described which, if actually obtained, would conclusively establish the truth of the sentence" (Hempel 1965: 103).

Given this background, we can be more specific about what it means to be operationally meaningful in Bridgman's sense. Like so many physicists and philosophers, Bridgman found Einstein's general theory of relativity in the early 1900s extremely disruptive; both the empirical basis and the theoretical concepts that had constituted our bedrock knowledge about the physical universe suddenly changed, and there was a strong desire to find something invariant—"permanent mental relations" (Bridgman

[4]See any of the traditional texts on so-called received view philosophy of science (e.g., Hempel 1965; Nagel 1961; Suppe 1977) or for a discussion of these issues with an eye toward economics, see Caldwell (1994: Chapters 2–4) or Hands (2001: Chapter 3).

1927: 2)—that would render physical science less easily disrupted. Bridgman found the desired invariants in the physical *operations* associated with various scientific concepts and terms. In particular, according to Bridgman's 1927 version of operationalism (the one relevant to Samuelson's methodological writings), a theoretical term or concept is *operationally meaningful* if and only if it can be characterized by a series of specific operations, and its meaning is *defined by*, and is thus *synonymous with*, that set of operations. Bridgman used "length" as an example:

> We may illustrate by considering the concept of length: what do we mean by the length of an object? … To find the length of an object, we have to perform certain physical operations. The concept of length is therefore fixed when the operations by which length is measured are fixed: that is, the concept of length involves as much as and nothing more than the set of operations by which length is determined. In general, we mean by any concept nothing more than a set of operations; *the concept is synonymous with the corresponding set of operations.* (ibid.: 5; italics in original)

So why did Bridgman think such operationalism made physics less susceptible to major disruptions? The stabilizing impact of operationalism is at least twofold. On the one hand, much of what was previously taken as the theoretical foundations of physics would need to be given up since it was not operational in this strict sense (ibid.: 28). Less would need to be sacrificed in future theory change because fewer concepts would be considered absolute or universal. Perhaps this is one way to interpret the motivations behind Samuelson's original revealed preference paper in 1938, a paper which also responded to a disruption: the ordinal revolution in consumer choice theory. Secondly, operationalist physics becomes less brittle because theoretical terms are more relative: defined *relative to a set of operations*. As Bridgman explained: "Relativity in the general sense is the merest truism if the operational definition of concept is accepted, and since our concepts are constructed of operations, all our knowledge must unescapably be relative to the operations selected" (ibid.: 25). Thus, the application of operationalism would mean more, and more relative, theoretical terms, which in turn implied that physics would be more flexible because it would no longer rest on a small number of universal foundational concepts.

Of course, there are many potential problems with operationalism,[5] but the one that seems to have received the most attention is the *uniqueness* of the operation-concept relation; each *operation* will define a different *concept* creating a plethora of different concepts. As Bridgman himself notes: "In *principle* the operations by which length is measured should be *uniquely* specified. If we have more than one set of operations, we have more than one concept, and strictly there should be a separate name to correspond to each different set of operations" (ibid.: 10; italics in original).

Having a theoretical term defined for each measurement operation might build in flexibility by distributing the epistemic responsibility over more, each less critical, theoretical concepts, but it also leads to less systematic science and more ambiguity. Another common criticism, closely linked to the uniqueness problem, is what might be called the progress incommensurability problem, a new operation that brings about an *improvement* in scientific measurement which also creates a new theoretical concept (see Gillies 1972: 6–7). Because of these and other problems, operationalism has always been a controversial position, so much so that it was eventually disowned by Bridgman himself: "I have only a historical connection with this thing called 'operationalism.' In short, I feel that I have created a Frankenstein, which has certainly got away from me. I abhor the word *operationalism* or *operationism*, which seems to imply a dogma, or at least a thesis of some kind" (Bridgman 1954: 224; italics in original).

In addition to the various logical and practical problems identified by philosophers of science, operationalism has also been a victim of broader historical changes. The intellectual, specifically epistemic, context that initially motivated Bridgman to endorse operationalist ideas, and initially encouraged scientists to find solace in such ideas, is no longer with us.

All this said, operationalism did have a profound impact on certain areas of the social sciences during the second quarter of the twentieth century.

[5]The literature is extensive, but a wide-ranging sample is Bergmann (1954), Chang (2009), Gillies (1972), Green (1992), Hempel (1954), Nagel (1961), and Suppe (1972, 1977).

One clear example is psychology. The philosopher Frederick Suppe offers particularly sharp comments on this influence:

> On the negative side, this century Positivistic philosophy of science has had a profound impact and influence on several of the less advanced branches of science such as behavioral psychology...with consequences that were arguably disastrous – though a strong case can be made that much of this was due largely to the uncritical and unsophisticated acceptance of outdated philosophical views (e.g. operationalism). (Suppe 1979: 330)[6]

One additional background point to be made about Samuelson's methodological arguments concerns his views on the nature of scientific theories and scientific explanation. Samuelson defended a *descriptivist* view of scientific theories and argued for a closely related position that *science does not provide explanations* (at least explanations that go beyond the re-description of observables). The descriptive view of theories requires the direct "translatability of theoretical statements into statements about observable things," and, as a result, it often carries with it the "conception that the sciences never 'explain' anything, but merely 'describe' in a 'simple' or 'economical' fashion the succession and concomitance of events" (Nagel 1961: 118–119). Samuelson repeated his position on description and explanation in his methodological writings throughout his career: "a description...that works to describe well a wide range of observable reality is all the 'explanation' we can ever get (or need desire) here on earth ... *An explanation, as used legitimately in science, is a better kind of description and not something that goes ultimately beyond description*" (Samuelson 1965: 1165; italics in original).

And:

[6]When one discusses operationalism in psychology and to a lesser extent economics, one immediately raises the question of the impact of *behaviorism* in these social sciences, since operationalism is frequently—sometimes correctly and sometime incorrectly—associated with behaviorism. But the impact of behaviorism and its relationship to operationalism in the social sciences is a very complex topic that has generated a massive literature in the history and philosophy of the social sciences. Given this, I will stay on task and defer the broader question of behaviorism for another time. Here, I will focus exclusively on Samuelson and his operationalist methodology sans behaviorism.

> Unpopular these days are the views of…crude logical positivists, who deem good theories to be merely economical descriptions of the complex facts … When we are able to give a pleasingly satisfactory 'HOW' for the way of the world, that gives the only approach to 'WHY' that we shall ever attain. (Samuelson 1991: 242; upper case in original)

Samuelson did provide some argumentation[7] for these positions, but they were never sustained or particularly rigorous philosophical arguments; they generally took the form of strongly worded statements of his own beliefs about scientific theories and explanations, beliefs about both what described (good) science and how it (good science) ought to be done.[8] While the descriptivist position on scientific theories and the reduction of explanation to description were certainly characteristic of early positivism, it is not at all clear how these views relate to operationalism. While descriptivism and operationalism are both strongly empiricist and positivist in spirit, they are not the same thing; being able to translate theoretical statements into purely observational statements is not equivalent to defining theoretical terms by physical operations. Bridgman's operations, as he himself noted (see above), are process-based and relativizing, and this is much more human-centered than the (presumed to be timeless) protocol language of the positivist empirical basis.[9] As Samuelson's biographer Roger Backhouse explains:

> Bridgman's operational methods were adopted by logical positivists and behavioral social scientists (notably Skinner), but were taken in directions

---

[7] Wong (1973: 319) discussed six of Samuelson's different arguments and raised reasonable concerns about each.

[8] In many ways, it is disappointing that Samuelson continued to say the same things about economic methodology in published work throughout his life. It is disappointing because there are a few places in his correspondence where he expressed not only understanding of, but sympathy for, some of the ideas in post-positivist philosophy of science. For example: "the real objection to positivism in philosophy, I suppose, is that when you get down to the nitty-gritty, at the very frontier of what you mean about meaning, it cannot deliver the goods. When I read…Quine on Two Dogmas…I am distressed – because the simple-minded distinctions that my youthful reading of Ayer and other such types made me think can be maintained turn out to be fuzzy and even self-contradictory. And most logical positivists of the 1930s, who have not gone senile have recanted on their faith in their simplicities" (Samuelson to Hahn, 14 January, 1972, Box 36).

[9] This human and intentional property of operations was precisely that which attracted pragmatists like John Dewey to operationalism even though they were generally anti-positivist. See Footnote 3.

> different from those in which Bridgman himself wished to go. Bridgman held that there was an irreducibly individual, subjective element in all knowledge, and he was critical of attempts…to equate his operational method with their attempts to derive rules by which the objectivity of knowledge could be ensured: that was an impossible goal. Given this ambiguity, we need to be careful in imputing to Samuelson a particular interpretation of operationalism, for though he was to make the idea central to his work, there is little evidence of how much he read and precisely what he made of it…or of personal interactions with Bridgman that might have colored his reading of his [Bridgman's] work. (Backhouse 2017: 200–201)

The bottom line is that although Samuelson consistently said that he endorsed an economic methodology that was positivist, operationalist, descriptivist, and reduced explanation to description, it was not clear exactly how he interpreted each of these terms or how his meaning related to the relevant philosophical literature. Even more importantly, it was not clear how these various philosophical ideas were supposed to hang together into a coherent methodological position.

This section has given us a fairly detailed background on operationalism. This background is useful for the re-examination in the rest of the paper, but that said, most of this information was available when Samuelson was debating various economists and philosophers about operationalism during the 1960s. It is now time to turn to some information that was not available at that time.

3 Samuelson, Bridgman, and Operationalism: A Thicker History

We now have much more information about Paul Samuelson's professional life and ideas than was the case a few decades ago. This is certainly a result of the extraordinary depth and breadth of the personal papers that he left behind (containing, e.g., nearly every draft and piece of professional correspondence from the 1940s on), but it is also due to the diligence of a number of historians of economic thought who have put these papers to very productive use. This is true in almost all areas of Samuelson's professional life—from empirical work, to service, to economic pedagogy, to the many different areas of economic theory where he made important contributions—but it is also true of his methodological ideas. The purpose of this section is to use these newer resources to get a better understanding of Samuelson's methodological thinking than what is available from just his writings on the subject.

As noted above, Samuelson was exposed to operationalist ideas as a Chicago undergraduate, but his main exposure came during his years at Harvard, particularly during his three years in the Society of Fellows. One of the important figures at Harvard during this time

> was physicist Percy Bridgman (1882-1961), a teacher at Harvard since 1910, whose reputation rested on his experimental work on thermodynamics, for which he later (1946) received the Nobel Prize for physics. He attracted the attention of philosophers and students of other disciplines with *The Logic of Modern Physics* (1927), which put forward the method of 'operational analysis'. Samuelson remembered having been introduced to operationalism by Henry Schultz…in Chicago. However, the development and spread of operational analysis was most closely linked to Harvard, where it proved particularly influential in psychology … Samuelson, who was to make much use of operationalism, had probably attended Percy Bridgman's lectures in the autumn term of 1936. In any case, he could hardly have avoided Bridgman, who had close connections with those involved in the Society of Fellows. (Backhouse 2017: 199)

Another aspect of Samuelson's professional life, particularly in the early years, that becomes much clearer from archive-based research is the profound impact that a number of his teachers and colleagues had on the development of his overall intellectual vision: scholars such as Alvin Hansen, Lawrence Henderson, Frank Knight, Joseph Schumpeter, and others. In the area of economic methodology, and particularly the scientific vision of *Foundations* and Samuelson's other early work, the most important such scholar was Edwin Bidwell Wilson (1879–1964) who had been a student of Josiah Willard Gibbs at Yale and tried to carry on Gibbs's mathematical and scientific tradition. Wilson was a mathematician with wide-ranging interests who taught Samuelson mathematical economics and mathematical statistics at Harvard during 1936–1937 and who became a very important influence on Samuelson's thinking about the relationship between science and mathematics (see Backhouse 2015, 2017; Carvajalino 2016, 2018). As Samuelson explains:

> Perhaps most relevant of all for the genesis of *Foundations*, Wilson was at Harvard. He was the great Willard Gibbs' last (and, essentially, only) protege at Yale. He was a mathematician, a mathematical physicist, a mathematical statistician, a mathematical economist, a polymath who had done first-class work in many fields of the natural and social sciences. I was perhaps his only disciple: in 1935-36, Abram Bergson, Sidney Alexander, Joseph Schumpeter, and I were the only students in his mathematical economics seminar. (Samuelson 1998: 1376)

Wilson had a unique take on the foundations of both science and mathematics. On the one hand, he was drawn toward mathematics directly connected to the practice of science and critical of purely formalist or logical approaches, such as those of David Hilbert or Bertrand Russell. But he was also skeptical about the statistical approaches associated with Karl Pearson and Ronald Fisher. Although much of mathematical economics could be done using traditional calculus-based techniques, Wilson worked, and pushed Samuelson to work, toward analysis in terms of finite differences and discrete mathematics. Unlike much of physical science, the empirical data of economic science is discrete, and developing mathematical techniques that could be used in such analysis was an important and original contribution to economics. It was precisely this project that Wilson encouraged Samuelson to pursue:

> Samuelson learned from Wilson the importance of basing economic theory on…the general case where functions were not necessarily smooth and differentiable. Their correspondence makes it clear that Wilson pushed Samuelson to analyze finite changes and, as Gibbs had done, to base conclusions on inequalities linked to generalized notions of convexity. Directing Samuelson to the types of mathematics on which he was to rely in much of his work…techniques that Samuelson was later to use in *Foundations*, and which marked his book out from previous work on the subject. (Backhouse 2015: 333)

Although *Foundations* ended up not being an entirely new approach to economic analysis based on discrete mathematics, which might have been Wilson's ideal case, it provided tools for translating important existing, calculus-based, comparative statics results into a mathematical framework that was closer to Wilson's discrete and more data-ready approach: "a way of mediating between the new and the old" (Carvajalino 2016: 144). Thus, in *Foundations* "Samuelson attempted, albeit in highly abstract and analytical ways, to connect extant economic theory with data, by means of establishing one-to-one correspondences between the continuous cases as found in marginal and differential calculus and the finite cases found in the discrete world of economic phenomena" (ibid.). While it remains an open question how much success Samuelson had in moving mathematical economics out of differential calculus and into discrete mathematics, either in *Foundations* or in later work,[10] there is no doubt that he was *trying* to move in that direction and that Wilson's influence was one of the reasons why.

Finally, it is important to remember that while Wilson's ideas were very important to the development of the young Samuelson's methodological thinking, they were certainly not the only ideas that mattered; his understanding of operational analysis and methodological issues was mediated by his discussions not only with Wilson, but also "Schumpeter, Henderson, and colleagues in the Society of Fellows, all of whom had strong views on scientific method" (Backhouse 2017: 201).

All of these things help us understand why Samuelson's operationalist methodology, although consistently maintained and assertively stated, was never particularly clear or coherent with respect to the philosophical details. A non-exhaustive list of these factors would include: (i) He was

---

[10] I would suggest that he was a little less successful than Backhouse and Carvajalino seem to argue. Two of the reasons for this are: (i) the sheer fact that the number of pages in *Foundations* (and Samuelson's later work) where the analysis is conducted in terms of derivatives and differential equations is significantly larger than the amount conducted in terms of discrete mathematics and (ii) also the fact that many of the linear inequalities are linear because they come from Jacobian or Hessian matrices and were thus also calculus-based. Note that this is not a criticism of the argument that Samuelson was *trying* to do mathematical economics in a Wilsonian way—it seems clear he was. It simply means that discrete mathematics was extremely difficult in the pre-computer age. Another factor may have been that Samuelson always saw his work as fitting into, and improving on, the grand flow of economic ideas, and doing that, and having it recognized as such, is much easier when the theory is couched in the same mathematical formalism.

very young when his methodological ideas were initially formed, (ii) he maintained a lifelong epistemic preference for the empiricism of Mach and other early positivists even though the prevailing philosophical trends ran against such ideas, (iii) he was profoundly influenced by Wilson, but Wilson himself had a fairly complex view of science and mathematics which, although it clearly nudged Samuelson in the direction of developing the mathematical tools of *Foundations*, did little to help clarify the relevant philosophical—as opposed to mathematical or structural—foundations of economic theory, (iv) operationalism itself is a position that is simultaneously ambiguous and problematic; Bridgman's own views evolved over time, philosophers were generally critical even when positivist ideas were still dominant (although many psychologists embraced it), and neither Wilson nor Samuelson (for different reasons) interpreted operationalism in exactly the way that Bridgman did in his original 1927 book, and finally (v) there were many other intellectual influences on Samuelson early in his career and all of those—Knight, Schumpeter, Henderson, Hansen, as well as others not mentioned above (Abram Bergson, Wassily Leontief, Paul Sweezy, etc.)—had quite different views on methodological issues than either Bridgman or Wilson.

While these factors can account for the various tensions and lack of clarity in Samuelson's methodological writings, they do not really explain why Samuelson failed to revise, or attempt to improve, his methodological arguments. Given that Samuelson's work helped bring about major developments in economics—the mathematical revolution, the Keynesian Revolution, the new welfare economics, a major change in economic pedagogy (initiated by *Economics* in 1948 Samuelson 1948a), and a host of other contributions—one would have expected his methodological ideas to have developed along with his economics, but at least with respect to what he wrote on methodology, they did not. What he said about methodological issues remained the same positivist-operationalist narrative that characterized what he said in the methodological debates of the 1960s as well as what he wrote about the basis of *Foundations* later in life.

Of course, Samuelson was extraordinarily busy doing economics, but so were other influential economists who found time for serious methodological research and supported methodological research among young economists; Lionel Robbins comes to mind. It is also telling that while most influential economic theorists of the middle of the twentieth century had little or no interest in the history of economic thought, it was actually a field where Samuelson made contributions (e.g., see Medema and Waterman 2015). So, yes, Samuelson had tight constraints on his time, but he also revealed a preference to work on things other than methodology. Another personal characteristic that might explain Samuelson's lack of interest in updating his early statements about operationalism may simply be that he did not admit changing his views on scholarly questions very often. There might be something to this, but Samuelson's views on various economic theories as well as his political views did actually change over time. They changed slowly, rather than abruptly, but they changed. A good example is his slow commitment to Keynesian macroeconomics—first critical, then sympathetic to certain specific aspects, then finally developing his own version of "a Keynesianism that was distinct from the one that came to dominate postwar macroeconomic theory" (Backhouse 2017: 525)—and given this, a general unwillingness to admit changing his views does not seem to be an adequate explanation of his methodological stasis.

So why then? I would suggest that much of the resistance came from the simple fact that Samuelson never had much interest in, or appreciation of, methodology or philosophy of science. He certainly was, and clearly thought of himself as, much more of a science *doer* than as a philosopher reflecting on how science should be done (note his comment about methodological prattle in the epigraph). One can find many Samuelson quotes that suggest a low regard for the philosophy of science, but his comment on a 1963 paper by Ernst Nagel is illustrative: "Methodological discussion, like calisthenics and spinach, is good for us, and Dr. Nagel deserves our thanks for taking the time away from other sciences to help straighten us economists out. It is the Lord's work, and we are grateful" (Samuelson 1963: 231).

We actually find this attitude throughout his life, and it helps explain both the amount of ambiguity he was willing to live with in his methodological writing—certainly far more than he would let pass in his economic theory—as well as his tendency to not update or revise what he had written. One particular example, two years before *Foundations* was published, provides additional evidence for this.

Samuelson was presented with an…opportunity to become involved with scientists (and philosophers) when Leontief conveyed to him an invitation to join the Inter-Scientific Discussion Group. This group was a part of the Unity of Science movement … A common theme among those behind the discussion group was an affinity with Bridgman's operationalism … Given Samuelson's emphasis on operationalism in his thesis and the book he was currently writing, it would be natural to deduce that it was these links that induced him to accept Leontief's invitation (Backhouse 2017: 450).

But Samuelson attended only a handful of meetings over the next two years and showed little interest in the discussion group. Given this, Backhouse concludes:

> Samuelson was busy, but given his capacity for fitting commitments into his schedule, it is hard not to conclude that, despite his emphasis on operationalism in his thesis and in *Foundations*…he had no deep interest in the philosophy of science…although he chose to use the term *operationalism* – rather than alternatives such as *testability*, *refutability*, or *falsificationism* – there is no evidence that he engaged seriously with the related philosophical issues. (ibid.: 450–451; italics in original)

4 Samuelson, Operationalism, and Empirical Revealed Preference Theory

As noted above, Samuelson considered revealed preference theory (hereafter RPT) to be an exemplar of operationalist practice in economics. This section will discuss the development of RPT and attempt to trace whatever operationalist thread runs through it. I will try to make the history of RPT relatively brief since I have discussed it in other contexts (see Hands 2013, 2014, 2017a).

Samuelson (1938b) was critical of ordinal utility theory—particularly Hicks and Allen (1934)—because it did not go far enough to eliminate utility/preference from the theory of consumer choice. He sought to replace utility-preference-based theory with an alternative theoretical framework: “I propose, therefore, that we start anew in direct attack upon the problem, dropping off the last vestiges of the utility analysis” (Samuelson 1938b: 62). The goal was to develop an alternative theory of consumer behavior that would have the same implications as ordinal utility theory—negative substitution effects and the symmetry and negative semidefiniteness of the Slutsky substitution matrix—but without assuming the consumer had a well-behaved ordinal utility function or well-ordered preferences.[11]

The specific condition that Samuelson introduced came to be called the *Weak Axiom of Revealed Preference* (WARP). The intuition behind the axiom is that if an individual chooses x_0 when x_1 is available (x_0 is revealed preferred to x_1), then x_1 would only be chosen if x_0 were not available (e.g., if x_0 were no longer affordable). In particular, if p_0 and p_1 are n-dimensional price vectors, and $h(p)$ is the consumer's demand function, so $h(p_0)$ is the quantity purchased at p_0 and $h(p_1)$ is the quantity purchased at p_1, then the consistency condition was given by:

$$\sum p_0 h(p_1) \leq \sum p_0 h(p_0) \rightarrow \sum p_1 h(p_0) > \sum p_1 h(p_1)$$

It is clear this condition would hold if the consumer were maximizing a well-behaved ordinal utility function subject to the standard linear budget constraint, but Samuelson's 1938 results demonstrated that WARP—along with a binding budget constraint—implied all of the standard restrictions on consumer demand functions, at least all except one (Slutsky symmetry), without the consumer maximizing, or even having, a utility function. Samuelson's original paper demonstrated that: (i) WARP was necessary for ordinal utility theory (hereafter OUT) so WARP $\leftarrow$ OUT

[11]Since this chapter is primarily concerned with Samuelson's methodology and not his economic theory, it is useful to note that RPT was fundamentally a *methodological* program. Samuelson did not introduce RPT because of some practical problem with ordinal utility theory, for example, to correct for particular empirical refutations or anomalies or to extend the possible range of application of the theory. He was trying to develop a theory that would have the same empirical implications as ordinal utility theory—the exact same Slutsky conditions—but one that would rest on more epistemically palatable foundations. As Daniel Hausman explains: “The *raison d'être* of revealed-preference theory was philosophical. It was supposed to enable economists to rid economic theory of references to subjective preferences or to make those references respectable” (Hausman 2000: 112).

and (ii) that WARP was almost sufficient for OUT (one implication was missing, that one implication being, not coincidentally, the integrability condition that guaranteed the existence of an underlying utility function). The revealed preference condition that was both necessary and sufficient for ordinal utility theory did not come until 1950 with Houthakker's strong axiom of revealed preference (SARP). Since SARP $\longleftrightarrow$ OUT and the two approaches have exactly the same implications, the two theories of consumer choice are *equivalent*; "the 'revealed preference' and 'utility function'...approaches to the theory of consumer's behaviour are therefore formally the same" (Houthakker 1950: 173). So, by the early 1950s the majority of economic theorists were "treating the revealed preference and utility approaches as complements rather than substitutes" (Pollak 1990: 144).

There are contemporary versions of RPT that are direct descendants of WARP and SARP, but the literature that involves Samuelson's original and direct contribution to RPT effectively ends with the papers Samuelson (1948b, 1950). He continued to talk about RPT in various contexts—including the methodological debates of the 1960s, various retrospective papers, and even his Nobel Lecture (Samuelson 1972)—but made no more substantive contributions to the theory of revealed preference and he also never published any empirical studies which applied revealed preference analysis to practical or policy questions.

How does WARP stand up to Samuelson's positivist and operationalist methodological standards? Can the theoretical concept of WARP be translated into statements in the purely observational language of prices and quantities purchased, as positivist strictures require? Does revealed preference analysis produce operationally meaningful theorems? Is the theoretical concept "revealed preferred" defined by, and equivalent to, a series of systematic operations? Or, since the practical question is not whether WARP does all these things perfectly, but whether it does them better than OUT, perhaps these questions should all be reframed in contrastive terms using standard consumer choice theory as the reference point.

It is certainly clear that Samuelson thought his RPT was valid operationalist science or at least more scientifically adequate than OUT. He closed the 1938 paper on precisely these points. His postulates

> are less restrictive than the usual setup, and logically equivalent to the reformulation of Hicks and Allen. It is hoped, however, that the orientation given here is more directly based upon those elements which must be taken as *data* by economic science, and is more *meaningful* in its formulation. Even if this will not be granted, the results...are a useful extension of the restrictions in the older analysis, being directly related to the demand functions. (Samuelson 1938b: 70–71; italics added)[12]

There is a draft of the original revealed preference paper in the archives,[13] and although it is longer and differs in various ways, it closes with the same statement about data and meaningful implications.

In a few places, Samuelson even argued that the Wilson-inspired mathematics of finite differences—which is clearly closer to the structure of data than functions defined over real numbers—was a characteristic of both *Foundations* and his papers on RPT. As he explains in his introduction to the 1983 revised version of *Foundations*:

> [The book] began the systematic use of *finite inequalities* in modern economics. To say that raising price from p_1 to p_2 will lower quantity bought from q_1 to q_2 along a demand curve, $q = f(p)$, one need not be able to say that $f'(p)$ is almost everywhere negative on the interval (p_1, p_2). It will do to know that $(p_2 - p_1)(q_2 - q_1) = \Delta p \Delta q < 0$ for every two distinct points on the demand curve. Where Newtonian calculus helps, economists are grateful. But where it doesn't apply, as when price can take on only integral (or rational) values, we are even more grateful for more general methods. When I stumbled on the notion of revealed preference in 1937, I was shoved into the task of trying to free classical mathematical analysis from its calculus corsets. (Samuelson 1983: xvii–xviii; italics in original)

---

12 Samuelson says that WARP was "logically equivalent to the reformulation of Hicks and Allen," but that is not the case in general (although it is true for only two goods), although Samuelson did not know this at the time (and nor did anyone else). It was not until Houthakker's paper that it became clear that it was SARP, not WARP, that was equivalent to OUT. It was not until, as Samuelson put it: "Mr. Houthakker's paper arrived in the daily mail" (Samuelson 1950: 370).

13 Samuelson "New Foundations for the Pure Theory of Consumer's Behavior," Box 152 (no date, but definitely from the 1930s; it says "Paul A. Samuelson Harvard University"). Backhouse says the paper "is undated but is assumed to be 1937" (Backhouse 2017: 652, fn. 40).

Given all this, it certainly seems clear that Samuelson thought his work on RPT was quite consistent with, even exemplary of, the positivist and operationalist methodology he endorsed. But was he right? The short answer clearly seems to be "no." The first and probably most important problem is that Samuelson did not start with data; there are no tables of numbers in *Foundations* or in his revealed preference papers. But not only is there no actual data, there are no variables that could be placeholders for future data, because the relevant independent variables are not finite, they are real numbers. Samuelson 1938 starts with continuous, in fact differentiable, demand functions with prices as vectors of real numbers:

> I assume in the beginning as known, i.e., *empirically determinable under ideal conditions*, the amounts of n economic goods which will be purchased per unit time by an individual faced with the prices of these goods and with a given total expenditure. It is assumed that prices are taken as given parameters not subject to influence by the individual … For mathematical convenience we assume that all our functions and their derivatives of the desired order are continuous with no singularities in the region under discussion. (Samuelson 1938b: 62–63; italics added)

Samuelson says these functions are "empirically determinable under ideal conditions," but it is not clear how one could "determine" differentiable functions defined over (infinite) real variables from discrete choice data. One could statistically estimate the functions from such data, but the result would require statistical inference and a number of theoretical commitments that go beyond the strict reduction of all theoretical terms to purely observational statements as required by the narrow positivist interpretation of correspondence rules. As Robert Pollak aptly suggested, it would require a "miraculous revelation of consumer demand functions to the economist-observer" (Pollak 1990: 150). The "observables" that serve as epistemic grounding are demand functions given as purely mathematical objects: $\psi_i = h^i(p_1, \ldots p_n, I)$ for all i, and $\sum_i \psi_i p_i = I$ (see Samuelson 1938b: 62).

However, this concern is with a violation of strict positivist notions of what counts as observational. There seems to be an even bigger problem with respect to the operational meaningfulness of the results. WARP implies that the (own) Slutsky terms are negative and that the Slutsky matrix is negative semidefinite. But what "operation" defines these theoretical terms? The Slutsky matrix consists of derivatives of income-compensated demand functions which are purely mathematical transformations of the given abstract demand functions. This all seems far too purely mathematical and far too remote from any empirical measurement operation to be operationally meaningful. Finally, given the formalist origins of all these transformations, in what sense could the laws (the sign restrictions on the Slutsky matrix) be considered purely *descriptive*?

Since SARP gives both necessary and sufficient conditions, it is a stricter version of RPT, but it starts from the same abstract continuous demand functions and inherits all of the same problems about requiring the miraculous revelation of those, assumed to be observable, functions. Also, given the equivalence of OUT and SARP, the explanatory power of the two theories will be the same. Samuelson notes early on in the original 1938 paper that moving from cardinal to ordinal utility "robbed it of its only possible virtue as an *explanation* of human behaviour in other than a circular sense" (ibid.: 61; italics in original), so given its identity with OUT, the strong axiom seems to be without explanatory power as well (see Wong 1973: 317). Of course, explanation was not something that Samuelson was looking for in demand theory anyway, but it is clear that since SARP inherited WARP's domain restrictions, it also inherited its methodological issues, in particular the inability to describe consumer behavior in a way that would live up to strict positivist standards.

This seems to be a negative conclusion about the scientific contribution of Samuelson's RPT, but it need not be. It is important to be clear about exactly what is being argued here and perhaps, more importantly, about what is *not* being argued. The argument is *not* that there was (or is) no possible way to empirically test Samuelson's RPT. Although extensive empirical research in RPT did not appear until the end of the twentieth century—a literature that will be discussed in the conclusion—there was some earlier experimental work that tried to empirically test versions of RPT. Such tests were difficult and the experimental setups often rudimentary, given the equivalence of OUT and SARP (and how close WARP is to SARP) it was often unclear which version of the rational consumer was actually being tested, and the empirical results were often ambiguous, but such a literature *did* exist (see Moscati 2007; Moscati and Tubaro 2011). In any case, the argument here is *not* that RPT was an inadequate empirical theory according to *any/every* sense of empirical; it is only that in its WARP and SARP form, it was not empirical in the very strict sense required by the early positivist standards that Samuelson identified as necessary for operationally meaningful economics. The point is the failure of Samuelson's RPT to live up to the strict methodological standards he explicitly endorsed—and thus *inconsistency* between his methodological prescriptions and his theoretical practice—and not necessarily the failure of RPT to live up to other, more reasonable, empirical standards.

So, what are we to make of this? I put the responsibility on philosophical problems with Samuelson's stated methodology rather than on any scientific problems with his theory of revealed preference. In other words, the inconsistency is simply a result of Samuelson's commitment to early positivist and operationalist methodological standards, and those standards are problematic.[14] This is certainly the conclusion that the vast majority of philosophers of science have reached about operationalism and the strictest forms of positivism, the views that Samuelson seemed to be most attracted to. In other words, they provided neither a good *description* of what has gone on in the best science nor a reasonable *normative standard* for what ought to be done in scientific practice.

Samuelson committed to these philosophical views early in his professional life—for a number of different reasons—as well as the belief that economics should be guided by these standards. This was consistent with Wilson's view, and it was a motivating scientific impulse behind much of Samuelson's early work. He was skeptical to some degree about the usefulness of philosophy of science even when positivist ideas were dominant and grew more so as philosophy moved away from these views. As a result, he had little interest in correcting the ambiguities of the methodological positions he originally defended. To have seriously revised his

[14]My assessment is thus similar to what Hausman calls the "methodological schizophrenia" of economics, whereby "methodological doctrine and practice regularly contradict one another. This schizophrenia is a symptom of the unsound philosophical premises underlying…economic methodology" (Hausman 1992: 152). I would also note that Samuelson's use of abstract mathematical functions presumed to be "empirically determinable under ideal conditions" was typical of the theoretical economics of his day. It may not seem very "empirical" today, but it was standard practice then. See Hands (2017a) for more details.

stated methodological position was simply not something he was interested in doing. Such "prattle" was neither his comparative advantage nor very rewarding (personally or professionally) and besides, dwelling on the fact that the "simple-minded distinctions" of his youthful views had turned out "to be fuzzy or even self-contradictory" was distressing (see Footnote 8). It was better to stick with economics where he had a clear comparative advantage and where his work was so well received. After all, early in his career was a great time to be an economist and he made the most of it:

> The times were ripe for *Foundations.* Nature abhors a vacuum, and *Foundations* helped fill the vacuum. I have written elsewhere about how much there was back in the 1930s waiting to be discovered and aching to be codified. I was like a fisher for trout in a virginal Canadian brook. You had only to cast your line and the fish jumped to meet your hook. (Samuelson 1998: 1377)

For Samuelson, economics was not only exciting and rewarding, but also socially important. Philosophy of science, on the other hand, was *distressing.* In economics, Samuelson was Mr. Science: "For among economists, Samuelson is Mr. Science. He is widely credited with establishing the scientific ideal in economics at the graduate and professional level with his 1947 *Foundations of Economic Analysis*" (Pearce and Hoover 1995: 184).

For Samuelson, real scientists *do* science, but they do not pick at it. In addition, whatever philosophers of science thought about the methodological positions he defended, or for that matter what other economists thought about them, Samuelson firmly believed that "the scientific guys who win the prizes still judge matters…the way I do" (epigraph).

5 Conclusion

Since I have nothing significant to add to the preceding paragraphs in the way of a conclusion, I will use this section to talk about some developments in RPT during the last few decades that seem to move it more in the methodological direction that Samuelson endorsed.

Despite Samuelson's desire for RPT to be "more directly based upon those elements which must be taken as *data* by economic science" (Samuelson 1938b: 71; italics in original), that was not the case for the RPT of the next few decades. Both Samuelson's WARP and Houthakker's SARP were initially presented as restrictions on abstract demand functions and that is how they were used by economists. An extensive literature developed in mathematical economics—a literature elsewhere that I have called "traditional revealed preference theory" (see Hands 2013)—which treated RPT as one of many useful mathematical restrictions—like gross substitutes, homogeneity, Walras' law, etc.—that could be used to generate useful results in demand theory and Walrasian general equilibrium theory. RPT had almost no contact with, or role in, applied empirical economics, which at the time was exclusively econometrics-based. Houthakker had proven a utility function *rationalization* result—for any demand function satisfying SARP, there always exists a utility function that if maximized subject to the standard budget constraint would generate that demand function—but it was not an empirically useful result, and there was no way to find such a utility function.

An extraordinary paper by Sidney Afriat in 1967—along with some user-friendly simplifications by Diewert (1973), Varian (1982), and others—changed this. What came to be called Afriat's theorem brought two important changes to RPT. First, the relevant revealed preference axiom—what came to be called the Generalized Axiom of Revealed Preference (GARP)—could be used for finite data, the kind of price-quantity data available in consumer choice theory, and second, it provided a way of determining the utility function that could have generated it. As Hal Varian explains:

> Most of the theoretical work [in RPT] starts with a demand function: a complete description of what would be chosen at any possible budget. Afriat (1967) offered quite a different approach to revealed preference theory. He started with a finite set of observed prices and choices and asked how to actually construct a utility function that would be consistent with these choices … This makes Afriat's approach much more suitable as a basis for empirical analysis. Afriat's approach was so novel that most researchers at the time did not recognize its value … Several years later Diewert (1973)

> offered a somewhat clearer exposition of Afriat's main results. (Varian 2006: 101)

Over time, these results opened up a new field of empirical revealed preference theory which has, during the last few decades, expanded into a number of different areas of applied economic analysis.[15] These empirical techniques start from (discrete) empirical choice data—in the consumer case, prices, and quantities, but applications have expanded beyond consumer choice theory—and if the data satisfies a version of GARP (there are a number of such restrictions), then it can be rationalized and a rationalizing utility function determined. These results can then be used in a number of ways in empirical-based economic analysis. Although a discussion of this empirical RPT, or the associated methodological issues, is beyond the scope of the current chapter, it does raise a number of interesting methodological questions, the most obvious being: Is this newer empirical RPT more consistent with Samuelson's methodological standards than traditional RPT was? It is a complex topic and certainly deserves a serious investigation, but let me just close with my own opinion about the answer. It seems to me that with respect to the connection between the empirical data and theoretical terms, the answer is clearly "yes." The newer GARP-based empirical RPT may not be consistent with the strictest version of the positivist empirical-to-theoretical relation—no science is—but it is certainly much closer than the abstract mathematical demand functions that were the starting point for Samuelson and others working in traditional RPT. This is of course consistent with contemporary philosophy of science where the observation-theoretical distinction is still important, but it is also much less rigid and more dependent on the local characteristics and pragmatic constraints of the relevant scientific community than it was for the positivists who imprinted their epistemic vision on the young Paul Samuelson. That said, having a unique physical operation define every theoretical term still seems to be very impractical, even if one starts with

[15]See Varian (2006) or Vermeulen (2012) for a general discussion of the GARP-based literature and the importance of Afriat's work in its development. Moscati and Tubaro (2011) discuss some of the early applications of these techniques, while Andreoni et al. (2013), Cherchye et al. (2009), and Crawford and De Rock (2014) provide accessible discussions of the empirical revealed preference literature. Various aspects of this literature are discussed in Hands (2013, 2017a, b).

finite price-quantity choice data. But then given what we know about operationalism—its history and philosophical standing—that is probably a good thing.

References

Afriat S.N. (1967) "The Construction of Utility Functions from Expenditure Data," *International Economic Review*, 8: 67–77.

Andreoni J., B.J. Gillen and W.T. Harbaugh (2013) "The Power of Revealed Preference Tests: Ex-Post Evaluation of Experimental Design," Working Paper, Department of Economics, University of Oregon.

Archibald, G.C. (1963) "Problems of Methodology—Discussion," *American Economic Review*, 53: 227–229.

Backhouse, R.E. (2015) "Revisiting Samuelson's Foundations of Economic Analysis," *Journal of Economic Literature*, 53: 326–350.

Backhouse, R.E. (2017) *Founder of Modern Economics: Paul A. Samuelson, Volume I: Becoming Samuelson, 1915–1948*. New York, Oxford University Press.

Bergmann, G. (1954) "Sense and Nonsense in Operationism," *The Scientific Monthly*, 79: 210–214.

Blaug, M. (1992) *The Methodology of Economics: Or How Economists Explain*. Second edition. Cambridge, Cambridge University Press. First edition, 1980.

Boumans, M. and J. Davis (2015) *Economic Methodology: Understanding Economics as a Science*. Second edition. New York, Palgrave. First edition, 2010.

Bridgman, P.W. (1927) *The Logic of Modern Physics*. New York, Macmillan.

Bridgman, P.W. (1954) "Remarks on the Present State of Operationalism," *The Scientific Monthly*, 79: 224–226.

Caldwell, B.J. (1994) *Beyond Positivism: Economic Methodology in the Twentieth Century*. Reissued with new preface. London, George Allen & Unwin. First edition, 1982.

Carvajalino, J. (2016) *Edwin B. Wilson at the Origin of Paul Samuelson's Mathematical Economics: Essays on the Interwoven History of Economics, Mathematics and Statistics in the US: 1900–1940*. PhD dissertation, University of Montreal at Quebec.

Carvajalino, J. (2018) "Samuelson's *Operationally Meaningful Theorems*: Reflections of E.B. Wilson's Methodological Attitude," *Journal of Economic Methodology*, 25: 143–159.

Chang, H. (2009) "Operationalism," in E.N. Zalta (ed.) *The Stanford Encyclopedia of Philosophy*. Fall 2009 edition. Available at https://plato.stanford.edu/archives/fall2009/entries/operationalism/.

Cherchye, L., I. Crawford, B. De Rock and F. Vermeulen (2009) "The Revealed Preference Approach to Demand," in D.J. Slottje (ed.) *Quantifying Consumer Preferences*. Bingley, UK, Emerald Group Publishing: 247–279.

Cohen, J. (1995) "Samuelson's Operationalist-Descriptivist Thesis," *Journal of Economic Methodology*, 2: 57–78.

Crawford, I. and B. De Rock (2014) "Empirical Revealed Preference," *Annual Review of Economics*, 6: 503–524.

Diewert, W.E. (1973) "Afriat and Revealed Preference Theory," *Review of Economic Studies*, 40: 419–425.

Friedman, M. (1953) "The Methodology of Positive Economics," in M. Friedman (ed.) *Essays in Positive Economics*. Chicago, University of Chicago Press: 3–43.

Garb, G. (1965) "Professor Samuelson on Theory and Realism: Comment," *American Economic Review*, 55: 1151–1153.

Gillies, D.A. (1972) "Operationalism," *Synthese*, 25: 1–24.

Gordon, D.F. (1955a) "Operational Propositions in Economic Theory," *Journal of Political Economy*, 63: 150–161.

Gordon, D.F. (1955b) "Professor Samuelson on Operationalism in Economic Theory," *Quarterly Journal of Economics*, 69: 305–310.

Green, C.D. (1992) "Of Immortal Mythological Beasts: Operationism in Psychology," *Theory & Psychology*, 2: 291–320.

Hands, D.W. (2001) *Reflection without Rules: Economic Methodology and Contemporary Science Theory*. Cambridge, Cambridge University Press.

Hands, D.W. (2004) "On Operationalisms and Economics," *Journal of Economic Issues*, 38: 953–968.

Hands, D.W. (2013) "Foundations of Contemporary Revealed Preference Theory," *Erkenntnis*, 78: 1081–1108.

Hands, D.W. (2014) "Paul Samuelson and Revealed Preference Theory," *History of Political Economy*, 46: 85–116.

Hands, D.W. (2017a) "The Road to Rationalization: A History of 'Where the Empirical Lives' (or has Lived) in Consumer Choice Theory," *European Journal of the History of Economic Thought*, 24: 555–588.

Hands, D.W. (2017b) "Revealed Preference, Afriat's Theorem, and Falsifiability: A Review Essay on *Revealed Preference Theory* by C.P. Chambers and F. Echenique," *Oeconomia*, 7: 409–438.

Hausman, D.M. (1992) *The Inexact and Separate Science of Economics.* Cambridge, Cambridge University Press.

Hausman, D.M. (2000) "Revealed Preference, Belief, and Game Theory," *Economics and Philosophy*, 16: 99–115.

Hempel, C.G. (1954) "A Logical Appraisal of Operationism," *The Scientific Monthly*, 79: 215–220. Reprinted as Chapter 5 of C.G. Hempel (1965) *Aspects of Scientific Explanation and Other Essays in the Philosophy of Science.* New York, The Free Press: 123–133.

Hempel, C.G. (1965) *Aspects of Scientific Explanation and Other Essays in the Philosophy of Science.* New York, The Free Press.

Hicks, J.R. and R.G.D. Allen (1934) "A Reconsideration of the Theory of Value, Parts I and II," *Economica*, New Series, 1: 52–76, 196–219.

Houthakker, H.S. (1950) "Revealed Preference and the Utility Function," *Economica*, New Series, 17: 159–174.

Lerner, A.P. (1965) "Professor Samuelson on Theory and Realism: Comment," *American Economic Review*, 55: 1153–1155.

Machlup, F. (1964) "Professor Samuelson on Theory and Realism," *American Economic Review*, 54: 733–735.

Machlup, F. (1966) "Operationalism and Pure Theory in Economics," in S.R. Krupp (ed.) *The Structure of Economic Science: Essays on Methodology.* Englewood Cliffs, NJ, Prentice-Hall: 53–67.

Massey, G.J. (1965) "Professor Samuelson on Theory and Realism: Comment," *American Economic Review*, 55: 1155–1164.

Medema, S.G. and A.M.C. Waterman (eds.) (2015) *Paul Samuelson on the History of Economic Analysis.* New York, Cambridge University Press.

Moscati, I. (2007) "Early Experiments in Consumer Demand Theory: 1930–1970," *History of Political Economy*, 39: 359-401.

Moscati, I. and P. Tubaro (2011) "Becker Random Behavior and the As-If Defense of Rational Choice Theory in Demand Analysis," *Journal of Economic Methodology*, 18: 107–128.

Nagel, E. (1961) *The Structure of Science: Problems in the Logic of Scientific Explanation.* New York, Harcourt, Brace & World.

Nagel, E. (1963) "Assumptions in Economic Theory," *American Economic Review*, 53: 211–219.

Pearce, K.A and K.D. Hoover (1995) "After the Revolution: Paul Samuelson and the Textbook Keynesian Model," in A.F. Cottrell and M.S. Lawlor (eds.) *New Perspectives on Keynes.* Annual supplement to *History of Political Economy*, 27. Durham, Duke University Press: 183–216.

Pollak, R.A. (1990) "Distinguished Fellow: Houthakker's Contributions to Economics," *Journal of Economic Perspectives*, 4: 141–156.

Samuelson, P.A. (1938a) "The Empirical Implications of Utility Analysis," *Econometrica*, 6: 344–356.

Samuelson, P.A. (1938b) "A Note on the Pure Theory of Consumer's Behaviour," *Economica*, New Series, 5: 61–71.

Samuelson, P.A. (1940) *Foundations of Analytical Economics: The Observational Significance of Economic Theory* PhD dissertation, Harvard University. Box 91 of Samuelson Papers, Duke University.

Samuelson, P.A. (1947) *Foundations of Economic Analysis*. Cambridge, MA, Harvard University Press.

Samuelson, P.A. (1948a) *Economics: An Introductory Analysis*. New York, McGraw-Hill.

Samuelson, P.A. (1948b) "Consumption Theory in Terms of Revealed Preference," *Economica*, New Series, 15: 243–253.

Samuelson, P.A. (1950) "The Problem of Integrability in Utility Theory," *Economica*, New Series, 17: 355–385.

Samuelson, P.A. (1955) "Professor Samuelson on Operationalism in Economic Theory: Comment," *Quarterly Journal of Economics*, 69: 310–314.

Samuelson, P.A. (1963) "Problems of Methodology—Discussion," *American Economic Review*, 53: 231–236.

Samuelson, P.A. (1964) "Theory and Realism: A Reply," *American Economic Review*, 54: 736–739.

Samuelson, P.A. (1965) "Professor Samuelson on Theory and Realism: Reply," *American Economic Review*, 55: 1164–1172.

Samuelson, P.A. (1972) "Maximum Principles in Analytical Economics," *American Economic Review*, 62: 249–262.

Samuelson, P.A. (1983) *Foundations of Economic Analysis*. Enlarged edition. Cambridge, MA, Harvard University Press.

Samuelson, P.A. (1991) "My Life Philosophy: Policy Credos and Working Ways," in M. Szenberg (ed.) *Eminent Economists: Their Life Philosophies*. Cambridge, Cambridge University Press: 236–247.

Samuelson, P.A. (1998) "How Foundations Came to Be," *Journal of Economic Literature*, 36: 1375–1386.

Simon, H.A. (1963) "Problems of Methodology—Discussion," *American Economic Review*, 53: 229–231.

Suppe, F. (1972) "Theories, Their Formulations, and the Operational Imperative," *Synthese*, 25: 129–164.

Suppe, F. (ed.) (1977) *The Structure of Scientific Theories*. Second edition. Urbana, University of Illinois Press.

Suppe, F. (1979) "Theory Structure," in P. Asquith and H. Kyburg (eds.) *Current Research in Philosophy of Science*. East Lansing, MI, Philosophy of Science Association: 317–338.

Varian, H.R. (1982) "The Nonparametric Approach to Demand Analysis," *Econometrica*, 50: 945–973.

Varian, H.R. (2006) "Revealed Preference," in M. Szenberg, L. Ramrattan and A.A. Gottesman (eds.) *Samuelsonian Economics and the Twenty-First Century*. Oxford, Oxford University Press: 99–115.

Vermeulen, F. (2012) "Foundations of Revealed Preference: Introduction," *Economic Journal*, 122: 287–294.

Wong, S. (1973) "The 'F-Twist' and the Methodology of Paul Samuelson," *American Economic Review*, 63: 312–325.

Wong, S. (2006) *The Foundations of Paul Samuelson's Revealed Preference Theory: A Study by the Method of Rational Reconstruction*. Revised edition. London, Routledge. Originally published in 1978.

4

The Young Paul Samuelson: Mathematics as a Language, the Operational Attitude, and Systems in Equilibrium

Juan Carvajalino

1 Samuelson's Dissertation: A Harvard Story

In the opening page of his doctoral dissertation (Samuelson 1941), defended in 1940 at Harvard University, Paul Samuelson wrote: "Mathematics is a Language." He attributed this motto to Josiah Willard Gibbs, an American mathematician and physicist who had spent his whole career at Yale University and who contributed significantly to traditional nineteenth-century applied mathematics in the USA (Parshall and Rowe 1994). When he defended his dissertation, Samuelson was 25 years old. His young age belied the strong argument that he advanced in its pages: Economics lacked the sound scientific foundations that he was proposing. Subsequently, from the Department of Economics at the Massachusetts Institute of Technology (MIT), which he joined after he left Harvard,

J. Carvajalino (✉)
University Paris VIII, Vincennes-Saint-Denis, Saint-Denis, France
e-mail: juan.carvajalino-florez@univ-paris8.fr

R. A. Cord et al. (eds.), *Paul Samuelson*, Remaking Economics: Eminent Post-War Economists, https://doi.org/10.1057/978-1-137-56812-0_4

Samuelson added two new chapters and submitted his expanded dissertation to Harvard University Press in 1945. Two years later, his *Foundations of Economic Analysis* (Samuelson 1947) appeared. In its opening page, one can still read: "Mathematics is a Language."[1]

It is difficult to determine whether Gibbs actually defined mathematics as a language or not. He was the mentor of Edwin Bidwell Wilson, Samuelson's professor of advanced mathematical and statistical economics at Harvard. Moreover, as is well known, Wilson's ideas about mathematics and science significantly influenced Samuelson's early mathematical economics. Wilson was an American polymath who obtained his Ph.D. in mathematics at Yale, where he met Gibbs, and conducted postdoctoral research in Paris between 1902 and 1903 (Hunsaker and Mac Lane 1973). Around 1905, Wilson, then a professor at the Department of Mathematics at Yale (1903–1907), was one of the most active members of the modern mathematical research community in the USA (Fenster and Parshall 1994). During these years, mathematics in America was emerging as an autonomous academic discipline. Feeling that his mathematician colleagues tended to overemphasize pure abstraction, Wilson gradually withdrew from that community. At the same time, he became professionally involved with mathematical physics at MIT (1907–1922) and then with statistics and social science at the Harvard School of Public Health (1922–1945). In this process of self-alienation from the community of mathematics and concomitant association with other academic communities, Wilson fully engaged with Gibbs's applied mathematics, willing to bridge mathematics and science. Deeply concerned with foundational questions and by introducing himself as the true representative of Gibbs's mathematics, Wilson eventually defined mathematics as a language, which conveyed meaning and structure (Carvajalino 2018a).

During the 1920s and 1930s, Wilson gravitated toward highly influential circles at Harvard. In particular, he developed his ideas about mathematics and science in an operational way and in a similar spirit to Percy Bridgman, a physicist at Harvard who defined something he called the *operational attitude* in science. Operationalism would subsequently be

[1] For the first volume of a detailed and comprehensive intellectual biography of Samuelson, see Backhouse (2017).

attributed to Bridgman. At Harvard, Wilson also became a close friend of Lawrence Henderson, a physiologist who believed that society and the economy could be regarded as *systems in stable equilibrium.* During the 1930s, Henderson became one of the most influential figures at Harvard. Wilson, Bridgman, and Henderson had strong ideas about what should be scientists' practices and developed a coherent discourse about science (Isaac 2012). Their activism significantly framed the development of natural and social sciences at Harvard during the 1920s and 1930s. Of particular relevance for this account, during the 1930s, hand with hand with Henderson, Wilson played a major role in the rise of mathematical economics in the USA. He notably promoted and established the first program in advanced mathematical economics and statistics at Harvard. In 1936 and 1937, Samuelson, then a Harvard Ph.D. student in economics, attended Wilson's courses in advanced mathematical statistics and mathematical economics (Carvajalino 2018b).

In his dissertation, the young Samuelson did not simply use Gibbs's name and the "Mathematics is a Language" motto as rhetorical arguments of authority. He also used them to introduce the reader to the attitude by which he was influenced when writing the different parts of his texts. In his dissertation and *Foundations*, by following Wilson's ideas about mathematics and science, Samuelson connected mathematics and economics, adopting an operational attitude while treating the individual and aggregate levels of the economy as systems in stable equilibrium.

It remains difficult to reconstruct the precise connection between Samuelson and Henderson, as well as that between Samuelson and Bridgman (Backhouse 2017). In this chapter, we will argue that Wilson acted as a mediator between his Harvard colleagues and the young Samuelson. We will show how Wilson interacted with Bridgman and Henderson and trace Wilson's influence on Samuelson's dissertation and *Foundations.* With this in mind, Wilson's definition of mathematics as a language will be discussed first. We then compare Wilson's and Bridgman's ideas about the operational attitude. Then, the Wilson-Henderson connection will be mapped out. Finally, we will analyze Samuelson's dissertation and *Foundations* from the perspective of Wilson's influence.

2 Wilson: *Much Science with Little Mathematics*

By defining mathematics as a language, Wilson was reacting to the foundational debates in mathematics and science that emerged around 1900, just as he started his professional career in academia. He was also staking out a position regarding the emerging relationship between departments of mathematics and departments of science in American universities. For Wilson, the recent departmentalization of mathematics and what he regarded as an overemphasis on pure abstraction in the curriculum offered by his mathematician colleagues had led to a dislocation between mathematics and science: Young mathematicians knew much about pure mathematics, but did not know how to apply it to science, for they had received no training in science. At the same time, young scientists barely knew mathematics because they had stopped taking courses in mathematics since pure mathematicians did not adapt their teachings to scientists. As a consequence, Wilson claimed, mathematics and science in American universities were developing disjointedly. There was too much mathematics in departments of mathematics and too little mathematics in departments of natural and social science (Wilson 1903a, 1911).

In general terms, for Wilson, defining mathematics as a language primarily meant that mathematics and science were necessarily indispensable to each other. This indispensability argument implied that mathematics became unintelligible when it was practiced and developed without having in mind immediate applications to a subject matter. Mathematics could only gain meaning when it was connected with the natural or social sciences. At the same time, the indispensability argument implied that a subject matter could hold legitimate scientific status only if it was structured by mathematics. A subject matter that was not sufficiently mathematized, Wilson believed, was not a legitimate scientific endeavor. In other words, he defined mathematics as a language because he believed that, as with language, in mathematics there was one aspect—pure mathematics—which provided structure, like grammar, and another aspect—the subject matter—which provided meaning, like semantics. More specifically, by defining mathematics as a language, Wilson wanted to interconnect mathematics and science while taking into account the distinct practices of modern mathematicians and scientists. For this purpose, and as he was taking part in foundational discussions, he sought to define the basic and distinct kinds of hypotheses with which his mathematician and scientist colleagues worked (Wilson 1904a, 1906). For this purpose, Wilson adopted the terminology of one of his American mathematician colleagues at Harvard, Edward Huntington, who believed that the word that best characterized the kind of hypotheses that were used in mathematics was "postulate" and not "axiom" (Huntington 1904, 1911).[2]

On one side, Wilson thought, along with Huntington, that pure mathematicians based their work on hypotheses that he called postulates, which represented (algebraic and logical) structures existing in the minds of pure mathematicians who knew them because they had studied them in a classroom. Postulates did not have any empirical existence. They were abstract conditions that pure mathematicians imposed on given systems in order to structure them as wanted. Thanks to the work of David Hilbert in pure mathematics (Hilbert 1899) and of Bertrand Russell in logic (Russell 1901, 1903), Wilson believed that the postulational aspect of mathematics had been well developed and so could be trusted. The problem in mathematics, due in large part to Hilbert himself, Wilson claimed, was that modern mathematicians were interested only in abstract mathematical systems (Wilson 1903b, 1904a).

On the other side, Wilson suggested that scientists worked with hypotheses that he called axioms, which, for him, represented convenient conventional working explanations found in subject matter. With axioms, scientists sought to establish the best possible mediation between theory and data relative to the phenomena at hand. For Wilson, this meant that with axioms, scientists sought to develop meaning relative to their subject matter by combining theoretical and empirical aspects. Furthermore, during their careers, Wilson believed, scientists accumulated experience, which eventually helped them improve their intuition and judgment about the systems that they studied. Hence, experience assisted them in establishing better ways of mediating between theory and data, in turn allowing

[2]Huntington was reacting to foundational debates in mathematics and science as these debates were developing in the USA around 1910.

for more meaningful scientific statements. The problem in science, Wilson claimed, was that most scientists did not know mathematics and so did not structure their work in a postulational fashion.

For Wilson, mathematics as a language implied connecting the postulates of pure mathematics and the axioms of science. More precisely, it implied imposing certain mathematical demands on particular working hypotheses found in subject matter in order to postulate them. These working hypotheses may or may not satisfy these conditions. If they did, Wilson claimed, the mediation between theory and data would be improved. In this process of structuring specific systems of subject matter, Wilson stressed that axioms prevailed over postulates. By this, he meant that the mathematician/scientist should develop his work in an operational spirit, namely in such a way that the convenient conventional hypotheses prevailing in the field of study guided the postulational development of the field and not the other way round. In Wilson's operational attitude, axioms, not postulates, provided meaning (Wilson 1904a). Wilson did not hesitate to praise scientific contributions, which had been developed in a postulational spirit but which still may contain some mathematical gaps. In these cases, he believed that if these gaps could be filled with intuition of the subject matter, mathematically incomplete contributions are to be preferred to scientific contributions, which were only concerned with pure mathematical consistency (Wilson 1904b, 1912a, 1928a).

In brief, by defining mathematics as a language, Wilson suggested that mathematics had three distinct but interrelated levels: one postulational, which provided structure, like a sort of grammar; one axiomatic, which conveyed meaning, like a sort of semantics; and one operational, which consisted of connecting the first two levels. In this operational aspect, if some mathematical gaps appeared but could be filled with intuition relative to the subject matter, then the correspondence established between mathematics and the subject matter could be based on a solid foundation.[3]

Wilson was sympathetic to the work of scholars who bridged mathematics and science in this operational sense. Jacques Hadamard's work on the theory of waves illustrated his operational attitude. In the study of the

[3]See Papers of Edwin Bidwell Wilson (hereafter PEBW), Harvard University Archives (HUA), HUG4878.214, Box 3, Folder Miscellaneous Papers, Chapter I. General Introduction (unpublished and undated).

propagation of waves, some mathematical series were often used in order to evaluate certain quantities. These series were traditionally thought to converge to a specific value. But contemporary developments had shown that they eventually diverged from this value. Their use implied a lack of mathematical rigor and created mathematical gaps. Hadamard, a French mathematician, employed these kinds of series to structure the system with which he studied the dispersion of light. For Wilson, Hadamard's research, despite the fact that it was not complete mathematically, was scientifically well founded because Hadamard used his intuition and judgment about the atomic nature of matter to fill the mathematical gaps. Indeed, Hadamard worked like Gibbs: He emphasized meaning and not just mathematical structure, and he thus offered *much science with little mathematics* (Wilson 1904b). Wilson's influence on Samuelson, which will be described in Sect. 5, will lead us to suggest that *Foundations* could be regarded as a contribution that offered *much economics with little mathematics*.[4]

3 Wilson and Bridgman: The *Operational Attitude*

When Wilson joined the Harvard School of Public Health in the early 1920s, he became a colleague of physicist Percy Bridgman. Over the next few years, Wilson and Bridgman moved within the same intellectual circles and developed their ideas about the operational attitude in a similar spirit. Yet they diverged slightly on the elements that determined the meaningfulness of scientific statements.

Wilson and Bridgman were both concerned with Albert Einstein's recent works on general relativity. As a result of these developments, which threw into question the traditional foundations of physics and knowledge, Wilson and Bridgman felt, in Wilson's words, that "we need a scientific attitude

[4]On Wilson's ideas about too much or too little mathematics, see Wilson (1928b). More generally, for a full account of Wilson's definition of mathematics as a language, see Carvajalino (2018a).

towards the study of the history of philosophy."[5] For them, this was necessary in order to develop a new attitude in which new and old works and practices were reconciled. In this vein, Bridgman, in his *The Logic of Modern Physics* (Bridgman 1927), defined the operational attitude in physics. Physicists used certain concepts in their work and Bridgman characterized these concepts by the sets of operations that had been necessary to develop them. These operations embodied the operational attitude. They involved actual physical measurements and/or mathematical calculations. In order to be meaningful, Bridgman suggested, a concept needed to be established on the basis of a unique rule of equivalence between the concept and its relative set of operations. However, in cases when such unique equivalence was established on mathematical grounds, a concept developed in this way could only be regarded as partially meaningful. It could be used as a working hypothesis, but it would require experimental justification to be validated and thus become fully meaningful.[6]

Wilson identified with Bridgman's operational ideas. As Wilson had done when defining mathematics as a language, Bridgman adopted an a-philosophical attitude. In their discussions about philosophy of science and epistemology, Wilson and Bridgman did not aim at offering a comprehensive philosophy of knowledge. They wanted rather to define and establish a new scientific attitude in which the methodological and epistemological question was resolved, ultimately, at the individual level. For both, the free choice of scientists was central. Wilson's and Bridgman's operational attitude, however, also aimed at disciplining free scientists. Their new attitude involved more empirical methods and practices as well as more rigorous and postulational habits. At the same time, they also insisted that their new attitude implied a sort of self-control that individual scientists could adopt in their working practices, which consisted of being systematically aware of the limits of pure experimentation and of pure abstraction.[7]

---

[5]Wilson to Hoernlé, 4 March 1920, PEBW, HUA, HUG4878.203, Box 2, Folder 1917–1920 H.

[6]On Bridgman's operational attitude, see Isaac (2012), Hands (2004), and Walter (1990) as well as Hands in this volume.

[7]Wilson's and Bridgman's ideas about science significantly reflected the ideas of American pragmatism. During the 1920s, Wilson was asked to write the biographical memoir of Charles Sanders

Notwithstanding the similarities between Wilson's and Bridgman's ideas about the operational attitude, there was a fundamental difference between them. For Bridgman, who wanted to describe the recent development of physics, mathematics represented a set of concepts useful for physics (Bridgman 1927: 60–65). At the same time, his ideas about the intelligibility of mathematics in physics somehow reflected ideas developed by mathematicians: Even in cases where pure mathematics was not immediately applicable, it would probably be useful in specific applications to solve practical problems in the future. In contrast, Wilson, who felt that mathematics and the natural and social sciences were evolving independently of each other (in the USA), claimed that they needed to be defined as interconnected. Further, he insisted that the structure (postulates) and meaningfulness (axioms) of specific subject matter had to be operationalized systematically. For Wilson science could not be based on uncertain future validations. If convenient conventional working hypotheses of a subject matter were mathematically structured by postulates and with an operational attitude, then the subject matter could be regarded immediately as scientifically well founded (Carvajalino 2018c).

Another difference between Wilson's and Bridgman's views about the operational attitude lay in the fact that while Bridgman's account of the history of physics was mainly descriptive, Wilson's definition of mathematics as a language had a clearly normative character. Wilson's description of the development of mathematics and science in the USA led him to repeatedly plea for the reform of the mathematics curriculum in American colleges. With such changes, he wanted to encourage young pure mathematicians to take a greater interest in practical applications. At the same time, he wanted to encourage young natural and social scientists to offer, as quickly as possible, better ways of mediating between theory and data relative to their subject matter. In other words, with his proposed educational reforms, Wilson hoped that he could help reconcile mathematics and science (Wilson 1911, 1913, 1915, 1918).

Peirce, one of the most important American pragmatists. Wilson never finished the memoir. However, he read some of Peirce's work and eventually engaged with some aspects of it. Wilson was particularly impressed by Peirce's ideas on statistical inference (Wilson 1923a, b, 1926a, b, 1927a, b).

Wilson's courses in economics during the 1930s were part of his program of educational reforms. With his courses, he hoped that some young Harvard economists would eventually adopt his operational attitude and thus offer *much economics with little mathematics*. For this purpose, and starting in the 1920s, Wilson closely collaborated with another of his colleagues at Harvard, the physiologist Lawrence Henderson (Carvajalino 2018b).

4 Wilson and Henderson: *Systems in Stable Equilibrium*

When Wilson was still working at MIT during the 1910s, he received a visit from Henderson. Henderson had been an undergraduate at Harvard at approximately the same time as Wilson. He later obtained a Doctor of Medicine degree at Harvard and had conducted postdoctoral research in physiology in France (Dill 1977; Mayer 1968; Cannon 1943; Ferry 1942). In the 1910s, the two Cambridge (USA) scholars had similar academic backgrounds, although they were active in different fields. They were also both significantly impressed by Gibbs. When Henderson visited Wilson in December 1915, the former wanted to talk about Gibbs, as he had "been trying to get something out of Gibbs's Statistical Mechanics and out of the papers on Thermodynamics, and he believes he has found in those papers an idealization of nature which will take its place in [the] principal rank of philosophical ideas just as the line, time, and mass have their place there. The idea he finds is that of A System."[8]

Henderson developed a theory of organisms as systems in equilibrium (Henderson 1913, 1917). He regarded Gibbs's concept of systems as an original and genuine working hypothesis valid in physiology. Systems were bounded and represented a distinct proportion of a whole in which all factors—variables—were mutually dependent. Working along these lines, Henderson connected the abstract theory of closed equilibrium, as

[8] Wilson to Bumstead, 18 December 1915, PEBW, HUA, HUG4878.203, Box 1, Folder 1914–1916 B; underlining in original.

found in physics, with the descriptive and intuitive approach of open equilibrium, as found in biology. Henderson was of the view that equilibrium was a factual requirement for living organisms. For a living organism, living meant to be in equilibrium; it also meant to be in constant exchange with the environment. Henderson believed that the relationship between a living organism and its environment further determined the evolution of a dynamic equilibrium (Weintraub 1991; Russett 1966). Wilson sympathized with Henderson's work, as he believed that "Nature had a way of correcting excessive conditions, whether those conditions were departures above or below the normal; that life was in the main so far as the individual was concerned, a state of equilibrium from which no great departures either way toward better or worse were possible."[9]

At the beginning of the 1920s, Henderson turned his attention to social science, impressed by his reading of Vilfredo Pareto's 1917 *Traité de Sociology Générale.* During the 1920s, Henderson developed the idea that the social stability observed in most societies implied that they were in equilibrium. On this basis, he argued that society could be regarded as an organic system of individuals who shared a similar culture and which could be analyzed in terms of stable equilibrium. For Henderson, the idea of a stable equilibrium in the study of society was empirically evident and, thanks to Pareto, theoretically founded (Russett 1966; Parascandola 1971, 1992).

During these years, Henderson's interest in the social sciences and Pareto in particular acted as a reinforcement to his friendship with Wilson, who, during the 1910s, had praised Pareto's economics. For Wilson, even though economics was in its infancy as a scientific discipline (because it lacked consensus and mathematical structure), Pareto's (as well as Irving Fisher's) mathematical economics was the path to follow. Wilson was of the view that Pareto worked on the basis of a relatively well-defined hypothesis, which consisted of regarding the economy as a system in stable equilibrium that could be structured with the mathematics of optimization systems. If economists adopted Pareto's attitude while seeking to connect their work with economic data, as the economist Wesley Mitchell would later do, they would eventually base economics on sound scientific

[9] Wilson to Cannon, 8 May 1923, PEBW, HUA, HUG4878.203, Box 4, Folder C, 2).

grounds. Economists would in particular be able to achieve consensus about fundamental working hypotheses and thus improve their intuition and judgment regarding economic affairs and social life (Wilson 1909, 1912b).

Wilson and Henderson shared the prevailing idea in American social science and economics[10] which viewed social and economic issues as engineering/medico-quantitative problems. This, they felt, could be useful for planning and controlling social and economic affairs. However, as Wilson (and most probably Henderson) felt that these fields had not yet achieved real scientific status, neither social scientists nor economists could be trusted in their attempt to plan and control such affairs. Wilson argued that any such planning and control should be subtle and indirect (Wilson 1918). Scientific planning, for him, consisted first of reforming the curriculum of social scientists and economists, and instructing them in the "right" scientific operational attitude, as found in the work of Pareto, Mitchell, Henderson, and Gibbs. Eventually, Wilson believed, these social scientists and economists would offer *much social science and economics with little mathematics*, and would be able to deal with social and economic affairs as engineering problems in a sound scientific way (Carvajalino 2018a).

In the 1920s and the 1930s, Wilson and Henderson played a central role in framing the development of the social sciences and economics at Harvard (Isaac 2012). Their efforts were undoubtedly made easier by the fact that during these years both scholars became renowned academic figures. Wilson gained influence at the national level, as he joined a number of executive committees in associations and academies promoting science in the USA. In particular, he served as President of the American Academy of Arts and Sciences (1927–1931), of the American Statistical Association (1929), and of the Social Science Research Council (1929–1931), and later as Vice President of the National Academy of Sciences (1949–1953). At around the same time, Henderson emerged as one of the most important and influential figures at Harvard and the National Academy of Science. He also founded the Harvard Fatigue Laboratory in 1927 and the Harvard Society of Fellows in 1933.

[10]See Leonard (2016) and Rutherford (2011).

At the beginning of the 1930s, Wilson started participating in the meetings of the Departments of Sociology and of Economics at Harvard. In the Department of Sociology, he promoted the establishment of a course on Pareto's methods, which would be taught by Henderson.[11] In 1932, Henderson began lecturing on "Pareto and Scientific Methods."[12] A few years later, the famous Pareto Circle would emerge from these lectures. At the same time, Wilson started teaching a course on "Quantitative Problems of Population" to sociologists. In the Department of Economics, as already mentioned, Wilson established the first program of advanced mathematical and statistical economics. During the 1930s at Harvard, Henderson promoted the methodology of case studies (Isaac 2012) while in his courses to economists, Wilson emphasized the mathematical notion of generality. Wilson also taught graduate students in economics that Gibbsian mathematics was useful for the analysis of the economy, at the individual and aggregate levels, which could be regarded as systems in stable equilibrium. This framework, he insisted, could/should still be better connected with data (Carvajalino 2018b).

5 Samuelson's Dissertation and *Foundations*: *Much Economics with Little Mathematics*

Samuelson became a student at the Department of Economics at Harvard in 1935. He was then 20 years old, a recent graduate from the University of Chicago, and had been awarded a predoctoral scholarship by the Social Science Research Council. When he attended Wilson's course in advanced "Statistical Mathematics" in 1936, he was still preparing his general exams. The next year he attended Wilson's course in advanced "Mathematical Economics." Wilson's courses were extremely difficult for most graduate students in economics. But Samuelson, who had followed

---

[11]Wilson to Henderson, 25 January 1932, PEBW, HUA, Box 19, Folder H.

[12]See Isaac (2012), Cot (2011) and Heyl (1968).

extra-curricula mathematical courses, was well trained in college mathematics, and he impressed Wilson. Thanks to Wilson and his close relationship with Henderson, who headed the Harvard Society of Fellows, Samuelson was elected a Junior Fellow of the Society in 1937. This election came with a comfortable scholarship that Samuelson put to good use.

During his fellowship years, Samuelson wrote a number of papers, many of which were published before he defended his dissertation and some of which became influential almost immediately.[13] Samuelson did not write all of these papers as if he were following a particular common thread. Instead, they emerged in a rather disparate way. Despite this, when it came the time to submitting his dissertation around 1940, Samuelson took the different projects in which Wilson had had the greatest influence, put them together and added some introductory chapters and a mathematical appendix. These projects were related to Samuelson's work on consumer theory, on production and cost theory of the firm, as well as the comparative statics and dynamics at the aggregate level of the economy. In these projects as in the dissertation, echoing Wilson, Samuelson argued that he offered *operationally meaningful* theorems. Wilson himself chaired the committee that evaluated Samuelson's doctoral defense. He would also be involved in Samuelson's hiring at the Department of Economics at MIT (Backhouse 2014). At the Institute, between 1940 and 1945, Samuelson extended his dissertation with a couple of chapters. Two years later, *Foundations of Economic Analysis* was published. As in his dissertation, Samuelson argued that he was putting forward operationally meaningful theorems.

With Gibbs's motto "Mathematics is a Language," with which he started his dissertation and *Foundations*, Samuelson introduced his readers to the Wilsonian style that he had adopted in these contributions. Wilson defined mathematics as a language and presented himself as the true mathematical heir of Gibbs. Samuelson's operationally meaningful theorems embodied Wilson's emphasis on three distinct but interconnected aspects: the postulational, the axiomatic, and the operational (Carvajalino 2018c, 2019).

[13]A non-comprehensive listing includes Samuelson (1937a, b, 1938a, b, c, d, e, 1939a, b, c, d, e, 1940), Schumpeter et al. (1939), and Nixon and Samuelson (1940).

Samuelson's operationally meaningful theorems had clear postulational and axiomatic ambitions in a Wilsonian vein. For Samuelson, these particular theorems were not mere mathematical or purely abstract entities. Neither were they pure theoretical or pure empirical elements of economics disconnected from mathematics. These theorems were mathematical elements full of economic meaning. These meaningful theorems embodied Samuelson's effort to connect the mathematical "structural characteristics of the equilibrium set" (Samuelson 1941: 15) with convenient conventional working hypotheses in economics. In a Wilsonian-Hendersonian-Paretian spirit, Samuelson regarded the individual and the aggregate levels of the economy as systems that could be analyzed as being in stable equilibrium. In this way, Samuelson assumed that it was conventional in economics that individuals, who behave to optimize a given quantity, as well as the intertemporal interrelations between aggregate variables, could both be regarded as systems in stable equilibrium. Further, with his meaningful theorems, Samuelson suggested, economists could better mediate between economic theory and data. He argued that the greatest difficulty in economics resulted from there not yet being enough data about economic phenomena. Another difficulty resulted because in standard contemporary mathematical economics, the structural characteristics of optimization problems and functional analysis—which were based on continuous mathematics—had left the discipline with no clear connection to data and so without empirical foundations.

Samuelson developed his meaningful theorems with a self-avowedly Wilsonian attitude: They were operationally established. Samuelson's operational solution to the difficulties mentioned above consisted of developing formulas defined with discrete magnitudes, which could be translated into the standard formulas of his contemporary mathematical economics, defined as continuous elements. These discrete magnitudes, Samuelson implicitly suggested, could be regarded as the data of economics, as they were observable in idealized conditions.

In his operationally meaningful theorem in consumer theory, which he referred to as the consistency postulate, Samuelson played with elements found in expenditure, demand functions and preference fields, and then deduced a certain inequality of discrete elements. From it, he showed that the standard restrictions of maximization procedures of demand functions could be derived. Also, in his operationally meaningful theorems in the theory of the firm, Samuelson used the Le Châtelier's Principle, which was a principle of stability of equilibrium in cases of marginal changes, and generalized it to cases of finite changes of a parameter. With this Principle, Samuelson was able to study the optimization exercise of the firm as a problem that involved certain discrete relationships as, for example, when discontinuous production functions were assumed. Finally, in his operationally meaningful theorems in comparative statics and dynamics, Samuelson used the Principle of Correspondence, which established a one-to-one correspondence between comparative statics and dynamics of the aggregate system of the economy. With it, Samuelson presented the static problem of individuals' optimizing behavior as a discrete problem and the dynamics of the aggregate system as a continuous problem. Comparative statics and dynamics were therefore interconnected as the discrete and the continuous; it was only a matter of emphasis. In this vein, Samuelson developed certain correspondences between systems of differential equations and systems of difference equations.[14]

Other aspects of Samuelson's meaningful theorems further reveal his engagement with Wilson's "operational" ideas. Samuelson's mathematics was not systematically complete. He filled the mathematical gaps in his work with economic intuition while emphasizing and reinforcing conventional working hypotheses in contemporary mathematical economics. For example, with his consistency postulate in consumer theory, he claimed that he was offering the empirical foundations of the subfield. He did not, however, offer the mathematical apparatus required to develop his theory on the basis of actual economic information. In a similar vein, in his theory of the firm, Samuelson did not mathematically prove that the Le Châtelier's Principle could be generalized into discrete cases. At one point, he even realized that this generalization was impossible to prove.[15] Further,

[14]Wilson's influence on Samuelson's dissertation was not only relevant from the perspective of the operational attitude. Wilson was also significantly influential at the theoretical level. In his courses, Wilson had defined equilibrium in consumer theory precisely with time-independent inequalities of discrete magnitudes, which he called the Gibbs conditions. He had also mentioned the Le Châtelier's Principle and had explained that the continuous and the discrete could be interconnected by a one-to-one correspondence, as suggested in Samuelson's use of the Correspondence Principle.

[15]Samuelson to Wilson, 25 January 1939, Paul A. Samuelson Papers, David M. Rubenstein Rare Book & Manuscript Library, Duke University, Box 77.

in his comparative statics and dynamics, Samuelson used the Correspondence Principle in a highly intuitive way. He did not put corresponding comparative statics and dynamics on a clearly defined mathematical basis, but rather on an intuitive one, which let him connect individuals' optimizing behavior, as a discrete problem, with the dynamics of the aggregate system, as a continuous one. Although he suggested that individuals' optimizing behavior "affords a unified approach" in economics (Samuelson 1947 [1983]: 23), he did not provide the microfoundations for the macroeconomics.

Notwithstanding these mathematical gaps, Samuelson presented his operationally meaning theorems, embodied in his postulate of consistency, the Le Châtelier's Principle and the Principle of Correspondence, as being mathematically well structured, theoretically well founded, and empirically based. In this way, he succeeded in reinforcing the conventional working hypotheses in his contemporary mathematical economics that the individual and the aggregate levels of the economy could be regarded as systems in stable equilibrium. With his work, the notion of stable equilibrium could be, and would henceforth be, regarded as being mathematically, theoretically, and empirically sound. As such, it can be argued that in his dissertation and in *Foundations*, Samuelson offered *much economics with little mathematics*.

6 Concluding Remarks

In his dissertation (Samuelson 1941) and in *Foundations* (Samuelson 1947), Samuelson claimed that he was offering operationally meaningful theorems. In the opening pages of these two documents, he also wrote: "Mathematics is a Language." These elements, it has been argued in this chapter, reflected Samuelson's personal commitment to Wilson's ideas about mathematics and science. Wilson, a protégé of Gibbs, defined mathematics as a language, meaning that mathematics and science were reciprocally indispensable. His definition also implied that mathematics consisted of three interconnected aspects: the postulational, which provided structure, like grammar; the axiomatic, which provided meaning, like semantics; and the operational, which consisted of connecting the former two aspects. For Wilson, this operational aspect implied that scientists/mathematicians should create *much science with little mathematics.* This meant that if they were able to fill in the mathematical gaps in their research with intuition and judgment relative to their subject matter, then their work could be regarded as mathematically and scientifically sound.

Wilson joined Harvard at the beginning of the 1920s. From then on, he moved in influential circles at the prestigious university. In particular, he developed his ideas about the *operational attitude* in a similar spirit to Bridgman's operationalism. Yet, Wilson and Bridgman differed regarding the way science and mathematics actually interacted and/or should interact. Bridgman believed that the meaningfulness of physical concepts, which were based on mathematical techniques, could only be validated by future experiments, while Wilson thought that mathematics, thanks to its operational aspect, could offer immediately valid foundations for science. For Wilson, the development of science could not be based on uncertain promises to be realized in the future but on what scientists/mathematicians could/should actually *do* in the present. At the same time, Wilson developed his ideas about social science and economics hand with hand with Henderson, a Harvard physiologist. During the 1920s and 1930s, Henderson developed the idea that society could be studied as a *system in stable equilibrium.* Simultaneous to this, Wilson and Henderson initiate significant developments in the social science and economics curricula at Harvard. In particular, with Henderson's help, Wilson established the first program in advanced mathematical and statistical economics at the Department of Economics in the 1930s. Notably, in 1936 and 1937, the young Samuelson attended Wilson's courses.

Wilson acted as a mediator between the young Samuelson and his Harvard colleagues. In his dissertation and in *Foundations*, Samuelson adopted Wilson's *operational attitude*, which was similar but not identical to Bridgman's. Samuelson believed that his work could immediately serve as a new scientific foundation for economics. Further, he suggested that he was offering the new empirical, theoretical, and mathematical foundations of the discipline, even if he was not offering a complete mathematical apparatus to argue such a thing: He filled the mathematical gaps with a significant amount of intuition relative to economics. It can thus be argued that he offered *much economics with little mathematics.* At the same time, by following Wilson's lectures, Samuelson studied the individual and the aggregate levels of the economy as *systems in stable equilibrium*.

During the twentieth century, Samuelson became a "towering figure in economics" (Backhouse 2017: xi). In the final analysis, it can be suggested that such success was not completely independent of the fact that he embodied a particular form of the Harvard discourse about science that prevailed throughout the 1930s, a discourse which was represented perhaps most prominently by Wilson, Henderson, and Bridgman.

References

Backhouse, R.E. (2014) "Paul A. Samuelson's Move to MIT," *History of Political Economy*, 46: 60–77.

Backhouse, R.E. (2017) *Founder of Modern Economics: Paul A. Samuelson, Volume 1: Becoming Samuelson, 1915–1948*. New York, Oxford University Press.

Bridgman, P. (1927) *The Logic of Modern Physics*. New York, Macmillan.

Cannon, W. (1943) "Biographical Memoir of Lawrence Joseph Henderson 1878–1942," *National Academy of Sciences of the United States*, 23: 31–58.

Carvajalino, J. (2018a) "Edwin Bidwell Wilson and Mathematics as a Language," *Isis*, 109: 494–514.

Carvajalino, J. (2018b) "Edwin B. Wilson and the Rise of Mathematical Economics in America, 1920–1940," *History of Political Economy*, 50: 229–259.

Carvajalino, J. (2018c) "Samuelson's Operationally Meaningful Theorems: Reflections of E.B. Wilson's Methodological Attitude," *Journal of Economic Methodology*, 25: 143–159.

Carvajalino, J. (2019) "Edwin B. Wilson, More Than a Catalytic Influence for Paul Samuelson's Foundations of Economic Analysis," *Journal of the History of Economic Thought*, 41: 1–25.

Cot, A. (2011) "A 1930s North American Creative Community: The Harvard 'Pareto Circle'," *History of Political Economy*, 43: 131–159.

Dill, D. (1977) "L.J. Henderson, His Transition from Physical Chemist to Physiologist; His Qualities as a Man," *The Physiologist*, 20: 1–15.

Fenster, D.D. and K. Parshall (1994) "A Profile of the American Mathematical Research Community: 1891–1906," in E. Knobloch and D. Rowe (eds.) *The History of Modern Mathematics: Images, Ideas, and Communities*. Boston, Academic Press: vol. 3, 179–227.

Ferry, R.M. (1942) "Lawrence Joseph Henderson: 1878–1942," *Science*, New Series, 95: 316–318.

Hands, D.W. (2004) "On Operationalisms and Economics," *Journal of Economic Issues*, 38: 953–969.

Henderson, L. (1913) *The Fitness of the Environment: An Inquiry into the Biological Significance of the Properties of Matter*. New York, Macmillan.

Henderson, L. (1917) *The Order of Nature: An Essay*. Cambridge, MA, Harvard University Press.

Heyl, B.S. (1968) "The Harvard 'Pareto Circle'," *Journal of the History of the Behavioral Sciences*, 4: 316–334.

Hilbert, D. (1899) *Grundlagen Der Geometrie*. Leipzig, Teubner.

Hunsaker, J. and S. Mac Lane (1973) "Edwin Bidwell Wilson, 1879–1964, A Biographical Memoir," *National Academy of Sciences (US)*, 43: 283–320.

Huntington, E. (1904) "Sets of Independent Postulates for the Algebra of Logic," *Transactions of the American Mathematical Society*, 5: 288–309.

Huntington, E. (1911) "The Fundamental Propositions of Algebra," in J. Young (ed.) *Monographs on Topics of Modern Mathematics*. New York, Longmans, Green and Co.: 151–207.

Isaac, J. (2012) *Working Knowledge: Making the Human Sciences from Parsons to Kuhn*. Cambridge, MA, Harvard University Press.

Leonard, T. (2016) *Illiberal Reformers: Race, Eugenics, and American Economics in the Progressive Era*. Princeton and Oxford, Princeton University Press.

Mayer, J. (1968) "Lawrence J. Henderson," *Journal of Nutrition*, 94: 1–5.

Nixon, R.A. and P.A. Samuelson (1940) "Estimates of Unemployment in the United States," *Review of Economics and Statistics*, 22: 101–111.

Parascandola, J. (1971) "Organismic and Holistic Concepts in the Thought of L.J. Henderson," *Journal of the History of Biology*, 4: 63–113.

Parascandola, J. (1992) "L.J. Henderson and the Mutual Dependency of Variables: From Physical Chemistry to Pareto," in C. Elliott and M. Rossiter (eds.) *Science at Harvard University: Historical Perspectives*. London and Toronto, Associated University Presses: 146–190.

Parshall, K. and D. Rowe (1994) *The Emergence of the American Mathematical Research Community, 1876–1900: J.J. Sylvester, Felix Klein, and E.H. Moore*. Rhode Island, American Mathematical Society.

Russell, B. (1901) *Essai Sur Les Fondements de La Géométrie*. Translated by A. Cadenat. Paris, Gauthier-Villars.

Russell, B. (1903) *The Principles of Mathematics, Volume 1*. Cambridge, Cambridge University Press.

Russett, C.E. (1966) *The Concept of Equilibrium in American Social Thought.* New Haven, CT, Yale University Press.

Rutherford, M. (2011) *The Institutionalist Movement in American Economics, 1918–1947: Science and Social Control.* Cambridge, Cambridge University Press.

Samuelson, P.A. (1937a) "A Note on Measurement of Utility," *Review of Economic Studies,* 4: 155–161.

Samuelson, P.A. (1937b) "Some Aspects of the Pure Theory of Capital," *Quarterly Journal of Economics,* 51: 469–496.

Samuelson, P.A. (1938a) "A Note on the Pure Theory of Consumer's Behaviour," *Economica,* New Series, 5: 61–71.

Samuelson, P.A. (1938b) "Welfare Economics and International Trade," *American Economic Review,* 28: 261–266.

Samuelson, P.A. (1938c) "The Empirical Implications of Utility Analysis," *Econometrica,* 6: 344–356.

Samuelson, P.A. (1938d) "The Numerical Representation of Ordered Classifications and the Concept of Utility," *Review of Economic Studies,* 6: 65–70.

Samuelson, P.A. (1938e) "Cost Theory and the Theory of International Trade: Reply by Mr. Samuelson," *American Economic Review,* 28: 746–747.

Samuelson, P.A. (1939a) "The End of Marginal Utility: A Note on Dr. Bernardelli's Article," *Economica,* 6: 86–87.

Samuelson, P.A. (1939b) "The Rate of Interest Under Ideal Conditions," *Quarterly Journal of Economics,* 53: 286–297.

Samuelson, P.A. (1939c) "Interactions Between the Multiplier Analysis and the Principle of Acceleration," *Review of Economics and Statistics,* 21: 75–78.

Samuelson, P.A. (1939d) "The Gains from International Trade," *Canadian Journal of Economics and Political Science,* 5: 195–205.

Samuelson, P.A. (1939e) "A Synthesis of the Principle of Acceleration and the Multiplier," *Journal of Political Economy,* 47: 786–797.

Samuelson, P.A. (1940) "The Theory of Pump-Priming Reexamined," *American Economic Review,* 30: 492–506.

Samuelson, P.A. (1941) *Foundations of Analytical Economics: The Observational Significance of Economic Theory.* PhD dissertation, Harvard University.

Samuelson, P.A. (1947) *Foundations of Economic Analysis.* Cambridge, MA, Harvard University Press.

Samuelson, P.A. (1947) [1983] *Foundations of Economic Analysis.* Enlarged edition. Cambridge, MA and London, England, Harvard University Press.

Schumpeter, J.A., I. Fisher, J. Marschak and P.A. Samuelson (1939) "The Pure Theory of Production," *American Economic Review,* 29: 118–120.

Walter, M. (1990) *Science and Cultural Crisis: An Intellectual Biography of Percy Williams Bridgman (1882–1961)*. Stanford, CA, Stanford University Press.

Weintraub, E.R. (1991) *Stabilizing Dynamics: Constructing Economic Knowledge*. Cambridge, Cambridge University Press.

Wilson, E.B. (1903a) "Review: Émile Borel, *Leçons Sur Les Fonctions Méromorphes*," *Bulletin of the American Mathematical Society*, 9: 506–507.

Wilson, E.B. (1903b) "The So-Called Foundations of Geometry," *Archiv Der Mathematik Und Physik*, 6: 104–122.

Wilson, E.B. (1904a) "The Foundations of Mathematics," *Bulletin of the American Mathematical Society*, 11: 74–93.

Wilson, E.B. (1904b) "The Theory of Waves," *Bulletin of the American Mathematical Society*, 10: 305–317.

Wilson, E.B. (1906) "The Foundations of Science," *Bulletin of the American Mathematical Society*, 12: 187–193.

Wilson, E.B. (1909) "Economics," *Bulletin of the American Mathematical Society*, 15: 169–186.

Wilson, E.B. (1911) "Mathematical Physics for Engineers," *Bulletin of the American Mathematical Society*, 17: 350–361.

Wilson, E.B. (1912a) "The Fourth Dimension as a Text," *Science Conspectus*, 2: 104–107.

Wilson, E.B. (1912b) "Mathematical Economics," *Bulletin of the American Mathematical Society*, 18: 462–474.

Wilson, E.B. (1913) "Let Us Have Calculus Early," *Bulletin of the American Mathematical Society*, 20: 30–36.

Wilson, E.B. (1915) "Some Books on Calculus," *Bulletin of the American Mathematical Society*, 21: 471–476.

Wilson, E.B. (1918) "Insidious Scientific Control," *Science*, New Series, 48: 491–493.

Wilson, E.B. (1923a) "First and Second Laws of Error," *Journal of the American Statistical Association*, 18: 841–851.

Wilson, E.B. (1923b) "The Statistical Significance of Experimental Data," *Science*, 58: 93–100.

Wilson, E.B. (1926a) "Empiricism and Rationalism," *Science*, 64: 47–57.

Wilson, E.B. (1926b) "Statistical Inference," *Science*, 63: 289–296.

Wilson, E.B. (1927a) "Probable Inference, the Law of Succession, and Statistical Inference," *Journal of the American Statistical Association*, 22: 209–212.

Wilson, E.B. (1927b) "What Is Statistics?" *Science*, 65: 581–587.

Wilson, E.B. (1928a) "Review of *The Abilities of Man, Their Nature and Measurement*, by C. Spearman," *Science*, 67: 244–248.
Wilson, E.B. (1928b) "Too Little Mathematics—And Too Much," *Science*, 67: 52–59.

5

Paul Samuelson and My Intellectual Development

Gregory C. Chow

1 Introduction

During his lifetime, Paul Samuelson made significant contributions to more areas of economics than any other economist in the world. In such a position, he undoubtedly influenced many economists. I am fortunate to be one of the beneficiaries. In this chapter, I will describe Samuelson's influence in three sections. The first is his influence on my intellectual development when I was an undergraduate student before meeting him in person. The second is his influence on me while I was a junior colleague of his at MIT. The third is our exchanges on the topic of dynamic economics after I left MIT.

G. C. Chow (✉)
Princeton University, Princeton, NJ, USA
e-mail: gchow@Princeton.EDU

R. A. Cord et al. (eds.), *Paul Samuelson*, Remaking Economics:
Eminent Post-War Economists, https://doi.org/10.1057/978-1-137-56812-0_5

2 Influence of Paul Samuelson's Work on Me While I Was an Undergraduate Student

When I was an undergraduate student majoring in economics at Cornell University, I became interested in mathematical economics, although I knew almost nothing about the subject. All I knew was that mathematics can be applied fruitfully to study economics. This knowledge was very exciting because most people did not think so at that time. I came to realize this mainly from my discovery of a journal known as *Econometrica* which I could read in the Cornell University Library. When I examined a copy of this journal, I was impressed and excited by the topics of some of the articles and the mathematics used to discuss them, although I did not understand the contents. In 1950, I decided to join the Econometric Society and discovered that it had been founded in 1930 by a small group of distinguished economists including Joseph Schumpeter, Ragnar Frisch, Harold Hotelling, and Henry Schultz, among others.

At about the same time, I discovered Samuelson's *Foundations of Economic Analysis*. I was excited just by looking at its table of contents and the mathematics used to study different topics cited in the table, although again I could not understand most of the material. There are two parts to the volume, one on static economics and the second on dynamic economics. Mathematics is used throughout the book. There are also two mathematical appendices. In writing this article, I re-examined my copy of the book and found many marginal notes covering almost the entire volume. These notes show my attempts to understand, as well as my failures to understand, the content of the volume.

Having been exposed to *Econometrica* and Samuelson's *Foundations*, I decided to study econometrics, a term defined at the time to include both mathematical economics and statistical economics, and now to include only the latter. When I applied to graduate schools in the spring semester of 1951, I discovered that the Economics Department at the University of Chicago was the only one in the USA (and probably in the world) which offered a course in econometrics. I applied to Chicago and started my graduate program in the fall of 1951.

After learning some mathematical economics at Chicago, I tried to read Samuelson's *Foundations* again. I saw my marginal notes written when I was an undergraduate student at Cornell and discovered how little I had understood the book. Having read more of it when I was a graduate student, I began to understand that it was the first book to cover so many important topics in economics using mathematical tools written in English. Hicks's *Value and Capital* had mathematical appendices using similar mathematical tools to discuss some of the topics covered by Samuelson, but Samuelson covered more topics using mathematics.

A distinguishing feature of *Foundations* was its discussion of dynamic economics using differential and difference equations. A similar discussion was absent in *Value and Capital*. In *Foundations*, differential and difference equations were used to model dynamic economic behavior but, unlike more recent discussions, these equations were not derived from maximizing behavior, as is done in the study of static economics in *Foundations*. It is fair to say that more than any other book, *Foundations* promoted and influenced the development of mathematical economics in the USA and the rest of the English-speaking world. (Perhaps the entire world, but my knowledge of the non-English literature in economics is very limited.)

3 My Experience as a Junior Colleague of Paul Samuelson

After receiving my Ph.D. from the University of Chicago, I became an assistant professor at the Sloan School of Management at MIT in 1955. I received an offer as an assistant professor mainly because of a strong letter of recommendation from Milton Friedman. I looked forward to be on the faculty at MIT because this would provide me with an opportunity to get to know and to learn from Samuelson, among other distinguished economists at MIT.

In the first half of the twentieth century, John Maynard Keynes was recognized as the most influential economist. In the second half, I believe that this honor was shared by Friedman and Samuelson (listed alphabetically). I was fortunate to be a student of Friedman and a junior colleague of Samuelson.

During the fall semester of 1955, I attended the economic theory seminar run jointly by Samuelson and Robert Solow. The seminar was conducted casually as compared with the Money Workshop led by Friedman at Chicago. Friedman would announce a topic well in advance and give the students time to prepare. Sometimes the seminar was about some preassigned reading material. Sometimes a student was asked to present their research results from his/her ongoing dissertation. I was fortunate to present drafts of my doctoral thesis on the demand for automobiles in the USA and benefited a great deal from comments made by Friedman. Research in progress by Friedman himself was also discussed. One well-known piece was the study by Friedman and David Meiselman which compared autonomous expenditure and money supply as alternative variables to explain GNP. Friedman coined the terms M1 and M2 casually in the Money Workshop for the purpose of that study.

By comparison, Samuelson and Solow did not seem to prepare for their economic theory seminar. Many MIT faculty members had lunch at the faculty dining room on the top floor of the Sloan Building which housed the Sloan School of Management and the Department of Economics. There was one round table occupied by the economics faculty members. Samuelson was the natural leader of this group. The other, and perhaps less well-known, economists tended to listen to his ideas and observations. On one day, when the Samuelson-Solow seminar was to be held after lunch, I followed them walking downstairs to the classroom. I heard Paul asking Bob, "Bob, what should we talk about today?" "How about expected utility?" was Bob's reply. When I entered the seminar room, about fifteen to twenty students were already there. Paul started telling the students that expected utility was to be the topic of the day. Expected utility was introduced by John von Neumann and Oscar Morgenstern in their 1944 book *Theory of Games and Economic Behavior.* Paul made a few introductory remarks about expected utility. Bob continued the discussion by adding a few more observations. I still remember Paul asking Bob a question because he was not sure of the answer. Paul remarked, "Anyone is entitled to learn something from Bob." As is well known, the two were very good friends. They were the leaders of the MIT School of Economics. Bob was the junior member of the team. Both had received their Ph.D. degree in economics from Harvard. Bob had studied and conducted research in mathematical statistics at Columbia University before joining MIT in 1949. While at MIT, I benefited a great deal from exchanges with Samuelson and Solow, among other economists.

There were regular seminars at MIT on different topics. One that I remember well was on international economics. The most distinguished scholar in this field was Charles (Charlie) Kindleberger. Not only were his remarks penetrating but he had a sense of humor, often speaking softly with a smile. Samuelson and Solow also attended some of these seminars. The friendly exchanges in these meetings were in sharp contrast with the critical and sometimes even unfriendly sounding remarks of faculty members in seminars at Chicago. Giving a seminar at Chicago one had, and still has, to be ready for attacks by faculty members. For many years, it has been a tradition for the attending faculty members to criticize seminar speakers especially those from outside the department. This tradition started at least at the time when I was a graduate student in the 1950s. Friedman set the example and many others followed. Such an atmosphere is not easily found in economics departments in other universities. In addition, participants of seminars at Chicago were more active and well prepared as they were supposed to have read any preparatory material carefully and be ready to make critical comments. The chair of the seminar would allow the author of a paper that was being presented to speak for about five minutes. Then he would say, "page 1, any comments… page 2, any comments…"

Students attending Friedman's Money Workshop were fortunate to learn from his wisdom. As noted, I presented parts of my Ph.D. on the demand for automobiles in the USA and benefited a great deal. Students attending the Samuelson-Solow seminar were equally fortunate, although the styles of teaching in the two seminars were very different. The most important common feature of these gatherings was the quality of the faculty members. To be a top economist, one has to be exposed to great minds and to learn their way of thinking. Needless to say, the comments of great economists may be critical remarks to correct the mistakes of a researcher or complimentary remarks to encourage further research.

Besides the different styles of teaching of the leaders at Chicago and MIT, their viewpoints about the use of economic analysis and the role of government were different. Friedman placed less emphasis on the use of mathematics as compared with Samuelson and Solow. He concentrated more on partial equilibrium than general equilibrium analysis. The Chicago School advocates less government intervention in a market economy while MIT considers government intervention as more important and necessary. To reduce macroeconomic fluctuations, Friedman advocated the use of monetary policy by controlling the supply of money while Samuelson and Solow preferred the use of fiscal policies by controlling government expenditures. Friedman's view on the importance of monetary policy was derived, at least partly, from his study with Meiselman referred to above. A major finding of that study is that national income is more highly correlated with money supply than with government expenditures. Besides advocating the use of monetary policy, Friedman championed the policy of keeping the rate of increase in money supply constant rather than setting the amount of money supply in response to economic circumstances. Samuelson and Solow were influenced by Keynes who had suggested increasing government spending in order to combat the Depression of the 1930s.

After learning the viewpoints of the MIT School, I was no longer a strict adherent of Chicago. I came to believe that both money supply and government expenditures affect national output in important ways. There is no need to select only one of these two sets of instruments in the conduct of macroeconomic policy. After having been at MIT for several years, I met a distinguished economist who had been a fellow student at Chicago. I expressed my belief in some of the viewpoints advocated by Samuelson and Solow. My friend remarked, "We should take back your Chicago PhD degree." Other friends in the economics profession often did not realize that I had a Ph.D. degree in economics from Chicago. Some even thought that I had received my doctorate from MIT!

There is a divergence of viewpoint between the two schools concerning the role of economic theory. The key issue is the relative merits of a theory that embraces many areas in economics verses a theory that explains a narrower range of areas but has more to say about these areas than the general theory. For example, the theory of maximizing behavior covers consumer behavior, behavior of the firm, etc. The theory of consumer behavior may include a particular utility function or special constraints such as a rationing constraint. Both the more general theories and the specific theories are useful in economics. Samuelson seemed to emphasize the theories which are more general and Friedman championed the more specific. Both the general theory, such as the theory based on constrained maximization and the specific theory of consumer behavior with a particular utility function, are useful tools of economic analysis. Samuelson has contributed more to the first kind of theory and Friedman more to the second kind.

4 Samuelson on Dynamic Economics

Dynamic programming is the most important tool used by economists today. It was first proposed by Richard Bellman in his well-known Rand monograph entitled *The Theory of Dynamic Programming* published in 1954. In the summer of 1956, I was one of the instructors of a summer course on operations research organized by Philip Morse, professor of physics at MIT. The course was designed for and attended by researchers working in industry. I had not studied operations research at that time but had learned some of the topics, such as linear programming and other mathematical tools, required as a graduate student in economics at Chicago. In this summer course, Bellman was invited to give a lecture on dynamic programming. I still remember his remark on what motivated him to call the subject "dynamic programming." He said, frankly and proudly, that both words, "dynamic" and "programming," would attract attention. "Dynamic" is certainly an eye-catching word as dynamic analyses were flourishing in many fields in the 1950s. "Programming" is equally eye-catching since linear and nonlinear programming had been developed a few years before and had attracted much attention in academic research all over the world. However, I could not understand Bellman's lecture and failed to understand dynamic programming at the time. I only began to understand the subject several years later.

Samuelson was responsible for introducing dynamic programming as an important tool for economic analysis. As is fairly well known, dynamic programming was introduced to the economics profession by two lead articles published in the August 1969 issue of the *Review of Economics and Statistics*, one by Samuelson and the other by Robert Merton, his Ph.D.

student. Samuelson's article, "Life-Time Portfolio Selection by the Use of Dynamic Stochastic Programming," introduced dynamic programming in discrete time, while the article by Merton solved the same problem in continuous time. Beginning with these articles, the use of dynamic programming for economic analysis has flourished.

Without understanding the method of dynamic programming, I was trying to solve a problem in the design of optimum monetary policy and discovered that the elementary and well-known method of Lagrange multipliers could be applied to solve it. The method I applied was explained in Chow (1970). In this paper, I set up a linear macroeconomic model for the macro-economy and assumed a multi-period quadratic objective function to be maximized. Given the objective function and the macroeconomic model, I applied Lagrange multipliers to solve this dynamic optimization problem.

Beginning with my 1970 paper, research on the use of models for the purpose of designing optimal macroeconomic policies began to take hold in the economics profession. One can Google "optimal macro-economic policies by Lagrange multipliers" to get a glimpse of the literature on this topic. By adding "Gregory Chow" at the end of this Google search, one still finds a fairly large number of references. The momentum of this line of research was, however, interrupted by Robert Lucas's article "Macroeconomic Policy Evaluation: A Critique" (Lucas 1976). Lucas had reservations on the application of optimum control techniques to the design of optimum economic policy because when a policy changes the parameters of the econometric model may change. In my opinion, the Lucas critique gained fairly wide acceptance in the economics profession because the use of optimum control techniques for the design of macroeconomic policies was unsuccessful, the reason being the low quality of most of the macroeconomic models being used. If the models used are good, optimum control techniques can be fruitfully applied to obtain optimum economic policies. When the optimal policies change, the parameters of the econometric model may change slightly but not by enough to invalidate the optimum control policy.

Returning to the method for dynamic optimization, there is still the choice between the Lagrange method and the method of dynamic programming. Samuelson introduced dynamic programming into the economics profession. I had a set of lengthy exchanges with him on the relative merits of dynamic programming verses the Lagrange method for the purpose of solving a given dynamic optimization problem. This discussion was recorded in nearly 100 pages of private correspondence, now contained in Box 22 of the Samuelson Papers at Duke University.

Samuelson changed his view in favor of the method of Lagrange multipliers, as partly revealed in his paper "The Irreducible Role of Derived Marginal Utility in Dynamic Stochastic Programming" (Samuelson 1996). Its abstract states:

> Using the important case of multi-period investing between a safe asset with a low mean return and an equity basket with a higher total return but a riskier one, this analysis demonstrates that the relevant stochastic programming involves irreducibly recursive variational relations. The 'direct' Lagrange-Chow procedure is related to the derivatives of the Bellman 'indirect' algorithms and shown to require essentially the same computations save only for standard integrations or taking of first derivatives. To demonstrate that the comparison is unchanged when a vector of control variables must be optimized in a many-period stochastic scenario, the problem is solved for a rentier to both decide how much to save in each period and how much to put of each period's investment into risky securities. (ibid.: 3)

Note that Samuelson refers to the Lagrange-Chow procedure as direct and the use of the Bellman equation as indirect. In his 1996 paper, Samuelson further stated:

> Dr. Chow points out that the too-little-known direct Lagrangian procedure delivers all the optimal solutions that the indirect-utilities method can deliver, and does so more economically in the sense that redundant laborious calculations of any indirect utilities can be avoided... [I]t is regrettable if the popular indirect method has eclipsed attention by scholars from the

> efficient and effective direct Lagrangian approach. We are all in Gregory Chow's debt for a cogent and needed important. reminder (ibid.)

The discussion with Samuelson on dynamic optimization continued with my note "Comments on 'The Irreducible Role of Derived Marginal Utility in Dynamic Stochastic Programming'," also published in *Pacific Economic Review* (Chow 1996). My note shows why the Lagrange method can be simpler than dynamic programming in solving dynamic optimization problems. A demonstration of the advantages of Lagrange multipliers as compared with dynamic programming can be found in Section 1.2 of my book, *Dynamic Economics: Optimization by the Lagrange Method* (Chow 1997). Here, I simplify the discussion in that volume by considering the problem of maximizing the following two-period objective function subject to the constraint as given on the right-hand side of the equation below. This is only a two-period problem, but its discussion suffices to show the merit of the Lagrange method.

$$\text{Max}\, r(x_1, u_1) + \beta r(x_2, u_2) - \lambda(x_2 - f(x_1, u_1)) \tag{1}$$

where x is a state variable and u is a control variable with subscript denoting the time period. We assume all functions are differentiable. By the method of dynamic programming, we first find the optimum value of u_2 as a function $g_2(x_2)$ of x_2 and substitute the result for u_2 in the objective function for the last period, now called the value function of the last period:

$$V_2(x_2) = r(x_2, g_2(x_2)) \tag{2}$$

Having solved for the optimization problem for the last period 2, we reduce the function to be maximized to

$$r(x_1, u_1) + \beta V_2(x_2) \tag{3}$$

After maximizing the above function with respect to u_1, we call it the value function at period 1, namely

$$V_1(x_1) = \max u_1(r(x_1, u_1) + \beta V_2(x_2)) \tag{4}$$

The above is known as the Bellman equation. To solve it, we first find the optimum value of the control variable u_{t+1} that maximizes the value of the objective function from period $t + 1$ onward and then repeat the same process backward in time.

By the Lagrange method, we simply differentiate the Lagrange expression given above with respect to all control and state variables (in this case u_2, u_1, and x_2), obtaining three first-order conditions for the solution of these three variables. Since the Lagrange method does not require the calculation and utilization of the value function for each period, it is simpler than the method of dynamic programming. If the problem is formulated in continuous time, the method used to solve it is to apply Pontryagin's maximum principle. This method is the same as the Lagrange method in discrete time.

5 Conclusion

Much of the economics profession today applies the method of dynamic programming for the solution of dynamic optimization problems for the reasons pointed out above. Paul Samuelson was the leader of this approach. While the Lagrange method is simpler if one wants to find the solution to a dynamic optimization problem, the value function itself is useful in presenting one important characterization of the solution; this characterization can be useful in many applications.

In this chapter, I have shown Samuelson's important contribution to the method of dynamic optimization and its applications. I have also tried to explain my indebtedness to him for his influence on my intellectual development. The topics treated in this volume cover Samuelson's many and varied contributions to economics, in terms of both the development of theories to explain economic phenomena and the methods of economic analysis. No one has contributed as much to the entire field of economics. In this chapter, I have discussed only one aspect of his extensive contributions to the methods of economic analysis.

Acknowledgements I am indebted to Benjamin Moll for critical comments which led to improvement of this paper, although many shortcomings may remain which are my own responsibilities. I would like to thank the Gregory C. Chow Econometric Research Program at Princeton University for financial support in the preparation of this paper.

References

Chow, G.C. (1970) "Optimal Stochastic Control of Linear Economic Systems," *Journal of Money, Credit and Banking*, 2: 291–302.

Chow, G.C. (1996) "Comment on 'The Irreducible Role of Derived Marginal Utility in Dynamic Stochastic Programming'," *Pacific Economic Review*, 1: 251–252.

Chow, G.C. (1997) *Dynamic Economics: Optimization by the Lagrange Method.* New York, Oxford University Press.

Lucas, R.E., Jr. (1976) "Econometric Policy Evaluation: A Critique," in K. Brunner and A.H. Meltzer (eds.) *The Phillips Curve and Labor Markets.* Carnegie-Rochester Conference Series on Public Policy. Amsterdam, North-Holland: 19–46.

Samuelson, P.A. (1996) "The Irreducible Role of Derived Marginal Utility in Dynamic Stochastic Programming," *Pacific Economic Review*, 1: 3–11.

6

Some Correspondence with Paul Samuelson on Economic Theory: An Intimate Memoir

Donald A. Walker

1 Introduction

This memoir presents some extracts from the correspondence and conversations between Paul Samuelson and me about topics in economic theory over a period of fifty-three years.[1] The reader will find his communications of interest because, as a matter of style, they have a frankness, immediacy, and uninhibited quality uncharacteristic of his published writings and

[1] Samuelson's letters and copies of mine are in my possession. My letters and copies of Samuelson's are in the Duke University David M. Rubenstein Rare Book & Manuscript Library. The archived papers do not include some of my early letters to him because he wrote his reply on them and sent them back to me. The archives do not include the other autograph notes and autograph letters that he sent to me, nor transcripts of our conversations. As with my other chapter included in this volume, the letters to me from Samuelson are documented by the date of his letter, without writing "PAS to DAW." When my letters to him are quoted or cited, they are referenced as "DAW to PAS" followed by their date.

D. A. Walker (✉)
Indiana University of Pennsylvania, Indiana, PA, USA
e-mail: dawalker@iup.edu

R. A. Cord et al. (eds.), *Paul Samuelson*, Remaking Economics: Eminent Post-War Economists, https://doi.org/10.1057/978-1-137-56812-0_6

public addresses; and because, as a matter of content, they contain perceptive and illuminating comments and opinions on significant theoretical issues.

The extracts from Samuelson's letters include passages drawn from his commentaries on the work and personalities of notable economists, many of whom he knew personally. The extracts exclude many personal matters that he enjoyed conveying to me and that I enjoyed receiving, such as a conversation with his mother, accounts of his car trips with friends, comments on our conversation when he was a guest in my home, the middle name chosen for him, the last name chosen by members of his extended family and by some of his friends, his Asian commodity broker's aversion to cemeteries, and his comments on events in my life. The extracts from my letters exclude passages on economic theory that are not an integral part of our mutual discourse, and passages with personal content. The memoir avoids our discussions of the history of economic thought insofar as I was able to separate them from our discussions of current economic theory.[2] Inasmuch as such separation was not always possible, there occurs some slight overlap in the content of this memoir and the one in this volume that I devoted to our correspondence on the history of economic thought.

This is an informal intellectual biography, restricted to the presentation of contents of our communications. It is not a research paper. It does not consider views and comments that Samuelson or I made in publications, unless such commentary is also quoted verbatim in our correspondence. It does not have or need bibliographic documentations appended to each name or topic or publication that we mentioned. The reader will know the first name of the economists that we mentioned, and the research to which we made reference. Citation of documents is provided only if it is required to make a letter intelligible. The extracts from our communications are presented exactly as they appear in the originals. For example, uses of tenses that may seem dubious are presented as they were uttered in the unedited context of conversation; underlinings, erroneous dates, parentheses, italics, and question marks are those that are in our letters.

[2]See my "Some Correspondence with Paul Samuelson on the History of Economic Thought: An Intimate Memoir," in the current volume.

2 On Various Economists

Samuelson's interests and intellectual curiosity led him to deal with a wide variety of topics. For example, the character, work, and intellectual interrelationships of Swedish economists deeply interested him and were frequently mentioned by him. Regarding the view that Cassel had developed a revealed preference theory of demand, I asked:

> Tell me what you think of his just leaving out considerations of utility entirely and just passing directly to what you might call phenomenological supply and demand functions in his *Theory of social economy*? What do you think of that as a technique for avoiding the problems of non-quantifiable marginal utility? (conversation, 18 June 1991)

Samuelson answered:

> Well, I think it was more than that. It was a manifesto in its own right. But what he didn't realize, and I think I have made some slanting remarks on this, what he didn't realize was that the utility convention is not purely formalistic, that it does make restrictions.
>
> I replied: "It places restrictions on demand curves," and he agreed. "I think pretty highly of Cassel as a mind," he said, "but he was a rotten person". (ibid.)

He did not similarly value Oskar Morgenstern's rejection of his theory of revealed preference or Morgenstern's contention that mainstream theory is wrong to assume that individuals try to maximize utility (see Morgenstern 1972). Considering the importance to Samuelson of revealed preference theory and his then-recent contentions in his Nobel laureate address (see Samuelson 1972), I had suggested that Morgenstern's views deserved an answer (DAW to PAS, 16 February 1973). Samuelson disagreed. He recognized and explained to me a case of indeterminacy of a game-theoretic type, but remarked that otherwise "most of what Morgenstern says I don't find very interesting" (30 May 1973).

Samuelson was impressed with Bertil Ohlin's 1924 doctoral dissertation.[3] PAS: "In particular, it has a Walrasian system in much better form than Cassel's version, which assumed fixed coefficients of the factors of production" (18 June 1991). Samuelson continued by remarking that Ohlin has variability of coefficients, which Eli Heckscher successfully urged Ohlin to use. As a result, "Cassel was very angry at Ohlin. He said to him: 'Why do you put all that Heckscher nonsense into your thesis?' which is the essence of the thesis." As a consequence of the variability assumption, "the slightly inaccurate Schlesinger-Wald stuff was really all unnecessary" (ibid.). I responded: "Cassel must have known something because he was an advisor to just about every central bank in Europe. He had a very productive career." Samuelson pointed out that,

> Just before my time, like 1925, Cassel would probably have been the world-famous economist that Keynes became after about 1932 or 1933. Well, I think he [Cassel] was quite a productive economist, but because he was so bad as a person and Wicksell was so good as a person, everyone takes revenge against Cassel. (ibid.)

In 1980, I recalled to Samuelson a conversation we had in 1956 in which we had discussed Clarence Ayres's work, remarking that, "I finally got around to dealing with Ayres in a systematic way" (DAW to PAS, 16 December 1980) in articles that Samuelson said that he enjoyed (25 June 1981). Agreeing with my negative conclusion on Ayres's version of institutionalism, Samuelson observed that, "All in all, his formal paradigms were thin, and he did a lot of graduate students career harm. But he had verve and good aims" (ibid.). I had nevertheless thought it worthwhile to draw attention to the fact, as I believe it to be, that Ayres "had the right of priority in proposing a negative income tax" (DAW to PAS, 16 December 1980). In the same letter, I mentioned Robert Clower's work in connection with my project to edit his essays on money (see Walker 1984), and his debate with Samuelson on the issue of the optimum size of the quantity of money. Samuelson replied that, "Clower revived the

[3]This appeared in an English translation in Heckscher and Ohlin (1991).

study of the nature of money: his quarrel with me does not do justice to his original breakthroughs" (25 June 1981).

Regarding Dutch scholars, Samuelson noted that he "knew best (and revered) Jan Tinbergen and Tjalling Koopmans; neither brimming over with a sense of humor" (21 April 1998), and he also knew the distinguished scholar Arnold Heertje. He wanted to know about the Heertje *Festschrift* that I was editing. For a possible contribution, he was seeking to "identify a topic congenial to me [himself]" (17 December 1997). He asked for my opinion on "an experimental paper under the approximate title: 'Sherlock Holmes and the Swarthy German: The 'Transformation' Processes as Backing Out of Marx's Gratuitous *Mehrwert* Cul de Sac'" (21 April 1998). Of course, I accepted his offer to send me an early draft of that paper (DAW to PAS, 4 May 1998) and subsequently included the final text in the Heertje volume (see Fase et al. 1999).

Samuelson mentioned other names when he "sampled the new issue of your journal[4] with respect," although his comments did not evince precisely that quality:

> As it happened, the two items I know most about – Wolfson on Marx's transformation problem and Negishi on Morishima on Ricardo – left me unenthusiastic. Morishima did good work in pure theory: I gave up long ago reading his historical reconstructions. It is as if he makes up the rules as he goes along. According to the Keynes-Kahn multiplier, one bad work generates two bad works – a divergent series that sums to minus infinity. (21 December 1990)

Rephrasing what I had written in a review of Morishima's book on Walras (see Walker 1980), I commented: "I think there is general agreement, excepting, of course, on the part of Morishima himself, that his work on the history of thought is not closely tied to subjects named in the titles of his books" (DAW to PAS, 23 July 1991).

Along with the above-mentioned paper on Marx, Samuelson submitted some suggestions for referees of it:

[4] *Journal of the History of Economic Thought*, the journal of the History of Economics Society.

> Here are a few possibilities. Ian Steedman is one of the few sympathetic to Marx who is competent. Morishima will be infuriated by my footnote 6; I fear my unruly pen will ruin a friendship. Blaug and Hollander would be possibilities, although they too, find me irritating. Negishi – the richest economist in the world with the exception of David Rockefeller – might be a possibility. (18 June 1992)

That comment about "the richest economist in the world" became a running joke. I replied: "I don't think Negishi is the richest economist in the world. I think you are. I could prove this by circumstantial evidence to any impartial observer," and I proceeded to do that, starting with Samuelson's Nobel prize, and making allowances for the proceeds of his textbook (DAW to PAS, 29 June 1992). Samuelson would have none of it:

> Arithmetic is not your strong suit. Stick to economic theory. Your estimates of my net worth are way off the mark … Negishi, I seem to have been told, is son-in-law of a fabulous real-estate tycoon. When Otto Eckstein sold DRI to M-H for $102 million, more than a fifth being his, he probably registered the highest earnings of any economist from his economics … (When that old fool H.H. Burbank died he left Harvard enough for two chairs. Since he never drove a car, I thought we should never underestimate the power of thrift. But when I thought to ask Ed Mason how it all happened, he laughed: 'Burbie made money the old-fashioned way. He married it.' So two fools were involved.) (15 July 1992)

I reported to Samuelson that in editorial correspondence with Negishi, I had expressed

> my admiration of his [Negishi's] great wealth. Sometime later I received a letter from him. At the end of it he apologized for being tardy with some material, explaining that he had been busy with some jobs around the house because, he said, he was unable to afford a housekeeper. (DAW to PAS, 9 December 1999)

Samuelson was active in supporting the research of many scholars, with recommendations, forewords, and publishers' blurbs. An example, described in a letter to me (9 June 1993) and therefore qualifying for mention in this memoir, was his recommendation that a translation of H.-H. Gossen's book be published by The MIT Press, which was done in 1983: "The translator was Rudolph Blitz of Vanderbilt, and I think it cost him a friendship (and vice versa?) with the prickly Nicolas Georgescu-Roegen. Georgescu is a near-genius with intimations that he is a far-genius." Samuelson also, he recounted in his letter, recommended that a collection of Georgescu's papers be published by Harvard University Press and wrote a foreword for them. That book paved the way for the publication, also by Harvard, of Georgescu's book on economic entropy (ibid.).

Samuelson was unfailingly supportive of my own efforts, as shown by the jackets of my books and by his letters. I inscribed one book to "my revered mentor and cherished friend" (DAW to PAS, 15 September 1997). He thanked me

> for the inscribed copy of your new *Walras's market models*. Years ago when Bob Mundell in a huff left the University of Chicago to go to Waterloo, Canada, some wag (I think it may have been Jagdish Bhagwati) aptly said: 'At last Waterloo is meeting its Napoleon.' I am serious when I say, at last Léon Walras has been given an ideal critic. (25 September 1997)

Samuelson noted the work of a variety of other economists in papers that he sent me. One batch included "Conversations with My History of Economics Critics," and "for your algebraic enthusiasm, an ms. to appear in the Blaug *Festschrift*, and an essay on Fisher" (26 June 1991). He mentioned the work of Tobin, Tochtermann, and Recktenwald and commented on work done on applied economics. That led me to send him a copy of a letter I had written to Pascal Bridel

> because I wanted to remark upon how much mischief can be done by listening to methodologists. In this case, Pascal is having conversations with Vaclav Klaus, the minister of finance of Czechoslovakia. Pascal is conveying to him Weintraub's opinion that general equilibrium modeling is nothing but a thought experiment, irrelevant for any applied purposes and therefore irrelevant for the economies of eastern European countries. I am trying to persuade him to examine what economists are doing rather than to read methodologically and philosophically inspired commentaries. (DAW to PAS, 29 June 1992)

My point, I wrote to Samuelson, was that there are many fruitful applications of computable general equilibrium models that have irrevocable disequilibrium transactions, and that Bridel must not have been referring to them but to virtual models, like those constructed by Debreu, Arrow, and Hahn. Their models cannot be used for econometric or planning purposes because they exclude real disequilibrium behavior and variables, which are, of course, the data of real economies. Samuelson replied:

> Your letter to Pascal Bridel helps in the Lord's work. I am reminded of a story about the harm that an economic 'authority' can do, told to me by a Swede visiting Yale around 1955. The economists in the Swedish government had finally persuaded the Labour Government to begin to use a higher interest rate as a device to help ration the very scarce capital there. Along came Ken Galbraith as a visiting V.I.P. His opinion was asked. With a monosecond of 'thought,' he replied: 'Nonsense. Pick some fixed interest rate. Preferably a very low one. And announce that it will be fixed to prevail for the indefinite future.' Two good years were lost! (15 July 1992)

3 On the Uniqueness of Equilibrium

Samuelson reflected on the uniqueness of equilibrium in a number of his communications. One of our exchanges on this topic went as follows (18 June 1991).

PAS: Of course, there isn't any reason why in the real world there should be a uniqueness.

DAW: I have argued that of course if the real world goes to an equilibrium, it's a unique path that it follows.

PAS: That could still involve hysteresis from what the initial conditions were, and there could be more than one equilibrium. In fact, you get all kinds of – I was going to say chaos theory [behavior], but more correctly, – catastrophe theory, bifurcation, where a finite small impulse can have an effect much bigger than its own multiple can. We have to accept the real world as it is and not fight it. Of course, there is a different possibility you might have been stating: given an initial condition, there can be only one equilibrium reached asymptotically from it.

DAW: That is what I was saying, except that I didn't use the word 'asymptotic.' The consequences of hysteresis strengthen the view that, whatever the path may be, it is the one and only determinate path.

PAS: There are systems like that, but there are different regions. If the initial conditions came from different regions, its rendezvous would be with a different equilibrium.

DAW: Yes, but in the real economy there aren't different possible initial conditions; the initial conditions are what they are. And in the real world there are historical and institutional and other conditions which make it true that whatever equilibrium the economy is going to, it is a unique equilibrium. And the possibility of multiple equilibria is an indeterminacy in knowledge, not an indeterminacy in the nature of the real world.

PAS: Modern chaos theory is instructive because implicit [in it] is that even in an exact system, if we have the knowledge of initial conditions, we would be able to predict indefinitely into the future the whole evolution of the system. If it is a dynamic system with strange attractors then the slightest alteration of the initial conditions leads to a divergence from the previous path, which grows chaotically and indefinitely.

DAW: But you don't think the real world is like that, 'chaotic', do you?

PAS: Yes, I do. Chaos was invented by my colleague Ed Lorenz, in weather forecasting. And it's exactly that. What he showed in effect was that if you want to do more than get five days of weather forecasting, it does not help to get 10 more decimal places of accuracy in initial conditions, because the sensitivity of the transformation is such that you lose all precision for practical purposes.

DAW: O.K. I see we are saying slightly different things. I am not contesting the well-known fact that different initial conditions, even slightly different ones, can lead to widely different paths of the variables, notably weather patterns. What I mean is that the real economy doesn't show behavior in the chaos theory sense of the physical systems in which the variables start following patterns of greater and greater divergency. We have at any time a unique set of initial conditions, and they lead in the ongoing course of time to a pretty highly damped economic system.

PAS: I think you have to be very careful. The essence of chaos isn't explosive differences. I don't know if you are a cook, but it's like this: If you take some dough and put a little egg yellow in it and spread it out with a roller and fold it back and spread it out and fold it back, then in the limit the yellow is shot through the loaf. That's the essence of chaos. It's both spreading and bending back on itself, and I think there are a lot of things like that in economic life. However, after the stock market crash of 1987, there was a whole crew of people who thought the chaos theory might give us a handle on it, but I think the stock market kind of uncertainty is the opposite of chaos theory. Chaos theory is based upon things which are completely determined in the short run, but which fritter away in the long run. Whereas, in the stock market, the essence of the phenomena is that you can't know what is going to happen in the short run or it would have already happened. (18 June 1991)

Samuelson made a partial concession to the view I espoused:

> Suppose you contemplate 1879 Marshall's offer curves that intersect three times. Yes, in some real world situation where it is specified that the system begins at an indicated initial disequilibrium point in just one of the four possible areas of the plane – then yes, under specific dynamic laws of correction, only one final 'equilibrium' point will be reached. But <u>that</u> is a different kind of 'uniqueness' than what obtains when the offer curves intersect only once. (15 July 1992)

"Yes," I replied,

> it is the difference between uniqueness in a model and uniqueness in reality. Naturally we can and do define 'uniqueness' as, for example, a single intersection of offer curves, and say that equilibrium is not unique if there

> is more than one intersection. That is a feature of the model, using conventional terminology. My comment in my review [of a book on dynamics] related to two other issues. First, I remarked on allegations which go beyond an economic model to make an assertion about the real world, namely that the pure or econometric model has multiple equilibria so the real world must have them... The real economy has only one path and can go toward only one [moving] equilibrium...completely determined by many conditions, including institutional and historical ones ... It is wrong to say, on the grounds of the non-uniqueness of equilibrium in a model...that predictions about the directions of change of variables cannot be made in reference to the real world ... Second, since a multiplicity of possible points of equilibrium occurs only in a model and is a result of insufficient knowledge, not something in rerum natura, it follows that to advance understanding we should introduce more assumptions and historical conditions to render determinate the actual path of the model. (DAW to PAS, 14 August 1992)

I was criticizing the modeling that concluded that existence had been proved for a competitive economy but that uniqueness and stability cannot be proved and therefore that competitive-economy research had reached a dead end. Debreu, like other theorists, stated that his competitive model had an abstract theoretical nature that was unrelated to empirical considerations (see Debreu 1959: 35). The resulting modeling, I wrote to Samuelson, reached its adverse conclusion about competitive-analysis proofs because it suffered from "insufficient assumptions and detail, except that it is, of course, difficult to understand the economy and society and their history sufficiently well to find realistic additional conditions" (DAW to PAS, 14 August 1992).

Samuelson replied: "When more leisure offers itself, we can discuss further 'multiplicity of equilibrium'; and the usefulness of Debreu stuff" (19 August 1992).

4 On the Stability Conditions

What follows is some of that discussion relating to stability. "You see," I wrote (DAW to PAS, 27 October 2005), "the highlighted statement on the attached page copied from Ingrao and Israel's *The Invisible Hand*," namely: "In fact, the matrix of the second partial derivatives completely controls the local stability of equilibrium (i.e., in a neighborhood of it) and it is therefore immediately possible to supply examples of excess demand vector fields whose equilibria are locally unstable and thus repel trajectories, thereby making global stability impossible" (Ingrao and Israel 1990: 346). I wrote to Samuelson that "I cannot get past the reasoning and the conclusion that the matrix of the *second* partial derivatives of the excess demand functions cannot specify anything about local stability. Will you please help me to see the light on this matter?" (DAW to PAS, 27 October 2005). I sent him three examples of stable equilibria, each with necessarily negative first partial derivatives of the excess demand functions, and three examples of unstable equilibria, each with necessarily positive first-degree partial derivatives: "When the equilibrium is stable, the second order partial derivative x'' can be > 0 as, in (1); or < 0, as in (2); or = 0, as in (3) [the linear case]. When the equilibrium is unstable, x'' can be > 0, as in (5), or < 0, as in (4), or = 0, as in (6)" (ibid.). So, I continued, the second-order partials can be positive or negative or zero when the first-order partials are negative, i.e., when the equilibrium is stable; the second-order partials can also be positive or negative or zero when the first-order partials are positive, i.e., when the equilibrium is unstable. In other words, I wrote, specifying the signs of the x''s puts no restrictions upon the signs of the first partial derivatives and therefore the x''s do not control local stability: "Whereas the first partial derivatives are *always* negative when the equilibrium is stable, and *always* positive when the equilibrium is unstable," so it is the matrix of the first partial derivatives that "completely controls the local stability of equilibrium" (ibid.).

Samuelson's initial response did not clarify matters. He faxed me an exposition of a cobweb process, whereupon I answered as follows:

> I sent you a number of examples that have the effect of showing that the second partials do not place any restrictions on the stability behavior; their signs are compatible with anything. You sent me an exposition of a cobweb process, and with it and in your accompanying discussion you seemed to say that I am wrong, and to suggest that if I understood the process, I would understand why I am wrong. I do understand the cobweb process, and I believe that I am right. In fact, in your exposition, you indicate precisely

> what I contended. You write that one must evaluate the derivative of the function $p_t = f(p_{t-1})$ at p^*. That is the *first* derivative. In your examples, it is -1/2 and -2, giving respectively the stable and unstable cases. The *second* derivative is in *both* cases *zero*, showing in your examples once more that the *second* derivative doesn't imply what is the case in regard to stability. (DAW to PAS, 16 November 2005)

I went on to express the truth (for a proof of which I am indebted to Alan Kirman) of what I contended is the case of equilibria that are, to put it briefly, stable on one side and unstable on the other:

> The conclusion is still that the second order partial doesn't tell anything because [in that case] it is everywhere positive. The first derivative, on the other hand, must be negative on the stable side and positive on the unstable side, just as in the cases of normal stability and normal instability. Same conclusion regarding pathological relationships in a two-good case, etc. (ibid.)

Two days later, Samuelson responded critically by fax (18 November 2005). I replied immediately:

> Your counterexample is undoubtedly correct, but it does not deal with my situation. You show that the 2nd derivative of the monopolist's profit function dictates whether a point at which mc=mr is a maximum or a minimum. But I am concerned only with *market excess demand functions* in a *purely competitive market system*, and for them, it must be the 1st partials that determine stability, whether the equations are dynamic or static. I think you state that. (DAW to PAS, 18 November 2005)

And there we let the matter rest.

5 An Auctioneer

Those issues arose many times, in different contexts. I alluded to the question of the first appearance in the literature of the concept of a "Walrasian auctioneer," who does not appear in any of Walras's writings and who performs functions that are unlike those performed by any real auctioneer (DAW to PAS, 20 September 1991). That led Samuelson to recall his early use of computers to explore the issues of stability and uniqueness:

> We hard-wired our robots so that determinate functional equations could define the time profiles of approach to equilibrium. (We applied the methodology to bilateral monopoly, too. In 1935 Leontief asserted – wrongly as I now conjecture – that the following algorithm would stably converge to the same equilibrium if the rivals met again and again and started out each morning with last night's asymptotic P_{nuts}/P_{apples} ratio: at any point in the Edgeworth-Bowley square, the two chaps' respective indifference slopes are generally unequal; they trade at the average until the first one finds himself tangent to his contour; at this new point, repeat; by late night you will be somewhere on [on? nearly on][5] the contract curve; next morning start them off at their usual point, but begin with last night's price ratio. The point of the recollection is not that the algorithm makes much sense or is correctly described: the point is that we sensed the need for a dynamic rule and only sometimes invoked a human auctioneer or referee.) (26 September 1991)

Samuelson contended: "But, in connection with each good's and service's market in general equilibrium, there had to be a separate auctioneer, all presided over by a grand referee for all markets" (ibid.). I responded with a critique of that view (DAW to PAS, 28 October 1991). It did not, I wrote, draw upon the behavior of the real perfectly competitive organized markets of the nineteenth and twentieth centuries. The behavior that Samuelson thought needed to be linked with theory—buyers and sellers not changing the price—is not a feature of real purely competitive markets.[6] In a long handwritten reply, Samuelson insisted once more upon the necessity of an auctioneer:

> An auctioneer-angel has a useful ring to it because you want a deus ex machina that is distinct from 'demanders' and from 'suppliers.' It is natural,

[5]The brackets and the words inside them are Samuelson's.

[6]For a correction of the notions about the behavior of the French securities markets expressed by Keynes and Kregel, among a host of others, see Walker (2001). I sent Samuelson an off-print of that article, which, I think, he did not read.

> and not unnatural, to try to construct a link between real life and the ideal construct of the elementary textbook...the price being the one at which the supply and demand quantities are equal. (6 November 1991)

He continued with an account of the kind of model that he thought illuminating:

> Already in 1881 Edgeworth conceived of hypothetical contracting and recontracting. Marshall's 1879 offer curves, translated from Mill, called for an algorithm to find their intersection(s), 'stable' and/or 'unstable.' For my classes, I would speak of all-morning-long dry-run explorations of p that would or wouldn't clear markets. Then by 11 A.M. when the trial runs had located p^*, everybody would adjourn for coffee. At exactly 12 noon, they'd exchange the q^* of producers for the q^* of consumers at the uniform p^* price. When I was publishing my (1940 Econometrica?) articles on 'dynamic stability,' I (and later Lange) invoked a law of gradual price adjustment by the hypothetical auctioneer
>
> $$dp/dt = k[D(p) - S(p)],\ k > 0$$
>
> being careful not to specify what was happening to actual q inventories at times when D(p) and S(p) did not match. (6 November 1991)

Thus it appears that, at least in the case of competitive market-day pricing, Samuelson did not accept that the true linkage between a well-constructed model and reality is the elements of reality that are put into the model. His fanciful model was the consequence of the supposition that buyers and sellers are purely price-takers. Inasmuch as he put that supposition into his model, he had to add a means by which prices are quoted and changed. The answer, he thought, is to create a central authority to do that, defying the fact that the most important feature of a market system is that it gets pricing and production done without a central authority.

I remarked on the obvious necessity in this context of recognizing the different types of "real life" purely competitive markets (DAW to PAS, 28 October 1991). Each type should have the properties of the reality it is modeling. Here, I noted, are the two relevant ones. First, in the many markets in which there really is an auctioneer, there is only one seller.

A single batch of a commodity is put up for sale by the seller, the price is always raised by the auctioneer (or always lowered in Dutch auctions), and there are no disequilibrium transactions. Second, in organized purely competitive markets, like stock exchanges, there is no auctioneer, there are transactions at disequilibrium prices, and many buyers and sellers are represented by relatively few agents. The agents change the price, up or down depending upon the state of their individual excess demands, acting for the buyers and sellers, and they communicate their offers, prices, and acceptances directly to each other. There is no need to shy away from considering inventories; they do not constitute a problem. Inventories are assets that appear as arguments in demand and supply functions. If disequilibrium transactions occur, inventories change, thus contributing to the shifting of static supply and demand functions. To trade is to change inventories. In Samuelson's model, nothing happens to them when desired supply and demand "do not match" because no trade occurs when that is the case.

As I have recorded elsewhere,[7] after more than a decade of intermittent discussions on the issue of the necessity of an auctioneer, Samuelson essentially conceded my point when he acknowledged that, "Institutional factors that depart from nice auction behavior in the realistic labor market are not irrationalities which we should try to get rid of in a better theory" (27 October 2003).

6 Returns to Scale

Complicating matters was Samuelson's view of the work of Walras in regard to returns to scale:

> If we had time for informal talk, I hope I could soften your pejorative views on Debreu and Arrow-Hahn. Much of economic reality – on either side of the iron curtain – is illuminated by constant-returns-to-scale technologies; and those works simply carry to completion the kind of analysis L.W. began in 1874. (15 July 1992)

---

[7] See my other essay in the current volume.

I replied by referring to the virtual character of the modern theory, which, by eliminating real irreversible disequilibrium production and exchange, excluded it from mimicking or explaining the real economy:

> If you will show me one practical application of the Debreu-Arrow-Hahn purely competitive general equilibrium model, I will reduce by one my strictures on the uselessness of the theory. I have no fear on that score, however, because in the nature of the case no such application is possible and that model is not used in econometric modeling. Also, I invite you to review once more the Arrow-Hahn book on general comparative equilibrium and its open admission, in the introduction and conclusion and in every chapter, of the general uselessness of what they were doing [see Arrow and Hahn 1971]. To me, that book is almost movingly pathetic in the apologetic attitude that two such brilliant and distinguished authors felt they had to take. Furthermore, we should remember Debreu's own comments about his construction having nothing to do with reality, his disregard of empirical relevance, and his purposeful severing of his model from empirical connections. I had always supposed that your lack of participation in the existence and stability work on general competitive equilibrium in the vein of Walras-McKenzie-Arrow-Debreu-Hahn was fundamentally motivated by a feeling that it is, as Clower has said, "science fiction." In your last letter you indicated that you do not have that feeling. (DAW to PAS, 14 August 1992)

Moreover, "You describe the W-M-A-D-H literature as just the working out of Walras's assumption of constant returns to scale. That sounds so reasonable, as though the authors were like engineers doing a practical job of work. Not so. You must remember the character of the hypothetical world they created" (ibid.).

Samuelson stated not only that constant returns to scale are a logical implication of Walras's analysis but also, I think, that Walras overtly made that assumption. I tried to explain that the latter was certainly not true:

> I just want to state that Walras did not assume constant returns to scale. He assumed firm and industry partial-equilibrium long-run supply curves that are positively inclined in reflection of average costs that rise with output. He states that many, many times and makes his entire analysis of the adjustment process depend on it. (ibid.)

Samuelson replied:

> If you say Walras did not assume constant returns to scale, who am I to protest? I only say for now this: Entrepreneurs who make 'neither gain nor loss' (and who made Edgeworth's mind boggle) make strict sense only in a c.r.t.s. universe… When L.W. in 1874-78 [sic] and later wrote equilibrium conditions in terms of *intensive* technical coefficients, then that implied in extensive-variable space first-degree-homogeneous functions. QED. See H. Schultz, *JPE* (1932? Or 1929?) for an Ynetema theorem to this effect. (19 August 1992)

Nevertheless, Walras, in his treatise in 1874–1877 and in the 1889 and 1896 editions, assumed only initially that the coefficients of production are constant and are given independently of the system of equations of equilibrium, "all the while," Walras wrote, "stating that they are not. Indeed they are not, neither with respect to their value nor with respect to their nature. This circumstance," Walras continued, "is decisive; it has far-reaching consequences" (Walras 2014: 320). Accordingly, he deduced that firms' long-run average cost increases or decreases as a result of the increase or decrease in the prices of inputs in the irreversible tatonnements carried out by entrepreneurs,[8] the proportions of the factors of production entering into the production of one unit of output being variable. Reflecting that condition, he drew positively inclined long-run market supply curves (graphical plates in all French editions). He explained that, at the intersection of such a curve with the market demand curve, price equals the average cost depicted by the former, so the entrepreneur makes zero Walrasian profit (Walras 2014: 254, 210). Wicksteed, Walras pointed out, wrote equations that are "homogeneous and linear and identical to mine" but failed to adopt Walras's general assumption of production equations that are, as Walras explained, "neither homogeneous nor linear; that is

[8]On page 269 of my *Walras's Market Models*, this analysis is scrambled by a printer's error that omitted a crucial part of my sentence, making it say the opposite of what Walras wrote, but the extensive references cited at the end of the sentence on that page are correct and there are many correct presentations of Walras's ideas on that issue in that book. For example, in disequilibrium "the average cost of that capital good is appreciably increased or decreased" as output is increased or decreased thereby raising or lowering input prices (Walras 1877: 297 and passim).

to say, for the case in which the coefficients of production vary with the quantity produced" (ibid.: 507).

7 Market Structures

Samuelson had a great deal to say about theories of the economics of the firm formulated during the first half of the twentieth century:

> I must remember to add that Knight's thesis on Risk and Uncertainty was also widely attributed to Allyn Young, his mentor at Cornell. Tosh. Still, Young somewhere felt it necessary to state publicly that this was not so. I never knew Young: he died in London seven years before I arrived at the Harvard Yard. But his long shadow still stretched across the grass ... I knew Young's work well. My own introduction to microeconomics came at Chicago from the theory chapters he wrote for Old Ely's Outline of Economics. He was a great mind. (In 1913 his QJE review of [Pigou's] Wealth and Welfare was the first to point out the idiocy of wanting to tax industries with rising supply price because increased demand had induced a rise in inputs they used intensively. In 1924 Robertson and Knight, in one of his best papers on social cost, elaborated on Young's point.) On the evidence I have to be skeptical that, had he lived into the 1950s, there was a great book in him [Young]. (31 July 1991)

Samuelson's approach was very different from Chamberlin's. Samuelson "was asked to give a lecture on the use of mathematics in economics ... It was an innocuous lecture," he remembered. Chamberlin was preparing to leave the lecture room when Bob Bishop asked him: "Well, Ed, how did you like Paul's lecture?" and Ed said, "I didn't like it," and Bob said, "What didn't you like about it?" and Ed thought for a moment and said, "Well, it wasn't what he said but it was what I knew he was thinking" (4 November 1990). Samuelson wanted to explore the issue. He asked me: "Do I vaguely recall that you thought I was hard on Ed Chamberlin in some connection. Remind me when and where so that I can ponder whether my judgment would be otherwise today" (21 December 1990). I belatedly replied that "I remember that [in class lectures in 1956] you criticized Chamberlin's work, but I don't have the impression that you spoke harshly of it" (DAW to PAS, 23 July 1991).[9] That led Samuelson to produce a major summary of his views on the issue (31 July 1991):

> Before Kaldor used les mots justes – 'Professor Chamberlin is guilty of the crime of over-differentiating his product' – I formed that view from his Socratic seminar. Joan was his bête noire. Perfect competition has a clear-cut meaning, and both would be realistic to insist that it is only a polar limit to the real world. Surely there is nothing inferior to Imperfect Competition as against Monopolistic Competition. Actually, 'monopoly' is a harder and less interesting pole to define; and, as Ed used to admit, people always made him insist explicitly that there was nothing felonious about situations where it had a presence… Both books are less than perfect. But indeed it is not true that Joan writes of a world of monopolies. She had entrants of rival imperfect-competitors, and tangency of AC to DD was not something Ed could have deserved a patent on. (Schumpeter, God knows why, always called that tangency Kahn's Theorem.) It is true that Joan weasels on the indeterminate behavior responses of rival game-players. But Ed, for all the excellence of his (not-complete) Appendix on duopoly, has no solution for that problem. His large-group paradigm is a classroom tour de force for sidestepping those complications; it is not a real-world tour de force… You correctly emphasize[10] an important aspect of Chamberlin. Whereas many economists regard differentiation of product as a regrettable pathology, he was less judgmental. Indeed he came to love his own baby and at one point gratuitously speaks of his large-group tangency as 'kind of an ideal' (compromise between variety and cheapness). There is no cogency in that judgment, since we are never given the chance to choose between all the combinations of the tradeoff; and, even if we were too alike in our tastes for variety and uniformity, our voting of dollars in the marketplace would not be led by some Smithian invisible hand to Chamberlin's alleged ideal or to our own true one… Chamberlin understood but insufficiently stressed the role of departures from first-degree-homogeneity of production technology in creating imperfections of competition. Whereas a Kaldor expected a sufficient increase in demand to exhaust increasing returns stages and thus approach the competitive asymptote, Chamberlin hypothesized that further differentiation of product could (and, sic, would) be induced,

---

[9] Samuelson's other comments to me on Chamberlin's work are chronicled in my other chapter in the current volume.

[10] In Walker (1989).

> thereby denying Kaldor's asymptote. The agnostic view – maybe yes, maybe no – I think to be a better view than either of theirs. (ibid.)

I had mentioned in my article that Chamberlin said in class that he had conversed with Joan Robinson when he was in England in 1956 and that she had admitted that his monopolistic competition theory was superior to her imperfect competition concept, but declined to say so publicly. Samuelson did not believe that was accurate: "This was not a subject on which Ed was cool and reliable. Even an honest man can be misled; and being Napoleonic does not lessen that possibility." There is "precious little in Chamberlin's pages that she at any date would deem superior to her own Weltanschauung. I would find it credible if she were tape-recorded as saying, 'Yes, I did not exhaust the topic of irrational and rational differentiation of tastes.' Much beyond that would surprise me and require confirming evidence" (ibid.).

8 Welfare Economics

Samuelson returned many times to the topic of maximizing social utility, and, in his letters to me, he discussed it with reference to the neoclassical economists' thoughts on the matter. He could not be dissuaded from the suspicion that Walras harbored religious views that impeded his search for truth in the matter of the best social rules to follow regarding property rights. "I have to ask you a question about Walras," Samuelson said: "What kind of a Catholic was he?" (14 November 1990). I replied: "Not a good Catholic. He was not really a believer" (ibid.). Samuelson continued:

> The reason I ask is [to learn] what the importance might be in his thinking of the concepts of commutative justice and distributive justice, because I once suggested to a Jesuit Boston College student…that he write on modern welfare economics from the viewpoint of commutative justice and distributive justice, and he said 'I wouldn't touch the topic with a ten foot pole.' And I thought maybe I could make some sense about this fairness notion – that everybody should be charged the same price – and that although the rich man's marginal utility is lower than the poor man's, that doesn't entitle the poor man to come off the street and steal the furniture

> in my house. That sounded to me as if it might be a Catholic training. (14 November 1990)

We returned to the topic a year later. I commented that Walras spent a great deal of intellectual energy working out a definition of economic justice and writing down its meaning and applications (DAW to PAS, 28 October 1991). Samuelson reiterated his view. "It is odd," he wrote,

> that Knight, who was unlikely to have known W's [Walras's] text, should resort to the same quibble: 'subject to exchange at a single price, competition maximizes Benthamite Total Utility.' It is odd that W did not dig deeper into what we should mean by 'justice.' When and why is it a good thing that you should not be able to plunder my house just because you are poor and I am rich? When should enlightened citizens form a social contract (perhaps by unanimity) permitting public utilities to depart from uniform pricing for the first, second, and third train trips? Squatters' rights on the common is not inexpedient because it violates God's edicts on justice: it is bad because it tramples the grain; because it equates average labor productivity everywhere and not marginal labor productivity; etc.… Pareto, after 1894, proves something (albeit somewhat obscurely) about the efficiency-optimality of laissez faire pricing when technology is suitable and tastes are individualistic (sans envy or altruism). W could have read him (in Italian? after 1898 in French); but I suppose W was too old by then. The old Catholic. Distributive VS. Commutative Justice may have confused Walras?… By 1900 I think Wicksell sensed that, with 'proper' initial income endowments, competitive p's could attain maximal $\sum U_j$? (6 November 1991)

I defer a question about welfare economics to Sect. 10 where it is an integral part of the exposition.

9 Economics and Physics

I often questioned Samuelson on methodological matters. For example, we discussed them in connection with letters sent to each other by Samuelson, Patinkin, and Blaug (see Samuelson et al. 1991). Another exchange went like this: DAW: You have been charged by one writer with being "extremely disingenuous and how you purposely misrepresent the relationship of physical science to economics, and how you play 'one big shell game.'" PAS: "He's got me as an energeticist?" DAW: "A dissimulating one." PAS: "I happen not to be one of those. Whatever my physicalisms are, that's not it" (14 November 1990). Similarly, I noted that a critic had suggested that "you derived your inspiration and many ideas for the Foundations from Lotka and 'the beliefs and prejudices of E.B. Wilson,' in addition to the work of Birkhoff and Piccard ... If I were to formulate a couple of clear questions on the matter, would you answer them?" (29 June 1991). These exchanges led Samuelson unnecessarily to ask: "Do you think your journal would have an interest in a piece that testifies from the horse's mouth on matters that future scholars can only guess at once the horse is dead or gaga?" (15 July 1992).

I reminded Samuelson that

> On June 29, 1992, I asked: If I draft some questions about the influences on your work, would you answer them: You replied that you would testify 'from the horse's mouth on matters that future scholars can only guess at once the horse is dead or gaga' and would even add and answer some questions of your own devising ... There is no great hurry about your response, but don't wait too long, if you know what I mean. Just joking! And then, as PAS would say, not a peep from the universe. I'd sure like to see your answers! (DAW to PAS, 14 October 2003)

Samuelson had answered:

> Yes, I would welcome your putting to me key questions about my own evolution and what people and notions influenced me. I would even add some further illuminating questions and answer them. Ironically, I have been defending the house of economics from uninteresting notions of 'entropy' and physicists' conservation laws. I include a copy of a paper I wrote for a recently-published Harsanyi Festschrift. It takes seriously the task of investigating whether Hungarian Brody is right to agree with von Neumann's notion that his minimax expression in his general equilibrium model is truly a 'potential function' like that in classical thermodynamics. It turns out not to be. But I am so thorough and polite that someday [someone] will

> enunciate the innuendo: 'Samuelson rides again trying to fob off physicisms on honest economic peasants'. (15 July 1992)

10 Some Later Research Interests

I was eager to assure Samuelson that I would be more than glad to publish his answers to my questions and proceeded to pose three additional questions. I enumerated them, and he answered in kind:

1. Do you believe that Arrow's Impossibility Theorem destroyed the Bergson-Samuelson social welfare function and rendered progress in welfare generalizations about collectivities impossible? (DAW to PAS, 14 October 2003)

I had struck a nerve. Samuelson shot back his answer, which was "NO":

> Now for your Question 1. In my National Academy of Sciences eulogy for Abram Bergson, who died recently, I tried to correct an important injustice. Ken Arrow uncharacteristically deserves some blame in this matter. I've not sounded out on that because he is so noble a guy and so deserving of fulsome praise. (I don't understand it: Bergson, Little, and I independently pointed out around 1953 that Ken had hijacked the term 'welfare function' and applied it to a 'Constitution for Voting function'—not at all the same thing. Yet in Arrow's revised edition he admits nothing at all.)
>
> Several of the papers in *The Collected Scientific Papers of Paul A. Samuelson* correct Kemp-Ng and others for confusing 'single profile Bergson-Samuelson SWFs and Arrow so-called multiple-profile SWFs.' Bergson's excellence in no way diminishes Arrow's important insights on another matter. (Example: Any ethical credo is 'imposed' in Arrow's lingo. A bad thing?) (27 October 2003)

Here is my next question:

2. Do you believe that the Sonnenschein-Mantel-Debreu results regarding the arbitrariness of aggregate excess demand functions despite the existence of well-behaved individual excess demand functions means that the Arrow-Debreu-Hahn type of general equilibrium research has reached a dead end, i.e. that no general results about uniqueness and stability are

possible? (I don't classify the case of all commodities being gross substitutes a general result for uniqueness.) (DAW to PAS, 14 October 2003).

I do not understand Samuelson's answer, which was:

> 2. I lack minutes to deal with this. Face and accept the fact (you have no choice) that the two-person demand functions of the best-behaved person's one-person demand functions can generate multiple competitive equilibria. Don't fight it. Or airbrush out this inconvenience, known since 1869 Marshall, if not already known to 1829[11] J.S. Mill. (27 October 2003)

Here is my third question:

3. Do you believe that it is impossible to provide logically consistent microeconomic foundations for macroeconomic propositions? (DAW to PAS, 14 October 2003).

Here is his answer:

> 3. Institutional factors that depart from nice auction behavior in the realistic labor market are not irrationalities which we should try to get rid of in a better theory. Before you were in grade school, the 1932 unemployment surrounding me was never explained by Knight's lectures on Say's Law. So to speak, while I spent four summer vacations on the beach, I knew 50 pairs of identical twins: half of each pair was grateful to have a job; the other half envied then and would gladly have changed places with them. But they had no way to get the work by offering to work for considerably less. That's why, after a struggle, by mid-1936 I had accepted Neanderthal Keynes *General Theory* models. (27 October 2003)

The character of our communications changed somewhat toward the end of Samuelson's life. We talked more on the telephone and wrote less. We had extensive discussions about his then-current research, and about our preparation of a volume of his selected essays on the history of economic thought.[12] He supplied me with biographical details to help me to write the citation on the occasion of my university conferring an honorary degree on him, which was done on 15 May 1993. That was also his birthday, and

[11] Samuelson probably meant to write "1848."

[12] See my other chapter in the current volume.

"the birthday cake was a happy inspiration for which I take full credit. We have a photograph of you blowing out the candles, and I'm still curious as to what wish you could have made. Except for youth, what could you possibly want that you haven't got?" (DAW to PAS, 3 June 1993). Never at a loss for an instructive comment, he replied: "On what to wish for, youth is overrated. It would be nice to stay 70 for a long, long time. And to have a mathematician slave to do my bidding" (9 June 1993).

He congratulated me on my post-retirement activities and commented on his own:

> Your present life is like being a Junior Fellow at Harvard, as I was in 1937–1940. I could have done that forever.[13] Later as an MIT Institute Professor, I returned to heaven. Being Emeritus means only being less overpaid. Like Einstein I could wish for a clever assistant to speed up and check my calculations. That would give me back my earlier speed[14] … Good health is good luck. And my luck, in all things, has been many standard deviations above the mean. However, the small hand of the clock, which appears to be stationary, always does move. (23 February 2000)

Samuelson had good health during his eighties and remained active intellectually until very shortly before his death. He explained:

> Today I turn 88. My rational expectations based on male genealogy were to die around age 53, much like FDR who died of generalized arteriosclerosis around age 65. However, around 1950 medical technology innovations suspended my sentence. So every day is a new day, as I perform about as always except at a somewhat slower pace. My tennis, age corrected, remains undeservedly good. (15 May 2003)

In his research, Samuelson became much occupied with miniature abstract economic models that could be tested for various properties by using computer programs, some results of which eventuated in his last publications.

---

[13] I know how he felt. I was a Harvard University Fellow of Faculty of Arts and Sciences, 1956–1957, and a Henry Lee Memorial Fellow, 1957–1958.

[14] He was fortunate, in his later years, to have the help of Erkko Etula, a talented computer programmer.

He asked me some difficult questions, some of which I present in order to show the type of problems that concerned him:

> My present major interest is how Walras would derive the interest rate in the *stationary state*, with zero net accumulation and perfect replacement of used-up inputs already being carefully subtracted out of gross output to leave him with *net stationary* product. Only when his competitive supply and demand have fixed on (1) a unique interest rate and (2) unique real wage rates for different goods—I omit land rents by supposing Ben Franklin's new continent has redundantly free land. What kind of technology background between inputs and outputs of cornseed and corn does he envisage? How does more labor supply relative to the same stock of (replaced) cornseed depress the equilibrium real wage rate (W/P)* and raise the safe rate of interest i*? Can you find specificity on all that in his exposition? (16 June 2005)

Samuelson enlarged upon that theme:

> Maybe you can find and point out to me words of Walras that cater to *my* curiosity. When Etula and I specify a technology where labor, wheat, and iron inputs can produce either or both of wheat and iron one period later, we are able to generate a unique stationary-state triplet [of the interest rate, and prices of the two products] just from exogenous knowledge of permanent labor supply, permanently replaced iron endowments; and wheat endowments. (16 June 2005)

I [DAW] was unable to understand how that would be possible without introducing the demand functions for the products.

Samuelson thanked me for the "specific Walras references" on the topic in my reply and continued:

> The words there are not without interest. But we are left with various vagueness(es):
>
> 1. Too bad that Walras did not put a microscope on say, a 2-good consumption model where each good is produced by, say, labor, land and a *single* K good. (It could be that the one consumable good, wheat, is produced in one period by labor, wheat-seed itself, and land.) Then

Walras could augment the intertemporal production story by people's intertemporal utility story:
Total U = say $\{\log \text{Wheat}(t) + 1/(1 + p) \log \text{wheat}(t + 1) + \ldots\}$

2. I had hoped that the pre-calculus Walras might have specified two or more different (L, wheatseed) mixtures to produce wheat. One mixture only precludes *any* unique set of distributional pricings.
3. Maybe somewhere else in 1874 or later Walras did deal with non-temporal joint products? Sheep species A that produces wool and mutton in *different* proportions than B species does. Then the Gordian Knot of P_{mutton}/P_{wool} might be cut by supply and demand clearings?

A forlorn hope, I fear. (29 June 2005)

11 Pareto, Keynes, and Allais

One of my questions concerned Lawrence J. Henderson's Pareto Seminar in the 1930s at Harvard. At a meeting in Lausanne in 2006, Annie Cot had given an excellent paper that did, however, in one respect conflict with Samuelson's views. I asked him for his opinion regarding her contention that the Seminar played a role in "the dissemination and development of the notion of general equilibrium in many disciplines in the U.S. You're familiar with the contents of her paper, except the part especially devoted to you" (DAW to PAS, 10 December 2006). Cot contended, in her words, that "Samuelson is partly right and partly wrong when he claims, in the 1990s, that the conception of his *Foundations* had no relation to the Pareto seminar." I wrote to Samuelson: I "thought you might be 'partly interested'" (ibid.), and indeed he evidently enjoyed the opportunity to express his opinion, which he did three days later, providing an interesting view of accounts of intellectual history:

> Each letter from you splashes me with both consumers and producers surplus. You remain incredibly active, and your being well-organized provides an extra multiplier to your inputs… I learned at the age of 14 or 15 that history never gets things right. But at a time of greater leisure I'll relate that story to you. Much of what Annie Cot wrote on the Harvard Pareto seminar bears zero relation to the 20th century conquest of economic theory

> by general equilibrium paradigms in competition with Marshallian partial equilibrium. Only Rip van Winkles like M. Friedman and G. Stigler had good words to say about Marshall's partial equilibrium in 1990, the hundredth anniversary of the 1890 Marshall *Principles*. Concerning Cot's quoted words about 'boundary objects' and 'nomade' concepts, Dickens would say, 'Bah! Humbug!' I am speechless. (13 December 2006)

I wanted to get Samuelson's opinion on the determinateness of the Keynesian model that, I wrote to him, "you polished and packaged in your textbook.[15] You present the intersection of a saving and an investment function. Then you shift, for example, the investment function and point to the new intersection and state it is the new equilibrium to which the globally and locally stable economy moves" (DAW to PAS, 6 December 2007). I went on to note, as I summarize here, that it cannot, however, logically be assumed that simultaneously the array of asset holdings is constant and net investment changes. A change in investment is a change in the array of asset holdings, regardless of whether or not the investment is small relative to the total existing capital stock. It entails a change in saving, consumption, and the amounts and distribution of firms' and individuals' inventories and financial assets. Those alterations change their supply and demand functions. As a result, "the Keynesian functions you presented are part of a path-dependent system." The new investment function that Samuelson posits is transitory. It gives rise to subsequent continuously shifting functions, and whether a stable final set emerges, and hence whether equilibrium exists, "cannot be demonstrated with the model" (ibid.).

In the hope of getting a reply to that statement, I repeated it (DAW to PAS, 28 September 2008). I pointed out again that the source of indeterminacy in his textbook models is his ceteris paribus assumption, namely that the array of assets is constant while investment, saving, and consumption vary. Samuelson had, as indicated above in regard to an earlier letter, defended his acceptance of "Neanderthal Keynes models" on practical and pragmatic grounds, but I was unable to persuade him to discuss their indeterminacy. Nevertheless, he evinced, I think, his sympathy for my point

[15]See Samuelson (1948: Chapter 12, and specifically for investment shifts, p. 267).

of view by his "Neanderthal" remark and when he wrote, in his answer to my 28 September letter, that he had written "a beginner's book that reeked of partial equilibrium" (7 October 2008).

Another of my questions concerned the contributions of Maurice Allais. I had learned, I told Samuelson, that he was going to write a homage to Allais. I reported that I had agreed to write an essay on Allais's influence on US economists and wanted to benefit from Samuelson's view of his work (DAW to PAS, 9 September 2008). Samuelson responded by sending me a typescript draft of his homage (17 September 2008), along with a cautionary observation:

> Your September 9 note about Allais reminds me to keep you on my worry list whenever tropical storms bypass Longboat Key, Florida, on their way to harass bayou country… Allais spells his name Napoleon. If he had not done pendulum experiments to disprove Einstein's 1905 special theory of relativity, he might have become professor at École Polytechnique. (When I asked a physicist what might have produced Allais' result(s), he said, 'Maybe it was the metro.')… Here is the brief homage I wrote for a collective book on Allais' contributions. When you read it remember Dr. Samuel Johnson's words: At funerals and honorific occasions, speakers are not under oath. (ibid.)

Eventually, I told Samuelson that I had finished my research on Allais and had concluded, after an exhaustive review of 70 years of publications, that apart from whatever influence the Allais Paradox of 1953 may have had, he did not influence economics in the United States Samuelson had written—I quoted his words in my letter to him—that "a whole generation of economic theory would have taken a different course" if Allais had written in English. I answered: Which of the two very different courses would theory have taken?—a pertinent question because, in the last part of his career, Allais had rejected the body of theory which he had helped to construct and for which he had received the Nobel Prize and had espoused a quite different theory. In my summary to the conference organizer,

> I say that Allais's impact has not been aided by the fact that he has changed his opinions and his theory. If both his original and his new ideas had been accepted, the course of economic theory would have been quite messy. Furthermore, the possibility that some of his ideas have been plagiarized cannot be established scientifically. I conclude that Allais did not have an influence on Anglophone economists, and therefore I cannot contribute a paper on the subject for the Allais conference. (DAW to PAS, 16 September 2009)

12 Homage

At the end of that letter, I acknowledged that in a previous communication, Samuelson had "posed some difficult questions, which I'll try to answer in my next letter," but further communication was not to be. Samuelson passed away in the early morning of 13 December 2009.

Some years earlier I had wanted to send Samuelson a copy of one of my books, namely Walker (1997). I thought, however, I should make excuses for having suggested in it "qualifications to the proposition, expressed so clearly by Willard Gibbs and yourself, that mathematics is language" (DAW to PAS, 4 May 1998),[16] a tiresome and fruitless question dependent on definitions of terms. Samuelson replied: "I like people to be different from me. So shame the devil and send me your new book – an inscribed copy, please" (4 May 1998). I did as he asked, with an inscription that I reproduce here as a fitting close to this memoir:

> Dear Paul,
> Mathematics may be language and words are certainly language, but neither mathematics nor words can express the depth of my appreciation for having had the benefit of your contributions, tutelage, and friendship throughout my entire career. (DAW to PAS, 20 May 1998)

[16]See the title page of Samuelson's *Foundations of Economic Analysis.*

References

Arrow, K.J. and F.H. Hahn (1971) *General Competitive Analysis.* San Francisco, Holden-Day.

Debreu, G. (1959) *Theory of Value: An Axiomatic Analysis of Economic Equilibrium.* Monograph 17, Cowles Foundation. New York, Wiley.

Fase, M.M.G., W. Kanning and D.A. Walker (eds.) (1999) *Economics, Welfare Policy, and the History of Economic Thought: Essays in Honor of Arnold Heertje.* Cheltenham, UK, Edward Elgar.

Heckscher, E.F. and B. Ohlin (1991) *Heckscher-Ohlin Trade Theory.* Edited by H. Flam and M.J. Flanders. Cambridge, MA, The MIT Press.

Ingrao, B. and G. Israel (1990) *The Invisible Hand: Economic Equilibrium in the History of Science.* Cambridge, MA, The MIT Press. Original Italian version, 1987.

Morgenstern, O. (1972) "Thirteen Critical Points in Contemporary Economic Theory: An Interpretation," *Journal of Economic Literature,* 10: 1163–1189.

Samuelson, P.A. (1948) *Economics.* New York, McGraw-Hill.

Samuelson, P.A. (1972) "Maximum Principles in Analytical Economics," *American Economic Review,* 62: 249–262. Nobel Memorial Lecture. Reprinted in *The Collected Scientific Papers of Paul A. Samuelson, Volume 3* (1972). Cambridge, MA, The MIT Press: 2–17.

Samuelson, P.A., D. Patinkin and M. Blaug (1991) "On the Historiography of Economics: A Correspondence," *Journal of the History of Economic Thought,* 13: 144–158.

Walker, D.A. (1980) "Review of *Walras' Economics: A Pure Theory of Capital and Money,* by M. Morishima," *History of Political Economy,* 12: 131–135.

Walker, D.A. (ed.) (1984) *Money and Markets: Essays by Robert W. Clower.* Cambridge, UK, Cambridge University Press.

Walker, D.A. (1989) "Monopolistic Competition: An American Contribution," *Storia del Pensiero Economico,* 16: 3–9.

Walker, D.A. (1997) *Advances in General Equilibrium Theory.* The Hennipman Lectures. Cheltenham, UK, Edward Elgar.

Walker, D.A. (2001) "A Factual Account of the Functioning of the Nineteenth-Century Paris Bourse," *European Journal of the History of Economic Thought,* 8: 186–207.

Walras, L. (1877) *Éléments d'Économie Politique Pure.* Lausanne, Corbaz.

Walras, L. (2014) *Elements of Theoretical Economics, or The Theory of Social Wealth.* Third edition, 1896, translated and edited by D.A. Walker and J. van Daal. Cambridge, UK, Cambridge University Press.

7

Some Correspondence with Paul Samuelson on the History of Economic Thought: An Intimate Memoir

Donald A. Walker

1 The Purpose of This Memoir

This memoir provides information about Paul A. Samuelson's ideas on the history of economic thought that is not to be found in published documents. That is done in two ways. First, the memoir presents extracts from correspondence between Samuelson and me,[1] and from some of the notes

[1]The letters to me from Samuelson are documented by the date of his letter, without writing "PAS to DAW." When my letters to him are quoted or cited, they are referenced as "DAW to PAS" followed by their date. I have not changed the wording of the letters in any way and have not annotated them except in some instances in which the text demands a reference. Italics and underlines are those that are in the original documents. The readers for whom this memoir is intended will know the first names of the persons mentioned, and inserting dozens of bibliographical citations and biographical facts about the persons to whom Samuelson referred are also unnecessary given its readership and informal nature, and would make it unacceptably long. Samuelson's letters and copies of mine are in my possession; my letters and copies of Samuelson's are in the Duke University David M. Rubenstein Rare Book & Manuscript Library.

D. A. Walker (✉)
Indiana University of Pennsylvania, Indiana, PA, USA
e-mail: dawalker@iup.edu

R. A. Cord et al. (eds.), *Paul Samuelson*, Remaking Economics: Eminent Post-War Economists, https://doi.org/10.1057/978-1-137-56812-0_7

I made of our telephone conversations. The memoir recounts our communications that deal with the history of economic thought, excluding recent issues in economic theory insofar as it is possible to disentangle them from the former. That condition required the selection of parts of letters and the elimination from consideration of entire letters. Naturally, I have on occasion referred to my writings, "naturally," I say, because I was one of the two parties to the correspondence and conversations, so without some of my remarks some of Samuelson's would be obscure. Samuelson's communications are of interest because they have analytical content regarding past doctrines, and because they are enlivened by stories, commentaries, and amusing facts. They differ qualitatively from anything he published, having a freshness, spontaneity, and frankness of expression that derive from the circumstance that they were communications to a friend, not written for appearance in a research paper. The inclusion of two passages that are in Samuelson's publications is justified on the grounds that they appear in our letters and are essential to the discourse in them. The extracts from our correspondence are representative but not exhaustive because of limitations of space.

Second, the memoir presents a previously unpublished list of the articles that Samuelson chose, circa the years 2000–2003, for reprinting in a volume that was to be devoted to his writings on the history of economic thought. The list is prefaced by some of Samuelson's reflections on its composition.

2 Samuelson's Interest in the History of Economic Thought

2.1 Lectures and Publications

Samuelson expressed a conviction of the importance of a knowledge of the history of economic thought. He was concerned to show how past economic doctrines have influenced why and how present doctrines have taken their form. That included showing the linkages between earlier theories and his own contributions in order to make clear his place in the evolution of the discipline. He manifested his conviction in his lectures, conversations, and correspondence. When I was Samuelson's student in 1956—he was taking Edward Chamberlin's place in the first semester of the first-year graduate economic theory class at Harvard while the latter was on sabbatical—I was struck by the historical context into which he placed his lectures. Blessed with an extremely retentive memory of the literature, he would introduce the theoretical topic at hand with a review of its history, with names and dates and a brief account of the evolution of the doctrine. He brought to bear a firm grasp of the past analytical framework in which each specific part of the literature had its place. At 41 years of age, he was a joy to watch, just as he was decades later, brimming with intellectual energy and self-confidence in navigating the vast waters of economic thought.

Samuelson manifested his conviction also in his publications, producing insightful articles, reviews, eulogies, and forewords written from the viewpoint of consideration of the history of economic thought. Those writings examine the ideas of classical and neoclassical economists, and expositions of more recent economists, including Jacob Viner, Frank Knight, John Hicks, Harold Hotelling, Dennis Robertson, Abba Lerner, Maurice Allais, Seymour Harris, Alvin Hansen, Joseph Schumpeter, Wassily Leontief, Milton Friedman, Franco Modigliani, Abram Bergson, and Walt Rostow. He knew most of these scholars personally. Moreover, in many articles the body of which is not on the history of economic thought, Samuelson revealed his conviction of its importance with footnotes and appendixes in which his scholarship regarding that history is of the highest quality. For example, the appendix to his 1974 article on complementarity[2] is a condensed but incisive and instructive review of the history of thought on that topic.

It was in order to express his conviction that, in December of 1961, he chose the topic "Economics and the History of Ideas" for his Presidential Address to the American Economic Association.[3] The history of economic thought, Samuelson contended, should be important, for the reasons just given, not only to historians but also to economic theorists generally. Similarly, he responded positively to my invitation that he give

[2] See Samuelson (1974).

[3] Published in 1962 as referenced in Sect. 4.

the keynote address to the History of Economics Society in 1987.[4] Samuelson chose to argue the desirability of eschewing antiquarianism, except for personal pleasure, like a hobby, and of studying "past intellectual activity that appears to have been significant in leading to the current state of the discipline" (DAW to PAS, 28 September 1987). It must be added that he had a clear-eyed view of the limitations of the relevance of long-past economic doctrines. For example, he cautioned that "the notion that wisdom in such matters" as the study of large private fortunes and income inequality "begins with the study of Sir William Petty, Smith," etc., "is laughable on its face."[5]

2.2 Characteristics as a Writer and as a Person

Samuelson lectured and wrote in a manner uniquely his own. His way of dealing with his subjects enabled rapidity of reference and concision but correspondingly made considerable demands upon his reader. I wanted to make sure that he knew that I appreciated the way he expressed himself:

> Apart from the intellectual core of your address, I greeted the style as I would a cherished friend. The asides, the anecdotes, the intricate and allusive texture, the erudite embellishments are so unmistakably yours that I recognized your work with the same readiness with which one can recognize a piece by Mozart or an intermezzo by Brahms. (DAW to PAS, 28 September 1987)

Who else would write in the following way?

> Mine is a skeptical mind. But I suspect I put more credence in equilibrium theory as an idealized model of reality than you do. In today's ruthless global competition, I infer that oligopoly rents are lower than they used to be; dynamic Darwinism dampens down quasi-random aberrations of price and production patterns. I've been known to be wrong. (23 February 2000)

---

[4] Referenced in Sect. 4.

[5] In a draft of an essay edited by me and attached to DAW to PAS, 14 August 1992.

Samuelson was confident in the superlative quality of his scholarship, a quality resulting in part from his being unstintingly self-critical. For example, he contended, regarding his paper "Marx on Rent"[6] that I was editing for publication in the *Journal of the History of Economic Thought*, that his "present effort is obviously only a speedy sortie into the heart of Marx's purported novel rent doctrines." I told him:

> It is not accurate to characterize your fine paper as "only a speedy sortie." It is a full-scale rigorous treatment of the problem, and to describe it in the way that you have would only give critics an excuse to be critical of it. They would say PAS himself describes it as only a speedy sortie. Perhaps I'm being overly protective, which is quite unnecessary, because you are perfectly capable of taking care of yourself. (DAW to PAS, 13 August 1992)

Samuelson also wrote, in reference to his topic, that "Just as war is too important to be left to generals, historians of economic thought cannot be counted on to do the tasks like this one. (As an example, how long must we wait for a proper appraisal of the classical theories of commodity moneys?)" (in attachment to DAW to PAS, 14 August 1992).

That was too much. I had to caution him:

> Second, it is speculative in the extreme to say that historians of thought cannot be counted on to do one or another particular task. I would prefer, in a journal that is the official organ of the History of Economics Society and that is read by 500 dedicated historians of economic thought, not to insert [that sentence]. Moreover, whether or not you are right, the sentence doesn't have anything to do with the body of your paper. Third, the reference to classical theories of commodity monies is a purely parenthetical aside that may be provocative to some people and that in any case does not have anything to do with your thesis regarding Marx. (DAW to PAS, 14 August 1992)

I asked him either to accept the elimination of those statements or to direct me to reinstate them (ibid.). The passages do not appear in his

---

[6] Referenced in Sect. 4.

article because, without hesitation, he chose the former option, adding only: "I take your points" (19 August 1992).

Samuelson's receptivity to well-reasoned and principled evaluations of his work shown in the case just mentioned was an important and consistent aspect of his scholarly approach. He actively sought opinions on his work on the history of economic thought, as when he wrote about another projected paper on Marx: "With encouragement from you, I could send you an early draft of this item. With your good sense you could advise: (a) publish it elsewhere than in the Heertje *Festschrift*; (b) abort it" (21 April 1998). Other examples are shown in the course of this memoir.

Samuelson's acceptance on 15 May 1993, of an honorary degree from Indiana University of Pennsylvania gave me an opportunity to witness again his gracious and unaffected demeanor, and to remark in the citation I wrote for the occasion and in a letter that "You long ago passed through the portals of the Pantheon of the Greats on which someone once said you were knocking, but to achieve scientific immortality without becoming narcissistic and pompous is a challenge that many great persons have failed" (DAW to PAS, 3 June 1993). Unlike many eminent scientists who become almost totally self-referential in their later years, absorbed in thoughts about their own research and in some cases about their own eminence, Samuelson remained deeply interested in the work and experiences of others. He spoke and wrote to me on many occasions about my actual and possible research. He asked questions about Walras's ideas. He recommended that I investigate Cassel's intellectual debt to Walras. He was interested to learn that Gerard Debreu had fulfilled his acceptance of my invitation to speak to the International Walras Society and suggested that I write an account of our conversations (23 February 2000). He wanted to know my opinion of Herbert Gintis's computerized model of market behavior (15 October 2007; DAW to PAS, 9 November 2007). He urged me to examine the Stigler-Friedman letters on partial equilibrium analysis and report my findings to him (7 October 2008). He advised: "Your extreme youth makes you the guy to defend Jevons and Walras. (Walras wouldn't like my pairing. That was *his* Napoleonism!)" (7 October 2008). He endorsed my books on their jackets, and he commented on the offprints and books that I sent him over the years.

2.3 On Marshall and Walras

Samuelson respected the neoclassicals. He thought that it is important to study them in order to clarify their accomplishments and the respects in which they were limited in their views. He commented frequently on Marshall, often critically, as when he took issue with Marshall's claims that Ricardo anticipated marginalism:

> Hollander sent me a reprint of an article with a title like "Marshall was Right about Ricardo". It amounts to: One, Tolstoy did not beat babies or whip dogs. Therefore, Two, Tolstoy understood Newtonian mechanics. What the whole world has always found laughable in Marshall's words on Ricardo was his pretence that the marginal utility notions of Jevons, Walras, and Menger are already implicitly there in 1817. Hollander compliments Ricardo for his understanding of resource allocation and for being more than a pre-Sraffian. O Tempora! O Mores! (31 July 1991)

On occasion, Samuelson derived some innocent pleasure from having fun with Marshall. The remark about Samuelson knocking on the door of greatness led him to this thought: "Were you aware that Marshall knocked on the door of the One-Joke Club? But as far as I know, A.M. never passed out of it. Do you know what his one joke was?" [Francis is all right but you have to watch out for Ysidro] (9 June 1993).[7]

Yes, having read Keynes's *Essays in Biography*, I knew that Marshall had made that quip, but I was glad to learn the name of the Club. Samuelson was interested in other Marshallian details, generally not trivial, such as whether the condition of Marshall's copy of Léon Walras's treatise (in the Marshall Library in Cambridge, England) was evidence that Marshall had not devoted much effort to understanding Walras's ideas. Samuelson said in class in 1956 that the pages of Marshall's copy were, after the first few, still folded shut, subsequently writing to me that his authority for that information was William Jaffé (22 July 1969). In fact, Jaffé told me, years later, that he had discovered, upon examining the book, that the bindery had severely cropped all the pages, thus eliminating clues as to how much

[7]The sentence appears in brackets in the letter. Keynes reported the joke this way: "Francis is a charming fellow, but you must be careful with Ysidro."

of it Marshall had read, and eliminating any marginal notations (no pun intended) he may have made.

Samuelson was steadfast in his criticism of Marshall's partial equilibrium approach, applauding "the 20th century conquest of economic theory by general equilibrium paradigms in competition with Marshallian partial equilibrium. Only Rip van Winkles like M. Friedman and G. Stigler had good words to say about Marshall's partial equilibrium in 1990, the hundredth anniversary of the 1890 Marshall *Principles*" (13 December 2006).

Similarly, Samuelson cautioned me to

> Skip the *People* magazine stuff about the fiendish perfidies of Paul Samuelson. Concentrate on Friedman's conversion of Stigler to the view that Marshall's **d′d′ – s′s′** (partial?!) equilibrium is better than general equilibrium. Try to coax some further letters out of Steve Stigler. Friedman is utterly confused. Before his 1890 *Principles*, Marshall was obviously a general equilibrium guy and a good one. (His personal failing was to belittle Jevons and by innuendo puff up his own early originality.) If Friedman is not aiming at the partial equilibrium of Marshall, he is pushing at open doors. His way of defining *group* ss-dd is by postulating that they somehow sum up the curves that keep people at some same Slutsky-like tradeoff between corn and wheat on each person's indifference curve, not curve(s). I wrote to Milton but made no dent on him – an easy thing to do.

> Stigler thought Milton to be better than himself, better than anyone. Actually, Milton has a short publication list, containing not a few nutty analyses. His strong point was as a pied piper for libertarianism—economic libertarianism, not J. S. Mill liberal concern for freedom of speech and belief. (7 October 2008)

At the end of some additional remarks about the superiority of general equilibrium analysis, Samuelson nevertheless allowed that he had derived material benefit from the partial equilibrium approach: "I made a fortune in a beginner's book that reeked of partial equilibrium" (ibid.).

As for Walras, Samuelson recognized that among his contributions were literary studies as well as mathematical modelings. I quoted Samuelson's own words to him: "today there can be little doubt that most of the literary and mathematical economic theory appearing in our professional journals is more an offspring of Walras than of anyone else (and I stress the adjective *literary*)" (Samuelson 1962: 3; italics in original[8]; quoted in DAW to PAS, 28 August 2000). He remarked in a similar vein:

> The stock of Marshall declined on the market of reputations relative to those of Léon Walras, Stanley Jevons, Knut Wicksell, and Francis Edgeworth. After being underestimated as an eclectic, John Stuart Mill's terms of trade steadily appreciated vis-à-vis David Ricardo's. After Vilfredo Pareto succeeded to Walras's Chair at Lausanne, Pareto's reputation at first tended to eclipse that of his Master; but Schumpeter's championship of the unique and stellar worth of general equilibrium helped engineer a Kondratieff wave that brought Walras to the top of the microeconomic pole. (Samuelson quoted in DAW to PAS, 14 October 2002)[9]

He subsequently added:

> Here is a 2003 second thought. As I wrote more than once: "Lagrange said that Newton was not only the greatest, but he was also the *luckiest.* For he did discover the 'System of the World' and there is only one such system to be discovered". So with Walras who did first discover the one and only general equilibrium. Pareto should not eclipse him. However, it was time to move on *beyond* Walras, and Pareto did do important work deserving of judicious praise. (27 October 2003)

2.4 On Some Other Economists

Samuelson was knowledgeable about the work not only of major past economists, such as those just mentioned, but also of those less prominent. Drawing upon his vast network of acquaintances, he gleaned and related to me an extensive amount of biographical detail about them. For example, I sent him a postcard which, on the front, had a photograph of a smiling

---

[8] Referenced in Sect. 4.

[9] From an undated typescript that Samuelson sent to me that became Samuelson (1998).

Henry Simons, and, on the back, one of Simons's dictums: "The open season on consumers must be abolished." Samuelson answered:

> A short postcard induced a long multiplier chain in reply. But what a postcard! Henry Simons was a dear teacher of mine at Chicago and the likeness was a good likeness. He was a 33-year-old bachelor when I knew him and he lived in one room at the Quadrangles (faculty) Club, where he was a billiards champ. I saw him at the U.S. Treasury not long before he committed suicide and his old ebullience was not in evidence. (5 August 1998)

I wrote to Samuelson that

> One of my recent articles uses the work of Adolphe Landry to explore the theory of profit. I bet you don't know anything about him. I bet you don't know that he is the author of the French system of subsidies (allocations familiales) designed to increase the size of French families and having a number of other social objectives. I bet you don't know that the Landry family grows and bottles under their name some pretty good wines near Calvi. (DAW to PAS, 9 December 1999)

It was rash of me to make that bet. Except about the wine, I lost it. He replied:

> You underestimate me. Paul Douglas, at the University of Chicago, fall quarter 1934 mentioned Landry when lecturing on his new book *The Theory of Wages*. From that, or reading the book, I got the idea for my first article (*Review of Economic Statistics*, 1937: measuring cardinal utility by observing how people altered their lifecycle savings patterns when the market interest rate changed). But now I've shot my Landry bolt. (23 February 2000)

Samuelson knew about many relatively minor European economists. After a discussion of aspects of the history of marginalism, I suggested: "You seemed hesitant to accept that Hermann Amstein was the individual who first told Walras about marginal productivity, in 1877. Nevertheless it appears that was the case. Paul Piccard was the individual who told Walras how to derive a demand function. He did that in 1872" (DAW to PAS, 3 June 1993).

I thought Amstein's name was one that could be added to Piccard's as something that Samuelson did not already know, but I was soon corrected by his reply, in which he noted that he knew the first name of the person in question, even though he gave it only one "n":

> My hesitation about the 1877 help given to Walras was over the name of the helper: Herman What? Obviously Herman Amstein should have been German enough to be the correct name. Paul Piccard's 1872 derivation for L.W. of the demand function seems like fresh news to me. You learn something every day. (9 June 1993)[10]

On one occasion, Samuelson initiated this conversation:

PAS: Did you ever hear of a fellow named Antonelli?
DAW: Oh yes. Sure.
PAS: Which Antonelli?
DAW: There was an Antonelli who was a follower of Walras and who was a socialist and also a writer on topics of general equilibrium. He was also in the French central bank.
PAS: That's probably the one I mean – the one that actually taught it.
DAW: He was at the University of Montpellier and died about twenty years ago in Montpellier.
PAS: He considered himself the founder of the third Lausanne School. He was not a person of any competence really.
DAW: Not really – he was a politician, elected to the Assemblée nationale.
PAS: But there was an Antonelli who was lost in history, who found the integrability conditions in 1885.
DAW: He was in Italy.
PAS: Yes. Pareto must have known about him but forgot that several times. Pareto went forward and backward in understanding the integrability problem. (conversation, 14 November 1990)

Samuelson was personally acquainted with Continental economists that were active in the inter-war developments in general equilibrium theory:

[10] Actually, I had mentioned Piccard's contribution in 1990. See below.

> Hans Neisser was a gifted refugee from Hitler at the New School. (He told me that in the terrible days when Der Führer was perpetrating his early evils it was an anodyne to argue with Zeuthen and von Stackelberg about "the *determinacy* of the Walrasian price system." This was *before* Schlesinger and Wald, and like Wicksell-Fisher-Hicks, Neisser and Zeuthen had it right about *non-negative* prices for redundantly supplied goods.) (5 August 1998)

Samuelson had facts on so many economists stored away in his memory bank that he sometimes, he confessed, got "his wires crossed" (ibid.). Franco Modigliani, who had been a graduate student of Neisser's and Marschak's at The New School, told him in 1998 that speaking of "the late Neisser" could not be right; indeed, upon telephoning Hans Neisser, Samuelson learned it was another of his acquaintances, "Hans STAEHLE in Geneva" who had passed away (ibid.).

On some other Continental scholars, Samuelson remarked that

> Aside from Walras's contemporary, Bertrand, I am aware that Poincaré did have some interesting ideas about economics. (The great logician Gödel was personally kind of wacky and paranoid. However, in Karl Menger's Vienna seminar, where Abraham Wald was proposing proper foundations for Walras's general equilibrium à la Schlesinger, Gödel's intervention was very sensible. He asked why not specify supply of factors of production and deduce spendable incomes from their endogenous equilibria? Schumpeter was right that Cassel fraudulently plagiarized Walras. However, Cassel's protégé Ohlin, in his 1933 masterpiece, did adequately do independently just what Gödel suggested be done.) (20 June 2006)

2.5 Welfare Economics

On the issue of who coined the term "Pareto Optimality," Kenneth Arrow asked me if I knew the answer. He asserted that Gerard Debreu used that exact term in 1951 in a way that suggests that he thought it was in general use at that time, and that Debreu had confirmed both his use of the term and the generality of its use. That being so, Arrow reasoned, he should have been able to find its earlier appearances, but could not (Arrow to Walker, 3 September 1991). I did not know the answer, and after a long search and many inconclusive results, I was still without an answer, so I posed the question to Samuelson. "Someone told me," he answered, "it dates to 1950 Ian Little. I was surprised" (26 September 1991). Samuelson was ahead of Arrow in the timing of the search: "Bergson in 1937 had puzzled, with my help, over Pareto's obscure Cours and Manuale wordings," without finding a pre-1950 usage of the exact term "Pareto Optimality." However, "their meanings were often to be found. Indeed J.S. Mill, and no doubt Eve, has precise remarks on Pareto Optimality." Samuelson pointed out that the expression "optimum in the sense of Pareto" appears in his 1947 *Foundations*, "written probably in the 1937-40 period" (ibid.). I reported to Samuelson that Arrow and Debreu were mistaken. As elusive as the Scarlet Pimpernel, the term is not to be found in Debreu's article, and his three wordings are quite far from "optimality": "Pareto sense," "Pareto criterion," "Paretian philosophy" (DAW to PAS, 28 October 1991).[11] I like my [Walker's] concluding opinion: In Hla Myint's *Theories of Welfare Economics* (1948), an enlargement of his 1943 thesis, he wrote, among similar constructions, about "the Pareto Optimum" (Myint 1948: 173, 176, 197), which is close enough to "Pareto optimality" and early enough to earn Myint a generous degree of priority.[12]

Those reflections lead to a remembrance of Samuelson's concern, manifested time and again in our discussions, with the definition and maximization of societal welfare. He wanted to know about Walras's view of pure competition as a means of maximizing welfare:

> Let me ask you about Walras. To what degree is it your final opinion that he understood that the Pareto optimality necessary condition for an optimum was contained as a subset of his competitive conditions? This is something that my teachers didn't understand, great people like Knight and Viner. They all glimpsed that there is something optimal about competition but they couldn't state exactly what it was namely that if you could make the original endowment of the resources ethically optimal, then under a broad

[11] See Debreu (1951: 273, 278, 282, 286). I asked Debreu about this and he agreed—he could not have done otherwise—with *my* account of his article. Incidentally, for those who are concerned about the accent on his first name, he told me that he used it only in "*contextes francophones.*"

[12] As I documented in a letter to Arrow, there are a number of authors, such as Kenneth Boulding and Ragnar Frisch, who used terms similar to Myint's in the early 1950s (Walker to Arrow, 15 September 1991).

> set of conditions the device of competition could be used to achieve an ethical optimum. (conversation, 14 November 1990, quoted verbatim in DAW to PAS, 28 October 1991)

Not by accident, Pareto and Barone 100 years ago sketched how markets can achieve "efficiency"—a point Smith only glimpsed (15 July 1992).

> If you tried on Walras the Dupuit-like argument that in an increasing-return context where the total utility from having the product is greater than the total resources that the product would use up, but couldn't be achieved under marginal cost pricing but could be achieved under a multi-price system – what we would call discrimination – would he say that it would be so damned unfair that he wouldn't allow it even though by unanimous vote everybody would vote for it? (conversation, 14 November 1990, quoted verbatim in DAW to PAS, 28 October 1991)

I replied that I had wanted since our original conversation on the matter in 1990 to respond to those questions. I asserted that Walras was fully cognizant of the issue, and I supported this contention in a letter to Samuelson as follows:

> Here is what he wrote to Carl Launhardt on May 20, 1885 (Jaffé, Correspondence, vol. 2, p. 50, letter 652): "In representing as mine…the conclusion that "by the natural play of competition, the general interest is as completely satisfied as possible," you attribute to me an opinion that I have never proposed. I have stated that free competition would procure the maximum effect of utility subject to the limit of the condition of a single price, that is to say a relative maximum and not an absolute maximum. It is very clear that if one arranges matters so that commodities are sold at high prices to the rich and cheaply to the poor, the former will be forced to deprive themselves of superfluous goods and the latter will be able to furnish themselves with necessities, and there will be a great increase in effective utility … It remains only to be known if the condition of a single price [in each market] is or is not a condition of justice. That is a question which is not in the province of pure economic theory and which I treat in the part of the science which is occupied with the distribution of wealth and in which the principles of ethics intervene … [T]he goal for which to strive is not an absolute maximum of satisfaction, but the maximum satisfaction

> compatible with justice. The fact that you may be hungrier than me does not confer upon you, in and of itself, the right to eat my dinner" (ibid.). In other words, he [Walras] recognized that differential pricing could increase social utility, but he did not think it would be just to impose that type of pricing on the system. (DAW to PAS, 28 October 1991)

Samuelson sustained his curiosity about Walras's ideas. Shortly after his ninetieth birthday, he wrote to me: "My major present interest is how Walras would derive the interest rate in the *stationary* state" and asked whether I could "find and point out to me words of Walras that cater to *my* curiosity" (16 June 2005). Our subsequent discussions prompted Samuelson to write again on the ethical aspect of welfare maximization:

> You must tell me whether, and where, Walras did earlier do what Pareto (and Barone) did in the 1892-1899 period. Pareto called attention to the *fact*, that the conditions for competitive equilibrium were *the same* as the *normative* condition for what Bergson and I called Pareto optimality. There are an infinity of states where *no* movement from them can escape hurting someone. Adam Smith never got a clear understanding of his Invisible Hand. Most of the apologists for *laissez faire* from 1750 onwards took for granted its "optimality" or "efficiency" without knowing exactly how to define those loose terms; and of course no Russell-Whitehead logical proofs came from their quills. Von Wieser's natural state hinted at what Pareto did clarify. (Vilfredo was a deplorable human being, of course. Schumpeter independently had some of his faults.) (7 October 2008)

Both Walras and Samuelson, in the above passages, recognize what the former called the ethical dimension and the latter called the normative dimension of the maximization of social utility. Samuelson's quoted remarks on this topic are more interesting than the claim he appears to have made about the term "Pareto Optimality"—perhaps he meant simply that he used the term in some of his writings, not that he and Bergson were the first to use it.

It is a matter of concern that Walras and Samuelson indicated, without expressing a shadow of doubt, that they believed a multi-market system of price discrimination is possible. In fact, the proposal as applied to all consumer commodities is absurd because of the impossibility of making accurate or intelligible interpersonal comparisons of utility, and the difficulty of getting participants to declare and prove and present to sellers their income bracket and estimated expected gain of non-measurable utility each time they go to buy a quart of milk or a tank of gasoline. Sellers of goods and services, concerned with both cost and revenue and calculating prices in relation to income brackets, would find setting and resetting an array of prices an impossible task. Competition, changes of preferences, and failures to cover costs would undermine their arrays, leading to the horrors of government price controls. Samuelson was not kind to Walras on this subject. He wrote to me, in a long and forceful autograph letter, that "It is odd that Knight, who was unlikely to have known W's text, should resort to the same quibble: 'subject to exchange at a single price, competition maximizes Bentham's total Utility'" (6 November 1991). Samuelson called the constraint a quibble, but, in fact, Walras and Knight were simply stating the universally acknowledged condition that a single price for all buyers and sellers is an equilibrium condition in a purely competitive market. Whether the equilibrium maximizes aggregate satisfaction at all or uniquely or otherwise is, as Walras contended, another matter. Walras's and Samuelson's belief that it does not inasmuch as more utility would result from price discrimination falls into the category of indefensible suppositions.

2.6 The Auctioneer and Tatonnement

We were interested in the origin of the term "Walrasian auctioneer." Samuelson reported that: "Around 1935 Schumpeter's lectures at Harvard used to speak of 'an angel of the marketplace' or 'a Walrasian angel' or 'a Walrasian auctioneer,' who lowered price systematically in some proportion to the excess of supply over demand. In my 1941 MIT lectures, I continued the rhetoric" (26 September 1991).[13]

[13]As far as I can determine, the published use of the term "super-auctioneer" was first made by Kenneth Arrow and Frank Hahn in their *General Competitive Analysis* (Arrow and Hahn 1971: for example 269, 310–314, 324–325, 329). They did not attribute it to Walras and disclaimed using the word "tatonnement" in the way that he did.

Samuelson was thereby providing some dates and, more important, was indicating his belief that Walras assumed that there is an auctioneer in his tatonnement modeling. I replied that he did not make that assumption in any of his models:

> Walras showed that each individual market would reach equilibrium without a particular market price changer, simply by the interaction of the traders with each other in a situation in which all prices and offers are simultaneously known by all participants within the particular market. What he lacked was a mechanism by which traders would know what is happening in other markets, and that is what modern theory also needs ... Personally, I don't think it is worth the effort to build such a system ... To conclude, there is no need for a 'Walrasian' auctioneer in a model of a purely competitive economic system in which there are disequilibrium transactions...or no disequilibrium transactions. (DAW to PAS, 28 October 1991)

Samuelson went on to write that "in connection with each good's and service's market in general equilibrium, there had to be a separate auctioneer, all presided over by a grand referee for all markets" (26 September 1991). Samuelson thus joined others in saddling purely competitive general equilibrium theory with that monstrous assumption—monstrous because its workings are demonstrably impossible even in the science fiction in which it appears and it therefore does great harm to economic theory. I argued strenuously against that approach to modeling market processes: "Why didn't you," I asked him, "derive a notion of market adjustments and information dissemination from the actual technology and institutions that are used in the real world?" (DAW to PAS, 28 October 1991):

> Would the imaginary system of auctioneers that you propose mimic the equilibrating processes of a real competitive system? Of course not, because of the impossibility of constructing a central auctioneer model with the requisite means of information collection, processing, and distribution. The whole point of a system of purely competitive markets is that it performs the functions of internal and inter-market price adjustments that would be impossible for a central price setter to accomplish. Etc., etc. (ibid.)[14]

[14] See, for example, Walker (1996).

After more than a decade of intermittent discussions, Samuelson essentially conceded my point when he acknowledged that “Institutional factors that depart from nice auction behavior in the realistic labor market are not irrationalities which we should try to get rid of in a better theory” (27 October 2003).

“Incidentally,” I wrote, “I know perfectly well that when you say: ‘I was always hazy on what Walras meant by his tatonnement process’ (26 September 1991), you intend an implicit criticism of his work, namely that Walras was hazy on the matter” (DAW to PAS, 28 October 1991). Samuelson’s remark merits a comment. Prior to 1900, Walras presented what he intended to be a realistic non-virtual tatonnement process, devoting most of his treatise to it. It must be recognized, however, that what is in his original models is not a simple situation, because he assumed there are several different types of economic actors each performing a different type of tatonnement—some with prices and some with quantities. Moreover, he wrote about three other different subjects: the tatonnement within his models; another type of tatonnement when he was trying to devise a process of mathematical iteration to solve his equations; and a tatonnement in reference to what he took to be equilibrating processes in the real world. He often mixed those different subject matters together. Furthermore, Walras rejected his older model in favor of a sketch of a virtual tatonnement process, but its incompleteness, lack of content, and contradictions with the older model, many expositions of which he retained alongside the virtual sketch, produced a chaotic state of affairs. A thick haze therefore permeates the fifth edition of his treatise, the edition with which Samuelson was familiar because it was the one translated into English, so Samuelson’s comment was fully justified. My efforts to clarify the textual history were well received by him (24 May 1995), but many years after our initial discussion, I noted resignedly that Walras was still misunderstood by numerous other economists:

> I must also say that I am used to the colossal ignorance…about Walras’s tatonnement. It no longer perturbs me to see that a modeler has attained an advanced age without ever reading either as much as a word of the writings of Walras or the secondary history-of-thought literature on his work. I no longer flinch when I read, in a respected journal, that Walras devised

> an auctioneer to change prices, etc. (Did you read my article contrasting Keynes's description and Kregel's *Economic Journal* description of the Paris Bourse with the way it actually functioned?) (DAW to PAS, 9 November 2007)

2.7 Plagiarism and Other Faults

Samuelson identified and condemned false claims of originality and also defended originality against false charges of plagiarism. In this respect as in others, his conversation and letters were not only erudite; they were also entertaining. The following harmless examples illustrate that, in his mind and in his accounts of history, economists are not abstract intellects but humans with virtues and foibles and flaws. He questioned the degree to which Smith was a plagiarist and defended him by arguing that "if he was, he probably did not exceed the standard of his day. I am interested [in the case of Smith] because Coleridge was the greatest plagiarist that ever lived. If you call Smith a ten, then Coleridge would be five hundred" (conversation, 14 November 1990).

Regarding his own work on Smith, Samuelson wrote:

> Actually, if I am vulnerable, I am vulnerable to the general thrust that much that is attributed to Smith's successors is in Smith, but lacking the competence to know exactly what is in Cantillon or Turgot and the other heroes, I didn't ever comment in a professional way on his increments to them. But since I have elevated him to be the greatest of the classical economists, that would make [Smith's critics] angry because it must be that a two-way comparison is implied. (ibid.)

Marshall was not blameless, Samuelson believed, in regard to the issue of not acknowledging having copied the work of predecessors. "Bob Bishop wrote quoting the identity between Marshall's 1890 words and those of earlier minor unsophisticated men and women scholars, and evoked only the Chicago response that Bishop was egged on by me just as Huxley was egged on by Darwin to defend evolution" (7 October 2008). Samuelson observed that Walras "wasn't very good to his predecessors. He claimed at one point to have invented supply and demand functions, but then

Cournot's diagrams were pointed out to him, and that took the wind out of his sails" (conversation, 14 November 1990). To set the record straight, I said that Walras always recognized Cournot's contribution on demand, but argued that the latter's "demand curve was phenomenological, based on empirical considerations, not on marginal utility reasoning." "Walras," I continued—and here is where the issue of plagiarism arose—"said that he was the person who had rectified the problem, but in fact he took the solution from Paul Piccard, who provided him with the derivation of a demand curve from a utility function" (ibid.).

"I think," Samuelson continued, "Walras's paranoia about Edgeworth was a little excessive," and it seems "he did not feel warmly towards Pareto. He believed that Pareto did not acknowledge adequately his indebtedness." "Quite true," I interjected, "Walras wouldn't even comment on the *Cours d'Économie Politique* when it was published. Walras felt that Pareto was always talking about how this is *my* theory and so forth and referring to *my* work. Walras said once – this really bothered Pareto – that Pareto's writings were like Italian music: more froth than substance." Samuelson replied: "Of course, all of us mathematical economists say that about economists whose work is more mathematical than ours because we believe that we have arrived at exactly the optimum ratio of words to equations" (conversation, 14 November 1990).

Ten years later, Samuelson noted that:

> Your article,[15] to my mind, demonstrates *conclusively* that Walras did decline early in originality and creativity. (Nor had he been an early bloomer.) It seemed to me that already in the early 1890s, in his polemics with Wicksteed, that he never fully understood what Barone and Wicksteed were up to in production theory. (Carl Menger was an early fader; and so, they said, was his mathematician son Karl, the offspring from his loins with the help of his housekeeper. My teacher Gottfried Haberler, going pretty strong at 94-95, who was no malicious gossiper, is the source for my genealogy.) (23 February 2000)

Haberler was also my teacher, and I can vouch for the fact that he was the least likely person to engage in gossip of any kind.

[15] Walker (1999).

Samuelson remarked that somebody, probably me, should explain Cassel's "degree of plagiarism…of Walras.[16] You are probably aware, I presume, that it is widely and probably correctly believed that Cassel's system was stolen whole out of Walras." "Yes indeed," I replied, "With no acknowledgement whatsoever." Samuelson concurred: "With no acknowledgement. Schumpeter used to say that Cassel is 10 percent Walras and 90 percent water." Gerschenkron told Samuelson "that Cassel's secretary, who wrote a biography of him, explained that he got along so badly with his father that everything at that stage of his life was effaced from his memory, so he couldn't be expected to acknowledge anyone. However," Samuelson added dryly, "he never got over that habit." I interjected: "You know Cassel wrote an early article in which he made an exposition of the Walrasian system and waxed enthusiastic about Walras and gave him a lot of credit."[17] Then, staunchly agreeing with Samuelson, I added that Cassel subsequently suffered "some lapse of memory. He forgot that he had ever written that article" (ibid.). Samuelson wanted both to criticize Cassel and to avoid judging him too harshly, so he suggested that "plagiarism" was not quite the right word to describe his work on general equilibrium equations. "Unacknowledged intellectual borrowing," I suggested. "'Plagiarism' is too much like a literal transcription." Samuelson agreed and continued: "That's right. It could amount to the same thing. There are many ways of showing that you did benefit from somebody's work without revealing to the naive reader the degree of your indebtedness." I added: "I wonder why Cassel made such a blunder as not to acknowledge Walras in his treatise. Anybody can see where he was drawing the elements [of his system] from" (conversation, 18 June 1991).

Samuelson commented intermittently on the work of E. H. Chamberlin, whom he defended against the charge of plagiarism:

> I went to Harvard much because of him. He was a disappointment. But I never agreed with those who thought that Allyn Young must have written his theses. He was a one-accomplishment scholar and since he didn't die at

[16] I had done that in Walker (1988), did so in greater detail in Walker (2003), and in even greater detail in Walker (2006: 290–296).

[17] See Cassel (1899).

> 35, necessarily an element of anti-climax and condescension haunted his reputation. (21 December 1990)

> I read your piece on Chamberlin with much delight[18] ... I picked Harvard for graduate studies mostly because on my own I had read [his] book and been excited by it ... I must confess that Ed was a disappointment ... You are right that he was an American. Knight had been his undergraduate teacher at Iowa City. (Later, Knight, on no evidence, claimed that the little that was good in Chamberlin had come from him. What really boiled Knight was that Chamberlin was a Catholic. Worse still, a convert who took seriously Mary and all that. I am quoting from private conversations very characteristic of the town-pump atheist.) (31 July 1991)
>
> Even by the late Thirties E.C. was considered a one-idea scholar. The canard that would not die was that it was the genius of Allyn Young that had fashioned T.T.O.M.C. I never believed that for a moment. Ed was demonstrably capable of doing what he did. Joan [Robinson] and [Richard] Kahn always exaggerated the impact of the 1926 Sraffa article, excellent as it was when we stick to the critique of Marshal's fuzzy attempt to admit falling marginal cost into a firm's competitive (sic)[19] equilibrium. Actually, the Americans J. M. Clark, Viner, and Viner's student T. Yntema wrote with good instincts and were known to E.C. (ibid.)

2.8 Methodology

The foregoing reflections have touched upon the doctrinal component of Samuelson's articles on the history of economic thought; but it should also be remembered that he developed fruitful methodological approaches to analyzing it. He considered psychological aspects of the use of mathematics in those studies. He pondered the limitless topic of economic theory in relation to reality. He applied his concept of operationally meaningful

---

[18]I had responded to an invitation to write an essay on an *American* contribution to economic theory. Just like Samuelson, I had been Chamberlin's student and also knew him well personally, and so felt able to accept the assignment. See Walker (1989).

[19]Samuelson's "(sic)."

theorems to the evaluation of aspects of the ideas of past economists. He contributed to an understanding of how mathematics can be a useful tool in investigating certain aspects of economic behavior originally presented in literary and qualitative ways. He did this by developing the mathematical models that he found implicit in these works, and by examining those models to reveal and evaluate the consistency of their assumptions and the logical qualities of their deductions. He nonetheless recognized that economists, such as Schumpeter, had developed rigorous analyses of economic doctrines without the use of mathematics.

3 Development of a List of Preferred Essays

This section fills out the previously unpublished aspects of a portrait of Samuelson as historian of economic thought by providing an account of his preferences regarding his publications in that field. As it happens, there is no need to speculate about the matter. He worked on, circa 2000–2003, a list of his history-of-thought publications he considered most worthy of being reprinted in a dedicated volume. The genesis of the prospective collection was a conversation of mine with Edward Elgar on the occasion of a visit to his offices at Cheltenham, England, in May of 2000. I wrote to Samuelson about that exchange:

> Among other things, I told [Elgar] how I introduced you to the members of the History of Economics Society at its luncheon in 1987 as an economist who had received every conceivable honor *except* that of having been recognized as a great historian of economic thought.[20] Upon my return to the States, I received an e-mail from [Elgar] asking me if I would like to edit a volume of your essays on the history of economic thought. I immediately replied in the affirmative, and I am now asking you if you would like me to undertake the project. (DAW to PAS, 6 June 2000)

[20] In that same year, I nominated Samuelson for the award of Distinguished Fellow of the History of Economics Society, with supporting documentation, but the proposal was rejected by the Executive Committee of the Society.

Samuelson replied with his unfailing considerateness:

> Your June 6 letter was a very welcome one to me. If bringing out an Elgar volume of my articles in the History of Economic Thought would interest and please you, and not constrain your own research and career interests, then I am all in favor of it. With advance notice, I'd also offer to write some fresh stuff for it – after consultation with you. (13 June 2000)

He approved a suggested title: "You are right on target. I like the title *Selected Essays on the History of Economic Thought.* A *Selection* is good in principle since there is inevitably some repetitious coverage in the complete set of papers" (13 September 2000). I assured Elgar that "I have had a number of discussions with Paul about the project. We will be able to agree upon the items that should be included" (DAW to Elgar, 17 October 2000). Having a preferred set of articles on any topic implies placing a limitation on the number that can be included in the set. I had arrived at an initial total of about 700 pages. Reason prevailed, however, and Elgar, always striking precisely the right tone, wrote: "I am most grateful to you for giving such careful thought to the length. In view of Samuelson's reputation, we would be willing to support a volume of between 500 and 540 pages of which around 20 pages would be your introduction" (Elgar to DAW, 25 October 2000).

This restriction meant that there were many of Samuelson's articles that were meritorious but that could not be included. Our solution was to draw up a list of "Supplementary Readings," a list that would be published in the volume. In a fairly definitive form, that list included 29 articles, so the total on the two lists is exactly 60. For example, David Ricardo's work was especially interesting to Samuelson and is included on his preferred list, but he also liked "A Modern Treatment of Ricardian Economics," so he included his two articles with that title in the group of "Supplementary Readings." Some exclusions were agreeable to Edward Elgar because, for obvious reasons, he did not like to republish articles, like a number of Samuelson's, that had already appeared in the Elgar series of collected articles on the history of economic thought.

We eventually classified Samuelson's writings into seven categories. He considered the details of the project carefully. For example:

> I would advise skipping "A Classical Theorem for John Chipman". Sraffian economics and revisionist stuff of Sraffa is another matter. The problem will be to reduce overlap and maximize substantive completeness. Same will be a problem in dealing with Irving Fisher, Böhm-Bawerk, Smith and Ricardo. (I think there are two Viner pieces. At least two on Ricardo's admission that machinery can hurt wages, etc.) Whig history may reoccur? You will have to "satisfice" rather than "maximize". (13 September 2000)

Other communications reflected Samuelson's deep interest in the character and limitations of Karl Marx's economics, covering such topics as the notion of exploitation, a theory of prices, and the labor theory of value. He published seven papers on Marxian economics during the years 1972 through 1975 alone. In one exchange in 2000, Samuelson inquired about an article on Marx: "I cannot imagine," I responded, "why I forgot to include your 1999 article 'Sherlock Holmes and the Swarthy German…'[21] That represents your most recent published thought on the subject of transforming values and should be included" (DAW to PAS, 23 November 2000). In a similar vein, Samuelson noted:

> Already I have wondered about saving ten pages devoted to "What Keynes Would Think About Rational Expectations". Maybe one or another Marx item could be triaged? Subject to a year 2001 brief addendum by me, certain dispensable self-contained parts of some included items might be omitted – but only if the editor's sensibilities permit. (13 December 2000)

At the end of the year 2000, Samuelson felt that he was going to have to slow down the pace of his consideration of the project, but wanted it to be kept alive: "I am not being a bad boy. This Saturday we go to Florida for the long hibernation. Then life will become less hectic and in my daily communications with Janice Murray I hope to take seriously how to use best Elgar's strict page limitation" (13 December 2000). "Never refrain from nagging me (through my MIT office). I thrive on that and will endeavor to ration your time and energy. Janice and I try never to use

---

[21] Referenced in Sect. 4. My error was all the more egregious in that I had invited Samuelson to submit his article (DAW to PAS, 4 May 1998) and had accepted it for publication as Samuelson (1999).

e-mail: remember I was born in 1915" (ibid.). Finally, however, the press of his commitments to other projects, more important and time-sensitive, forced a recognition that the volume of selected essays would have to be put aside. Samuelson remarked: "Alas, later I failed you. It is hard to deal with past writings in economics while being busy with writing new economics. So your efforts to collect selectively my papers on the history of economics got aborted by my repeated missing of deadlines. Do not excuse. But do forgive" (15 May 2003).

I assured him:

> You didn't fail me in the matter of the collection of your history of economic thought articles. No need for forgiveness. I think your course of action is right. You have to be careful about the allocation of your time, and that means prioritizing wisely. I too am busy, finishing the tenth of a twelve-chapter book titled *Walrasian Economics*. Maybe we'll return to the collection when we want some relaxation. (DAW to PAS, 14 October 2003)

There was nothing to forgive. We had achieved the immediate objective of our research, namely the list of Samuelson's preferred writings as of 2000–2003 in as nearly a finished form as could be expected. If we had both been less occupied with other matters, we could have proceeded to publication. Although we remained in close contact during the remaining years of his life, increasingly conversing rather than writing letters, we did not revisit the project, and, indeed, we did not need to do so. In the early years of the present century, our project of republishing Samuelson's preferred essays had the justification that volume 5, the last one of Samuelson's *Collected Scientific Papers* that appeared during his lifetime, had been published in 1986,[22] fifteen years before we contemplated our project; the publication of the next volumes was nowhere in sight. The situation today is much different. All of his essays appear in journals published shortly after he wrote them, and they have all been reprinted in one or another

[22] Samuelson (1966–2011).

of the volumes of his *Collected Scientific Papers*.[23] Many of Samuelson's essays have been reprinted in volumes edited by other scholars.[24] All his articles on the history of economic thought are therefore readily available and can be studied individually or in any grouping that the researcher finds interesting.

The accomplishment of the project therefore turns out not to have been a volume of essays but rather the value of Samuelson's list of his preferred articles circa 2000–2003. Of course, he wrote eleven history articles after 2003, which may have resulted in differences in his preferences. Nevertheless, the list sheds light on his evaluations of the majority of his essays on the history of economic thought.

4 Samuelson's Preferred Essays as of 2003

Part I: Historiography

1. (1962) "Economists and the History of Ideas," *American Economic Review*, 52(1): 1–18.
2. (1987) "Out of the Closet: A Program for the Whig History of Economic Science," *History of Economics Society Bulletin*, 9(1): 51–60.
3. (1991) "Conversations with My History-of-Economics Critics," in G. K. Shaw (ed.) *Economics, Culture and Education: Essays in Honour of Mark Blaug*, Aldershot, UK: Edward Elgar: 3–13.
4. (1998) "How *Foundations* Came to Be," *Journal of Economic Literature*, 36(3): 1375–1386.

Part II: Classical

5. (1977) "A Modern Theorist's Vindication of Adam Smith," *American Economic Review*, 67(1): 42–49.

---

[23]The organization of volume 6 (2011), devoted to the history of economic thought, was "worked out with Professor Samuelson" with the aid of Janice Murray (Murray to DAW, 18 July 2000) and was edited by her.

[24]For example, see the selections made in Blaug (1991a, b, 1992) and Medema and Waterman (2015).

6. (1978) "The Canonical Classical Model of Political Economy," *Journal of Economic Literature*, 16(4): 1415–1434.
7. (1982) "Quesnay's 'Tableau Économique' as a Theorist Would Formulate It Today," in I. Bradley and M. Howard (eds.) *Classical and Marxian Political Economy: Essays in Honor of Ronald L. Meek*, New York: St. Martin's Press: 45–78.
8. (1989) "Ricardo Was Right!" *Scandanavian Journal of Economics*, 91(1): 47–62.
9. (1992) "The Overdue Recovery of Adam Smith's Reputation as an Economic Theorist," in M. Fry (ed.) *Adam Smith's Legacy: His Place in the Development of Modern Economics*, London and New York: Routledge: 1–28.
10. (1994) "The Classical Classical Fallacy," *Journal of Economic Literature*, 32(2): 620–639.

Part III: Marxian

11. (1967) "Marxian Economics as Economics," *American Economic Review*, 57(2): 616–623.
12. (1971) "Understanding the Marxian Notion of Exploitation: A Summary of the So-Called Transformation Problem Between Marxian Values and Competitive Prices," *Journal of Economic Literature*, 9(2): 399–431.
13. (1972) "The Economics of Marx: An Ecumenical Reply," *Journal of Economic Literature*, 10(1): 51–57.
14. (1974) "Marx as Mathematical Economist: Steady-State and Exponential Growth Equilibrium," in G. Gorwich and P. Samuelson (eds.) *Trade, Stability, and Macroeconomics: Essays in Honor of Lloyd A. Metzler*, New York: Academic Press: 269–307.
15. (1982) "The Normative and Positivistic Inferiority of Marx's *Values* Paradigm," *Southern Economic Journal*, 49(1): 11–18.
16. (1991) "Logic of the Historical Transformation Problem: Exchange Ratios Under Simple Commodity Production," in G.A. Caravale (ed.) *Marx and Modern Economic Analysis: Values, Prices and Exploitation*, Aldershot, UK and Brookfield, VT: Edward Elgar: 145–168.

17. (1992) "Marx on Rent: A Failure to Transform Correctly," *Journal of the History of Economic Thought*, 14(2): 143–168.
18. (1999) "Sherlock Holmes and the Swarthy German: The Case of Inanely 'Transforming' *Mehrwert* to Prices," in M.M.G. Fase, W. Kanning and D.A. Walker (eds.) *Economics, Welfare Policy and the History of Economic Thought: Essays in Honour of Arnold Heertje*, Cheltenham, UK and Northampton, MA: Edward Elgar: 345–363.

Part IV: Neoclassical

19. (1967) "Irving Fisher and the Theory of Capital," in W. Fellner et al. (eds.) *Ten Economic Studies in the Tradition of Irving Fisher*, New York: Wiley: 17–39.
20. (1993) "Gustav Cassel's Scientific Innovations: Claims and Realities," *History of Political Economy*, 25(3): 515–527.
21. (1994) "Two Classics: Böhm-Bawerk's *Positive Theory* and Fisher's *Rate of Interest* Through Modern Prisms," *Journal of the History of Economic Thought*, 16(2): 202–228.

Part V: Sraffian

22. (1990) "Revisionist Findings on Sraffa," in K. Bharadwaj and B. Schefold (eds.) *Essays on Piero Sraffa*, London: Unwin Hyman: 263–279.
23. (1991) "Sraffa's Other Leg," *Economic Journal*, 101(406): 570–574.
24. (1998) "Report Card on Sraffa at 100," *European Journal of the History of Economic Thought*, 5(3): 458–467.

Part VI: Schumpeterian

25. (1981) "Schumpeter's *Capitalism, Socialism and Democracy*," in A. Heertje (ed.) *Schumpeter's Vision: Capitalism, Socialism and Democracy After 40 Years*, London: Praeger: 1–21.
26. (1982) "Schumpeter as an Economic Theorist," in H. Frisch (ed.) *Schumpeterian Economics*, London: Praeger: 1–27.

27. (1983) "Marx, Keynes and Schumpeter," *Eastern Economic Journal*, 9(3): 166–180.

Part VII: Keynesian

28. (1964) "The General Theory," in R. Lekachman (ed.) *Keynes' General Theory: Reports of Three Decades*, New York: St. Martin's Press: 315–331.
29. (1975) "The Balanced Budget Multiplier: A Case Study in the Sociology and Psychology of Scientific Discovery," *History of Political Economy*, 7(1): 43–49.
30. (1983) "What Would Keynes Have Thought of Rational Expectations? Comment," in D. Worswick and J. Trevithick (eds.) *Keynes and the Modern World*, Cambridge: Cambridge University Press: 212–222.
31. (1995) "Who Innovated the Keynesian Revolution?" in M. Dutta (ed.) *Economics, Econometrics and the LINK: Essays in Honor of Lawrence R. Klein, Contributions to Economic Analysis*, Vol. 226, Amsterdam: Elsevier, North-Holland: 3–19.

5 Epilogue

The high quality of the friendship that Samuelson extended to me was manifested in kindness, thoughtfulness, and generosity, sustained for half a century, and I cherish each word that he wrote to me in that vein: "I can refuse old students almost nothing," he told me, "particularly when they are distinguished scholars and good friends" (15 April 1986).

> I have had many warm friends on the firing line in economics and I count you as one of the warmest. Also, I had meant to write long ago to say how important and unique have been your creative analyses of the Walras corpus. God is indeed in the details and where Léon Walras has been concerned, most of us have stayed at a more superficial level. (24 May 1995)

"I like people to be different from me. So shame the devil and send me your new book – an inscribed copy, please" (7 May 1998). "Each letter from you splashes me with both consumers and producers surplus" (13 December 2006).

Fortunately for me, I took advantage of all opportunities to express my appreciation of Paul's work and friendship publicly[25] and in my letters. In what was to be my penultimate recognition to him of his stature as an economist, I reacted as follows to a ranking that he pointed out in a letter to me:

> You report Schumpeter as having said that, of the four most important economists of all time, three were French: Quesney, Cournot, and Walras. What ignorant nonsense. One can speculate about obvious choices he implicitly made for the fourth, probably himself, but I'm not interested in doing that. [He] was wrong about all but Walras. It is obvious to me, after 55 years in the history-of-thought business, that the pride of place goes to Adam Smith, Léon Walras, J.M. Keynes, and P.A.S. I mean it; the face of modern economics is cast in your image. Your contributions are everywhere in it. In about 1958, I was talking to Gerschenkron in his office. He told me that he had just finished reading your *Economics* text. He admired it, but confided that History would judge that you were a figure like Edgeworth. I suppose he meant a sort of narrow mathematical specialist. How wrong he was! But, I'm preaching to the choir! (DAW to PAS, 28 September 2008)

We discussed Schumpeter's ranking. The topic, we agreed, has complex facets. I regretted the word "ignorant" in application to Schumpeter, although I could not find one to replace it that would retain the impression of lack of sufficient knowledge or lack of sufficient reflection and also retain consistency with "nonsense," which I would not abandon. What, we asked, are the measures of importance? Can any reasonable argument be made that Quesney was more important than Smith, whom Paul had called the greatest of the classicals? Or Quesnay or Cournot more important than Keynes? Etc., etc. Paul speculated: "I think Schumpeter's fourth great guy might have been Marshall" (7 October 2008), not supporting

[25] I am grateful that I was able to do so publicly in Samuelson's presence in my homage delivered to the audience at the History of Economics Society meeting on 20 June 1987, to graduating economics majors at my University on 15 May 1993, to the assembled university community on the occasion of Paul's receipt of a Doctorate of Humane Letters on that same date, and to the audience celebrating his ninetieth birthday on 15 May 2005.

that thought with references to Schumpeter's writings and, as has been seen, elsewhere arguing against Marshall's central analytical perspective. Paul did not endorse Schumpeter's choices, but neither did he reject mine.

Paul's health deteriorated significantly after the first quarter of 2009. I wrote to him, but I understood that he could not reply. On 12 December 2009, I attempted to telephone him and was told that he could not converse. With a sense of urgency, and not knowing that he had passed away on the early morning of 13 December, I faxed my last words to him on 14 December, asking that they be read to him:

> Dear Paul,
> I want to thank you for fifty-three years of friendship and professional relationships. I have enjoyed and benefited so greatly from our many conversations and extensive correspondence. For me, and for thousands of others, you have been, and will always be, a source of inspiration and of economic truths.
> More than fifty years of the study of the history of economic thought has made plain to me that the name to be added to those of Adam Smith, Léon Walras, and J.M. Keynes is yours. It is an honor to be your student and a great comfort to be your friend.
> There is no standard complimentary close to this letter that can convey the depth of my admiration and respect for your imperishable contributions to our science and for your remarkable personal qualities. (DAW to PAS, 14 December 2009)

References

Arrow, K.J. and F. Hahn (1971) *General Competitive Analysis.* San Francisco, Holden-Day.

Blaug, M. (ed.) (1991a) *Elgar Reference Collection Series: Pioneers in Economics Series, Volume 14.* Aldershot, UK, Edward Elgar.

Blaug, M. (ed.) (1991b) *Elgar Reference Collection Series: Pioneers in Economics Series, Volume 21.* Aldershot, UK, Edward Elgar.

Blaug, M. (ed.) (1992) *Elgar Reference Collection Series: Pioneers in Economics Series, Volume 24.* Aldershot, UK, Edward Elgar.

Cassel, K.G. (1899) "Grundriss einer Elementaren Preislehre," *Zeitschrift für die Gesamie Staatswissenschaf,* 55: 395–458.

Debreu, G. (1951) "The Coefficient of Resource Utilization," *Econometrica*, 19: 273–292.

Medema, S.G. and A.M.C. Waterman (eds.) (2015) *Paul Samuelson on the History of Economic Analysis: Selected Essays*. New York, Cambridge University Press.

Myint, H. (1948) *Theories of Welfare Economics*. Cambridge, MA, Harvard University Press.

Samuelson, P.A. (1962) "Parable and Realism in Capital Theory: The Surrogate Production Function," *Review of Economic Studies*, 29: 193–206.

Samuelson, P.A. (1966–2011) *The Collected Scientific Papers of Paul A. Samuelson, Volumes 1–7*. Cambridge, MA, The MIT Press.

Samuelson, P.A. (1974) "Complementarity: An Essay on the 40th Anniversary of the Hicks-Allen Revolution in Demand Theory," *Journal of Economic Literature*, 12: 1255–1289.

Samuelson, P.A. (1998) "Samuelson, Paul Anthony, as an Interpreter of the Classical Economists," Chapter 146 in H.D. Kurz and N. Salvadori (eds.) *The Elgar Companion to Classical Economics, Volume 2*. Cheltenham, UK, Edward Elgar: 329–333.

Samuelson, P.A. (1999) "Sherlock Holmes and the Swarthy German: The Case of Inanely 'Transforming' *Mehrwert* to Prices," in M.M.G. Fase, W. Kanning and D.A. Walker (eds.) *Economics, Welfare Policy and the History of Economic Thought: Essays in Honour of Arnold Heertje*. Cheltenham, UK and Northampton, MA, Edward Elgar: 345–363.

Walker, D.A. (1988) "The Vision of Léon Walras: Markets Interacting in an Equilibrium System," in *Great Economic Thinkers*. Audio Classics Series. Nashville, TN, Knowledge Products.

Walker, D.A. (1989) "Monopolistic Competition: An American Contribution," *Storia del Pensiero Economico*, New Series, 16: 3–9.

Walker, D.A. (1996) *Walras's Market Models*. Cambridge, Cambridge University Press.

Walker, D.A. (1999) "Some Comments on Léon Walras's Health and Productivity," *Journal of the History of Economic Thought*, 21: 437–448.

Walker, D.A. (2003) "Early General Equilibrium Economics: Walras, Pareto, and Cassel," in W.J. Samuels, J.E. Biddle and J.B. Davis (eds.) *A Companion to the History of Economic Thought*. Malden, MA, Blackwell: 278–293.

Walker, D.A. (2006) *Walrasian Economics*. Cambridge, Cambridge University Press.

8

The Samuelson Revolution in Australia

Alex Millmow

1 Introduction

Contemporary Australian university economics instruction is dominated by best-selling American economics textbooks to the exclusion of local-produced texts. A big step in the internationalisation of Australian economics began in 1970 with the Australian adaption of Paul Samuelson's *Economics: An Introductory Analysis*. Samuelson's classic volume adapted for local conditions taught more Australians than any other textbook. The story of how it came to Australia is the purpose of this chapter. The Samuelson text was extensively adapted to fit Australian conditions by two local economists and would quickly take local university economics instruction by storm. It was the first attempt at adapting an overseas text to suit Australian institutions, conventions and customs, and in this, it was never bettered by any subsequent adaptation of an American text.

A. Millmow (✉)
Federation University Australia, Ballarat, VIC, Australia
e-mail: a.millmow@federation.edu.au

R. A. Cord et al. (eds.), *Paul Samuelson*, Remaking Economics: Eminent Post-War Economists, https://doi.org/10.1057/978-1-137-56812-0_8

What will not be discussed is how the text sidetracked the true interpretation of Keynes as put forward by his Cambridge followers.

2 Paul Samuelson in Australia

When Samuelson arrived in Australia in March 1973, it was the first time an economics Nobel Prize winner had graced Australian shores. It was something of a media event since Australia was a long detour from the transatlantic lecture circuit. Samuelson's arrival made front-page news in Australia's business daily *The Australian Financial Review (AFR)*. He was there not to promote his textbook but to undertake a brief lecture tour to mark the 25th anniversary of the Fulbright Scholarship scheme. Bemused by Australia's centralised wage arbitration system, Samuelson told reporters at Sydney Airport: "You in Australia don't realise how remarkable it is. It is so remarkable that you didn't get into trouble with it", before adding that he hoped to learn more about the arbitration apparatus (Samuelson quoted in Haupt 1973a: 1). It was to be, in hindsight, a classic Ides of March comment because in the space of a year that same system, through an ill-advised decision of a double-digit pay rise for federal public servants, thrust the Australian economy into full-blown stagflation. His other airport comment was that the last third of the twentieth century was going to be an Asian one, with Japan at the forefront. This was, he thought, good news for Australia. He had arrived at an interesting time, just before the global economy was to be buffeted by turbulence from inflation caused by rising commodity prices and the first international OPEC oil price shock. A new Labor government, led by Gough Whitlam, had been in power for just four months after spending twenty-three years in the electoral wilderness. At the University of Sydney, there was an ongoing clash between some economics students and their mainstream professors about allowing more pluralism or what was then called "radical economics" into the economic syllabus. Samuelson was scheduled to give a public lecture there the day after he arrived. Unwittingly, his lecture was to fan the flames of rebellion.

During his visit, Samuelson was briefed by academic and official economists in closed-door sessions. He came away from such counsel making something of a significant reassessment of Australia's economic future. In one lecture, he now warned against "nationalistic bombast" (Haupt 1973b: 22) regarding foreign investment. These comments were reproduced in an editorial in the *AFR*. He also sounded some vague warnings about the new Labor government's more interventionist style, especially its mineral development policies. It was apparent, according to the *AFR* journalist Robert Haupt that local economists had not been unwilling in pouring out their grievances and misgivings about the intentions of the Labor administration. Haupt had also noticed, too, that Australian university economists were too deferential to their visitor in not challenging any of the sweeping statements Samuelson made at a lecture at the University of Sydney on the evening of 22 March 1973 (see Haupt 1973c).

Unbeknownst to Samuelson, his lecture at Sydney took place when there was an ongoing battle within the Sydney Economics Faculty and student dissidents over the introduction of heterodox economics courses. Samuelson had been invited by the mainstream economists heading the Faculty to speak on some aspect of orthodox economic theory. Samuelson agreed to speak on a complex mathematical model of a dynamic market for commodities incorporating storage costs, speculation and interest rates. However, it was something of a disappointment, with the subject matter too esoteric for most of the audience, some of whom left early. At the end of the lecture, there was a solitary question from a student activist named Richard Fields who asked why Samuelson had not spoken on "the aims and orientation of economics" and meeting the radical challenge to orthodoxy rather than "an academic model of strictly limited interest" (Fields quoted in ibid.: 21). Fields asked this question because Samuelson had been known to address this issue in other forums around the world and indeed had included some material on it in his best-selling textbook (see Butler et al. 2009: 9). Samuelson could only defend his model and justified its worth to economic science but did not disclose that the head of the Economics Faculty, Professor Simkin, who was chairing the event, had suggested the topic. If this was the case the world's, then most famous economist was left "illustrating the very problem" with which dissident economics students, like Fields, were up in arms (see ibid.). Sitting in the audience was Evan Jones who had just joined the Faculty after returning from Michigan with a doctorate in orthodox microeconomics and econometrics. He had gone through Samuelson's *Foundations* in his studies. However, attending the Samuelson lecture had left him drained and despondent. He noted in his diary:

> A tremendous emotional reaction to the talk of Paul Samuelson, the greatest living economist. 150-200 people listened for over an hour and a half to a lecture – that only half a dozen came close to understanding. An exercise in absurdity. And they think of Kafka as unreal! It is evident that the general understanding of economics as a field has to be revamped. It is no longer within the realm of the average intelligence. It joins physics on a higher plane... Evidence also that we've been sold a great bill of goods on the scientific nature of economic problems.[1]

Whether Samuelson knew of the poor reaction to his lecture is unknown, but it is interesting to note that in his very next public speech, given at the Australian National University in Canberra five days after Sydney, he chose as his subject "Mainstream Economics and its Critics". It met with a less hostile reception.

3 The Economist with the Golden Pen

One journalist, Tony Thomas, from *The Age* newspaper who attended the Canberra lecture, had hailed Samuelson's visit with the headline "The Prof. with the Golden Pen" (Thomas 1973). This was a reference to the fact that Samuelson was the author of the legendary textbook which had sold four million copies. Australian economics students, both at secondary school and university, had already been using a locally adapted version of Samuelson since 1970. In Samuelson's only television appearance in Australia, the talk show host, Robert Moore, held aloft a resplendent olive green and gold covered copy of the volume, saying that more Australians had drawn their education of economics from this source than from any

[1] This is an extract from Evan Jones's personal diary. Personal communication with the author.

other text. This in itself was noteworthy because it marked the first attempt at a successful adaptation of a best-selling overseas text.

It allowed Samuelson to market the forthcoming (ninth) edition of the textbook. He said: "I am told the book is well written. It should be. I sweated blood over it. I am like Oscar Wilde. I spent a morning putting in a comma, and an afternoon taking it out" (Samuelson quoted in Thomas 1973: 23). However, for the Australian version of the book, which had been published three years earlier, there had to be some major work on the narrative to fit the local audience. As Keith Hancock, one of those tasked with adapting the volume, put it, they had "to tone down Professor Samuelson's language in the revision. It was too racy for Australian students" (ibid.). In Sydney, Samuelson met his two Australian co-authors, Hancock and Robert Wallace, both from Flinders University in South Australia. When they met Samuelson, he paid them a bitter-sweet compliment by remarking that, "Just as Hegel said that he had not fully understood Hegelian philosophy until he read the French translation so I am led to believe that I will not understand Samuelson's *Economics* until I read the Australian version" (Samuelson quoted by Robert Wallace 2011, personal communication). It left the two adaptors red-faced. Samuelson was directing a mild barb at them for their considerable re-engineering of his text. That said, his Australian co-authors doubt Samuelson ever read their version of his canon. In that sense, then the Australian version of *Economics* played little role in how Samuelson changed the regimen, style and accent of the text over its many subsequent editions (see Smith 2000). Indeed, Samuelson had his own team of advisers and consultants at McGraw-Hall regarding design and content changes (see Giraud 2013). At the time, North American texts dominated Australian first-year economics teaching (see Groenewegen 1997: 69). In their *History of Australian Economic Thought*, Peter Groenewegen and Bruce McFarlane (1990) concluded that American textbooks were eroding the authenticity of Australian economics. One could contend, however, that Hancock and Wallace mounted an excellent rearguard effort in at least preserving a local voice in conveying economic principles but also presenting them in a historical light. At a more doctrinal level, it has been argued that the success of Samuelson's text, both in Australia and elsewhere, snuffed out authentic interpretations of what the true Keynes was all about (see Harcourt et al. 2018: 50–53).

Older Australian economists can still recall, perhaps favourably, being introduced to the subject by reading the first Australian edition of Samuelson issued in 1970. As noted, it came in a magnificent patriotic olive green and gold cover; inside, the pages were smooth with a monochrome print, replete with diagrams, summaries of chapter texts and emboldened capsules. Before Samuelson, there had been no adaptation in Australia of American texts for economics education.

The remaining parts of this chapter discusses how the Australian adaptation of *Economics* came about, with the latter parts looking at how it differed, in some places significantly from the master copy. Sections 5 and 6 of the chapter discusses the legacy of the Samuelson project, in particular how it shaped the Australian economics textbook market.

4 Genesis

The inspiration to launch an Australian version of *Economics* appears to have been the brainchild of Kenneth Pearson, an editorial director at McGraw-Hill who had helped orchestrate the production of a Canadian adaptation; it had enjoyed great success. Anthony Scott, a professor of economics at the University of British Colombia, was Samuelson's offsider for the Canadian edition. In May 1969, Scott wrote to Samuelson to ask about the revisions to the next edition of his book. Samuelson's reply was very interesting. He promised to take "the complacency" out of the text that essentially Hancock and Wallace would be working from. Samuelson went on:

> I sense the students are restless. They are radical. Many of them are anti-establishment. This means lots of economics on the problems of poverty. Of the race problem. Of economics of the cold war. If I can make it seem more like Galbraith, without sacrificing correctness I shall be happy. (Samuelson to Scott, 12 May 1969, Paul A. Samuelson Papers, Duke University [hereafter PASP, DU])[2]

[2]Samuelson's marketing input was valued by McGraw-Hill, but on one occasion it led to a disaster heavy in bathos. McGraw-Hill asked Samuelson whether there should be an American edition of Joan Robinson and John Eatwell's *An Introduction to Modern Economics*. Samuelson encouraged

It seems that from as far back as 1965 staff at McGraw-Hill's head office in New York had been contemplating launching an Australian adaptation. Market research undertaken by the publishers estimated that before the Canadian version was prepared, the American edition of *Economics* had secured 43% of the Canadian market. After the Canadian edition was complete, it took 75% of the market.

In 1967, two executives from McGraw-Hill re-examined the likely sales potential of an Australian version. Denis Hinton reported to his American manager, Bruce Kezer, that if McGraw-Hill continued to rely on the International Student Edition of *Economics* it would not match "Australian authored economic texts which are being planned" (Hinton to Kezer, 8 February 1967, PASP, DU). Hinton wanted the McGraw-Hill management to study the market appraisal. McGraw-Hill staff, using the experience of the Canadian case, made a market projection about how many copies of an Australian adaptation would be sold and the royalties that would flow to Samuelson who had the ultimate sanction on whether the project would go ahead or not. McGraw-Hill estimated that sales of the 1967 International Student Edition, which by 1969 had reached a respectable 10,000 copies in Australia, was projected to plateau as other competitors hit the market.

McGraw-Hill listed their competitors and their respective market shares of the Australian market as Reynolds 15%, Ferguson 15%, Bach 10% and the third edition of Richard Lipsey's *An Introduction to Positive Economics*, first published in 1963, which was described as a "promising" English import. It held just 5% of the market. Lipsey was the successor to the Stonier and Hague textbook, the last of the British texts that had dominated economics teaching in Australia since the 1930s.

The annual enrolment in economics at tertiary and secondary level in Australia at the time was estimated at 25,000 students. The Australian

---

them, saying Robinson had a great reputation and name recognition and that there was a "latent demand for books that are not ultra-conservative" (Samuelson to Harcourt, 2 November 1995, PASP, DU). As Samuelson admits, his name became mud as the text bombed in the US market with more copies given away than sold. Robinson had squarely written her text to supplant Samuelson (see King and Millmow 2003).

market was estimated to be growing at 12% per annum and McGraw-Hill noted that the International Student Edition of Samuelson still commanded an astonishing 40% of the local market, but that an Australian version would increase this to 50% and ultimately 75%.[3]

The relaunched McGraw-Hill market appraisal, completed by Pearson from a template prepared by Bruce Kezar at the New York office, noted that Heinz Arndt at the Australian National University's Research School of Pacific Studies and Peter Karmel, vice chancellor of the recently established Flinders University, were the most prestigious figures in the Australian economics community. Pearson added that they had not yet been approached, but suggested there was a good chance that they would ally themselves with Samuelson.

Pearson's report closed with summaries of Karmel's and Arndt's resumes. Interestingly, the brief summation of Karmel's output mentioned his book on *Applied Statistics for Economists*, the first edition of which appeared in 1958 (Karmel 1958), and his co-authored work with Maureen Brunt, *The Structure of the Australian Economy* (Karmel and Brunt 1962) but did not list his macroeconomics primer *Economic Activity* which he wrote with Geoff Harcourt and Bob Wallace. Karmel might have lightly dismissed the latter as "a week-end project" because it was partly based on his first-year lectures given at the University of Adelaide, but the text did take some time in preparation and did win a substantial share of the tertiary market (see Harcourt 1995: 239; see also Cockburn 1966: 8).[4]

When Roy Webb (1967: 119) reviewed *Economic Activity* in the *Economic Record* he prefaced his critical commentary with the remark that the book signified "the growing movement towards import replacement in the Australian economics textbook market" and that the book "draws upon Australian experience for illustration of argument".

In his memoirs, Arndt recalls that when visiting Boston in the 1960s Samuelson asked him to produce an Australian version of his textbook.

---

[3]Australia's two oldest universities had differing views on its suitability for first-year economics. The University of Sydney used Samuelson from 1962 but there were objections to its use at the University of Melbourne.

[4]*Economic Activity* was hardly "a week-end book" Based on the 'Karmel' lectures which both Harcourt and Wallace also gave at Adelaide, the book was put together by the two while Karmel was pre-occupied running a new university. The authentically Australian text did very well in Australia and was even used at Cambridge. It was also translated into Italian.

Arndt (1985: 35) demurred, saying he had neither the time nor "the confidence" to do the job. In September 1967, Pearson visited Arndt to broach again the idea of an Australian adaptation. He told Arndt that McGraw-Hill was "expanding their indigenous publishing program" with an Australian version of Samuelson's *Economics* (Pearson to Arndt, 28 September 1967, Heinz W. Arndt Papers, National Library of Australia [hereafter HWAP, NLA]). Quickly ruling himself out of the undertaking, Arndt briefed Pearson about finding the most suitable person to take on the task. Arndt recalls in his memoirs that he "persuaded" Hancock to undertake the task. Arndt told Pearson that he wanted to keep in touch with the project and was to play no small part in the writing of it.

Nothing was heard from Pearson until almost a year later when he wrote to Arndt informing him that he had found a writing team to undertake the task. In the meantime, McGraw-Hill had approached Harcourt to take on the task after he had returned to Adelaide from Cambridge in 1967. However, Harcourt, recalling the toils of writing *Economic Activity*, resisted. He told Samuelson that it would have been a case anyway of "odd bedfellows" given his Post Keynesian orientation, though he much later joked "Ex post, I find it was rather a costly decision in terms of income forgone as the Australian edition has sold like hot cakes" (Harcourt to Samuelson, 25 January 1973, PASP, DU). Some 80,000 copies of the Australian *Economics* had been sold by the mid-1970s. Harcourt attributed this to the excellent work undertaken by Hancock and Wallace. On Arndt's recommendation, Hancock had been invited to take up the challenge. He, in turn, invited his colleague, Bob Wallace, as an equal partner in the venture. As mentioned, Wallace had already helped co-write an economics text with Karmel and Harcourt. Wallace received a warm, welcoming letter from Samuelson (personal communication with Wallace, June 2011). McGraw-Hill wanted the volume completed in 1969, in little less than a year. Pearson stressed the importance of the task in terms of educating young students. Samuelson wrote to the two Australian adaptors making it clear that they had "a free hand" where they wished but it was to be made clear to the reader that Samuelson was still the lead author and that all variations were the responsibility of Hancock and Wallace (ibid.). Drafts of the revised chapters were sent to Samuelson in Boston but no response ever came back. There would be no direct contact between the Australian writing team and Samuelson until 1973 when, on Samuelson's visit to Australia, McGraw-Hill arranged a meeting. The two Australians had the great fortune that the copy editor, Jenny Walker, who had worked on the Canadian version of *Economics*, had returned to live in Adelaide (ibid.). Pearson, too, was based in Sydney while the project was undertaken.

While Pearson had no reservations about Hancock and Wallace's ability, he asked Arndt to become a consultant to the project, to proofread and, more importantly, "to ensure the book is technically correct, readable and at the appropriate level" (Pearson to Arndt, 14 August 1968, HWAP, NLA). Ahead of the two authors lay some 40 chapters with varying degrees of alteration needed given their descriptive setting or the level of exposition. They also had a deadline of July 1969 so that the text would be ready for the 1970 academic year.

Arndt accepted the brief to overview the revision but warned Pearson that occasionally he would be out of the country involved with his work on the Indonesian economy. He told Pearson that with the team of Hancock and Wallace, McGraw-Hill could not have done any better (Arndt to Pearson, 16 August 1968, HWAP, NLA).

5 The Reconstruction

Hancock and Wallace's reconstruction of the Samuelson text would amount to a major overhaul, one of the boldest and imaginative ever undertaken with an overseas textbook. It would be more than just changing settings and the institutional framework. In some parts of the text, the two authors spliced some of Samuelson's chapters to give it a better flow to Australian readers. They rearranged sections, adding details where it was relevant to Australian students and highlighted the contributions of Max Corden (effective rate of protection), L. F. Giblin (the export multiplier) and Trevor Swan's external and internal balance diagram—one of the most overlooked Australian contributions to economic science. The diagram integrated the two aspects of macroeconomic theory, namely aggregate demand determined by fiscal and monetary policy and relative costs determined by exchange rate policy and wage policy. The three chapters on the banking and monetary system had to be recast by Wallace.

There were entirely new sections of chapters written on the Australian tariff, the Australian external account and a long applied chapter on growth and inflation experience in the Australian economy. These additions were written by Hancock. Some of these chapters Arndt did not have time to scrutinise fully. Hancock and Wallace also localised some of the opening quotes that decorated the Samuelson text and the end of chapter questions. There was no senior partner in the enterprise; each would review and edit each other's work, resulting in a seamless product. However, they did allocate chapters roughly according to their expertise and specialisation.

The first chapter rolled over the Hancock-Wallace assembly line in August 1968 and was forwarded to Pearson who would act as an intermediary between the adaptors and Arndt.[5] Arndt would comment on each chapter especially on stylistic features if he felt it was warranted. Pearson duly forwarded the chapter to Arndt (Pearson to Arndt, 22 August 1968, HWAP, NLA). The introductory chapter was not a mere overlay job. Hancock and Wallace basically rewrote the chapter from scratch, telling Arndt, that after seven editions, Samuelson's text had "drifted into a rather bad condition" (Hancock to Arndt, 2 September 1968, HWAP, NLA). Arndt expressed his delight at Hancock's revamping of Chapter 1 both in what he had added and what he had deleted. Arndt continued: "To my un-American mind, the new version is much more economical in words and more elegant. I have gone through it fairly carefully comparing successive paragraphs of the old and the new versions and have found myself applauding your changes in practically every case" (Arndt to Hancock, 27 August 1968, HWAP, NLA).

Arndt went on to recommend a few grammatical and literal changes. Hancock told Arndt that he could not afford the time necessary to revise and recast all 40 chapters given time constraints (Hancock to Arndt, 2 September 1968, HWAP, NLA). Consequently, Chapter 2, as Pearson informed Arndt, was the same as the original bar an added piece on Australian population growth. Chapters 3 and 4 also ran close to the original

[5] Arndt was given an honorarium of $150 by McGraw-Hill for reviewing the manuscript (see Pearson to Arndt, 14 August 1969, HWAP, NLA).

Samuelson narrative, but the appendix to Chapter 4 on the stock exchange was localised. Apart from minor quibbles on population and immigration, Arndt did have a minor quarrel with Samuelson over his rendition of the law of diminishing returns and how it was conveyed to the student.

Chapter 4 must have been revised by Hancock because Arndt sent him some comments on the "new version", mostly queries (Arndt to Hancock, 31 October 1968, HWAP, NLA). Arndt also enclosed some comments on Chapter 3 which was initially entitled "Price Functioning of a 'Mixed' Capitalistic Enterprise System". Arndt called the title "ghastly", preferring instead "The Price Mechanism in a Mixed Economy". So it became, along with a legion of rewritten headings and sentences.

The New Year saw Arndt congratulating the authors on the revised version of Chapter 6 on "Affluence and Poverty". He continued to praise the effort resulting in "an entirely new piece which brings out all the issues discussed by Samuelson in relation to Australian conditions and data and, once again, does so with much more economy and elegance of style" (Arndt to Hancock, 2 January 1969, HWAP, NLA).

Appreciative of Arndt's input behind the scenes, Pearson suggested to Hancock the idea of getting Arndt to write a Foreword for the text. Pearson was looking to have half the manuscript by the end of March 1969. The delivery of chapters resumed with Chapter 7 arriving on Arndt's crowded desk. Hancock and Wallace, realising that a tight deadline was looming, had begun to mark up chapters from the International Student Edition of Samuelson which were to be sent direct to Arndt, with Pearson kept in the picture.

As originally written, Chapter 7 was an account of Australia's unique centralised wage arbitration system that had so intrigued Samuelson in 1973. Arndt wondered whether students "at this stage" needed quite so much institutional background. Nevertheless, he was for retaining it and forwarded some minor grammatical points. Arndt closed, noting that there was an awfully long way to go and that he was bound for another overseas trip in May until July (Arndt to Hancock, 13 February 1969, HWAP, NLA). Unhappy with his first effort, Hancock sent Arndt a revised copy of Chapter 7, but did not expect Arndt to comment on it (Hancock to Arndt, 26 February 1969, HWAP, NLA). In the meantime, Arndt had sent back to the authors Chapters 27, 28 and 29 with only a few comments on each of them.

The assiduous Arndt quickly returned the chapters on microeconomics which were done by Wallace. Arndt was finding it rather a mammoth job and he could not pretend to have read every line of Samuelson. Arndt was soon sending back more draft chapters to Hancock. He took issue with Samuelson over blurring the difference between capital goods and capital. Pearson was content that the project was still on time and that the authors had begun to copy edit the remaining chapters. Pearson continued to emphasise the original objective of the task, namely to "make the book as relevant as possible to the Australian situation without altering the scope and direction" of the original (Pearson to Arndt, 6 March 1969, HWAP, NLA). By this time, Arndt was able to confidently reply that the textbook would better fit Australian conditions "and in some respects be better – period". He noted that the adaptation could not be entirely the same, but it was in approach, tenor and quality (Arndt to Pearson, 9 March 1969, HWAP, NLA). In closing, Arndt felt that the chapters requiring the most revision—especially chapters on income determination theory—were still to come. Hancock acknowledged the work ahead, but noted that 65% of the project was done (Hancock to Arndt, 11 March 1969, HWAP, NLA).

There was a minor hiccup. When Arndt received a further three chapters on the theory of income determination undertaken by Wallace, he objected that they were at odds with Hancock's standard of editing. In particular, Arndt was concerned that Wallace had not "picked up some of Samuelson's more dubious formulations" (Arndt to Hancock, 19 April 1969, HWAP, NLA). Arndt complained that Wallace had retained Samuelson's "horrible folksy verbosity, almost baby language which is the very least attractive feature of Samuelson's style" and attributed it to careless editing. In short, Arndt was worried that the adaptation would come across as "two clearly distinguishable parts" and that Hancock needed to re-edit some of Wallace's work (ibid.). This proved unnecessary as Wallace rewrote them. In the same letter, Arndt informed Hancock that time and logistics meant this was his last editing work as he was bound to go overseas and would not be back until 20 July. He regretted this because he had a "strong avuncular (if not paternal)" interest in the enterprise (ibid.). It meant that Arndt would not see the chapters on forecasting and the business cycle, banking and fiscal policy and also chapters on trade and protection, international accounts, growth and development, the macroeconomic performance of the Australian economy and alternative economic systems. These were areas he noted that were more suitable to his own expertise. He did, however, get a chance to forensically go through the chapter on trade and the international economy and list some 23 suggested changes. The international economy matters far more for a small, open economy like Australia than it did for the United States. Arndt was happy with the rewrite, telling Hancock: "Gone is not only all of Samuelson's playfulness but even most of his patient spelling out of every point. The subject matter is so difficult in parts that it is probably impossible in a reasonable compass to be both reasonably rigorous and reasonably simple" (Arndt to Hancock, 21 April 1969, HWAP, NLA).

Arndt was back in September and was sent galley proofs of the remaining chapters (Stephen (Pearson's secretary) to Arndt, 4 September 1969, HWAP, NLA). These proofs would only allow him to make minor changes. His last act in the venture was to write the Foreword which he was cajoled into writing by Pearson not because he found disfavour with the finished product but rather because he felt it unnecessary. Although Arndt relented, he asked Pearson for some points that might be expanded upon (Arndt to Pearson, 6 February 1969, and Pearson to Arndt, 15 January 1969, HWAP, NLA). Arndt would only write the Foreword in September 1969. He recorded that the Samuelson text had a number of rivals, but that three outstanding merits lay behind its popularity: first, Samuelson's mastery of every aspect of theory, second, his intense concern with social and economic problems and, third, his ability to express to readers his excitement and enjoyment of the subject. He then listed the benefits of having an Australian version of *Economics* which included local data and institutional detail. Arndt joked that this was the first time he had been "personally involved in the establishment of an Australian subsidiary by an American industry" (Arndt to Pearson. 6 February 1969, HWAP, NLA). In the early draft of the Foreword, Arndt made a crack about how the project would yield pecuniary benefits to its creators. He told Hancock that this was intended specifically for Samuelson who had mentioned it in his own Preface (Arndt to Hancock, 24 September 1969, HWAP, NLA).

The finished product looked almost identical to the International Student Edition in terms of parts, chapters and sub-headings. Moreover, some chapters, like those in Part III on microeconomic issues, were almost identical. There were, however, some key differences on the nature of the trade cycle, the efficacy of fiscal policy, the open economy and the application of the neoclassical synthesis; Samuelson had toned down the synthesis from earlier editions. Hancock and Wallace were less confident than Samuelson that the business cycle had been tamed. Moreover, in the important early chapter on income determination, they extended the existing analysis by stressing how international trade both in terms of quantity and price might affect Australian economic activity and brought in a treatment of the multiplier earlier than did Samuelson.

6 Aftermath

The Australian version of textbook made its baptism in January 1970. It conquered the domestic textbook market and easily met the expectations of its publishers.[6] Indeed, they had not anticipated how much effort Hancock and Wallace had invested in the project. The fact that Samuelson would win the Nobel Prize that same year gave pedigree to the text and impetus to sales. Samuelson became the market leader and its predominance was to last through the 1970s (see Maxwell 1999: 119–120). Economics courses in Australia became, in effect, Samuelson courses. Flinders University, not more than five years old, could lay claim to be at the forefront of Australian economics education in terms of setting the definitive university economics textbook.

Owen Covick, a young lecturer from England who arrived at Flinders University in 1973, was told that he would be using what sounded to him like a Japanese-authored text by the name of *Sahawa*. It was, of course, the coda for the text adapted by Hancock and Wallace, and Covick, having read it cover to cover in five days, found it an excellent text (personal communication with Covick, April 2011). Like the Canadian issue, a study guide to the volume was commissioned and undertaken by

---

[6]The Australian adaption also sold in New Zealand and Papua New Guinea.

Barry Hughes and John Hayles. This was supplemented in 1972 when Hancock, Wallace and Hughes produced *Applied Economics: Readings for Australian Students*. Each of the readings had cross-references to *Economics*, but the volume was intended for general use. It also reflected the Flinders approach to economics education. As Wallace put it: "We treated the students as serious inquirers, not just passive vessels to be stuffed with enough narrowly defined economics to jump through exam hoops". The selected readings included extracts from Keynes, Gregory, Marshall, Malthus, Robbins, Brigden, Giblin and Wicksteed, and "reflected the role the history of economic thought played in the course we developed at Flinders" (personal communication with Wallace, March 2011).

A few years later, Hancock and Wallace revised their text for the second edition using the ninth Samuelson edition as the text to work from. Stressing commitments elsewhere, Arndt had opted out of the reviewing work (Arndt to Gardner, 12 October 1973, HWAP, NLA). The two Australian authors won a greater share of the royalties (from 3 to 5%) from the project which both Samuelson and his wife Marion consented to (Aksen to Samuelson, 28 March 1972, PASP, DU). The second edition was launched in 1975.

Hancock and Wallace would have been unaware that one of their competitors, Weidenfeld & Nicolson had been exploring the possibility of an Australian adaptation of Lipsey's textbook. A representative of the publisher approached Richard Downing, Ritchie Research Professor of Economics at the University of Melbourne, about publishing a local version with applied material relating to Australia (Wheatcroft to Downing, 9 August 1974, Richard Downing Papers, University of Melbourne Archives (hereafter RDP, UMA)). While the British version of Lipsey had been growing in a "flourishing" Australian market, a representative of Weidenfeld & Nicholson, Andrew Wheatcroft, told Downing, "We feel we would attract a wider spectrum of buyers if we could produce an Australianised edition of the book. Despite its failings, Samuelson has been successful in this respect". Wheatcroft asked Downing if he was interested in undertaking a revision of Lipsey even "if only slight alterations" were envisaged. He closed, "We do feel it would add considerably to the character and appeal of the book in its Australian edition if you were to be connected with the revisions" (Wheatcroft to Downing, 27 September 1974, RDP, UMA). Downing found the proposal "a most attractive proposition", believing the text could stand "largely untouched except perhaps for some extensive re-writing" and some Australian experience of some of the macroeconomics and international material. He went on to remark: "The Hancock-Wallace Australian edition of Samuelson did, I think, involve much more rewriting – but it was such a bad book to begin with that I did expect it to need much more" (Downing to Wheatcroft, 21 August 1974, RDP, UMA). Ultimately, however, Downing was not interested in participating in the venture, referring Wheatcroft to Roy Webb, who had taken first-year economics classes at La Trobe University and who therefore had a captive market at his mercy (Downing to Wheatcroft, 21 October 1974, RDP, UMA). In the end, an Australian version of Lipsey did not appear until 1981 when two La Trobe economists, Paul Langley and Dennis Mahoney, turned out *Positive Economics for Australian Students* (see Lipsey et al. 1981). They had however been beaten by the appearance the year before of the Australian adaptation of the Campbell McConnell best-selling text, *Economics: Principles, Problems, and Policies*, which was aimed at students at Colleges of Advanced Education or polytechnics. It also was published by McGraw-Hill, but that did not bother Hancock and Wallace. The McConnell text also gave a fair allowance to Australia's institutional framework, would soon replace Samuelson as market leader partly because the third edition of Samuelson was delayed (see Maxwell 1999: 120).

7 Conclusion

While the Australian version of Samuelson only attracted one review (see Stonham 1970), the text would spark a number of imitators albeit none arguably with the same verve of readability, enrichment and application to Australian economic problems. So successful was the venture that, as Maxwell (1999: 120) finds, there would be no comparable Australian economics principles text, written solely by Australian economists, that would achieve a similar degree of market penetration. Later adaptations of overseas textbooks would not be as diligent as the Hancock and Wallace makeover of *Economics*.

Acknowledgements Alex Millmow is associate professor of economics at Federation University Australia. He is also the current President of the History of the Economic Thought Society of Australia. I am indebted to the critical input of Keith Hancock and Bob Wallace in the writing of this paper. Thanks are due also to Owen Covick, Evan Jones, Geoff Harcourt, Neville Norman and Frank Stilwell.

References

Primary

Heinz Arndt Papers, National Library of Australia.
Paul A. Samuelson Papers, Duke University.
Richard Downing Papers, University of Melbourne Archives.

Secondary

Arndt, H. (1985) *A Course Through Life: Memoirs of an Australian Economist.* Canberra, National Centre for Development Studies.

Butler, G., E. Jones and F. Stilwell (2009) *Political Economy Now! The Struggle for Alternative Economics at the University of Sydney.* Sydney, Darlington Press.

Cockburn, S. (1966) "Uni has Brilliant Mind," *The Adelaide Advertiser*, 12 February: 8.

Giraud, Y. (2013) "The Political Economy of Textbook Writing: Paul Samuelson and the Making of the First Ten Editions of *Economics* (1945–1976)," Thema Working Paper No. 2011-18, Universite de Cergy Pontoise.

Groenewegen, P. (1997) "The Australian Experience," in A.W. Coats (ed.) *The Post-1945 Internationalization of Economics.* Durham, Duke University Press: 61–79.

Groenewegen, P. and B. McFarlane (1990) *A History of Australian Economic Thought.* London, Routledge.

Harcourt, G.C. (1995) "Recollections and Reflections of an Australian Patriot and a Cambridge Economist," *Banca Nazionale del Lavoro Quarterly Review*, 195: 225–254.

Harcourt, G.C., P. Kriesler and J.W. Nevile (2018) "The Attacks on *The General Theory*: How Keynes's Theory was Lost," in S. Dow, J. Jespersen and G. Tily (eds.) *The General Theory and Keynes for the 21st Century*. Cheltenham, Edward Elgar: 44–56.

Haupt, R. (1973a) "A Free Floater Comes to Australia," *Australian Financial Review*, 22 March: 1, 23.

Haupt, R. (1973b) "How Australia Could Go Sour," *Australian Financial Review*, 29 March: 22.

Haupt, R. (1973c) "Lack of Antagonists Takes Sting from Samuelson Tour," *Australian Financial Review*, 30 March: 21.

Karmel, P. (1958) *Applied Statistics for Economists*. Melbourne, Pitman.

Karmel, P. and M. Brunt (1962) *The Structure of the Australian Economy*. Melbourne, F.W. Cheshire.

King, J.E. and A.J. Millmow (2003) "Death of a Revolutionary Textbook," *History of Political Economy*, 35: 105–134.

Lipsey, R., P. Langley and D. Mahoney (1981) *Positive Economics for Australian Students*. London, Weidenfeld & Nicolson.

Maxwell, P. (1999) "The Economic Principles Text: Its Evolution and Influence in Australia," *Journal of Economic and Social Policy*, 3: 117–132.

Samuelson, P.A., K. Hancock and R.H. Wallace (1970) *Economics: An Introductory Analysis*. Sydney, McGraw-Hill.

Smith, L.M. (2000) "A Study of Paul A. Samuelson's *Economics*: Making Economics Accessible to Students," PhD dissertation, Massey University.

Stonham, P. (1970) "Review of Economics—Australian Edition by P.A. Samuelson, K Hancock and R. Wallace," *Economic Record*, 46: 271–272.

Thomas, T. (1973) "The Prof with the Golden Pen," *The Age*, 27 March: 23.

Webb, L.R. (1967) "Review of G.C. Harcourt, P. Karmel and R.H. Wallace *Economic Activity*," *Economic Record*, 44: 119–122.

Part II

Samuelson's Contribution to Economics: Microeconomics and Finance

9

Samuelson's Approach to Revealed Preference Theory: Some Recent Advances

Thomas Demuynck and Per Hjertstrand

1 Introduction

In January 2005, Hal Varian (2006) searched the JSTOR business and economics journals and Google Scholar for the phrase 'revealed preference'. He reports to have found 997 articles in JSTOR and approximately 3600 works on Google Scholar containing this phrase. Based on this result, he concluded that '*Surely, revealed preference must count as one of the most influential ideas in economics*' (ibid.: 99; italics added). A March 2018 search of the same phrase over the period from January 2005 to March 2018 found an additional 996 articles in JSTOR business and economics

T. Demuynck
ECARES, Université Libre de Bruxelles, Brussels, Belgium
e-mail: thomas.demuynck@ulb.ac.be

P. Hjertstrand(✉)
Research Institute of Industrial Economics, Stockholm, Sweden
e-mail: per.hjertstrand@ifn.se

R. A. Cord et al. (eds.), *Paul Samuelson*, Remaking Economics: Eminent Post-War Economists, https://doi.org/10.1057/978-1-137-56812-0_9

journals and an additional 22,200 works on Google Scholar.[1] Echoing Varian's view, we can confidently state that revealed preference continues to be an important and influential concept in economics.

Since its introduction by Paul Samuelson in 1938, revealed preference has been applied to a vast number of different areas. Varian (ibid.) surveys the early history of the literature that evolved from Samuelson's initial contribution. The aim of this chapter is to continue where Varian left off and survey some of the more recent advances in the theoretical and applied revealed preference literature.[2]

2 Testing for Rationality

Revealed preference theory, initiated by Samuelson (1938, 1948), provides a structural approach to analyze demand behavior. Its main underlying principle is that a consumer's observed choices provide information about her underlying preferences. If a consumer is observed to have chosen a certain consumption bundle x,[3] while another bundle y was also available (e.g., because it was less expensive), then she reveals her preference for x over y. Equivalently, we say that x is revealed preferred over y. In this manner, choices say something about the underlying preferences of the consumer. Samuelson (1938) introduced the weak axiom of revealed preference (WARP), which provides a test of the simplest form of the utility maximization hypothesis: If a bundle x is revealed preferred over a bundle y, then at some other instances, y should not be revealed preferred over x. WARP requires the revealed preference relation to be asymmetric. Houthakker (1950) generalized WARP by introducing the strong axiom of revealed preference (SARP) which states that the revealed preference relation is acyclic. Interestingly, he also showed that this gives

---

[1] The more refined search 'revealed preference' + samuelson returned approximately 4460 works on Google Scholar over the period from 2005 to 2018.

[2] Other recent surveys or overviews of revealed preference, some with a different focus, are Cherchye et al. (2009a), Diewert (2012), Crawford and De Rock (2014), and Chambers and Echenique (2016).

[3] By a bundle we mean an N-dimensional vector that gives the various quantities over the N goods that the consumer chooses.

the strongest test for the consistency of choice behavior under the utility maximization hypothesis.

2.1 Afriat's Theorem

Samuelson and Houthakker derived their results under the assumption that one can observe the entire demand function of a consumer. In a subsequent seminal contribution to the literature, Afriat (1967) considered the more realistic setting where the researcher only observes a finite set of choices. Starting from such a finite data set, Afriat showed that a slight relaxation of SARP, which he calls cyclical consistency, provides the necessary and sufficient conditions for the existence of a utility function whose imposed choice behavior is consistent with the data. Diewert (1973) and Varian (1982) made Afriat's approach more transparent and gave complete proofs. It was also Varian (ibid.) who used the term general axiom of revealed preference (GARP) instead of cyclical consistency.

Before we present a more formal exposition of Afriat's results, we need to introduce the concept of a revealed preference relation.

Definition 1 (Revealed Preference): Given a finite data set $S = (p^t, x^t)_{t=1,\ldots,T}$ of prices $p^t \in \mathbb{R}^N_{++}$ and consumption bundles $x^t \in \mathbb{R}^N_{+}$, we say that x^t is directly revealed preferred to a bundle x (written $x^t R_D x$) if $p^t x^t \geq p^t x$.[4] We say that x^t is revealed preferred to x (written $x^t R x$) if there is some (possibly empty) sequence $u, v, \ldots, s$ such that $p^t x^t \geq p^t x^u$, $p^u x^u \geq p^u x^v$, $\ldots$, $p^s x^s \geq p^s x$. The revealed preference relation R is the transitive closure of the direct revealed preference relation R_D.

The intuition behind the revealed preference relation is simple. If $p^t x^t \geq p^t x$, then x^t was chosen (at observation t) while the bundle x was not more expensive to buy. Given that the consumer chose the bundle x^t and not x, it must have been her preferred option.

[4] By px, we mean the dot product $\sum_{i=1}^N p_i x_i$.

Theorem 1 *(Afriat's Theorem): Given a finite data set of observed prices and choices* $S = \left(p^t, x^t\right)_{t=1,\dots,T}$, *the following conditions are equivalent:*

1. *There exists a locally non-satiated*[5] *utility function* $u(x)$ *that rationalizes the data set* S, *i.e. for all observations* t *and all bundles* x, *if* $p^t x^t \geq p^t x$ *then,* $u(x^t) \geq u(x)$.
2. *The data set* S *satisfies the generalized axiom of revealed preference (GARP), i.e. for all observations* t *and* s, *if* $x^t R x^s$ *then,* $p^s x^s \leq p^s x^t$.
3. *For all observations* t, *there exists a number* U^t *and a number* $\lambda^t > 0$ *such that the Afriat inequalities hold, i.e. for all observations* t *and* s,

$$U^s - U^t \leq \lambda^t p^t \left(x^s - x^t\right).$$

4. *For all observations* t, *there exists a number* V^t *such that the Varian inequalities hold, i.e. for all observations* s *and* t,

$$\text{if } p^t x^t \geq p^t x^s \text{ then, } V^t \geq V^s, \tag{1}$$
$$\text{if } p^t x^t > p^t x^s \text{ then, } V^t > V^s. \tag{2}$$

5. *There exists a continuous, monotone and concave utility function* $u(x)$ *that rationalizes the data.*

Conditions 1, 2, 3 and 5 give the standard version of Afriat's theorem. The equivalence between Conditions 1 and 5 shows that continuity, monotonicity, and concavity are non-testable properties in settings with linear budgets.[6]

Afriat's theorem suggests various procedures to test the utility maximization model. First, the GARP in Condition 2 offers a simple combinatorial test on observed prices and quantities. Varian (1982) provides a simple and fast algorithm to implement GARP based on Warshall's (1962) algorithm to compute the transitive closure of a relation.[7]

---

[5]A function $u : \mathbb{R}^N_+ \to \mathbb{R}$ is locally non-satiated if for all $x \in \mathbb{R}^N_+$ there exists a neighborhood $\mathcal{N}_x$ around x and a vector $y \in \mathcal{N}_x \cap \mathbb{R}^N_+$ such that $u(y) > u(x)$.

[6]With nonlinear budgets, the property of quasiconcavity is testable (see Cherchye et al. 2014).

[7]Varian's algorithm is widely available in many programming languages. See, for example, www.revealedpreferences.org for codes.

The Afriat inequalities in Condition 3 give an alternative equivalent condition that takes the form of a set of linear inequalities. The variables U^t and λ^t can be interpreted as the utility and marginal utility of income values at the observation t. To see this, suppose that the data $S = \left(p^t, x^t\right)_{t=1,\ldots,T}$ were generated by a differentiable and concave utility function $u(x)$, in which case, by the properties of concavity, it must be that for all observations t, s:

$$u(x^s) - u(x^t) \leq \nabla u(x^t)\left(x^s - x^t\right).$$

Additionally, the first-order conditions for utility maximization subject to a linear budget constraint (excluding boundary conditions) yield:

$$\nabla u(x^t) = \lambda^t p^t,$$

where λ^t is the marginal utility of income (i.e., the Lagrange multiplier). If we substitute this into the concavity inequalities and define $U^t = u(x^t)$, we effectively obtain the Afriat inequalities. Diewert (1973) and Fleissig and Whitney (2005) propose linear programing (LP) procedures to check whether there exists a feasible solution to the Afriat inequalities.

Condition 4 is usually omitted from Afriat's theorem, but it turns out to be a key formulation for various more recent developments in revealed preference theory. It was originally introduced in the nonparametric production literature by Varian (1984), which motivates the use of the term 'Varian inequalities'.

The intuition behind the Varian inequalities is straightforward if one interprets V^t as the utility of bundle x^t. Then, if $p^t x^t \geq p^t x^s$, we have that x^t is directly revealed preferred to x^s, so $V^t = u(x^t)$ should be at least as large as the utility $V^s = u(x^s)$. If $p^t x^t > p^t x^s$, then a similar reasoning (together with local non-satiation) guarantees that $V^t > V^s$.

A second intuition for why V^t can be interpreted as the utility value at observation t follows a similar reasoning as for the Afriat inequalities. Suppose that the data $S = \left(p^t, x^t\right)_{t=1,\ldots,T}$ were generated by a non-satiated, differentiable and quasiconcave utility function $u(x)$.[8] Differentiability

[8]A non-satiated and quasiconcave function is also called semistrict quasiconcave (see Ginsberg 1973).

and quasiconcavity imply:

$$\text{if}\, u(x^s) - u(x^t) \geq 0, \quad \text{then} \quad \nabla u(x^t)\left(x^s - x^t\right) \geq 0,$$

while non-satiation further implies:

$$\text{if}\, u(x^s) - u(x^t) > 0, \quad \text{then} \quad \nabla u(x^t)\left(x^s - x^t\right) > 0.$$

Substituting the first-order conditions for utility maximization and defining V^t for all observations t as utility values, i.e., $V^t = u(x^t)$, yields:

$$\begin{aligned} &\text{if}\, V^s - V^t \geq 0, \quad \text{then} \quad \lambda^t p^t \left(x^s - x^t\right) \geq 0, \\ &\text{if}\, V^s - V^t > 0, \quad \text{then} \quad \lambda^t p^t \left(x^s - x^t\right) > 0. \end{aligned}$$

However, since $\lambda^t > 0$, we can without loss of generality drop it from the inequalities. Taking the contrapositive, the Varian inequalities follow.

Analogous to the Afriat inequalities, it is possible to check whether the Varian inequalities have a feasible solution by solving an LP problem.[9] Interestingly, this LP problem only has T parameters, which is T fewer than the LP procedure to test the Afriat inequalities.

Cherchye et al. (2015a) show that the Varian inequalities can be equivalently formulated in terms of the following feasibility problem:

There exist numbers $V^t \in [0, 1]$ and $X^{t,s} \in \{0, 1\}$ such that for all observations t, s:

$$\begin{aligned} &V^t - V^s < X^{t,s}, \\ &(X^{t,s} - 1) \leq V^t - V^s, \\ &p^t(x^t - x^s) < X^{t,s} A^t, \\ &(X^{t,s} - 1)A^s \leq p^s(x^t - x^s). \end{aligned}$$

[9]Without loss of generality, the strict inequality on the right-hand side in the second row can be converted to a weak inequality by noticing that the inequalities are homogeneous of degree one in V^t. Thus, the second row may be written as if $p^t\left(x^t - x^s\right) > 0$, then $V^t - V^s \geq \varepsilon$, for any $\varepsilon > 0$ (the standard choice is to set $\varepsilon = 1$).

Here, A^t is a fixed number greater than $p^t x^t$. The variables $X^{t,s}$ are either 0 or 1. The interpretation is that $X^{t,s}$ should be equal to one if and only if $V^t \geq V^s$. This condition is guaranteed by the first and second inequalities: the first inequality ensures that $V^t \geq V^s$ implies $X^{t,s} = 1$, while the second condition inequality that $X^{t,s} = 1$ implies $V^t \geq V^s$. The third inequality guarantees that if $p^t x^t \geq p^t x^s$, then $X^{t,s} = 1$ (i.e., $V^t \geq V^s$). This constitutes the first Varian inequality (i.e., Condition [1]). The last inequality guarantees that $X^{t,s} = 1$ (i.e., $V^t \geq V^s$) implies $p^s x^t \geq p^s x^s$, which is the contrapositive of the second Varian inequality (i.e., Condition [2]).

The above feasibility problem cannot be verified using LP methods because the variables $X^{t,s}$ are restricted to be either 0 or 1. On the other hand, they can be verified using mixed integer linear programing algorithms (MILP). Similar to a standard LP problem, an MILP problem minimizes a linear objective function subject to a set of linear constraints. However, in contrast to an LP problem, the variables in an MILP problem may also take integer values. From a computational perspective, MILP algorithms are much less efficient than LP algorithms.[10] Even so, this MILP formulation has been shown to be very useful in practice. Its main advantage is that the system of inequalities remains linear even if some prices or quantities become unobserved (i.e., are treated as parameters in the problem). This is the case for many revealed preference characterizations of more complicated behavioral models as we will illustrate below.

3 Extensions and Generalizations

A sizable part of the revealed preference literature has focused on enlarging the class of economic models to which the revealed preference methodology can be applied. As the present space is too limited to discuss all of them, we will focus in this section on two of these models: the weakly separable utility maximization model and the collective household model.

[10]From a computational perspective, we have that LP problems are solvable in polynomial time, while MILP problems are in general NP-hard.

At the end of the section, we provide a brief, non-exhaustive overview of other recent contributions to the literature.

3.1 Revealed Preference Tests for Weak Separability

Weak separability is a key property in economics. Every empirical study involving consumption, macro or financial data is based, either explicitly or implicitly, on the assumption that preferences are at least weakly separable. A standard example is when non-durable goods are analyzed without reference to durable goods or when consumption is analyzed without reference to labor supply. In such settings, the former set of goods is assumed to be weakly separable from the latter. We say that a group of goods is weakly separable from all other goods when the marginal rate of substitution between any two goods in the separable group does not depend on the quantities consumed of the goods outside the group. Hence, weak separability implies that the demand functions for the goods in the separable group depend only on the prices of those goods and total expenditure allocated to this group.

Revealed preference methods are a particularly suitable means of testing for weak separability and other forms of separability. The revealed preference conditions for separability were derived by Afriat (1969), Varian (1983a), and Diewert and Parkan (1985). Suppose that we partition the quantities x into two mutually exclusive and collectively exhaustive groups, given by y and z. Denote the corresponding prices of y by q and those of z by r, respectively. We say that the utility function $u(y, z)$ is weakly separable in the y-goods if there exists a macro (aggregator) function v and a sub-utility function w such that

$$u(y, z) = v(w(y), z).$$

We have the following revealed preference characterization.

Theorem 2: *For any finite data set $S = ((q^t, r^t), (y^t, z^t))_{t=1,\ldots,T}$, the following conditions are equivalent:*

1. *There exists a continuous, monotone, concave and weakly separable utility function* $v(w(y), z)$ *that rationalizes the data, i.e. for all observations* t *and all* (y, z), *if* $q^t y^t + r^t z^t \geq q^t y + r^t z$, *then* $v(w(y^t), z^t) \geq v(w(y), z)$.
2. *For all observations* t *there exist numbers* V^t *and* W^t *and numbers* $\mu^t > 0$ *and* $\lambda^t > 0$ *such that for all observations* t *and* s,

$$W^s - W^t \leq \mu^t q^t \left(y^s - y^t\right), \tag{3}$$

$$V^s - V^t \leq \lambda^t r^t (z^s - z^t) + \frac{\lambda^t}{\mu^t}(W^s - W^t). \tag{4}$$

This theorem is analogous to Afriat's theorem. In fact, it is easy to see that Condition 2 mirrors Condition 3 in Theorem 1. To grasp the intuition behind Condition 2, consider the two concavity restrictions:

$$\begin{aligned} v(w(y^s), z^s) - v(w(y^t), z^t) &\leq \frac{\partial v(w(y^t), z^t)}{\partial w}\left(w(y^s) - w(y^t)\right) \\ &\quad + \nabla_z v(w(y^t), z^t)(z^s - z^t), \\ w(y^s) - w(y^t) &\leq \nabla_y w(y^t)(y^s - y^t), \end{aligned}$$

and the (interior) first-order conditions

$$\begin{aligned} &\frac{\partial v(w(y^t), z^t)}{\partial w} \nabla_y w(y^t) = \lambda^t q^t, \\ &\nabla_z v(w(y^t), z^t) = \lambda^t r^t, \\ &\nabla_y w(y^t) = \mu^t q^t. \end{aligned}$$

From the first and third first-order conditions, we have $\frac{\partial v(w(y^t), z^t)}{\partial w} \mu^t q^t = \lambda^t q^t$, which implies that for any good in the separable y-group:

$$\frac{\partial v(w(y^t), z^t)}{\partial w} = \frac{\lambda^t}{\mu^t}.$$

Substituting this and the other first-order conditions into the concavity inequalities, and setting $v(w(y^s), z^s) = V^s$, $v(w(y^t), z^t) = V^t$, $w(y^t) = W^t$ and $w(y^s) = W^s$ gives the inequalities (3) and (4).

Although Condition 2 provides a clear set of inequalities that need to be verified, doing so in practice is far from trivial. The problem concerns inequality (4), which is no longer linear because it contains the term λ^t/μ^t. Nevertheless, Swofford and Whitney (1994) proposed to jointly check whether there exists a solution to inequalities (3) and (4). Their procedure is further extended to allow for incomplete adjustment of expenditure and therefore to account for various forms of habit persistence such as adjustment costs and the formation of expectations. However, because it is based on finding a solution to the nonlinear inequalities (3) and (4), any implementation is based on solving a complex nonlinear optimization problem, which may be computationally difficult even for medium-sized data sets.[11]

An alternative sequential approach was proposed by Varian (1983a). This two-step method is based on the fact that W^t and $1/\mu^t$ can be interpreted as quantity and price indices for the separable y−group of goods. The first step consists of finding numbers W^t and μ^t that satisfy the Afriat inequalities (3), and the second step consists of using these numbers as plug-ins to check whether inequality (4) holds. Since W^t and μ^t are known variables in the second step, verifying whether (4) holds is a linear problem and, by Theorem 1, is equivalent to testing whether the data set

$$S' = ((r^t, 1/\mu^t), (z^t, W^t))_{t=1,\dots,T} \text{ satisfies GARP.}$$

Varian (1983a) suggested a combinatorial algorithm to calculate the numbers W^t and μ^t in the first step while Fleissig and Whitney (2003) proposed a linear programing procedure to find these numbers.

Unfortunately, this sequential approach is biased toward rejecting weak separability (see, e.g., Hjertstrand 2009). The bias arises because the numbers W^t and μ^t in the first step are constructed without reference to the GARP test in the second step. Specifically, the degree of the bias is related

[11]Cherchye et al. (2015a) showed that verifying Conditions (3) and (4) is an NP-hard problem, meaning that it is computationally intractable for very large datasets. See also Echenique (2014).

to the choice of W^t and μ^t, and since these numbers are not unique, some choices may cause a violation of weak separability while others may not. Using Monte Carlo experiments, Hjertstrand (2009) found that Varian (1983a)'s procedure is heavily biased while Fleissig and Whitney (2003)'s procedure is considerably less so.

However, all is not lost. As shown in Cherchye et al. (2015a), we can use the MILP formulation of the Varian inequalities in Theorem 1 to derive an exact test of Conditions (3) and (4). To see this, first note that the data set S' satisfies GARP even if all prices $(r^t, 1/\mu^t)$ are multiplied by a common number (i.e., the GARP test is homogeneous of degree zero in prices). Thus, the data set S' satisfies GARP if and only if

$$S'' = ((\mu^t r^t, 1), (z^t, W^t))_{t=1, \dots, T} \text{ satisfies GARP.}$$

By the equivalence of GARP and the Varian inequalities in Theorem 1, it is then easy to see that the Varian inequalities are linear even if we do not observe the 'prices' $\mu^t r^t$ or the 'quantities' W^t. Thus, the MILP formulation of the Varian inequalities gives the following practical test of the weak separability conditions in Theorem 2:

There exist numbers $0 \leq V^t \leq 1$, $0 \leq W^t \leq 1$ and $0 < \mu^t \leq 1$ and binary numbers $X^{t,s} \in \{0, 1\}$ such that the following inequalities hold for all observations s and t,

$$\begin{aligned}
&W^s - W^t \leq \mu^t q^t \left(y^s - y^t\right), \\
&V^t - V^s < X^{t,s}, \\
&\left(X^{t,s} - 1\right) \leq V^t - V^s, \\
&\mu^t r^t \left(z^t - z^s\right) + \left(W^t - W^s\right) < X^{t,s} A^t, \\
&\left(X^{t,s} - 1\right) A^s \leq \mu^s r^s \left(z^t - z^s\right) + \left(W^t - W^s\right),
\end{aligned}$$

where $A^t > r^t z^t + 1$. The first inequality equals the Afriat inequalities (3) in Theorem 2, while the last four inequalities ensure that the data set S'' satisfies GARP.

The revealed preference conditions of Theorem 2 have been applied in different areas. Swofford and Whitney (1987), Belongia and Chrystal (1991), and Fisher and Fleissig (1997) apply Varian (1983a)'s procedure, while Jones et al. (2005) and Elger et al. (2008) apply the procedures developed by Fleissig and Whitney (2003) and Swofford and Whitney (1994) to test whether various monetary aggregates are weakly separable to analyze what monetary assets the public is including in their definition of 'money.'

More recently, Hjertstrand et al. (2016) apply the MILP procedure to identify monetary aggregates. Using the same data, Hjertstrand et al. (2019) modify the MILP procedure to check how close monetary and consumption aggregates calculated from superlative and other index numbers are to being weakly separable. These recent papers show that Cherchye et al.'s (2015a) MILP procedure can be effectively implemented on medium- and large-scale data sets.

Hjertstrand and Swofford (2012) derive revealed preference conditions for weak separability of the indirect utility function. In Cherchye et al. (2015a), it is also shown how the MILP procedure can be modified to test for weak separability in the indirect utility function and how the procedure can be adapted when the sub-utility function $w(y)$ is assumed to be homothetic. Hjertstrand and Swofford (2019) apply these test procedures to check whether some monetary and consumption aggregates are indirectly and homothetically weakly separable.

3.2 Collective Household Models

The traditional literature on household consumption behavior assumes that households behave as single agents. This unitary model of household consumption imposes empirically testable restrictions on consumption behavior (e.g., Slutsky symmetry or GARP) that are frequently rejected empirically. Because of this, the literature has shifted to models that explicitly take into account the fact that households are composed of distinct individuals and that each member has his or her own preferences. Household decisions are then determined by an underlying intra-household bargaining process. Following Apps and Rees (1988) and Chiappori (1988, 1992), the intra-household process is usually assumed to produce a Pareto efficient allocation of resources in the household.

Consider a household with two members, A and B, with utility functions u_A and u_B over own consumption. The benchmark model assumes that goods can be partitioned into private goods and (household-level) public goods. Private goods are exclusive, meaning that a good can only be consumed by one household member (e.g., food, clothing). Public goods are non-exclusive and are jointly consumed by both members (e.g. housing, heating, cleaning). Denote private goods by q and public goods by Q with prices p and P. Assuming Pareto efficient household decision making, the household chooses the allocation (q_A, q_B, Q) that maximizes a weighted sum of utilities.

$$\max_{q^A, q^B, Q} \; u_A(q_A, Q) + \mu \; u_B(q_B, Q) \text{ s.t. } p(q_A + q_B) + PQ \le Y,$$

where Y is the household income and μ is the Pareto weight that might depend on prices and income.

The characterization of this collective model was established in a series of papers by Cherchye et al. (2007, 2009b, 2011a).

Theorem 3 *(Cherchye et al.): For any finite data set* $S = \left((p^t, P^t), (q^t, Q^t)\right)_{t=1,\dots,T}$*, the following conditions are equivalent:*

1. *There exist continuous, monotone and concave utility functions u_A and u_B, Pareto weights μ^t and private consumption bundles q_A^t and q_B^t that rationalize the data, i.e. for all observations t, $q_A^t + q_B^t = q^t$, and for all (q_A, q_B, Q) if $p^t q^t + P^t Q^t \ge p^t(q_A + q_B) + P^t Q$, then*

$$u_A(q_A^t, Q^t) + \mu^t u_B(q_B^t, Q^t) \ge u_A(q_A, Q) + \mu^t u_B(q_B, Q).$$

2. *For all observations t, there are numbers U_A^t, U_B^t and $\lambda_A^t, \lambda_B^t > 0$, consumption bundles q_A^t, q_B^t and prices P_A^t, P_B^t such that for all observations t and s:*

$$\begin{aligned}
&U_A^s - U_A^t \le \lambda_A^t p^t(q_A^s - q_A^t) + \lambda_A^t P_A^t(Q^s - Q^t),\\
&U_B^s - U_B^t \le \lambda_B^t p^t(q_B^s - q_B^t) + \lambda_B^t P_B^t(Q^s - Q^t),\\
&q_A^t + q_B^t = q^t,\\
&P_A^t + P_B^t = P^t.
\end{aligned}$$

3. *There exist private consumption bundles* q_A^t, q_B^t *and public prices* P_A^t, P_B^t *such that for all observations* t,

$$q_A^t + q_B^t = q^t,$$
$$P_A^t + P_B^t = P^t,$$

and the data sets $S_A = \left((p^t, P_A^t), (q_A^t, Q^t)\right)_{t=1,\dots,T}$ *and* $S_B = \left((p^t, P_t^B), (q_B^t, Q^t)\right)_{t=1,\dots,T}$ *satisfy GARP.*

Condition 2 gives the usual Afriat inequalities. As before, they can be obtained by using concavity inequalities together with the first-order conditions for the household maximization problem. The numbers P_A^t, P_B^t should be interpreted as the marginal willingness to pay (MWTP) at observation t for public goods by members A and B. Condition 3 uses Theorem 1 to translate the Afriat inequalities into equivalent GARP conditions. The intuition behind the revealed preference restrictions can be clarified by making use of the second fundamental theorem of welfare economics. This theorem states that any Pareto efficient allocation can be decentralized by making use of Lindahl prices for public goods, where the Lindahl prices sum to the market price. In our setting, these Lindahl prices are given by the MWTP vectors P_A^t and P_B^t. Thus, by the second fundamental theorem the Pareto optimal allocation is equivalent to a situation where each household member is maximizing his or her own utility utility function subject to the observed prices p^t for private goods and the Lindahl prices P_A^t (P_B^t) for public goods.

The GARP conditions in Theorem 3 are not directly verifiable because neither the Lindahl prices P_A^t, P_B^t nor the private quantities q_A^t, q_B^t are observed. However, the Varian inequalities corresponding to the GARP conditions in Condition 3 do remain linear in prices and quantities, and therefore, the MILP procedure provides a feasible way to check the revealed preference conditions.

The model above assumes that household allocations are Pareto optimal. An alternative approach is to assume that household allocations are determined through a noncooperative Nash equilibrium where each member chooses her/his own amount of private goods (q^A, q^B) and her/his own contribution to the level of public goods (Q_A, Q_B). The total level of public goods in the household is then $Q_A + Q_B$. In this case, member A solves

$$\max_{q_A, Q_A} u_A(q_A, Q_A + Q_B) \text{ s.t. } pq_A + PQ_A \leq (Y - pq_B - PQ_B).$$

A similar maximization problem holds for member B. As shown by Cherchye et al. (2011b), the revealed preference conditions for this noncooperative model are very similar to those of the cooperative model except that in this case, the MWTP adding up condition,

$$P_A^t + P_B^t = P^t,$$

is replaced by a condition where the maximum MWTP should equal the market price, i.e.,

$$\max\{P_A^t, P_B^t\} = P^t,$$

where the maximum operator is element-wise, and the numbers P_A^t, P_B^t are the MWTP at observation t for public goods by members A and B. The noncooperative model is analogous to the public goods model with voluntary contributions to the public good (Bergstrom et al. 1986). In this model, the usual equilibrium will exhibit free riding, meaning that there is a household member who abstains from contributing to the public good. In this case, the MWTP for the non-contributing member will be below the market price, while the MWTP for the contributing member will equal the market price. If, for a public good, both MWTP values are equal (and therefore equal to the market price), there will be a joint contribution to the particular public good. Interestingly, as shown by Cherchye et al. (2011b), this max condition can also be implemented using linear inequalities (containing integer variables). As such, the noncooperative model is also verifiable using MILP methods.

The revealed preference model of household behavior has recently been incorporated into a broader marriage market model by Cherchye et al. (2017). The marriage market, which contains all potential partners, defines the 'outside options' of existing households. As these outside options give a lower bound on the utility each partner receives in his/her marriage, they will impact the intra-household allocation. The standard way to conceptualize the marriage market is as a two-sided matching model. In these models, the outside options are determined by the *individual rationality* and *no blocking pairs* conditions. Individual rationality imposes that no member of an existing household would prefer being single to staying married. The no blocking pairs condition requires that no currently unmarried couple would prefer to divorce their current partners and form new households. Cherchye et al. (ibid.) showed how these restrictions can be formalized as revealed preference restrictions on observed matching and consumption patterns. As an example, take a man A and woman B who are both married but not to each other. Let A consume the bundle (q_A, Q_A) in his current marriage, and let B consume (q_B, Q_B). Assume that if A and B were to form a couple, they would generate total income $Y_{A,B}$. Then, one revealed preference restriction that follows from this is:

$$Y_{A,B} \leq p(q_A + q_B) + P \max\{Q_A, Q_B\},$$

where again max is the element-wise maximum operator. To see that this restriction must hold, assume for a moment that the inequality is reversed, i.e., $Y_{A,B} > p(q_A + q_B) + P \max\{Q_A, Q_B\}$. In this case, the 'new couple' (A, B) could buy the bundle $(q_A, \max\{Q_A, Q_B\})$ for A and $(q_B, \max\{Q_A, Q_B\})$ for B and still have some money left to buy additional goods. In other words, by forming the couple (A, B), both A and B can improve upon their current consumption bundle, which means that they form a blocking pair.[12]

3.3 Other Recent Contributions

In this subsection, we provide a brief (non-exhaustive) list of other contributions to the revealed preference literature.

[12]Of course, this disregards the fact that there are many other things in addition to the consumption of goods that influence the utility that partners derive from marriage.

Functional Form Restrictions: Matzkin and Richter (1991) show that SARP is necessary and sufficient for the existence of a monotone, continuous, and strictly concave utility function that rationalizes a data set. Chiappori and Rochet (1987) add differentiability to the rationalizing utility function and provide a necessary and sufficient condition for this case, which they call strong-SARP (SSARP). Varian (1983a) considers homothetic and additively separable utility functions. The first leads to the well-known homothetic axiom of revealed preference (HARP). Brown and Calsamiglia (2007) obtained revealed preference conditions for quasi-linear utility functions. This result is extended by Cherchye et al. (2015b), who examined the revealed preference conditions that are consistent with the generalized quasi-linear utility specification.

Uncertainty: Varian (1983b, 1988) and Green and Osband (1991) derived revealed preference conditions for the expected utility model. These were generalized to other models of decision making under uncertainty by Echenique and Saito (2015), Heufer (2014), and Polisson et al. (2017).

Intertemporal: Browning (1989) derived the revealed preference conditions for the standard life-cycle intertemporal consumption model. These were generalized to include models of habit formation and rational addiction by Crawford (2010) and Demuynck and Verriest (2013). Adams et al. (2014) derived the revealed preference conditions for the collective intertemporal model.

Behavioral Conditions: Chambers et al. (2010) examined revealed preference conditions for complementarity in choice behavior. Chambers et al. (2011) derived revealed preference conditions for substitutability, and Cherchye et al. (2018) obtained the revealed preference conditions under the assumption that goods are normal.

Stochastic Revealed Preference: The theory of stochastic revealed preferences was developed by McFadden and Richter (1971) (see McFadden 2005 for an overview). Stochastic revealed preference theory departs from the random utility model in which at each decision problem an individual draws a utility function at random and chooses the best option according to this utility function. However, random utility models also have a population interpretation: There are many people with a fixed utility function, but each observation is obtained using a random draw from the population. Recently, there has been considerable interest in applying these revealed preference models to consumption data. Blundell et al. (2003, 2008) use nonparametric Engel curve estimation with revealed preference restrictions to obtain tight bounds on welfare and demand counterfactuals. Hoderlein and Stoye (2014) propose tests for the weak axiom of stochastic revealed preference (WASRP), which is a stochastic revealed preference version of Samuelson's WARP condition. Kitamura and Stoye (2018) and Kawaguchi (2017) verify stochastic revealed preference conditions that also take into account transitivity. Cosaert and Demuynck (2018) show how the WASRP can be used to derive counterfactual welfare and demand analysis.

Other Models: Brown and Matzkin (1996), Brown and Shannon (2000), and Brown and Kannan (2008) derived revealed preference conditions for general equilibrium models. Cherchye et al. (2011c) and Carvajal and Song (2018) provided simpler testable conditions for these models by exploiting the Varian inequalities. Demuynck and Seel (2018) derived revealed preference conditions for models with limited consideration. Cherchye et al. (2013), Carvajal and Gonzáles (2014), and Chambers and Echenique (2014) examined the revealed preference conditions for (Nash) bargaining models. Polisson and Quah (2013), Forges and Iehlé (2013), Forges and Iehlé (2014), and Cosaert and Demuynck (2015) considered revealed preference characterizations of discrete choice models. Matzkin (1991), Forges and Minelli (2009), Cherchye et al. (2014), and Nishimura et al. (2017) analyzed models with nonlinear budgets. Finally, van Bruggen and Heufer (2017) showed that GARP is a valid test of the utility maximization hypothesis in lab environments.

4 Evaluating Revealed Preference Tests

The ultimate objective of a revealed preference application is, of course, its implementation on real-life (or experimental) data. This means that the results of these applications have to be analyzed and evaluated. Fortunately, there exists a large array of tools to do so. We divide this section into three parts. First, we provide a brief overview of various goodness-of-fit measures that are used to evaluate the fit of a single particular data set to the revealed preference conditions. Next, we provide a discussion of three useful concepts that can be used to evaluate the fit of a revealed preference test to a collection of data sets, i.e., pass rate, power and predictive success. Finally, we show how the revealed preference tests can be accommodated to take into account measurement error.

4.1 Goodness-of-Fit Measures

Revealed preference tests are 'sharp' tests: They only tell us whether or not observed choices are consistent with some underlying model. In practice, however, it may well be that the test is very close to satisfying the revealed preference restrictions. As noted by Varian (1990), for most purposes, nearly optimizing behavior is just as good as exactly optimizing behavior. This calls for a goodness-of-fit measure that tells us how close observed behavior is to actually pass the revealed preference test. In this section, we discuss several such measures.

Efficiency Indices: The most popular goodness-of-fit measure is called the critical cost efficiency index (CCEI) or the Afriat efficiency index (AEI) (Afriat 1972). The AEI measures the severity of GARP violations by calculating the minimal expenditure adjustment necessary to render the choices consistent with GARP. Before, we defined the revealed preference relation R_D in the following way:

$$x^t R_D x^s \leftrightarrow p^t x^t \geq p^t x^s.$$

The AEI works by relaxing this condition to

$$x^t R_D(e) x^s \leftrightarrow e p^t x^t \geq p^t x^s.$$

where $e \in [0, 1]$. When $e = 1$, we obtain the usual revealed preference restriction, $R_D(1) = R_D$. The lower the value of e, the less stringent the revealed preference relation, i.e., for $e \leq e' : R_D(e') \subseteq R_D(e)$. Similarly, we can define GARP using the relation $R_D(e)$ instead of R_D. This gives us a GARP test, conditional on some value of e, denoted by GARP(e). The AEI is the highest value of e such that the data set passes GARP(e). In practice, the AEI is easily calculated using a binary search algorithm (Varian 1990).

Varian (ibid.) also proposes a generalization of the AEI (called the Varian efficiency vector [VEV]) by letting the adjustment differ between observations. For a vector $E = (e^1, \ldots, e^T)$ of numbers in [0, 1], we define the relation

$$x^t R_D(E) x^s \leftrightarrow e^t p^t x^t \geq p^t x^s.$$

A data set satisfies GARP(E) if GARP holds when it is defined over the relation $R_D(E)$. The VEV is defined as the vector E closest to the unit vector in some norm subject to the data satisfying GARP(E). Thus, in practice, the VEV may differ for different norms. By exploiting the equivalence between GARP and the Varian inequalities in Theorem 1, Heufer and Hjertstrand (2019) proposed a computationally simple method to calculate the VEV by minimizing the linear objective function (i.e., in the L1-norm) $\frac{1}{T}\sum_{t=1}^{T}(1 - e^t)$ subject to the MILP formulation of the Varian inequalities:

There exist numbers $V^t \in [0, 1]$ and $e^t \in [0, 1]$ and $X^{t,s} \in \{0, 1\}$ such that for all observations t, s:

$$\begin{aligned}
&V^t - V^s < X^{t,s},\\
&(X^{t,s} - 1) \leq V^t - V^s,\\
&e^t p^t x^t - p^t x^s < X^{t,s} A^t,\\
&(X^{t,s} - 1) A^s \leq p^s x^t - e^s p^s x^s.
\end{aligned}$$

It is easy to see that the AEI is a special case of the VEV, in which all adjustments are equal, i.e., $e = e^t$ for all $t = 1, \ldots, T$. The AEI and VEV are both measures of wasted expenditure due to inconsistency with GARP: if the consumer has an AEI (VEV) less than one, then he could have obtained the same level of utility by only spending a fraction 1−AEI (1−VEV) of expenditures. In this regard, Varian (1990) interprets the AEI/VEV as measures of goodness-of-fit of the utility maximization model.

Heufer and Hjertstrand (2019) propose analogous indices for homothetic utility maximization, which they call the homothetic efficiency index (HEI) and the homothetic efficiency vector (HEV). Like the AEI/VEV, these measures can be interpreted as the amount of wasted expenditure. They also introduce the misspecification index (MSI), which is the additional adjustment required to make data that have already been adjusted to fit the utility maximization model also fit the homothetic utility maximization model. The MSI is defined as:

$$\text{MSI} = \frac{\text{AEI} - \text{HEI}}{\text{AEI}}.$$

As with the AEI, the HEI can be easily calculated using a binary search algorithm. Heufer and Hjertstrand (2019) also propose a procedure to calculate a first-order approximation to the HEV by solving an LP problem.

The Houtman–Maks Index: Houtman and Maks (1985) proposed measuring the degree of inconsistency as the maximal subset of observations consistent with revealed preference. Like the VEV, the Houtman–Maks (HM)-index is defined as the vector E closest to the unit vector conditional on the data satisfying GARP(E). However, while the vector E takes on continuous values in the VEV, it is restricted to be binary for the HM-index, i.e., $e^t \in \{0, 1\}$ for all t. Heufer and Hjertstrand (2015) propose two methods to calculate the HM-index. One method is based on a simple modification of the combinatorial algorithm in Gross and Kaiser (1996) and is applicable when the data consist of two goods. The second method is analogous to calculating the VEV and applicable to any number of goods. In this method, the HM-index is the value that minimizes

$\frac{1}{T}\sum_{t=1}^{T}(1 - e^t)$ subject to the MILP restrictions derived from the Varian inequalities, with the additional restriction that the vector E be binary.

The Money Pump: Echenique et al. (2011) proposed an index based on the idea of the money pump called the money pump index (MPI). The basic idea is that if an individual violates GARP, then she has a revealed preference cycle. This means that she is open to exploitation. Assume that a consumer has a revealed preference cycle, i.e., a set of observations $1, \ldots, J$ such that, for all $j \leq J - 1$,

$$p^j q^j \geq p^j q^{j+1} \text{ and } p^J q^J > p^J q^1.$$

Intransitivity means that the consumer would also prefer q^{j+1} to q^j, so a trader can easily give q^{j+1} to the consumer in return for q^j and cash the surplus $p^j(q^j - q^{j+1})$. The total amount this trader can extract from the cycle is given by $\sum_{j=1}^{J-1} p^j(q^j - q^{j+1}) + p^J(q^1 - q^J)$. Echenique et al. (2011) suggests interpreting the total amount of money that can thus be generated (divided by the total income over the cycle) as a measure of failure of the GARP test. The MPI index is the average of this measure over all cycles. Computing the MPI index, however, is computationally very cumbersome, i.e., NP-hard (Smeulders et al. 2013).[13]

Minimum Cost Index: Dean and Martin (2016) suggest measuring violations of GARP by considering the minimum cost necessary to break all revealed preference cycles, where the cost of removing a revealed preference comparison $x^t R_D x^s$ is given by

$$p^t(x^t - x^s).$$

The idea of this index, called the minimum cost index (MCI), is that if a cycle can be broken by removing only low-cost comparisons, then this is less serious than a cycle that involves only high-cost comparisons. Although the MCI is computationally hard, Dean and Martin (ibid.) show how it can be computed using off-the-shelf algorithms.

[13]Computing the maximum or minimum of the measure over all cycles can be done in a computationally efficient manner (i.e. in polynomial time).

4.2 Pass Rate, Power, and Predictive Success

Revealed preference tests are not traditional tests. The reason is that revealed preference conditions are essentially set predictors: For a specific behavioral model, the revealed preference test predicts that observed choice behavior will lie within a certain bounded region of the consumption outcome space, namely the collection of all datasets that satisfy the particular revealed preference test.

For a traditional revealed preference test, the outcome space, Ω, contains the set of all possible consumption bundles $(q^t)_{t=1,\ldots,T}$ that exhaust the consumer's budget at every observation t. The revealed preference test under consideration, e.g., GARP, then effectively bounds a region within this outcome space, say A,

$$A = \{(q^t)_{t=1,\ldots,T} : (p^t, q^t)_{t=1,\ldots,T} \text{ satisfies GARP}\}.$$

Now, assume that we observe a collection of data sets where each data set is considered as an observation in the set Ω. We find that some data sets are consistent with GARP, i.e., lie within the set A, while some other data sets are not consistent with GARP and therefore lie outside the set A. Of course, the higher the proportion of data sets in A, the better the model is supported empirically. The pass rate quantifies this empirical support as the fraction of data sets that are situated in the set A, i.e., satisfy GARP.

When treating observed data sets as random observations, the observed pass rate $\hat{\pi}$ will not be equal to the population pass rate π, although its asymptotic distribution is well known:

$$\sqrt{n}(\hat{\pi} - \pi) \sim^a N(0, \pi(1 - \pi)),$$

where n denotes the number of observations. However, pass rates only capture one dimension of the empirical performance of a revealed preference test. In general, the pass rate of the model will be higher the larger the set A. Therefore, for a revealed preference test to be meaningful, we would like this set to be sufficiently small. The smallness of the set A defines the discriminatory power of the GARP test. The power is commonly expressed as the relative size of the complement of A. This immediately allows for an intuitive probabilistic interpretation: The power measures the probability that a data set generated by irrational behavior (i.e., behavior that is inconsistent with the underlying model of choice) violates the revealed preference condition. To quantify this power, we therefore need a model of irrational behavior. The most common practice in revealed preference theory defines irrational behavior as random draws from the outcome space Ω. This generates the power measure as defined by Bronars (1987). Bronars motivated his measure as an operationalization of Becker (1962)'s theoretical notion of irrational behavior that states that consumers randomly (uniformly) choose consumption bundles that exhaust their available budget. It has become standard practice in empirical applications of revealed preference to report the Bronars power measure, although other power measures are also available (see Andreoni et al. 2013).

In general, the pass rate and the power are two sides of the same coin. A favorable pass rate for a specific model provides convincing support only if the associated test has high enough power. In practice, the two measures are almost always inversely correlated, which makes it interesting to define a summarizing measure that combines the two into a single metric. Beatty and Crawford (2011) suggest such a measure based on an original idea of Selten (1991). This measure is called the predictive success and is defined as:

$$\text{predictive success} = \text{pass rate} - (1 - \text{power}).$$

Pass rates and power are always between 0 and 1, which means that the predictive success is bounded between -1 and 1. A value close to 1 indicates a model that is consistent with a large fraction of the observations and also has high power. By contrast, a value close to -1 implies a model with very low power and low pass rate. In this case, the revealed preference model allows for almost all (random) behavior and yet the observed data fails to pass the test. Finally, a predictive success close to 0 corresponds to a model where the pass rate for the observed behavior is more or less equal to what the expected pass rate would be if behavior were random. Essentially, it implies that the rationality test does not allow us to distinguish observed behavior from random (irrational) behavior. In general, for a model to be meaningful, the predictive success should be above 0. Demuynck (2015) shows how to conduct statistical inference on predictive success measures to compare the empirical fit between different revealed preference models.

4.3 Measurement Errors

The presence of measurement errors in observed data may erroneously result in a violation of revealed preference even when the 'true' data (without errors) satisfy the revealed preference restrictions. Suppose that the observed quantity data $x^t \in \mathbb{R}^N$ is measured with error and let us denote the 'true' (unobserved) data by q^t.[14] Following Varian (1985), we assume that the observed and 'true' data are related via the multiplicative Berkson measurement error model:

$$q^t = x^t(1 + \varepsilon^t), \tag{5}$$

where the random measurement errors at observation t are denoted by $\varepsilon^t \in \mathbb{R}^N$. We wish to test the following hypothesis:

$$\mathrm{H}_0 : \text{The data set } \left(p^t, q^t\right)_{t=1,\ldots,T} \text{ satisfies GARP.} \tag{6}$$

If the observed data $\left(p^t, x^t\right)_{t=1,\ldots,T}$ violate GARP but one fails to reject H_0, then it means that failure of the GARP test might be attributed to measurement error. In contrast, if H_0 is rejected, then it means that the violation of GARP is too strong to be attributed to measurement error alone.

Varian (ibid.) departs from the assumption that $\varepsilon_n^t \sim N(0, \sigma^2)$ are i.i.d.[15] Then, under H_0 and this distributional assumption, we have that $(p^t, x^t(1 + \varepsilon^t))_{t=1,\ldots,n}$ satisfies GARP and the statistic,

$$M = \sum_{t=1}^{T} \sum_{n=1}^{N} \frac{\varepsilon_n^t \varepsilon_n^t}{\sigma^2},$$

[14] It is straightforward to modify the exposition and instead allow for measurement error in prices (see, e.g., Jones and Edgerton 2009).

[15] We use superscripts to refer to observations, while subscripts refer to the goods.

has a χ^2 distribution with TN degrees of freedom. Let c_α be the $(1 - \alpha) \times 100$th percentile of this distribution. If measurement errors were observed, we would reject H_0 if

$$M > c_\alpha.$$

Unfortunately, we do not observe the measurement errors, ε_n^t, which means that we cannot compute M. Instead, Varian proposed looking for the errors e_n^t that solve

$$\widehat{M} = \min \sum_{t=1}^{T} \sum_{n=1}^{N} e_n^t e_n^t, \text{ s.t. } \left(p^t, x^t(1 + e^t)\right)_{t=1, \ldots, T} \textit{ satisfies GARP.} \tag{7}$$

$\widehat{M}$ gives the minimal distance (in a squared Euclidean sense) from the observed dataset to the collection of data sets that satisfy GARP. Under H_0, the true data satisfy GARP, which means that:

$$\widehat{M} \leq \sum_{t=1}^{T} \varepsilon^t \varepsilon^t,$$

This shows that we can form a conservative test that rejects H_0 whenever

$$\frac{\widehat{M}}{\sigma^2} > c_\alpha.$$

This test still hinges on the condition that the error variance σ^2 is known. Of course, in empirical applications, this is never the case. Varian therefore proposed an alternative 'Bayesian'-style approach. Notice that the rejection criterion can be restated as

$$\sigma^2 < \frac{\widehat{M}}{c_\alpha}.$$

Varian defined the statistic $\overline{\sigma^2} = \frac{\widehat{M}}{c_\alpha}$, which provides the largest value of σ^2 for which H_0 would be rejected. In other words, if $\overline{\sigma^2}$ is smaller than your prior belief concerning the variance σ^2, you may want to accept the hypothesis that the 'true' data $\left(p^t, q^t\right)_{t=1,\dots,T}$ satisfy GARP.

A main difficulty in implementing the test involves solving (7). Varian (1985)'s implementation is based on the Afriat inequalities, which would require solving a highly nonlinear optimization problem. However, by exploiting the equivalence between GARP and the Varian inequalities in Theorem 1, we obtain a considerably simpler problem, since the variables e_n^t enter the Varian inequalities linearly. This means that we can use the MILP formulation of the Varian inequalities when solving problem (7). This amounts to minimizing a quadratic (and convex) objective function subject to a set of linear constraints, which can be done using off-the-shelf algorithms.

The Upper Bound Test: Fleissig and Whitney (2005) proposed an alternative procedure to test hypothesis (6) that was further modified by Jones and Edgerton (2009). The test statistic of Jones and Edgerton's procedure is defined as the smallest value of F such that the following adjustments of the Afriat inequalities hold:

$$U^s - U^t - \lambda^t p^t \left(x^s - x^t\right) \leq \lambda^t F.$$

Assuming that the observed and 'true' data are related via the multiplicative Berkson measurement error model (5), Jones and Edgerton show that under H_0:

$$F \leq C \equiv \max_{s,t=1,\dots,T} \{p^t \left(x^s \circ \varepsilon^s - x^t \circ \varepsilon^t\right)\},$$

where $\circ$ denotes the Hadamard (element-wise) product. For a given distribution of the measurement errors, it is straightforward to simulate the distribution of C and obtain its $(1-\alpha) \times 100$th percentile c'_α. The null of rationality, H_0, is then rejected whenever F exceeds this critical value, i.e. $F > c'_\alpha$. Compared to the MILP procedure above, the upper bound procedure is much easier to compute. However, the test is more conservative than Varian's.

Hjertstrand (2013) pointed out that the test statistic F can be calculated by solving a sequence of linear programming problems in the form of a binary search. He also noted that this is the most computationally expensive part of the implementation. By exploiting the equivalence between the Afriat inequalities and GARP in Theorem 1, Hjertstrand showed that F can be calculated using a combinatorial algorithm very similar to GARP. This allows for a very efficient implementation of the procedure and, consequently, its applicability to large data sets.

Finally, Hjertstrand (ibid.) noted that the Berkson measurement error model in (5), where the 'true' variable of interest is predicted (or caused) by the observed variable and a random error, may be inappropriate to describe many economic data sets. Instead, the classical measurement error model, where the observed variable is predicted by the 'true' variable and a random error, i.e.

$$x^t = q^t(1 + \epsilon^t),$$

is widely considered a more appropriate model in economic applications. Hjertstrand showed how the upper bound test can be modified to test H_0 under the assumption of this classical multiplicative measurement error model.

5 Conclusion

Revealed preference theory has expanded considerably since Samuelson's seminal contribution more than 80 years ago. Nowadays, revealed preference theory has grown into a very versatile theoretical and empirical toolbox that can be used to study a wide variety of decision-making models.

In this chapter, we have provided a brief survey of several recent contributions to the literature with a special emphasis on computational advancements. In particular, we have shown that many revealed preference models can efficiently be implemented using mixed integer linear programming procedures. This allows us to bring various popular decision-making models, that were previously thought as being unverifiable, to the data. As a result, this not only adds to the attractiveness of revealed preference theory as an empirical tool, but it also allows us to expand the revealed preference toolbox to new and unexplored models in economics. The next 80 years look promising indeed.

Acknowledgments Thomas Demuynck acknowledges financial support by the Fonds de la Recherche Scientifique-FNRS under grant nr F.4516.18. Per Hjertstrand acknowledges financial support from Jan Wallander och Tom Hedelius stiftelse, Marcus och Marianne Wallenbergs stiftelse and Johan och Jakob Söderbergs stiftelse.

References

Adams, A., L. Cherchye, B. De Rock and E. Verriest (2014) "Now or Later? Time Inconsistency, Collective Choice and Revealed Preference," *American Economic Review*, 104: 4147–4183.

Afriat, S.N. (1967) "The Construction of Utility Functions from Expenditure Data," *International Economic Review*, 8: 67–77.

Afriat, S.N. (1969) "The Construction of Separable Utility Functions from Expenditure Data," Tech. rep., University of North Carolina.

Afriat, S.N. (1972) "Efficiency Estimation of Production Functions," *International Economic Review*, 13: 568–598.

Andreoni, J., B.J. Gillen and W.T Harbaugh (2013) "The Power of Revealed Preference Tests: Ex-Post Evaluation of Experimental Design," Tech. rep., University of California, San Diego.

Apps, P.F. and R. Rees (1988) "Taxation and the Household," *Journal of Public Economics*, 35: 355–369.

Beatty, T.K.M. and I. Crawford (2011) "How Demanding Is the Revealed Preference Approach to Demand," *American Economic Review*, 101: 2782–2795.

Becker, G.S. (1962) "Irrational Behavior and Economic Theory," *Journal of Political Economy*, 70: 1–13.

Belongia, M.T. and K.A. Chrystal (1991) "An Admissible Monetary Aggregate for the United Kingdom," *Review of Economics and Statistics*, 73: 497–503.

Bergstrom, T.C., L. Blume and H.R. Varian (1986) "On the Private Provision of Public Goods," *Journal of Public Economics*, 29: 25–49.

Blundell, R., M. Browning and I. Crawford (2003) "Nonparametric Engel Curves and Revealed Preference," *Econometrica*, 71: 205–240.

Blundell, R., M. Browning and I. Crawford (2008) "Best Nonparametric Bounds on Demand Responses," *Econometrica*, 76: 1227–1262.

Bronars, S.G. (1987) "The Power of Nonparametric Tests of Preference Maximization," *Econometrica*, 55: 693–698.

Brown, D.J. and C. Calsamiglia (2007) "The Nonparametric Approach to Applied Welfare Analysis," *Economic Theory*, 31: 183–188.

Brown, D.J. and R. Kannan (2008) "Two Algorithms for Solving the Walrasian Equilibrium Inequalities," in D. Brown and F. Kubler (eds.) *Computational Aspects of General Equilibrium Theory: Refutable Theories of Value.* Lecture Notes in Economics and Mathematical Systems. Berlin, Springer.

Brown, D.J. and R.L. Matzkin (1996) "Testable Restrictions on the Equilibrium Manifold," *Econometrica*, 64: 1249–1262.

Brown, D.J. and C. Shannon (2000) "Uniqueness, Stability, and Comparative Statics in Rationalizable Walrasian Markets," *Econometrica*, 68: 1529–1540.

Browning, M. (1989) "A Nonparametric Test of the Life-Cycle Rational Expectations Hypothesis," *International Economic Review*, 30: 979–992.

Carvajal, A. and N. Gonzáles (2014) "On Refutability of the Nash Bargaining Solution," *Journal of Mathematical Economics*, 50: 177–186.

Carvajal, A. and X. Song (2018) "Testing Pareto Efficiency and Competitive Equilibrium in Economies with Public Goods," *Journal of Mathematical Economics*, 75: 19–30.

Chambers, C.P. and F. Echenique (2014) "On the Consistency of Data with Bargaining Theories," *Theoretical Economics*, 9: 137–162.

Chambers, C.P. and F. Echenique (2016) *Revealed Preference Theory.* Cambridge, UK, Cambridge University Press.

Chambers, C.P., F. Echenique and E. Shmaya (2010) "On Behavioural Complementarities and Its Implications," *Journal of Economic Theory*, 145: 2332–2355.

Chambers, C.P., F. Echenique and E. Shmaya (2011) "Testable Implications of Gross Substitutes in Demand for Two Goods," *American Economic Journal: Microeconomics*, 3: 129–136.

Cherchye, L., B. De Rock and F. Vermeulen (2007) "The Collective Model of Household Consumption: A Nonparametric Characterization," *Econometrica*, 75: 553–574.

Cherchye, L., I. Crawford, B. De Rock and F. Vermeulen (2009a) "The Revealed Preference Approach to Demand," in D. Slottje (ed.) *Quantifying Consumer Preferences: Estimating Demand Systems.* Contributions to Economic Analysis. Bingley, UK, Emerald Press.

Cherchye, L., B. De Rock and F. Vermeulen (2009b) "Opening the Black Box of Intra-Household Decision-Making: Theory and Nonparametric Empirical Tests of General Collective Consumption Models," *Journal of Political Economy*, 117: 1074–1104.

Cherchye, L., B. De Rock and F. Vermeulen (2011a) "The Revealed Preference Approach to Collective Consumption Behavior: Testing and Sharing Rule Recovery," *Review of Economic Studies*, 78: 176–198.

Cherchye, L., T. Demuynck and B. De Rock (2011b) "Revealed Preference Analysis of Noncooperative Household Consumption," *Economic Journal*, 121: 1073–1096.

Cherchye, L., T. Demuynck and B. De Rock (2011c) "Testable Implications of General Equilibrium Models: An Integer Programming Approach," *Journal of Mathematical Economics*, 47: 564–575.

Cherchye, L., T. Demuynck and B. De Rock (2013) "Nash Bargained Consumption Decisions: A Revealed Preference Analysis," *Economic Journal*, 123: 195–235.

Cherchye, L., T. Demuynck and B. De Rock (2014) "Revealed Preference Analysis for Convex Rationalization on Nonlinear Budget Sets," *Journal of Economic Theory*, 152: 224–236.

Cherchye, L., T. Demuynck, B. De Rock and P. Hjertstrand (2015a) "Revealed Preference Tests for Weak Separability: An Integer Programming Approach," *Journal of Econometrics*, 186: 129–141.

Cherchye, L., T. Demuynck and B. De Rock (2015b) "Is Utility Transferable? A Revealed Preference Analysis," *Theoretical Economics*, 10: 51–65.

Cherchye, L., B. De Rock, T. Demuynck and F. Vermeulen (2017) "Household Consumption When the Marriage Is Stable," *American Economic Review*, 107: 1507–1534.

Cherchye, L., T. Demuynck and B. De Rock (2018) "Normality of Demand in a Two-goods Setting," *Journal of Economic Theory*, 173: 361–382.

Chiappori, P.-A. (1988) "Rational Household Labor Supply," *Econometrica*, 56: 63–89.

Chiappori, P.-A. (1992) "Collective Labor Supply and Welfare," *Journal of Political Economy*, 100: 437–467.

Chiappori, P.-A. and J.-C. Rochet (1987) "Revealed Preferences and Differentiable Demand," *Econometrica*, 55: 687–691.

Cosaert, S. and T. Demuynck (2015) "Revealed Preference Theory for Finite Choice Sets," *Economic Theory*, 59: 169–200.

Cosaert, S. and T. Demuynck (2018) "Nonparametric Welfare and Demand Analysis with Unobserved Individual Heterogeneity," *Review of Economic and Statistics*, 100: 349–361.

Crawford, I. (2010) "Habits Revealed," *Review of Economic Studies*, 77: 1382–1402.

Crawford, I. and B. De Rock (2014) "Empirical Revealed Preference," *Annual Review of Economics*, 6: 503–524.

Dean, M. and D. Martin (2016) "Measuring Rationality with the Minimum Cost of Revealed Preference Violations," *Review of Economics and Statistics*, 98: 524–534.

Demuynck, T. (2015) "Statistical Inference for Measures of Predictive Success," *Theory and Decision*, 79: 689–699.

Demuynck, T. and C. Seel (2018) "Revealed Preference with Limited Consideration," *American Economic Journal: Microeconomics*, 10: 102–131.

Demuynck, T. and E. Verriest (2013) "I'll Never Forget My First Cigarette: A Revealed Preference Analysis of the Habits as Durables Model," *International Economic Review*, 54: 717–738.

Diewert, W.E. (1973) "Afriat and Revealed Preference Theory," *Review of Economic Studies*, 40: 419–425.

Diewert, W.E. (2012) "Afriat's Theorem and Some Extensions to Choice Under Uncertainty," *Economic Journal*, 122: 305–331.

Diewert, W.E. and C. Parkan (1985) "Tests for the Consistency of Consumer Data," *Journal of Econometrics*, 30: 127–147.

Echenique, F. (2014) "Testing for Separability Is Hard," Tech. rep., Caltech.

Echenique, F., S. Lee and M. Shum (2011) "The Money Pump as a Measure of Revealed Preference Violations," *Journal of Political Economy*, 119: 1201–1223.

Echenique, F. and K. Saito (2015) "Savage in the Market," *Econometrica*, 83: 1467–1495.

Elger, C.T., B.E. Jones, D.L. Edgerton and J.M. Binner (2008) "A Note on the Optimal Level of Monetary Aggregation in the United Kingdom," *Macroeconomic Dynamics*, 12: 117–131.

Fisher, D. and A.R. Fleissig (1997) "Monetary Aggregation and the Demand for Assets," *Journal of Money, Credit and Banking*, 29: 458–475.

Fleissig, A.R. and G.A. Whitney (2003) "A New PC-Based Test for Varian's Weak Separability Condition," *Journal of Business and Economic Statistics*, 21: 133–145.

Fleissig, A.R. and G.A. Whitney (2005) "Testing for the Significance of Violations of Afriat's Inequalities," *Journal of Business and Economic Statistics*, 23: 355–362.

Forges, F. and V. Iehlé (2013) "Essential Data, Budget Sets and Rationalization," *Economic Theory*, 54: 449–461.

Forges, F. and V. Iehlé (2014) "Afriat's Theorem for Indivisible Goods," *Journal of Mathematical Economics*, 54: 1–6.

Forges, F. and E. Minelli (2009) "Afriat's Theorem for General Budget Sets," *Journal of Economic Theory*, 144: 135–145.

Ginsberg, W. (1973) "Concavity and Quasiconcavity in Economics," *Journal of Economic Theory*, 6: 596–605.

Green, E.J. and K. Osband (1991) "A Revealed Preference Theory for Expected Utility," *Review of Economic Studies*, 58: 677–695.

Gross, J. and D. Kaiser (1996) "Two Simple Algorithms for Generating a Subset of Data Consistent with WARP and Other Binary Relations," *Journal of Business and Economic Statistics*, 14: 251–255.

Heufer, J. (2014) "Nonparametric Comparative Revealed Risk Aversion," *Journal of Economic Theory*, 153: 569–616.

Heufer, J. and P. Hjertstrand (2015) "Consistent Subsets: Computationally Feasible Methods to Compute the Houtman-Maks-Index," *Economics Letters*, 128: 87–89.

Heufer, J. and P. Hjertstrand (2019) "Homothetic Efficiency: Theory and Applications," forthcoming in *Journal of Business and Economic Statistics.*

Hjertstrand, P. (2009) "A Monte Carlo Study of the Necessary and Sufficient Conditions for Weak Separability," *Advances in Econometrics*, 24: 151–182.

Hjertstrand, P. (2013) "A Simple Method to Account for Measurement Errors in Revealed Preference Tests," IFN Working Paper 990, Research Institute of Industrial Economics, Stockholm.

Hjertstrand, P. and J.L. Swofford (2012) "Revealed Preference Tests for Consistency with Weakly Separable Indirect Utility," *Theory and Decision*, 72: 245–256.

Hjertstrand, P. and J.L. Swofford (2019) "Revealed Preference Tests of Indirect and Homothetic Weak Separability of Financial Assets, Consumption and Leisure," forthcoming in *Journal of Financial Stability.*

Hjertstrand, P., J.L. Swofford and G.A. Whitney (2016) "Mixed Integer Programming Revealed Preference Tests of Utility Maximization and Weak Separability of Consumption, Leisure and Money," *Journal of Money, Credit and Banking*, 48: 1547–1561.

Hjertstrand, P., J.L. Swofford and G.A. Whitney (2019) "Index Numbers and Revealed Preference Rankings," forthcoming in *Macroeconomic Dynamics.*

Hoderlein, S. and J. Stoye (2014) "Revealed Preference in a Heterogeneous Population," *Review of Economics and Statistics,* 96: 197–213.

Houthakker, H.S. (1950) "Revealed Preference and the Utility Function," *Economica,* 17: 159–174.

Houtman, M. and J.A.H. Maks (1985) "Determining All Maximal Data Subsets Consistent with Revealed Preference," *Kwantitatieve Methoden,* 89: 89–104.

Jones, B.E., D. Dutkowsky and C.T. Elger (2005) "Sweep Programs and Optimal Money Aggregation," *Journal of Banking and Finance,* 29: 483–508.

Jones, B.E. and D.L. Edgerton (2009) "Testing Utility Maximization with Measurement Errors in the Data," *Advances in Econometrics,* 24: 199–236.

Kawaguchi, K. (2017) "Testing Rationality Without Restricting Heterogeneity," *Journal of Econometrics,* 197: 153–171.

Kitamura, Y. and J. Stoye (2018) "Nonparametric Analysis of Random Utility Models," *Econometrica,* 86: 1883–1909.

Matzkin, R.L. (1991) "Axioms of Revealed Preference for Nonlinear Choice Sets," *Econometrica,* 59: 1779–1786.

Matzkin, R.L. and M.K. Richter (1991) "Testing Strictly Concave Rationality," *Journal of Economic Theory,* 53: 287–303.

McFadden, D.L. and M.K. Richter (1971) "On the Extension of a Set Function on a Set of Events to a Probability on the Generated Boolean σ-Algebra," Tech. rep., University of California, Berkeley.

McFadden, D.L. (2005) "Revealed Stochastic Preference: A Synthesis," *Economic Theory,* 26: 245–264.

Nishimura, H., E.A. Ok and J.K.H. Quah (2017) "A Comprehensive Approach to Revealed Preference Theory," *American Economic Review,* 107: 1239–1263.

Polisson, M. and J.K.H. Quah (2013) "Revealed Preference in a Discrete Consumption Space," *American Economic Journal: Microeconomics,* 5: 28–34.

Polisson, M., J.K.H. Quah and L. Renou (2017) "Revealed Preferences Over Risk and Uncertainty," School of Economics and Finance Discussion Paper 1706, University of St Andrews.

Samuelson, P.A. (1938) "A Note on the Pure Theory of Consumer's Behavior," *Economica,* 5: 61–71.

Samuelson, P.A. (1948) "Consumption Theory in Terms of Revealed Preference," *Economica,* 15: 243–253.

Selten, R. (1991) "Properties of a Measure of Predictive Success," *Mathematical Social Sciences,* 21: 153–167.

Smeulders, B., L. Cherchye, B. De Rock and F.C.R. Spieksma (2013) "The Money Pump as a Measure of Revealed Preference Violations: A Comment," *Journal of Political Economy*, 121: 1248–1258.

Swofford, J.L. and G.A. Whitney (1987) "Nonparametric Tests of Utility Maximization and Weak Separability for Consumption, Leisure and Money," *Review of Economics and Statistics*, 69: 458–464.

Swofford, J.L. and G.A. Whitney (1994) "A Revealed Preference Test for Weakly Separable Utility Maximization with Incomplete Adjustment," *Journal of Econometrics*, 60: 235–249.

van Bruggen, P. and J. Heufer (2017) "Afriat in the Lab," *Journal of Economic Theory*, 169: 546–550.

Varian, H.R. (1982) "The Nonparametric Approach to Demand Analysis," *Econometrica*, 50: 945–974.

Varian, H.R. (1983a) "Non-Parametric Tests of Consumer Behavior," *Review of Economic Studies*, 50: 99–110.

Varian, H.R. (1983b) "Nonparametric Tests of Models of Investor Behavior," *Journal of Financial and Quantitative Analysis*, 18: 269–278.

Varian, H.R. (1984) "The Nonparametric Approach to Production Analysis," *Econometrica*, 52: 579–597.

Varian, H.R. (1985) "Non-Parametric Analysis of Optimizing Behaviour with Measurement Error," *Journal of Econometrics*, 30: 445–458.

Varian, H.R. (1988) "Estimating Risk Aversion from Arrow-Debreu Portfolio Choice," *Econometrica*, 56: 973–979.

Varian, H.R. (1990) "Goodness-of-Fit in Optimizing Models," *Journal of Econometrics*, 46: 125–140.

Varian, H.R. (2006) "Revealed Preference," in M. Szenberg, L. Ramrattan and A.A Gottesman (eds.) *Samuelson Economics and the Twenty-First Century*. Oxford, Oxford University Press.

Warshall, S. (1962) "A Theorem of Boolean Matrices," *Journal of the American Association of Computing Machinery*, 9: 11–12.

10

Paul Samuelson and the Economics of Pass-Through and the Envelope Theorem

Joseph Farrell

1 Introduction

In August 1979, I became a very junior faculty member at MIT's distinguished Economics Department. This gave me the privilege of getting to know Paul Samuelson, then in his sixties. As the world knows, he was exceptional in his combination of rigor and breadth. He was also very willing to tutor a young colleague in a bewildering range of topics. Here, I briefly describe two topics that I especially associate with those discussions.

2 Revealed Preference and Cost Pass-Through

I particularly recall his enthusiastically explaining to me—I had not seen it before—the revealed-preference argument that a profit-maximizing firm,

J. Farrell (✉)
University of California, Berkeley, CA, USA
e-mail: farrell@econ.berkeley.edu

R. A. Cord et al. (eds.), *Paul Samuelson*, Remaking Economics: Eminent Post-War Economists, https://doi.org/10.1057/978-1-137-56812-0_10

faced with higher marginal costs, will choose (weakly) lower output and higher price. Consider a firm facing inverse demand $p(x)$. Initially, it has constant marginal cost c_0, and optimally chooses the output and price combination $(x_0, p(x_0))$. Now its constant marginal cost c_0 is exogenously replaced by a higher constant marginal cost c_1, where $c_1 > c_0$, and it optimally chooses a new output and price combination $(x_1, p(x_1))$. The claim is that $x_1 \leq x_0$.

As i recall Paul expounding the proof to me, we write out two revealed-preference inequalities:

$$(p(x_0) - c_0)x_0 \geq (p(x_1) - c_0)x_1;$$

$$(p(x_1) - c_1)x_1 \geq (p(x_0) - c_1)x_0.$$

Adding these two inequalities, all the terms involving the inverse demand function $p(.)$ cancel out, and (collecting terms) we are left with:

$$(c_1 - c_0)(x_0 - x_1) \geq 0.$$

As promised, for $c_1 > c_0$, it follows that $x_1 \leq x_0$. The lower output will normally go along with a higher price, which we describe as the pass-through of the firm's now higher marginal cost.

Strikingly, no assumption need be made about the inverse demand function. This was mind-expanding, not because anyone had really thought higher marginal costs might maybe lead to higher output (though it sometimes seems that 'anything can happen' results abound in economics), but because it gloriously vaulted above the widespread use of functional-form assumptions that would enable explicit calculation, or of smoothness assumptions that would enable the use of calculus (in this instance the implicit-function theorem); and unlike a calculus approach, it gets us directly to the effects of finite (versus infinitesimal) changes. Intellectually glorious vaulting-above indeed—but also a bit magical and mysterious. I at least, and I think many others, had trouble correlating the slick 'add two inequalities and collect terms' wave of the wand with the highly intuitive—and, we learn, very general—result.

For the past almost 40 years, I have believed that the argument was one of the gems of Samuelson's 1947 *Foundations of Economic Analysis*. In writing this chapter, however, I went to look it up—and failed to find it there.[1] However, Samuelson does give the revealed-preference argument that a price-taking firm's profit-maximizing output is weakly increasing in the output price.[2]

These seem at first blush like quite different results. The first concerns the response to cost shocks on the part of a firm facing a given demand curve, not necessarily a price-taker. The second concerns the response to a change in output price on the part of a price-taking firm with a fixed cost function (I will call it the 'second firm'). However, they are in fact closely related, and in an instructive way. To see this, reframe the revealed-preference argument more transparently as follows.

Given constant marginal cost c_0, the first firm prefers its optimal choice x_0 over (of course) all alternative output choices, and in particular over all *higher* levels of output, i.e. above x_0. Now when the firm's marginal costs are *increased*, increasing its output to one of those higher levels obviously cannot become *more* appealing than it was. Thus, the firm's preference of x_0 over all higher levels of output, a fortiori, must continue. If its optimal choice changes, it must be to a lower level of output.

Similarly, and using overlapping notation to stress the parallel even at the slight risk of confusion, our second firm, facing a given output price p_0, prefers its optimal output x_0 over (of course) all alternative output choices, and in particular over all *lower* levels of output. Now present the firm with a higher given output price, $p_1 > p_0$, and that preference for x_0 over lower levels of output clearly cannot be reversed, only strengthened. Thus, if its optimal choice changes, it must be to a higher level of output.

I call these 'the a fortiori arguments,' and they can be systematized as follows. For any two output choices, (x, y), define the incremental profit of y versus x, say $f(x, y)$, to be just what it sounds like: the profit from

[1] Neither the index nor the table of contents gives me much guidance or assurance that I have looked in the right places, but I have tried. Perhaps also relevant is the fact that *Foundations* does give a calculus-based argument for the result—with differentiability of course assumed—at page 16 and again at page 40.

[2] See Samuelson (1983: 51).

choosing y minus the profit from choosing x.[3] For concreteness, focus on pairs (x, y) with $y \geq x$. For such pairs, the upward shift in marginal costs for the first firm unambiguously shifts f downwards, while the increase in output price for the second firm unambiguously shifts f upwards.[4] When f shifts upwards, that makes the profit comparison if anything less favorable to reducing output and more favorable to raising it. Of course, the reverse occurs when f shifts downwards. In particular, it does not matter whether the shift in the incremental profit function comes from a shift in marginal costs, holding the revenue side constant, or from a shift in marginal revenues, holding costs constant. In this sense, the price-taking supply response result is equivalent to the pass-through result we began with.

These observations help to demystify the revealed-preference pass-through argument. It is not surprising that all the terms involving $p(x)$ drop out: those terms are of course important to calculating profits from any given output choice, or even to calculating the difference in profits between two output choices—that is, if we were calculating $f(x_0, x_1)$. However, since all we need to know is the shift in f, that amounts to the impact on the additional cost of one output level versus the other. The comparison of revenues at the two candidate output levels does not change. The 'shift in comparison' reasoning is a little subtle, and might even feel treacherous; some readers might prefer the firm foundation of the calculation. Nevertheless, calculation without understanding can also be a bit treacherous. I like to think that with the spread of difference-in-difference estimation techniques in econometrics, and the more directly related theoretical work on supermodularity in economics,[5] perhaps more students will readily grasp it more intuitively than did my generation, let alone most of Professor Samuelson's.[6] Moreover, it has the great aesthetic virtue

---

[3] As a general matter, a good case can be made that the difference in profit between two choices is conceptually more solidly defined than is the level of profit from one choice, but I do not pursue this here.

[4] By construction, the function f is anti-symmetric, meaning that $f(y, x) \equiv -f(x, y)$. Thus, there can be no non-trivial upward shift in f over its full range, but of course when we restrict as in the text, it works.

[5] For an exposition, including the pass-through result, see Amir (2005).

[6] As he was fond of quoting, 'science progresses funeral by funeral' (attributed to Max Planck.)

of not mentioning the $p(x)$ function that otherwise laboriously and mysteriously turns out to play no role.[7]

It is worth commenting on the relevant ranges for the incremental profit function f. As one might expect, a global shift is not essential to the arguments. For our first firm, facing a higher marginal cost, recall that the result is that its output will not rise to, say, $y > x_0$. What is needed for the argument is that $f(x_0, y)$ has shifted down for those higher values y. Concretely, this means an upward shift in the incremental costs of expanding output from x_0 to higher levels y, or in marginal costs on intervals (x_0, y), or one might say for output above x_0. It is a little confusing because intuitively what actively drives the output reduction is the increase in marginal cost *at and somewhat below* x_0. That, after all, is what pushes the optimizing firm to reduce output first slightly below x_0 and then to keep going down to the lower new optimal level. The logic of the result, however, does not track this driver of output reduction, but focuses on the absence of a new reason to increase output.

Similarly, for our second firm, the output expansion when its output price p increases is, of course, economically driven by the higher incremental profit at output levels at and somewhat above its initial output x_0. However, the proof centers on explaining that, a fortiori, output reductions below x_0 that were by construction unappealing at the lower output price remain (and become more) unappealing at the higher output price—that is, incremental profit of additional output at levels *below* x_0 is higher than it was.

One could argue that this mismatch between the real economic forces and the players in the proof is an aesthetic flaw in what is nevertheless a beautiful piece of mathematical economic logic. It arises because the proof does not exactly study the effects but rather rejects the possibility of perverse effects, a strategy that involves focusing on things other than those that will happen!

What concretely shifts the incremental profit function? As is well understood, on the cost side it is incremental or marginal costs over relevant ranges. On the demand side, it is incremental or marginal revenue, not

---

[7]I am fairly sure that at this point Samuelson would remind us of the dramatic principle of Chekhov's gun: every element in a story ought to turn out to be necessary.

price—the result for the price-taking firm (our firm 2) relies on the fact that among horizontal (price-taking) demand curves, marginal revenue and average incremental revenue coincide with price.

We can use the incremental-profit approach to generalize the pass-through result that we started with. From a modern point of view, it might seem unduly limiting to assume uniform pricing against a simple demand curve. What about nonlinear pricing, private information, price discrimination, follow-on sales, and mechanism design by the seller? A range of such extensions yield themselves up very easily. What is required is (a) a separation between costs and marketing: specifically, that the set of marketing options open to the firm is unaffected by the cost shift, as would in many cases be true of the extensions just mentioned; and (b) information on the relative impact of a cost shock on the profitability of different options.

Suppose that the seller can pick a marketing strategy (perhaps involving price discrimination, etc.) indexed by say $m \in M$, which could be a price but might be multidimensional or non-numerical. Each such strategy m involves costs $c(m)$ and profits gross of costs (traditionally we might think gross revenues) $g(m)$. Assume that we can partially order the marketing strategies such that if $m \preccurlyeq n$ then the cost shock weakly raises $c(n) - c(m)$: this is the appropriate generalization of ordering quantity choices in the usual way and considering an upward shift in the marginal cost curve. Then the cost shock yields a downward shift in $f(m, n)$ for $m \preccurlyeq n$, so that if m is preferred to n prior to the shock, it is, a fortiori, preferred after the shock. More concretely, an upward shift in marginal costs pushes output weakly downward even if pricing and output choices are more complex than choosing a point on a traditional demand curve relating linear price to output. Since (or in cases for which) the g function does not shift, it plays no role in how preferences might change with the cost shift, and that is equally true whether it is simple and intuitive like a demand curve, or complex and subtle like optimal nonlinear pricing and price discrimination constrained by some threat of arbitrage. Again, this is why the terms in $p(x)$ dropped out above. We can focus only on what changes.

3 The Envelope Theorem

Let us return to our first firm, choosing output levels x_i in response to different levels of cost c_i. In this section, I consider revealed preference and the envelope theorem, which concerns the overall impact on the firm's profits.

The prevailing way to give the theorem assumes (or in some cases proves) differentiability and gives the result in terms of derivatives. Write $\pi(c, x)$ for the firm's profit when it faces costs c and chooses output x, and write $x(c)$ for the value of x that maximizes π given c. Then we have:

$$\frac{\mathrm{d}\pi(c, x(c))}{\mathrm{d}c} = \frac{\partial\pi(c, x)}{\partial c} + \frac{\partial\pi(c, x)}{\partial x}\frac{\mathrm{d}x(c)}{\mathrm{d}c}.$$

Here the partial derivative with respect to c involves holding x fixed, and conversely. The 'total derivative' on the left-hand side refers to the change in profits when c exogenously changes and x is optimally adjusted to the change. All the terms are evaluated at the point $(c, x(c))$.[8]

This equation superficially appears to teach us that we would need to study how a change in c affects x or (more or less equivalently) affects the price $p(x)$. As most readers will be aware, that 'rate of cost pass-through' can be calculated from partial derivatives of the profit function in a now familiar way explored in Samuelson's *Foundations*,[9] but it is not simple (it depends on the slope of the marginal revenue curve, which of course implicates the second derivative of the demand curve).[10] It is thus a relief to note that the first factor of the final term is zero, by the first-order condition for the optimal choice of x. Thus, for an infinitesimal change in c, only the direct impact, holding fixed the firm's optimal choices such as output or price, affects payoff. This is the usual calculus formulation of the envelope theorem.

Samuelson noted that it is natural to ask about 'finite,' meaning bigger than infinitesimal, changes in the parameter, here c. He pursued the

---

[8] The exposition assumes that c is a scalar, which might be a (constant) cost 'level' or a parameter indexing more general cost functions.

[9] See Samuelson (1983: 34). Oddly, the term 'envelope theorem' does not appear in the index!

[10] See, for instance, Bulow and Pfleiderer (1983) and Weyl and Fabinger (2013).

approach of examining higher derivatives. Seemingly he missed an opportunity to relish applying his revealed-preference approach. Consider our shift from c_0 to c_1. The overall impact on profits (when x has been reoptimized) is $\pi(c_1, x_1) - \pi(c_0, x_0)$. The revealed-preference inequalities are $\pi(c_1, x_1) \geq \pi(c_1, x_0)$ and $\pi(c_0, x_0) \geq \pi(c_0, x_1)$. Using the inequalities, we get the discrete revealed-preference envelope theorem, bounding the profit impact both from below and from above:

$$\begin{aligned}\pi(c_1, x_0) - \pi(c_0, x_0) &\leq \pi(c_1, x_1) - \pi(c_0, x_0)\\ &\leq \pi(c_1, x_1) - \pi(c_0, x_1).\end{aligned}$$

In words, the overall impact on profits lies between the partial impact calculated as if x stayed at its pre-shift optimum, and the partial impact calculated as if x stayed at its post-shift optimum.

One way to reframe this is to imagine first starting at (c_0, x_0) and leaving x fixed as c changes from c_0 to c_1; the impact on profits will obviously be less favorable with that failure to readjust x, and this yields one of the revealed-preference inequalities. To see the other inequality imagine starting at (c_1, x_1) and leaving x fixed as c changes from c_1 to c_0; the impact on profits will again obviously be less favorable than the impact of that 'reverse shock' with readjustment.

This inequality formulation of the envelope theorem recovers the calculus formulation when those values of x differ only infinitesimally. In practice, economists often write down the first-order calculus formulation and (one hopes) keep in mind that it is an approximation for small changes and a starting point for larger ones—and I will succumb to this short-cut below. The inequality formulation offers more precision and rigor in addressing discrete changes. It can be especially helpful when the shift in c and hence (often) in x is moderate, since then the bounds will be relatively tight, and can thus give a good sense of the discrete impact of the cost shift and help diagnose when more information is needed for a closer estimate.

This inequality or revealed-preference formulation surely must be fairly widely known, but perhaps mostly as a 'folk theorem'—it does not show up in several graduate economics texts I consulted. I think that is too bad, and I like to think that Samuelson would agree.

4 Incidence and the Apportionment Theory

We can now bring together the impact of a cost shift on the firm's profits and on downstream customers. When the cost shift is driven by a change in input prices from an upstream industry, antitrust economics may be interested in the harm or 'damages' to the firm and to its customers, for instance if the upstream industry starts to collude, raising the input prices. For concreteness (the discussion could be generalized considerably), suppose upstream collusion raises the cost of producing any quantity x by $x \cdot \Delta c$. Without the collusively higher cost, the firm would produce x_0 and price its output at p_0; facing that higher cost, the firm would produce x_1 and price its output at p_1.

4.1 Apportionment and Cost Changes for a Single Firm

Some discussion of this problem assumes an 'apportionment' of an 'overcharge.' The overcharge approach calculates damages at $x_1 \cdot \Delta c$, assuming no pass-through, and the apportionment theory posits that the actual harm to the firm, with pass-through of $p_1 - p_0 \equiv r \cdot \Delta c$, is only $x_1 \cdot (\Delta c - [p_1 - p_0]) = x_1 \cdot (1 - r)\Delta c$, the other $x_1 \cdot r \cdot \Delta c$ being borne instead by the downstream customers. The apportionment theory thus asserts that total harm adds up to the overcharge, and the pass-through rate r affects only how that total harm is distributed: a fraction $(1 - r)$ is borne by the firm, the remaining fraction r being borne by its customers.

That theory is wrong.[11] By the envelope theorem (together with the intermediate value theorem), the impact of the cost shift on the firm's profits is the 'full' $x \cdot \Delta c$ for some $x \in (x_1, x_0)$, independent of the pass-through rate r. Effects on the firm's customers, via pass-through, are in addition, for a total impact $(1 + r) \cdot x \cdot \Delta c$. When our firm's costs rise, it loses an amount equal to (in the calculus formulation, for a small

[11] Disappointing in this regard is the US Supreme Court's repetition in the 2019 Apple case of the apportionment error from its 1970s Hanover Shoe and Illinois Brick cases.

cost change) the extra costs holding fixed its output, and its downstream customers also lose an amount equal to their extra spending on the passed-through price change, holding fixed their quantity.[12]

To some, that fact seems (when $r > 0$) to violate a basic adding-up constraint. This reaction reflects zero-sum thinking, and in the special case of fixed output and zero pass-through, such as with a sufficiently kinked demand, the apportionment theory holds. However, in general, there is no adding-up constraint: the total harm often exceeds the overcharge. Indeed, if we identify the overcharge with initial upstream gains from collusion, that fact merely recites that collusion is economically inefficient in a way (perhaps among others) tied to a quantity effect, as might be expected from basic undergraduate microeconomics.

4.2 Apportionment and Cost Changes for a Price-Taking Industry

While it usually fails, the apportionment theory does also hold in a second special case: perfect competition. Instead of one firm's costs changing, think of a cost change that applies across a perfectly competitive (price-taking) industry. The envelope theorem applies again, but differently.

First, because each firm's quantity of output maximizes its profits in price-taking competitive equilibrium, the envelope theorem implies that the impact on its profits is equal to the direct impact on its costs at fixed quantity, plus the change in output price multiplied by that quantity. Extending our notation above, we have, for each such firm, $\Delta\pi = x \cdot (\Delta p - \Delta c)$.

Moreover, since consumers choose total quantity (and its allocation among consumers) in a way that maximizes consumer gains given the price p that they face, a second application of the envelope theorem implies that their loss is equal to $X \cdot \Delta p$, where X is total quantity across all such firms.

Summing across the firms, the price change apportions between firms and consumers a total impact that is equal to the direct impact of the cost

12 Adjustments of quantities increase these gains further, although by a second-order amount.

change on the firms, holding outputs fixed. The apportionment theory holds for this case!

Another nice way to see this point is that by standard welfare theorems, the perfectly competitive industry plus consumers, as a whole production-and-consumption coalition, maximizes its total surplus given the costs it faces upstream. Consequently, by the envelope theorem applied yet again, the aggregate impact on this coalition's surplus is as if it did not change its surplus-maximizing choices, including total quantity and its allocation among producers.

5 Demand Shifts, Competition and Pass-Through

For each firm in the competitive industry, not only do its own costs go up, but so do those of its rivals. The latter effect shifts upward the residual demand function that the firm faces (or, for a price-taker, the output price that it commands), and (by the envelope theorem) it is really this impact on rivals' supply, not the own-supply response, that puts the Δp term into each competitor's $\Delta \pi$. Here I apply a folk theorem that I was first shown by Jeremy Bulow[13] regarding the 'pass-through' or pricing consequences of a shift in a firm's residual demand.

Consider a profit-maximizing price-setting firm, facing a marginal cost function $c(x)$ and inverse demand function $p(x)$, where x is its output. If these are replaced by $c(x; h) \equiv c(x) + h$ and $p(x; h) \equiv p(x) + h$, respectively—that is, if both the marginal cost curve and the inverse demand curve are shifted up by h—it makes no difference to the profit resulting from any choice of x, and hence is completely neutral in its impact on profit-maximizing x.

In effect, this is a mere relabeling. A picturesque way to see this is to imagine taping some cash to each unit of the product. Taping $\$h$ to each widget increases both marginal cost and willingness to pay by $\$h$, but of course nothing real has changed: every allocation involving price

[13] The result plays a role in the economic analysis of payment systems and interchange: see, for instance, Gans and King (2003) and Farrell (2006).

p, quantity x, etc., is the same as the no-tape allocation involving price $p - h$, quantity x, etc.

An immediate but not obvious implication is: if shifting the marginal cost curve upward by h (without changing demand) yields a price increase of rh, where $r \geq 0$ is the standard own-pass-through rate as above, then shifting the firm's residual demand curve upward by h (without changing its costs) must yield a price increase of $(1 - r)h$. That is, the pass-through of a cost increase, plus the pass-through of a demand increase, adds to 100%, so the latter can be expressed in terms of the former.

While I am not aware of any conclusive results, it seems promising to apply this to explore relationships between firm-specific and industry-wide pass-through. In a competitive industry, each firm's residual demand shifts up when rivals' costs go up. Indeed, one might argue that a feature of a 'competitive' market is that each firm's demand responds largely to comparisons between its price and its rivals,' rather than by the absolute level of its price or its comparison against outside goods.[14]

In such an industry, let r denote the pass-through of an upward shift in one firm's costs into that firm's price, and R the pass-through of an upward shift in all firms' costs into that same firm's price. It follows that the difference, $R - r$, is the impact on this firm's price of an upward shift in all other firms' costs. However, at the same time, the pass-through of a unit upward shift in residual demand for this firm is, by the observation above, just $1 - r$. Thus, the upward shift in all other firms' costs raises residual demand for this firm by $(R - r)/(1 - r)$.

[14]One might argue that this merely means that we have included almost all plausible substitutes in the 'market,' suggesting that this is a diagnostic for an inclusive category rather than for a competitive market. However, merely including a wide qualitative range of substitutes would usually make market-wide cost shifts implausible. So, the proposed criterion (as used below) does capture the idea that products very similar (on the supply side, or perhaps descriptively) to this one include almost all plausible substitutes for this one.

6 Conclusion

In this chapter, I hope I have illustrated just a few of the insights one can derive from simple versions of some fundamental microeconomics that Paul Samuelson relished and admired.

Acknowledgements I thank Christopher Kilgore for his assistance in collating presentations of the envelope theorem.

References

Amir, R. (2005) "Supermodularity and Complementarity in Economics: An Elementary Survey," *Southern Economic Journal*, 71: 636–660.

Bulow, J.I. and P. Pfleiderer (1983) "A Note on the Effect of Cost Changes on Prices," *Journal of Political Economy*, 91: 182–185.

Farrell, J. (2006) "Efficiency and Competition Between Payment Instruments," *Review of Network Economics*, 5: 1–19.

Gans, J. and S. King (2003) "The Neutrality of Interchange Fees in Payment Systems," *Journal of Economic Analysis & Policy*, 3: 1–18.

Samuelson, P.A. (1983) *Foundations of Economic Analysis*. Cambridge, MA, Harvard University Press. Enlarged edition.

Weyl, E.G. and M. Fabinger (2013) "Pass-Through as an Economic Tool: Principles of Incidence Under Imperfect Competition," *Journal of Political Economy*, 121: 528–583.

11

Not a Behaviorist: Samuelson's Contributions to Utility Theory in the Harvard Years, 1936–1940

Ivan Moscati

1 Introduction

When economists, historians of economics, and economic methodologists refer to the work of Paul Samuelson in choice and demand theory, they typically cite the "Note on the Pure Theory of Consumer's Behaviour" and its Addendum that he published when he was a twenty-two-year-old graduate student at Harvard University (Samuelson 1938a, b). In these articles, Samuelson put forward an approach to demand analysis, later called revealed preference theory, whose postulates concern choice behavior, rather than, as was common among other economists of the period, the properties of ordinal utility functions or the shape of indifference curves. The typical reference to Samuelson's 1938 "Note" includes the following quotation: "I propose, therefore, that we start anew in direct attack

I. Moscati (✉)
Department of Economics, University of Insubria, Varese, Italy
e-mail: ivan.moscati@uninsubria.it

R. A. Cord et al. (eds.), *Paul Samuelson*, Remaking Economics: Eminent Post-War Economists, https://doi.org/10.1057/978-1-137-56812-0_11

upon the problem, dropping off the last vestiges of the utility analysis" (Samuelson 1938a: 62).

The steady association of Samuelson with the 1938 "Note" in general and this quotation in particular has had two interrelated effects. First, it has contributed to an image of Samuelson, and specifically of the young Samuelson, as a committed behaviorist who wanted to free economic analysis from the psychological concepts of utility and preference and give demand theory a purely behaviorist configuration centered on those choice postulates later called the Axioms of Revealed Preference (see, e.g., Wong 1978 [2006]). Second, when this behavioristic image of the young Samuelson was juxtaposed with his later presentation of revealed preference theory as equivalent to ordinal utility theory (Samuelson 1948, 1950), the question arose of whether he had changed his mind between 1938 and 1948–1950. Wade Hands (2014: 86–87) gives a name to this question: "Did he [Samuelson] change his mind about revealed preference, particularly between the time he was writing the original 1938 paper [the "Note"] and his second round of contributions (Samuelson 1948, 1950) I will call this…question *Das Paul Samuelson Problem*."[1]

In this chapter, I do three things. First, I review the several contributions to utility theory that Samuelson made when he was a Ph.D. student at Harvard, from the first scientific papers he began writing in 1936 to the doctoral dissertation he submitted in November 1940. In his first article, composed in 1936 and published in February 1937, Samuelson put forward a seminal model for intertemporal choices that relies on what today we call cardinal utility (Samuelson 1937). In the "Note" (Samuelson 1938a, b), I will argue, Samuelson did not want to eliminate utility from consumer choice theory but presented his revealed preference approach as complementary to the utility-based approach. In a paper published in October 1938, he explored the empirical implications of ordinal utility theory (Samuelson 1938c). In another paper, also published in October 1938, he

[1]The reference is to *Das Adam Smith Problem*, that is, the extensive late nineteenth-century German debate over the apparent inconsistency between the "sympathetic" conception of human nature put forward by Smith in his *Theory of Moral Sentiments* (Smith 1759 [1976]) and the "selfish" conception advanced in the *Wealth of Nations* (Smith 1776 [1976]). More discussion of the *Das Adam Smith Problem* can be found in Tribe (2015).

stated the conditions that make utility cardinal rather than just ordinal—thereby popularizing the expression "cardinal utility"—but judged these conditions implausible (Samuelson 1938d). In a brief comment published in February 1939, he opposed Harro Bernardelli's attempt to reintroduce the non-ordinal notion of diminishing marginal utility (Samuelson 1939). In a paper completed in the fall of 1939, but published only three years later, Samuelson (1942) criticized the non-ordinal assumption that the marginal utility of monetary income is constant. Finally, in his Ph.D. dissertation, entitled "Foundations of Analytical Economics" (Samuelson 1940), which later became *Foundations of Economic Analysis* (Samuelson 1947), he downplayed the revealed preference approach and presented the theory of consumer behavior by adopting an ordinal utility approach. A comprehensive review of Samuelson's early work in utility analysis has hitherto been missing in the rich literature about him; the present chapter fills this lacuna.[2]

Second, based on this review of Samuelson's early contributions to utility theory, I contend that the image of the young Samuelson as a committed behaviorist who consistently attempted to eliminate notions of utility and preference from economic analysis is misleading. Rather, I will argue that in 1936–1937, he was exploring different research paths, that is, more prosaically, he was a young man who wrote different things in different papers. However, Samuelson's stance on utility analysis quickly stabilized,

[2] In the first volume of his impressive intellectual biography of Samuelson, covering the period 1915–1948, Roger Backhouse (2017) discusses most of the research in utility analysis that Samuelson carried out between 1936 and 1940. However, Samuelson's utility theory plays only a marginal role in Backhouse's narrative and perhaps gets lost in his encyclopedic study. Moreover, I do not always share Backhouse's interpretation of Samuelson's stance on utility. Wade Hands (2001, 2010, 2013, 2014, 2017) has thoroughly discussed Samuelson's revealed preference theory between 1938 and 1950, but has never explicitly examined Samuelson's early work in utility analysis. John Chipman's essay on Samuelson's consumption theory (Chipman 1982) is very helpful in many respects, but examines Samuelson's work from an economic-theoretic rather than a historical perspective. In an illuminating article on Samuelson's revealed preference theory, Philippe Mongin (2000) rejected the behaviorist interpretation of Samuelson's 1938 "Note" but did not examine the other contributions to utility theory that Samuelson made between 1936 and 1940. Even Jean-Sébastien Lenfant, in his acute study of the stabilization of indifference curves (Lenfant 2012), says little about Samuelson's early work on utility analysis. In previous research, I have discussed individual parts of Samuelson's early work on utility theory (Moscati 2013, 2018), but this is my first attempt to connect the different pieces in a systematic fashion.

and from around mid-1938, he became a consistent advocate of an ordinal utility approach to choice theory.[3]

Samuelson's intellectual trajectory—*from exploration to ordinalism*—is in fact similar to that of another eminent demand theorist of the period, namely the English economist John Hicks. In a famous paper co-authored with Roy Allen, Hicks put forward a utility-free approach to demand analysis based on the notion of indifference curves (Hicks and Allen 1934). In subsequent works, however, Hicks (1937, 1939) set forth his analysis in terms of ordinal utility indices, and in *Value and Capital* (Hicks 1939), he fine-tuned the ordinal approach to utility theory.

Third, I argue that the answer to *Das Paul Samuelson Problem* is either negative or the question itself is ill-posed. It is negative in the sense that Samuelson did not change his mind between 1938 and 1948–1950, since he had already changed it in 1938. Alternatively, the problem is ill-posed in the sense that the claim of a change of mind in Samuelson's exploratory path between 1936 and 1937 and mid-1938 is incorrect.

2 Setting the Stage: Utility and Demand Theory in the 1930s

To understand Samuelson's early work on utility and demand, it is essential to bear in mind the state of the theory in the 1930s. That period was one of intense debates associated with the conclusive phase of the so-called ordinal revolution.

[3] In this chapter, I focus on Samuelson's early work on utility analysis and do not discuss the several articles he published on various other subjects between 1937 and 1940 (for an overview, see Backhouse 2017). This focus on a subset of Samuelson's scientific output appears legitimate because almost all the other papers he published in his Harvard years did not deal with utility theory at all. The few times that Samuelson touched upon the subject, such as in his paper on "Welfare Economics and International Trade" (Samuelson 1938e), he adopted the ordinal utility approach he was using in his contemporary papers on utility analysis. Therefore, discussing the whole of Samuelson's publications between 1937 and 1940 would have not modified my reconstruction of his early stance on utility analysis.

2.1 From Pareto to Hicks and Allen, 1900–1934

The ordinal revolution, initiated by Vilfredo Pareto around 1900, consisted of the gradual construction of a theory of demand and equilibrium independent of the assumption that utility is measurable. Pareto and subsequent "revolutionaries" pursued the goal of superseding measurable utility along two distinct lines that, using more modern terminology, can be called the preference-based approach and the choice-based approach. Pareto explored both lines of research, and in this, he was followed by Samuelson and Hicks.

In the *Manual of Political Economy* (Pareto 1906/1909 [2014]), Pareto adopted the preference-based approach. In this approach, the primary concept is that of preference: Individuals have well-behaved preferences between commodity bundles and are able to rank bundles according to their preferences. Utility is just an ordinal numerical index that represents the individual's preference ranking between bundles by assigning higher numbers to more preferred bundles. In mathematical terms, the ordinal nature of utility is expressed by the fact that, if the utility function $U(x)$ represents the individual's preference ranking, any other utility function $U^*(x) = F[U(x)]$, where F is any increasing function, also represents the individual's preference ranking.

In other writings, Pareto (1900 [2008], 1911 [1955]) advocated a choice-based approach in which the primary element is the individual's indifference curves. Pareto conceived of an indifference curve as something that can be elicited experimentally by observing the individual's choices, that is, without any reference to psychological introspection or the notion of utility. More precisely, Pareto imagined an experiment in which the individual is asked to choose between two commodity bundles x and y. If the individual chooses bundle x, the composition of y is changed up to the point where the individual becomes indifferent between x and y, thus determining two points on the indifference curve. This procedure can be repeated until a sufficient number of points on the same indifference curve are identified. Pareto's experiment, however, was hypothetical; there was no actual experimental subject and no commodity bundles.

Pareto's analysis was highly innovative but, as observed by many authors from the 1930s on, defective with respect to both the preference-based and the choice-based lines of attack. In the 1910s, 1920s, and early 1930s, Pareto's idea of restating demand and equilibrium analysis independently of measurable utility found many supporters, especially in terms of its preference-based version (see, e.g., Johnson 1913; Slutsky (1915 [1952]); Amoroso 1921; Bowley 1924; Schultz 1933). However, these supporters did not address the problems that Pareto had left open. Things changed abruptly in the mid-1930s, when a new generation of economists solved most of Pareto's unanswered problems. The conclusive phase of the ordinal revolution was initiated in 1934 by an article jointly co-authored by John Hicks and Roy Allen, two members of the circle of brilliant young economists who formed around Lionel Robbins at the LSE in the early 1930s.

Hicks and Allen (1934) followed the choice-based approach and attempted to construct demand theory without introducing utility indices. As for Pareto, the cornerstone of Hicks and Allen's analysis was the indifference curve and more precisely the marginal rate of substitution (MRS), which corresponds to the slope of the indifference curve. Hicks and Allen defined the MRS between commodities x and y as the quantity of commodity y that just compensates the individual for the loss of a marginal unit of x. This is a definition in terms of commodity quantities and is independent of utility. Based on the MRS so defined, and the assumption that it is diminishing or, equivalently, that the indifference curves are convex, Hicks and Allen were able to determine the relationships between the demand for goods, their price, and consumer income in terms of elasticity and to decompose the effect of a price change on demand into what in current microeconomics are called the substitution effect and the income effect. Hicks and Allen's 1934 article quickly became the new reference point for utility and demand theorists.

2.2 The Debate on the Determinateness of the Utility Function, 1934–1936

For our narrative, it is important to call attention to a less well-known part of the conclusive phase of the ordinal revolution, namely the debate on the determinateness of the utility function. In one digression in his

Manual, Pareto (1906/1909 [2014]: 132–133) suggested that individuals are not only able to rank combinations of goods (an assumption that in the 1930s was labeled "Pareto's postulate 1") but might even be capable of ranking transitions from one combination to another (as an assumption this suggestion became "Pareto's postulate 2"). Moreover, Pareto argued, if an individual prefers passing from combination x to combination y over passing from combination y to combination z, then for that person the utility difference between x and y is larger than the utility difference between y and z, that is, $U(y) - U(x) > U(z) - U(y)$.

From the mid-1910s to the early 1930s, a number of eminent economists from different quarters picked up on Pareto's discussion about the ranking of transitions and endorsed his postulate 2 (see Osório 1913; Edgeworth 1915; Amoroso 1921; Bowley 1924; Rosenstein-Rodan 1927 [1960]; Morgenstern 1931). In an article published in 1934, however, the Polish-American economist Oskar Lange of the University of Chicago argued that, when added to postulate 1, postulate 2 implies a return to measurable utility or, as he called it, "determinate" utility. More precisely, Lange (1934) claimed that postulate 2 restricts the admissible transformations of the utility function representing the individual's preferences to a subset of the increasing transformations, namely the positive linear transformations. This means that if the utility function $U(x)$ represents the individual's preferences, only utility functions $U^*(x)$ obtained by multiplying $U(x)$ by a positive number α and then adding any number β, that is, transformations $U^*(x) = \alpha U(x) + \beta$, with $\alpha > 0$, also represent the individual's preferences. Today, we call a utility function with this feature a cardinal utility function, although Lange did not employ that expression.

Lange's article initiated a significant debate between 1934 and 1936. In particular, Henry Phelps Brown (1934) of Oxford University pointed out that ranking transitions from one combination to another is different from ranking utility differences. That is, even if an individual prefers passing from combination x to combination y over passing from combination y to combination z, this does not imply that for him $U(y) - U(x) > U(z) - U(y)$. Therefore, Phelps Brown continued, Lange's claim that postulates 1 and 2 are sufficient to restrict the admissible transformations of the utility function to the positive linear ones was unwarranted. Phelps Brown did not, however, investigate what assumptions, if any, should be added to postulates 1 and 2 to obtain measurable or "determinate" utility. This issue was addressed by Viennese mathematician Franz Alt. In an article in German, published in the Austrian journal *Zeitschrift für Nationalökonomie* and escaping the attention of many Anglo-American economists, Alt (1936 [1971]) showed that in order to obtain a utility representation of preferences that is unique up to positive linear transformations, Pareto's postulates 1 and 2 must be integrated by five additional assumptions regarding an individual's preferences.

2.3 Supporters of Measurable Utility

One final element of utility analysis and demand theory in the 1930s should be noted here, namely that not everybody was in favor of abandoning measurable utility and embracing an ordinal utility approach. At the University of Cambridge, for instance, economists such as A. C. Pigou and Dennis Robertson ignored the ordinal approach and continued teaching Alfred Marshall's (1920 [1961]) theory of utility and demand, which largely relied on measurable utility.

Harro Bernardelli, a Viennese of Italian extraction who studied economics in Germany before joining the Robbins circle at LSE in 1933, criticized Pareto as well as Hicks and Allen because their theories entailed "the relinquishing of many propositions which until now have been considered as undoubtedly belonging to the body of Economic Theory" (Bernardelli 1934: 71), such as the principle of diminishing marginal utility.[4] For Bernardelli, the theories of Pareto and Hicks-Allen were "axiomatic experiments" that showed how much our knowledge of economics depends only on the assumption that individuals are able to rank combinations of goods. As axiomatic experiments, these theories resembled "the behaviour

[4]As noted by Hicks and Allen (1934: 55–57), an ordinal approach to utility implies the dismissal of notions that are not invariant to increasing transformations of the utility function, such as the principle of diminishing marginal utility. To see this, let $U(x_1, \ldots, x_n)$ be the utility function, and denote U_i the first-order partial derivative of U with respect to x_i, and U_{ii} the second-order partial derivative of U with respect to x_i. The principle of diminishing marginal utility implies that $U_{ii} < 0$. Consider now an increasing transformation $F(U)$ of U with $F' > 0$. The second-order partial derivative of $F(U)$ is $F' \times U_{ii} + F'' \times (U_i)^2$. Now, even where $U_{ii} < 0$, if $F'' \times (U_i)^2$ is large enough, $F' \times U_{ii} + F'' \times (U_i)^2$ can be positive.

of a man who cuts off one of his legs, in order to see how he gets on as a cripple" (Bernardelli 1934: 71). For Bernardelli, such amputation was of course unnecessary.

The Norwegian Ragnar Frisch also continued to believe that utility is measurable, and, in a pioneering econometric study, he attempted to actually measure the marginal utility of monetary income (Frisch 1932). In the early 1930s, Frisch's work was widely discussed, but most commentators stressed that his utility measurements relied on doubtful assumptions, most notably that the marginal utility of each commodity does not depend on the quantities of other commodities, that is, that the utility function is additively separable (see, e.g., Bowley 1932; Schultz 1933; Allen 1933).

With this picture of the state of utility theory in the 1930s before us, we now turn to Samuelson and his formative years at Chicago and Harvard.

3 Samuelson's Training in Utility and Demand Theory

Paul Samuelson entered the University of Chicago in January 1932 and then in fall 1935 moved on to graduate school at Harvard. Roger Backhouse's (2017) intellectual biography of Samuelson makes clear that when he began writing research papers on utility theory around mid-1936, he was familiar with the state of utility theory sketched in the previous section.

In the winter quarter of 1935, his senior year at Chicago, Samuelson took the graduate course in Price and Distribution Theory taught by Jacob Viner. As Samuelson (1972: 7–8) later wrote, Viner covered the subject by using indifference curve analysis, which was then exceptional at Chicago: "Although I had the best undergraduate education in economics that opportunity could provide at that date, only once, and then in Viner's graduate course, was I exposed to the mysteries of indifference curves and the production possibility frontier."

A more systematic introduction to the recent theory of utility demand came from Wassily Leontief's seminar in Price Theory, which Samuelson attended in fall 1935 during his first term at Harvard. Leontief, who had recently published an article in which he used indifference curves to analyze international trade (Leontief 1933), presented demand theory according to an indifference curve approach that was analogous to that of Hicks and Allen. Moreover, like the two English economists, Leontief avoided introducing utility indices into the picture. As Samuelson recalled in an unpublished note on the origin of revealed preference theory: "Leontief went deliberately slowly, eschewing use of 'utility' functions, and steadfastly adhering to 'marginal rate of substitution' concepts" (Samuelson 1996). Leontief's seminar had a great impact on Samuelson, who declared that "no other course I ever took so profoundly set me on the way of my life career" (Samuelson 2004: 6).

Samuelson's assimilation of utility and demand theory continued in the spring of 1936, when he took the course Topics in Statistical Theory taught by polymath Edwin Bidwell Wilson. Wilson also covered some utility theory, using as a textbook *The Mathematical Groundwork of Economics* (1924) by the English economist and statistician Arthur Bowley. This was a slender treatise in mathematical economics that attempted to harmonize traditional utility analysis *à la* Marshall with Pareto's novel ordinal approach. In an article published in 1935, Wilson had criticized Bowley for making an erroneous point about the implications of a change in the marginal utility of money (Wilson 1935). He repeated this criticism in the course attended by Samuelson (see Backhouse 2017: 151–152; Carvajalino 2018).

For the development of Samuelson's ideas on demand and utility theory, the course on International Trade he took with Gottfried Haberler in the fall of 1936 was also important. Unlike Leontief, Haberler did not use indifference curves to analyze international trade because, among other reasons, he did not see any compelling reason to assume that the curves have the curvature required to identify a unique equilibrium point in international trade (see Backhouse 2017: 180–181). As we will see, Haberler's skepticism about the curvature of indifference curves was at the origin of Samuelson's 1938 "Note" on the theory of consumer behavior.

To summarize, through Viner's course at Chicago and the courses by Leontief, Wilson, and Haberler at Harvard, between 1935 and 1936 Samuelson became familiar with up-to-date utility analysis and demand theory and was thereby prepared to contribute to the subject.

4 Discounted Utility, February 1937

It seems likely that Samuelson began writing what came to be his first published article during the summer of 1936, completing it the following fall (Backhouse 2017: 168). The article appeared in the February 1937 issue of the *Review of Economic Studies* under the title "A Note on Measurement of Utility" (Samuelson 1937). The *Review* was the junior LSE economics journal, founded in 1933 by Abba Lerner, who belonged to the Robbins circle, Paul Sweezy, a Harvard graduate student who visited the LSE in the academic year 1932–1933, and Ursula Webb, another member of the Robbins group, who in 1935 married Hicks.

In his 1937 article, Samuelson adopted a traditional, almost pre-Paretian approach. This work is based not on preference rankings represented by ordinal utility functions, nor on indifference curves and marginal rates of substitution. The declared goal of the paper is to delineate a method to measure the marginal utility of money that provides an alternative to, and is arguably more effective than, the method proposed by Frisch (1932; see Sect. 2.3 above). In order to measure the marginal utility of money, Samuelson (1937: 156) put forward a model of choice over time according to which the individual behaves so as to maximize the discounted sum of all future utilities. Basically, this means that, if $(x_0, x_1, x_2, \ldots, x_T)$ is a stream of monetary payments from the present time $t = 0$ until a future time $t = T$, the individual behaves so as to maximize the discounted sum of future utilities $\sum_{t=0}^{T} U(x_t)e^{-\pi t}$, whereby π is a parameter capturing how the individual discounts the future. Samuelson claimed that, if this model correctly describes the intertemporal choice behavior of an individual and if we have sufficient observations about the individual's actual choices, we can inductively measure his marginal utility of money.[5]

The details of the method Samuelson suggested to measure utility need not detain us here. For us, it is more important to note that he was well aware that his discounted utility model relied on a number of questionable assumptions, such as: "[A]t every instant of time the individual's satisfaction depends only upon the consumption at that time" (ibid.: 159).

[5] Further discussion of the discounted utility model and its shifting fortunes can be found in Frederick et al. (2002).

Samuelson also remarked that the maximization of the discounted sum of future utilities implies that the individual is able to rank utility differences, that is, Pareto's assumption 2: "Reflection as to the meaning of our Assumption Two [that the individual maximizes the sum of future utilities] will reveal that…we must invoke Pareto's postulate Two, which relates to the possibility of ordering *differences* in utility by the individual" (ibid.: 160–161; italics in original). Following Lange (1934), for Samuelson, postulate 2 implies that the utility function $U(x)$ featured in the discounted utility model is not ordinal but "determinate," that is, unique only up to positive linear transformations. However, in his 1937 article, Samuelson did not profess himself scandalized by this implication. In the three articles on utility theory and demand analysis that Samuelson published in 1938, he took a different approach.

5 The "Note," February–August 1938

In September 1937, Samuelson was appointed a Junior Fellow in Harvard's prestigious Society of Fellows (Samuelson 1998; Backhouse 2017: 193–198). The Society had been created by Lawrence Henderson and other Harvard professors to give a select group of promising Harvard students the possibility of pursuing their own research without the formal obligations associated with a standard Ph.D. program. The fellowship lasted three years and fellows were forbidden to work toward a Ph.D. degree. Samuelson took full advantage of the opportunity represented by the fellowship, and during his three years in the Society, he published thirteen articles in major economic journals on topics ranging from consumer theory to international trade. The first article in this impressive series was the celebrated "Note on the Pure Theory of Consumer's Behaviour," which appeared in the February 1938 issue of *Economica*, the senior LSE economics journal; Samuelson was still only twenty-two years old (Samuelson 1938a). In the August 1938 issue of the journal, Samuelson published a brief Addendum that corrected his theory and provided an alternative definition of its key postulate (Samuelson 1938b).

On various occasions, Samuelson (1950, 1996, 1998, 2004) recounted that the "Note" grew out of a remark made to him by Haberler in his 1936 course on International Trade. In international trade theory, indifference curves were used to represent the preferences of a country but, as mentioned in Sect. 3, Haberler did not use indifference curves because he was skeptical about assumptions concerning their curvature. So, he asked his student, Samuelson, who was then enthusiastic about Leontief indifference curve analysis: "How do you know indifference curves are [convex]?" (Samuelson 1950: 369).[6]

Samuelson gave a quick response, but then came to see that Haberler's question had in fact wide-ranging implications, not only for international trade theory but also for consumer theory: How do we know that the indifference curves of individuals are convex? The convexity assumption made by Hicks and Allen now became suspect in Samuelson's eyes, relying on dubious introspective considerations. In the "Note" he wrote: "Just as we do not claim to know by introspection the behaviour of utility, many will argue we cannot know the behaviour of…indifference directions. Why should one believe in the [diminishing] rate of marginal substitution?" (Samuelson 1938a: 61).

Haberler's remark was made at some point in the fall of 1936, but the "Note" was written later, probably in the second half of 1937. Originally, it bore a title more explicit that the final one: "New Foundations for the Pure Theory of Consumer's Behavior."[7] According to Samuelson (1996), the final version was completed in early 1938: "I wrote all this up for publication early in 1938. Marion Crawford, soon to become Marion Samuelson, wrote up my dictation. It was all done in great haste at the insistence of the Editors of *Economica*, who wished to include it in an early issue." Samuelson never saw the proofs of the article and had to accept that the editors had deleted some sections of the manuscript.[8]

---

[6]Haberler in fact asked Samuelson how he knew that indifference curves are *concave* rather than convex. But this was only a terminological issue. A curve is labeled as convex or concave according to the reference point from which it is considered. If, as Hicks and Allen did, we take the origin of the Cartesian plane as the reference point, Haberler's indifference curves should be labeled as convex.

[7]An undated draft of the "Note" bearing this title is contained in Box 152 of the Samuelson Papers. The published article is shorter than the draft, but there are no significant conceptual differences between the two.

[8]Given what Samuelson (1996) remarks about the alphabetical symbols used in the paper ("x's which Marion had written down…appeared in print as Greek ψ's"), it appears likely that the typescript sent to *Economica* in early 1938 is the draft of the paper contained in Box 152 of the Samuelson

As an alternative to Hicks and Allen's convex indifference curve approach, in the "Note" Samuelson proposed working out consumer theory on the basis of three postulates that directly related to an individual's demand behavior. In the Addendum of August 1938, these postulates were reduced to one, which was later called the Weak Axiom of Revealed Preference. In particular, Samuelson proved that almost all the restrictions on the demand functions that derive from the constrained maximization of an ordinal utility function can also be obtained starting from the Weak Axiom.[9] The only restriction on demand functions that derives from utility maximization but not from the Weak Axiom is the so-called integrability condition for demand functions, that is, the symmetry of the compensated variation of the demand for a good when the price of another good varies. However, Samuelson (1938a: 68) did not consider this fact relevant: "Concerning the question of integrability I have little to say. I cannot see that it is really an important problem."[10]

This is not the place for a discussion of the descriptive validity or the normative plausibility of the Weak Axiom, nor, more generally, to appraise the pros and cons of the revealed preference approach to choice theory.[11] Here, I would like to make only three relevant points.

First, even in the "Note," that is, even in the most behavioristic paper—in which he proposed to drop "the last vestiges of the utility analysis" (Samuelson 1938a: 62)—Samuelson did not completely preclude the introduction of the utility notion, nor did he intend to contradict the

---

Papers (see footnote 7). One of the parts that was significantly shortened in passing from the draft to the published article is the reconstruction of the history of utility theory and demand analysis that opens the paper.

[9] These restrictions are expressed as features of certain mathematical matrices, but their economic meaning can be summarized as follows: (i) The substitution effect is negative, that is, when the price of a good increases, the compensated demand for that good decreases; (ii) the income effect, that is, the effect of a price increase on demand due to the decrease of purchasing power, can be either positive or negative; (iii) when the price of a good increases, the uncompensated demand for the good can either decrease or increase, where the latter case is that of so-called Giffen goods; and (iv) if the prices of all commodities and the consumer's income change in the same proportion, the quantities of goods demanded by the consumer do not change.

[10] For a further discussion of the importance of the integrability condition in the history of demand analysis, see Mongin (2000), Hands (2006), and Hands (2014).

[11] On these issues, see, for example, Sen (1973), Wong ((1978) [2006]), Pollack (1990), Sen (1997), Spiegler (2008), Hausman (2012), and Hands (2013).

results obtained by using utility-related constructs. Rather, he took a pluralist stance and argued that his novel approach allowed a more direct analysis of consumer behavior than did the utility-based analysis. This pluralist stance is evident in the two sentences of the "Note" that follow the sentence about the removal of the last vestiges of the utility analysis. Here is the complete paragraph:

> I propose, therefore, that we start anew in direct attack upon the problem, dropping off the last vestiges of the utility analysis. This does not preclude the introduction of utility by any who may care to do so, nor will it contradict the results attained by use of related constructs. It is merely that the analysis can be carried on more directly and from a different set of postulates. (ibid.: 62)

As remarked in the introduction to this chapter, scholars who claim that the young Samuelson was a committed behaviorist typically quote the first sentence of this paragraph. However, they typically omit the rest of the paragraph and thus provide an incomplete picture.

Second, in the Addendum of August 1938, the Weak Axiom is presented in terms of preference, rather than choice. In the "Note," Samuelson explained the postulate in terms of selection, i.e., choice, of one batch of goods over another: "In words this [the postulate] means that if an individual selects batch one over batch two, he does not at the same time select two over one" (ibid.: 65). However, in the Addendum, Samuelson switched to a preference terminology and explained the Weak Axiom as imposing a consistency condition over preferences: "The individual always behaves consistently in the sense that he should never 'prefer' a first batch of goods to a second at the same time that he 'prefers' the second to the first" (Samuelson 1938b: 353). This explanation of the Weak Axiom in terms of the consistency condition over preferences supports the idea that, even in the "Note," Samuelson did not want to eliminate utility and preference from consumer choice theory. Rather, he conceived of his revealed preference theory as an approach compatible with, and to some extent complementary to, utility-based analysis.

Third, the "Note" is a purely theoretical contribution that does not deal with observed human behavior. It contains neither statistical data about demand, like those used by Frisch in his econometric study of the marginal utility of money (Frisch 1932), nor experimental data, like those obtained by the American psychologist Louis Leon Thurstone (1931) in a pioneering laboratory experiment to elicit the indifference curves of an individual.[12] Moreover, in the "Note," Samuelson did not attempt to test his choice postulate, i.e., the Weak Axiom, against actual data on choice behavior but took its validity as self-evident. Therefore, I contend, if any behaviorism is present in the "Note," it is little more than a rhetorical behaviorism.

The two papers on consumer theory that Samuelson published in October 1938 support the view that, even in 1937–1938, he did not oppose utility analysis and, more specifically, ordinal utility analysis, but considered it as a scientifically legitimate approach to the study of consumption choices. Indeed, both papers feature the word "utility" in their titles.

6 Empirical Implications of Ordinal Utility, October 1938

One of the two papers was titled "The Empirical Implications of Utility Analysis." Samuelson probably wrote it in late 1937 and presented it on 27 December of that year at a meeting of the Econometric Society held in Atlantic City (see Leavens 1938). Around the same time, Samuelson also sent the paper to Wilson, his teacher at Harvard, who sent back comments. In early 1938, that is, at almost the same time he sent the final version of the "Note" to *Economica* (see Sect. 5), Samuelson submitted the paper to *Econometrica*, the Econometric Society's journal. The paper was in fact reviewed by Wilson, who recommended publication (see Backhouse 2017: 201–202). The paper was published in the October 1938 issue of *Econometrica* (Samuelson 1938c).

Although the paper on the empirical implications of utility analysis is almost contemporary with the "Note," its stated goals are quite different. Here, Samuelson did not argue that the last vestiges of utility analysis

---

[12]For a further discussion about Thurstone's experiment and its reception among utility theorists in the 1930s, see Moscati (2007).

should be dropped. Rather, he claimed that ordinal utility theory is scientifically sound because it has refutable implications in terms of demand behavior: "It is the purpose here to demonstrate that the utility analysis in its ordinary form does contain empirically meaningful implications by which it could be refuted" (ibid.: 345). By "utility analysis in its ordinary form," Samuelson meant ordinal utility theory plus the assumption that, in the "Note," he criticized for relying on dubious introspective considerations, namely that indifference curves are convex: "Only the most general assumptions are made: that there exists an ordinal preference field satisfying everywhere curvature conditions [i.e. convexity conditions] sufficient to insure a proper relative maximum under the constraint of a fixed total budget" (ibid.).

In the *Econometrica* paper, Samuelson derived the empirical implications on demand behavior of ordinal utility theory, such as the negativity of the substitution effect, and then stressed that the same implications can be derived more easily and directly from the postulates on choices he put forward in the "Note": "Recently I proposed a new postulational base upon which to construct a theory of consumer's behavior. It was there shown that from this starting point could be erected a theory which included all the elements of the previous analysis [ordinal utility analysis]" (ibid.: 346).

Samuelson saw no inconsistency between his *Econometrica* article and his "Note." In the "Note," he criticized the convex indifference curve assumption and explored the implications for demand behavior of a set of postulates that do not concern utility, preference, or the shape of indifference curves. In the *Econometrica* article, he adopted the ordinal utility framework, assumed that indifference curves are convex, and explored the implications for demand behavior of this approach. The conclusions of the two articles are similar: The ordinal utility or indifference curve approach and the approach based on the choice postulates have almost the same empirical implications for demand behavior.

My point here is not to criticize Samuelson's "explorative" method as bad scientific practice. From the viewpoint of the philosophy of science, in fact, investigating the empirical implications of different sets of assumptions can readily be defended as good scientific method. Even from the viewpoint of the psychology of science, the fact that a twenty-two-year-old scientist explores different research paths is difficult to criticize. The only point I want to make is that the fact that Samuelson adopted both the ordinal utility approach and the choice-based approach, in two separate papers that were submitted almost at the same time (both in early 1938), is incompatible with the picture of the young Samuelson as a committed and consistent behaviorist who wanted to free economic analysis from the utility concept. This image is also incompatible with the content of the other article Samuelson published in October 1938. It was called "The Numerical Representation of Ordered Classifications and the Concept of Utility" and appeared in the October 1938 issue of the *Review of Economic Studies*.

7 Conditions for Cardinal Utility, October 1938

His *Review of Economic Studies* article was Samuelson's contribution to the debate on the determinateness of the utility function initiated by Lange in 1934. As discussed in Sect. 2.2, Lange (1934) had claimed that Pareto's postulate 1, according to which individuals can rank combinations of goods, and postulate 2, according to which individuals can even rank transitions from one combination to another, restrict the admissible transformations of the utility function to the positive linear ones. Phelps Brown (1934) had pointed out that Lange's claim was based on an incorrect implicit assumption and that postulates 1 and 2 are not sufficient to obtain "determinate" utility. Then, Alt (1936 [1971]) had showed that, in order to restrict the admissible transformations of the utility function to the positive linear transformations, postulates 1 and 2 must be integrated with five additional postulates. Without mentioning Alt's paper, Samuelson (1938d) took up the problem where Phelps Brown had left it, first providing alternative conditions that make utility unique up to positive linear transformations and then criticizing them from an ordinal utility viewpoint.

7.1 Equation 15

Following Phelps Brown, Samuelson noted that postulates 1 and 2 concern only preference order. Postulate 1 refers to preference order over combinations of goods and allows for the introduction of a numerical index U that assigns larger numbers to more preferred combinations. Thus, if an individual prefers combination z to combination y and combination y to combination x, then postulate 1 implies that $U(z) > U(y) > U(x)$. Postulate 2 refers to the preference order over transitions from one combination to another and allows for the introduction of another index that Samuelson called G. The index G assigns larger numbers to more preferred transitions: If the individual prefers the transition from x to y to the transition from y to z, then postulate 2 implies that $G(x, y) > G(y, z)$. Phelps Brown had stressed two main issues with the indices U and G. First, the numbers associated by G with transitions need not be equal to the differences between the numbers associated by U to combinations. That is, postulate 2 does not imply that $G(x, y) = U(y) - U(x)$ or that $G(y, z) = U(z) - U(y)$.[13] More generally, since postulate 2 refers only to the ranking of transitions and G numbers, it has no implications for the differences between the U numbers. Second, since the G numbers have only an ordinal meaning, it does not make sense to sum them. Thus, for instance, if the individual considers the transition from x to y to be equally preferable to the transition from y to z, then the G number associated with both transitions is the same, say, 7. But postulate 2 does not warrant that the G number associated with the transition from x to z is $7 + 7 = 14$.

To solve these two issues, Samuelson assumed that the preference order over combinations and the preference order over transitions are both transitive. He connected them by arguing that if an individual prefers the transition from x to y to the transitions from x to z, that is, if $G(x, y) > G(x, z)$,

[13] Consider the following numerical example. If an individual prefers z to y and y to x, we can assign the following U numbers to the three combinations: $U(z) = 10$, $U(y) = 3$, and $U(x) = 1$. If an individual prefers the transition from x to y to the transition from y to z, we can assign to the two transitions the G numbers $G(x, y) = 5$ and $G(y, z) = 2$. Although these U numbers and G numbers are perfectly consistent with postulates 1 and 2, it turns out that $U(y) - U(x) = 2$ while $G(x, y) = 5$ and $U(z) - U(y) = 7$ while $G(y, z) = 2$.

then combination y must be preferred to combination z, that is, $U(y) > U(z)$. Subsequently, Samuelson introduced the key postulate of his article as equation 15 (Samuelson 1938d: 68). This equation overcomes the problem that G numbers cannot be summed by simply assuming that G numbers can indeed be summed. That is, if $G(x, y)$ is the number associated with the transition from x to y, and $G(y, z)$ is the number associated with the transition from y to z, Samuelson's equation 15 requires that the number $G(x, z)$ associated with the transition from x to z is equal to the sum of $G(x, y)$ and $G(y, z)$, that is, $G(x, y) + G(y, z) = G(x, z)$.

One may discuss whether the postulated equation 15 simply begs the issue posed by Phelps Brown. For our purposes here, however, this point is not relevant. More important is that Samuelson showed that his postulate, together with the other assumptions mentioned above, is necessary and sufficient to make the G numbers associated with transitions equal to the difference between the U numbers associated with combinations, that is, to have $G(x, y) = U(y) - U(x)$. In turn, and as Lange had already showed, $G(x, y) = U(y) - U(x)$ if and only if the utility function U is unique only up to linear increasing transformations (ibid.: 69–70).

In the final part of his paper, Samuelson discussed the plausibility of the condition $G(x, y) + G(y, z) = G(x, z)$ from the viewpoint of the ordinal approach to utility and preference: "What is the meaning of this condition in terms of the individual's ordinal classification of movements? Can such a relationship in general be satisfied?" (ibid.: 70). His answer was negative. He saw "no a priori reason why the individual's preference scale…should obey this arbitrary restriction," and he regarded the chance that some individuals actually satisfy it as "infinitely improbable" (ibid.).

7.2 Samuelson, Lange, and Alt

As noted above, Samuelson (1938d) did not mention the 1936 piece by Alt, in which the Viennese mathematician had provided a different solution to the issue posed by Phelps Brown. One question that naturally arises is whether Samuelson knew of Alt's article. We can say that he was at least aware of its existence.

It seems reasonable to suggest that in early 1938, Samuelson sent a draft of his paper to Lange, who replied in a letter dated 10 May 1938 (Samuelson Papers, Box 48). Lange declared Samuelson's manuscript to be "a contribution which really helps to clarify the subject" and judged Samuelson's equation 15, that is, his postulate $G(x, y) + G(y, z) = G(x, z)$, a satisfactory condition for restricting the admissible transformations of the utility function to the positive linear ones. Moreover, Lange was more positive than Samuelson about the validity of the condition: "I do not share your object[ion] to Equation (15). ... Acceptance of (15) neither runs us into contradictions or violates observations" (underlining in original).

In the same letter, Lange also explicitly invited Samuelson to look at Alt's article and pointed out the possible relationship between Samuelson's postulate 15 and Alt's postulates: "I would suggest that you look up the article of Alt, Über die Messbarkeit des Nutzens, Zeitschr. F. Nat.-Oeconomie, Bd. VII (1936). If I am not mistaken your Equation (15) corresponds to his postulates IV and V." We know from a letter of one of the editors of the *Review of Economic Studies* to Samuelson that he did not see the proofs of his article.[14] Therefore, even if he did look at Alt's article between May and October 1938, he could not have added a reference to Alt. Be that as it may, in his subsequent writings of the 1930s and 1940s, Samuelson did not refer to Alt's 1936 article.

7.3 Naming Cardinal Utility

A final, terminological feature of Samuelson's (1938d) article should be mentioned. In current economic theory, a utility function representing the preferences of an individual is called "ordinal" if it is unique up to any increasing transformations and "cardinal" if it is unique only to positive linear transformations. While the notion of ordinal utility had already been accepted in the writings of Pareto, that of cardinal utility only secured a similar status much later.

---

[14] Webb Hicks to Samuelson, 4 October 1938, Samuelson Papers, Box 37.

In effect, until Hicks and Allen (1934: 54–55) referred to "a 'cardinal' conception of utility" in a passage of their celebrated paper, the very expression "cardinal utility" was not used in economics, and even Hicks and Allen did not make clear what they meant by it. Apparently, they used cardinal as a residual notion, in the sense that they considered cardinal everything that was not ordinal, that is, not invariant to increasing transformations of the utility function. Certainly, Hicks and Allen did not associate cardinal utility with positive linear transformations of the utility function, not least because in their article there is no sign of them.

The first article in which utility unique up to positive linear transformations was explicitly and consistently coupled with the terms "cardinal" and "cardinal measurability" was Samuelson's *Review of Economic Studies* article of October 1938. The association occurs ten times in this paper, of which here is one example: "Dr. Lange has not proved satisfactorily that from these two assumptions [Pareto's assumptions 1 and 2] can be derived the cardinal measurability of utility (subject to a linear transformation involving scale and origin constants)" (Samuelson 1938d: 66). I argue, therefore, that cardinal utility acquired its current technical meaning in Samuelson's 1938d article.

7.4 Summing up

The papers on intertemporal choice and consumer behavior that the young Samuelson wrote between mid-1936 and early 1938, which were published between February 1937 and October 1938, reveal him as very far from a committed behaviorist who aimed at dropping the last vestiges of utility analysis. In contrast, he dealt intensively with utility theory and made important contributions to it: He put forward a model for intertemporal choices based on the maximization of cardinal utility (Samuelson 1937), explored the empirical implications of ordinal utility theory on demand behavior (Samuelson 1938c), and stated conditions that make utility cardinal rather than just ordinal, yet judged these conditions implausible (Samuelson 1938d). Even in the "Note" (Samuelson 1938a, b), Samuelson took a pluralist stance and presented his revealed preference approach as compatible with, and to some extent complementary to, ordinal utility analysis.

Arguably, in the years 1936–1938 the young Samuelson was exploring different research paths, ranging from cardinal utility analysis to the revealed preference approach, passing through ordinal utility theory. His explorations, however, display a definite trend in the direction of a refusal of cardinal utility assumptions, which are accepted in the February 1937 article but rejected as "infinitely improbable" in the October 1938d article, and endorsement of the ordinal utility approach, which is adopted in the two articles of October 1938 (Samuelson 1938c, d). As for the revealed preference approach, Samuelson advocated it in the "Note" (Samuelson 1938a, b), but played it down in the two articles of October 1938 (Samuelson 1938c, d). As we will see in the following sections, in the papers and the Ph.D. dissertation that he wrote in 1939–1940, Samuelson also played down the revealed preference approach and presented the theory of consumer demand according to ordinal utility theory. Before discussing these works, however, a brief overview of the main developments in utility analysis after the publication of Hicks and Allen's 1934 article is in order.

8 Further Developments in Utility and Demand Theory, 1935–1939

8.1 Slutsky and Allen

Russian economist and statistician Eugen Slutsky was an admirer of Pareto. In 1915, he published an article in the *Giornale degli Economisti*, the Italian journal in which Pareto had published most of his contributions, which anticipated many of the results later obtained by Hicks and Allen (Slutsky 1915 [1952]). Unlike the two LSE economists, however, Slutsky expressed his theory in terms of a utility function and its derivatives. He did not make clear whether his results were ordinal in nature, that is, whether they were invariant to increasing transformations of the utility function. At any rate, for reasons about which we can only speculate, for almost twenty years Slutsky's paper was completely neglected. It was rediscovered only in the early 1930s by Valentino Dominedò (1933) in Italy, Henry Schultz (1935) in the USA and Allen in England.[15]

In an article published in the *Review of Economic Studies*, Allen (1936) called attention to Slutsky's paper, acknowledged his priority with respect to a number of results, and stressed the differences between Slutsky's utility-based approach and the utility-free approach he and Hicks had put forward in 1934: "Slutsky's starting point is different from that of Hicks and myself. Our theory was constructed so as to be independent of the existence of an index of utility. … Slutsky expresses his theory in terms of one selected utility function and its partial derivatives" (ibid.: 127). Allen showed, however, that Slutsky's results are in fact independent of measurability assumptions on the utility function and hold also in a purely ordinal framework.

8.2 Hicks the Ordinalist

Allen's article paved the way for the ordinal restatement of Slutsky's findings and the subsequent establishment of ordinal utility theory as the mainstream approach to demand analysis. Although for a while Allen (1938) insisted on the utility-free approach, after 1936, Hicks (1937, 1939) set forth his analysis in terms of ordinal utility indices.[16] Most notably, in *Value and Capital* (Hicks 1939), Hicks fine-tuned the ordinal approach to utility theory. He now re-presented Slutsky's results in a systematic and mathematically clear way and demonstrated, more thoroughly than had Allen, that these results were ordinal in nature. Hicks also showed that the results he and Allen had obtained in 1934 using the marginal rate of substitution could be obtained through ordinal utility indices in a theoretically rigorous and much simpler way.

Hicks's intellectual trajectory—from the choice-based approach explored in the article with Allen to the fully-fledged ordinalism expounded in *Value and Capital*—was thus similar to the intellectual trajectory of Samuelson as reconstructed in this chapter.

---

[15]On the rediscovery of Slutsky's 1915 article, see Chipman and Lenfant (2002).

[16]For more discussion on the differences between Hicks's and Allen's approaches, see Fernandez-Grela (2006).

9 Samuelson's Ordinalism Stabilizes, 1938–1939

Between the fall of 1938 and the fall of 1939, Samuelson wrote two papers related to consumer and demand theory. Both works confirm the stabilization of his ordinal approach to utility analysis.

9.1 The Dispute with Bernardelli on Diminishing Marginal Utility

The first paper was titled "The End of Marginal Utility: A Note on Dr. Bernardelli's Article" and was published in the February 1939 issue of *Economica*. As its title indicates, the article was a comment on a paper published by Harro Bernardelli, one of the opponents to the ordinal utility approach mentioned in Sect. 2.3.[17]

In his paper, Bernardelli (1938) had defended the scientific legitimacy of the principle of diminishing marginal utility and argued that it can be obtained by a novel and plausible set of postulates that are invariant to increasing transformations of the utility function. This would render the principle of diminishing marginal utility consistent with the ordinal approach to utility analysis. In his comment, Samuelson (1939: 87; italics in original) claimed that in fact Bernardelli's postulates "are *not* invariant under a monotonic renumbering of the indifference loci," and, therefore, the principle of diminishing marginal utility remained incompatible with the ordinal utility approach.

Bernardelli (1939) replied that Samuelson had misconstrued his postulates. Without entering here into the details of the Samuelson-Bernardelli exchange, we can say that, although in effect Samuelson missed Bernardelli's main point, Bernardelli's mathematical demonstrations were nonetheless flawed.[18] More important for us is that Samuelson criticized Bernardelli's postulates from a purely ordinalist viewpoint and without any

---

[17]In the mid-1930s, Bernardelli left LSE for the University of Liverpool, and in 1937, he moved eastward, to universities in, first, Burma (Rangoon) and then New Zealand (Otago). More on Bernardelli can be found in Donoghue (2007).

[18]On the limits of Bernardelli's approach, see Lancaster (1953).

reference to the revealed preference approach put forward in the "Note" of February 1938.

9.2 Against the Constancy of the Marginal Utility of Income

In the fall of 1939, Samuelson completed a further paper on utility. It discussed the marginal utility of monetary income, that is, the marginal utility a consumer can obtain by spending an additional unit of his income, and the assumption, often made by Marshall and other demand theorists, that the marginal utility of income is constant. Samuelson sent the paper to Oskar Lange, who was editing a volume of essays in memory of Chicago economist and statistician Henry Schultz, who had died in a car accident in 1938 (see Backhouse 2017: 209–210). The volume, which included Samuelson's paper, was published three years later (Samuelson 1942).

Samuelson began his essay by observing that the very notion of the marginal utility of income is not invariant to increasing transformations of the utility function and is in fact cardinal, rather than ordinal, in nature (ibid.: 76–77). Subsequently, he showed that the assumption that the marginal utility of income is constant implies that the income elasticity of demand for each commodity is unitary, that is, that a given percentage increase in the consumer's income is reflected in an equal percentage increase in the consumer's demand for each commodity. However, Samuelson stressed that consumers typically do not react to income increases in this way: "As far as I know, every investigation contradicts flatly this basic assumption" (ibid.: 81). Finally, he investigated what happens when the assumption of constant marginal utility of income is combined with another typically Marshallian assumption, namely that the marginal utility of each commodity is independent of the quantities of other commodities, that is, the utility function is additively separable. Samuelson proved that in this case the consumer would spend a fixed fraction k_i of his income on each commodity x_i. Again, this conclusion appeared implausible to him: "It need hardly be said that no empirical observations justify the imposition of such a definite form upon the…demand functions" (ibid.: 83).

Samuelson's endorsement of the ordinal utility approach found its most systematic expression in the Ph.D. dissertation he wrote between mid-1940 and November 1940.

10 The "Foundations of Analytical Economics," 1940

In the middle of 1940, the prohibition of work toward a Ph.D. degree imposed by Harvard's Society of Fellows expired, and Samuelson began writing his doctoral dissertation. The writing proceeded at "fever pace" (Samuelson 1998: 1377), with some parts dictated to Marion, who had married Samuelson in July 1938. The dissertation was entitled "Foundations of Analytical Economics" (Samuelson 1940), and Samuelson submitted it in November 1940, after he had already left Harvard for the Massachusetts Institute of Technology (MIT), the institution where he would spend the rest of his academic life.[19]

Samuelson successfully defended his dissertation on 4 December 1940. His examiners were Harvard economists Joseph Schumpeter, Edward Chamberlin, and Overton Taylor. Edwin Wilson, Samuelson's mathematics mentor, was also on the examination panel (Backhouse 2017: 453–454). After a seven-year delay, partly due to the war, the thesis was published as *Foundations of Economic Analysis* (Samuelson 1947). The book contained some new chapters not in the dissertation, although the dissertation material itself was incorporated into the book with few modifications. This is particularly true for the parts on consumer and demand theory.[20]

In the dissertation and, in identical form, in *Foundations*, Samuelson further downplayed the revealed preference approach he had proposed in his 1938 "Note" and, in chapter five (of both the dissertation and the book), he presented the theory of consumer behavior following an ordinal utility approach substantially equivalent to that used by Hicks in

[19]For more on Samuelson's move to MIT, see Backhouse (2014).

[20]For more on the relationship between the dissertation and the book, and the reasons for the book's delayed publication, see Samuelson (1998) and Backhouse (2015).

Value and Capital (Samuelson 1940: 110–146, 1947: 90–124). The starting point of his analysis was the consumer's ordinal preferences, represented by a utility function that is invariant to any increasing transformation. Samuelson then expressed the equilibrium conditions for the consumer in terms of the determinants of the matrix of the second-order derivatives of the ordinal utility function. Only at the end of chapter five did Samuelson mention the postulate of the 1938 "Note," that is, the Weak Axiom, and then only as an alternative way of characterizing one of the implications of ordinal utility analysis, namely that the substitution effect is negative (ibid.: 1940: 139–146, 1947: 111–117).[21]

In chapter six of the dissertation (which became chapter seven of *Foundations*), Samuelson discussed "Special Aspects of the Theory of Consumer's Behavior" (ibid.: 1940: 147–164, 1947: 172–202). At the beginning of the chapter, he argued that "the content of utility analysis in its most general form [involves] only an ordinal preference field," and he dismissed "the cardinal measure of utility" as a "special and extra" assumption by which "nothing at all is gained" (ibid.: 1940: 147–150, 1947: 172–173). Samuelson then discussed other special and extra assumptions of utility theory, such as the additive separability of the utility function and the constancy of the marginal utility of income and showed that these assumptions often imply cardinal utility. However, he rejected these other special assumptions, too, judging them "not generally applicable," "arbitrary," "dubious," "highly unrealistic," "superfluous," and leading to "really fantastic conclusions" (ibid.: 1940: 150–189, 1947: 174–202).

11 The Alleged *Das Paul Samuelson Problem* and Conclusions

Samuelson's ordinalist stance did not change during the 1940s. As discussed above, *Foundations of Economic Analysis*, published in 1947, reproduced the ordinal utility approach to consumer and demand theory expounded in the Harvard dissertation of 1940. *Foundations* quickly

[21] On Samuelson's approach to consumer choice theory in the Ph.D. dissertation and the *Foundations*, see Hands (2014), especially p. 102.

became a reference book for postwar students of economics of no less importance than Hicks's *Value and Capital*. The two books provided a systematized version of the ordinal utility approach to consumer and demand theory that has remained canonical up to this day.

In November 1948, Samuelson published an article entitled "Consumption Theory in Terms of Revealed Preference," which consolidated the bridge between the choice-based and the preference-based approaches to demand theory. At the theoretical level, Samuelson (1948) showed that, in the case of only two goods, the observation of a sufficient number of a consumer's choices satisfying the Weak Axiom makes it possible to elicit the consumer's indifference curves. At the terminological and conceptual level, by introducing the very expression "revealed preference," Samuelson suggested that consumer's preferences exist prior to consumer's choices and in fact cause them.

In 1950, an article by the Dutch-American economist Hendrik Houthakker (1950), and a prompt follow-up by Samuelson (1950), transformed the bridge between the two approaches into a revolving door. Houthakker introduced a coherence assumption on consumer behavior stronger than Samuelson's Weak Axiom—the so-called Strong Axiom of Revealed Preference—and proved that if the choices of a consumer satisfy the Strong Axiom, these choices can be interpreted as the result of the constrained maximization of the consumer's well-behaved ordinal preferences. Samuelson (1950) completed Houthakker's contribution by showing that the reverse is also true, that is, if a consumer maximizes his well-behaved ordinal preferences under the budget constraint, his choices satisfy the Strong Axiom. Houthakker's and Samuelson's articles showed that the choice-based approach and the preference-based approach to demand theory are substantially equivalent and thus eliminated the opposition between the two approaches.

Samuelson interpreted this equivalence result not as a refutation of the revealed preference approach he had advanced in the 1938 "Note," but as a full realization of it. As noted in Sect. 5, the Weak Axiom does not imply all the empirical restrictions on demand functions that are implied by the constrained maximization of an ordinal utility function. In particular, the Weak Axiom does not imply the so-called integrability condition for demand functions, that is, the symmetry of the compensated variation of the demand for a good when the price of another good varies. In his 1950 article, Samuelson claimed that in 1938 he had conjectured about the existence of a strengthened version of the Weak Axiom that had exactly the same empirical implications of the constrained maximization of ordinal utility, including the integrability conditions. However, he was unable to find such a strengthened version of the Weak Axiom, which was eventually provided by Houthakker. The relevant passage from Samuelson's 1950 article is worth quoting at some length:

> We are now in a position to complete the programme begun a dozen years ago of arriving *at the full empirical implications for demand behaviour of the most general ordinal utility analysis* … I soon realised that this [the Weak Axiom] could carry us almost all the way along the path of providing new foundations for utility theory. But not quite all the way … I held up publication on the conjecture that if the axiom were strengthened…then non-integrability could indeed be excluded … But no proof was forthcoming for all these years, until Mr. Houthakker's paper arrived in the daily mail. Not only had he provided the missing proof, but in addition he had independently arrived at precisely the same strong axiom as I had hoped would save the day. (Samuelson 1950: 369–370; italics in original)[22]

Based on this claim, several interpreters of Samuelson's economic thought have argued that, between 1938 and 1948–1950, he changed his mind about the utility concept and ordinal utility analysis: While in 1938 he wanted to free the theory of consumer behavior from the last vestiges of the utility concept and saw revealed preference theory as a research program wholly alternative to ordinal utility theory, in 1948–1950 he conceived of revealed preference theory as wholly equivalent to ordinal utility theory (for this interpretation, see, e.g., Houthakker (1983), and Wong (1978 [2006]). Hands (2014) has labeled *Das Paul Samuelson Problem* the question of whether Samuelson changed his mind between 1938 and 1948–1950. Based on the present review of the contributions to utility theory that Samuelson made when he was a Ph.D. student at Harvard,

---

[22]Samuelson made similar claims also in correspondence; see in particular a letter to Houthakker of 23 December 1949 and a letter to Hicks of 25 January 1952. Relevant passages from both letters are quoted in Hands (2014: 99).

I argue that *Das Paul Samuelson Problem* has either a negative answer or is ill-posed.

We saw that during 1936–1938, Samuelson explored different research paths, which ranged from cardinal utility analysis to the revealed preference approach, passing through ordinal utility theory. Around mid-1938, however, his stance on utility analysis became more settled: He firmly refused cardinal utility assumptions, downplayed the revealed preference approach, and fully endorsed ordinal utility theory. The articles on utility theory he published after mid-1938, as well as his Harvard dissertation of November 1940, clearly express this position. Therefore, Samuelson did not change his mind between 1938 and 1948–1950. If he changed his mind, he did so much earlier on, namely between 1936 and mid-1938. In this sense, *Das Paul Samuelson Problem* has a negative answer.

Alternatively, *Das Paul Samuelson Problem* is ill-posed in the sense that it is incorrect to represent the intellectual trajectory of the young Samuelson—which took him from the explorations of the period mid-1936 to mid-1938 to the ordinalist stance maintained after mid-1938—as involving a change of mind. As noted above, Hicks's ideas followed a similar trajectory—from the utility-free approach to demand analysis pursued in the 1934 paper co-authored with Allen to the fully-fledged ordinal utility approach expounded in *Value and Capital*. However, and rightly, nobody has argued that there exists a *Das John Hicks Problem*!

In my opinion, *Das Paul Samuelson Problem* is an artifact that draws from the erroneous conviction that the young Samuelson was a committed and consistent behaviorist. This conviction, in turn, draws from two main errors of interpretation: (1) neglect of the several, important contributions to utility analysis that Samuelson made during his years at Harvard and (2) an incomplete reading of his "Note" of 1938, in which revealed preference theory is already presented as compatible with, and to some extent complementary to, utility-based analysis. In this chapter, I have attempted to refute the image of the young Samuelson as a committed behaviorist and thus to show that *Das Paul Samuelson Problem* is a false one.

Acknowledgements I am grateful to Wade Hands and Philippe Mongin for several discussions on Samuelson's theory of choice; these discussions were the main motivation for writing this paper. I also thank Juan Carvajalino, Jean-Sébastien Lenfant, and other participants at the 2019 meeting of the European Society for the History of Economic Thought for helpful comments on a previous draft. Some portions of this chapter draw in part on work previously published, namely Moscati (2013) and Moscati (2018). Any errors are mine.

References

Allen, R.G.D. (1933) "On the Marginal Utility of Money and Its Application," *Economica*, 40: 186–209.

Allen, R.G.D. (1936) "Professor Slutsky's Theory of Consumer's Choice," *Review of Economic Studies*, 3: 120–129.

Allen, R.G.D. (1938) *Mathematical Analysis for Economists*. London, Macmillan.

Alt, F. (1936) [1971] "On the Measurability of Utility," in J.S. Chipman, L. Hurwicz, M.K. Richter and H.F. Sonnenschein (eds.) *Preferences, Utility, and Demand*. New York, Harcourt Brace Jovanovich: 424–431.

Amoroso, L. (1921) *Lezioni di Economia Matematica*. Bologna, Zanichelli.

Backhouse, R.E. (2014) "Paul A. Samuelson's Move to MIT," *History of Political Economy*, 46: 60–77.

Backhouse, R.E. (2015) "Revisiting Samuelson's *Foundations of Economic Analysis*," *Journal of Economic Literature*, 53: 326–350.

Backhouse, R.E. (2017) *Founder of Modern Economics: Paul A. Samuelson, Volume 1: Becoming Samuelson, 1915–1948*. New York, Oxford University Press.

Bernardelli, H. (1934) "Notes on the Determinateness of the Utility Function, II," *Review of Economic Studies*, 2: 69–75.

Bernardelli, H. (1938) "The End of the Marginal Utility Theory?" *Economica*, New Series, 5: 192–212.

Bernardelli, H. (1939) "A Reply to Mr. Samuelson's Note," *Economica*, New Series, 6: 88–89.

Bowley, A.L. (1924) *The Mathematical Groundwork of Economics*. Oxford, Clarendon Press.

Bowley, A.L. (1932) "Review of *New Methods of Measuring Marginal Utility*, by R. Frisch," *Economic Journal*, 42: 252–256.

Carvajalino, J. (2018) "Edwin B. Wilson and the Rise of Mathematical Economics in America, 1920–40," *History of Political Economy*, 50: 229–259.

Chipman, J.S. (1982) "Samuelson and Consumption Theory," in G.R. Feiwel (ed.) *Samuelson and Neoclassical Economics*. Boston, Kluwer: 31–71.

Chipman, J.S. and J.-S. Lenfant (2002) "Slutsky's 1915 Article: How It Came to Be Found and Interpreted," *History of Political Economy*, 34: 553–597.

Dominedò, V. (1933) "Considerazioni Intorno Alla Teoria Della Domanda," *Giornale Degli Economisti e Rivista di Statistica*, 73: 30–48, 765–807.

Donoghue, M. (2007) "Harro Bernardelli (1906–1981)," in J.E. King (ed.) *A Biographical Dictionary of Australian and New Zealand Economists*. Cheltenham, Edward Elgar: 25–28.

Edgeworth, F.Y. (1915) "Recent Contributions to Mathematical Economics," *Economic Journal*, 25: 36–63, 189–203.

Fernandez-Grela, M. (2006) "Disaggregating the Components of the Hicks-Allen Composite Commodity," *History of Political Economy*, 38: 32–47.

Frederick, S., G. Loewenstein and T. O'Donoghue (2002) "Time Discounting and Time Preference: A Critical Review," *Journal of Economic Literature*, 40: 351–401.

Frisch, R. (1932) *New Methods of Measuring Marginal Utility*. Tübingen, Mohr.

Hands, D.W. (2001) *Reflection Without Rules*. Cambridge, Cambridge University Press.

Hands, D.W. (2006) "Integrability, Rationalizability, and Path-Dependency in the History of Demand Theory," *History of Political Economy*, 38: 153–185.

Hands, D.W. (2010) "Economics, Psychology, and the History of Consumer Choice Theory," *Cambridge Journal of Economics*, 34: 633–648.

Hands, D.W. (2013) "Foundations of Contemporary Revealed Preference Theory," *Erkenntnis*, 78: 1081–1108.

Hands, D.W. (2014) "Paul Samuelson and Revealed Preference Theory," *History of Political Economy*, 46: 85–116.

Hands, D.W. (2017) "The Road to Rationalisation: A History of 'Where the Empirical Lives' (or Has Lived) in Consumer Choice Theory," *European Journal of the History of Economic Thought*, 24: 555–588.

Hausman, D.M. (2012) *Preference, Value, Choice, and Welfare*. Cambridge, Cambridge University Press.

Hicks, J.R. (1937) *Théorie Mathématique de la Valeur*. Paris, Hermann.

Hicks, J.R. (1939) *Value and Capital*. Oxford, Clarendon Press.

Hicks, J.R. and R.G.D. Allen (1934) "A Reconsideration of the Theory of Value, Parts I and II" *Economica*, New Series, 1: 52–76, 196–219.

Houthakker, H.S. (1950) "Revealed Preference and the Utility Function," *Economica*, New Series, 17: 159–174.

Samuelson, P.A. (1998) "How *Foundations* Came to Be," *Journal of Economic Literature*, 36: 1375–1386.

Samuelson, P.A. (2004) "Portrait of the Master as a Young Man," in E. Dietzenbacher and M.L. Lahr (eds.) *Wassily Leontief and Input-Output Economics*. Cambridge, Cambridge University Press: 3–8.

Schultz, H. (1933) "Frisch on the Measurement of Utility," *Journal of Political Economy*, 41: 95–116.

Schultz, H. (1935) "Interrelations of Demand, Price, and Income," *Journal of Political Economy*, 43: 433–481.

Sen, A. (1973) "Behaviour and the Concept of Preference," *Economica*, New Series, 40: 241–259.

Sen, A. (1997) *Choice, Welfare and Measurement*. Cambridge, MA, Harvard University Press.

Slutsky, E. (1915) [1952] "On the Theory of the Budget of the Consumer," in G.J. Stigler and K.E. Boulding (eds.) *Readings in Price Theory*. Homewood, IL, Irwin: 27–56.

Smith, A. (1759) [1976] *The Theory of Moral Sentiments*. Oxford, Oxford University Press.

Smith, A. (1776) [1976] *An Inquiry into the Nature and Causes of the Wealth of Nations*. Oxford, Oxford University Press.

Spiegler, R. (2008) "On Two Points of View Regarding Revealed Preference and Behavioral Economics," in A. Caplin and A. Schotter (eds.) *The Foundations of Positive and Normative Economics*. New York, Oxford University Press: 95–115.

Thurstone, L.L. (1931) "The Indifference Function," *Journal of Social Psychology*, 2: 139–167.

Tribe. K. (2015) *The Economy of the Word: Language, History, and Economics*. New York, Oxford University Press.

Wilson, E.B. (1935) "Generalization of Pareto's Demand Theorem," *Quarterly Journal of Economics*, 49: 715–717.

Wong, S. (1978) [2006] *The Foundations of Paul Samuelson's Revealed Preference Theory*. New York, Routledge.

12

A Short History of the Bergson–Samuelson Social Welfare Function

Herrade Igersheim

1 Introduction

The so-called Bergson–Samuelson social welfare function was first introduced in 1938 by Abram Bergson and subsequently developed by Paul Samuelson in his 1947 *Foundations of Economic Analysis*. Although it is intended primarily to clarify the works of Pareto and the studies which belong to the New Welfare Economics, the function developed by Bergson and Samuelson also sheds light on the close connections between the Old and the New Welfare Economics, and, above all, on the fact that social welfare requires value judgments in order to be defined. It is from this that it became one of the main tools of welfare economics, as stressed for instance by Pattanaik (2008). However, only four years after the publication of *Foundations*, the very existence of the social welfare function was called into question by Arrow's landmark impossibility theorem, which

H. Igersheim (✉)
University of Strasbourg, Strasbourg, France
e-mail: igersheim@unistra.fr

R. A. Cord et al. (eds.), *Paul Samuelson*, Remaking Economics: Eminent Post-War Economists, https://doi.org/10.1057/978-1-137-56812-0_12

states that under a set of reasonable conditions, the social welfare function can be shown not to exist. Samuelson retorted that:

> [Arrow] used the same name for his unicorn that Bergson and other writers had used for their existent animals. So it is not particularly surprising that Arrow's readers, learning that he had proved the impossibility of a 'social welfare function,' should have formed the mistaken inference that there cannot exist a reasonable and well-behaved Bergsonian social welfare function. (Samuelson 1981: 228)

Yet social welfare functions are today still widely used in tax-optimal theory, environmental economics, agricultural economics and in measuring poverty and economic inequalities. It thus seems that the use of social welfare functions outside its initial remit has flourished independently of the heated theoretical debate—which lasted for more than sixty years—about their existence, which followed the publication of Arrow's *Social Choice and Individual Values.*

The objective of this chapter is to offer a short history of this concept, from its origins in the late 1930s up to the present day.

2 The Bergson–Samuelson Social Welfare Function: An Edifice Constructed by Two Harvard Friends

Abram Bergson (1914–2003) came to Harvard in 1933 after undergraduate training at Johns Hopkins. From 1933 to 1940 he was, according to Samuelson, Wassily Leontief's first protégé at Harvard, before moving to the University of Texas, then to Columbia after the Second World War, and finally to the Harvard Russian Research Center from 1965 where he became "the world's leading authority on the Soviet economy" (Goldman et al. 2005: 493). Sons of Jewish Russian immigrants, he and his brother Gus (who was a graduate physics student at Harvard at the same time), both born Burk, changed their surname to Bergson at the end of the 1930s in order to lay emphasis on their origins. This eloquent tale regarding Bergson's character was frequently recalled by Samuelson after his death in 2003, "both as a reflection of what American academic and ordinary life was like 70 years ago and for what it tells about his own straight-arrow character" (Samuelson 2004: 24).

Bergson's meeting with the future Nobel Prize winner Paul Anthony Samuelson (1915–2009) in 1935 is part of the Harvard legend: "Abram Bergson was my closest friend at Harvard. Waiting in the 1935 line to collect my fellowship, I met him as a tall preppy type on my first day in Cambridge" (Goldman et al. 2005: 497). Also a son of Jewish immigrants, Samuelson completed his undergraduate studies at the University of Chicago at the age of 20. He was awarded a Social Science Research Council Fellowship to pursue graduate studies in economics and first intended to go to Columbia but finally changed his mind "by nonrational process and miscalculation…in search of green ivy" and went to Harvard, despite warnings from his teachers and friends that he "would not learn any modern statistics at Harvard if [he] passed up the chance to attend Hotelling's Columbia lectures" (Samuelson 1977a: 887–888). Almost fifty years later, Samuelson's move led Bergson to speculate "on what might have become of Paul, Columbia, Harvard, and contemporary economics if his decision had been otherwise" (Bergson 1982: 331). On similar lines, Samuelson remarked simply that "Harvard made us. Yes, but we made Harvard" (Samuelson 1977a: 889).

Bergson's and Samuelson's interest in welfare economics thus began soon after their meeting, despite the fact that "welfare economics enjoyed little favor at Harvard at the time. Among faculty who were inclined to formal analysis, Haberler was almost alone in being particularly attentive to work in welfare economics. For Schumpeter, that branch of economics held no interest to speak of. Leontief seemed rather ambivalent regarding it" (Bergson 1982: 333). As suggested by Backhouse (2013, 2017), Frank Knight's influence over Samuelson when he was in Chicago might explain, at least partly, his route into questioning welfare economics, especially when he came to pointing out the profound distinction between utility and welfare: "[N]othing said here in the field of consumer's behavior affects in any way or touches upon at any point the problem of welfare economics, except in the sense of revealing the confusion in the traditional theory of these distinct subjects" (Samuelson 1938: 71, quoted by Backhouse 2013: 6, 2017: 187). Regarding Bergson, it seems that his move toward welfare economics was probably motivated by his desire "to clarify [his] thoughts about optimal resource allocation in a planned economy" (Bergson 1982: 333). The development of what would become a landmark paper in welfare economics is evoked both by Bergson and Samuelson in their writings. Signed by Bergson (still Burk at that time) as the sole author, the exact paternity of the 1938 *Quarterly Journal of Economics* article is still rather unclear even today. According to Bergson (ibid.):

> I wrote the paper on my own, rather than for a course, and must have done practically all of my work on it in the year after I took the Leontief seminar – that is, during 1936-37. It was only natural, though, that as my work progressed, I should discuss it with Paul. He was, I think, the first person to whom I presented my idea of introducing a social welfare function into the analysis and using it to demonstrate the value judgements underlying previous formulations.

On the other hand, Samuelson's memories of this episode suggest that he had a more active role in Bergson's writing process than simply as a discussant. In fact, Bergson and Samuelson were both engaged in interrogating Pareto's writings: "Bergson would read to me a passage from Pareto and ask: 'What do you think is being said there?'" (Samuelson in Suzumura 2005: 334). Moreover, Samuelson pointed out that "this is where my association with Bergson becomes relevant," at the same time stressing that, "I was not an independent co-author of Abram Bergson's 1938's paper … I was a helpful midwife in helping to pull the baby out. I felt once the baby was pulled out, I had reached perfect clarification of the so-called 'new' welfare economics" (ibid.).

Bergson's aim was to "state in a precise form the value judgments required for the derivation of the condition of maximum economic welfare which have been advanced in the studies of the Cambridge economists, Pareto, and Barone, and Mr. Lerner" (Bergson 1938: 310). He thus proposes an "Economic Welfare Function" whose purpose is to define the welfare of the community and which depends on the set of resources of the society. Bergson then defines three groups of value propositions then being used to study maximum economic welfare. He makes it clear that "the maximum conditions presented in the welfare studies relate to a particular family of welfare functions. Their derivation thus requires the introduction of restriction on the shape of the Economic Welfare Function" (ibid.: 315–316). He first examines the Lerner Conditions, which focus on the production functions of the Economic Welfare Function; then the Pareto-Barone-Cambridge Conditions, which amount to saying that "in the maximum position it is impossible to improve the situation of any one individual without rendering another worse off" (ibid.: 320); and finally, the Cambridge Conditions which lead to the Propositions of Equal Shares. Bergson stresses that "the three groups of value proposition are not only sufficient for the derivation of the maximum conditions presented in the welfare studies. They are necessary for this procedure" (ibid.: 322), knowing that each of them corresponds to particular value judgments and that "the selection of one of them must be determined by its compatibility with the values prevailing in the community the welfare of which is being studied" (ibid.: 323).

After finally accepting a position at the Massachusetts Institute of Technology, Samuelson pursued his friend's work by adding a whole chapter on welfare economics to his 1940 Wells Prize-winning Ph.D. dissertation subsequently published as the *Foundations of Economic Analysis* (see Backhouse 2014, 2015). As with Bergson, Samuelson's main ambition was to clarify the welfare studies regarding the definition of maximum welfare. He notably stresses that: "[T]he most important objection to Pareto's exposition is his lack of emphasis upon the fact that an optimum point, in his sense, is not a unique point ... His optimum points constitute a manifold infinity of values" (Samuelson 1947: 214). He then emphasizes the significance of Bergson's 1938 paper:

> [Bergson] is the first who understands the contributions of all previous contributors, and who is able to form a synthesis of them. In addition, he is the first to develop explicitly the notion of an ordinal social welfare function in terms of which all the various schools of thought can be interpreted ... The analysis that follows is an enlargement and development of his important work. (ibid.: 219)

He then defines a social welfare function as "a function of all the economic magnitudes of a system which is supposed to characterize some ethical belief – that of a benevolent despot, or a complete egotist, or 'all men of good will', a misanthrope, the state, race, or group mind, God, etc." (ibid.: 221). If one adds to this well-known assumption that "individuals' preferences are to count," i.e., "if any movement leaves an individual on the same indifference curve, then the social welfare function is unchanged, and similarly for an increase or decrease" (ibid.: 223), then one obtains a so-called individualistic social welfare function which in fact corresponds to the classic Bergson–Samuelson social welfare function to which most subsequent authors would later refer. Like Bergson, Samuelson sheds light on the connection between the New and the Old Welfare Economics, stressing that it is "clear that [Pareto] is included in [Pigou], but not vice versa" (ibid.: 249). Further, and again following Bergson, he shows that if one only considers the set of optimality conditions put forth by the New Welfare Economics, the social welfare remains undefined. One needs further conditions which reflect ethical judgments.

It is commonly emphasized that there are two different streams of research within the New Welfare Economics: the compensationist school represented by authors such as Hicks, Kaldor or Scitovsky (termed the "British" approach by Baujard [2016]) and the approach followed by Bergson and Samuelson with their social welfare function (termed the "American" approach by the same author). This now well-established distinction is made by Samuelson in the 1981 Bergson Festschrift:

> For a long time scholars confused two versions of the New Welfare Economics: 1. The narrow version that emphasized and stopped short at 'compensation payments' made by gainers to losers … 2. Bergson's synthesis of the Old Welfare Economics of the additive-hedonistic type with the more general notion of a Social Welfare Function that introduces, from outside positivistic economic science, ethical norming of alternative states of the world. (Samuelson 1981: 225)

He thus suggested that the second approach by Bergson and himself should be considered to be more general than the former. Indeed, Samuelson specified that:

> Bergson not only clarified the relationship of this general New Welfare Economics to the previous Old Welfare Economics; but, as well, his 1938 analysis enabled scholars to understand how the narrow 'New Welfare Economics' of Hicks, Kaldor, Scitovsky, and a dozen others reached only the state of necessary conditions rather than that of necessary-and-sufficient conditions. By means of Bergson's analysis, the practitioners of the narrow welfare economics could not only apprehend the crucial distinctions between necessary condition(s) and sufficient condition(s) – but he also provided them with an understanding of for what the sufficient conditions may suffice. (ibid.)

The very same idea of an expanded approach proposed by Bergson and Samuelson is also present in the British economist Ian Little's 1950 *Critique of Welfare Economics* as compared to the "Kaldor-Hicks school of thought" (Little 1950: 114–115). In fact, Little explicitly adopts the same approach as Bergson and Samuelson by introducing "a value judgement about welfare distribution in the Kaldor-Hicks-Scitovsky 'situational', or 'partial', analysis" (ibid.: 117). All these assertions amount to showing that the compensationist school should be seen as just one of the possible forms that a Bergson–Samuelson social welfare function can have. However, the very basis of the New Welfare Economics, and especially the expanded approach were about to be challenged by Arrow's Theorem.

3 Arrow's Theorem and Its Connections to Welfare Economics

In a 1975 unpublished manuscript, Samuelson commented that:

> During the first 13 years of its life a Bergson Social Welfare Function (or, by courtesy, a Bergson-Samuelson SWF) was pretty well understood – both by those who thought it a useful concept, and those who had their doubts. It was an ethical norming of ordinal ordering of all the states of the world, provided from outside of positivistic economics. (Box 148, Paul A. Samuelson Papers (hereafter PASP), Economists' Papers Archive, David M. Rubenstein Rare Book & Manuscript Library, Duke University)

Indeed, according to Samuelson, Arrow's famous impossibility theorem, notably disseminated via his 1951 book *Social Choice and Individual Values*, is responsible for the confusion regarding the very existence of the so-called Bergson–Samuelson social welfare function.

Kenneth Arrow (1921–2017) was born into a rather poor Jewish Romanian immigrant family established in New York. First more interested in mathematics and statistics, Arrow enrolled in the Economics Department at Columbia under the guidance of Harold Hotelling and Abraham Wald. It was during the summer of 1948, spent at the RAND Corporation in Santa Monica, that Arrow developed his famous theorem. In the first volume of his *Collected Papers* (Arrow 1983: 1–4), and in many places subsequently, he documented very precisely where the initial spark came from (see, e.g., Kelly 1987; Arrow 1991; Horn 2009; Arrow et al. 2011; Maskin and Sen 2014). During a RAND coffee break, the German philosopher Olaf Helmer asked how a country could have a utility function seen as an aggregation of individual utility functions. Arrow replied that this "had been answered by Abram Bergson's notion of the social welfare function" (Arrow 1983: 3) and promptly began to study the topic: "About three or four days later, I saw that the voting paradox would be replicated, no matter what you did" (Arrow in Horn 2009: 76). The RAND report dated 26 September 1948, entitled "The Possibility of a Universal Social Choice Welfare Function," contained the main elements of the theorem and showed that the connection immediately made by Arrow between this issue and Bergson's and Samuelson's works was still explicit in his study, as well as the intricate links between the compensationist school and the Bergson–Samuelson approach:

> A. Bergson has reintroduced the social welfare function and has pointed out that it need only depend on the preference schedules of individuals and not on the measurability of individual utility. Also, of course, no assumption need be made as to the measurement of social utility; the social welfare function need be unique only up to a monotone transformation. Bergson's approach has been accepted by Samuelson and Lange. The only concrete form that has been proposed for Bergson's social welfare function is the compensation principle developed by Hotelling. Suppose the current situation is to be compared with another possible situation. Each individual is asked how much he is willing to pay to change to the new situation;

> negative amounts mean that the individual demands compensation for the change. The possible situation is said to be better than the current one if the algebraic sum of all the amounts offered is positive. Unfortunately, as pointed out by T. de Scitovsky, it may well happen that situation B may be preferred to situation A when A is the current situation, while A may be preferred to B when B is the current situation. Thus, the compensation principle does not provide a true ordering of social decisions. It is the purpose of this note to show that this phenomenon is very general. Under certain very reasonable restrictions, there is no method of aggregating individual preferences which leads to a consistent social preferences scale, apart from certain trivial methods which violate democratic principles. (Arrow 1948: 2–3)

This report would go on to be the main foundation of his Ph.D. thesis defended in January 1949, in front of a jury including Bergson himself: "I certainly do remember your PhD oral. I must sadly admit, though, that I did not really grasp at the time I was witnessing the birth of a new discipline" (Bergson to Arrow, 4 January 1982, Box 32, Kenneth J. Arrow Papers, Economists' Papers Archive, David M. Rubenstein Rare Book & Manuscript Library, Duke University). Soon after his recruitment at Stanford a few months later, Arrow published his theorem in a 1950 issue of the *Journal of Political Economy*, and then (and more significantly) in his *Social Choice and Individual Values*, published in 1951 as a monograph for the Cowles Commission.

Compared to Bergson and Samuelson, who claimed that some ethical judgments are necessary to obtain a complete social ordering but do not specify them, Arrow's objective was slightly different, since his setting does include some value judgments supposed to be shared by all the members of a society. He is thus examining if there exist methods able to aggregate the preferences of many individuals into a social choice on the basis of these shared value judgments. In doing so, he claimed that his research focused on the methods able to be used by capitalist democracies ("voting, typically used to make 'political' decisions, and the market mechanism, typically used to make 'economic' decisions" [Arrow 1963: 1]) as compared to two other methods such as dictatorship and convention which lead to consistent outcomes for they do not rely on conflicting individual tastes but rather on a unitary will—either the dictator's or the common will.

Arrow further introduced a new formalism based on symbolic logic, which marks out a clear distinction from "the more conventional representations in terms of indifference maps or utility functions" (ibid.: 16) used by pre-war economists.

This new approach included several definitions. The fixed set of the different states of the world or social states is named $X = \{x, y, z\ldots\}$, while the finite number of individuals in the society are enumerated 1, …, n. Each individual i has a preference ordering over X. $x R_i y$ means that individual i prefers x over y or is indifferent between them. R_i is assumed to be complete (for all x, y in X, either $x R_i y$ or $y R_i x$, or both) and transitive (for all x, y, z in X, if $x R_i y$ and $y R_i z$, then $x R_i z$). With this framework, no interpersonal comparisons of utility are allowed. A profile R is the list of the preference orderings of all the individuals $(R_1, \ldots, R_n)$. Finally, Arrow's social welfare function is a process which assigns a social ordering to each profile.

Arrow then introduces four conditions that ought to be satisfied by any social welfare function, since all four correspond to value judgments supposedly shared by all the individuals of a society.[1]

1. Universal domain (condition U), that is all logically possible orderings of the states of the world that can be chosen by any member of society.
2. Weak Pareto principle (condition P), that is if every member of society prefers a state of the world x to another state of the world y, then so does the social welfare function: for any profile R, for any x, y in X, if for all i $x P_i y$, then $x P y$.
3. Independence of irrelevant alternatives (condition I), that is for any x, y in X, for any profiles R, R', if [for all i, $x R_i y \Leftrightarrow x R'_i y$] then $[x R y \Leftrightarrow x R' y]$.
4. Non-dictatorship (condition D), that is there is no individual i such that for any profile R, for any x, y in X, if $x P_i y$, then $x P y$.

In a society with at least two individuals and three social states, Arrow then proves that there is no social welfare function which satisfies conditions

[1] Note that these conditions are those described in the second edition of *Social Choice and Individual Values* published in 1963, since the first version contained some mistakes identified by Blau in 1957.

U, I, P and D. In his 1951 volume as well as his 1950 paper, Arrow remains firm on the idea that the social welfare function developed by Bergson and Samuelson is directly impacted by his result: "[T]he Bergson social welfare function is mathematically isomorphic to [Arrow's] social welfare function ... Hence, the Possibility Theorem...is applicable here; we cannot construct a Bergson social welfare function" (Arrow 1950: 346, 1963: 72).

In the same period, Arrow wrote a review of Little's *A Critique of Welfare Economics* (1950) published in the *American Economic Review*. Arrow was rather critical of Little's proposal to go beyond the Kaldor-Hicks criterion in order to focus on distribution issues:

> [W]here Mr. Kaldor and Professor Hicks seek to compare different production levels independently of income distributions, Little wants to compare different distributions independently of income. I am afraid that, desirable though such separation would be from the viewpoint of simplification, no such separation is likely to be valid. We come back to Bergson's original formulation of the social welfare function; we simply must rank in order of preference absolute welfare distributions and cannot simplify the comparison in any way by analyzing such a distribution into 'total income' and 'relative income distribution'. Little's conclusions from his discussion of welfare distribution are somewhat contradictory. On the one hand, he concludes that the concept of an 'ideal' distribution is meaningless because of the vagueness involved in the concept of distribution; on the other hand, he believes that it is possible to compare any two distributions independently of total real income. It would certainly seem that if we can make the second statement, we can find a distribution which is better than any other. (Arrow 1951: 928)

Beyond this critical assessment, it should be noted here again that Arrow posits a strong connection between Little's proposal, which follows the lead of the compensationist approach, and Bergson–Samuelson's. Little's proposal is therefore subject to Arrow's impossibility theory, as Arrow explicitly states:

> Little's general conclusion seems to be the same as Bergson's; we start with a value judgement that one situation is better than another if everyone is

> better off in the first case than in the second, and in any given context we can order welfare distributions according to our value judgements … As I have shown elsewhere, the above viewpoint is contradictory to some very reasonable value judgements. (ibid.: 927)

4 The Theoretical Controversy Between Welfare Economists and Social Choice Theoreticians

As the above quotes suggest, Arrow's landmark theorem would engender a virulent controversy between welfare economists and the new community to which this negative result would give birth, the social choice theoreticians. Although the importance of the term "social welfare function" in this controversy is obvious—for Arrow used the very same terminology as Samuelson, and stated explicitly that he had proven the failure of the New Welfare Economics project—the ins and outs of the debate are more difficult to circumscribe, for it has several dimensions (see Igersheim 2019). This is why the controversy between two Nobel-winning economists, Arrow and Samuelson, and their respective camps, lasted so long: from 1951 right up to the beginning of the twenty-first century. As claimed by Samuelson in a 2005 interview: "I have never heard of Arrow saying that it was a linguistically unfortunate abuse of those three words – the same three words [social welfare function]. I think he was sort of reaffirming his right to have done it" (Samuelson in Suzumura 2005: 339).

Shortly after the publication of *Social Choice and Individual Values*, Bergson and Little wrote papers critical of Arrow's theorem. After Arrow's 1950 review, Little was especially careful in what he wrote, not wanting anyone to conclude that his assessment was motivated by personal issues: "I don't want to commit myself to commenting on Arrow until I am quite sure in my own mind – this especially in view of his review of my book!" (Little to Samuelson, 9 February 1952, Box 48, PASP). Samuelson promptly replied: "As you say, you will want to lean over backwards so as not to give an erroneous impression of personal animus" (Samuelson to Little, 13 February 1952, Box 48, PASP).

As a matter of fact, Little's 1952 paper in the *Journal of Political Economy* discusses Arrow's theorem with deep precision and convincing arguments. In a nutshell, Little—soon followed by Bergson (1954), then Samuelson (1967)—claims that Arrow's impossibility theorem has no bearing on welfare economics, and a fortiori none on the Bergson–Samuelson social welfare function, basing his statement on two main arguments. First, Little points out that the Bergson–Samuelson social welfare function is "a process or rule which would indicate the best economic state as a function of a changing environment (i.e. changing sets of possibilities defined by different economic transformation functions), *the individuals' tastes being given*" (Little 1952: 423; italics in original), while Arrow's social welfare function is "a process or rule which will produce a social ordering as a function of the tastes themselves" (ibid.: 424). The difference between the functions on this matter corresponds to one of the main dimensions of the controversy: the technical one. While the individual preferences or tastes are given in the welfare economics framework, Arrow deals with any possible profile of preferences. But the point here is that Arrow requires a continuity condition across the profiles via the condition of independence of irrelevant alternatives: if the profiles change, Arrow's social welfare function is expected to guarantee a kind of continuity between the social orderings it leads to. It is precisely this continuity that Little rejects:

> If tastes change, we may expect a new ordering of all the conceivable states; but we do not require that the difference between the new and the old ordering should bear any particular relation to the change of tastes which have occurred. We have, so to speak, a new world and a new order; and we do not demand correspondence between the change in the world and the change in the order. (ibid.: 423–424)

He thus adopts a clear consequentialist viewpoint: "[I]t is foolish to accept or reject a set of ethical axioms one at a time. One must know the consequences before one can say whether one finds the set acceptable" (ibid.: 426). But welfare economists, and Little in particular, had not realized that the Bergson–Samuelson social welfare function could perfectly well fit into an environment with changing tastes but with no continuity condition (see Sen 1976; Fleurbaey and Mongin 2005; Morreau 2016). The refusal of welfare economists to deal seriously with the apparent difference between Bergson's and Arrow's settings regarding this issue would eventually debar them from further questioning the condition of the independence of irrelevant alternatives, and thus from offering a convincing response to social choice theoreticians, thus accelerating the deterioration of their discipline (see Mongin 2002; Amadae 2003).[2]

Little's second argument relates to another dimension of the controversy: the conceptual. Indeed, it is now rather well established in the literature that the formalism devised by Arrow led to another kind of conception of social welfare (see Amadae 2003; Saito 2011; Cherrier and Fleury 2017). For Arrow, social welfare is seen as the outcome of his social welfare function, i.e., it is generated by the aggregation of individual preferences. On the contrary, welfare economists such as Bergson and Samuelson strongly believed that social welfare required judgments of value to be defined externally. In this regard, Little claims that Arrow's social welfare function is nothing more than a "machine" which produces a "sentence," say x is better than y. If an individual is in disagreement with this sentence, he has to contradict his own value judgment, thus leading to a contradiction with the idea of non-dictatorship. Regarding this second issue, Bergson's 1954 paper in the *Quarterly Journal of Economics* introduces an important distinction between the real aim of welfare economics—i.e. "to counsel individual citizens generally" on the basis of their own value judgments, to which he adds that "I believe I am only expressing the intent of welfare writings generally; or if this is not the intent, I think it should be"—and Arrow's view, which amounts to counseling public officials whose "aim in life is to implement the values of other citizens as given by some rule of collective decision-making." Regarding the latter view, Bergson stresses that "If anyone wishes to call this welfare economics, he is welcome to do so, but he should be clear that he is back in the realm of political theory" (Bergson 1954: 242).

Arrow agreed with some of Little's and Bergson's arguments in the second edition of his *Social Choice and Individual Values* published in 1963, notably assenting to use the term "constitution" as suggested by

[2]For a more technical analysis of the implications of the condition of independence of irrelevant alternatives in this debate, particularly in connection with the issue of interpersonal comparisons of utility, see Fleurbaey (2003) and Fleurbaey and Mongin (2005).

Kemp and Asimakopulos (1952) and no longer referring to the "social welfare function"; yet still he stressed that "the difference, however, is largely terminological; to have a social welfare function in Bergson's sense, there must be a constitution" (Arrow 1963: 105). The important distinction between the two different conceptions of social welfare was simply ignored by Arrow: "'Social welfare' is related to social policy in any sensible interpretation; the welfare judgments formed by any single individual are unconnected with action and therefore sterile" (ibid.: 106), adding that "one can hardly think of a less interesting question about my theorem than whether it falls on one side or another of an arbitrary boundary separating intellectual provinces" (ibid.: 108), and finally concluding that "The area of fundamental disagreement thus narrows down to this one assumption [independence of irrelevant alternatives]" (ibid.: 105).

It appears that the two issues—the two kinds of formalism, two different conceptions of social welfare—are intrinsically imbricated, along with the third: the battle between two academic communities. After a first short and rather unconvincing defense by Samuelson in a volume edited by Sidney Hook in 1967, and the notable impossibility result developed by Kemp and Ng for fixed preferences (1976) aiming at explicitly showing the impossibility of Bergson–Samuelson social welfare functions, social choice theoreticians seem to have won the battle of ideas. As stressed by Fleurbaey and Mongin (2005: 382), "The message got across to the non-specialists, and it became part of the official history of economics that a major refutation had taken place. If the official death of welfare economics were to be dated with some precision, the years 1976-1979 would suggest themselves." Amadae (2003: 87) shares this point of view, emphasizing that the decline of the discipline is especially caused by their failure to take Arrow's result into account in their research program:

> Welfare economists were wholly unimpressed with Arrow's theorem, finding it irrelevant to their concerns. Yet their tradition floundered as it failed to attract a new generation of adherents, while scholars adopting the methods of Arrow's social choice theory were able to build up a new disciplinary standard. With Amartya Sen's being awarded the 1998 Nobel Prize in economics, social choice theory can be seen to have achieved the status of a global standard for addressing questions of social welfare and justice.

These three dimensions (technical, conceptual, battle of communities) are the key factors to understanding the strange dynamic of this controversy, as well as its protracted length. Samuelson's own culpability in this story should also be acknowledged, for he took some time to realize how widespread the misunderstanding was, and above all that Arrow, "his most-admired contemporary" (Samuelson to Suzumura, 7 May 2003, Box 67, PASP, not sent, not finished), disagreed with his exposition in the Hook volume:

> I wonder whether there is any substantive disagreement between you and my Hook text (which I believe captures the exact content of the Little and Bergson critiques, which in point of fact I had discussed with both of them before their wrote their reviews, and which it never entered my mind to doubt that you would fully agree with). (Samuelson to Arrow, 30 April 1976, Box 12, PASP)

We may illuminate the close overlap between the technical.and the conceptual dimensions by examining the statement regarding Pareto-optimality which Samuelson addressed primarily in his correspondence and, eventually, in the 2005 Suzumura interview. This is expressed, for instance, in a letter to Kemp where Samuelson literally orders him to add some clarificatory formula to his 1976 paper with Ng (which the authors did not do): "What appear as 'plausible' restrictions or axioms on an Arrow Constitutional Function simply have no meaning as applied to a Bergson-Samuelson Social Welfare Function. Thus, Pareto-optimality for Arrow has an entirely different meaning than for Bergson-Samuelson" (Samuelson to Kemp, 22 August 1975, Box 43, PASP). A few months later, the same idea appears in a letter Samuelson sends to Arrow:

> Any reader of my Hook exposition will realize that in it 'the Pareto principle', applied to the f(.) defined on the Bergson domain, is simply not logically isomorphic with the 'xPz Pareto principle' as applied to the f(.) defined on the Arrow domain. I wonder therefore if, in a third edition, you would really want to write: 'the area of fundamental disagreement thus narrows down to this one assumption'... the assumption of Independence of Irrelevant Alternatives. (Samuelson to Arrow, 30 April 1976, Box 12, PASP)

Years later, one again finds the same idea in the Suzumura interview, where Samuelson declares that:

> Bergson's Individualistic Social Welfare Function, by definition, must have the mathematical property of 'weak separability'. Without this, there may indeed exist no meaningful Pareto optimal conditions ... I recall that, at the NYU Sidney Hook conference on Philosophy and Economics, Kenneth Arrow startled the philosophers present (and me, too) when he declared something like: 'Surely when all the individuals agree that situation A is better than situation B, any admissible ethical system must not second guess their desires.' I don't recall Bergson as ever going to that extreme, even though to make sense of well-known Pareto optimality conditions he did include in his admissible Social Welfare Functions the weakly separable species in which those conditions did make sense. But never did he make the following common error: If situation A is Pareto optimal and B is not, then always society should prefer A to B. And when asked to also contemplate situation C which like A is Pareto optimal, never did he pronounce on how one could deduce which of A and C was the better ethically. (Samuelson in Suzumura 2005: 336)

In his earlier correspondence with Suzumura in 2003, one can find the same attack on the Pareto principle and the ways it is used on the one hand by welfare economists, and by social choice theoreticians on the other:

> Sen sometimes inveighs against the Pareto Principle. What's the big deal? It's only for what Bergson clearly delineated as Individualistic B-S SWF's that we can know what it means to say that Situation A is non-Pareto optimal in the sense that there is a different Situation B that is equally feasible and which makes both 1 and 2 better off. (Samuelson to Suzumura, 7 May 2003, Box 67, PASP, not finished, not sent)

The link with imposition and thus with the conceptual dimension of the controversy is now apparent:

> Too briefly, under the same name but with a new meaning, Arrow proved that no voting system or constitutional agreement could exist and at the same time satisfy several seemingly innocent and desirable properties such as: if every voter prefers A to B then the outcome A should be chosen over

> B for the polity. Also, no single John Doe should be able to 'impose' his coherent preference structure on everybody in society. (Samuelson to Little and Suzumura, 15 April 2005, Box 48, PASP)

Hence, closely scrutinized, the problem Samuelson encountered with Arrow's use of Pareto-optimality seems to have some relationship with the "independence" property of the Pareto principle revealed by Sen in his "Paretian epidemic" (Sen 1976). Samuelson's focus on Arrow's Pareto condition seems to harbor the same kind of criticisms formulated by Sen, but in relation to the domain in which Pareto optimality conditions make sense.

From the end of the 1970s onwards, Samuelson would insist unceasingly on the importance of Bergsonian welfare economics (see Samuelson 1977b, 1981, 1987, 2004; Suzumura 2005), which he thought should have earned Bergson a Nobel Prize:

> Many of the cognoscenti at the frontier of modern welfare economics – I being one of them – expected Stockholm to wake up to Bergson's merits. Alone, along with Ian Little or John Harsanyi or John Rawls, a Bergson prize could have added luster to the new post-1968 Alfred Nobel awards in economics. My tentative guess as to why that never did happen goes as follows. Kenneth Arrow's monumental work on the impossibility of any constitutional method of voting that would satisfy half-a-dozen plausible desirable axioms, that great theorem somehow got confused in nonspecialists' minds as being a proof against the possible existence of the quite different animal of the Bergson Ethical Normative Function. The history of every science contains some history of confusions, and economics is no exception to this. (Samuelson 2004: 25)

According to Samuelson, Arrow's result had irremediably damaged the Bergson–Samuelson social welfare function in the eyes of the next generation of economists. But, as stressed by Mongin (2002: 147), one must not forget that Arrow's theorem did result in a splitting of welfare economics

> into two different forms of normative economics, that is, social choice on the one hand, public economics on the other … It is often said that Arrow's *Social Choice and Individual Values* in 1951 gave a fatal blow to the

> new welfare economics. However, this claim has been disputed violently by the welfare economists. Whatever its intended meaning, it cannot be that social choice theory superseded welfare economics in its traditional role of assessing the working of markets and proposing improvements in terms of corrective taxes and the like. The agenda of social choice theory is to investigate the various abstract methods of evaluating social states. Applications may or may not be market-related and anyhow enter social choice theory mostly by way of examples. From the 1970s onwards, it has been incumbent to the newly created discipline of public economics to discuss market optimality and policy corrections. According to an insider's suggestion, public economics absorbed much of the content of the 'new welfare economics' that had survived social-choice-theoretic criticism. Thus, there are two quite distinct forms of normative economics being currently practiced in parallel.

In fact, while the concept of the Bergson–Samuelson social welfare function had indeed suffered from the theoretical dispute between welfare economists and social choice theoreticians at the very heart of the discipline, this was not the case outside social choice theory, in particular not in public economics, and in yet other domains this concept has retained its followers and continues to find adherents outside its initial realm.

5 The Flourishing of Social Welfare Functions Outside the Initial Theoretical Realm: The Key Role of Ian Little

As stressed by Adler (2012, 2017), the Bergson–Samuelson social welfare function has been widely used since the 1970s in a range of fields in order to formulate policy ends: "Perhaps the most important example is the field of 'optimal tax theory', spurred by James Mirrlees' 1971 article, 'An exploration in the theory of optimum income taxation', for which he ultimately won the Nobel Prize" (Adler 2012: 87). In this famous paper, Mirrlees attempted to define the tax schedule which will maximize a social welfare function, with individual utilities as arguments. He thus opened a wide stream of literature which is still very active today (see Tuomala 2016). But, as Adler noted, social welfare functions have also been used in many other realms: optimal growth theory, environmental economics, agricultural economics, health economics, as well as measures of poverty and economic inequalities with the seminal 1970 paper by Atkinson in the *Journal of Economic Theory*.

Yet the Bergson–Samuelson social welfare function per se is not used by most government agencies, which have historically resorted to cost-benefit analysis (CBA) instead. In the United States, the appeal to CBA is notably due to the emergence of Lyndon Johnson's Great Society programs which reshaped public policy: "Johnson's War on Poverty, then, 'virtually created a new and well-funded discipline: policy analysis'," and thereby strongly supported the development of CBA (Cherrier and Fleury 2017: 34; Jardini 2013: 302). As such, one can claim, as does Adler (2012: 88–89), that "CBA is the foundation for modern applied welfare economics." We must also recall the well-known link between CBA and the compensationist school à la Kaldor-Hicks: "The application of welfare economics in a piecemeal manner – that is, the application of welfare economics – has come to be called social cost-benefit analysis" (Little 1999: 54). Furthermore, it has been argued that while the compensationist school could be seen as a narrow version of the New Welfare Economics, the approach proposed by the Bergson–Samuelson social welfare function should be interpreted as a more comprehensive framework, coming to mark the distinction between the necessary conditions and the necessary and sufficient conditions.

One can infer from the above that CBA and the Bergson–Samuelson social welfare function actually have a close relationship as well, since the former was generated from the compensationist school. Indeed, scholars such as Adler (2012: 88) have taken care to stress that CBAs with distributive weights are indeed "a variation" of the Bergson–Samuelson social welfare function:

> The 'Green Book' (the official policy-assessment document in the UK, applicable to regulations as well as other types of governmental interventions, such as infrastructure spending) generally instructs decisionmakers to conduct CBA with 'distributive weights'. CBA with distributive weights is a refinement of the standard unweighted technique, and can be used to

> approximate an SWF. (Adler 2017: 4; on this issue, see also Adler 2016; Boadway 2016; Fleurbaey and Abi-Rafeh 2016)

Therefore, we should not be surprised if the same kind of conclusions are reached regarding the difference between the Bergson–Samuelson social welfare function and the compensationist school, as we find between the Bergson–Samuelson social welfare function and the CBA: "The SWF framework is sensitive to distributional considerations, while CBA is not" (Adler 2017: 2), which very precisely echoes Little's claim in his 1950 *Critique.*

One cannot but notice the key role of Ian Little in our narrative. Indeed, this British economist (1918–2012), whose focus moved from welfare economics in the early stages of his life to development economics after the mid-1960s is present in each stage of this story. Scion of a very rich and ancient family, he first attended Eton and left as soon as he was admitted to Oxford in order to avoid making the ritual Eton speech. Mostly focused on hunting, drinking and gambling, Little confessed that he went through an identity crisis when he arrived at university. Then, under the guidance of his tutor Isaiah Berlin, he took an interest in philosophy, but finally opted for economics on the grounds that "philosophers were cleverer than economists and so the competition would be more severe" (Little 1999: 8). After his 1950 *Critique of Welfare Economics* sold 70,000 copies, he taught until 1953 before joining the Treasury for two years. He was progressively becoming convinced that his "minimal mathematics precluded [him] from making any contribution to economic theory" (ibid.: 20) when development economics offered him a new escape after a trip to India at the end of the 1950s.

In welfare economics, Little made two main contributions (see ibid.: 13–15): first, his *Critique* questions the usage of "persuasive language in economics" and particularly in welfare economics. Economists have to acknowledge that many economic statements "which appear at first sight to be merely descriptive, have value implications." Little thus claims that ethical discussions must be brought into the "limelight" by economists.[3]

[3]Note that Little is the first to have introduced into the literature the term "Pareto optimality" (see Suzumura 2005: 335).

Second, and as already stressed above, Little proposed to go beyond the Hicks–Kaldor compensation criterion to focus on distributional concerns. This aim led him to the so-called Little criterion which includes two value judgments and can be stated as follows: "An economic change is desirable if (a) it would result in a good redistribution of wealth, and if (b) the potential losers could not profitably bribe the potential gainers to oppose the change" (ibid.: 40).[4,5]

In development economics, Little focused his efforts on developing methods of social CBA (see, e.g., Little and Mirrlees 1974). In so doing, he emphasized that he was still partly in favor of the social welfare function along the lines of Bergson and Samuelson: "I am not against using distributional or 'social' weights, and Little and Mirrlees (*Project Appraisal and Planning for Developing Countries*, 1974), showed how a decision-maker might do so" (Little 1999: 16–17). Indeed, the links forged by Little between his former discipline and development economics can be easily evidenced. In the interview of Little conducted by Pattanaik and Salles published in 2005 in *Social Choice and Welfare*, this is crystal clear:

> PKP/MS: Do you think that welfare economics has contributed anything to our understanding of problems of economic development? IL: In the most general sense, welfare economics would be any economics which is aimed at policy in any way. Welfare economics would include devaluing a currency. Anything where government decisions are in question is welfare economics I suppose. (Little in Pattanaik and Salles 2005: 366–367)

Although his last works and correspondence (notably with Samuelson) show that Little was not really aware of the latter episodes of the long-running theoretical controversy between Arrow and Samuelson, he did not change his mind on the subject or on the bearing of Arrow's result on welfare economics. Indeed, a whole page of his 1999 *Collections and Recollections* is devoted to this issue, pointing out the connection between

[4] After Arrow (1951), the Little criterion was further analyzed and criticized; see, in particular, Meade (1959), Sen (1963), and Chipman and Moore (1978).

[5] Although the aims of the Little criterion and the Bergson–Samuelson social welfare function are conceptually similar, i.e. to go beyond Pareto optimality, it must be stressed that they can be seen as alternatives (see, for instance, Schofield 1987; Little 1999: 16–17).

the Little criterion and Bergson's ideas regarding the aim of welfare economics (see Little 1999: 18). Further, in the Pattanaik and Suzumura interview, Little was still in total agreement with his initial statement regarding Arrow's theorem. He reiterated his firm commitment to consequentialism as expressed in 1952:

> I think I say somewhere in that article [Little 1952] that you don't know whether you accept a particular axiom until you know what all its consequences are. You don't accept an axiom out of the blue; you want to know what it's being combined with and what the consequences are … I reread my article, the 'Arrow' one, and I must say I think it's the best thing I ever wrote. (Little in Pattanaik and Salles 2005: 362)

6 Conclusion

This chapter provides a brief overview of one of the most famous tools in welfare economics: the Bergson–Samuelson social welfare function. Elaborated in 1938 by Abram Bergson trying to make sense of the theoretical tools of welfare economics, then developed by Paul Samuelson in 1947, it has been the subject of a long and complex controversy mainly between Samuelson and the father of social choice theory, Kenneth Arrow. This controversy, which accompanied the ascent of social choice theory and the decline of welfare economics, has only recently had light shed upon its several dimensions (technical, conceptual, the battle of scientific communities). Arrow's negative result would eventually diminish the status of the Bergson–Samuelson social welfare function in the eyes of social choice theoreticians, seemingly indicating that it was doomed. But, as we have seen, outside of social choice theory the concept is still alive and well. In particular, we have underlined the key role in this narrative of the British economist Ian Little, who transitioned from welfare economist to development economist and firm advocate of CBA.

As Samuelson would, perhaps sadly, claim up until the very end:

> Kenneth Arrow, like the Columbus who set out for the East Indies only to discover the different and richer domain of the New World, set out to

> explain to Rand non-economists what policy devisers might be maximizing. With the words 'Welfare Function' ringing in his mind, Arrow (in my interpretation) pursued a different Holy Grail … He did not knowingly hijack the nomenclature that Bergson and earlier post-Bentham writers had used. I've never found evidence that he then noticed the difference … As one who lived and worked in that earlier truly golden age, I have a duty to bear witness and help set the record straight. (Samuelson to Suzumura, 7 May 2003, Box 67, PASP, not sent, not finished)

Above all, the present contribution can be seen as an attempt to "set the record straight."

References

Adler, M.D. (2012) *Well-Being and Fair Distribution: Beyond Cost-Benefit Analysis.* New York, Oxford University Press.

Adler, M.D. (2016) "Benefit-Cost Analysis and Distributional Weights: An Overview," *Review of Environmental Economics and Policy*, 10: 264–285.

Adler, M.D. (2017) "A Better Calculus for Regulators: From Cost-Benefit Analysis to the Social Welfare Function," Working Paper, Duke University.

Amadae, S.M. (2003) *Rationalizing Capitalist Democracy.* Chicago, University of Chicago Press.

Arrow, K.J. (1948) "The Possibility of a Universal Social Welfare Function," P-41, RAND Corporation.

Arrow, K.J. (1950) "A Difficulty in the Concept of Social Welfare," *Journal of Political Economy*, 58: 328–346.

Arrow, K.J. (1951) "Little's Critique of Welfare Economics," *American Economic Review*, 41: 923–934.

Arrow, K.J. (1963) *Social Choice and Individual Values.* Second revised edition. New York, Wiley. First edition, 1951.

Arrow, K.J. (1983) *Collected Papers of Kenneth J. Arrow, Volume 1: Social Choice and Justice.* Cambridge, MA, Belknap.

Arrow, K.J. (1991) "The Origins of the Impossibility Theorem," in J.K. Lenstra, A.H.G. Rinnooy Kan and A. Schrijver (eds.) *History of Mathematical Programming.* Amsterdam, North-Holland: 1–4.

Arrow, K.J., A. Sen and K. Suzumura (eds.) (2011) *Handbook of Social Choice and Welfare, Volume 2*. Amsterdam, North-Holland.

Atkinson, A.B. (1970) "On the Measurement of Inequality," *Journal of Economic Theory*, 2: 244–263.

Backhouse, R.E. (2013) "Scientific Welfare Analysis: The Origins of Bergson-Samuelson Welfare Economics, 1936–1947," mimeo.

Backhouse, R.E. (2014) "Paul A. Samuelson's Move to MIT," *History of Political Economy*, 46: 60–77.

Backhouse, R.E. (2015) "Revisiting Samuelson's *Foundations of Economic Analysis*," *Journal of Economic Literature*, 53: 326–350.

Backhouse, R.E. (2017) *Founder of Modern Economics: Paul A. Samuelson, Volume 1: Becoming Samuelson, 1915–1948*. Oxford University Press, New York.

Baujard, A. (2016) "Welfare Economics," in G. Faccarello and H. Kurz (eds.) *Handbook of the History of Economic Analysis, Volume 3*. Cheltenham, Edward Elgar: 611–623.

Bergson, A. (1938) "A Reformulation of Certain Aspects of Welfare Economics," *Quarterly Journal of Economics*, 52: 310–334.

Bergson, A. (1954) "On the Concept of Social Welfare," *Quarterly Journal of Economics*, 68: 233–252.

Bergson, A. (1982) "Paul A. Samuelson: The Harvard Days," in G.R. Feiwel (ed.) *Samuelson and Neoclassical Economics*. Boston, Kluwer: 331–335.

Blau, J.H. (1957) "The Existence of Social Welfare Functions," *Econometrica*, 25: 302–313.

Boadway, R. (2016) "Cost-Benefit Analysis," in M.D. Adler and M. Fleurbaey (eds.) *The Oxford Handbook of Well-Being and Public Policy*. New York, Oxford University Press: 47–81.

Cherrier, B. and J.B. Fleury (2017) "Economists' Interest in Collective Decision After World War II: A History," *Public Choice*, 172: 23–44.

Chipman, J.S. and J.C. Moore (1978) "The New Welfare Economics 1939–1974," *International Economic Review*, 19: 547–584.

Fleurbaey, M. (2003) "On the Informational Basis of Social Choice," *Social Choice and Welfare*, 21: 347–384.

Fleurbaey, M. and R. Abi-Rafeh (2016) "The Use of Distributional Weights in Benefit-Cost Analysis: Insights from Welfare Economics," *Review of Environmental Economics and Policy*, 10: 286–307.

Fleurbaey, M. and P. Mongin (2005) "The News of the Death of Welfare Economics Is Greatly Exaggerated," *Social Choice and Welfare*, 25: 381–418.

Goldman, M., J. Sachs, P.A. Samuelson and M. Weitzman (2005) "Testimonials," *Comparative Economic Studies*, 47: 492–502.

Horn, K.I. (2009) "Kenneth J. Arrow," in *Roads to Wisdom: Conversations with Ten Nobel Laureates in Economics.* Cheltenham, Edward Elgar: 58–84.

Igersheim, H. (2019) "The Death of Welfare Economics: History of a Controversy," *History of Political Economy*, 51: 827–865.

Jardini, D. (2013) *Thinking Through the Cold War: RAND, National Security, and Domestic Policy, 1945–1975.* Meadow Lands, PA, Smashwords.

Kelly, J.S. (1987) "An Interview with Kenneth J. Arrow," *Social Choice and Welfare*, 4: 43–62.

Kemp, M.C. and A. Asimakopulos (1952) "A Note on 'Social Welfare Functions' and Cardinal Utility," *Canadian Journal of Economics and Political Science*, 18: 195–200.

Kemp, M.C. and Y.-K. Ng (1976) "On the Existence of Social Welfare Functions, Social Orderings and Social Decision Functions," *Economica*, 43: 59–66.

Little, I.M.D. (1950) *A Critique of Welfare Economics.* Oxford, Clarendon Press.

Little, I.M.D. (1952) "Social Choice and Individual Values," *Journal of Political Economy*, 60: 422–432.

Little, I.M.D. (1999) *Collections and Recollections: Economic Papers and their Provenance.* Oxford, Clarendon Press.

Little, I.M.D. and J.A. Mirrlees (1974) *Project Appraisal and Planning for Developing Countries.* London, Heinemann Educational Books.

Maskin, E. and A.K. Sen (2014) *The Arrow Impossibility Theorem.* New York, Columbia.

Meade, J.E. (1959) "Review of *A Critique of Welfare Economics*, Second Edition, by I.M.D. Little," *Economic Journal*, 49: 124–129.

Mirrlees, J.A. (1971) "An Exploration in the Theory of Optimum Income Taxation," *Review of Economic Studies*, 38: 175–208.

Mongin, P. (2002) "Is there Progress in Normative Economics?" in S. Boehm, C. Gehrke, H.D. Kurz and R. Sturn (eds.) *Is there Progress in Economics? Knowledge, Truth and the History of Economic Thought.* Cheltenham, Edward Elgar: 145–170.

Morreau, M. (2016) "Arrow's Theorem," in E.N. Zalta (ed.) *The Stanford Encyclopedia of Philosophy.* Winter edition. Available at https://plato.stanford.edu/archives/win2016/entries/arrows-theorem.

Pattanaik, P.K. (2008) "Social Welfare Function," in S.N. Durlauf and L.E. Blume (eds.) *The New Palgrave Dictionary of Economics, Volume 7.* Houndmills, Basingstoke, Hampshire, Palgrave Macmillan: 662–667.

Pattanaik, P.K. and M. Salles (2005) "An Interview with I.M.D. Little," *Social Choice and Welfare*, 25: 357–368.

Saito, N. (2011) "Arrow's Social Ordering as Moral Obligation," G-COE GLOPE II Working Paper Series, No. 51.

Samuelson, P.A. (1938) "A Note on the Pure Theory of Consumer's Behaviour," *Economica*, 5: 61–71.

Samuelson, P.A. (1947) *Foundations of Economic Analysis*. Cambridge, MA, Harvard University Press.

Samuelson, P.A. (1967) "Arrow's Mathematical Politics," in S. Hook (ed.) *Human Values and Economic Policy*. New York, New York University Press: 41–51.

Samuelson, P.A. (1977a) "Economics in a Golden Age: A Personal Memoir," in H. Nagatani and K. Crowley (ed.) *The Collected Scientific Papers of Paul A. Samuelson*. Cambridge, MA, The MIT Press: 881–896.

Samuelson, P.A. (1977b) "Reaffirming the Existence of 'Reasonable' Bergson-Samuelson Social Welfare Functions," *Economica*, 44: 81–88.

Samuelson, P.A. (1981) "Bergsonian Welfare Economics," in S. Rosefielde (ed.) *Economic Welfare and the Economics of Soviet Socialism: Essays in Honor of Abram Bergson*. Cambridge, Cambridge University Press: 223–266.

Samuelson, P.A. (1987) "Sparks from Arrow's Anvil," in G.E. Feiwel (ed.) *Arrow and the Foundations of the Theory of Economic Policy*. New York, New York University Press: 154–178.

Samuelson, P.A. (2004) "Abram Bergson 1914–2003," *Biographical Memoirs*, 84. Washington, DC, National Academies Press: 23–34.

Schofield, J.A. (1987) *Cost-Benefit Analysis in Urban & Regional Planning*. London, Routledge.

Sen, A.K. (1963) "Distribution, Transitivity and Little's Welfare Criteria," *Economic Journal*, 73: 771–778.

Sen, A.K. (1976) "Liberty, Unanimity and Rights," *Economica*, 43: 217–245.

Suzumura, K. (2005) "An Interview with Paul Samuelson: Welfare Economics, 'Old' and 'New,' and Social Choice Theory," *Social Choice and Welfare*, 25: 327–356.

Tuomala, M. (2016) *Optimal Redistributive Taxation*. New York, Oxford University Press.

13

Climbing Mount Everest: Paul Samuelson on Financial Theory and Practice

Jeremy J. Siegel

1 Introduction

My first contact with Paul Samuelson was most unexpected. It was March of 1967, the spring of my senior year at Columbia. The phone in the corridor of our dormitory rang. "Jeremy," my dorm mate yelled, "It's for you – someone from MIT." Puzzled, I took the receiver. Paul Samuelson was on the line. "Jeremy," Paul barked, "We mailed your acceptance to our PhD program two weeks ago and you haven't responded yet! What's the matter? We think you'd be a great match for our program." Stunned that Samuelson would call me personally, I bumbled some excuse and said I'd promptly send in my acceptance. It was good that I did. Pursuing my doctoral degree in economics at MIT was one of the best choices I made. Over the next four years, I was blessed to be Samuelson's student, interact with his keen intellect, and enjoy his guidance as my dissertation adviser. Years later, Samuelson expressed great interest in my long-term asset return

J. J. Siegel (✉)
University of Pennsylvania, Philadelphia, PA, USA
e-mail: Siegel@Wharton.upenn.edu

R. A. Cord et al. (eds.), *Paul Samuelson*, Remaking Economics: Eminent Post-War Economists, https://doi.org/10.1057/978-1-137-56812-0_13

series which showed the dominance of equity returns over other financial assets. He also strongly warned against a bubble that may be caused in the stock market if investors rushed into equities, ignoring their valuation.

Now, more than half a century later, I have been asked to write a review of Samuelson's contributions to the field of finance. To do so is a distinct honor. Not only do I regard Samuelson as the greatest economist of the twentieth century,[1] but his contributions to the field had an enormous impact on financial practice and the portfolios of countless investors. Indeed, it could be argued that of all of Samuelson's path-breaking research in economics, those with the greatest practical impact were in finance.

2 Samuelson's Early Works

I write this review in the shadow of a masterful summary of Samuelson contributions to finance published by Robert Merton in 2006 (Merton 2006).[2] It was written in honor of Samuelson's 90th birthday, a celebration I had the pleasure of participating in. Merton was my classmate at MIT, we both received our Ph.D.s in 1971, and I was well aware that at that time he was working closely with Samuelson on the option pricing problem.[3]

Merton stated that most of Samuelson's best papers in finance were done after he had reached the age of 50. But Samuelson dates his earliest foray into finance as his 1937 publication, at the age of 22, entitled "Some Aspects of the Pure Theory of Capital" (Samuelson 1937). There he generalized the relations between the interest rate, the value of investment, and economic profits.[4] The field of finance was virgin when Samuelson wrote

---

[1] Although Samuelson was not the economist with the greatest political impact, in my opinion, that honor goes for John Maynard Keynes in the first two-thirds of the twentieth century, and Milton Friedman in the last third.

[2] See also an earlier review by Merton (1983).

[3] This was evident by Merton's 1969 class paper, "An Empirical Investigation of the Samuelson Rational Warrant Pricing Theory," which became part of his MIT Ph.D. dissertation in 1970.

[4] This article, published while a student at Harvard, was the second of nearly 1000 scholarly pieces that Samuelson published in his lifetime. The David M. Rubenstein Rare Book & Manuscript Library at Duke University contains almost 89,000 items (printed and teaching materials, correspondence, speeches and interviews, and other audiovisual materials) related to the work of Paul Samuelson, which they claim occupy 119 linear feet of shelf space!

this piece and he reveled in the fact that his lifetime spanned virtually all the theoretical developments in the field. In "An Enjoyable Life Puzzling Over Modern Finance Theory," Samuelson stated that he regarded capital theory as the "Mount Everest" of economic science and was puzzled that many other great economists, particularly Milton Friedman, considered finance as a sideshow of little economic interest (see Samuelson 2009: 20).[5]

3 Option Pricing Theory

Much of Samuelson's research in finance in the 1960s was on option pricing. Merton (2006) showed that Samuelson's 1965, "Rational Theory of Warrant Pricing," which appeared eight years before the famous Black–Scholes formula, derived the critical equations of option pricing (Samuelson 1965a). Although it did not provide a closed-form solution, Merton claimed the paper was a "near miss" (Merton 2006: 21).

However, "near misses" did not count for much for Samuelson. In December 1996, I flew up to Boston to have lunch with Paul and to discuss several topics in my book, *Stocks for the Long Run.* Samuelson surprised me when, after a brief pause in our conversation about non-economic topics, he blurted, "You know, I just didn't see that arbitrage condition." I knew he was referring to the insight that made the solution to the option pricing formula tractable and provided Black and Scholes (1973) with the key to solving the option equations. I realized then how deeply this failure disturbed him.[6] Nevertheless, Merton, who received the Nobel Prize in 1997 with Myron Scholes for his contribution to solving the

---

[5]It is well known that Friedman opposed approving Harry Markowitz's Ph.D. dissertation, which was the foundation of modern portfolio theory and later worthy of a Nobel Prize in economics. Friedman regarded it as a statistical exercise, not an economic contribution. In contrast, Samuelson praised Markowitz in a 2010 article entitled, "On the Himalayan Shoulders of Harry Markowitz." Friedman's resistance to analyzing stock prices possibly arose from his work on the monetary history of the United States, which debunked the popular explanation that the stock market crash of 1929, not the collapse of the banking system, caused the Great Depression.

[6]He understates his disappointment in his personal reminisces on modern finance theory (Samuelson 2009: 19) where he contends that his attempts to establish pricing theory for options fell "a bit short of the Black-Scholes-Merton Holy Grail."

option pricing equation, gives Samuelson enormous credit for bringing that problem to the brink of a solution.

4 Random Walks and Efficient Markets

The same year his "Rational Theory" was published, Samuelson wrote "Proof That Properly Anticipated Prices Fluctuate Randomly" (Samuelson 1965b). This work was pivotal in establishing the random nature of speculative prices and formed the basis of the "efficient market hypothesis" that was contemporaneously developed by Eugene Fama of the University of Chicago (see Fama 1970).

In retrospect, the random nature of stock market prices may seem almost trivial to finance economists. In a freely competitive, frictionless market all known information must already be incorporated into prices, so that price movements can only be caused by unexpected, uncorrelated, and unforeseen information; otherwise arbitrage profits would exist. But the randomness of prices is counter-intuitive when applied to the prices of goods and services. If all prices are random walks, it can easily be proved that the relative price of two goods can drift arbitrarily far apart and reach any ratio as time goes to infinity. However, economic prices clearly do not do so—the price of a Rolls-Royce will not decline to the price of a green pea no matter how much time elapses, as Samuelson clearly stated (Samuelson 2009: 24). Samuelson carefully showed that it is the *total return*, price plus cash flow (or imputed utility), that displays random walk characteristics, not the price itself. Indeed, the price of economic goods does not wander to arbitrary levels and can be highly correlated from one period to another.

Samuelson was quick to share his belief in the randomness of stock prices with the public. In a September 1966 column for *Newsweek*, entitled "Science and Stocks," he states: "When statisticians feed equity price changes into an electronic computer, it literally cannot distinguish them from [random] coin tossings. Try it on your IBM 7090" (Samuelson 1973: 112). The same column contains one of Samuelson's most quoted statements about the stock market. He writes, "Commentators allege that market downturns predicted four out of the last five recessions. That is an understatement. Wall Street indexes predicted nine of the last five recessions! And its mistakes were beauties" (ibid.: 111).

5 Challenge to Judgment

The random nature of speculative prices led Samuelson to the conclusion that in order to "beat the market" an investor would have to possess special information or insight that was not already in the price of the asset. He was careful to indicate that the efficient market theory did *not* prove that professional money managers could not outperform market. But in order to justify their existence, these money managers had to outperform the market by more than the fees that they charged, a feat he claimed they failed to perform.

In one of Samuelson's most famous articles, entitled "Challenge to Judgment," published in 1974 in the inaugural issue of *Journal of Portfolio Management*, he asked whether there exist decision makers "capable of doing better than the averages on a repeatable, sustainable basis?" He claimed that highly respected economists, such as "Irwin Friend, William Sharpe, Jack Treynor, James Lorie, Fischer Black, Myron Scholes," and others, "are quite unable to find them" (Samuelson 1974: 17). Samuelson forcefully asserted: "Any jury that reviews the evidence, and there is a great deal of relevant evidence, must at least come out with the Scottish verdict: Superior investment performance is unproved" (ibid.).

Samuelson beseeched the profession to create a simple bogey against which these money managers could be measured. His recommendation: an open-ended mutual fund that would hold 500 firms chosen by Standard & Poor's to represent the market, in proportion to their market value: the S&P 500 Index. He concluded: "The ball is in the court of the practical men [who believe in the superior performance of managed money]: it is the turn of the Mountain to take a first step toward the theoretical Mohammed" (ibid.).

6 Jack Bogle and Vanguard

One such "practical man" was Jack Bogle, an investment professional and a graduate of Princeton University. He had just been removed as CEO and Chairman of the Wellington Management Company and, looking for more creative portfolios that would serve investors, described his reading of Samuelson's "Challenge to Judgment," as a "bolt of lightning" (Bogel 2014: 42).

Against much ridicule and active discouragement from his colleagues, on 31 August 1976, Bogle, now the head of his newly created firm, Vanguard, established the First Index Investment Trust designed to mimic the performance of the S&P 500, just as Samuelson had sought. When the Trust's prospectus hit Samuelson's desk, he was ecstatic. In a August 1976 *Newsweek* column, he said "My implicit prayer has been answered" (Samuelson 1976: 22).

The relationship between Samuelson and the leader of Vanguard evolved, to use Bogle's own words, into "a mutual admiration society" (Bogle 2005: 5). In 2005, Samuelson, not generally one for hyperbole, spoke before the Boston Security Analysts Society. He claimed: "I rank this Bogle invention [the S&P 500 Index Fund] along with the invention of the wheel, the alphabet, Gutenberg printing, and [I am sure he said this with a twinkle in his eyes] wine and cheese" (ibid.). Bogle claimed he owed a momentous debt to Samuelson. But Samuelson responded that such a debt was more than paid back by "what Vanguard has done for my 6 children and 15 grandchildren. May Darwin bless you!" (ibid.).

Bogle basked in the adoration, replying modesty, "Those words from an intellectual giant to a mere mortal who has scraped by without a great intellect…are among the greatest rewards of my long career" (ibid.).[7]

On the twentieth year anniversary of "Challenge to Judgment," Samuelson wrote that further research confirmed that actively managed portfolios underperformed the averages: "By and large, the ball that was put in the court of the would-be judgment-mongers never did get returned with point-winning velocity" (Samuelson 1994: 15). In other words, money

---

[7]Vanguard's index funds had an enormous impact on college pension practices as faculty agitated for inclusion of these funds to supplement TIAA-CREF, which had held a virtual monopoly.

managers were not presented with systemic inefficiencies which they could exploit for financial gain.

Nearly a quarter century later, the same conclusion holds. Over the last two and a half decades, hundreds of billions of dollars have flowed out of actively managed portfolios into index funds, reflecting the latter's superior performance.[8]

7 Other Efforts on Behalf of Individual Investors

Before Samuelson challenged money managers to create an index fund, he railed against other practices on Wall Street that hurt ordinary investors. He sharply criticized the oligopolistic system of fixed commissions rates (Samuelson 1973: 114–116), called the New York Stock Exchange an "island of privileged monopoly," and blasted "rigged commission schedules," and "powerful vested interests" (ibid.: 117–118). When former Fed Chairman William McChesney Martin Jr. was assigned to look into these issues, he called Martin's report a "grievous disappointment" that whitewashed Wall Street practices which hurt ordinary investors (ibid.: 123).

Samuelson praised Professor Irwin Friend for leading the Wharton Report that showed that mutual funds which charged a "load" or sales fee for investors did no better than funds that did not (ibid.: 129). A fan of diversification, Samuelson convinced the College Retirement funds to include foreign stocks in their portfolios and always counseled that investors choose a well-diversified "no-load" funds for their equity investments (ibid.: 132–134). He also beseeched the government to issue "stable-purchasing power bonds," to help investors protect themselves from inflation without taking risky positions in stocks or real estate (ibid.: 144). Finally, Samuelson called it a "scandal" that so few mutual funds had been established to enable middle classes to earn ever-rising interest rates

[8]See S&P Dow Jones Indices (2016). According to Thomson Reuters, ICI (topdowncharts.com), since the 2009 financial crisis about $750 billion of funds have moved out of actively managed accounts and over $1 trillion have moved into passive (indexed) accounts.

while constraining financial institutions from paying higher rates because of "Regulation Q" ceilings (ibid.: 140).[9]

8 Can *Samuelson* Beat the Market?

Although Samuelson championed index investing, this did not stop him for seeking superior returns in the market. In a little-known, but significant episode in Samuelson's life, he was one of two founders of perhaps the first "hedge fund," called the Commodities Corporation of Princeton.

The only mention I find in Samuelson's works of his association with this organization is in his 2009 musings about his life in finance where he states: "I skip here my long years as activist charter investor and Board of Directors member for the Commodities Corp. in Princeton. Space does not allow me to go into that intricate story" (Samuelson 2009: 26). However, his role in this venture is ably told by Sebastian Mallaby in a chapter entitled "Paul Samuelson's Secret" (Mallaby 2010: 62–88). Samuelson and his MIT colleague Paul Cootner each contributed $125,000 to capitalize a hedge fund in 1970 with the sole purpose of "beating the market."[10] Ironically, Samuelson was lured into this adventure by former student F. Helmut Weymar, a strong *disbeliever* in the random walk theory. Samuelson had supervised Weymar's prize-winning thesis a couple of years earlier on predicting cocoa prices using fundamental analysis.[11]

At first, Weymar crunched tons of data into a computer to predict the fundamentals of supply and demand for various commodities. But the computer models that he built and the macroeconomic views Samuelson offered did not track commodity prices. The capital of the Commodities Corporation fell abruptly, threatening dissolution of the fund. Weymar

---

[9] Milton Friedman also railed against those ceilings in a *Newsweek* article entitled "The Bank Depositor," 7 November 1966.

[10] Samuelson's stake is worth about $750,000 in 2018 dollars. He was very comfortable financially, having earned millions from his bestselling textbook, *Economics* (Samuelson 1948). This text, through its 19 editions, has sold nearly 4 million copies and has been translated into 40 languages.

[11] Weymar told Mallaby (2010: 64), "I thought random walk was bullshit. The whole idea that an individual can't make serious money with a competitive edge over the rest of the market is wacko."

shifted gears, forsook fundamental analysis, and took positions in "trending markets," which met with far more success. Samuelson's experience with the fund led him to confess:

> I never considered myself to be an A+ trader. What I did become was a useful monitor of traders. ... I learned to carefully abstain from influencing successful traders by offering them my macroeconomic views. Star traders...somehow had the knack to go beyond what was already in today's financial pages. To maintain their positive alphas required a concentration that for me had to be devoted to *avant garde* scientific economic discoveries. (Samuelson 2009: 26)[12]

Despite the fund's early problems, by the end of the 1970s it had become a prodigious success: Its capital grew to $30 million and its profits in 1980 were $42 million after $13 million were paid in bonuses (see Mallaby 2010: 76–77). Many of its traders earned returns of 50% a year by using strategies very different from what they—and Samuelson—had first imagined.

The Commodities Corporation was not the only attempt by Samuelson to outperform the market. He was also a significant investor in Berkshire Hathaway, the investment fund run by the famed Warren Buffett. Samuelson stated, "Investors such as Warren Buffett are strong and rare exceptions to the efficient market dogma" (Samuelson 2009: 26).[13] Nevertheless, Samuelson claimed emphatically that "*There are no easy pickings on Wall Street.* ... Such talents are hard to find. And they don't provide their services on the cheap" (ibid.; italics in original). Furthermore, as easy as their trading techniques may look, or as easy as these successful traders say their principles are, Samuelson cautioned that they are *not* easy, asserting that these superior investors have a special flare which the vast majority cannot hope to replicate (see ibid.).[14] Lastly, Samuelson averred even those

---

[12]In other words, Samuelson considered his "comparative advantage" was tackling tough economic problems, not trading strategies.

[13]He also claimed that commodity trader Amos Hostetter Sr. (whose picture was on the wall of the Commodities Corporation) garnered positive returns over virtually every year in the half century before his death, a performance which would have virtually zero chance of being the result of random outcomes. See Samuelson (1989a: 7).

[14]Samuelson cites Buffett's: "Aw shucks, just buy a good business franchise at a favorable price!" See Samuelson (1993: 3).

"hot hands" often do turn cold. He warned that Buffett himself said it was not likely that he could match his past performance.[15]

Perhaps the best summary of Samuelson's advice to individual investors appears in the subtitle of his article commemorating the 15th anniversary of "The Challenge to Judgment": "*Forsake searching for needles that are so very small in haystacks that are so very large*" (Samuelson 1989a: 4; italics in original).

9 Stock Valuation and the Equity Risk Premium

Although Samuelson had considerable belief in the microefficiency of "liquid, organized markets," he was "doubtful about any great *macro*efficiency" (Samuelson 1994: 23). In the 1970s, he was attracted to his colleague Franco Modigliani's (and later fellow Nobelist) contention that the stock market was reacting far too negatively to inflation, discounting future profits at the soaring *nominal* interest rates of interest instead of the correct *real* rates (see Modigliani and Cohn [1979]; also see Samuelson's memoriam to Modigliani [Samuelson 2005: 6]). He stood firmly with Robert Shiller in the view that non-fundamental factors, such as fads and fashions, frequently influence market prices far more than earnings and discount rates (see Samuelson 1994: 23; Shiller 1981, 1984).

Samuelson was frequently asked whether he thought the stock market was too high or low. To this question he professed ignorance, proclaiming:

> *Although…corporate profits are admittedly the most important determinant of…market movements, no way exists to determine what is the proper price-earnings ratio…* I doubt that the devil himself knows what is the equilibrium price earnings ratio on stocks. Eighteen to 1, as so long held? Fifteen to 1, as [Treasury] Secretary Douglas Dillon once rashly averred? Twenty-five to 1. Or 14 to 1, as the tape enunciates now… No one knows. (Samuelson 1973: 112; italics in original)

[15] Indeed, over the past 10 years, Berkshire Hathaway has underperformed the S&P 500.

However, we do know that these price-to-earnings (P-E) ratios, if maintained, do translate into identifiable returns for stocks. It can be shown that at a constant P-E ratio, the *earnings yield*, or the reciprocal of the P-E ratio, becomes the real forward-looking return on equity (see Siegel 2014: Chapter 11). The 15-to-1 ratio that Samuelson cites produces a 6.7% annual real return on stocks. Not surprisingly, this is precisely the long-run historical return on equities that I calculated in my own work, *Stocks for the Long Run*, and nearly identical to that found by other economists who have calculated long-term equity returns (see Dimson et al. 2002).

Despite Samuelson's wide-ranging research in financial economics, the one area that he never addressed was the "equilibrium" return on stocks nor the expected return on stocks over bonds, which is called the *equity risk premium*. This premium has been the subject of enormous debate, especially since the path-breaking work of Mehra and Prescott in 1985 (Mehra and Prescott 1985).

The nearly 7% real annual return on equities over the last two centuries (and the post-war period in the United States) is at least 4 percentage points above the real return on Treasury bills, with the spread becoming even higher in recent decades.[16] Mehra and Prescott showed that this premium is far greater than can be explained by standard economic models except with levels of risk aversion that are far higher than seem reasonable.

Although Samuelson never ventured into this debate, he did give us some thoughts on how investors should think about stock market valuations. In a 1970 *Newsweek* column, he claimed that the much-watched relation between *dividends yields* and *bond yields*—overweight stocks when the dividend yield is above the interest rate and underweight them otherwise—was likely inaccurate since part of the earnings of the stocks that are not paid as dividends is used to finance growth, generating "systematic capital gains" (Samuelson 1973: 122).[17] Stocks are more dangerous, Samuelson claims, when the *earnings yield* on them falls below the interest rate on bonds, a yardstick that has been called the "Fed Model" of

[16]The real return on short-term fixed income assets has fallen dramatically in recent years and has been less than zero over the past decade.

[17]Today a large part of earnings is deployed for stock buybacks, also generating "systematic capital gains."

stock valuation (ibid.).[18] However, Samuelson was quick to note that in an inflationary environment, even that criterion may not hold, especially if inflationary pressures arose from excess demand and not from the cost side of the corporation's income statement.

On the question of what fraction of one's assets should be in equity, Samuelson's early recommendations tended to be aggressive. In a 1967 column, he asked, "Is 100 percent wise?" and answers, "Surprisingly, perhaps yes," but then states that an investor would probably sleep better if he only puts 60–80% of surplus savings—defined as liquid assets minus life insurance—into common stocks (Samuelson 1973: 132). He continues: "I know older trust officers will raise an eyebrow at this departure from 50-50. But remember, we live in an age of growth and inflation" (ibid.: 132–133).

Later, Samuelson retreated a bit from this aggressive equity allocation. In 1970, he stated: "Unexciting as it may sound, deciding on some general ratio – such as 60-40 [stock/bond ratio] – may be the path of prudence" (ibid.). Although Samuelson never subsequently opined on the proper ratio of stock and bonds, he wrote extensively on whether the makeup of an investor's portfolio should be influenced by the holding period.

10 Time Horizon and Portfolio Allocation

The one area of finance which Samuelson perhaps took his early conclusions too literally concerned the relation of the stock-bond allocation to the investor's holding period. He became a strong advocate of maintaining a constant allocation in equity regardless of the holding period, contrary to the recommendations of a vast proportion of financial advisers who believed in a higher allocation to stocks as the investor's horizon increased.

Samuelson's path to this conclusion came quite serendipitously. In the early 1960s, he asked a colleague whether he would take a bet that had

[18] The "Fed Model" received its name from a graph in the 22 July 1997 Fed Monetary Policy ("Humphrey-Hawkins") Report to Congress. It was popularized by Edward Yardeni, then at Deutsche Morgan Grenfell.

a 50% chance of winning $200 and a 50% chance of losing $100. His colleague responded that he would not take that bet just one time, but if Samuelson offered him the bet 100 or a 1000 times, he would take it.[19] Samuelson was intrigued with this response. His colleague's intuition was that over many periods, the riskiness of these bets would tend to "cancel out" and the positive expected value of the proposition would dominate. However, Samuelson showed that this intuition is incorrect. To be sure, the probability that one would lose did decline rapidly as the number of bets rose. But in those cases where the bettor had a run of bad luck, losses would be significant, if not devastating. Samuelson (1963) showed that if you did not take the bet once, you should *never* take the bet, no matter how many times it was offered. This conclusion had an immediate application to investing. If investors face the same uncertainty at the beginning of each period and return realizations are independent from one period to the next, as the efficient market hypothesis argued, then there is no reason to increase one's allocation to equities as the holding period increased. As noted, this conclusion flew in the face of virtually every financial adviser and investment counselor who recommended higher equity allocations for younger investors than older investors.

Samuelson readily admitted that as the time period lengthens, the *percentage* of times in which stock returns beat bonds increases. Indeed, as the time period becomes very large, the percentage of times that stocks will outperform bonds approaches (but never reaches) unity. Samuelson repeatedly stressed that this does not mean that over the long run stock risks "cancel out" and that stocks would *always* beat bonds. Even a small probability of a huge underperformance must be calculated in the portfolio of a risk averter.[20]

---

[19]He finally identified his colleague 28 years later in Samuelson (1989b: 292) as E. Cary Brown (one of my professors at MIT), referring to him as his "long-time boss." Brown was chairman of the Economics Department for 18 years.

[20]Zvi Bodie, who crusaded with Samuelson against the belief that in the long run stocks would always beat bonds, often mentioned my book, *Stocks for the Long Run*, as providing the basis for this incorrect belief (Bodie 1995). When I confronted Zvi and said that I never claimed that in my book, he agreed and replied, "I know you don't, Jeremy, but everyone thinks you do!"

11 Comments on *Stocks for the Long Run*

Samuelson's emphasis on long-term risks in the equity market was made very clear after I published my research on long-term returns on stocks, bonds, and bills in the early 1990s, culminating in my book, first published in May 1994, entitled *Stocks for the Long Run*.[21] I asked Samuelson if he would write a blurb for my cover, and he happily consented. On 1 February 1994, he faxed me the following, in his own handwriting:

> Jeremy Siegel makes a persuasive case for a long-run buy-and-hold stock investment strategy. Read it. Profit from it. And even when short-run storms rock your ships, sleep well from a rational conviction that you have done the prudent thing. And if you are a practitioner of economic science like me, ponder as to when this new philosophy of prudence will self-destruct after Siegel's readers come someday to be universally imitated.

Until the last sentence, his contribution could not have been a better endorsement. My editor, Amy Gabor from Dow Jones-Irwin, wondered whether we could truncate the last sentence. "No!" Samuelson responded, but gave me an alternative, which, like the first, he insisted must be quoted in its entirety: "Jeremy Siegel gives persuasive evidence for a long-run buy-and-hold stock policy. Read and profit from it, even when short-run storms rock your ships. But be warned that, on this theory becomes universally acted on, it must self-destruct in the 1990 Japanese manner."

Since the Japanese stock collapse of 1990–1992 deeply spooked stock investors, we quickly decided to use Samuelson's first endorsement in its entirety.[22]

Samuelson repeated his warning in 1994 in "The Long-Term Case for Equities (And How It Can Be Oversold)." Under a section entitled "Self-Destruction of a Dogma," he wrote: "Finally, let me explain why this hold-for-the-long-pull tactic will self-destruct if ever it becomes universally believed. If you adhere to the dogma that stocks *must* beat bonds in the

---

[21] Research was initially undertaken as a project with Marshall Blume supported by the New York Stock Exchange in anticipation of its 200-year anniversary in 1987 (see Siegel 1992, 1994).

[22] I retold this story at Samuelson's 90th birthday celebration. It received loud chuckles from the audience and even Samuelson smiled.

long-enough run, there is no P/E level that the market averages out to at which you will take in sail" (ibid.: 17–18; italics added).

Samuelson's statement is true if the word "must," instead of, say, the words "most likely" is used. It is certainly true that if stock prices are bid up, forward-looking stock returns, and the percentage of long periods in which stocks beat bonds, will fall. My book concurred with all these conclusions. However, if the equity premium has historically been too large to be derived from most risk-return models, then perhaps investors *should* bid equity prices to a higher level and thereby lower their forward-looking return.[23]

I put this issue in a letter to Paul several days later. Back came a long (typed) letter (dated 17 February 1994), which did not address my query about the equity premium. In fact, he wrote:

> Today's newest bandwagon is to become a long-term investor in order to benefit. Books like yours will help recruit new fellow travelers on the bandwagon. Many, maybe most, of your readers will after the fact be entitled to bless you for pushing them toward emphasizing more the long view. There is a non-zero probability, however, that all of your readers will someday have reason to curse your name.

He softened these words at the end by wishing me "Good luck" with my new book.[24] Clearly, Samuelson was worried about a "bandwagon" effect and feared that "can't-lose-in-the-long-run" equity advocates, such as myself, would push investors into stocks and send their prices too high. He interpreted the 1980s Japanese stock market "bubble" as built on that psychology.[25]

---

[23] For example, if we assume a long-run real rate on bonds of 2%, and an equity premium of 2% (which is still much larger than Mehra and Prescott propose), we get a real return on stocks of 4%, which corresponds to a 25 price-to-earnings ratio. These are all geometric returns.

[24] Fortunately, a quarter of a century after receiving this letter I am basking in the "blessed territory." From the date of this exchange through 31 July 2018, the US stock market has returned over 9.4% per year (about 7.1% after inflation is taken into account), more than its historical average. In contrast, a 25-year US government bond would have returned about 6%, and rolling over in bills, less than 2.5%. However, the ride to these great stock returns was rocky. I clearly would have been in the "cursed territory" at the bottom of the bear market in March 2009.

[25] In January 1997, one month after Alan Greenspan, Chairman of the Federal Reserve, made his famous "Irrational Exuberance" speech, Samuelson wrote a short piece, "Dogma of the Decade:

12 Mean Reversion of Equity Returns

Samuelson was fond of saying that we have only one sample of history. It may be true, he declared, that stocks have historically never given investors negative real returns over 15- or 20-year periods, as *Stocks for the Long Run* claims. But that does not mean that it cannot happen in the future. He claimed if you put the 150 years or 1800 months of stock return data in an urn and pick out a thousand replications, with replacement, of those 1800 months, one will find a not-insignificant percentage of negative returns for stocks over 15- and 20-year periods.[26]

However, two words in Samuelson's urn example significantly strengthen his contention, namely *with replacement.* Returning each period's outcome to the urn implies that each period's return is completely independent of any prior period's return. This implies that right after a severe bear market, the probability that investors *immediately* experience another severe bear market is not diminished. But if a series of negative returns is instead more likely to be followed by a period of positive returns, then Samuelson's conclusion does not necessarily hold. This would be the case if stock returns followed a process called *mean reversion* instead of a random walk. Indeed, I found that the standard deviation of the total return to stocks as the time period increased rose less than the "random walk" theory would predict.[27] If this is the case, then the probability that stocks beat bonds over longer-term holding periods is greater than the Law of Large Numbers would predict from the random walk hypothesis.

It would seem that mean reversion of stock returns would *always* tilt longer-term investors into holding more stock. But Samuelson showed that this was not always so. Among the class of investors with constant relative risk aversion, which was by far the most popular (and tractable)

Sure-Thing Risk Erosion for Long-Horizon Investors" (Samuelson 1997) claiming that the "can't-lose-in-equity" philosophy was flawed.

[26] These returns can be simulated by a "bootstrapping" technique.

[27] I was not the first to suggest that stock returns followed a mean-reverting process. Poterba and Summers (1988) and Fama and French (1988) showed that long-term stock returns did not conform to the random walk hypothesis. Mean reversion became even more apparent when I extended the stock return series back to 1802.

characterization of risk preferences, only those more risk averse than logarithmic utility would own more stocks if the holding period were longer.[28] At the same time, Samuelson was quick to concede that empirical evidence appeared to confirm higher risk aversion, so the case for larger equity holdings for longer horizons hinged on the existence of mean reversion in equity returns.[29]

Despite the growing empirical evidence, Samuelson was skeptical about the long-term mean reversion of equity returns. In 1992, he cautioned:

> Since it takes a long time to duplicate statistical samples of long-term epochs, our confidence in the strength of the rebound [red noise] deviation from the random walk must be guarded. Moreover, the size of the alleged effect, particularly after we discount for the possible one-time nature of the 1920-1945 swings of the Great Depression and the Second World War, may not be great quantitatively. For these reasons, a certain caution toward the new results would seem prudent. (Samuelson 1992: 415–416)

He further writes: "We have only one history of capitalism. Inferences based on a sample of one must never be accorded sure-thing interpretations. How did 1913 Tsarist executives fare in their retirement years on the Left Bank of Paris?" (Samuelson 1994: 17).

However, in the UK, the greatest (real) decline in stock prices was in the early 1970s, a period of high-inflation, labor strikes, and industrial paralysis, and not the Great Depression or the Second World War. Yet stock prices in Britain reverted to the mean in the 1980s and 1990s. Also, stock prices reverted to the mean in the United States following the Internet mania of the late 1990s and the Great Financial Crisis of 2008–2009. Furthermore, the large equity premium was not just a US phenomenon. In a study of 16 world equity markets from 1900, Dimson et al. (2002: 62) stated:

---

[28] Analytically, if $U(c) = c^{1-\gamma}/(1-\gamma)$, the class of investors who would hold more stocks are those with a risk coefficient $\gamma > 1$, i.e., those more risk averse than $U(c) = \log(c)$.

[29] In Samuelson (1989a: 10; italics in original), he states that "the bulk of the empirical evidence, cross-sectional and from time series, is that real life investors are *more risk-averse* than Bernoulli utility function log(c)."

> while we find the US stocks have performed well, the United States has not been the best performing equity market, nor are its returns especially out of line with the world averages. The real return on equities was positive in all sixteen countries, typically at a level of 4 to 6 percent compounded over the period 1900-2000.[30]

In early 1996, Zvi Bodie of Boston University invited me to a debate about the long-term risks and returns of stocks and bonds. Bodie took Samuelson's side, proclaiming that mean reversion was not certain and emphasizing that the Law of Large Numbers did not cancel equity risks in the long run (see Bodie 1995). I took the position that mean reversion was definitely present in the long-term stock market data. I was surprised that Samuelson showed up at this meeting. At the end, he asked for a show of hands from the audience to the question: "How many believed in mean reversion of equity returns?" The audience was split, about 50–50. But the consensus of the profession was shifting. In 1999, John H. Cochrane wrote: "The last 15 years have seen a revolution in the way financial economists understand the investment world. We once thought that stock and bond returns were essentially unpredictable. Now we recognize that stock and bond returns have a substantial predictable component at long horizons" (Cochrane 1999: 36). In a recent email to the author (12 April 2018), he indicated that over 90% of financial economists would agree that equity returns display long-term mean reversion.

Even as he expressed his doubts about mean reversion, Samuelson softened his stance against age-based asset allocations. Noting that there are other rational reasons (such as the existence of labor income, or a minimum required level of consumption) that might rationally persuade younger investors to hold a larger fraction of their portfolio in equities, he titled his 1992 piece "At Last, a Rational Case for Long-Horizon Risk Tolerance and for Asset-Allocation Timing" (see also Samuelson 1991).[31]

---

[30] In their 2018 yearbook, Dimson et al.'s sixteen country sample was expanded to 21, and stock returns still dominated in all countries. Equities outperformed bonds by 4.3 percentage points per year and bonds by 3.2 percentage points. They state that "this provides a reassuring reminder that, over the long run, there has been a reward for the higher short-term risk from stocks" (Dimson et al. 2018: 24).

[31] The importance of labor supply flexibility is found in Bodie et al. (1992).

13 Conclusion

Paul Samuelson's contributions to financial theory were prodigious. He launched the random walk theory, played an indispensable role in the creation of index funds, and brought the option pricing problem to the brink of solution—and these are just a few of his wide-ranging accomplishments in the field of finance.

Many try to climb the slopes of Mount Everest. Few reach the top, and fewer still reach the top by scaling virtually all the mountain's many faces. Samuelson was one who conquered Everest from all its angles, providing the essential foundations for establishing both the theory and practice of financial economics.

14 Postscript

A year before Samuelson passed away, the phone rang in my Wharton office. It was Samuelson. "Jeremy, I read your op-ed in the *Wall Street Journal* today on gains from trade. Interesting, but you forgot that improved productivity does not always make workers better off and that the gains from trade are not always fairly distributed. Remember the case of Immiserizing Growth!"

> "Oh, yes," I responded, barely remembering that odd case from my international trade studies nearly a half century earlier. "I'll be more careful next time – thanks for calling."

It had been more than 40 years between my first and what proved to be the last time I talked with Samuelson. I marveled that anyone who was in his nineties could stay so sharp and on top of his game. I also felt honored that I was able to rub shoulders with such an intellectual giant who contributed so much for so long.

Acknowledgements The author is the Russell Palmer Professor of Finance at the Wharton School of the University of Pennsylvania and a student of Paul Samuelson from 1967 through 1971. I would like to thank Robert Cord for offering me the opportunity to write about this iconic economist and Michal Kolakowski for valuable research support.

References

Black, F. and M. Scholes (1973) "The Pricing of Options and Corporate Liabilities," *Journal of Political Economy*, 81: 637–654.

Bodie, Z. (1995) "On the Risks of Stocks in the Long Run," *Financial Analysts Journal*, 51: 18–22.

Bodie Z., R.C. Merton and W. Samuelson (1992) "Labor Supply Flexibility and Portfolio Choice in a Life Cycle Model," *Journal of Economic Dynamics and Control*, 16: 427–449.

Bogle, J.C. (2005) "The Professor, the Student, and the Index Fund," comments delivered at the Boston Security Analysts Society, 15 November. Available at http://johncbogle.com/wordpress/wp-content/uploads/2011/09/The-Professor-The-Student-and-the-Index-Fund-9-4-11.pdf.

Bogle, J.C. (2014) "Lightning Strikes: *The Creation of Vanguard, the First Index Mutual Fund, and the Revolution It Spawned*," *Journal of Portfolio Management*, 40: 42–59.

Cochrane, J.H. (1999) "New Facts in Finance," *Economic Perspectives*, 23: 36–58.

Dimson, E., P. Marsh and M. Staunton (2002) *Triumph of the Optimists: 101 Years of Global Investment Returns*. Princeton, NJ, Princeton University Press.

Dimson, E., P. Marsh and M. Staunton (2018) *Credit Suisse Global Investment Returns Yearbook 2018*. Zurich, Credit Suisse Research Institute.

Fama, E.F. (1970) "Efficient Capital Markets: A Review of Theory and Empirical Work," *Journal of Finance*, 25: 383–417.

Fama, E.F. and K.R. French (1988) "Permanent and Temporary Components of Stock Prices," *Journal of Political Economy*, 96: 246–273.

Mallaby, S. (2010) *More Money Than God: Hedge Funds and the Making of a New Elite*. New York, Penguin Press.

Mehra, R. and E.C. Prescott (1985) "The Equity Premium: A Puzzle," *Journal of Monetary Economics*, 15: 145–161.

Merton, R.C. (1969) "An Empirical Investigation of the Samuelson Rational Warrant Pricing Theory," class paper, included as Chapter V in *Analytical Optimal Control Theory as Applied to Stochastic and Non-Stochastic Economics*. Unpublished PhD dissertation (1970), MIT.

Merton, R.C. (1983) "Financial Economics," in E.C. Brown and R.M. Solow (eds.) *Paul Samuelson and Modern Economic Theory*. New York, McGraw Hill: 105–140.

Merton, R.C. (2006) "Paul Samuelson and Financial Economics," *American Economist*, 50: 9–31.

Modigliani, F. and R.A. Cohn (1979) "Inflation, Rational Valuation and the Market," *Financial Analysts Journal*, 35: 24–44.

Poterba, J.M. and L.H. Summers (1988) "Mean Reversion in Stock Returns: Evidence and Implications," *Journal of Financial Economics*, 22: 27–59.

S&P Dow Jones Indices (2016) "SPIVA Institutional Scorecard – How Much Do Fees Affect the Active Versus Passive Debate?" July. Available at https://us.spindices.com/documents/research/research-spiva-institutional-scorecard-how-much-do-fees-affect-the-active-versus-passive-debate.pdf.

Samuelson, P.A. (1937) "Some Aspects of the Pure Theory of Capital," *Quarterly Journal of Economics*, 51: 469–496.

Samuelson, P.A. (1948) *Economics*. First edition. New York, McGraw-Hill.

Samuelson, P.A. (1963) "Risk and Uncertainty: A Fallacy of Large Numbers," *Scientia*, 57: 108–113.

Samuelson, P.A. (1965a) "Rational Theory of Warrant Pricing," *Industrial Management Review*, 6: 13–31.

Samuelson, P.A. (1965b) "Proof That Properly Anticipated Prices Fluctuate Randomly," *Industrial Management Review*, 6: 41–49.

Samuelson, P.A. (1973) *The Samuelson Sampler*. Glen Ridge, NJ, T. Horton.

Samuelson, P.A. (1974) "Challenge to Judgment," *Journal of Portfolio Management*, 1: 17–19.

Samuelson, P.A. (1976) "Index-Fund Investing," *Newsweek*, 16 August: 66.

Samuelson, P.A. (1989a) "The Judgment of Economic Science on Rational Portfolio Management: Indexing, Timing, and Long-Horizon Effects," *Journal of Portfolio Management*, 16: 4–12.

Samuelson P.A. (1989b) "The $\sqrt{N}$ Law and Repeated Risktaking," in T.W. Anderson, K.B. Athreya and D.L. Iglehart (eds.) *Probability, Statistics, and Mathematics: Papers in Honor of Samuel Karlin*. San Diego, CA and Orlando, FL, Academic Press: 291–306.

Samuelson P.A. (1991) "Long-Run Risk Tolerance When Equity Returns Are Mean Progressing: Pseudoparadoxes and Vindication of 'Businessman's Risk'," in W.C. Brainard, W.D. Nordhaus and H.W. Watts (eds.) *Money, Macroeconomics, and Economic Policy*. Cambridge, MA, The MIT Press: 181–204.

Samuelson P.A. (1992) "At Last, a Rational Case for Long-Horizon Risk Tolerance and for Asset-Allocation Timing?" in R.D. Arnold and F.J. Fabozzi (eds.) *Active*

Asset Allocation: State-of-the-Art Portfolio Policies, Strategies & Tactics. Chicago, Probus Publishing: 411–416.

Samuelson, P.A. (1993) "Reflections on Investing for Foundations and Colleges," Rutgers Conference, New York, 17 November.

Samuelson, P.A. (1994) "The Long-Term Case for Equities (And How It Can Be Oversold)," *Journal of Portfolio Management,* 21: 15–24.

Samuelson P.A. (1997) "Dogma of the Decade: Sure-Thing Risk Erosion for Long-Horizon Investors," originally published as "Dogma of the Day"), *Bloomberg Personal,* 33–34.

Samuelson, P.A. (2005) "Franco: A Mind Never at Rest," *BNL Quarterly Review,* 58: 5–9.

Samuelson P.A. (2009) "An Enjoyable Life Puzzling Over Modern Finance Theory," *Annual Review of Financial Economics,* 1: 19–35.

Samuelson P.A. (2010) "On the Himalayan Shoulders of Harry Markowitz," in J.B. Guerard (ed.) *Handbook of Portfolio Construction: Contemporary Applications of Markowitz Techniques.* New York, Springer: 125–132.

Shiller, R.J. (1981) "Do Stock Prices Move Too Much to Be Justified by Subsequent Changes in Dividends?" *American Economic Review,* 71: 421–436.

Shiller, R.J. (1984) "Stock Prices and Social Dynamics," *Brookings Papers on Economic Activity,* 2: 457–498.

Siegel, J.J. (1992) "The Equity Premium: Stock and Bond Returns Since 1802," *Financial Analysts Journal,* 48: 28–38.

Siegel, J.J. (1994) *Stocks for the Long Run.* First edition. Burr Ridge, IL, Irwin Professional Publishing.

Siegel, J.J. (2014) *Stocks for the Long Run.* Fifth edition. New York, McGraw-Hill.

14

Paul Samuelson: Three Key Contributions to Finance

Ronald MacDonald

1 Introduction

Paul Samuelson's Ph.D. dissertation is generally regarded as a milestone in the development of modern economics as a social science, in that he brought the mathematical toolkit of the natural sciences to bear on a wide range of key economic issues and topics. The application of this toolkit was reflected throughout Samuelson's professional career and indeed underpins his seminal book, the *Foundations of Economic Analysis.* Samuelson's huge array of scientific papers covers just about every area of economics. In this chapter, we consider some of Samuelson's key contributions to the area of finance. Given that he made such wide-ranging contributions to finance, in addition to his broad and eclectic contributions elsewhere in economics, we focus here on the three that the profession, and indeed it seems he himself (see, e.g., Merton [1983, 2006]), seem to regard as his key contributions to this discipline, namely the development of the

R. MacDonald (✉)
University of Glasgow, Glasgow, Scotland, UK
e-mail: Ronald.MacDonald@glasgow.ac.uk

R. A. Cord et al. (eds.), *Paul Samuelson*, Remaking Economics: Eminent Post-War Economists, https://doi.org/10.1057/978-1-137-56812-0_14

efficient markets hypothesis (EMH), the pricing of options and portfolio theory.

In considering Samuelson's contributions to finance, it is necessary first to take a brief historical step back in time to the French scholar Louis Bachelier, and the rediscovery of his work described in Samuelson (1972: 6):

> In 1900, a French mathematician, Louis Bachelier, wrote a Sorbonne thesis on the Theory of Speculation. This was largely lost in the literature, even though Bachelier does receive occasional citation in standard works on probability. Twenty years ago, a circular letter by L.J. Savage (now, sadly, lost to us) asking whether economists had any knowledge or interest in a 1914 popular exposition by Bachelier led to his being rediscovered. Since the 1900 work deserves an honoured place in the physics of Brownian motion as well as in the pioneering of stochastic processes, let me say a few words about the Bachelier Theory.

In essence, Bachelier applied the concept of Brownian motion to describe the behaviour of financial asset yields as a random walk and, as a result, also made important contributions to the theory of option pricing. Although many have seen Bachelier's work as "merely" describing the time series properties of financial market returns, Samuelson recognised it as much more profound and significant than that. Specifically, he saw Bachelier's contribution as capturing the notion that Adam Smith described in The *Wealth of Nations* of how markets clear by the device of the invisible hand, a concept that was later rigorously defined and elaborated by Kenneth Arrow in his proof (see, e.g., Arrow and Debreu [1954]) of the existence of a competitive equilibrium and how this could be extended to financial markets with various future states of nature. It was the reintroduction of Bachelier's work in the 1960s by Samuelson that led to his own interest in these fundamental aspects of finance and resulted in him producing the theoretical justification for what is now referred to as the EMH.

Given that Bachelier's work underpins much of Samuelson's early thinking on finance, and the use of mathematical rigour (in his Ph.D.) must have also had an influence too, it is worth briefly detailing Bachelier's key contribution. There were two vital themes that underpinned Bachelier's career as a scholar and brought mathematical rigour to bear on his work:

a keen interest in games of chance, particularly the concept of a martingale, alongside probability theory and particularly the concept of random motion, an area that had fascinated scientists and scholars for many centuries. Bachelier's interest in random motion was further underpinned by an exposure to mathematical physics at the Sorbonne, specifically the diffusion theory of heat and gases.

Bachelier's specific contribution was to apply mathematical and statistical methods to the pricing of put and call options on French government perpetual bonds—rentes—which had been traded on the Paris Stock Exchange since the 1850s. By so doing, he demonstrated that, although the price or yield of a financial instrument may be close to its fair, or fundamental, value on average, it can randomly drift away from this value with a probability due to a Gaussian distribution. The randomness was formally modelled using the concept of Brownian motion which had previously been used to model the random motion of particles suspended in a fluid (be it liquid or gas) resulting from their collision with the fast-moving molecules in the fluid. In this application, Bachelier was able to describe the resulting distribution function, which today is referred to as a Weiner stochastic process, and, in turn, to link this to the standard second-order partial differential process that was in his day known for the description of diffusion processes.

In the remainder of this chapter, we consider Samuelson's contribution to the three areas in finance noted above. It is noteworthy that at the time of his early work in applying mathematical and statistical rigour to economic topics, there were also parallel developments in mathematics and finance which allowed Samuelson to push the boundary/frontier of the discipline. For example, Norbert Weiner produced the continuous time equivalent to the discrete time random walk model of Bachelier, and, additionally, Kiyoshi Ito published the new tool of stochastic calculus in 1951 (Ito 1951), allowing Samuelson to use this powerful tool in his own work.

2 Efficient Markets Hypothesis (EMH)

In thinking about Samuelson's contribution to the EMH, it is worth making the distinction between the underlying value of an asset and its market price. Are the two always one and the same or do they differ? In corporate finance, security analysis and international finance, the underlying value of an asset is labelled fair or intrinsic value, and this, in turn, is determined by the underlying fundamental determinants of the asset in question, such as a firm's earnings or broader macro-fundamentals. The intrinsic value can then be used to create trading signals in portfolio management decision-making of, say, buying when the market price is lower than the intrinsic value or selling when the price is above the intrinsic value.

The concept of value that Samuelson used, however, was a much broader measure and consisted of the "shadow value" of an asset. A shadow value is that placed on an asset by an idealised central planner who can, in principle, efficiently allocate society's resources. Given this, the question that arises is: In what sense are observable market prices in a decentralised capital market structure the best estimate of that shadow value? Since such values are not observable in any market place and indeed are clearly idealised prices, the issue that Samuelson was addressing was the extent to which market prices provide the best estimate of the shadow values. One well-known interpretation of this was given by Keynes who argued that the time series properties of financial asset prices are simply a reflection of the casino-like behaviour of speculators and that such markets simply transfer wealth between the lucky and unlucky. Hence, in Keynes's view, market prices do not necessarily bear any relationship to the shadow value. Set against this, however, is the view of Working (1960) who demonstrated that futures prices moved randomly around paths that a technocrat might deem optimal.

Since most finance models use underlying fundamental factors (such as GDP, money supply, unemployment and earnings) as the key drivers of financial prices and since these fundamentals are often serially correlated and quite persistent, it might therefore be expected that the changes in the prices of financial assets would exhibit similar kinds of intertemporal dependencies. This was one of the issues that Samuelson's seminal 1965 paper, "Proof that Properly Anticipated Prices Fluctuate Randomly" (henceforth Samuelson 1965a), sought to address. This paper brought together a number of the ideas that he had previously articulated regarding the behaviour and pricing of asset prices. It provides the foundation for the EMH that many others, such as Eugene Fama, would develop into the paradigm that we are familiar with today.

The main conclusion of Samuelson (1965a) would seem to contradict the notion that asset price changes should exhibit the same serial dependencies as the underlying fundamental variables. His modelling, based on the work of Bachelier noted above, demonstrated that in a well-informed and competitive speculative market, any intertemporal changes in prices will effectively be random. However, the considerable insight that Samuelson gives in his paper is that there is basically no inconsistency between the stylised empirical result that the market prices of assets follow a random walk with a finding that changes in macro-fundamentals are not random and that therefore the fair value of an asset is also likely to be non-random.

The basic intuition of Samuelson's results will be familiar to those versed in the textbook version of the EMH and its counterpart in macroeconomics, the rational expectations hypothesis. In the context of a competitive market, if investors know that the price of a speculative asset is expected to rise or fall by more or less than the expected fair value rate of return, then the return would already be bid up or down to negate that outcome. Therefore, at each point in time, assets will be priced at the expected fair value, and Samuelson proves that the changes in such asset prices around the fair return will be a martingale. In other words, the only source of movements of speculative prices will be the unanticipated changes in such variables.

To many, the randomness in price movements was seen as evidence that financial markets are efficient. However, Samuelson was keen to emphasise that a test that relies on the lack of autocorrelation of the change in asset yields is a weak test "to appraise the efficiency of market prices." In the penultimate paragraph of his "Proof" paper, Samuelson cautions against inferring too much from his results:

> It does not prove that actual competitive markets work well. It does not say that speculation is a good thing or that randomness of price changes would be a good thing. It does not prove that anyone who makes money in speculation is *ipso facto* deserving of the gain or even that he has accomplished something good for society or for anyone but himself. All or none of these

> may be true, but that would require a different investigation. (Samuelson 1965a: 48)

In other words, Samuelson's proof does not provide support for the Keynesian view that such price movements reflect casino-like behaviour in the determination of such prices or indeed the alternative view that such price behaviour reflects the outcomes of a competitive, efficiently functioning market.

In the final paragraph of the "Proof" paper, Samuelson goes on to note that in formulating his proof, he says nothing about where the underlying probability distributions come from. Do they belong just to a group of investors, the market as a whole or a "representative individual," and "is there any *ex post* validation of them?" Furthermore, his proof says nothing about whether the price outcomes from his modelling produce a Pareto-optimal configuration.

Fama (1970) builds on the unanswered questions in the final paragraph of Samuelson (1965a). Specifically, he defines the full information set available to investors and shows that if changes in speculative prices form a martingale around their fair value expected returns, then the price should also exhibit a martingale property for any distribution generated by an information set which is a subset of the full information set. The fact that Fama's tests, and nearly all subsequent tests of the EMH, rely heavily on the martingale property of speculative prices underscores the importance and significance of Samuelson's proof.

The early evidence on the EMH, which largely involved using auto-correlation tests and return comparisons between a buy and hold strategy and various simple trading rules, gave support to the EMH and this led Samuelson (1974) to issue a "challenge." Although he clearly recognised the distinction between "not rejecting" and "accepting the EMH," he interpreted the balance of evidence as putting the onus on those who believe the EMH to be invalid to prove their case.

Samuelson's most up-to-date pronouncement on market efficiency is contained in Samuelson (1994: 15) where he states in his response to his earlier challenge that "The jury of history did not find systematic inefficiency that exercisers of judgement could use to achieve excess risk corrected returns. We can expect the debate to go on. And that tells you something about the approximate micro efficiency of the organised markets where widely owned securities are traded."

Although post his 1994 paper mainstream academic research has moved against the micro-efficiency case for the EMH, it is nonetheless clear that Samuelson's work in this area is seminal and profound and continues to be influential.

3 Option Pricing

The second key contribution of Paul Samuelson to the finance literature considered in this chapter concerns his work on the pricing of options (or warrants, which is a call option). It is important to stress that the concept of an option is much wider than that of simply a derivative asset based on a stock and covers a whole range of financial assets from currencies to fixed income securities, bonds and beyond, such as commodities, real estate publishing and motion picture rights. As in the case of his efficient markets contribution, Samuelson's research on options had its starting point in the work of Bachelier.

As we have seen, Bachelier demonstrated that stock prices follow a random walk which implies that the expected change in the stock price over time is zero. Additionally, he postulated that the price of a warrant gives the owner the right to buy the underlying stock at some future time T for an exercise price of $\$a$ that must ensure that the expected change in the option price is also zero. From this, Bachelier inferred that the option price $W(X; T, a)$ must satisfy the following partial differential equation:

$$1/2\sigma^2 W_{xx}(X; T, a) - W_T(X; T, a) = 0,$$

subject to the boundary condition $W(X; 0, a) = \text{Max}\,[0, X-a]$, where X is the price of the stock and σ^2 is the variance rate on the stock. The solution of this equation is given by

$$W(X; T, a) = (X - a)\Phi\left(\frac{X - a}{\sigma\sqrt{T}}\right) + \frac{1}{\sqrt{2\pi}} exp\left[\frac{-(X - a)^2}{2\sigma^2 T}\right]\sigma\sqrt{T},$$

where Φ () is the standard normal cumulative density function. For an option that is at-the-money with a relatively short time to expiry, Bachelier's rule is that the value of the option grows as $\sqrt{T}$ is a good approximation to observed options prices. However, as Samuelson pointed out, for long-lived options, Bachelier's formula implies that the option will sell for more than the underlying stock itself in the case of perpetuities ($T = \propto$), i.e. the value of the option will be unbounded.

Samuelson was able to resolve this apparent paradox by postulating a geometric Brownian motion process to describe logarithmic stock price changes. In this case, the derived partial differential equation of the option price eliminates the Bachelier paradox since the solution satisfies $W()$, for all X and T.

From Bachelier's initial and indeed subsequent work on option pricing up to Samuelson's contribution focused on the evaluation of what he referred to as "European" options, that is, an option that can only be exercised on the expiration date. However, since the terms of most options that trade today can be exercised prior to the exercise date and contain potentially extra value due to the possibility of an early exercise, it is important to price these too. Samuelson referred to these early exercise options as "American" options and showed that the correct formula for such an option would satisfy his partial differential equation subject to four boundary conditions which he refers to as the "high contact" principle. Although closed-form solutions to such boundary conditions are not straightforward to derive, Samuelson additionally develops a recursive integral method that is a forerunner to the numerical methods used today to price such options.

Without doubt, the publication of the Black–Scholes pricing model in 1973 was the breakthrough that resulted in the creation of the significant sub specialism of derivative pricing within finance. Given this, and in the context of Samuelson's contribution to finance, it is worth discussing the link between his work on option pricing and the seminal contribution of Black and Scholes. Central to the Black–Scholes formula is the concept of a dynamic hedging strategy which can be used to form a riskless portfolio of the underlying stock, the option and riskless bonds. In a market with free arbitrage, the creation of such a portfolio must yield a return that is exactly equal to that earned on a riskless bond, and it therefore follows that there must be a unique relationship among the option price, the stock price and the riskless interest rate.

It is noteworthy that in Samuelson (1965b) hedging strategies are discussed, with specific numerical examples, between the option and stock as a way of deriving bounds on the discrepancies between alpha and beta. Using Samuelson's option pricing formula, these bounds translate into bounds on the range of rational options prices. In the context of this discussion, he also notes that the opportunity cost for the hedge should be included, which brings in the riskless interest rate as in Black–Scholes. Hence, all of the ingredients of the Black–Scholes formula are in Samuelson (1965b), although he did not push his analysis far enough to obtain the Black–Scholes formulation. That said, there remains a strong resemblance between the option pricing formula of Black–Scholes and Samuelson (1965b). Specifically, Black and Scholes make an identical assumption about stock returns to that in Samuelson by assuming a non-dividend paying stock with price dynamics described by a geometric Brownian motion and the associated lognormal distribution of stock returns. Additionally, as Merton (2006: 22) notes, "virtually all of the mathematical analysis in the 'Rational Theory' paper can be used to determine the prices of many types of options within the Black Scholes methodology." He gives a number of examples of these. Merton concludes his discussion of this contribution of Samuelson with the statement: "In light of these consequences, Samuelson's 'Rational Theory of Warrant Pricing' is some near miss!" (ibid.).

4 Portfolio Theory

Samuelson also made important contributions to the field of portfolio theory. The first contained in Samuelson (1960, 1977) was to support the use of the hyperbolic absolute risk aversion (HARA) class of utility functions in the research of the economics of uncertainty and thereby not rule out the use of unbounded utility functions in such research. In so doing, Samuelson emphasised that undue weight should not be given to the maximisation of the log return of portfolio utility, a member of the HARA family of utility functions. The use of such an approach could lead to false outcomes, as the title and contents of Samuelson and Merton (1974) illustrate.

A further fallacy in portfolio theory that Samuelson addressed has a strong resonance currently in real-world finance and specifically the view, which will be familiar to many, that investors who hold a significant proportion of equities in their portfolio can essentially regard the portfolio as riskless if a sufficiently long horizon is considered. To put this differently, over long horizons, stocks will outperform risk-free long-maturity bonds, and so both individuals and corporate pension funds should invest their retirement contributions in equities.

Samuelson's insight into this particular issue was to recognise the effect of age on risk-taking and optimal portfolio selection. In Samuelson (1969), stochastic dynamic programming along with a constant relative risk aversion (CRRA) utility function is utilised to demonstrate the important result that an investor facing identical investment opportunities in each period of their investment life would allocate the same fractions of their optimal portfolio between risky equities and a riskless short-term debt irrespective of their age. However, despite this proof, few in the "real world" heeded Samuelson's sage advice and the mantra that "equity investment is not risky in the longer term" prevailed in investor folklore until the early noughties. Indeed, the behaviour of stock markets in the 1990s, particularly in the USA, seemed to suggest that this mantra applied in the medium run, too. Although the 2007–2008 financial crisis seemed to challenge this view for many, the recent global equity boom perhaps suggests that financial markets have short memories. That said, no bull market lasts for ever, as previous experiences clearly demonstrate, and once again the truth of Samuelson's position on this issue will be demonstrated.

5 Closing Remarks

Without doubt, Samuelson's contribution to the finance literature is every bit as bold, innovative and cutting edge as his contributions across the gamut of specialisms within economics. In this chapter, we have sought to give a flavour of some of his key contributions to finance. Hopefully, we have demonstrated just how important and significant his contributions have been in the areas of the EMH, option pricing and portfolio theory. Although Paul Samuelson is no longer with us, his legacy lives on and the current generation of economists and doubtless future generations too will continue to deepen our understanding of the way financial assets behave and are priced.

References

Arrow, K.J. and G. Debreu (1954) "Existence of an Equilibrium for a Competitive Economy," *Econometrica*, 22: 265–290.

Fama, E.F. (1970) "Efficient Capital Markets: A Review of Theory and Empirical Work," *Journal of Finance*, 25: 383–417.

Ito, K. (1951) On Stochastic Differential Equations. *Memoirs of the American Mathematical Society*, 4: 1–51. New York, American Mathematical Society.

Merton, R.C. (1983) "Financial Economics," in E.C. Brown and R.M. Solow (eds.) *Paul Samuelson and Modern Economic Theory*. New York, McGraw Hill: 105–140.

Merton, R.C. (2006) "Paul Samuelson and Financial Economics," *American Economist*, 50: 9–31.

Samuelson, P.A. (1960) "The St. Petersburg Paradox as a Divergent Double Limit," *International Economic Review*, 1: 31–37.

Samuelson, P.A. (1965a) "Proof That Properly Anticipated Prices Fluctuate Randomly," *Industrial Management Review*, 6: 41–49.

Samuelson, P.A. (1965b) "Rational Theory of Warrant Pricing," *Industrial Management Review*, 6: 13–31.

Samuelson, P.A. (1969) "Lifetime Portfolio Selection by Dynamic Stochastic Programming," *Review of Economics and Statistics*, 51: 239–246.

Samuelson, P.A. (1972) "Mathematics of Speculative Price," in R.H. Day and S.M. Robinson (eds.) *Mathematical Topics in Economic Theory and Computation*. Philadelphia, Society for Industrial and Applied Mathematics: 1–42.

Samuelson, P.A. (1974) "Challenge to Judgement," *Journal of Portfolio Management*, 1: 17–19.

Samuelson, P.A. (1977) "St. Petersburg Paradoxes: Defanged, Dissected, and Historically Described," *Journal of Economic Literature*, 15: 24–55.

Samuelson, P.A. (1994) "The Long-Term Case for Equities and How It Can Be Oversold," *Journal of Portfolio Management*, 21: 15–24.

Samuelson, P.A. and R.C. Merton (1974) "Fallacy of the Log-Normal Approximation to Optimal Decision-Making over Many Periods," *Journal of Financial Economics*, 1: 67–94.

Working, H. (1960) "Note on the Correlation of First Differences of Averages in a Random Chain," *Econometrica*, 28: 916–918.

Part III

Samuelson's Contribution to Economics: Macroeconomics, International Trade and Development

15

Paul Samuelson and Macroeconomics

K. Vela Vellupillai

> Alvin Hansen led the revolt, with lumpen lecturers, assistants, and students in support. Harvard's giants – Haberler, Schumpeter, Leontief, and others – resisted the new paradigm, but *the golden age of macroeconomics* emerged from the ferment. (PAS 1988a: 32; italics added)

By macroeconomics I shall mean, often, macroeconomic dynamics or, simply, macrodynamics, in the light of Paul Samuelson's incredible productivity on practically all aspects of economic theory. The seven volumes of *The Collected Scientific Papers of Paul A. Samuelson* (1966–2011) contain a total of 7068 numbered pages and 597 chapters, not counting the xii + 447 pages of the *Foundations of Economic Analysis* (PAS 1947) and (even) the first (or third—where the much-maligned phrase neoclassical synthesis was coined) edition of the stupendously successful textbook on *Economics*!

K. Vela Vellupillai (✉)
Stockholm, Sweden

R. A. Cord et al. (eds.), *Paul Samuelson*, Remaking Economics: Eminent Post-War Economists, https://doi.org/10.1057/978-1-137-56812-0_15

1 Introduction

> *More can be less* ... But the fine garments *sometimes* achieved fit only by chopping off *some* real arms and legs ... Easy victories over a science's wrong opponents are hollow victories – at least *almost* always. (PAS 1986a: 850; italics added)

I think this is what PAS[1] means (ibid.) when he refers to the "new" mathematical economics of the "theory of cones, polyhedral, and convex sets made possible". The qualified predicates—"can", "sometimes", "almost"—show PAS at his critical best; he is *almost* always[2] generous and measured in his evaluation of those who are, implicitly, critical of his chosen methodology.

Of the almost 95 years of his life, he wrote and rewrote about the macroeconomics of fluctuations and growth for 68 years of those, and also at least once every decade, since he began his scientific authorship. It was about deterministic, determined, fluctuations of aggregate income, consumption and investment, in the context of—mostly—discrete-, but also of continuous-time, fluctuations, within a growth framework, i.e. of growth cycles. The names of his elder, contemporaneous and younger colleagues, like Joseph Schumpeter, Maynard Keynes, Alvin Hansen, Roy Harrod, Ragnar Frisch, Michał Kalecki, Erik Lundberg and many others, dot these critical, appreciative and influential contributions by PAS.

On the words, "macroeconomic" and "macrodynamics", PAS (1986b: 858; italics added) writes, with disarming frankness:

> These papers [vol. 1 of the Japanese translation of *The Collected Scientific Papers of Paul A. Samuelson*] deal with what today we call *macroeconomics*—a surprisingly recent term. A dozen years ago, Dr. Edwin Nourse, President Truman's venerable first Chairman of the US Council of Economic Advisers, wrote to Professor Alvin Hansen of Harvard, asking: "Who invented the word '*macroeconomics*'?" Hansen wrote back: "I don't know. *Probably Samuelson.* I'll ask him"... I must answer for much. But *I don't believe it was I*

[1] I shall almost always refer to Samuelson as PAS in this chapter.

[2] With notable exceptions (especially those economists, and others, who are more or less contemporaneous)—see Samuelson (1983, 1986b: 858–859).

> *who coined the now-standard word* … [Frisch], Tinbergen, and Kalecki used the expression "*macrodynamic*" and had not yet contrasted *microeconomics* and *macroeconomics*".[3]

These modest pages contain the consideration—both economic and mathematical—of the analysis and extension of PAS's fundamental contributions of 1939, as it changed and evolved, during the period from 1939 to 2007, via his observations about Frisch's rocking horse methodology, allegedly following Wicksell (1907).[4] In the process, PAS aligned himself firmly as a Keynesian in the US and (eventual) Canadian traditions (see Timlin 1949)—very different from the (Cambridge) UK tradition of Kahn and Robinson. Although inspired by Alvin Hansen, it must be said that it was not an exclusively North American tradition—at least Pigou, Robertson, Hicks, Meade, Harrod and Lange[5] also interpreted Keynes's multiplier analysis of short-run equilibrium macroeconomics in a way that was congenial to PAS.

Hansen inspired PAS not only to become a Keynesian macroeconomist, but also decisively in the way he considered equilibrium fluctuations against a backdrop of (predicted) secular stagnation—i.e. as the obverse of growth—contexts (as Nikaido 1987 emphasizes).[6] Of course, Hansen (1939) was more influential than Harrod (1939) for PAS. The former was true to Schumpeter and Wicksell, and therefore the idea of "No Growth,

[3]Although Frisch did also use the word macroeconomics, it was in an internal university memorandum. Lindahl (1939: 52) did use the word macroeconomics, in contrast with microeconomics (cf. PAS 1997: 157).

[4]Samuelson (1939a, b, 1974, 1988b, 2005). Wicksell (ibid.) does not refer to any rocking horse.

[5]However, the economics of the Stockholm School, led by the neo-Wicksellians (PAS (1952a) [1966]: 591), Lindahl, Myrdal, Hammarskjöld and Lundberg, was a combination of short-run and long-run analysis, with disequilibrium and equilibrium dynamics, respectively. PAS (1959: 183) acknowledged that the American Keynesians should take seriously the disequilibrium, model-sequences, general numerical, approach of Lundberg. Hansen adopted this numerical model-sequences approach because he did not know the elements of formal dynamics; Lundberg did so (partly) because he was not sure that the postulated relationships (between aggregates) can be assumed to be invariant. The formal dynamics of Lundberg's (and Lindahl's) numerical model sequences are best analysed in terms of general nonlinear dynamics (and structural stability).

[6]See, in particular, the chapters by Higgins and Goodwin in the Alvin Hansen Festschrift (Metzler et al. 1948a); PAS corresponded with his lifelong friend, Richard Goodwin, endorsing wholeheartedly this particular contribution (he—PAS—was one of the effective editors of the Festschrift, for his mentor and friend, but not, in any formal way, his teacher, Alvin Hansen).

No Fluctuations" (the title of Nikaido's unfortunately neglected paper); Harrod was trying to separate growth from cycles (Harrod 1936) despite the importance given to the relation, i.e. acceleration, in it.

In Sect. 2, the themes at the heart of PAS's contribution to economics, in general, and macroeconomics and macrodynamics, in particular, and ignored in this paper—and some of the reasons for ignoring them—are developed, no doubt inadequately. Section 3 is an examination of the background methodological discussion of dynamics in *Foundations of Economic Analysis*, its allied mathematics (and logic) and the way it (may have) influenced PAS's vision of macroeconomics. Several topics, all of them now part of the vocabulary of the macroeconomist, delineate this section, but all in the context of macroeconomics and macrodynamics. The different sections are, inevitably, uneven—perhaps not in quality, but in the pages involved and the underlying theoretical basis (the latter, perhaps, a reflection of my own narrow focus; after all, not all can be as universally competent in economics and classical mathematics[7] as PAS!).

Section 4 is on the macroeconomics of fluctuations and growth, within the context of PAS's vision of the interaction between the multiplier and the acceleration principle, as the mathematics of dynamical systems itself developed. The first part is written with a historical flavour, macrodynamically. PAS himself kept updating his knowledge of the changing horizons of dynamics, but somewhat classically. In the second part of Sect. 4, a more extensive and technical analysis of the Hansen–Samuelson multiplier-accelerator model(s) of 1939, as it became the Keynes–Hansen–Samuelson multiplier-accelerator model of secular stagnation, is the focus. I do not believe, even in this extension, PAS went beyond Nikaido (op. cit.); but PAS (1988b) is a splendid exercise in cyclical models with, first, a strict accelerator, and later, with a flexible accelerator,[8] leading to a stable (from the inside) limit cycle in phase space. However, in

[7] I should add modern physics, encompassing both classical and quantum aspects of the subject.

[8] Even though the paper, as a whole, brackets Goodwin, Hicks and Kaldor as simultaneous sources for nonlinear dynamical modelling of aggregate fluctuations, seeking limit cycle(s), this particular section is a handsome tribute to his friend, Richard Goodwin (see PAS 1988b: Section 2, p. 5 and Section 6, pp. 11–14).

PAS (1990) he had shown admirable familiarity with mathematical dynamics more intricate than limit cycles.[9]

In Sect. 5, I try to draw some threads together of the mathematical economics of this universal scientist. Of course, the limitations of my knowledge and ability in economic and mathematical analysis limits the scope and nature of what I can competently discuss the astonishing prowess and productivity of PAS. It is, therefore, nothing more than an outline—it cannot be anything else!

2 Some of the *Instruments* that *I* Don't *Sound*

> My soul is a hidden orchestra; I know not what instruments, what fiddlestrings and harps, drums and tambours I sound and clash inside myself. *All I hear is the symphony.* (Fernando Pessoa, *The Book of Disquiet*, 1930: 8; italics added)

A caveat on one of the (many) important "roads not taken" (pace Robert Frost), on PAS's monumental contributions even to the core of macroeconomics (and monetary theory) and its concepts and (mathematical) tools must be mentioned. I do not touch on the rich monetary macrodynamics of the famous overlapping generations, consumption loan model. As PAS (1986b: 860; italics added) himself acknowledged: "I took pride in the fact that my 1958 'Exact-Consumption Loan Model' had *immeasurably more depth and sophistication*..."[10] There are many expository and fundamental contributions to PAS's 1958 paper. I myself have found Blanchard and

---

[9]Although not existence (or uniqueness) proofs of dynamical systems, of any order from algorithmic or constructive mathematical viewpoints. This is what I mean by his focus on coming to terms with mathematical developments classically (see Hales [2014] and my comments on Flood [1950] in the next section).

[10]On this paper, Samuelson observes, in addition (ibid.: 861; italics added): "You might think that a scientist's best papers receive instant recognition and approbation. Actually, some of mine that have come to gain most renown were *first refused by editors and referees* ... ([T]he *1958 paper* mentioned above encountered *rough weather* from the *Journal of Political Economy*)". It is very similar to what Lucas experienced with his "Expectations and the Neutrality of Money", a foundational paper on new classical macroeconomics, at the hands of editors and referees (at the *American Economic Review*;

Fischer (1989, Chapter 3), Solow (2006) and Weil (2008) most illuminative—but there is the proverbial *L'Embarras des richesses* on this exceptional model. It leads, after Gale (1972), via the work of Day (1983)[11] and others, to a utilization of the mathematical tools of the frontiers of nonlinear dynamics,[12] to elucidate economics, in general, and macrodynamics, in particular. PAS did not take part in this adventure—perhaps a reflection of his fundamental philosophy, expressed in PAS (1959: 183): "Scientific theories are like children in that they have a life of their own. But, unlike children, they may have more than one father".

That it forms the foundation for the underpinning of the lack of the familiar welfare properties—particularly that of the first fundamental theorem of welfare economics, quite independent of the usual market-failure reasons of a competitive Arrow–Debreu economy—in a multiplier-accelerator model is, in my opinion, the reason for Samuelson adopting non-maximum systems for macrodynamic analysis (see below).

It is, however, woefully inadequate to only acknowledge, here, the solid and detailed work of Cord (2009: especially pp. 115–116) and Clower (1996: in particular pp. 42, ff),[13] on the next two topics, namely IS-LM and the Keynesian cross, and their important role in orthodox—i.e. American—textbook Keynesianism. My inadequate excuse for this is the lame one of blaming my personal interest in macrodynamics rather than orthodox macroeconomics.

Given this lame excuse, the other "instrument I don't sound", apart from the ramifications of the overlapping generations, consumption loan

---

see Gans and Shepherd 1994: 172), before it was, finally published in the *Journal of Economic Theory* in 1972. By the way 'Loan' is spelled 'Long' in the original of the quote above!

[11]I have chosen a late article by Day, who developed the ideas in Gale, Samuelson and nonlinear dynamics, from at least the early 1970s; in fact, Gale (ibid.) was published in a book (jointly) edited by Day.

[12]Barnett (2004: 538; italics added) speculates that PAS may not have mastered, or contributed to, "the recent literature on complex unstable nonlinear dynamics", but does cover himself by adding: "But I would not be surprised, if [PAS] were to *correct* those speculations as misperceptions, if I were to ask". Samuelson may cite PAS (1990), if asked, "to correct these…misperceptions". I had a minor role in getting PAS to write about complex unstable nonlinear dynamics, which was not difficult for someone like him who had heard the unstable nonlinear dynamical symphony played by Henri Poincaré, George Birkhoff, Alfred Lotka and Andrej Kolmogorov.

[13]Say's law—supply creates its own demand—is fruitfully, and in the context of PAS's stance on the Keynesian cross contrasted with Hansen's law—demand creates its own supply (at least in equilibrium states), and brilliantly espoused in Clower (ibid.: 44).

model, in the context of macroeconomics, leading to macrodynamics, is the framework of the neoclassical synthesis, encompassing the Hicks–Hansen (IS-LM) model,[14] augmented by the Samuelson–Solow work on the Phillips curve(s).

It was in the third edition of his famous textbook that a synthesis between Keynesian macroeconomics and Walrasian[15] microeconomics, called neoclassical[16] economics, was identified by PAS (1955: 282; italics added)

> In recent years, 90 per cent of American economists have stopped being "Keynesian economists" or "anti-Keynesian economists". Instead, they have worked towards a *synthesis* of whatever is valuable in older economics and in modern theories of income determination. The result might be called "*neoclassical economics*" and is accepted in its broad outlines by all but about 5 per cent of extreme left-wing and right-wing writers.

In Samuelson and Scott (1968: 226; italics added), the following is added to the paragraph above: "Modern economists are '*post-Keynesians*,' keen to render obsolete any theories that cannot meet the test of experience and applicability".

During a conversation with Robert Clower in the early 1970s, PAS confessed that the term "neoclassical synthesis" was coined primarily to get "McCarthy off my back"! The phrase did not signify anything dynamic, in particular, macrodynamic (at least according to Samuelson).

Finally, on the Keynesian cross, a staple of introductory texts on (neoclassical) macroeconomics (see Cord 2009: 110), PAS (1986b: 858; italics added) felt that he had to: "*[P]lead guilty to* when I approach St. Peter's Gate to Heaven—if it is a crime—*first devising the 45°-line diagrams* in which C + I Keynesian *schedules* of consumption-plus-investment intersect with the 45°-line to determine Keynes's simplest 'multiplier' model of (unemployment) equilibrium determination".

---

[14]Hicks, in his classic 1937 article labels IS-LM as SI-LL curves. In 1987, in Aalborg, I asked Hicks whether it stood for SILLY curves? His answer was to hide behind chuckles—and a pull of the pipe! Perhaps this is the reason for PAS referring to Hicks—after paying due respect—as an "egoist" (PAS 1998: 1381).

[15]With hindsight—it leads, via Clower, to the microfoundations of macroeconomics movement.

[16]The term neoclassical, hyphenated as neo-classical, was coined by Veblen (1900: 261).

If I had been literal in my interpretation of the static underpinnings of the Keynesian cross, as it became the core of the Hansen–Samuelson version of American Keynesianism, I would rely on the powerful critique of Clower (op. cit.) and dismiss this as an exercise in macroeconomics without macrodynamic implications. However, the above quote by Samuelson, buttressed by Fig. 1, on page 790, of PAS (1939b), provides an explicit way to understand the connection between the static and the dynamic in the Correspondence principle.[17]

To this, and other issues of a methodological[18] nature in macrodynamics, I now turn.

3 Mathematics, Logic, Proof, and *Foundations of Economic Analysis*

> On the title page of my *Foundations of Economic Analysis*, I quoted the only speech that the great Willard Gibbs was supposed ever to have made before the Yale Faculty … Gibbs, who was not a loquacious man, got up and made a four-word speech: 'Mathematics is ***a*** language' … I wish he had made it 25 per cent shorter – so as to read as follows: '***Mathematics is language***' … I mean this entirely literally … For ***in deepest logic***…the two media ***are strictly identical***. (PAS 1952b: 56; bold and italics added)

Neither Wittgenstein, representing, perhaps, the philosophy of mathematics, nor Brouwer, from a foundations of mathematics interpretation, would have agreed with this Samuelsonian viewpoint of the identity of logic and language. Brouwer, in particular, would not have agreed at all with Flood (1950: 267; italics added) that PAS (1947: 116, fn. 18) sketches "a *constructive proof*"; as a matter of fact, PAS's proof is not constructive in any sense, not just from the point of view of Brouwer's intuitionistic

[17]In this context, see Cord (ibid.: 116, fn. 53) on Swan's 1945 introduction of the AD/AS model.

[18]In the sense of Metzler et al. (1948b: 905; italics in original): "[*Foundations*], as its title indicates, is a study of the *foundations* of economic method, but it is by no means a book on methodology in the customary sense. It is methodological only in the sense that the author is more interested in illustrating a means of solving economic problems than in developing a complete and self-contained theory of the working of the economic system".

constructive proof. Samuelson's (mathematical) logic, mathematics and the proofs of his theorems—both mathematical and economic (broadly conceived)—were always classical.[19] However, it is necessary to point out that the proof of existence of general equilibrium in Walras and Pareto is mathematically constructive; the latter is for an analogical computable model, while the former could be for a digital or analogue model.

No competent mathematician (or physicist)—classical or not—(or even Samuelson) would agree with the misleading sketch of mathematics (and, by implication, mathematical physics) in Stigler (1948). Stigler's strictures on stability, differential and difference equations display his monumental ignorance of the distinction between linear and nonlinear systems (among other things of a similar nature, e.g., nonstationarity).[20] Stigler's ignorance of the homilies in Boulding (1948: 189, fn. 5) is fairly clear from the following two quotations: "It is the central task of…chapter [IX] to show how the problem of *stability* of equilibrium is intimately tied up with the problem of deriving fruitful theorems in comparative statics. This *duality* constitutes what I have called the *correspondence principle*" (PAS 1947: 258; italics added)[21] and "How many times has the reader seen an egg standing upon its end? From a formal point of view it is often convenient to consider the stability of *nonstationary* motions" (ibid.: 5; italics added). Metzler (1948b: 906; italics added), in a brilliant review of *Foundations*, refers to these quotes as, "[T]he part dealing with the *stability* of *a dynamic system* [being] its most novel feature and is perhaps *Samuelson's greatest contribution to economics*".

[19]Warts and all! PAS, himself, is on the record as acknowledging the mathematical mistakes in *Foundations* as well as confessing (PAS 1998: 1378; italics added): "Even the *book's mistakes generated a history*" and "[A] busy author who had no relish for proofreading *complicated mathematics*". Allen (1949) and Savage (1948) catalogue lists of the mistakes in *Foundations* illuminatingly. Incidentally, PAS writes, incorrectly, George Birkhoff, when he means, of course, Garrett Birkhoff (see PAS ibid.: 1377).

[20]Obviously, Stigler's ignorance of Boulding (1948: 189) and Hart (1948) does not embarrass him in the least. Hart (ibid.: 912; italics added), points out: "Broadly speaking, Samuelson is *not* out to discredit anybody". See also p. 911 of this splendid review of the classic PAS (1948), on the connection between the relentlessly (classical) mathematical and logical approach of *Foundations* and the predominantly (classical) geometric and verbal rendering of economic propositions in PAS (ibid.).

[21]Niels Bohr had defined a Correspondence principle, linking quantum and classical physics, at least as early as 1922 (see Velupillai 1973).

There were many competent, sympathetically critical and enlightening reviews of *Foundations*, by well-known economists, mathematical economists and statisticians, Allen (op. cit.), Baumol (1949), Carter (1950), Metzler (ibid.), Savage (op. cit.) and Tintner (1948) in addition to the dubious ones by Flood (op. cit.) and Stigler (op. cit.)[22]—all of them in leading journals. Savage (ibid.), in particular, concentrates on the mathematics of *Foundations* and observes, correctly in my view, that "In this book…[*mathematics*] is almost exclusively employed to *deduce qualitative* conclusions from *qualitative* assumptions" (ibid.: 201; italics added). This is most evident in PAS's propositions, conclusions and possible generalizations regarding the stability of dynamical systems, in a qualitative sense:

> [I]n the absence of *precise* quantitative data [the economist] must infer analytically the *qualitative* direction of movement of *a complex system.* What little success [the economist] has hitherto achieved can be classified *in large part* under two headings: (1) theorems proceeding from the assumption of *maximizing behaviour* on the part of firms or individuals and (2) *stability conditions* relating to the interaction between economic units. (PAS 1947: 258; italics added)

PAS was never tired of emphasizing the importance of initial conditions in the stability of generalized—i.e. even nonlinear—dynamical systems. Thus, implicitly, the future—and past, buried in the works of Poincaré and Cartwright-Littlewood—notions of stability, qualitatively conceived, of nonlinear dynamical systems, sensitive to initial conditions.

Figure 1, adapted from Ekeland (1988: 74), shows much—not all—of PAS's concept of stability and *SDIC*[23] of nonlinear dynamical systems. In view of *SDIC*, the (nonlinear) dynamical system, initialized at **P**, can lead to two trajectories that, in the *long-run*, diverge from each other (like the thick blue curve and the dotted curve). However, this dynamical system will also have trajectories (like the thin curve), although respecting *SDIC*,

[22]The reviews by Tintner and Stigler are in the same journal, but different numbers. It may be interesting, in this context, to mention that Hart (op. cit.) and Metzler (ibid.) are in the same issue of the *American Economic Review*—the former succeeds the latter!

[23]*SDIC*: Sensitive Dependence on Initial Conditions.

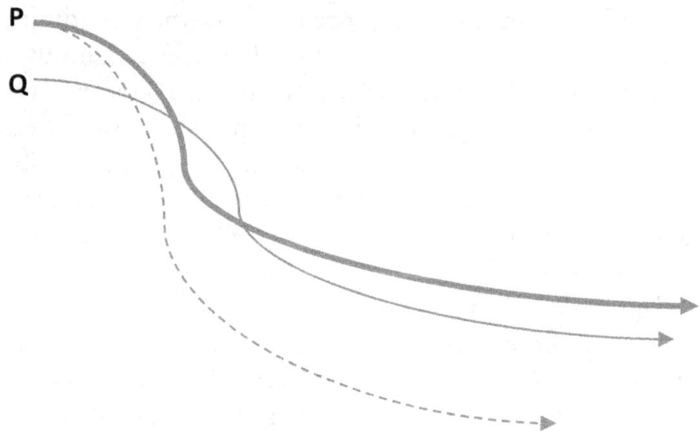

Fig. 1 Instability and approximate stability

will, in the long-run, be approximately (depending on the *quantitative* definition used) close to the thick curve. In other words, even though starting from an initial condition slightly different from **P**, say **Q**, it will, in a sense mathematically[24] definable, stay approximately close to the thick curve, starting from **Q**. One loses the possibility of exact short-term prediction of individual trajectories but gains long-term prediction feasibilities of a *whole* system of trajectories.

The notions of instability and approximate stability for dynamical systems subject to *SDIC*, summarized in the dynamics shown in Fig. 1, are based on Anosov's results of 1951 (which were inspired by Stephen Smale's invited lecture at Kiev in 1961). This is a perfectly appropriate way to honour Samuelson (cf., PAS 1986c). Thus, combining what Metzler (ibid.) calls the "greatest contribution to economics"—i.e. stability of a dynamic system—with Savage's characterization of the qualitative analysis of mathematical systems, one gets the above figurative and explanatory definitions implied in PAS's notions of the duality between stability and meaningful theorems—i.e. the Correspondence principle—as valid, but in terms of long-term feasibility of accurate (interval) predictions.

[24]Classically, constructively, infinitesimally, non-standardly or whatever mathematical framework one desires to use!

Perhaps PAS erred in not being specific about the time dimension of the dynamical system's predictability; but that does not mean his concepts are mathematically evanescent. PAS did not, however, err in the vistas of mathematical analysis that its future posed; he was fully aware of his own human short-term possibilities and the long-term possibilities of conceptual developments in mathematics. These are particularly evident in chapters 367 and 368 in PAS (1986b, 1986c), but it is also evident that he was constrained by the Gibbsian and (for want of a better name) Whitehead-Russell views of mathematics and logic, and the identity of the latter, by way of the use of classical mathematics, with language.

This did not entail a development of formal language theory, in the Chomskian sense, towards the mathematics of computability theory; nor did the role of theorems and proofs in the kind of mathematics he used in economics, lead to ideas on the alternative concepts of proof—or even the kind of mathematics he can use, in formalizing economics, beyond a future which, for example, emphasized Bourbakism—i.e. topology (mainly its combinatorial variety, leading to a specific kind of fixed-point theorem), group theory, manifold theory, etc. and non-standard analysis of the Abraham Robinson variety. He remained in the time warp that Bourbakism was in logic (see Matthias 1992). PAS did not foresee developments, at least, in the varieties of proof[25] (cf. Abramsky 2015).

I do not think this invalidates the mathematical and logical framework within which PAS formalizes dynamic economic concepts. On the other hand, I agree with Mas-Colell (1985) and Balasko (2009) that PAS (1947) is a culmination of a research programme in the application of calculus, from Cournot, via Marshall, Walras, Fisher, Pareto, Edgeworth and Hicks. It is a culmination with a continuation—say via a mastery of Spivak (1965) and Abraham and Marsden (1978)—with a resurrection of the fertility of calculus in formalizing economic concepts at the frontiers. This is, surely, what PAS (1986a: especially p. 849) means by *Newtonian Paradise Regained*.

The supreme knowledge PAS had in the mathematics of dynamical systems, of the time, and their applications in the foundational development

[25]Clower (op. cit., p. 5; italics added) is surely incorrect to state that: "If the argument is valid, *one proof should suffice*".

of economics, when *Foundations* was published,[26] became part of the core of analytical and mathematical macrodynamics for at least the proverbial Golden Age of (American) Keynesianism. Macroeconomics after *Foundations* became a fundamentally analytical subject.

4 The *Inexactness* of Macrodynamic Multiplier-Accelerator (M-A) Models

> In any sufficiently rich system
> including the present mire
> statements are possible
> which can neither be proved
> nor refuted within the system.
>
> *Those are the statements*
> *to grasp, and pull!*
>
> —(*Homage to Gödel* by Hans Magnus Enzensberger, translated from the original German by Enzensberger; italics added)

This first part of this section is partly historical, in which I deal with four aspects: the role of Harrod in dynamics, in general, and in M-A models, in particular; the Frischian framework for macrodynamics; the roles of Keynes and Hansen in making the M-A formalization a growth-cycle model; and the distinction between discrete- and continuous-time M-A models. The latter two parts are technical.

Let be begin with the declaration of what I call *inexactness*[27] in the macrodynamics of the M-A model by Samuelson in his Nobel Prize Lecture (PAS 1972: 258–259; italics added):

> My point in bringing up the *accelerator-multiplier* here is that it provides a typical example of *a dynamic system* that can in *no useful sense* be related to *a maximum problem* ... The fact that *the accelerator-multiplier cannot be related to maximizing* takes its toll in terms of the intractability of the

[26] See Samuelson (1998).

[27] I use the word inexactness in contrast to the way it is used in PAS (1958); hence, Enzensberger's '*statements to grasp, and pull*', against the backdrop of Gödel's (second) incompleteness theorem.

> analysis … [P]erhaps the hardest part of my 1947 *Foundations of Economic Analysis* had to deal with the statics and dynamics of nonmaximum systems.

As both Goodwin—in private correspondence with me—and Samuelson (PAS: 1939b: 795) emphasized, Roy Harrod's intuition was far ahead of his (technical abilities for) "reasoned conclusions".[28] His notions of dynamics never went beyond that which one obtains from classical mechanics (see, e.g., Harrod 1939: 14, fn. 1; 1937). Harrod did not have *any* understanding—either conceptual or technical (as he acknowledged to Tinbergen in Harrod ibid.)—of the nonlinear dynamics of Poincaré, van der Pol, Birkhoff, Levinson or von Kármán, or even Lotka, Volterra and Kolmogorov. Samuelson, through PAS (1947, 1967, 1971), makes clear that he is fully aware of the classical mathematical framework of the nonlinear dynamics of the above eight. I would even venture to say that Harrod's understanding of, and distinction between, statics and dynamics did not transcend that which was in the contemporary textbooks on these subjects by A. S. Ramsey.[29]

So, it is with surprise and bewilderment I read Heertje and Heemeijer (2002),[30] their reflections on PAS (1939a)[31] and propositions on Harrod. There are many inaccuracies in their paper, but I will point out only the glaring ones:

1. The (alleged) PAS M-A model they describe with the three equations and the fourth equilibrium relation, on p. 209, is *not* a differential model; Samuelson's reply (in his 87th year!), PAS (2002: 221), makes this very clear;
2. Obviously, these authors are *not* aware of Tinbergen (1937: especially p. 90), where it is shown that Harrod's model of the cycle in

---

[28] Quoted in Heertje and Heemeijer (2002: 214), but without a page source!

[29] A. S. Ramsey was the father of Frank Ramsey. His textbooks on statics and dynamics were those from which I was taught these subjects in high school in 'old' Colombo, now over fifty-five years ago.

[30] It is only because of PAS (2002) that I discuss here their paper. There are many other articles by Harrod (1936, 1937, 1939, 1948) that are equally worthy of comment, but Samuelson's role in them is minimal or non-existent (to the best of my knowledge).

[31] Or PAS (1939a).

> Harrod (1936), due to it being a (linear) first-order differential equation, cannot give rise to oscillations.

There are other—and many—infelicities in this paper, but let that pass.[32]

As for the Frischian framework for macrodynamics, in PAS (1974: 10; italics added) Samuelson confesses:

> In leaving Frisch's work of the 1930s on stochastic difference, differential and other functional equations, let me point out that a great man's work can, in its impact on lesser men, have bad as well good effects. Thus, by 1940, *Metzler and I* as graduate students at Harvard fell into the dogma…that all economic business-cycle models should have *damped* roots. *We* accepted Frisch's criticism of the Kalecki procedure of imposing constraints on his parameter-estimating equations so that roots would be neither damped nor undamped; to explain Kalecki's supposed constancy-of-amplitude-of-capitalism's-fluctuations, *Frisch's mechanism of exogenous shocks* seemed preferable.

Fourteen years later, in PAS (1988b: 17, fn. 2),[33] it became:

> I, and…Lloyd Metzler…took it more or less as a dogma that our dynamic systems should be 'stable', in the sense of having damped rather than anti-damped characteristic roots … [F]rom 1937 on, I rejected the multiplier-accelerator explosive exponentials that kept thrusting themselves at me in my research notebooks. My effect on Hansen in this regard was baneful.

Samuelson, in PAS (ibid.: especially Section 6), gave up the dogma; this may well be regarded as an atonement for the baneful effect on Hansen's stubborn refusal to accept the dogma, Frisch notwithstanding!

The vacuous nature of Frisch's mechanism of exogenous shocks generating observed oscillations, for the chosen values of the parameters and

---

[32]The authors use "none" and "all", in conjunction with "others", and given that the relevant time specified by them includes Kalecki (and the early Tinbergen of the ship-building cycle), makes their assertion on external shocks inaccurate (even Frisch's well-known—for all the wrong reasons—model in the Cassel Festschrift, does not oscillate, even with external shocks, as Zambelli (2007) has shown convincingly.

[33]Interestingly, in Section 9, titled, '*The road not taken*'!

initial conditions, has been amply demonstrated by Zambelli (2007).[34] However, the caveat(s) are cogently provided by PAS (2005),[35] in which, in the capacity of a generous referee at age 90, Samuelson wrote (bold and italics added): "More important at this date would be to show that *no* such [Frisch Mechanism] can ***exist***. (*That* is neither true ***nor*** I guess ***claimed by the author to be true***)".

The proof[36] of non-existence of such a Frisch Mechanism is impossible—unless the dynamical stochastic processes that it can give rise to, for given characterization of the mechanism, is well-defined (or definable). For now, such a definition of the entirety of possible stochastic processes that a Frisch Mechanism can generate is impossible.[37] It can be stated as a theorem, in honour of Samuelson, as follows:

Samuelson's Frisch Mechanism Theorem A Frisch Mechanism for the generation of a stochastic process, characterizing the macrodynamics of M-A models, is impossible.

Proof A Frisch Mechanism for the generation of any stochastic process is formally equivalent to an Oracle Turing Machine. It is then straightforward to derive a result on the non-deterministic halting problem for an Oracle Turing Machine (see also footnotes 40 and 41).

Remark The proof, as it stands, is incomplete for at least four reasons:

i. Where, and why, it is non-constructive, is not specified;
ii. The notion of Oracle Computations, and its relation with Turing Reducibility is not developed;
iii. The way non-determinism encapsulates stochastic and probabilistic formulations of sequences needs to be exactly defined; and

---

[34] As pointed out in fn. 32 above.

[35] I am greatly indebted to Professor Zambelli for providing me access to this letter/referee's report and also for giving me full permission to quote from it.

[36] I cannot envisage a constructive impossibility proof of this sort!

[37] This is akin to the proof of the halting problem for Turing Machines, based on the definability of algorithms, encapsulated by, for example, Hilbert's tenth problem (see Hilbert 1900: 21).

iv. The observation by Maury Osborne regarding nonstationarity and the way it relates to any kind of scientific computation of real sequences, has to be considered.

Detailed consideration of these issues will take us beyond the stunted Frisch Mechanism and Samuelson's own interests. Moreover, the proportion of pages of the overall chapter to the size of the full proof may not be useful.[38]

Samuelson, again in PAS (2005), delineates three possibilities for macrodynamics:

A. The M-A model(s) of PAS (1939a, b) in terms of damped linear difference equations;
B. Kaleckian (early) dynamics based on coefficient values that lead to centre-type dynamics;
C. The single limit cycle model (essentially of Goodwin 1951).

Figures 2 and 3, summarize the macrodynamics of (i) and (ii) above; (iii) cannot, even for a single limit cycle, be summarized in a figure in the coefficients plane. The general distinction to be respected, and observed, is that between (some kind of) linearity and nonlinearity. Moreover, the single limit cycle (in, say, Goodwin (ibid.: 15, Fig. 9) is entirely due to a truncated Taylor series approximation of a mixed difference-differential equation[39]; higher-order approximations of Taylor series expansions lead to a multitude of cycles, not necessarily finite (see Strotz et al. 1953).

Before I return to PAS (1988b), and the generalized Keynes–Hansen–Samuelson model—Samuelson calls it the *KHS model*—which is supposed to integrate Keynes (1937) and Hansen (1939) with the single limit cycle of the Goodwin (1951) model of the business cycle, I would like to point out the economic dubiousness of a (linear) discrete-time M-A model. In Goodwin (1989: 250–251; italics added), he wonders:

---

[38]These will be discussed, and elaborated, elsewhere.

[39]Of Eq. (5c), on p. 12, of Goodwin (ibid.), [y: income (real); O_A: "sum of the autonomous outlays β and l"; θ : "one half the construction time of new equipment"; $d\varphi(\dot{y})/d\dot{y}$: "is the acceleration coefficient". This gives: $\epsilon\dot{y}(t+\theta)+(1-\alpha)y(t+\theta)=O_A(t+\theta)+\varphi[\dot{y}(t)]$

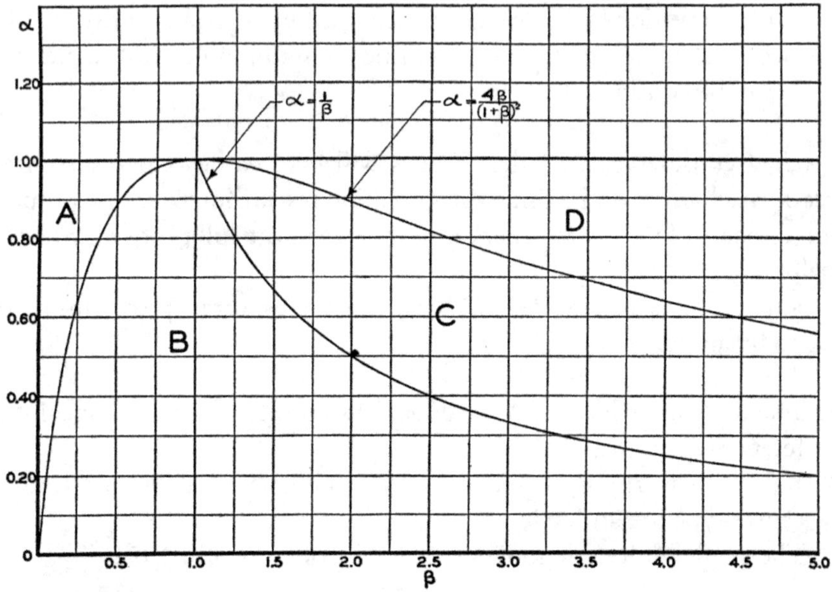

Fig. 2 Stability diagram for a linear difference equation (*Source* Samuelson [1939a: 78])

The problem with *difference equations* is: *What do we mean by them*? Is time a continuous or a discrete variable? *Does one assume that nothing happens between t and t + 1*? This is grossly unrealistic, but the alternative involved in a finite difference with continuous time, means horrendous difficulties. I find it acceptable *only if* we regard such *aggregative macromodels* not as realism, but as illustrative of the nature of the problem and indicative of possible *solution types.* With that proviso, we are then dealing with a discrete time dynamic model. It has in recent time become known, what was unsuspected in the great number of 'period' analyses, that frightful problems arise even with the simplest of such models. Such an endogenous, completely deterministic model…can give rise to highly erratic, totally unpredictable behaviour. [I]ts solution may *depend on initial conditions*; it can bifurcate from oscillatory to monotone behaviour and then bifurcate back again as also *from stability to instability.* This even in the absence of exogenous shocks, the solution can be erratic and quite unpredictable.

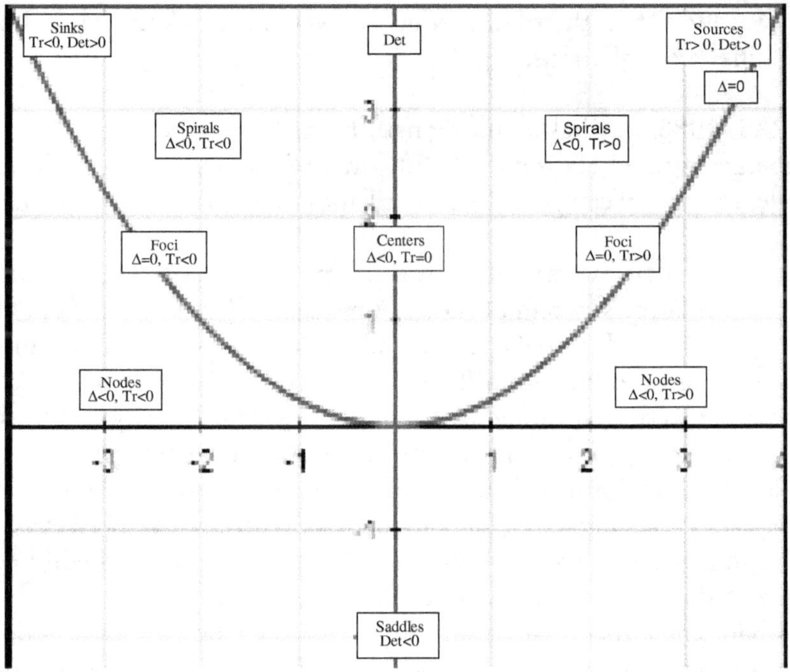

Fig. 3 Coefficients space of the phase portrait of a linearized nonlinear dynamics (*Source* Based on Hirsch and Smale [1974: 96])

Four Samuelsonian remarks, based on the above quote, may well be in order:

I. In a sense, the first part of this observation is a vindication of Harrod's disdain for lags and his relentless emphasis on differential equations, for the modelling of cycles and growth (I do not think he ever succeeded in integrating the two into a growth cycle).
II. The very last sentence of the Goodwin quote is the substance of what I have called Samuelson's Frisch Mechanism Theorem.
III. The substance of the penultimate sentence is that which was depicted in Fig. 1 and explained below it.
IV. Aggregative macro(dynamic) models, studied as solution types for illustrative problems is what was practiced by Samuelson—following Lundberg (1937: Chapter 8)—as studies of model sequences. He

> was lucky that the model sequences were for M–A models of linear difference equations.

In PAS (1988b: 8; italics in original), he makes the point that[40]: "[A]s Tinbergen warned Harrod in 1937, without time lags a *crude* multiplier-accelerator model can generate no oscillations but rather only exponential trends".

It is clear that by "crude" Samuelson means that Tinbergen's formalization of Harrod's system of the M-A model in Harrod (1936) is a first-order ordinary differential equation; adding time lags to the crude model makes it a linear difference-differential equation of appropriate order, i.e. depending on the nature and extent of the lags. The linearity makes every aspect of its dynamics (almost) completely characterizable (particularly if the lags are finite or its effects, if infinite, converge monotonely). On the other hand, referring to the KHS model, Samuelson observes (PAS: ibid.; italics in original): "For the KHS model it…*matters little* whether I use *differential equations* or *finite-lag difference equations*".

Whatever it is that "matters little for the KHS model", this proposition is true only if the differential equations or the finite-lag difference equations are linear. It is not true for the KHS–Goodwin M-A model, generating a single limit cycle.

The KHS-M-A version of the Goodwin-inspired single limit cycle model:

> The pure KHS-M-A model is a supposed integration of economic progress – in the form of stagnation – and fluctuations in (national) income (and unemployment), based on Keynes (1937) and Hansen (1939). In other words, it is Samuelson's integration of growth and fluctuations, i.e. growth cycles, where the former is of the order of decades and the latter of a time scale between the Schumpeterian Kitchin and Juglar cycles—approximately between inventory cycles of duration extending to a little beyond two years and the industrial cycle of (advanced) economies of an approximate period

[40]Referring to Tinbergen (1937: 90). However, see also Harrod (1937), especially the role of lags in his theory of the cycle, generated by multiplier-accelerator interaction. This letter to Tinbergen also reflects Harrod's ignorance of the mathematical properties of formal differential equations, the (formal) distinction between linearity and nonlinearity and that between difference and differential equations.

> length of ten years. I should observe that it should also be an integration of Keynes (1930), as long as its claims of being a growth cycle model is to be taken seriously. However, in spite of claims to the contrary – like the incorporation of Modigliani's life-cycle savings hypothesis to replace Harrod's purely exogenous propensity to save (shared with all the early neoclassical growth frameworks) – the KHS model (in any generalization) treats growth exogenously, especially in generating a limit cycle fluctuation in income and unemployment.

Therefore, I identify the key difference in the mathematics of PAS (ibid.) and the original PAS (1939a, b) as the transition to (nonlinear ordinary) differential equations modelling from a reliance on linear difference equations; as mentioned, almost in passing, thus downplaying its significance, Samuelson assumes (1988b: 4; bold and italics added): "What remains [in KHS] of the Harrodian razor's-edge is the inherent *anti-damped* instability of a laissez-faire equilibrium based on accelerator-multiplier ***differential equations***".

The significant economic change in assumptions (from a KHS model) is from a tight accelerator (ibid.: 8, Eq. 1) to a flexible accelerator (ibid.: 12, Eq. 15). These two assumptions—one mathematical, the other economic—generate the equilibrium single limit cycle fluctuation of the KHS model, but does not make the growth path endogenous. This—whether stagnation due to limits of population rise, or growth due to the obverse of this and the ensuing rate of accumulation[41]—remains exogenous (Fig. 4).

The only ordinary differential equation model of (macrodynamic) endogenous growth, but not necessarily generating a single, locally unstable, limit cycle, I know of is that of Nikaido (1987), who concludes:

> [C]apitalist economies are capable of evolution over time, but inevitably in the form of *cyclical growth*. This is not a pure cyclical movement superimposed on an autonomous growth trend, nor is the endogenously determined

[41] As Keynes (1930: Part II, p. 98; italics added) concludes: "[O]ur destination of economic bliss will be governed by four things — *our power to control population*, our determination to avoid wars and civil dissensions, our willingness to entrust to science the direction of those matters which are properly the concern of science, and *the rate of accumulation* as fixed by the margin between our production and our consumption; of which the last will easily look after itself, *given* the first three".

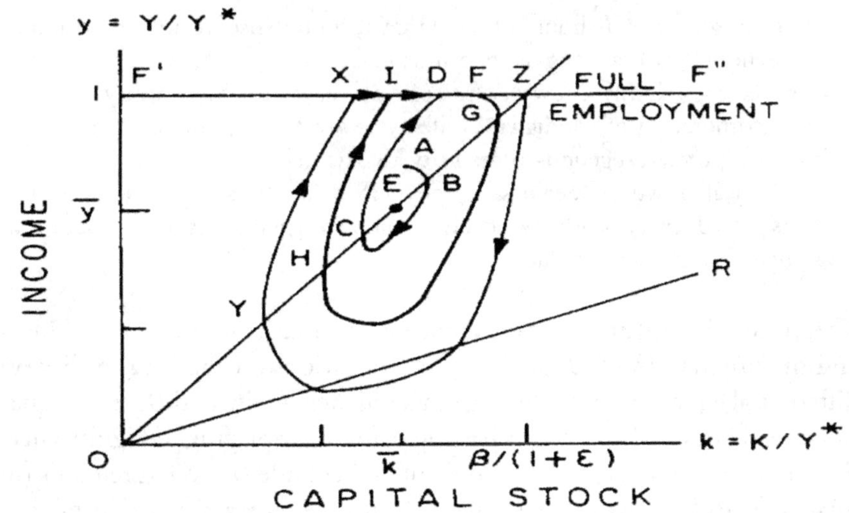

Fig. 4 The (one-sided) single, locally unstable, limit cycle (*Source* PAS [1988b: 13, Fig. 3])[42]

growth trend without cycles. Rather it ensues from the instability inherent in the workings of the capitalist economies as an entangled complex of growth and fluctuations mutually acting as causes and effects. (ibid.: 442–443; italics in original)

Thus, Nikaido – at least in this article – remains agnostic between Schumpeter's vision that "fluctuations are a form that any growth takes" (Ragupathy et al. 2013: 124) in an industrially capitalist economy and Hudson's precept that "growth is an inevitable consequence of the macrodynamic fluctuations of a capitalist economy". (ibid.)[43]

---

[42]The single, one-sided, locally unstable, limit cycle, in the phase space of capital and income, moving along the ceiling of full employment [given by XIDFZ], is shown as the trajectory, XZY. The phase space is reduced to a timeless ratio of $\frac{Y}{Y*} = y$ and $\frac{K}{Y*} = k$, where $y = n$. The latter assumption makes the growth part exogenous! I think the proper way to pay homage to Keynes and Hansen is to make sure that the [single] locally unstable limit cycle does not hit the full employment ceiling. After all, both Keynes and Hansen—especially after Hansen became the American Keynes—were of the unshakeable faith that a free enterprise economy will always be in a phase space with unemployment (see also PAS ibid.: 12, fn. 1).

[43]I am personally persuaded that Hudson allows non-industrial economies to be of a capitalist nature; cf. Ragupathy et al. (2013: especially p. 124).

5 Concluding Thoughts on a Universal Scientist

> Dynamics is a multidisciplinary study in mathematics and physics … In physics, *belief* is a strong principle: we *believe* in the laws of physics or we *believe* in the results of an *experiment. Proof* is more the concern of mathematicians; *logic* and *mathematics* enable the *possibility of proof*. When we work with *simulations* of *dynamical systems, question of belief and proof become confused.* (Weissert 1997: 133; italics added)

Paul Samuelson was a mathematical economist, in the mould of a mathematical physicist; he was neither a pure mathematician, nor a physicist, pure or applied. He believed in many of the observed facts of market capitalist macrodynamics; those he believed in, he tried to formulate as propositions or theorems—and thus, tried to prove them. Samuelson was admirably consistent in his search for rigour, in proving these propositions or theorems, but was fully aware that he failed in this endeavour.

He believed in the truth of the propositions or theorems about the market system that he formulated, but never displayed any dogmatism in defending the truth of them, if the proofs were shown to be mathematically incorrect or inadequate. Samuelson read widely, and absorbed deeply, the classical and neoclassical economists—Smith, Ricardo, Malthus, Marx and the two Mills; Jevons, Marshall, Walras, Pareto, Edgeworth, Fisher and Wicksell and many more; he was assiduous in mastering the economic works of his immediate predecessors and contemporaries—Schumpeter, Leontief, Robertson, Chamberlin, Keynes, Hansen and Hawtrey, but also Sraffa, Joan Robinson and Kahn, too—and, thus, also critically.

Samuelson was extremely generous to those younger than himself, especially when he disagreed with them. He neither did experiments with the market system, to test some of its properties, but studied, mostly theoretically, based on falsifiable hypotheses, the actual functioning of the market system, and extracted, in a Bayesian fashion, revised hypotheses, always relying on the principles of macro and micro that were enunciated in *Foundations*, i.e. maximization and equilibria for microeconomics, and stability of dynamical systems for aggregative economics (macrodynamics).

However, to the best of my knowledge, he did not ever even try to simulate the market economy or any aspect of it; so the kinds of questions asked by Weissert (ibid.), on the epistemology of simulation, were never asked in the Samuelsonian oeuvre. He was, of course, almost passionately interested in epistemological questions, but he was not averse to suspending hypothesis formation in the mathematical sense to try to answer them. His knowledge and understanding[44] of the philosophy underpinning the classics in economics was most helpful in these matters.

As pointed out above, he more or less specialized in classical mathematics that had at its core the differential and integral calculus—perhaps in the mould of a Hardy or Smirnov—of pure mathematics, in the physics of mathematics, so that he was comfortable with, say, Birkhoff on dynamical systems and familiar with something like the Hilbert-Courant two volumes on the *Methods of Mathematical Physics.* In applying this kind of mathematics and mathematical physics, he was explicitly influenced by E. B. Wilson and, implicitly, by Willard Gibbs.

Personally, I have only two regrets. Samuelson was a pioneer in the mathematics of Lotka–Volterra, struggle-for-existence, literature—as is evident from PAS (1967, 1971). His knowledge of this literature extended to a familiarity with the Kolmogorov (1936) classic. Kolmogorov inspired a definition of the structural stability of dynamical systems (in the phase plane).[45] Obviously, Samuelson was also fully aware, and familiar, with the economics of Goodwin (1967). Given all this, my first regret is, as an example of PAS (1985), he did not use his impeccable knowledge to model the KHS system, as giving rise to endogenous growth cycles.[46]

---

[44]Warts and all—*again,* I nearly said. Samuelson engaged with so-called specialists in classical and neoclassical economics, all the way from the mid-1930s to the end of his life. In my opinion, his stance on new classical economics was, at best sceptical; at worst, dismissive. He was critical of Chicago economics, so much so that, when he spoke to me, by phone, in early January 1987, when I had, for the first time, crossed the Atlantic and taken up a Visiting Professorship at UCLA, he asked (the bold in the word and phrase reflects the way he talked): "What is a person like **you**, doing in **a place like that**!" The composition of the Department of Economics at UCLA prompted it to be known, to many, as the University of Chicago at Los Angeles!

[45]Many macrodynamic models—by Yasui, Morishima, Ichimura, Rose, Schinasi, Chang and Smyth, for example—formalized as phase-plane models, assumed (implicitly and explicitly) structural stability of such systems (proceeding to use non-constructive proofs of the Poincaré-Bendixson theorem to demonstrate the existence of cycles in the plane).

[46]Growth is an exogenous factor, in the Harrod-Domar sense, in Goodwin (ibid).

My second regret, which is related to the first, at least mathematically, in the sense of interesting hypothesis formation of the behaviour of the stability (local and global) of dynamical systems, is that Samuelson does not seem to have been interested in Kolmogorov–Arnold–Moser (KAM) theories and theorems (see Abraham and Marsden 1978, particularly the appendix translation of Kolmogorov's 1954 lecture, Scott Dumas 2014 and Weissert 1997). Since the essence of KAM theory is to analyse the persistence of quasi-periodic motions under perturbations, it is eminently suitable for a Samuelsonian analysis of aggregate economic dynamics, especially those in which ergodicity is prevented and invariant tori can be observed.

Samuelson's esteem for Fermi, Kolmogorov[47] and Ulam is both legendary and well-recorded. His understanding of the mathematics of KAM, without any serious need for updating the classical mathematics of dynamical systems, would have been easy. The application of the dynamical hypothesis and theorems of KAM to the macrodynamics of *Foundations* may have shunted economists from concentrating on the economics of Bourbakian mathematics, quite apart from stimulating encouragement to simulational hypothesis testing of the stability of novel dynamical systems, thus avoiding the current dominance of experimental behavioural economics.

Paul Samuelson was a universal economist—he was interested in, and contributed to, every aspect of economics (of his time), but always within the framework he defined and explored in *Foundations.* I will always remember him, his many-faceted contributions, his generosity and his unsullied humanity, as I remember Rumi's verse, in his *Rubaiyat*:

> I sought a soul in the sea,
> And found a coral there;
> Beneath the foam for me,

[47]The Marshallian Samuelson may approve Shiryaev (2000: 5; italics added), quoting Kolmogorov: "In mathematics, I [Kolmogorov] was one of the first in my class, but *the principal more serious scientific passions* for me *in school* [the E. A. Repman private gymnasium] were initially *biology* and then Russian history". In relation to the topic of my first regret, see also Sigmund (2007). In fact, both of my regrets have, as a common element, Kolmogorov! The mathematics of population dynamics, as developed by Kolmogorov, must be embedded in KAM theory. In this way, macrodynamics can—must—be unified with biology and mathematics.

An ocean was all laid bare.
Into my heart's night,
Along a narrow way,
I groped; and lo! the light,
An infinite land of day.

References

Abraham, R. and J.E. Marsden, with the assistance of T. Ratiu and R. Cushman (1978) *Foundations of Mechanics.* Second edition, revised, enlarged and reset. Redwood City, CA, Addison-Wesley Publishing.

Abramsky, S. (2015) "Arrow's Theorem by Arrow Theory," in Å. Hirvonen, J. Kontinn, R. Kossak and A. Villaveces (eds.) *Logic Without Borders.* Berlin, Walter de Gruyter: 15–29.

Allen, R.G.D. (1949) "The Mathematical Foundations of Economic Theory," *Quarterly Journal of Economics,* 63: 111–127.

Balasko, Y. (2009) *The Equilibrium Manifold: Postmodern Developments in the Theory of General Economic Equilibrium.* Cambridge, MA, The MIT Press.

Barnett, W.A. (2004) "An Interview with Paul A. Samuelson: MD Interview," *Macroeconomic Dynamics,* 8: 519–542.

Baumol, W.J. (1949) "Relaying the Foundations," *Economica,* New Series, 16: 159–168.

Blanchard, O.J. and S. Fischer (1989) *Lectures on Macroeconomics.* Cambridge, MA, The MIT Press.

Boulding, K.E. (1948) "Samuelson's *Foundations*: The Role of Mathematics in Economics," *Journal of Political Economy,* 56: 187–199.

Carter, C.F. (1950) "Review of *Foundations of Economic Analysis,* by P.A. Samuelson," *Economic Journal,* 60: 351–355.

Clower, R.W. (1996) "On Truth in Teaching Macroeconomics," in D. Vaz and K.V. Vellupillai (eds.) *Inflation, Institutions and Information: Essays in Honour of Axel Leijonhufvud.* London, Macmillan: 35–61.

Cord, R.A. (2009) *The Keynesian Revolution: A Research School Analysis.* PhD dissertation, Cambridge University.

Day, R.H. (1983) "The Emergence of Chaos from Classical Economic Growth," *Quarterly Journal of Economics,* 98: 201–213.

Ekeland, I. (1988) *Mathematics and the Unexpected.* Chicago, University of Chicago Press.

Flood, M.M (1950) "Review of *Foundations of Economic Analysis*, by P.A. Samuelson," *Bulletin of the American Mathematical Society*, 56: 266–267.

Gale, D. (1972) "On Equilibrium Growth of Dynamic Economic Models," in R.H. Day and S.M. Robinson (eds.) *Mathematical Topics in Economic Theory and Computation*. Philadelphia, PA, Society for Industrial and Applied Mathematics: 84–98.

Gans, J.S. and G.B. Shepherd (1994) "How Are the Mighty Fallen: Rejected Classic Articles by Leading Economists," *Journal of Economic Perspectives*, 8: 165–179.

Goodwin, R.M. (1951) "The Nonlinear Accelerator and the Persistence of Business Cycles," *Econometrica*, 19: 1–17.

Goodwin, R.M. (1967) "A Growth Cycle," in C.H. Feinstein (ed.) *Socialism, Capitalism and Economic Growth: Essays Presented to Maurice Dobb*. Cambridge, Cambridge University Press: 54–58.

Goodwin, R.M. (1989) "Kalecki's Economic Dynamics: A Personal View," in M. Sebastiani (ed.) *Kalecki's Relevance Today*. New York, St. Martin's Press: 249–251.

Hales, T.C. (2014) "Mathematics in the Age of the Turing Machine," in R. Downey (ed.) *Turing's Legacy: Developments from Turing's Ideas in Logic*. Cambridge, Cambridge University Press: 253–298.

Hansen, A.H. (1939) "Economic Progress and Declining Population Growth," *American Economic Review*, 29: 1–15.

Harrod, R.F. (1936) *The Trade Cycle: An Essay*. Oxford, Clarendon Press.

Harrod, R.F. (1937) "Letter to Tinbergen," 1 July 1937.

Harrod, R.F. (1939) "An Essay in Dynamic Theory," *Economic Journal*, 49: 14–33.

Harrod, R.F. (1948) *Towards a Dynamic Economics: Some Recent Developments of Economic Theory and their Applications to Policy*. London, St. Martin's Press, Macmillan.

Hart, A.G. (1948) "Review of *Economics: An Introductory Analysis*, by P.A. Samuelson," *American Economic Review*, 38: 910–915.

Heertje, A. and P. Heemeijer (2002) "On the Origin of Samuelson's Multiplier-Accelerator Model," *History of Political Economy*, 34: 207–218.

Hilbert, D. (1900) *Mathematical Problems*. Lecture delivered before the International Congress of Mathematicians, Paris, 8 August.

Hirsch, M.W. and S. Smale (1974) *Differential Equations, Dynamical Systems, and Linear Algebra*. New York, Academic Press.

Keynes, J.M. (1930) "Economic Possibilities for our Grandchildren," *Nation and Athenaeum*, 46, Part I: 36–37, 11 October and Part II: 96-98, 18 October.

Reprinted in D. Moggridge (ed.) (1972) *Essays in Persuasion, Volume IX, The Collected Writings of John Maynard Keynes*. London, Palgrave Macmillan: 321–332.

Keynes, J.M. (1937) "Some Economic Consequences of a Declining Population," *Eugenics Review*, 29: 13–17.

Kolmogorov, A. (1936) "Sulla Teoria di Volterra della Lotta per l'Esistenza," *Giornale dell'Istituto Italiano degli Attuari*, 7: 74–80.

Lindahl, E. (1939) *Studies in the Theory of Money and Capital*. London, George Allen & Unwin.

Lundberg, E. (1937) *Studies in the Economic Theory of Expansion*. London, P.S. King & Son.

Mas-Colell, A. (1985) *The Theory of General Economic Equilibrium: A Differentiable Approach*. Cambridge, Cambridge University Press.

Mathias, A.R.D. (1992) "The Ignorance of Bourbaki," *The Mathematical Intelligencer*, 14: 4–13.

Metzler, L.A. et al. (eds.) (1948a) *Income, Employment and Public Policy: Essays in Honor of Alvin H. Hansen*. New York, W.W. Norton.

Metzler, L.A. (1948b) "Review of *Foundations of Economic Analysis*, by P.A. Samuelson," *American Economic Review*, 38: 905–910.

Nikaido, H. (1987) "No Growth, No Fluctuations," in G.R. Feiwel (ed.) *Arrow and the Foundations of the Theory of Economic Policy*. London, Macmillan: 421–445.

Ragupathy, V., S. Zambelli and K. Vela Velupillai (2013) "A Non-Linear Model of the Trade Cycle: Mathematical Reflections on Hugh Hudson's Classic," *Australian Economic Papers*, 52: 115–125.

Samuelson, P.A. (1939a) "Interactions Between the Multiplier Analysis and the Principle of Acceleration," *Review of Economics and Statistics*, 21: 75–78.

Samuelson, P.A. (1939b) "A Synthesis of the Principle of Acceleration and the Multiplier," *Journal of Political Economy*, 47: 786–797.

Samuelson, P.A. (1947) *Foundations of Economic Analysis*. Harvard, MA, Harvard University Press.

Samuelson, P.A. (1948) "The Simple Mathematics of Income Determination," in L.A. Metzler et al. (eds.) *Income, Employment and Public Policy: Essays in Honor of Alvin H. Hansen*. New York, W. W. Norton: 133–145.

Samuelson, P.A. (1952a) [1966] "'Dynamic Process Analysis' (Howard Ellis, ed., *A Survey of Contemporary Economics*. Homewood, IL, Richard D. Irwin, 1952'" in J. Stiglitz (ed.) *The Collected Scientific Papers of Paul A. Samuelson, Volume 1*. Cambridge, MA, The MIT Press: 590–625.

Samuelson, P.A. (1952b) "Economic Theory and Mathematics—An Appraisal," *American Economic Review*, 42: 56–66.

Samuelson, P.A. (1955) *Economics: An Introductory Analysis.* Third edition. New York, McGraw-Hill.

Samuelson, P.A. (1958) "An Exact Consumption-Loan Model of Interest with or Without the Social Contrivance of Money," *Journal of Political Economy*, 66: 467–482.

Samuelson, P.A. (1959) "Alvin Hansen and the Interactions Between the Multiplier Analysis and the Principle of Acceleration," *Review of Economics and Statistics*, 41: 183–184.

Samuelson, P.A. (1967) "A Universal Cycle," *Operations Research Verfahren*, 3: 307–320.

Samuelson, P.A. (1971) "Generalized Predator-Prey Oscillations in Ecological and Economic Equilibrium," *Proceedings of the National Academy of Sciences of the United States of America*, 68: 980–983.

Samuelson, P.A. (1972) "Maximum Principles in Analytical Economics," *American Economic Review* (Nobel Lecture), 62: 249–262.

Samuelson, P.A. (1974) "Remembrances of Frisch," *European Economic Review*, 5: 7–23.

Samuelson, P.A. (1983) "Comment [on Axel Leijonhufvud's 'What Would Keynes Have Thought of Rational Expectations?']," in D. Worswick and J. Trevithick (eds.) *Keynes and the Modern World.* Cambridge, Cambridge University Press: 212–217.

Samuelson, P.A. (1985) "Modes of Thought in Economics and Biology," *American Economic Review*, 75: 166–172.

Samuelson, P.A. (1986a) "Introduction to the enlarged edition of *Foundations of Economic Analysis*, Cambridge, MA: Harvard University Press, 1983, xv–xxvi," in K. Crowley (ed.) *The Collected Scientific Papers of Paul A. Samuelson, Volume 5.* Cambridge, MA, The MIT Press: 846–857.

Samuelson, P.A. (1986b) "Forewords to the Japanese edition of *The Collected Scientific Papers of Paul A. Samuelson*, vols. 1, 2, 4, 5, 6, 8, 9, M. Shinohara and R. Sato (eds.). Tokyo: Keiso Shobo, 1982," in K. Crowley (ed.) *The Collected Scientific Papers of Paul A. Samuelson, Volume 5.* Cambridge, MA, The MIT Press: 858–875.

Samuelson, P.A. (1986c) "Foreword to *Theory of Technical Change and Economic Invariance: Application to Lie Groups*, by Ryuzo Sato. New York, Academic Press: xi–xii," in K. Crowley (ed.) *The Collected Scientific Papers of Paul A. Samuelson, Volume 5.* Cambridge, MA, The MIT Press: 876–877.

Samuelson, P.A. (1988a) "In the Beginning," *Challenge*, 31: 32–34.

Samuelson, P.A. (1988b) "The Keynes-Hansen-Samuelson Multiplier-Accelerator Model of Secular Stagnation," *Japan and the World Economy*, 1: 3–19.

Samuelson, P.A. (1990) "Deterministic Chaos in Economics: An Occurrence in Axiomatic Utility Theory," in K. Vela Velupillai (ed.) *Nonlinear and Multi-sectoral Macrodynamics—Essays in Honour of Richard Goodwin*. Basingstoke, Hampshire, UK, Macmillan: 42–63.

Samuelson, P.A. (1997) "Credo of a Lucky Textbook Author," *Journal of Economic Perspectives*, 11: 153–160.

Samuelson, P.A. (1998) "How *Foundations* Came to Be," *Journal of Economic Literature*, 36: 1375–1386.

Samuelson, P.A. (2002) "Reply: Complementary Innovations by Roy Harrod and Alvin Hansen," *History of Political Economy*, 34: 219–223.

Samuelson, P.A. (2005) "Letter" (to Professor Craufurd D. Goodwin, *History of Political Economy*, on Zambelli 2007), 21 June.

Samuelson, P.A. and A. Scott (1968) *Economics: An Introductory Analysis*. Second Canadian edition. Toronto, McGraw-Hill.

Savage, L.J. (1948) "Samuelson's *Foundations*: Its Mathematics," *Journal of Political Economy*, 56: 200–202.

Scott Dumas, H. (2014) *The KAM Story*. Singapore, World Scientific Publishing.

Shiryaev, A.N. (2000) "Andreĭ Nikolaevich Kolmogorov (April, 25, 1903 to October 20, 1987): A Biographical Sketch of His Life and Creative Paths," in H.H. McFaden (trans.) *Kolmogorov in Perspective*. Volume 20 of *History of Mathematics*. Providence, RI, American Mathematical Society: 1–88.

Sigmund, K. (2007) "Kolmogorov and Population Dynamics," in É. Charpentier, A. Lesne and N.K. Nikolski (eds.) *Kolmogorov's Heritage in Mathematics*. Berlin, Springer: 177–186.

Solow, R.M. (2006) "Overlapping Generations," in M. Szenberg, L. Ramrattan and A.A. Gottesman (eds.) *Samuelsonian Economics and the Twenty-First Century*. Oxford, Oxford University Press: 35–41.

Spivak, M. (1965) *Calculus on Manifolds: A Modern Approach to Classical Theorems of Advanced Calculus*. Reading, MA, Addison-Wesley Publishing Company.

Stigler, G.J. (1948) "Review of *Foundations of Economic Analysis*, by P.A. Samuelson," *Journal of the American Statistical Association*, 43: 603–605.

Strotz, R.H., J.C. McAnulty and J.B. Naines, Jr. (1953) "Goodwin's Nonlinear Theory of the Business Cycle: An Electro-Analog Solution," *Econometrica*, 21: 390–411.

Timlin, M.F. (1949) *Keynesian Economics*. Toronto, University of Toronto Press.

Tinbergen, J. (1937) "Review of *The Trade Cycle*, by R. Harrod," *Weltwirtschaftliches Archive*, 45: 89–91.

Tintner, G. (1948) "Review of *Foundations of Economic Analysis*, by P.A. Samuelson," *Journal of the American Statistical Association*, 43: 497–499.

Veblen, T. (1900) "The Preconceptions of Economic Science," *Quarterly Journal of Economics*, 14: 240–269.

Velupillai, K.V. (1973) "A Note on the Origin of the 'Correspondence Principle'," *Swedish Journal of Economics*, 75: 302–304.

Weil, P. (2008) "Overlapping Generations: The First Jubilee," *Journal of Economic Perspective*, 22: 115–134.

Weissert, T.P. (1997) *The Genesis of Simulation in Dynamics: Pursuing the Fermi-Pasta-Ulam Problem.* New York, Springer.

Wicksell, K. (1907) "Krisernas Gåta," *Statsøkonomisk Tidsskrift*, 21: 255–286.

Zambelli, S. (2007) "The Rocking Horse That Never Rocked: Frisch's 'Propagation and Impulse Problem'," *History of Political Economy*, 39: 145–166.

16

Keynesian Uncertainty: The Great Divide Between Joan Robinson and Paul Samuelson in Their Correspondence and Public Exchanges

Harvey Gram with the collaboration of G. C. Harcourt

1 Introduction

The Joan Robinson/Paul Samuelson correspondence spans a period of thirty-six years.[1] An initial five letters are mutually flattering. Robinson begins, complimenting Samuelson (22 October 1946) on his "amusing and penetrating article on Keynes." Samuelson had joked, "I hasten to add – as who does not? – that I am not myself a Keynesian, although some of my

[1] Our main source of letters and other communications is Box 63 of the Paul A. Samuelson Papers, 1933–2010, located in the David M. Rubenstein Rare Book & Manuscript Library at Duke University. The Papers of Richard Ferdinand Kahn at King's College Archive, Cambridge University, contain some of that same correspondence.

H. Gram (✉)
City University of New York, New York, NY, USA
e-mail: HGram@gc.cuny.edu

G. C. Harcourt
UNSW Sydney, Sydney, NSW, Australia
e-mail: gch@unsw.edu.au

R. A. Cord et al. (eds.), *Paul Samuelson*, Remaking Economics: Eminent Post-War Economists, https://doi.org/10.1057/978-1-137-56812-0_16

best friends are" (Samuelson 1946: 188). He questions Keynes's analytical abilities: "Indeed, until the appearance of the mathematical models of Meade, Lange, Hicks, and Harrod there is reason to believe that Keynes himself did not truly understand his own analysis" (ibid.); and faulted Keynes's most famous work for failing to deliver on its promise: "As for expectations, the General Theory is brilliant in calling attention to their importance and in suggesting many of the central features of uncertainty and speculation. It paves the way for a theory of expectations, but it hardly provides one" (ibid.: 192). Samuelson acknowledged that Keynes, on at least one occasion, had shown interest in "an esoteric theoretical problem, [giving] a rather intricate interpretation in words of a calculus-of-variations differential-equation condition of equilibrium" (ibid.: 196, fn. 8). He was referring to Ramsey (1928), which presages Samuelson and Solow (1956) and Dorfman et al. (1958), a work referred to on numerous occasions in Samuelson's correspondence with Robinson. There is no mention of Keynesian uncertainty or speculation in this later work, whereas Ramsey is given star billing (see Samuelson and Solow 1956: 537).

Suggesting (2 January 1947) that Robinson make a "grand tour," Samuelson writes, "Along with all American economists, I have always been intensely interested in your writings." He repeats the invitation to "visit our shores" (23 May 1949), adding: "I read with great pleasure your review article on Harrod [Robinson 1949] … Perhaps if Harrod's lectures serve to provoke interesting discussions such as yours, I will have to modify my critical judgement." She returns the compliment (11 December 1950): "I much enjoyed your piece in *Economica* (I didn't try the appendix)." The charming style of Samuelson (1950) on the problem of integrability of utility functions involving more than two goods no doubt appealed to Robinson.

In the last of these initial letters (17 May 1951), Samuelson acknowledges hearing that Robinson is working on a new project: "I take it as the best possible news that we can soon look forward to another book of yours, and one on so interesting a subject." Her famous critique of the production function in the theory of capital (Robinson 1953–1954) was followed by that book, her magnum opus (Robinson 1956)[2] and its sequel

[2]For the long history behind this book, see Harcourt and Kerr (2013).

(Robinson 1962a). In all of this work, Keynesian uncertainty, though not always central to the discussion, is never lost sight of.

Seven years pass before the first rumblings of disagreements are heard in three rapid-fire letters in early 1958—disagreements that would, in the end, never be resolved. The last of these finds Robinson concluding on a despairing note (9 February 1958): "But I think you and Solow are a case of None so deaf as he who will not hear – so I shan't make myself hoarse shouting at you. Much look forward to seeing you later this year." A further pause ensued, followed by five letters from 1959 dealing with questions arising from Samuelson's famous paper on consumption loans (Samuelson 1958).

In 1961, Robinson finally made the "grand tour."[3] Following a seminar at MIT, Samuelson recorded that she had asked him "when you say the real wage is the marginal product of something, what is that something and what is it that is 'being held constant'?" His initial answer[4]: "Er, er. The

[3]Samuelson's attitude toward Robinson prior to her visit was revealed in a letter (14 August 1957) to the Rockefeller Foundation (concerning another visitor to MIT). In a postscript, he noted that Richard Kahn, unable to spend the 1958–1959 academic year at MIT, had asked, "Why not invite Joan Robinson?" Samuelson described her as "a top-notch scholar ... [A]lso controversial and would, I suppose, belong to the left wing of the labor party." He then comes to the point: "But of this I am sure. An actual visit to America she needs very badly. Naturally she doesn't know it. She can pontificate about the American peasant in a fashion that is often laughable. I think there is a sporting chance that a trip to this country might make a dent in her opinions, and since she is most definitely a leader of World opinion, this would be very much in our interest. Earlier I might have had some doubts whether it would [be] feasible for her to get a visa. Maybe such doubt still ought to prevail. I don't imagine that she has ever been a member of the Communist party, but there is no doubt that she did go to the Moscow conference of 1952, etc." He concludes, "From the standpoint of brain washing her, I think a stay at one place for some length of time is probably better than the quick tour, but naturally she would want to see the country in any case." Robinson did visit a number of other universities (see Turner 1989: 170–184).

[4]In a letter (31 March 1961) to Kahn following the MIT seminar, Robinson remembered it this way: "He replied – you have a point there – I do not know the answer ... [I]t seems he just was disconcerted ... [A]ll very amiable tho' hard hitting and plenty of good humoured banter." In a follow-up (2 April 1961) to Kahn, she added: "[I]t is remarkable that he should never have asked himself this simple question before...and turn it to a joke against himself. But I wonder if the point will sink in." Robinson's doubts are recalled in her 1977 Reminiscences: "It was great fun to tease Samuelson, but this debate took attention away from the main issue" (Robinson 1978: xviii, cited in Turner 1989: 171–172). There, she reported that "the answer [Samuelson gave to the question] is that either you keep all physical inputs constant or you keep the rate of interest constant." In the latter case, the main issue between them was what determined the rate of interest. For Samuelson, it was "the tradeoff twixt today's and tomorrow's consumption goods." This would never satisfy Robinson because it only made sense in a world where output is continuously constrained by an economy's production possibilities. She wanted a more general theory of the economy-wide rate

kings of England were William…and besides the interest rate or profit rate is identifiable as a certain physical marginal product concept, namely the tradeoff twixt today's and tomorrow's consumption goods." Her response: "Come, come, sir. Answer the question." Samuelson's memo set forth three answers dated 6:30 a.m. on the day after the seminar, implying a sleepless night struggling to cover all his bases! The protagonists were evidently enjoying the joust, but whether Samuelson's answers satisfied Robinson is unclear.[5] In any case, over the following six years, some thirty-four letters attest to the seriousness with which each attempted to understand and to criticize the other's positions on various matters relating to capital theory and the distribution of income. It all came to naught. On 11 May 1967, Robinson dashed off a final volley, "I fear it's hopeless. Goodbye."

Four years later, communication resumed in some two dozen letters written over the period 1971–1975. Robinson argued for an essential difference between various systems of prices and their associated schools of thought. Samuelson saw only a set of variations on a general equilibrium theory of supply and demand. In a response to her published note on model types (Robinson 1973), he threw up his hands, empowering "the reader…to strike out the label 'Walrasian,' substituting for it 'Ricardian,' 'Bortkiewiczian,' 'Sraffian,' or other similar adjectives" (Samuelson 1973: 1367). His well-known penchant for stringing together the names of famous progenitors of modern theory was only intended to give credit where credit was due. He did not agree with Robinson that different types of problems required different theories of price. Her own fully developed thesis first appeared in Robinson (1958) to which she made reference (21 January 1972; underlining in original): "I would be very much obliged if you would read a piece called The Philosophy of Prices." Samuelson wrote

---

of profits, such as she would offer in Robinson (1962a: 48–51). As for the short run, "keeping all physical inputs constant" was not the traditional basis upon which to define the marginal product of labor. Indeed, it was an old question, long discussed in Cambridge and elsewhere. Stigler (1952: 117, 1987: 136), echoing Robertson (1931: 48), found it reasonable to hold constant total *expenditure* on non-labor inputs while allowing their *form* to vary. Whether or not one accepts this way around the problem, estimates of, say, the marginal rate of substitution between more and less computer-literate workers—the ratio of their marginal products—would be quite meaningless without *also* knowing the prior level of investment in computer equipment (for empirical work, see Lichtenberg 1995).

[5]In her own theory of marginal productivity pricing, under conditions of imperfect competition, "the marginal net product of labour (after allowing for raw materials, power and maintenance of plant) is equal to the wage plus profit" (Robinson 1967: 77).

back (29 January 1972) saying only that he had "found it as I remembered it."

Much attention was paid in the letters of this period to the problem of constant returns in Sraffa. Samuelson initially asked Robinson in early 1972 if Sraffa's "constant returns" means constant returns to *scale* or (as becomes clear in a subsequent letter) constant *opportunity* cost. A notation in the margin, "What else could it mean?" is in Sraffa's hand and initialled "P." Exasperation soon set in on both sides. Robinson wrote (18 April 1972), "There is none so blind as he who will not see." Samuelson responded, "I feel I am wasting time better spent on other things. Here are my final words on this matter." But this was not the end of it. Robinson had submitted "The Unimportance of Reswitching" to the *Quarterly Journal of Economics* (Robinson 1975a) and sent a draft to Samuelson (15 June 1973). For her, it marked a final turning away from many of the formal problems that had so interested protagonists on both sides of the capital theory controversy. Samuelson saw the article as an opportunity for him and Solow to set matters straight in the pages of the journal wherein the famous "Paradoxes in Capital Theory: A Symposium" had first appeared.[6] In one of four long letters, Samuelson remarked to Solow: "[A]s any examination of the dirt on the pages of the bound volumes of the QJE…will verify, [the 1966 *Symposium* issue] was in fact one of the most read in its history." These letters were, indeed, drafts of their replies to Robinson (Samuelson 1975; Solow 1975). Another, longer paper (Samuelson 1976) also emerged from this correspondence with Solow, filling out Samuelson's response to what he had described to Solow (9 July 1973) as Robinson's "disconnected remarks."

Again, it all came to naught. Asking Samuelson for permission to include part of his response to "The Unimportance…" in her *Collected Economic Papers*, Robinson again despaired (30 March 1978): "I am sorry we have never been able to get to the bottom of this dispute." Samuelson replied: "You would not believe the hours I spend reading your writings … You should take satisfaction that you have had a major impact on three

---

[6]The Editor of the *Quarterly Journal of Economics*, Richard Musgrave, wrote to Samuelson (3 July 1973), in reaction to Robinson's submission: "We don't think it very novel, but suppose that the prominence of the author suggests we take it in any case. We shall, of course, be glad to have a brief rejoinder by you, Bob [Solow] or, perhaps, the two of you jointly."

generations of economists. Ever, Paul." Four years later (12 March 1982), upon her return from India, Robinson sent her last letter to Samuelson, evidently puzzled by what he had written: "I was somewhat mystified…but I am glad to know there is no ill will. Yours, Joan Robinson."

Section 2 of this chapter takes up the five letters between Robinson and Samuelson concerning his consumption-loan model. Section 3 covers the bulk of their letters, setting forth conflicting points of view in three overlapping areas, all concerned in one way or another with capital theory and the distribution of income. What often gets lost in the weeds of their back and forth is the simple fact that Keynesian uncertainty is central to Robinson's understanding of what constitutes an acceptable economic theory of accumulation and growth within a capitalist system. Samuelson, on the other hand, sees the same problem as one to be addressed with the tools of dynamic programming, which inevitably involves an embrace of the curious notion—for economics, at least—of perfect foresight. Section 4 considers the role of mathematics in explaining this conundrum.

2 Pure Consumption Loans or Saving Without Investment

Shortly after the publication of his classic paper on consumption loans,[7] Samuelson wrote to Robinson (18 May 1959): "I have been rather inundated by correspondence concerning my JPE article." He thanked her for her own reaction, "A Simpler Way of Putting It,"[8] noting that "a comment from you is always most welcome and I am looking forward

---

[7]Karl Shell (1971: 1002) expressed the view of many: "Paul Samuelson's (1958) paper on consumption loans is to my mind one of the most original and stimulating contributions to modern economic theory." It has long since become standard textbook fare (e.g., Azariadis 1993) and remains a stimulus for research (e.g., Azariadis and Smith 1993; Azariadis and Lambertini 2003). Samuelson's purpose, it should be recalled, was "to give a complete general equilibrium solution to the determination of the time-shape of interest rates [associated with] a rational consumer's lifetime consumption-saving pattern … This sounds easy, but actually it is very hard, so hard that I shall have to make drastic simplifications in order to arrive at exact results" (Samuelson 1958: 219).

[8]There is a brief indication in an accompanying (undated) note that Robinson's comment had been sent to the *Journal of Political Economy*. The note included a diagram, constructed with the help of Richard Kahn (as may be inferred from Kahn's papers in the King's College Archives), showing lending minus borrowing and income minus consumption as functions of the interest rate. It was

to reading it with the usual benefit and enlightenment." At the time, Samuelson was working on a response to Abba Lerner who "has written no less than two comments, each revised twice and I gather that the editors have already accepted some other comment." That response (Samuelson 1959) to Lerner (1959), who wrote a "Rejoinder," and another (Samuelson 1960) to Meckling (1960), who also fired back, were just the beginning of a burgeoning literature.

In two further exchanges, Robinson (22 May 1959) insisted that "the system requires excess consumption by the young adults." Samuelson (29 May 1959) answers a different question, stating that "any pure loan scheme is very likely to produce a negative interest rate." This prompted Robinson (12 June 1959) to write again: "If the young…don't want to overspend, it won't work," at which point, Samuelson (30 June 1959) simply answered: "I agree with your recent statement." This typifies the way in which their questions and answers often seemed to elide one another. In any case, Robinson's main point was straightforward. Retirees (assumed to have no income) cannot borrow because lenders know they will not be alive to honor their debts (assumed to be zero at the end of life).[9] To survive, they must have assets to liquidate and so, as middle-aged adults in the previous period, they must be lending—but to whom?

> The essential feature of the situation is the excess consumption of young Jones. If there are no spendthrifts and all are determined to start saving up as soon as they begin to earn, there is no equilibrium and there is an indefinitely great negative rate of interest [minus 100% per diem]…making it impossible to carry consumption forward from one day to the next. (Robinson 1960: 192)

It was this dire situation that prompted Samuelson to ask, "Is it true, in a growing or in a stationary population, that twenty-year-olds are, in fact, overconsuming so that the middle-aged can provide for their retirement?"

---

not included in the final version which appeared only in Robinson's *Collected Economic Papers* under the title "Saving Without Investment" (Robinson 1960).

[9] Robinson put it this way, focusing on the late stage of working life: "An elderly man cannot afford to borrow even at a negative rate, for he has little time left to repay and to save up for his retirement" (Robinson 1960: 192).

(Samuelson 1958: 474). Using the simplest example, he gave a negative answer and then proved his famous Impossibility Theorem: "*[T]he social optimum configuration can never here be reached by the competitive market, or even be approached in ever so long a time*" (ibid.: 477–478; italics in original). A further example showed that the only meaningful and locally stable solution "implies that consumption-loans lose about two-thirds of their principal in one period. This is here the competitive price to avoid retirement starvation" (ibid.: 478).

Samuelson's model

> points up a fundamental and intrinsic deficiency in a free pricing system, namely, that free pricing...by itself has no tendency to get you to positions on the [efficiency] frontier that are ethically optimal in terms of a social welfare function; only by social collusions – of tax, expenditure, fiat, or other type – can an ethical observer hope to end up where he wants to be. (ibid.: 479)

In the same vein, Robinson concluded: "When conditions are such that the free market rate of interest is heavily negative, the social insurance system seems more humane than the consumption-loan system, and more consonant with traditional morality" (Robinson 1960: 196).

In a discursive penultimate section, "Social Contracts and the Optimum," Samuelson also alluded to a social insurance system:

> Once social coercion or contracting is admitted into the picture, the present problem disappears. The reluctance of the young to give to the old what the old can never themselves directly or indirectly repay is overcome. Yet the young never suffer, since their successors come under the same requirement. Everybody ends better off. It is as simple as that. (Samuelson 1958: 480)

A coercive transfer by the State is not, however, the note on which the article ends. Rather, it is the use of Money as a Social Contrivance: "In our consumption-loan model nothing kept. All ice melted, and so did all chocolates ... There is no arguing with Nature. But what is to stop man – or rather men – from printing oblongs of paper or stamping circles of shell. These units of money can keep" (ibid.: 481). Robinson offers a Keynesian caveat: "The introduction of money tokens which could be hoarded would be disastrous unless the first generation of retired men were given a free issue" (Robinson 1960: 195). By spending it, the retired cohort guarantees what Samuelson then asserts: "Now the young and middle-aged do have something to hold and to carry over into their retirement years" (Samuelson 1958: 481). He adds another condition: "[A]s long as the new current generations of workers do not repudiate the old money, this gives the workers of one epoch a claim on workers of a later epoch, even though no real *quid pro quo* (other than money) is possible" (ibid.: 482). Thus, coercion may still be necessary to ensure that all follow the traditional golden rule: "Do [as workers] unto others [now retired] as [the older] you would have them [future workers] do unto [the retired] you" (after Matthew 7:12).

Besides adhering to the rules of the game, there is a further matter of theoretical importance—the amount of money introduced into the system must be *exactly* right. As David Gale showed, with too much money, "the model heads toward a kind of economic collapse in which eventually people will be demanding more consumption than the economy can provide … [Unless the issue of money is exactly right], the model will move back away from the golden rule toward the balanced steady state" (Gale 1973: 16–17). In Gale's terminology, a "balanced" steady state is one in which the aggregate of assets is zero. Samuelson alludes to the problem of getting the money injection just right at the beginning of his article: "Some interesting mathematical boundary problems, a little like those in the modern theories of dynamic programming, result from this analysis" (Samuelson 1958: 467). Writing to Robinson (29 May 1959), he is a little more explicit: "[T]he pure loan system if somehow engineered into the optimum configuration would generally be highly unstable," as is also true of convergent yet *unstable* saddle paths in neoclassical models of capital accumulation.

So-called boundary problems in infinite time horizon models received a great deal of attention in the subsequent literature.[10] Less attention was paid to Abba Lerner's insistence that, with either positive or negative interest, there will be less *total* utility than under an optimum zero rate of interest, owing to the wedge that is driven between marginal utilities of

[10]For a summary of results for the consumption-loan model, see Azariadis (1993: 245–247).

consumption of contemporaneous workers of various ages (young, older, and retired, in his three-period model). Consumption is the same thing as real income in this model. Thus, Lerner is taking the old-fashioned, radical view that social welfare is made higher by equating marginal utilities of income across individuals. Otherwise, "much of the good juice of utility [simply evaporates]" (Robinson 1962b: 52).

For Lerner, the concept of a biological rate of interest equal to the growth rate of population merely allows "the authorities [to] pretend that 'social security' is not a 'socialistic' tax and give-away program by the government but a 'saving' by each worker out of his current income to provide for his old age" (Lerner 1959: 514). In a stationary economy, the imaginary rate of interest associated with an imaginary transfer over time just happens to equal "the zero biological rate of increase in population" (ibid.). With a population that doubles every twenty-year period the

> proportions of the populations in the three age groups would be 4:2:1 ... [so that] the one-seventh of his wage that a young worker pays grows to four-sevenths of the wage during the two periods that elapse before he gets his pension ... The true reason for this wonder is that there are at every point of time *six* workers to support each pensioner. The fictitious nature of the 'biological' interest stems from the impossibility, by assumption, of transporting consumption through time in an economy where no products are durable. (ibid.: italics in original)

Lerner elaborates, noting that:

> In our society many people feel that social security by redistribution of income by the government is alien to the pure essence of the individualist capitalist system so that, if 'social security' has to be provided, it should take the form of individual saving for old age. This has led to the belief that a social security system cannot operate honestly unless it has acquired a fund actuarially corresponding to the savings of all those members of society who have paid in their contributions in the past and who will be taking them out as benefits in the future ... The essence of the matter is that the fable of the time-travel of consumption is accepted with implicit faith by the accountants, as guardians of the private point of view ... It is the duty of economists, as guardians of the social point of view, to explode

> this fairy tale ... The only real problem from the social point of view is the allocation of current output of consumption goods between current consumers of different ages. This can never be achieved by any kind of trading or lending, but only by a one-way transfer...with no genuine quid pro quo. (ibid.: 516–517)

All this suggests that Samuelson (1958) may not have provided a sound social justification for national superannuation schemes, whatever other merits the paper may have had.[11] Certainly, the myth of a "trust fund" backing US pay-as-you-go social security benefits attests to the "fairy tale" nature of the scheme that Lerner was eager to explode.

In writing to Robinson (29 May 1959), Samuelson observes that, "Lerner would probably argue that you should see that pensions and taxes are right and not worry about what the *quid pro quo* is between youthful payment and aged receipts." He says nothing about Lerner's main argument concerning the *fragility* of a system in which the interest rate is not effectively set equal to zero. Nor does he remind Robinson of what he saw as the important theoretical problem motivating his analysis: "[I]n order to define an equilibrium path of interest in a perfect capital market endowed with *perfect certainty*, you have to determine *all* interest rates between now and the end of time; every finite time period points beyond itself!" (Samuelson 1958: 467; italics in original). This may explain why Robinson titled her response, "A Simpler Way of Putting It." Samuelson stays the course, replying to Lerner: "Such a dynamic problem, involving as it does the infinity of time and the almost philosophical problems raised by the presence or absence of 'perfect certainty,' is to me one of the most difficult in all economics" (Samuelson 1959: 518). The same issues—an infinite time horizon and perfect foresight—would arise in his analysis of capital accumulation[12] and, yet, in his often long letters to Robinson, Samuelson mentions his denial of uncertainty on just two occasions (23 October 1961 and an undated communication of early 1972). There is far

---

[11] For further arguments along these lines, see Asimakopulos and Weldon (1968: 704, fn. 9) who wrote: "We have found the Lerner way of looking at the problem persuasive."

[12] Samuelson (1958), it may be noted, is reprinted under "The Pure Theory of Capital and Growth" in his *Collected Scientific Papers*, rather than in the sections concerned with consumption theory.

more candor expressed in communications with Solow during the summer of 1973 when their response to a draft copy of Robinson (1975a) was under intense discussion (see Sect. 4).

Samuelson returned to Lerner's critique, which had been further analyzed and supported by Asimakopulos (1967),[13] acknowledging:

> It is indeed paradoxical that the policy which maximizes social utility in every period should, when applied to a permanently growing exponential, result in a configuration such that every man who ever lives is worse off. This paradox, like most paradoxes,[14] arises from the infinity assumption involved ... Lerner presumably would bypass the pitfalls of divergent geometric series by insisting that the assumption of a permanently growing exponential is an absurd and monstrous one, involving a Ponzi-game or chain-letter swindle. If golden-age assumptions are successfully ruled out by Lerner as monstrous, he will in one swoop kill off a sizable fraction of the modern growth-theory literature. (Samuelson 1967a: 270)[15]

3 Capital Theory and Income Distribution

Samuelson's correspondence with Robinson on matters relating to capital theory and income distribution began about ten years after their first exchange of letters following the death of Keynes. Samuelson repeatedly made three points. First, the mathematical theory of dynamic optimization is the proper foundation for a theory of capital accumulation, the pricing of capital goods, and the determination of the spectrum of own rates of interest. Second, constant returns to scale leave indeterminate the number of transactions in final goods taking place between owners of various

---

[13]Cited by Samuelson (1967a: 280), this paper was written in 1966 (see Asimakopulos 1967: 189).

[14]Remarkably, Samuelson acknowledges that, "Up to *any* instant of time, the L-A [Lerner-Asimakopulos] state has produced more social utility than the S-D [Samuelson-Diamond] state. And departing from an ever-held S-D state in favor of an L-A state leads to an increase in social utility in *every* subsequent period" (Samuelson 1967a: 270, fn. 2; italics in original).

[15]Samuelson went on to outdo Lerner-Asimakopulos by proving a Catenary Turnpike Theorem. The most efficient path to a welfare-maximizing golden-rule equilibrium at some finite future date entails just such over-accumulation of capital as to bring the rate of interest down to *zero* for most of the path: "The optimum...presupposes direct intervention by the state to redistribute consumption by lump-sum taxation". (Samuelson 1967a: 279)

produced and non-produced inputs. Third, reduced consumption at a point in time causes a subsequent outward shift in production possibilities, under conditions of near enough full employment.

3.1 Dynamic Optimization as the Foundation for Capital Theory

Robinson (22 January 1958) thought the assumptions she discerned in Samuelson's "piece on Marx" (Samuelson 1957) were "very unnatural" and wrote that he had merely "escaped[d] the puzzles connected with measuring capital" by making the length of life of all capital goods "uniform and very short." Samuelson (3 February 1958; underlining and upper case in original) answered the charge by referring to his work on dynamic optimization, eschewing any concern with the value of capital as a whole:

> I avoided all puzzles connected with the measurement of capital…by specifying a complete (albeit simple) technological model. The world never grapples with the problem of reducing capital to a homogeneous measure: it uses complicated vectors of inputs to produce complicated vectors of output … [I]n the November 1956 QJE Solow and I showed how any number of heterogeneous capital goods are to be handled; and also in our Dorfman-Samuelson-Solow book LINEAR PROGRAMMING AND ECONOMIC ANALYSIS (1958), of which I've sent Richard Kahn a copy.

Without taking a stance "on the question as to whether it was natural or unnatural to consider a model in which…the system remains not too far from full employment," Samuelson made his objective clear: "I do consider it a highly interesting problem to analyze the probable pattern of goods and factor pricing of a model in which activist fiscal and monetary policies did succeed in keeping chronic unemployment from being large and growing."[16]

Following Robinson's 1961 visit to MIT, Samuelson (10 October 1961; underlining in original) again writes: "The MIT School view that I have

[16]Citing Meade (1961), Hahn (1966: 646) also suggests that the assumed success of Keynesian demand management policies is an "alternative interpretation" of a competitive equilibrium growth path under conditions of full employment.

always adhered to maintains that one has to work with vectors of heterogeneous physical capital goods and time-consuming processes – that use of a homogeneous capital stuff is never necessary even though the parable[17] may have some useful pedagogical functions." He concludes on a somewhat patronizing note: "I do not enclose a copy of the Dorfman-Samuelson-Solow book showing how programming handles such diverse vectors of goods because no one can be expected to read so big a book."

The determining role of "existent supplies of physical capital goods" (23 October 1961; underlining in original) is repeatedly emphasized, in opposition to the aggregate value of capital (3 May 1965; 13 August 1965; 5 May 1967). Answering Robinson's query (14 October 1971) concerning the difference between "what Marx called 'prices of production'…[and] what you now propose to call Walrasian prices based on supply and demand for scarce means with alternative uses," Samuelson wrote in the same vein:

> [I]n the DOSSO book [an acronym for Dorfman et al. (1958)], if you look carefully, you will find examples of complete, logically non-contradictory models in which heterogeneous capital-goods' pricing and interest rate determinations are defined over time. Whether these models are realistic or even interesting depends on the eyes of the reader.

He maintained this position—with its hint of ambivalence—throughout their correspondence, adopting Harrod's terminology (23 April 1973;

[17]When the "parable" was published, Samuelson expressed his gratitude to Pierangelo Garegnani "for saving me from asserting the false conjecture that my extreme assumption of equi-proportional inputs in the consumption and machine trades could be lightened and still leave one with many of the surrogate propositions" (Samuelson 1962: 202, fn. 1). See also Asimakopulos and Harcourt (1974: 483), where it is pointed out that, "If there are many techniques, the differences in the value of output per head and the value of capital per man between adjacent points may be very small … These small differences in value may mask substantial differences in the types and composition of capital goods in each system. Hence, if an attempt were made to move from one long-period equilibrium position to another, much more than a marginal change in the capital goods would be required. The existing equilibrium would be ruptured, and there is no guarantee that the behavior of the individual decision-makers in the economy would be such as to enable the transition to the new equilibrium position to be made." Robinson put it this way: "[T]he machines…may be completely different for each [technique]…[so that to] 'change' the technique in use…it would be necessary…to go back into the past and rewrite the history of the investment" (Robinson 1975a: 34, 53). Rewriting history is *her* way of ensuring equilibrium, but not, of course, Samuelson's.

underlining in original) when he wrote of "the optimal-programming rules for describing accurately a warrantable dynamic accumulation process from one steady state to another."

Samuelson was no doubt aware that a non-mathematically trained economist would be unable to follow the argument in Samuelson and Solow (1956), which forms the basis for Chapters 11 and 12 of DOSSO. However, neither the paper nor the book is entirely mathematical. There is, for example, a half-page of interpretation in DOSSO at the end of a section entitled *Competitive Markets and Dynamic Efficiency*:

> The truly remarkable thing about the intertemporal invisible hand is that while it results in efficiency over long periods of time, it requires only the most myopic vision on the part of market participants. Just current [equilibrium] prices and [their] current rates of change need to be known, and at each moment long-run efficiency is preserved. But for society as a whole there is need for vision at a distance. (Dorfman et al. 1958: 321)

Had Samuelson drawn attention to these few lines in his correspondence with Robinson, she would surely have pressed him to explain what society's "need for vision at a distance" actually entailed. The authors of DOSSO are clear on this; namely, setting the initial price of each capital good exactly right so that the equilibrium trajectory of accumulation will follow a convergent saddle path,[18] or, in language that Robinson would have understood, a knife-edge. Samuelson nowhere acknowledges a connection between this formal problem—the problem of ensuring that *transversality* conditions are satisfied—and the literary arguments set forth in Robinson (1953–1954) concerning the problem of reconciling past, present, and future valuations of capital. Robinson (1959) clarified the issues from a Keynesian perspective (part of her effort to extend Keynesian analysis of effective demand to the long period). Samuelson, in contrast, acknowledges no formal connection between dynamic optimization and Keynesian analysis. He simply assumes that fiscal and monetary policy

[18] In Dorfman et al. (1958: 321), capital-good prices at some *terminal* date must be set precisely—hence the "need for vision at a distance," but a footnote states that setting *initial* prices *correctly* will do just as well.

actions—Keynesian aggregate demand policies—always succeed in keeping the economic system operating at (or near enough to) a point on its production possibility frontier, a standard assumption of neoclassical capital theory (see Solow 1956: 91–94; Swan 1956: 335).[19]

In their correspondence, Samuelson often tells Robinson how much he has learned from her published work, but on the matter of making clear the role of perfect foresight in his own theory, he is less than candid.[20] She addressed the issue directly in a response to Samuelson's suggestion (27 May 1964; underlining in original) that she write an essay on the question:

> What difference does it make for the behavior of a mixed economy if its book of technological blue prints has a great many pages of slightly varied technical opportunities…as compared to an economy whose technology has great 'gaps' and which has choice only of a limited number of fixed coefficient alternatives?

Robinson answered (1 June 1964; italics added):

> [S]o long as we are concerned with the positions of equilibrium where each economy has become adjusted to its own rate of interest with *correct foresight*, it does not make the smallest difference to the argument how large or small are the steps in the book of blue-prints. What is important is the actual collection of physical capital goods, knowledge and qualities of labor produced by the past history in which there has *not been correct foresight* or a *single* book of blue-prints. The response of the economy to monetary policy and questions of that kind depend upon this short-period situation.

As for eschewing the importance of "reducing capital to a homogeneous measure" (22 January 1958), it is curious that Samuelson also fails to alert Robinson to a point that he and his co-authors had made:

---

[19] For extensive commentary on the differences between the growth models of Solow and Swan, see Pitchford (2002) and Dimand and Spencer (2009).

[20] Solow does not mince his words: "[T]he real difficulty…comes not from the physical diversity of capital goods. It comes from the intertwining of past, present and future, from the fact that while there is something foolish about a theory of capital built on the assumption of perfect foresight, we have no equally precise and definite assumption to take its place" (Solow 1955–1956: 102).

> One interesting sidelight before we leave the subject of intertemporal pricing: Consider any efficient capital program and its corresponding profile of prices and own-rates [of change of prices]. *At every point of time the value of the capital stock at current efficiency prices, discounted back to the initial time, is a constant,* equal to the initial value. This law of conservation of discounted value of capital (or discounted Net National Product) reflects, as do the grand laws of conservation of energy in physics, the maximizing nature of the path. (Dorfman et al. 1958: 321–322; italics in original)

An interest in "Conservations Laws" marks his later research,[21] and yet Samuelson granted no importance to the "conservation" of aggregate capital value in Dorfman et al. (1958) or elsewhere. He simply responded (3 May 1965) to Robinson's question concerning the relationship between the aggregate capital-output ratio and the interest rate by saying: "As soon as one leaves the simplest model, we need a general equilibrium approach in which everything depends upon everything else (but in a virtuously-Walrasian way and not in a viciously-circular way). The system cares nothing for aggregative totals and few invariant relations can be found for them." The exception, for "even the most complicated set of blueprints," is that "if intrinsic joint-products…are ruled out, it remains true that: 'The higher the interest rate r the lower the real wage expressed in terms of any (and hence every) consumption good.'"

Interpretive passages in other published work reinforce the view that Samuelson might well have met Robinson on her own ground, but, for whatever reason, did not do so. A clear case arises in connection with one of two articles Samuelson published in the 1967 volume edited by Karl Shell entitled *Essays on the Theory of Optimal Economic Growth.* Under the heading, "Re-aiming Behavior of Speculators," Samuelson sets forth, with

---

[21] Samuelson (1990) proves a theorem on the constancy of the capital-output ratio along an optimal path, where *both* prices and quantities of capital goods are changing continuously, i.e., along a non-steady-state path of accumulation. He then asks, recalling Robinson's arguments: "Will these neoclassical results hold for a neo-classical model of Joan Robinson type, where marginal productivities in the form of partial derivatives are not definable because only a finite number of activities are technologically possible?" (ibid.: 58). His affirmative answer is qualified, and so "this law is not trivially true … I conclude that, at best, if discrete-time intervals can be taken so small that there is little error in approximating the system by a continuous-time model, we can hope to state an 'almost-constancy' of the capital-output ratio along any optimal path" (ibid.: 69). Champernowne (1953–1954) had also faced the problem of dealing with discrete versus smooth changes.

striking imagery, his own misgivings concerning the "MIT School view that [he had] always adhered to"[22]:

> My analysis…has confirmed Hahn's finding[23] that merely to postulate overall saving propensities leaves a heterogeneous system indeterminate in its development … Now how do actual economic systems resolve these indeterminacies? … The image in my mind is that of a bicycle. The rider of the bicycle is the bulk of the market, a somewhat mystical concept to be sure – like its analogue, the well-informed speculator who gets his way in the end because his way is the correctly discerned way of the future … Even if there is something valid in this heuristic reasoning, one must admit that the system need not – and, generally, will not – move from its present position to the golden age in the most efficient way: it will harc after false goals, get detoured, and begin to be corrected only after it has erred … One feels that the real world of tools, plant, and inventory contrasts with the purely financial dream world of indefinite group self-fulfillment. But can this feeling be given documentation and plausible explication? (Samuelson 1967b: 228–230)

The pages from which this passage is taken—had they been sent to his sparring partner—might have opened up a more fruitful dialogue. Obfuscation may actually have been a strategy, however, as suggested in a letter to Solow (19 July 1973; underlining in original)[24]:

---

[22]A *belief* in the stabilizing role of speculators—neither backed up by an argument nor questioned in the way that Keynes (1936 [1973]) and Kaldor (1939) had done—informs Samuelson's other published work with Solow: "This re-aiming is, so to speak, what an optimizing society is constantly doing" (Samuelson and Solow 1956: 548). How such "re-aiming" occurs and what damage is done before the ship is righted are, of course, the fundamental questions that Robinson wanted to discuss.

[23]The issues raised by Hahn recall the theoretical stance taken by Irving Fisher: "When prices find their normal level at which costs plus interest are covered, it is not because the past costs of production have determined prices in advance, but because the sellers have been good speculators as to what prices would be" (Fisher 1906: 188). "Thus Fisher shifted all economic reasoning to the future … It was a complete reversal of the classical causation, as Fisher himself put it" (Bharadwaj 1985: 18). Hahn found in this reversal a profound problem: "The fact that the description of the present involves the future in an essential way must bear the responsibility for the unsatisfactory behavior of the equilibrium path" (Hahn 1966: 645–646). Samuelson quickly realized the importance of Hahn's argument, but nowhere is it mentioned in his correspondence with Robinson.

[24]In an addendum to an earlier letter (9 July 1973), Samuelson provides Solow with a list of eleven points he is considering in connection with a response to Robinson. There, he states categorically: "I doubt that she understands what a price-quantities warranted dynamic path is or that it is logically

> [W]hen we face up to heterogeneous capital goods, we do get into terrific problems of needed foresight (and indeed the 'Hahn' problem of how to cut the indeterminacy of the detailed composition of capital goods within the aggregate saving-investment budget set by baby-simple class propensities to save). Of course, Joan can't understand, or at least never keeps in mind for as long as 30 s running, that there is a logical way of defining warrantable dynamic paths that are not balanced exponentials (sometimes for a socialist planned society she concedes a little) ... And think how horribly difficult it would be to get this into a reasoned discussion of the so-called Two Cambridges issues ... Perhaps never admit anything and claim everything?

Certainly, Samuelson alludes to assumptions that he knows are unacceptable to Robinson, but they are not spelled out in his letters to her. Earlier (10 October 1961; underlining in original), he had written:

> One of the few apparent differences that still remain is that I think the study of transition states is not a hopeless one for the economic theorist. I am prepared to make certain assumptions about uncertainty and expectations in the presence of fast and slow changes that you will think useless assumptions; I expect some little light to be reflected on such transient dynamic states by the study of stationary states, and I understand you to be more skeptical in this regard. I think we can hope to make some slow progress toward understanding the behavior of an economy undergoing technological change by first isolating some of the properties of a system that undergoes no technical change. In all this I may be wrong, and time may tell.

It is rather in his correspondence with Solow concerning the draft of Robinson (1975a) where one finds (19 July 1973) a clear statement of Samuelson's position on the relationship between equilibrium theory and the market process:

> What you and I realize is that it is a tough problem for a market economy to have all the perfect futures markets that are needed for Arrow-Debreu

---

possible – albeit not always [if ever] realized in real life." The eleven points, plus two more, are found in Samuelson (1976).

> optimal dynamic paths. Yet, when you review the Pareto-Mises-Lerner-Lange-Hayek debates about socialism versus capitalism, one realizes that Hayek's point about the need to mobilize and utilize imperfect information actually wins the debate: no planning algorithm or computer can come anywhere close to approximating intertemporally-efficient paths, whereas the market (helped by the Justice Department and bankruptcy) makes a workably-adequate pass at the problem.

It is hard to countenance the suggestion at the beginning of this passage that lessor mortals—including Robinson—are quite unable to appreciate the fact that intertemporally efficient paths entail a set of perfect futures markets. As for allusions to actions by the Justice Department and to bankruptcy, these bring into question the whole theoretical argument, yet Robinson was never brought into Samuelson's confidence on this fundamental caveat.

3.2 Constant Returns to Scale Eliminates the Need for Transactions in Final Goods

On the theoretical implications of constant returns to scale, Samuelson (28 January 1972) wrote to Robinson:

> For 70 years at least students of Wicksell have realized that in a world of constant returns to scale, there is no need for exchange of final goods. I see no contradiction to that in the view of Smith, Ricardo, Sraffa and me that the equilibrium price ratio of goods readily reproducible at constant costs (and produced in positive amounts) is their cost ratio, without regard to the number of transactions that take place at that equilibrium ratio.

Samuelson was referring to Knut Wicksell's *Lectures on Political Economy*, in particular, "The Landowner as Entrepreneur," and "The Labourer (or a Third Party) as Entrepreneur," which, it should be noted, fall under the heading "Non-capitalist Production" (Wicksell (1934) [1977]: 110–133). Samuelson (1953–1954) had also granted the indeterminate *organization* of production under constant returns to scale, arguing that it is immaterial which "factor" hires the other(s):

> Throughout I make the simplifying assumption most appropriate for viable perfect competition – namely constant-returns-to-scale...; under this strict assumption the composition of industry output among firms becomes indeterminate and of no importance, so that the factors can be thought of as hiring each other in a Darwinian process of ruthless natural selection which severely punishes any momentary deviation from the statical optimum ... [T]he *same results* would follow if I supposed, with Leontief and others, that each good requires in its production every *other* good as an input. Goods would then have a double function – as inputs as well as outputs, as intermediate as well as final goods. Moreover, the only way to characterise a 'primary factor' in such a system would be by the fact that it cannot be produced and reproduced by a homogeneous production function. (ibid.: 1; italics in original)

Constant returns to scale is, for Samuelson, theoretically tractable rather than empirically justified, as is clear from his further remarks about additivity[25]:

> Alternative hypothesis: We can always independently carry on production in two separate processes and there will not be any necessary 'external' interaction between these processes that prevents us from getting as a total the sum of their separate outputs. Like the assumption of constant-returns-to-scale this is an empirical hypothesis rather than a truism; not only are both of these hypotheses conceptually refutable, but in addition there is considerable empirical evidence, in connection with technology and the breakdown of perfect competition, that in large realms of economic life these are poor hypotheses to make. (ibid.: 2)

In other communications as well, Samuelson had already gone to considerable lengths to insist that, under constant returns to scale, no transactions are strictly required. He sent Robinson (3 April 1971) a numerical example of an economy using coal and corn to produce coal and corn. In a familiar notation, the price equations (not given by Samuelson) are:

$$(.5p_2 + 2w)(1 + r) = p_1$$

---

[25]"Conservation Laws," too, require the assumption of constant returns to scale (see Samuelson 1990).

$$(.5p_1 + 2w)(1 + r) = p_2$$

Neither good is a direct requirement in its own production, but both are basic in the sense of Sraffa. The wage is paid at the beginning of the production period. Samuelson sets the steady-state rate of profit at 50% to obtain a real wage of 1/12 in terms of either good, and a relative price of 1. Each price is $12, given a $1 nominal wage. Quantity equations (also not given) are:

$$X_1 = .5X_2(1 + g) + C_1$$

$$X_2 = .5X_1(1 + g) + C_2$$

$$2X_1 + 2X_2 = 1200$$

There are 100 workers, each providing 12 hours of work per day; the growth rate is zero. Gross outputs are set equal: $X_1 = 300 = X_2$, so that the gross value in each sector is $3600, for a total of $7200. Workers spend their whole $1200 income on corn, for a total of 100 units, or 1 for each worker. Circulating capital is replaced using 150 units of each good, accounting for $1800 of each sector's output. This leaves $600 worth of corn (50 units) and $1800 worth of coal (150 units) for consumption. Samuelson assumes that capitalists spend their profit in such a way as to create an equilibrium of supply and demand. As a check, profit income is $1200 in each sector for a total of $2400 (50% of the sum of the value of circulating capital plus the wage bill). In terms of corn, this is 200 units. In equilibrium, one-quarter of profit must be spent on corn (the above 50-unit residual). In terms of coal, total profit is also 200 units. In equilibrium, three-quarters must be spent on coal (the above 150-unit residual). These are the fractions in Samuelson's example.

Samuelson posits a no-transactions "island of feudalism" headed by one (of ten) capitalists who "uses 10 workers 12 hours a day" to produce outputs for replacement of used-up corn and coal, as well as consumption for himself and his workers, exactly equal to 1/10 of the steady-state quantities already set forth. (No mention is made of the fact that the capitalist also needs 15 units of coal and 15 units of corn to produce 30 of each good, plus enough corn to pay wages "at the beginning of the period." Simply having 120 worker-hours at his disposal is not enough to operate in isolation from other capitalists, whether or not corn wages are paid in advance.) Samuelson then remarks that, "If the rest of society used competitive capitalist exchange, this island of feudalism could not be tempted out of its isolation by economic advantage." His main point, however, concerns the alternative arrangement in which "workers want the illusion of autonomy." Now, ten workers form a "cooperative or kibbutz." To get started, "They find a rentier-capitalist and strike an arms-length bargain or social contract with him once and for all in the year 1066: He gives them 15 initial corn + 10 [corn subsistence] and 15 initial coal, in return for their remitting forever 15 coal per period plus 5 corn per period."

Nothing has really changed, for, "As Wicksell put the matter so long ago, once interesting matters of uncertainty, change, and deviations from constant returns to scale are idealized away, the perfect competition that remains is indifferent as to which factors 'hire' the others." Importantly, there is no acknowledgment that Wicksell's argument concerned *non*-capitalist production or that, when Wicksell does take up capitalist production, he does *not* repeat or refer to the argument set forth earlier.[26]

Robinson's reaction (11 April 1972) is brief, reflecting her view that economic theory ought to recognize an essential difference between various systems of prices—in particular, Walrasian versus Sraffian (see Robinson 1962a: 1–21). In their correspondence, she repeatedly asks Samuelson for his theory of the rate of profit and, in this letter, asks: "What determines the rate of interest when workers hire inputs from capitalist-rentiers and why do they pay in perpetuity for an advance made in 1066?" In the example, the rate of profit (interest) is simply given, and the assumption

[26] Samuelson also ignored Wicksell's remarks on capital as a factor of production: "Whereas labour and land are measured each in terms of its own technical unit (e.g. working days or months, acre per annum), capital, on the other hand, as we have already shown, is reckoned, in common parlance, as a sum of exchange value – whether in money or as an average of products. In other words, each particular capital good is measured by a unit extraneous to itself. However good the practical reasons for this may be, it is a theoretical anomaly which disturbs the correspondence which would otherwise exist between all factors of production… If capital also were to be measured in technical units, the defect would be remedied and the correspondence would be complete. But, in that case, productive capital would have to be distributed into as many categories as there are kinds of tools, machinery, and materials etc., and a unified treatment of the role of capital would be impossible" (Wicksell (1934) [1977]: 149, cited by Eatwell 2012: 5, fn. 3).

of perpetual payments eases the calculation of implied capitalized values of the associated income streams. In this exchange, neither protagonist dwells on the implicit assumption of perfect foresight of those income streams.

Samuelson then addresses (14 April 1972; underlining in original) what he likely regarded as the underlying political problem at the heart of Robinson's queries:

> There is no disagreement that, in a stationary state with only one page-of-blue-print technology which has long been giving to workers only a fraction of the total net product, an act of political expropriation that gave the workers collectively ownership in the raw materials would successfully result in euthanasia of the capitalist class. But Allende will of course face a more complicated model.[27]

In cases

> with many pages of technology, a once and for all expropriation which was shared equally by all workers might well, if each worker was subsequently permitted to sell off his share of intermediate goods, result after a time in unequal ownership as between the more- and less-thrifty and the lucky or unlucky ... If the system ever comes into a new steady state – which I would regard as doubtful – it could be one again with positive profit rate (not necessarily unique) just high enough and just low enough so that the capitalized market value of non-labor resources averaged over people of all ages (the retired dissavers and working savers) would work out to equality with their cost of production total values. In short, Modigliani's life-cycle

---

[27] Samuelson wrote in the same vein to Solow in his letter of 19 July 1973 (underlining in original): "[R]eswitching and backward switching and all the important things that are possible in n-vector models but not in 1-vector models, do not provide a powerful test or refutation of 'marginal-productivity income determination' or of what is even more basic of the fundamental insight that supplies of capital goods, relative to unproducible labor, do importantly affect the pricing of the owned factors of production and the market-imputed income of property-less laborers in comparison with propertied people. This is the basic denial of Robinson, Kaldor, Pasinetti, etc. Only if they assume their overly-simple models – fixed capital/output ratio, etc. – do they get the indeterminacies that leave a way for simple power acts by unions to drastically alter distribution and the indeterminacies that can be filled in only by macroeconomic tautologies of the Kalecki-Robinson-Kaldor type." See Asimakopulos (1975, 1980–1981) for a discussion of how accounting identities—presumably what Samuelson was referring to as "tautologies"—provide a starting point for non-tautological macroeconomic theories of distribution.

> model of saving provides <u>one possible</u> way of finding the missing equation [for the profit rate]. But there are others.

A final, undated letter (underlining in original)[28] on this topic begins, as in the above numerical example, by assuming that "the rate of profit is (provisionally) taken as given." Samuelson reviews his "non-substitution theorem" (steady-state prices of final goods independent of the composition of final demand), emphasizing its dependence on the special assumption of a single non-produced input. With more than one such input, increasing opportunity cost immediately comes into play so that relative prices under competition do generally depend on the composition of final demand. However, the main thrust of the letter is to argue that in all cases where constant returns to scale prevail, there is "no occasion or necessity to trade" final goods, "since anyone can use his ownership of primary factors and of intermediate goods to hire all that is needed to produce the final goods." Regardless of the technological assumptions made, "what must be said is that, after a <u>single</u> initial exchange, ever after in the steady state each of us can exchange only primary factors against primary factors and can produce <u>all</u> of our unchanging final goods for ourselves." A footnote repeats a point made in connection with the numerical example, adding that "this initial exchange would consist of borrowing the wherewithal to buy the intermediate goods you will need forever, paying interest out of your gross sales; in exponential growth, a new act of borrowing will be needed to finance each increment of output reached for the rest of time thereafter." Finally, a brief answer is given to Robinson's repeated query on what determines Samuelson's "provisionally" given rate of profit[29]:

---

[28]The date is likely March or April 1972, as Samuelson is responding to a point that Robinson had made (15 March 1972) about labor-value prices in Smith.

[29]This is very much like the "provisional" assumption, in static theory, that relative prices are *given*. First, one works out what the value-maximizing composition of output *would* be; then, what the utility maximizing composition of demand *would* be, in light of the factor prices (and therefore the distribution of income, given factor ownership) implied by the given relative prices, assuming there is a unique answer. If they match, the "provisionally" given relative prices are equilibrium prices. If not, one tries again. Where no solution algorithm is known, i.e., in most cases of any degree of complexity, fixed-point theorems can establish existence, but not necessarily uniqueness. There may be multiple, isolated solutions or even a continuum (when a changing distribution of income just happens to leave the composition of final demand unchanged at the point where the value of output is maximized).

> To understand how the competitive rate of profit gets set under these conditions, whether high or low, one must weigh the conditions of supply that make intermediate goods available in plenitude or scarcitude [sic] as against the motivated commercial demand for them. The capitalists, like the landlords, have something the workers haven't got; the workers have something the others don't have, etc.

A generalized theory of supply and demand was always in the back of Samuelson's mind. Robinson, in contrast, insisted on distinguishing among various systems of prices, on one occasion (15 March 1972) setting forth a tripartite division, altered somewhat when later published (Robinson 1973). Robinson had written to Samuelson, "The important thing is to get the question clear before trying to answer it. Three cases have been mixed up in this correspondence." She then set forth her distinctions:

> (1) "Scarce means with alternative uses…, fixed amounts of specific factors and a production possibility frontier"; (2) "Sraffa. The composition of output is whatever it is. There is a single complex technique. Inputs in use, all produced within the system, are those appropriate to the technique and the composition of output; (3) "Beavers and deer [a reference to Smith]. There are constant returns for each separately in the sense that output per man hour is independent of the amount of labour engaged. If, furthermore, labour is interchangeable between occupations and divisible, there is no occasion to trade. Therefore, I say that Adam Smith was wrong in saying that trade takes place at labour value prices. On the other hand, if each kind of labour is fully specialized to its own product, there is no general unit of labour … If trade takes place, prices must be influenced by supply and demand.

There was no essential point of contention concerning Smith's deer and beavers, although Samuelson insisted that *if* trade did take place, it would have to be at labor-value prices, otherwise, "infinite arbitrage trade would be set into motion." Presumably, he also would have had no quarrel with Robinson's allusion, in the case of specialized types of labor, to his own comment on the role in trade of specifically localized factors of production: "We would be giving the show away if we were to descend to such fatuities as: the tropics grow tropical fruits because of the relative abundance there of tropical conditions" (Samuelson 1948: 182).

In her published list of model types, Robinson insisted that, in the case of scarce means with alternative uses, "there are 'rentals' for particular physical 'factors of production' but *no overall rate of profit.* This is the basis of Walras' general equilibrium" (Robinson 1973: 1367; italics added). She is here making no allowance for the possibility that particular physical factors of production may be reproducible, as in the world of Sraffa, where such inputs have prices, as *outputs* of the system, but no explicit rental rates for their services. It is in this world of production of commodities by means of commodities where one can find an overall rate of profit under conditions of competition, the starting point for an analysis of capitalism, which can then be modified to account for elements of monopoly power, among other complications to the basic model.[30]

Rental markets for the *services* of capital goods may, in fact, be thin or non-existent, but, for Samuelson, rental rates are *always* defined, if not observable, as *implicit* shadow prices. Each such rate, R_i, together with the price of the corresponding capital good, P_i, and its time derivative, $\dot{P}_i$, defines an own rate of return, net of (for simplicity, exponential) depreciation, δ_i. All rates of return are equalized under competition across the whole spectrum of capital goods[31]:

$$R_i/P_i + \dot{P}_i/P_i - \delta_i = R_j/P_j + \dot{P}_j/P_j - \delta_j$$
$$= R_k/P_k + \dot{P}_k/P_k - \delta_k = \cdots$$

[30] See, for example, Chapters 11 and 12 of Kurz and Salvadori (1995). An extensive discussion and critique of the classical "law of a uniform tendency in the rate of profit" is found in Harris (1988).

[31] See Bruno (1969: 49), where the *common* value of such rates of return is the growth rate of the labor force *plus* the rate at which future consumption is discounted, both in *and* out of steady-state equilibrium. In a footnote, Bruno states that, "an optimal growth model avoids some of the 'causal indeterminacy' problems recently raised by Hahn (1966)." Recent work undermines this optimism: "From the outset, it is admitted that, in all the models considered, the path of prices and quantities is, from the point of view of market adjustment, dynamically highly unstable – namely saddle-path stable" (Burgstaller 1994: 38). See also Gram (1996) and Burgstaller (2001). As for Robinson, Samuelson's remark to Solow (9 July 1973), doubting that she understood "what a price-quantities warranted dynamic path is," may not be quite fair. Referring to intertemporal equilibrium theory, she wrote: "[F]or my part, I have never been able to make that theory stand up long enough to knock it down" (Robinson 1980a: 128), an apt quip, in view of the knife-edge property of a convergent saddle path.

In short, where Robinson sees a basic difference between Walrasian and Sraffian prices—the former involving rental rates for scarce factor services along a production possibility frontier, the latter involving a uniform competitive rate of profits—Samuelson sees none. For him, only the special case of constant relative prices yields a simple proportional link between rental rates and prices: $R_i = rP_i$ for all i, where r is *the* rate of profit (interest) in a steady state.

Constant returns to scale is central to Samuelson's understanding of Sraffa, but not, it would seem, to Robinson's. Following Sraffa, she takes *both* the technique and the composition of output as given when referring to a Sraffian price system.[32] Sraffa himself equivocated on the role of returns to scale: "If [the assumption of constant returns in all industries] is found helpful, there is no harm in the reader's adopting it as a temporary working hypothesis. In fact, no such assumption is made" (Sraffa 1960: v). In correspondence, Samuelson did not engage Robinson on the essential/inessential role of constant returns to scale in Sraffa (ibid.). Yet, in his published work, he is adamant: "In sum, if a Sraffian denies constant returns to scale, the one-hundred-page 1960 classic evaporates into a few paragraphs of vapid chit-chat" (Samuelson 2000: 123). In "Sraffian economics" for *The New Palgrave*, he expressed the same viewpoint:

> Although Sraffa reserved judgment for half a century on whether he wanted to assume constant returns to scale, experiments with returns laws that depart from that property will be found to rob his algebra of any interesting economic applications, as the paucity of results on this point in the literature of the last quarter of a century attest. (Samuelson 1987: 455)

This indictment has not gone unchallenged. Dependence of prices and the wage on *both* outputs and the rate of profit in a Sraffian system is

[32]As noted in the Introduction, Samuelson had asked Robinson if, when Sraffa wrote "constant returns," he meant "to scale." It becomes clear (28 February 1972) that Samuelson took it to mean constant opportunity cost, i.e., a linear production possibility frontier, in contrast to "more general models." Robinson (1 February 1972), for her part, widened the question: "I do not know whether 'scale' applies to a plant, a firm, or an industry. I assume you mean the total output of a specified commodity, but then are you discussing a change in the composition of output or an increase in total output?" She reiterates her position that "there are two distinct kinds of prices."

recognized, formally, as a "correspondence…not yet fully explored" (Kurz and Salvadori [2000: 154], responding to Samuelson [2000]). More generally, this dependence is seen as an essential part of a reconstructed modern classical theory consisting of:

> [A] union of theories – theories of output, of accumulation, of technical development, of the real wage, and so on – from which the data of the theory of value are derived. A great strength of the classical framework derives from this separation between the determination of output and the theory of value. Not only does this separation free us from the need to assume constant returns, but also it embodies great potential for theoretical development. For example, the direct integration of the classical theory of value with Keynesian principles of effective demand presents none of the difficulties encountered in attempts to establish a relationship between the neoclassical theory of value, in which values and the employment of factors are determined simultaneously, and Keynesian analysis. (Eatwell 1977: 66; see also Eatwell 2012)

A "paucity of results" from Samuelson's vantage point is, at least for other students of Sraffa (1960), a potential not yet fully explored, a lacuna with rich and generative possibilities for the development of a classical theory of competition (see Harris 1988). In any case, reading Robinson (1956, 1962a) as a systematic effort to integrate the classical theory of value with Keynesian principles of effective demand is surely a more promising point of departure than one that holds her magnum opus up to the formal standards of intertemporal equilibrium analysis under perfect foresight, which, for Robinson, pulled the rug out from under any realistic analysis of capitalism.

3.3 Reduced Consumption Increases Future Production Possibilities

Toward the end of *The General Theory*, Keynes remarked, "[I]f our central controls succeed in establishing an aggregate volume of output corresponding to full employment as nearly as is practicable, the classical theory comes into its own again from this point onwards" (Keynes (1936) [1973]: 378). A door had opened to the development of what Robinson saw as a backward step: pre-Keynesian theory after Keynes. Thus, in the wake of Robinson's "memorable visit" to MIT, Samuelson wrote to her (10 October 1961), arguing, in effect, that the presumption of *successful* aggregate demand policies justified an intertemporal equilibrium analysis based on such traditional concepts as the production possibility frontier:

> But I assure you that whatever my delight in abstract models for their own sake, I have always in the front of my mind such important real questions as this: If by private thrift or Kennedy-overbalancing-of-the-budget-coupled-with-*successful*-expansionary-credit-policies a mixed economy succeeds in lowering the fraction that consumption is to its *full employment income,* how much will its *future* production possibilities improve as against what would be expected to happen under other policies. (italics added)

Later in the same month (23 October 1961), the connection between a change in the time profile of consumption and the average level of interest rates is referred to in a general way:

> [T]he rate at which the society is willing to consume below its potential in the interest of <u>physical</u> net capital formations could (as could any demand-composition factors) affect the average level and spread of (own) interest rates. You will realize that I do not mention <u>the</u> interest rate (or <u>the</u> profit rate) because in the regime I speak of there <u>is</u> no necessary equilibrium stationary over time which keeps relative prices the same and thereby turns the complex of own rates of interest into a single rate. (underlining in original)

He then "throw[s] in a bonus" on the overall *direction* in which interest rates will move:

> [A]ny society which stints itself in consumption goods, making sure that no Keynesian abortions of 'saving' result from induced unemployments [sic], can be expected to (1) increase its future production possibilities and

> (2) to lower the general position of its structure of own interest rates and (3) to find itself more easily in a position to swing into a new low-profit high-output high-wage stationary equilibrium if it should want to do so – all this in comparison with its having made the alternative decision to consume more generally. No more [is] implied by any position I have ever maintained – and I have maintained that general position for some decades now.

Samuelson's 1961 presumption that reduced consumption, under full employment, will lower interest rates in a new stationary equilibrium with expanded production possibilities is, by 1966, recognized as generally incorrect—a result that Samuelson came to regard as the sole significant theoretical advance to emerge from the capital theory controversy. In a footnote to his famous "Summing Up," he acknowledges that:

> The reversal of direction of the [interest rate, net national product] relation was, I must confess, the single most surprising revelation from the reswitching discussion. I had thought this relation could not change its curvature if the underlying technology was convex, so that there had to be a concave, basic Fisher (intertemporal) production-possibility frontier ... I had wrongly confused concavity of [the production possibility frontier] with concavity of the [interest rate, net national product] steady-state locus ... [R]eswitching reveals this possible curvature phenomenon, but is not necessary for it. (Samuelson 1966: 577, fn. 6)

Samuelson further acknowledged a general exception to the underlying idea of diminishing returns along the transition path to lower interest rates:

> Lower interest rates may bring lower steady-state consumption and lower capital/output ratios, and the transition to such lower interest rates can involve denial of diminishing returns and entail reverse capital deepening in which current consumption is augmented rather than sacrificed. There often turns out to be no unambiguous way of characterizing different processes as more 'capital-intensive,' more 'mechanized,' more 'roundabout,'

> except in the *ex post* tautological sense of being adopted at a lower interest rate and involving a higher real wage.[33] Such a tautological labeling is shown, in the case of reswitching, to lead to inconsistent ranking between pairs of unchanged technologies, depending upon which interest rate happens to prevail in the market. If all this causes headaches for those nostalgic for the old time parables of neoclassical writing, we must remind ourselves that scholars are not born to live an easy existence. We must respect, and appraise, the facts of life. (ibid.: 582–583)[34]

Samuelson was intent on correcting his own error concerning the direction in which interest rates were likely to move following an act of "abstaining" from consumption. He dubbed it "Samuelson's false theorem – the rate of interest will be (if anything) lower at the higher plateau of consumption" (Samuelson 1976: 14), acknowledging that "traces of this view" could be found in "my elementary *Economics*, somewhere around the sixth edition…in the appendix on interest theory [Samuelson 1964: 595-596, as noted in Samuelson 1966: 579, fn. 8] and in one or another of my letters to Robinson one might find this false theorem." His most detailed discussion is found in the published papers presented of a Conference on Capital and Macroeconomics held in Buffalo, New York, in March 1974:

> Even if that other false theorem, which for my sins I planted in the mind of Levhari, had not been false…Samuelson's false theorem would be false since indecomposability…cannot rule out the innumerable contradictions to Samuelson's false theorem. Why the false theorem is false, which is to

33 A year earlier, Samuelson wrote to Robinson (23 August 1965): "If the Levhari proof is valid, for such systems it is not possible to find contradictions and flaws in a definition of more-mechanized, more-round-about, more-capital-intensive configurations of the system at lower profit rates." The reference is to Levhari (1965), later shown to have contained an error (Levhari and Samuelson 1966). With the false proof withdrawn, the "contradictions and flaws" Samuelson had referred to were granted to be entirely possible, as shown by various examples of reswitching, using indecomposable technologies.

34 Robinson dismissed the possibility of finding empirical evidence of reswitching: "Nothing could be more idle than to get up an argument about whether reswitching is 'likely' to be found in reality" (Robinson 1975a: 38). She had earlier made the same point: "[E]quilibrium positions with different rates of profit and the same 'state of technical knowledge'…are not found in nature and cannot be observed". (Robinson and Naqvi 1967: 591)

> say why I should have discerned this fact from the beginning, is indicated briefly in footnotes 6 and 9 of Samuelson (1966: 577, 579). (Samuelson 1976: 14, fn. 5)

Mea culpa, on multiple occasions, meant only[35] that "the most general neo-neoclassical case of a concave homogeneous, Fisher-Solow intertemporal [production] frontier…does not, repeat not, have *all* the familiar properties of the simpler Clark-Ramsey-Solow-Swan-Meade parable" (ibid.: 15; italics in original).

Samuelson lists thirteen propositions true for the parable. Observing that only three can remain standing in his most general case, he goes on to say that, on the question of the relationship between steady-state consumption and steady-state interest rates, there is one definite result that emerged from the capital theory controversy. The *necessary and sufficient* condition for steady-state consumption to be higher, when the excess of the steady-state interest rate over the growth rate is also higher, is that the real Wicksell effect should "fail to be negative" (Samuelson 1976: 19), a result proved by Burmeister (1976). Samuelson takes pains to point out that an inverse relationship between the capital-output ratio (the capital-labor ratio) and the rate of interest is *not* the issue. Only the *sign* of the real Wicksell effect, which is the price-weighted sum of changes in the vector of physical capital goods, matters. When the effect is negative—as in the parable—the economy is "regular" (see ibid.).[36]

---

[35]Under the heading, WHAT THE CAPITAL THEORY CONTROVERSY TAUGHT ME, *only* this false theorem (Samuelson 1989: 137–139; upper case in original) is mentioned. None of the other issues—and certainly not the central problem of uncertainty in economics raised by Robinson in her published work and in her letters to Samuelson concerning the controversy—were deemed worthy of comment. This is remarkable in an article devoted entirely to his memories of their interactions!

[36]In more recent work, Burmeister observes: "There is some irony in the conclusion that a well-behaved aggregate production function exists when (and probably, for all practical purposes, only when) the Marx EOCC [equal organic composition of capital] condition holds. Unfortunately, the conditions required for EOCC are so exceedingly stringent that they are unlikely to be realized in any actual economy" (Burmeister 2008: 344). Nevertheless, the aggregate production function lives on as a seemingly valid theoretical construct in myriad textbooks.

4 General Assessment of the Correspondence

Robinson's arguments concerning income distribution and the meaning of capital, the process of capital accumulation, and, most importantly, the problem of "getting into equilibrium" were never fully embraced by Samuelson, but, in his correspondence with her, he was unfailingly polite—if a little wary of her influence. Certainly, he was taken aback by the interest of students in the capital theory controversy and what he saw as its political overtones, writing to Solow (9 July 1973):

> If this were all merely a tempest in the advanced seminar room of capital theory, it would all be comical. But, honest to goodness, the new left thinks that the 'other Cambridge' breakthroughs have shown up the emptiness of mainstream economics when it comes to a theory of distribution. Three times I've given general lectures on new trends in economics … The first two times, at the New School and Wisconsin, I never even mentioned the Robinson-Sraffa critique of marginal-productivity distribution; only to have students come up to me after the lecture and reproach me for not having mentioned this great new wave of the future. The third time I knew better and brought it up myself.

In a subsequent letter (19 July 1973), Samuelson muses on the best way that he and Solow might respond to the "misstatements" and "misrepresentations" he found in the draft of Robinson (1975a) which she had sent him:

> This could of course be done in a joint note…but that might be construable as a united front by a desperate and beleaguered official MIT and, to use Schumpeter's phrase, one wouldn't dream of using so big a cannon to crush so little a peanut … Murray Brown…is running next March a 2-day symposium on all this. I've little desire to go…the thought of being in a room with…some of those who've made a career of this subject will drive the strongest man into the field of plumbing.

Stepping back from the frustrations evident in some of their letters, the question remains: Why did Robinson and Samuelson fail to come to *any* sort of mutual understanding? The answer turns on the problem of uncertainty and how each protagonist viewed this long-standing bane of the formalist. Solow was clear: "The fundamental difficulty of uncertainty cannot really be dodged; and since it cannot be faced, it must simply be ignored" (Solow 1963: 15), while Samuelson, in a letter to Solow (19 July 1973), was uneasy about making such a drastic move, actually granting Robinson her point, while seeming to keep up the faith: "She is on to a real problem here; but she goes overboard in her nihilism that no kind of roughly good foresight is possible in dynamic paths outside golden age balanced growth."

Lack of candor aside, formalism also played a role. While Robinson acknowledged her limitations,[37] she understood that assumptions underlying a formal technique are not always recognized for what they are: "The account which the economist gives of the assumptions required for his technique is often very misleading. 'The formulae are wiser than the men who thought of them,'[38] and the technique knows a great deal more about the assumptions that it requires than the economist who is expounding it" (Robinson 1932: 8). Potts (2000: 73), referring once to Robinson (1962b), effectively addresses the point she had made thirty years earlier, arguing persuasively that in the algebraic structure known as a *field*, one

---

[37]When Ragnar Frisch invited her to be a Vice-President of The Econometric Society, "I said that it was no good for my name to appear on the cover of the journal when I could not understand anything inside it" (Robinson 1975b: iii). "The Rate of Interest" (Robinson 1951) was, however, published in *Econometrica* on the insistence of Frisch who wanted "to get more prose into [the journal, and who] paid me the very valuable compliment of saying that I had Ricardo's instinct for making realistic simplifications" (Robinson 1975b: iii). In "Thinking About Thinking," Robinson remarked that, "I had a very literary education and to this day I know only the mathematics that I was able to pick up in the course of trying to formalize economic arguments" (Robinson 1979: 115). She *did* seem to have had a knack for seeing "the resolution of complex logical and even mathematical problems without any knowledge of mathematics," as Richard Goodwin experienced first-hand (see Goodwin 1989: 916), but the mathematics that appeared in her writings was generally relegated to Appendices, written by others.

[38]Robinson was quoting Heinrich Hertz, who established the existence of electromagnetic waves, theorized by Cambridge mathematician James Clerk Maxwell. Hertz had written: "One cannot escape the feeling that these mathematical formulae have an independent existence and an intelligence of their own, that they are wiser than we are, wiser even than their discoverers, that we get more out of them than was originally put into them" (Hertz cited in Sheldrake 2012: 87–88). Hertz celebrated the power of mathematics to generate unexpected results and novel problems. Robinson was wary of the ways in which it can restrict the types of questions that can be asked in a subject like economics.

finds the root cause of many unresolved controversies.[39] The *field* concept is essential to the analytical economics Samuelson did so much to establish, but nowhere in discussions of its entailments (e.g., Samuelson 1983: 148–153; de la Fuente 2000: 24–37),[40] does one find a critical discussion of its implications for the *connections*—mutual and complete—that are assumed to *pre*-exist among all economic agents over space *and* time:

> Field theory allows complete off-the-shelf mathematical formalisms [e.g. dynamic programming] and analytical principles ... [I]ts appropriation was much influenced by the temptations of mathematical respectability, and, it must be acknowledged, this has...brought enormous success. But the fact remains that unlike physical space, economic space is not amenable to a field representation because it is not integral in the sense that every element (that is, agent) affects *every other element.* This is a wholly satisfied empirical condition for physical field theory but for reasons both definitional and observational it is a most audacious step to define an economic system as anything remotely resembling a perfect integral. (Potts 2000: 25; italics added)

A complete exegesis of Robinson's arguments with Samuelson in terms of this opposition between *field*-based theory and the imperfect, incomplete, mutable connections that characterize the economic life of firms, households, and other institutions would take us far afield. Nevertheless, this opposition—once appreciated in its full complexity—provides a clarifying backdrop to the otherwise ill-understood aspects of Robinson's efforts to grapple with "Time in Economic Theory" (Robinson 1980b) and with "History versus Equilibrium" (Robinson 1974). In the end, she did not think that she, or anyone else,[41] had accomplished much, concluding her

---

[39] His bold thesis is that *all* heterodox economics, of which he presents a sweeping survey, can be broadly understood as a rejection of the *field* concept as the foundation for analytical economics.

[40] For an everyman's guide to algebraic structures, rings, and fields, there is nothing to match the grace and elegance of Allen (1962), a book written with all the depth and insight of his better-known text, Allen (1938).

[41] Here, one must mention Brian Loasby, whose work was known to Robinson. She evidently enjoyed learning of his discovery that, "'Pretending to forecast the future' shall be classified as disorderly under...the [New York State] Code and liable to a fine of $250 and/or six months in prison" (Robinson 1977: 1322). There is, however, no evidence that Robinson had read the first of his many books (Loasby 1976) published during her lifetime. It offered just the sort of critique of the

life's work on a despairing note: "[T]he whole complex of theories and models in the textbooks is in need of a thorough spring cleaning. We should throw out all self-contradictory propositions, unmeasurable quantities and indefinable concepts and reconstruct a logical basis for analysis with what, if anything, remains" (Robinson 1985: 160).[42] Certainly, a never-ruptured equilibrium of supply and demand maintained over an infinite time horizon under conditions of perfect foresight would, for Robinson and others,[43] qualify on all three fronts! And, yet, one wonders, is there no *other* logical basis for analysis that mathematically oriented economists might embrace?

A resurgent evolutionary economics, relieved of its association with the now discredited biological notion of a competitive selection process effecting optimal outcomes (see Potts 2000: 34), treats *connections* among economic *objects* on a par with the objects themselves. Local and partial interactions are all that occur. Analysis of such *inter*-actions requires the use of a non-integral space, replacing the algebraic structure of a *field* with something else. As Robinson recognized, however, tractability of assumptions prompts "the optimistic, analytical…economist [to] choose the manageable set" (Robinson 1932: 6) and certainly the *field* assumption is manageable. Where would the differential and integral calculus be without it? But nowadays, combinatorics and, in particular, graph theory are sufficiently well developed to provide something else, a logical basis for a new type of economic analysis which casts aside the integral space[44] upon which so much current theory has been built (see Kirman 1987: 559). Of course, the path forward will not be an easy one, but with a

---

information structure of mainstream economic theory that would have addressed her Keynesian-inspired concerns about knowledge and expectations. Loasby's work is cited throughout Potts (2000).

42This posthumously published paper, originally dated December 1980, was a work-in-progress, "The Theory of Normal Prices, Spring Cleaning."

43"Should complete foresight be an indispensable postulate…there results that wider paradox that the science has already posited the object that it is first to investigate; that, without this assumption, the object could not exist at all" (Morgenstern 1935 [1976]: 175). "The intertemporal equilibrium is not an object of analysis, it is not a statement of what is to be determined. It is simply the name attached to the solution of a set of equations. Modify the equations – say by working with expected prices rather than a full set of futures markets – and a new 'equilibrium' emerges as the solution of the new equations" (Eatwell 2012: 3–4).

44The word "integral" sometimes appears in the context of evolutionary analysis so that the question of whether such analysis *requires* a non-integral space remains open. See Donkers (2016).

fuller understanding of how the *field* concept and associated integral space have restricted the types of economic questions that can be formulated, perhaps enough young economists will perceive another "lovely vacuum" (Samuelson 1983: xxv) into which to pour their energies. The potential payoff is enormous to the extent that it lays a foundation for an evolutionary growth theory[45] fulfilling Robinson's goal of generalizing Keynes's *General Theory*, a project that neither Samuelson nor Solow saw as having anything to do with the theory of capital accumulation.[46]

Acknowledgements We wish to acknowledge Donald J. Harris for insightful comments based in part on first-hand discussions he had with Joan Robinson and Frank Hahn, among others, during the time he spent at Cambridge University. Prue Kerr has also read our drafts and made important points about how mathematics has affected and infected methodological debates.

References[47]

Allen, R.G.D. (1938) *Mathematical Analysis for Economists.* London, Macmillan.
Allen, R.G.D. (1962) *Basic Mathematics.* London, Macmillan.

---

[45]The traditional foundation for increasing returns as found in Smith (1776 [1976]) and Young (1928) is described as "wholes into parts" or *downward* complementary by Dopfer et al. (2016: 757), who then place "parts into new wholes" or *upward* complementary on the same footing.

[46]Samuelson makes one concession in a letter (9 July 1973) to Solow: "If from relative factor supply side no distribution of income theory is possible, then a Kaldor-Keynes macro theory might be in order to try to fill the vacuum. That's the only sense in which 'generalizing the General Theory' and 'post-Keynesian versus pre-Keynesian processes of accumulation' are relevant." Solow (3 July 1973) had been more adamant: "Keynes has nothing to do with it one way or the other, since nobody is being Keynesian in the sense of having output limited by effective demand rather than by supply side considerations."

[47]The dates of papers by Robinson are followed by corresponding volume and page numbers from her five volumes of *Collected Economic Papers*, published by Blackwell, Oxford, in 1951, 1960, 1965, 1973, and 1979; and reprinted with an index by The MIT Press, Cambridge MA, in 1980. New Introductions to volumes 2 and 3 are reprinted as Chapters 9 and 10 in Robinson (1980a). Robinson added occasional postscripts or addenda to her reprinted papers. Among Robinson's cited papers, two were shortened in their reprinted versions (Robinson 1953–1954; Robinson 1958). For assessments of the work of Robinson and Samuelson, see, respectively, Harcourt and Kerr (2002) and Backhouse (2017), the first volume to be published of a multi-volume work.

Asimakopulos, A. (1967) "The Biological Interest Rate and the Social Utility Function," *American Economic Review*, 57: 185–190.

Asimakopulos, A. (1975) "A Kaleckian Theory of Income Distribution," *Canadian Journal of Economics*, 8: 313–333.

Asimakopulos, A. (1980–1981) "Themes in a Post Keynesian Theory of Income Distribution," *Journal of Post Keynesian Economics*, 3: 158–169.

Asimakopulos, A. and G.C. Harcourt (1974) "Proportionality and the Neoclassical Parables," *Southern Economic Journal*, 40: 481–483.

Asimakopulos, A. and J.C. Weldon (1968) "On the Theory of Government Pension Plans," *Canadian Journal of Economics*, 1: 699–717.

Azariadis, C. (1993) *Intertemporal Macroeconomics*. Oxford, Blackwell.

Azariadis, C. and L. Lambertini (2003) "Endogenous Debt Constraints in Life-cycle Economies," *Review of Economic Studies*, 70: 461–487.

Azariadis, C. and B.D. Smith (1993) "Adverse Selection in the Overlapping Generations Model: The Case of Pure Exchange," *Journal of Economic Theory*, 60: 277–305.

Backhouse, R.E. (2017) *Founder of Modern Economics: Paul A. Samuelson, Volume I: Becoming Samuelson, 1915–1948*. Oxford, Oxford University Press.

Bharadwaj, K. (1985) "Sraffa's Return to Classical Theory: Change and Equilibrium," *Political Economy, Studies in the Surplus Approach*, 1: 3–31.

Bruno, M. (1969) "Fundamental Duality Relations in the Pure Theory of Capital and Growth," *Review of Economic Studies*, 36: 39–53.

Burgstaller, A. (1994) *Property and Prices: Toward a Unified Theory of Value*. Cambridge, Cambridge University Press.

Burgstaller, A. (2001) "Some Metatheoretical Reflections and a Reply to Critics," *Metroeconomica*, 52: 197–216.

Burmeister, E. (1976) "Real Wicksell Effects and Regular Economies," in M. Brown, K. Sato and P. Zarembka (eds.) *Essays in Modern Capital Theory*. Amsterdam, North-Holland: 145–164. Reprinted in *Capital Theory, Volume 3* (2005). Edited by C. Bliss, A.J. Cohen and G.C. Harcourt. Cheltenham, Edward Elgar: 112–134.

Burmeister, E. (2008) "Equal Organic Composition of Capital," *Metroeconomica*, 59: 323–346.

Champernowne, D.G. (1953–1954) "The Production Function and the Theory of Capital: A Comment," *Review of Economic Studies*, 21: 112–135.

de la Fuente, A. (2000) *Mathematical Methods and Models for Economists*. Cambridge, Cambridge University Press.

Dimand, R.W. and B.J. Spencer (2009) "Trevor Swan and the Neoclassical Growth Model," *History of Political Economy*, 41: 107–126.

Donkers, H. (2016) "Integral Dynamics: A New Integration Between Wilber's Integral Theory and Spiral Dynamics," *International Journal of Humanities and Social Science*, 6: 86–106.

Dopfer, K., J. Potts and A. Pyka (2016) "Upward and Downward Complementarity: The Meso Core of Evolutionary Growth Theory," *Journal of Evolutionary Economics*, 26: 753–763.

Dorfman, R., P.A. Samuelson and R.M. Solow (1958) *Linear Programming and Economic Analysis*. New York, McGraw-Hill.

Eatwell, J. (1977) "The Irrelevance of Returns to Scale in Sraffa's Analysis," *Journal of Economic Literature*, 15: 61–68.

Eatwell, J. (2012) "The Theory of Value and the Foundations of Economic Policy," *Contributions to Political Economy*, 31: 1–18. Reprinted in *In Ricordo di Pierangelo Garegnani*. Rome, Centro per lo Studio di Roma: 11–31.

Fisher, I. (1906) *The Nature of Capital and Income*. New York, Macmillan.

Gale, D. (1973) "Pure Exchange Equilibrium of Dynamic Economic Models," *Journal of Economic Theory*, 6: 12–36.

Goodwin, R.M. (1989) "Joan Robinson—Passionate Seeker After Truth," in G.R. Feiwel (ed.) *Joan Robinson and Modern Economic Theory*. New York, New York University Press: 916–917.

Gram, H. (1996) "Review of *Property and Prices: Toward a Unified Theory of Value*, by A. Burgstaller," *Journal of Economic Behavior and Organization*, 31: 445–449.

Hahn, F.H. (1966) "Equilibrium Dynamics with Heterogeneous Capital Goods," *Quarterly Journal of Economics*, 80: 633–646.

Harcourt, G.C. and P. Kerr (2002) *Joan Robinson: Critical Assessments of Leading Economists*. London, Routledge.

Harcourt, G.C. and P. Kerr (2013) "Introduction," to the Palgrave Classics in Economics edition of *The Accumulation of Capital*, by J.V. Robinson (first edition 1956). Houndmills, Basingstoke, Palgrave Macmillan: vii–xxx.

Harris, D.J. (1988) "On the Classical Theory of Competition," *Cambridge Journal of Economics*, 12: 139–167.

Kaldor, N. (1939) "Speculation and Economic Stability," *Review of Economic Studies*, 7: 1–27.

Keynes, J.M. (1936) [1973] *The General Theory of Employment, Interest and Money, Volume VII, The Collected Writings of John Maynard Keynes*. London, Macmillan.

Kirman, A. (1987) "Graph Theory," in J. Eatwell, M. Milgate and P. Newman (eds.) *The New Palgrave: A Dictionary of Economics, Volume 2*. London, Macmillan: 558–559.

Kurz, H.-D. and N. Salvadori (1995) *Theory of Production: A Long-Period Analysis.* Cambridge, Cambridge University Press.

Kurz, H.-D. and N. Salvadori (2000) "Comment," in H.-D. Kurz (ed.) *Critical Essays on Piero Sraffa's Legacy in Economics.* Cambridge, Cambridge University Press: 152–163.

Lerner, A. (1959) "Consumption-Loan Interest and Money," *Journal of Political Economy*, 67: 512–518; and "Rejoinder": 523–525.

Levhari, D. (1965) "A Nonsubstitution Theorem and Switching of Techniques," *Quarterly Journal of Economics*, 79: 98–105.

Levhari, D. and P.A. Samuelson (1966) "The Nonswitching Theorem Is False," *Quarterly Journal of Economics*, 80: 518–519.

Lichtenberg, F. (1995) "The Output Contributions of Computer Equipment and Personnel: A Firm-Level Analysis," *Economics of Innovation and New Technology*, 3: 201–217.

Loasby, B.J. (1976) *Choice, Complexity, and Ignorance: An Enquiry into Economic Theory and the Practice of Decision-Making.* Cambridge, Cambridge University Press.

Meade, J.E. (1961) *A Neo-Classical Theory of Economic Growth.* London, Allen & Unwin.

Meckling, W.H. (1960) "An Exact Consumption-Loan Model of Interest: A Comment," *Journal of Political Economy*, 68: 72–76; and "Rejoinder": 83–84.

Morgenstern, O. (1935) [1976] "Perfect Foresight and Economic Equilibrium," translated by F.H. Knight and reprinted in A. Schotter and M.I. Nadiri (eds.) *Selected Economic Writings of Oskar Morgenstern.* New York, New York University Press: 169–183.

Pitchford, J.D. (2002) "Trevor Swan's 1956 Economic Growth 'Seminar' and Notes on Growth," *Economic Record*, 78: 381–387.

Potts, J. (2000) *The New Evolutionary Microeconomics: Complexity, Competence and Adaptive Behaviour.* Cheltenham, Edward Elgar.

Ramsey, F.P. (1928) "A Mathematical Theory of Saving," *Economic Journal*, 38: 543–559.

Robertson, D.H. (1931) "Wage-Grumbles," in *Economic Fragments*, by D.H. Robertson. London, P.S. King & Son: 42–57. Reprinted in W. Fellner and B.F. Haley (eds.) (1963) *Readings in the Theory of Income Distribution.* Irwin, Homewood, IL: 221–236.

Robinson, J.V. (1932) *Economics Is a Serious Subject: The Apologia of an Economist to the Mathematician, the Scientist and the Plain Man.* Cambridge, W. Heffer & Sons.

Robinson, J.V. (1949; **1**: 155–174) "Mr. Harrod's Dynamics," *Economic Journal*, 59: 68–85. Reprinted with a *Postscript*.

Robinson, J.V. (1951; **2**: 246–265) "The Rate of Interest," *Econometrica*, 19: 92–111. Republished with additional references in *The Generalisation of The General Theory and Other Essays*, by J.V. Robinson (1979). London, Macmillan: 137–168.

Robinson, J.V. (1953–1954; **2**: 114–131) "The Production Function and the Theory of Capital," *Review of Economic Studies*, 21: 81–106. Reprinted with a *Postscript*.

Robinson, J.V. (1956) *The Accumulation of Capital*. First edition. London, Macmillan. Second edition, 1965; Third edition, 1969.

Robinson, J.V. (1958; **2**: 27–48) "Some Reflections on the Philosophy of Prices," *Manchester School of Economic and Social Studies*, 26: 116–135.

Robinson, J.V. (1959; **2**: 132–144) "Accumulation and the Production Function," *Economic Journal*, 69: 433–442. Reprinted with a *Postscript*.

Robinson, J.V. (1960; **2**: 191–196) "Saving Without Investment." This is the published version of "A Simpler Way of Putting It."

Robinson, J.V. (1962a) *Essays in the Theory of Economic Growth*. London, Macmillan.

Robinson, J.V. (1962b) *Economic Philosophy*. London, C.A. Watts.

Robinson, J.V. (1967; **4**: 129–138) "Marginal Productivity," *Indian Economic Review*, New Series, 2: 75–84.

Robinson, J.V. (1973) "Samuelson and Marx," *Journal of Economic Literature*, 11: 1,367; with replies by P.A. Samuelson and M. Bronfenbrenner.

Robinson, J.V. (1974; **5**: 48–58) "History Versus Equilibrium," *Thames Papers in Political Economy*, Autumn. London, Thames Polytechnic.

Robinson, J.V. (1975a; **5**: 76–89) "The Unimportance of Reswitching," and "Reswitching: Reply," *Quarterly Journal of Economics*, 89: 32–39 and 53–55.

Robinson, J.V. (1975b; **2**: iii–xii) "Introduction," to a new edition of *Collected Economic Papers, Volume 2*. Oxford, Blackwell.

Robinson, J.V. (1977) "What Are the Questions?" *Journal of Economic Literature*, 15: 1318–1339. Reprinted in *What Are the Questions? and Other Essays: Further Contributions to Modern Economics*, by J.V. Robinson (1980). Armonk, NY, M. E. Sharpe: 1–32.

Robinson, J.V. (1978) *Contributions to Modern Economics*. New York, Academic Press.

Robinson, J.V. (1979; **5**: 110–119) "Thinking About Thinking," not published elsewhere.

Robinson, J.V. (1980a) *What Are the Questions? and Other Essays: Further Contributions to Modern Economics.* Armonk, NY, M. E. Sharpe.

Robinson, J.V. (1980b) "Time in Economic Theory," *Kyklos*, 33: 219–229. Reprinted in *What Are the Questions? and Other Essays: Further Contributions to Modern Economics*, by J.V. Robinson (1980). Armonk, NY, M. E. Sharpe: 86–95.

Robinson, J.V. (1985) "The Theory of Normal Prices and the Reconstruction of Economic Theory," in G.R. Feiwel (ed.) *Issues in Contemporary Macroeconomics and Distribution.* London, Palgrave Macmillan: 157–165.

Robinson, J.V. and K.A. Naqvi (1967; **4**: 74–86) "The Badly Behaved Production Function," *Quarterly Journal of Economics*, 81: 579–591.

Samuelson, P.A. (1946) "Lord Keynes and the General Theory," *Econometrica*, 14: 187–200.

Samuelson, P.A. (1948) "International Trade and the Equalisation of Factor Prices," *Economic Journal*, 58: 163–184.

Samuelson, P.A. (1950) "The Problem of Integrability in Utility Theory," *Economica*, New Series, 17: 355–385.

Samuelson, P.A. (1953–1954) "Prices of Factors and Goods in General Equilibrium," *Review of Economic Studies*, 21: 1–20.

Samuelson, P.A. (1957) "Wages and Interest: A Modern Dissection of Marxian Economic Models," *American Economic Review*, 47: 884–912.

Samuelson, P.A. (1958) "An Exact Consumption-Loan Model of Interest with or Without the Social Contrivance of Money," *Journal of Political Economy*, 66: 467–482.

Samuelson, P.A. (1959) "Consumption-Loan Interest and Money: Reply," *Journal of Political Economy*, 67: 518–522.

Samuelson, P.A. (1960) "Infinity, Unanimity, and Singularity: A Reply," *Journal of Political Economy*, 68: 76–83.

Samuelson, P.A. (1962) "Parable and Realism in Capital Theory: The Surrogate Production Function," *Review of Economic Studies*, 29: 193–206.

Samuelson, P.A. (1964) *Economics.* Sixth edition. New York, McGraw-Hill.

Samuelson, P.A. (1966) "A Summing Up," *Quarterly Journal of Economics*, 80: 568–583.

Samuelson, P.A. (1967a) "A Turnpike Refutation of the Golden Rule in a Welfare-Maximizing Many-Year Plan," in K. Shell (ed.) *Essays on the Theory of Optimal Economic Growth.* Cambridge, MA, The MIT Press: 269–280.

Samuelson, P.A. (1967b) "Indeterminacy of Development in a Heterogeneous-Capital Model with Constant Saving Propensity," in K. Shell (ed.) *Essays on the Theory of Optimal Economic Growth.* Cambridge, MA, The MIT Press: 219–232.

Samuelson, P.A. (1973) "Comment," *Journal of Economic Literature,* 11: 1367.

Samuelson, P.A. (1975) "Steady-State and Transient Relations: A Reply on Reswitching," *Quarterly Journal of Economics,* 89: 40–47.

Samuelson, P.A. (1976) "Interest Rate Determinations and Oversimplifying Parables: A Summing Up," in M. Brown, K. Sato and P. Zarembka (eds.) *Essays in Modern Capital Theory.* Amsterdam, North-Holland: 3–23.

Samuelson, P.A. (1983) *Foundations of Economic Analysis.* Enlarged edition. Cambridge, MA, Harvard University Press.

Samuelson, P.A. (1987) "Sraffian Economics," in J. Eatwell, M. Milgate and P. Newman (eds.) *The New Palgrave: A Dictionary of Economics, Volume 4.* London, Macmillan: 452–461.

Samuelson, P.A. (1989) "Remembering Joan," in G.R. Feiwel (ed.) *Joan Robinson and Modern Economic Theory.* New York, New York University Press: 121–143.

Samuelson, P.A. (1990) "Two Conservation Laws in Theoretical Economics," in S. Ryuzo and R.V. Ramachandran (eds.) *Conservation Laws and Symmetry: Applications to Economics and Finance.* Boston, Dordrecht and London, Kluwer Academic: 57–70.

Samuelson, P.A. (2000) "Sraffa's Hits and Misses," in H.-D. Kurz (ed.) *Critical Essays on Piero Sraffa's Legacy in Economics.* Cambridge, Cambridge University Press: 111–152.

Samuelson, P.A. and R.M. Solow (1956) "A Complete Capital Model Involving Heterogeneous Capital Goods," *Quarterly Journal of Economics,* 70: 537–562.

Sheldrake, R. (2012) *Science Set Free.* New York, Deepak Chopra Books. Originally published as *The Science Delusion: Freeing the Spirit of Enquiry* (2012). London, Coronet.

Shell, K. (1971) "Notes on the Economics of Infinity," *Journal of Political Economy,* 79: 1002–1011.

Smith, A. (1776) [1976] *An Inquiry into the Nature and Causes of the Wealth of Nations.* Volume 2 of *The Glasgow Edition of the Works and Correspondence of Adam Smith.* Edited by R.H. Campbell, A.S. Skinner and W.B. Todd. Oxford, Oxford University Press.

Solow, R.M. (1955–1956) "The Production Function and the Theory of Capital," *Review of Economic Studies,* 23: 101–108.

Solow, R.M. (1956) "A Contribution to the Theory of Economic Growth," *Quarterly Journal of Economics,* 70: 65–94.

Solow, R.M. (1963) *Capital Theory and the Rate of Return.* Amsterdam, North-Holland.

Solow, R.M. (1975) "Brief Comments," *Quarterly Journal of Economics*, 89: 48–52.

Sraffa, P. (1960) *Production of Commodities by Means of Commodities: Prelude to a Critique of Economic Theory.* Cambridge, Cambridge University Press.

Stigler, G. (1952, 1987) *The Theory of Price.* New York, Macmillan.

Swan, T.W. (1956) "Economic Growth and Capital Accumulation," *Economic Record*, 32: 334–361.

Turner, M. (1989) *Joan Robinson and the Americans.* Armonk, NY and London, M. E. Sharpe.

Wicksell, K. (1934) [1977] *Lectures on Political Economy, Volume I.* Fairfield, NJ, A.M. Kelley.

Young, A. (1928) "Increasing Returns and Economic Progress," *Economic Journal*, 38: 527–542.

17

Paul Samuelson, Government, and Monetary Policy: Some Evidence from the Archives

Robert A. Cord

1 Introduction

Discussions about Paul Samuelson's involvement in the US government usually centre on his relationship with John F. Kennedy, this beginning when Kennedy was a senator, candidate for president, president-elect and continuing when he became president. However, evidence from Samuelson's personal papers demonstrates that he gave economic advice to various presidential candidates and presidents. A potted history of the economic advice Samuelson gave to the Democratic Party is presented in this chapter, delineating the approaches that he took in order to get his hands dirty in the world of public policymaking. This together with some of his views

Research for this chapter was generously supported by a British Academy Small Research Grant. Any errors are my responsibility.

R. A. Cord (✉)
London, UK
e-mail: robert_cord@cantab.net

R. A. Cord et al. (eds.), *Paul Samuelson*, Remaking Economics: Eminent Post-War Economists, https://doi.org/10.1057/978-1-137-56812-0_17

on monetary policy suggests a much wider and richer contribution than has been previously assumed.[1,2]

Sections 2–4 of this chapter examines Samuelson's interactions with various Democratic presidents and presidential hopefuls, beginning with Adlai Stevenson, through John F. Kennedy and going up to Bill Clinton. In Sect. 5, we look at some of the archival evidence relating to Samuelson's views on monetary policy. Section 6 concludes.

2 Adlai Stevenson

Before his involvement with Kennedy, Samuelson's most important relationship in the political sphere was with the Democrat, Adlai Stevenson. This relationship appears to have begun in the opening months of 1955, with a note in the Samuelson Papers from Stevenson dated 30 March thanking Samuelson for his attendance and extensive participation in a seminar held at the home of Tom Finletter. The so-called Finletter Group was created in 1953 to advise Stevenson in the wake of his defeat to Dwight Eisenhower at the 1952 presidential election and with one eye on the 1956 election (where Stevenson would again secure the Democratic nomination but would for a second time lose to Eisenhower).

As well as attending the Finletter Group, Samuelson prepared two memoranda for Stevenson, one on tariff policy, dated 10 November 1955, and another on current economic developments as of late July 1956. In the former, Samuelson starts off by stressing that the American economy had benefitted a great deal from international trade and that there should be

---

[1]The focus in this chapter is mostly on the reporting of archival materials which may not be so well known to the interested reader. It does not endeavour to make any specific judgements about the relative success of Samuelson's policy advice. Of course, Samuelson also engaged in extensive economic journalism, notably his *Newsweek* columns, where he would often articulate his views on various government policies and the performance of different US administrations. For some of Samuelson's views on the role of the government in the economy and a debate he had with Milton Friedman on this question at Texas A&M University in 1980, see "The Economic Responsibility of Government" (25 March 1980, Box 119, Paul A. Samuelson Papers [hereafter PASP], Economists' Papers Archive, David M. Rubenstein Rare Book & Manuscript Library, Duke University).

[2]A "Fact Sheet 2005" contained in Box 131 of PASP lists Samuelson's extensive professional experience. His first position in government-related work was at the MIT Radiation Laboratory, 1944–1945, looking at secret military devices using high-frequency electronics.

a continuation of the "good work of the last 20 years aimed at reducing the artificial barriers to fruitful trade" (Box 70, "Memorandum on Tariff Policy," Folder "Stevenson, Adlai, 1955–1956," PASP). At the same time, there had to be a basic goal of maintaining employment opportunities and that any increase in trade must not be at the expense of workers being displaced. Following a section detailing some historical background, Samuelson discusses the problem of how foreign countries were to pay for American imports when these same countries had become, to a greater or lesser degree, dependent on US aid to help rebuild their economies following the end of the Second World War. Any imposition of import barriers by the USA would reduce the export revenues of countries selling into the American market, in turn reducing their ability to pay back loans. As Samuelson notes, the USA must "come into the world marketplace with clean hands" (ibid.: 4). He then considers some of the problems and pressures around tariff policy. Much like the dynamism that was seen in the American economy where some firms prospered and others failed, so it must be in the arena of international trade: competition from abroad will sometimes mean that domestic companies will be affected. Interestingly, Samuelson advocates the use of state aid to industries that have been subject to damaging foreign competition which was not necessarily their fault, this money to be used in helping developing other sectors which may be more efficient. Samuelson then asserts that there can be strong political pressure for more liberal trade and from business, even if the efforts by some firms and lobbyists for more protection is usually more concentrated than the calls for freer trade.

In conclusion, the main advice to McGovern is that the move towards greater trade liberalization must continue, this being not only in the interests of the USA but also of the world. Free trade leads to higher real wages and better living standards at home and abroad. Samuelson argues that although US trade barriers had been reduced over the previous 20 years, this was only because of the "militant vigilance" (ibid.: 7) of the Democratic Party.

In his second offering to Stevenson, Samuelson gave a summary of his views on where the US economy stood as of the middle of 1956. In a letter to Samuelson dated 10 July 1956, Stevenson admitted that he had been told to be "more concrete and less rhetorical…[and] should probably aim to err on the programmatic side!" (Stevenson to Samuelson, Box 70, Folder "Stevenson, Adlai, 1955–1956," PASP), the implication being that this may have been one of the reasons why he lost the 1952 presidential race. Either way, Samuelson obliged, providing Stevenson with a five-page account of economic conditions in the USA and how they might develop between then and election day in November. There were also suggestions for a Democratic economic programme and some thoughts on automation for a speech that Stevenson was planning to deliver in Detroit.

Describing the economy, Samuelson noted that although a recession might be imminent, another depression was not likely, thereby ruling out the possibility of Stevenson stressing the economic mismanagement of the Eisenhower administration. Samuelson was of the view that the coming months might see additional weakness in the housing sector, little change in car production and lower manufacturing output as a result of strike action. On the other hand, business investment spending was developing favourably, a factor which might mean, along with other things, that there would probably not be a sizeable decline in production and employment come early November.

Samuelson's advice for Stevenson and the Democrats was that the reforms pursued by Roosevelt and Truman had resulted in the landmark Employment Act of 1946 and that this piece of legislation should continue to be the guiding light for preserving American prosperity if economic circumstances were to become more difficult. Indeed, it had been increasingly accepted, Samuelson argued, that the course of the business cycle was something that could be altered by the sensible use of fiscal and monetary policies, countering the old view that the deleterious effects of a downturn simply had to be accepted. Samuelson goes on to emphasize the lack of economic ambition on the part of the Republicans, arguing that they were content merely with "rolling adjustments" (ibid.: 3) to the economy. Instead, "with population growing and technology ever improving, you must each year do better than the last or else men and women and children suffer" (ibid.).

In the final part of his briefing, Samuelson caveats his analysis by stating that he is no expert in the field of automation. Nevertheless, he does make some interesting points, even if they may seem a little mundane to the modern observer. Arguing that automation is simply a "continuation of the Industrial Revolution" (ibid.: 4), automation brings with it the promise of higher real wages and living standards. There is an acknowledgement that automation can sometimes result in significant transition costs as displaced workers seek out new employment and that the impact of this should be softened by expanding the existing programme of unemployment insurance, increasing severance pay and by guaranteeing wage income. Samuelson ends the document by reaffirming his support for Stevenson, stating that, "Your mission is such an important one" (ibid.: 5) and that he hopes that he has made "some small contribution to it" (ibid.).

3 John F. Kennedy

Samuelson's best-known association with US politics and government was his relationship with John F. Kennedy, an association which started towards the end of 1958 when Kennedy was a senator, then as a presidential candidate, president-elect and, finally, as president.[3] Some of these experiences were recorded by Samuelson in written evidence and speeches, a notable example being a talk he delivered to the Examiner Club in Boston in January 1994 entitled "Me and Kennedy," and which is reprinted in volume VII (Chapter 579) of the *Collected Scientific Papers.* In that speech, Samuelson detailed how his involvement with Kennedy first came about despite Samuelson admitting to Kennedy that he was in fact a supporter of Stevenson. His backing for Stevenson, however, started to ebb away after a meeting with Kennedy at which the future president told him that he did not need his vote but rather his expert advice on economic matters. Samuelson subsequently evolved into a Kennedy supporter.[4]

[3]Although Samuelson was an influential adviser to Kennedy, he never held an official post in the administration and turned down an offer to be the head of the Council of Economic Advisers (CEA).

[4]Advising Kennedy was not the only involvement that Samuelson had with the administration. For instance, he was one of a number of senior economists who were appointed as advisers to the Department of Treasury in May 1961. This group, which was headed by Seymour Harris, also included James Duesenberry, Alvin Hansen, Charles Kindleberger, Richard Musgrave and Walter Salant, plus a host of others. Its main task was to advise on fiscal policy, debt policy, the balance of payments and the forecasting of business conditions.

One of the most reported instances of Samuelson giving advice to Kennedy was on a log, Kennedy at one end, Samuelson at the other, at the Kennedy Compound at Hyannis Port, Cape Cod. This was a 40-minute tutorial where Samuelson articulated to the shortly-to-be-inaugurated president that the USA was struggling to recover from the 1958 recession and that action was needed. This meeting took place just a few weeks after an economic task force appointed by Kennedy and headed by Samuelson delivered a report, formally entitled "Prospects and Policies for the 1961 Economy," which argued, in a relatively moderate fashion in what was probably a deliberate bid to appease balanced-budget Democrats including Kennedy, that an increase in government spending of $3–5 billion was required as a first line of defence against any further economic weakening and that, if this did not do the trick, it should be augmented with tax cuts. This was the first time that the possibility of the tax reductions that would eventually follow would get their first airing, being passed into law in February 1964 under the Johnson administration.

However, the meeting at Hyannis Port was bookended by related and important events. On 3 August 1960, just a few days after Kennedy had secured the Democratic nomination for president, an economics seminar was held, also at Hyannis Port. Present at the meeting were Kennedy, Samuelson, the labour economist Richard Lester, and Kennedy advisers Archibald Cox and John Kenneth Galbraith, with Kennedy stating that he wanted the gathering to be one that focused on the basics of economics.[5] The details of what was discussed at this meeting have perhaps not been reported as widely as other interactions between Kennedy and Samuelson. However, the fact that shortly after Samuelson took it upon himself to write a nine-page memorandum[6] to Cox summing up the essence of what had been discussed points to the importance that Samuelson attached to the gathering.

The memorandum opens with a section on "Growth," outlining the three most important paths by which a stronger expansion can be achieved,

---

[5]Samuelson also fed into the Kennedy team ideas from other economists that he thought were worth pursuing. One instance of this was a proposal on farming by Hendrik Houthakker, which Samuelson brought to Kennedy's attention in June 1960 (see Samuelson to Kennedy, 22 June 1960, Box 43, Folder "Kennedy, J.F., 1958–2010 [2 of 2]," PASP).

[6]See Samuelson to Cox, undated, Box 43, Folder "Kennedy, J.F., 1958–2010 [2 of 2]," PASP.

namely a return to a higher level of utilization of unemployed human and capital resources, an increase in government backing of research and development and more investment in education and health and a move away from current consumption and, again, towards higher investment. One way of achieving this last goal would be to push easy money, Samuelson arguing that this would not be irresponsible (i.e. inflationary) if it were accompanied by an austere tax programme which reduced employees' after-tax income. He was perhaps emboldened to downplay the risk of upward price pressures resulting from excess demand by the fact that consumer price inflation was relatively benign at the time (1.4% in annual terms in July 1960 and below 3.0% since June 1958).

In the second section of the memorandum, called "Credit Policy and the Federal Reserve," Samuelson begins by noting that those in attendance at the Hyannis Port meeting were not in complete agreement about the relative importance of credit policy as a stabilization device (although he stopped short of naming names). Despite this difference of opinion, he does note that there was a consensus that credit conditions in the US economy were too tight. Interestingly, Samuelson then reports that there was also agreement that the conduct of economic policy should be based on a harmonious relationship between a strong president, a well-informed Congress and an independent Federal Reserve, with no designs by the government on the independence of the Fed; however, Samuelson is non-committal on whether Kennedy should or should not state this last point in public.

The third and final part of the Samuelson memorandum examines "Gold and the International Position." Samuelson states that Kennedy understood that the USA must accept constraints on economic policy resulting from its balance of payments position, a premise which had been lost sight of in the period leading up to Kennedy's presidency. Some of the policy implications of this revised approach are then underlined, including asking Europe and dollar-rich countries to share the burden of foreign aid and defence and that there was no reason to believe that a devaluation of the dollar was any more probable under the Democrats than the Republicans.

Once Kennedy was ensconced in the White House, Samuelson, with the help of selected others, ensured that the possibility of tax cuts remained firmly on the radar. In early June 1962, Samuelson and Solow had noted in a report to the administration that economic conditions had worsened to the point where a reduction in taxes had become more desirable. Samuelson and Solow quickly followed this up a few weeks later on 13 July 1962 with a memorandum to Kennedy entitled "That Second Look at Need for a Tax Cut" (Box 43, Folder "Kennedy, J.F., 1958–2010 (1 of 2)," PASP). Economic data for the second quarter had shown that conditions were worse than had been forecast, the peak of profits had passed, unemployment was expected to increase from its May level of 5.4%, production would struggle to maintain its prevailing level, and real GNP might not peak in mid-1963 but in 1962. Samuelson and Solow argued that recession could more or less be averted if tax cuts were sizeable ($8–10 billion), if the positive effects of an expansionary fiscal policy were not in large part cancelled out by a tightening of monetary policy and if lower taxes were not offset by a cut in public spending (the idea here being that expenditure has a greater impact than tax).

To further reinforce their case, Samuelson and Solow also addressed, in turn, the arguments that had been made in early June opposing a cut in taxes but which had subsequently become increasingly questionable. Among these was the notion that a request by the president to reduce tax would signal that the economy was in trouble and that this, by itself, would bring on a recession. Samuelson and Solow countered this argument by stating that the ordinary citizen was already worried about the US's short-term economic future. Moreover, accepting the idea that a tax cut would bring on a downturn through its psychological influence alone would mean that the role of stabilization policy would be significantly narrowed. The authors also noted that people did not believe something until it was done. In other words, the announcement today of a tax cut that will take place in the future is not the same as a cut now.

Even though Kennedy had publicly announced in August 1962 his intention to pursue cuts, Samuelson and Solow drew up yet another memorandum, entitled "Desirable Tax Policy in 1963,"[7] in mid-November 1962 to serve as an update on economic conditions and to reinforce their

[7] See "Desirable Tax Policy," 15 November 1962, Box 44, Folder "Reports to Kennedy, 1960–1962," PASP.

earlier message, this shortly before Kennedy presented his proposals to Congress in January 1963.[8] They began by arguing that the economic analysis that had been carried out a few months previously that was in favour of a cut continued to hold while at the same time admitting that it seemed unlikely that there would be a major economic downturn. Four reasons were given for this improved outlook, including that talk of a tax reduction was beginning to sink in with the public (although this contradicted the notion that cuts would only be believed once they had actually happened), car sales were buoyant, and the stock market had strengthened. Nevertheless, Samuelson and Solow went on to say that unemployment, profits and the outlook for production still looked difficult, one manifestation of this being a widening of the output gap.

Although the overall tenor of the memorandum was to reinforce the call for a cut, in the interests of balance, Samuelson and Solow also examined the case against reducing taxes. They considered five such arguments but find that only one of them had any validity. Among the arguments they dismissed was that consumers would save the windfall from a lowering of their taxes. This was countered by evidence which pointed to consumers spending 92–94% of such a windfall, assuming that the tax cut was a permanent one. In addition, the assertion that a reduction in taxes would cause a run on the dollar, lead to an outflow of gold and weaken the balance of payments, is answered with the argument that tax cuts were not peculiarly inflationary and that although import demand would increase, this would also be the case if there was a spontaneous recovery. The only argument against reducing taxes that is given any credence by Samuelson and Solow is that cuts might be regretted if the current strength of the economy was being underestimated and/or there might be a requirement for a rapid increase in government spending if the Cold War suddenly turned hot. The former idea is batted away with the argument that the economy could just as well be weaker at that point than stronger. The

[8]Kennedy wanted a reduction in the top rate of personal income tax from 91% to 65%, although the latter number was subsequently revised to 70%. A proposed cut in corporation tax from 52% to 47% was also pushed through but with a change in the lower figure to 48%. The Republicans insisted on spending cuts as a condition for their support. This aside, the cuts were widely regarded as a success, helping to boost private income and capital investment, reducing unemployment and actually increasing federal revenues.

authors deal with the latter possibility of a surge in Cold War military tensions by noting that Congress could usually be relied upon to raise taxes in the event of a national emergency and that the Fed would act, if required, to tighten monetary policy.

Apart from providing advice on economic policy, Samuelson was, on occasion, also asked for his views on the potential appointment of particular economists to senior positions within government. One of the most notable instances of this took place in late November 1960, a few weeks after Kennedy had won the presidential election. When it became clear that Samuelson himself did not want to take up an official position in the new administration, he was asked by Kennedy's speechwriter and close adviser, Theodore Sorensen, to compile a list of economists for possible government posts. Replying in two instalments, Samuelson applied himself with some zeal to the task, coming up with no fewer than 53 names, although he restricted himself to posts for the CEA, the Treasury, etc. rather than non-economic roles, such as State.

Before presenting his first list, Samuelson noted that he had intimately known the work of the CEA under both Truman and Eisenhower and that, in what was perhaps a criticism of the Council under those two presidents, it should not just be a body which monitors business conditions and produces an annual *Economic Report.* Rather, Samuelson argues that the staff of the CEA must be versatile enough to act as troubleshooters, able to deal with a broad range of issues, this helping to take at least some of the pressure off the White House staff.

With this move away from the then conventional view of the role and functions of the CEA, Samuelson proceeded to give his detailed opinion about the suitability of various economists for government posts. Heading his list was Charles J. Hitch, with Samuelson describing him as his first choice for chairman of the Council (see Box 43, "Possible Economists for Government Positions," Folder "Kennedy, J.F., 1958–2010 [1 of 2]," PASP). Samuelson would have known Hitch from his work at the RAND Corporation, where Hitch had been a long-serving head of the Economics Division. He had also been involved in various military and other projects and was described by Samuelson as a "good team man" (ibid.: 2). It was also the case that not many people knew what his views were on macroeconomic policy, suggesting that his appointment would not attract too much criticism at least on ideological grounds.

Despite Samuelson's strong recommendation and for reasons that are not entirely clear, Hitch was appointed neither as chairman of the CEA nor as one of its two other members. Instead, the accolade of chairman was given to Walter Heller, who appeared third on Samuelson's list. Samuelson believed that Heller would be a good member of the Council and even a good chairman, although he qualified the latter by stating that there might be some uneasiness about his [Heller's] "'unsoundness' of views" (ibid.). The two other members appointed to the CEA by Kennedy were James Tobin and Kermit Gordon. Tobin was second on Samuelson's list of recommendations, this in part based on Tobin being "a leader among economists…[who] could help recruit a prestige staff" (ibid.). Samuelson confirmed Tobin's Keynesian credentials, noting that "though he believes monetary policy has a role to play, he definitely is not a reactionary who would sacrifice full employment to price stabilization" (ibid.). However, Samuelson does go on to note that the one reservation he had was that Tobin had not made a significant impact on the Kennedy camp prior to the presidential election. Gordon does not appear on Samuelson's list, a somewhat surprising omission given Gordon's centre-left views, his service in the Office of Price Administration during the Second World War, a post-war appointment in the Department of State and a subsequent professorship at Williams College. Like Tobin, Gordon only served on the CEA from 1961 to 1962, leaving to become Director of the Bureau of the Budget.

In spite of Gordon's absence, Samuelson's list reads like a who's who of eminent contemporary US economists. Among those on the list who were appointed to the Kennedy administration were: Robert Roosa as Undersecretary for Monetary Affairs in the Department of the Treasury (Roosa had been vice-president of the Federal Reserve Bank of New York, with Samuelson suggesting that he should be considered as a candidate for chair of the Fed in the event of then Chairman William Martin's resignation); Walt Rostow as initially Deputy National Security Advisor and later Counsellor of the Department of State as well as Director of Policy

Planning (Samuelson recommended Rostow for either the State Department, the Bureau of Educational and Cultural Affairs or Defense rather than the CEA or the Treasury); and Robert Solow as a senior economist on the CEA staff (Samuelson described his colleague as MIT's "top troubleshooter" who could be placed "anywhere in economics if available" (ibid.: 6).[9]

There were also instances when Samuelson took a position on the economic views of senior economists working in government. Thus, in a revealing "Memorandum to President Kennedy: Who's Right: Heller or Burns?" dated 5 June 1961 (Box 19, Folder "Burns, Arthur, 1946–1965," PASP), Samuelson appears to have been asked by Kennedy or one of his officials to adjudicate on a difference of opinion over the future level of unemployment that had emerged between former head of the CEA and future governor of the Fed, Arthur Burns, who at the time was a member of the President's Advisory Committee on Labor-Management Policy, and Walter Heller. Burns argued that unemployment would be around 4.5% by July–October 1962 while, according to Samuelson, Heller's view was that joblessness would stand at 5.5%, there being "all the difference in the world between these estimates. Either could be right; either wrong" (ibid.: 1). Samuelson suggested that Burns was being overoptimistic and that Heller would be more nearly right, this based on three reasons: (1) if Burns had adopted the forecasting methods adopted by the National Bureau, of which he had been a member since 1930, his projection for unemployment would have been higher; (2) "Using his own [Burns's] diagnosis of the 1958-60 period, which he admits was a disappointing period, Burns should have shaded his own estimate of the future" (ibid.; underlining in original); and (3) Samuelson observes that although Burns was a "pretty smart cookie" (ibid.), he had bad days as well as good days when it came to economic forecasting.[10]

[9]Other luminaries on Samuelson's list included Seymour Harris, Richard Musgrave, Robert Triffin, Theodore Schultz, Robert A. Gordon, Gardner Ackley, Charles Kindleberger, Walter Salant, James Duesenberry and Herbert Stein.

[10]For what it's worth, the *Economic Report of the President* (*EROP*) 1964 reported the unemployment rate at an average of 5.1% for July–October 1962 (see *EROP* 1964: 230).

4 Post-Kennedy

Samuelson's subsequent interactions with senior US politicians were never as close as the relationship he had developed with Kennedy, although such interactions continued to be dominated by the giving of advice and opinions to Democrats as opposed to Republicans. In October 1964, Kennedy's successor at the White House, Lyndon Johnson, appointed Samuelson to lead one of fifteen taskforces, with Samuelson's group examining how US prosperity could be sustained. However, unlike with Kennedy, there appears to have been very little, if any, direct correspondence between Johnson and Samuelson. There was some contact with the Carter administration (see below), but again this seems to have somewhat limited.

President Kennedy was not the only Kennedy that Samuelson supported. As a resident of Massachusetts, Samuelson knew Senator Edward Kennedy, corresponding with him from 1968 to 1994. The Samuelson Papers show him backing the youngest of the Kennedy brothers during the 1970 Senate race in Massachusetts, which Kennedy was to comfortably win, arguing that he was a vital force in helping to protect and promote higher education in the state (Box 43, "Higher Education Leaders for Senator Kennedy," Folder "Kennedy, Edward M. correspondence, 1968–1994," PASP).

Of more interest was Samuelson's support for an attempt in 1979 by Kennedy to amend the Clayton Antitrust Act of 1914 to restrict the monopoly power of petroleum companies, in particular by restricting the ability of the 16 largest US firms from acquiring another company with assets in excess of $100 million. Samuelson states his general view that the government should not impose restrictions on investment decisions made by privately owned firms and that the efficiency of the private sector depends on capital being freely mobile. However, he was persuaded by the Kennedy proposal that the government would be justified in interfering in the private sector when it came to energy. He first asserts that petroleum companies had benefited from windfall revenues because of high world oil prices and that these firms had not achieved any greater efficiency or productivity. By alluding to this fairness argument, Samuelson was arguing that the petroleum majors did not deserve to mop up their competitors through the spending of windfall revenues. He then pointed out that the

USA was faced with an energy crisis of significant proportions and that there must be a move away from a reliance on the OPEC producers. However, this goal could not be achieved by a consolidation of the domestic petroleum industry as there was no reason to believe that such a process would necessarily result in higher overall oil output. In summary, the government should see to it that the executives of the oil majors concentrate on just their existing businesses.[11]

Another of the post-Kennedy Democrats that Samuelson actively threw his weight behind was George McGovern, the party's candidate in the 1972 presidential election. At least two pieces of related evidence exist in the archives. The first, dated 30 May 1972, is called "Statement for Democratic Platform on Unemployment, Prices, and Taxation" (see Box 52, Folder "George McGovern, 1972," PASP). Samuelson begins by stressing that the Democrats must continue to be the party of full employment and that it would be unacceptable to settle for the limited employment goals that had been pursued by the Nixon administration and, in particular, its CEA. In particular, Samuelson objected to what he regarded as the excuse given by Nixon for high levels of unemployment, namely the ending of the Vietnam War, the implication being that a Republican administration was not able to deliver prosperity during peacetime. In the second part of his analysis, Samuelson points out that the stagflation that was affecting the US economy was in part due to a neglect of incomes policy, with most macroeconomists agreeing that fiscal and monetary policies alone were not able to solve the dilemma between achieving full employment on the one hand and price stability on the other. Given this, Samuelson argued for the introduction of a militant incomes policy. Finally, he addresses the question of reforms to the tax system, complaining that it was full of loopholes and that the tax reform legislation introduced by Nixon had made the system less progressive. Closing loopholes and making tax more progressive should therefore be one of the first priorities for the Democrats should they secure the White House.

The second piece of archival evidence concerning Samuelson's support for McGovern is a seven-page document called "The Case for McGovern,"

[11] Samuelson went public with his support for Kennedy on this issue in his *Newsweek* column of 3 September 1979, entitled "Kennedy's Anti-Merger Initiative."

dated October 1972.[12] In this, Samuelson makes the economic case for McGovern over Nixon but also, and unusually for him, he also sets out why McGovern would be a better choice as president on political grounds especially when it came to foreign policy. In an echo of his May statement, Samuelson focuses on issues such as full employment, criticizing the Republicans for their position that America must settle for a peacetime unemployment rate of 5%, which meant a rate of anywhere between 6 and 25% for women, the young and non-whites. Tax reform is again emphasized by Samuelson, where he praises McGovern's plan to make changes to the tax system which would mean that nobody would have to pay more in tax than 48 cents on every dollar. Samuelson also expresses disappointment that McGovern had not been able to garner more support for his proposals to reform the welfare system, in particular the introduction of a negative income tax, an idea which had become more popular since its espousal by Friedman in 1962 in *Capitalism and Freedom.*

Turning to foreign matters, Samuelson notes that Vietnam was a moral and political disaster for the USA and that numerous opportunities to end the conflict had been thrown away. Adding that both Russia and China had become more concerned about Nixon's foreign policy stance, Samuelson notes that the chances of a nuclear war were no longer remote and that it was only McGovern who could address such issues at the same time as bringing American society closer together.

Other archival evidence shows that Samuelson was prepared to intervene on behalf of former students where there might have been a question mark over their suitability for an official position. Perhaps the clearest demonstration of this was the case of Lawrence Klein and the Carter administration. Klein was the chief economic adviser to Carter in the run-up to the November 1976 presidential election and was being lined up for a post should Carter win. However, there were lingering doubts in some quarters about Klein's alleged sympathies with Marxism, even though this was based on his very brief flirtation with the Communist Party in the 1940s. Aware of these concerns, Samuelson penned a letter

[12] It is unclear if this was a speech delivered by Samuelson or was related to his published pieces on McGovern.

to Stuart Eizenstat, head of Carter's presidential campaign, on 15 October 1976 stating that Klein, who would in fact ultimately turn down an offer to serve in the administration, had a "middle-of-the-road viewpoint, neither to the left nor to the right in the spectrum of the highest governmental and private economists" (Samuelson to Eizenstat, 15 October 1976, Box 21, Folder "Jimmy Carter, 1976–1979," PASP: 1) and that he recognized that "brute spending will not resolve the problems of stagflation and that structural unemployment can be made to yield only by new manpower and labor market programs" (ibid.).

Fast forward to the Clinton administration. Samuelson was a supporter of "Putting People First," the economic programme articulated by Clinton in 1992 shortly before he became president. Samuelson was one of the lead signatories of a list of no less than 555 economists, where he argued that what the USA needed most at that time was an increase in capital formation, including human and material capital as well as private and public capital. The money to pay for this, at least in the public sector, should be raised at least in part by a reversal of the tax cuts that those at the top of the earnings ladder had enjoyed under the Reagan-Bush governments when structural budget deficits had squeezed savings and therefore investment (see Box 22, "555 Economists [including nine Nobel laureates in economics] Support Bill Clinton's Plan for the US Economy," Folder "Clinton for President, 1992–1998," PASP).

Although he was not an adviser to Clinton, Samuelson did proffer his views on the conduct of economic policy early on in the administration. In a speech delivered to a Conference of Federal Judges held at George Mason University in May 1993, Samuelson set out a seven-point programme[13]: (1) the US economy was seeing slackness in terms of both labour and capacity. Under these circumstances, the optimal real growth rate for each of the following two years should be around 3.5%, but this could only be achieved, on balance, by some sort of macro stimulus; (2) the USA had become a low saving society, not helped, as noted, by the policies of the Reagan-Bush era. Samuelson argued that higher taxes should be used to wipe out the structural budget gap by 1999; (3) a temporary fiscal

[13]See Box 123, "Economic Advice to President Clinton," Folder "Economic Advice to President Clinton," "Conference of Federal Judges, Washington, DC, 17 May 1993," PASP.

stimulus designed to aid recovery would be, according to Samuelson, only a second-best option given points (1) and (2). He argued that a better option would be for the Fed to lower real rates of interest in an effort to boost investment; (4) a large budget surplus is the best budget target in the long run accompanied by a monetary policy stance which helps to channel resources not towards unemployment but increased investment with the aim of boosting real wages and productivity; (5) any new transfer initiatives, such as in health care, should be financed by higher taxes and a rationing of marginal spending programmes, a move which could help to address the growing inequality in wealth and income that was seen in the 1980s; (6) Samuelson argues that one of the reasons why Clinton was elected was to fulfil voter wishes for quality new jobs to be created. However, a mixed economy cannot conjure up such vacancies in the short run, with the wage rate clearing the market being determined by supply-side factors. Instead, quality jobs are more likely to be created by higher investment taking place over the long run; and (7) during a downturn, there can be a temptation to create good jobs by increasing protectionist barriers. However, such measures only serve to undermine the livelihoods of the less well paid. Not only was this bad economics but it was ethically wrong.[14]

5 Monetary Policy

As well as advising politicians, Samuelson had various interactions with other parts of American officialdom. Indeed, one of his longest associations with any organization external to MIT was with the Federal Reserve, lasting from 1941 to 2009 (see Box 30, Folders [two] "Federal Reserve, 1941–2009," PASP). Given his Keynesian beliefs, the common view is that Samuelson regarded fiscal policy as the main instrument of stabilization at the disposal of the authorities. As Tobin notes (1982: 4), "[Fiscal policy] was Samuelson's own emphasis in his first twenty-five years, both

---

[14]During Clinton's presidency, Samuelson also gave his personal support to the effort to establish NAFTA in 1994 and was also involved in the effort to push through the Uruguay Round of GATT, which came into effect in January 1995 and which replaced GATT with the WTO.

in his pathbreaking early papers on multiplier statics and dynamics and in his crystallization of the neoclassical synthesis after the Second World War." However, as Tobin went on to acknowledge, "At no stage was Samuelson a 'fiscalist'" (ibid.).

In terms of the role of monetary policy, Samuelson of course wrote various published pieces on the topic, notably in his *Newsweek* columns, confirming his view that he regarded the conduct of monetary policy as an important lever of economic management. An important part of Samuelson's association with the Fed was with its Board of Academic Consultants. An examination of some of the evidence that Samuelson gave to the Board reveals the deep understanding he had of the nuts and bolts of monetary policy and its interdependence with its fiscal counterpart.

In one set of notes for the Board entitled "Appropriate Monetary Policy" (12 September 1968, Box 30, Folder "Federal Reserve, 1941–2009 [2 of 2]," PASP), Samuelson closely examines the outlook for the US economy as of September 1968. He begins by noting that since the middle of 1968, a 10% tax surcharge, applicable to both individuals and corporations, had been in place and had been accompanied by major government spending cuts. The surcharge had been introduced by the Johnson administration in order to help pay for Vietnam. Samuelson noted that forecasters were expecting GNP to rise by $10 billion in each of Q3 and Q4 1968 compared to $20 in Q1 and Q2, with an even greater slowdown expected in the opening months of 1969, the implication being at least a temporary halting of real output growth and an increase in unemployment to least 4%. Given this fiscally induced weakening, an offsetting monetary easing by the Fed would be called for.

However, Samuelson notes three factors which might call into question the GNP forecasts: (1) the possibility that more money than planned would have to be spent on Vietnam; (2) in a nod to the monetarists, Samuelson stresses that the rate of money supply growth had been high in the preceding several months. Factoring in an impact lag of a minimum of 4–6 months, there might be strength in GNP growth in the second half of

1968[15]; and (3) Samuelson cites anecdotal evidence suggesting that business conditions may be better than expected, in particular car sales, which were at record levels in July and August, retail and housing starts. All of these factors taken together suggested that a recession was not imminent. A GNP growth figure of around $15 billion for Q3 is posited by Samuelson as a result of an increase in the propensity to consume driving more buoyant final demand. Samuelson also doubts the fashionable forecasts for Q4 1968 and Q1 and Q2 1969, putting his estimates $3–4 billion higher.

Given this backdrop, Samuelson then asks what the stance of the monetary authorities should be? He adopts a relatively orthodox position by asserting that the Fed should wait to see if any actual weakness in the economy develops and should counter any such weakening by cutting the discount rate, the prime rate and market bill rates. Importantly, Samuelson then acknowledges that in the year ahead, monetary policy would play an unusually important role, arguing that there should not be a deliberate attempt to push unemployment up in order to lower inflation expectations and restore balance of payments equilibrium.

On the back of this analysis, Samuelson posits a new theory of inflation. In the 1950s, Charles Schultze had proposed his theory of "demand-shift" inflation. Strong demand in certain sectors would push up prices and wages in those sectors. However, even where there was less strong demand in other sectors of the same economy, downward price stickiness would mean that average prices would drift up. In terms of policy, this would mean that monetary as well as fiscal policy would have to be even more restrictive, the risk being that unemployment would increase and production decline (see Samuelson and Solow 1960: 181–182). Samuelson propounds a theory of inflation which is the obverse of Schultze's: when the economy is near to a position of full employment and there is little appetite to increase unemployment in order to create disinflation, "it is highly appropriate

---

[15]Samuelson reveals that he had in fact sounded out strict monetarist and Friedman acolyte, Beryl Sprinkel, for his views on the likely development of GNP in the second half of 1968, with Sprinkel projecting growth of $17–18 billion in both the third and fourth quarters, well above the standard forecast. Contrast this consultation with Sprinkel with Samuelson's comment to *The Wall Street Journal* in 1984 that, "The day I become a monetarist is the day I have lost my marbles" (Samuelson quoted in Nelson 2005).

that different sectors undergo some relaxation at staggered periods of time" ("Appropriate Monetary Policy": 6). For instance, Samuelson argues that if, a year hence, manufacturing is marking time, there is no particular reason why housebuilding should be experiencing the same conditions, this of course only holding if there are no significant linkages between the sectors in question.

Much later, in October 1983, Samuelson wrote a detailed memorandum for a meeting of the academic consultants to the Boston Federal Reserve. Entitled "How the Fed Should Conduct Monetary Policy" (28 October 1983, Box 120, PASP), a key theme that Samuelson addresses in the memo is to what extent monetary policy should be guided by well defined and credible rules, the idea behind this being that policy is more effective the greater the understanding on the part of the public and open market operators as to how policy is made (rules vs. discretion). Samuelson expresses some sympathy for the rules approach but argues that the major faults with monetary policy, at least during the period that he had had an association with the Fed, could not be explained by violations of the rules-based approach. For instance, he argues that, "The disease of stagflation is real and has its source primarily outside of macroeconomic policy – namely in the fact that the mixed economy is a humane welfare state in which the divorce between income and work for pay alters fundamentally the downward pressure on price and wage levels that small amounts of slack used to exert under laissez-faire capitalism. No Martin, Burns or Volcker can alter this political fact of life" (ibid.: 2; underlining in original).

The main problem with the conduct of US monetary policy, Samuelson argues, is that there had been an underestimate in how high the trend had been in the natural rate of unemployment[16] and that this was not equivalent to setting too high money supply targets. The basic point is that there will always exist a temptation to overestimate the benefits of short-term economic gains against longer-term costs, even though economists had tried to temper this tendency through the use of optimal control models. Nevertheless, there remained an insufficient regard for end conditions.

[16]Samuelson avoids the question of whether or not the long-run Phillips curve is vertical.

Before questioning the usefulness of nominal GDP targeting, Samuelson notes that the US experience with monetarism from late 1979 to mid-1982 was not a fair one by which to judge the effectiveness of this approach to policy because many assets that were classed as M1 or M2 saw major swings in their rates of return relative to returns that could be secured by investment in assets not classed as M1 or M2. Following on, under a section named "The Game of Chicken," Samuelson throws doubt on the role of credibility in the operation of monetary policy, calling most of the rhetoric around the issue "naive" (ibid.: 11). By extension, Samuelson proceeds to challenge the existence of rational expectations, arguing that it is simply "not credible that the public should act as if they have a correct equilibrium model of the macroeconomy's future ... People do learn from experience ... Still, that's a far cry from the hypothesis that in the short run of a few years 'neutral (expected-) money' does obtain and Fed policy can't much alter real variables" (ibid.). Finally, in an acknowledgement that the Fed must try to keep all of its policy armour to hand in the fight against inflation and that some of these policies will be useful but at different times and in different combinations, Samuelson states that, "There is no once-and-for-all curing of inflation. The Fed's decision problems are never-ending" (ibid.: 12).[17]

6 Conclusion

This chapter has focused on only a small fraction of Paul Samuelson's public service, in its various guises. Additional highlights from his career include sitting on the Advisory Board of the important Commission on Money and Credit in the early 1960s, a near 20-year association with the Congressional Budget Office, in particular its Panel of Economic Advisers, and a long working relationship with the Congressional Joint Economic

[17] For Samuelson's later views on optimal monetary policy, see Samuelson (1993). In this testimony to the Senate Committee on Banking, Housing and Urban Affairs, he notes that, "After a dozen years of structural budget deficits and low private sector saving...economic history and economic science concur...that monetary policy rather than fiscal policy should be the major macroeconomics weapon for assuring a healthy 1993-1996 recovery and for restoring of the share of capital formation in the American economy" (ibid.: 1).

Committee. There were, of course, also numerous informal contacts with politicians and senior officials.

Although there is little doubt that Samuelson's most important relationship with a US politician was that with John F. Kennedy, he was also plugged in with various other senior actors in the political sphere and over a very long period. He was a strong supporter of the Democratic Party and was often highly critical of the policy positions and economic outlook of the Republicans. Despite being a Keynesian at heart, Samuelson was not afraid to put the case for monetary policy over fiscal policy where the circumstances, in his opinion, demanded it. Finally, when asked for advice and guidance, he often stressed the importance of fairness when it came to assessing the effects of economic policy.

References

EROP. (1964) *Council of Economic Advisers*. Washington, DC, United States Government Printing Office.

Nelson, E. (2005) "Paul Samuelson and Monetary Analysis," *Economic SYNOPSES*, 8. Federal Reserve Bank of St Louis. Available at https://files.stlouisfed.org/files/htdocs/publications/es/05/ES0508.pdf.

Samuelson, P.A. (1993, July 1) "Optimal Federal Reserve Policy for 1993–1994," testimony of Paul A. Samuelson, MIT, before the Senate Committee on Banking, Housing and Urban Affair. Paul A. Samuelson Papers, Box 123, Economists' Papers Archive, David M. Rubenstein Rare Book & Manuscript Library, Duke University.

Samuelson, P.A. and R.M. Solow. (1960) "Analytical Aspects of Anti-inflation Policy," *American Economic Review*, 50: 177–194.

Tobin, J. (1982) "Paul A. Samuelson and Modern Economics," Cowles Foundation Discussion Paper No. 616, Cowles Foundation for Research in Economics. New Haven, Yale University.

18

Paul A. Samuelson and the Foundation of International Economics

Lall Ramrattan and Michael Szenberg

1 Introduction

In today's global trade, driven by communication and digital technologies, Samuelson's position remains in support of free trade theory, but with some reservations. He wrote on international trade in the late 1930s, and in the 1940s he embraced another theorem called the Stolper–Samuelson theorem which was published in the article "Protection and Real Wages" (Stolper and Samuelson 1941 [1966]). Readers more concerned about the latter have occasioned people to think that he abandoned the notion of trade, but he did not. Those and other ideas on trade, as well as the tools that Samuelson forged, have stood him on a high pedestal along with other giants of international trade theory. His ideas provided the

L. Ramrattan
U.C. Berkeley Extension, Berkeley, CA, USA
e-mail: lallram@berkeley.edu

M. Szenberg (✉)
Touro College and University System, New York, NY, USA
e-mail: michael.szenberg@touro.edu

R. A. Cord et al. (eds.), *Paul Samuelson*, Remaking Economics: Eminent Post-War Economists, https://doi.org/10.1057/978-1-137-56812-0_18

foremost research program for over half a century and remain dominant in the current literature. He is acclaimed as going beyond his predecessors and teachers (Backhouse 2017: 233). This chapter presents those ideas of Samuelson along with other theories he has contributed to trade, such as the factor equalization theory and the transfer problem, and the tools he evolved to treat them from both the operational and the theoretical points of view.

2 Benefits from Trade

Samuelson was building on the Smith–Ricardo–Heckscher–Ohlin views of trade. Smith is included not so much for his absolute advantage theory but for his perfect competitive system that led to optimal conditions under free trade. Ricardo is known for his comparative advantage, premised on differences in countries' technologies; and Heckscher–Ohlin focuses on differences in countries' factor endowments. This model, in which cost is endogenous, became dominant in the post-Second World War period due mainly to the works of Samuelson (see Jones and Neary 1984: 14).

Samuelson developed trade theory from the equilibrium point of view, where one can do comparative analysis by changing parameters. An equilibrium viewpoint is optimal, so that one does not need concepts such as consumer surplus to measure benefits (see Samuelson 1990 [2011]: 931).

Samuelson viewed benefits from a social welfare function (SWF). He wrote: "[A]round 1938, Bergson (and I following him) had straightened out the interrelation: first, between the old, hedonistic welfare economics…second, between…necessary and sufficient conditions" (Samuelson 1958 [1966]: 1100). Samuelson thought that Bergson was giving meaning to the Pareto optimality concept, when he specified the Bergson-Samuelson individual social welfare function of the form:

$$W = w\ [U^1\left(x^1, y^1\right), U^2\left(x^2, y^2\right) \tag{1}$$

where x and y are commodities such as bread and wine, and W is a separable, as opposed to a joint, welfare indicator (see Samuelson 1986: 4).

This function specifies how private goods are distributed among individuals with a consumption function, given that a certain state of the world prevails. The social form of that function represents a complete order which determines an ethical order in the states of the world, meaning that for every pair of states, one can have preferences that are transitive (ibid.: 9). Samuelson proved that an individual form of that function always exists in a two-person-three-states world (ibid.: 39). He surveyed the evolution of this function in his *Foundations of Economic Analysis*, where he stated that Bergson "is the first who understands the contribution of all previous contributors, and who is able to form a synthesis of them" (Samuelson 1947 [1974]: 219).

One can begin to get a glimpse of the gains from trade by plotting the utilities of Eq. (1) for two persons on a Cartesian plane. SWF will be represented as indifference-like curves, where higher ones will be preferred to lower ones. They measure national welfare. Analysis such as income redistribution can also be inferred from such a diagram (see Corden 1984: 66–69).

3 General Equilibrium (GE) Basis of Samuelson's Trade Theory

Samuelson's GE approach was characterized by Paul Krugman as "Samuelson's angel" (Krugman 1995: 1246). It is a parable that reversed the traditional view of trade that starts from autarky and moves to trade. "Let us suppose that in the beginning all factors were perfectly mobile and nationalism had not yet reared its ugly head" (Samuelson 1949 [1966]: 882). Now let an angel appear and introduce nations and nationalities. Samuelson thinks that "just giving people and areas national labels does not alter anything: it does not change commodity or factor prices or production patterns" (ibid.: 882). This parable served as a springboard for the later development of integrated trade theory, which is achieved in a world economy without boundaries (see Krugman 1995: 1244).

Samuelson's approach to trade theory is through optimality, using indifference curves and production possibility analyses. This is something he picked up during his student days at the University of Chicago, mainly from his teacher Jacob Viner. He attained much success in putting those tools to work in trade theory, so much so that his name is often appended to the Heckscher–Ohlin model (see De Marchi 1976: 110). Samuelson used those tools in an early paper to show "how the new theories of revealed preference could be used to demonstrate important theorems in welfare economics,…the doctrine of opportunity cost in international trade and value theory" (1962 [1966]: 792).

4 Samuelson's 1938 Paper

Samuelson's 1938 paper that discussed welfare economics and international trade exemplifies his GE approach to trade. The model is built around given taste and technology, a one-person or one-country model, two goods,(x, y), and two kinds of productive services, (a, b) (Samuelson 1938 [1966]: 776). By permutation on the givens, we can find the optimum quantity to be produced. Given b, a, y, the maximum x is found, and given b, a, x, the maximum y is found. From the implicit function $\varphi(x, y, a, b) = 0$, the production possibility curve arises for given values of a and b and the indifference curve is found from assigning values for x and y, to solve for $b = a$. The equilibrium condition for each country under autarky occurs at the tangency of these curves for their respective countries. An intuitive view in this model is that gains can occur if a country can use less productive services (a, b), or other possibilities, to get on a higher indifference curve. Now a SWF is used in this apparatus, which is advantageous in performing the kind of analysis suggested above (see Corden 1984: 66–69). Samuelson concluded that

> it is demonstrable that free trade (pure competition) leads to an equilibrium in which each country is better off than in the absence of trade … Nevertheless, this does not prove that each country is better off than under any other kind of trade; indeed, if all others are free trading, it always pays [for] a single country not to trade freely. (Samuelson 1938 [1966]: 775)

Samuelson improved the results of his 1938 paper in his 1939 "The Gains from International Trade" article (Samuelson 1939 [1966]). Here the argument is not that free trade is better in some sense, but that free trade or some trade is better than no trade. To this position, he enunciated the following theorem:

> The introduction of outside (relative) prices differing from those which would be established in our economy in isolation will result in some trade, and as a result every individual will be better off than he would be at the prices which prevailed in the isolated state. (ibid.: 786)

The proof of this theorem uses simple arithmetic and inequalities in a small country model. Two sets of prices are considered: autarky prices and world prices. Trading at world prices would provide increased consumption activities that are the foundation of gains from trade. The benefits are not unique to free trade, but can arise from restricted trade as well.

One aspect of Samuelson's proof is based on counterexamples. He uses numbers for prices, p and quantities, q; three commodities; two factors prices, w; and factor quantities, a. He studied four scenarios or cases. One case applied to the Cairnes-Haberler model where factors remained invariant after trade. Changes in the terms of trade can also be accommodated. There is a unique case that examines whether more or less of all consumption and productive services will result with trade.

Another aspect of Samuelson's proof involves the solution of the following general model:

$$\sum p'x' - \sum w'a' \geq \sum p'x' - \sum w'a \ldots\ldots \text{(Objective)}$$

$$s.t. \sum px = \sum px' \ldots\ldots \text{(Constraint)}$$

In this model, the prime indicates preassigned prices and quantities, and the bar indicates optimal values. The summation runs over n commodities and s factors. The "subject to" condition of the constraint requires that exports must be equal to imports. Trade is introduced as the existence of "an outside market in which there prevail certain arbitrarily established (relative) prices at which this country can buy or sell various commodities in unlimited amounts without changing those quoted prices" (ibid.: 784–785) (see Letiche (1982: 126) for further implications).

From a vector notation perspective, the conclusion is that if at the primed set of prices, the individual would have bought the original combination of goods $[X^0]$ and provided the original amounts of productive services $[A^0]$, the total algebraic cost would have been less than that of what he actually bought and sold $[X', A']$ . . . It must necessarily follow from our inequality that $[X', A']$ is better than $[X^0, A^0]$. Thus, our theorem is proved (Samuelson 1939 [1966]: 788–789).

In his "The Gains from International Trade Once Again" paper in 1962, Samuelson used the Baldwin envelope model to prove gains from trade (Samuelson 1962 [1966]). This method looks at trade as "a technology of transforming one good into another" (Bhagwati et al. 1998: 266), so it starts out with a production possibility curve (PPC) in two goods. The envelope is a straight line or a curve concave to the origin that lies above the PPC and tangent to it at one point. While the PPC curve makes production and consumption possible under autarky, the Baldwin envelope provides the consumption possibilities for a country embarking on trade. In its derivation, Baldwin assumed that one country takes another country's behavior as given in making its optimal trade decision (see Baldwin 1948: 749).

Samuelson's envelope analysis extended his 1938 paper from small to large country cases. The main distinction between the large and small countries' models is that large countries can influence world prices. The consumption possibility occasioned by the envelope curve can now affect the terms of trade. The new conclusion is that "*society is potentially better off in the sense that there is a way of reallocating the enlarged totals of goods so as to make every person better off*" (Samuelson 1962 [1966]: 795; italics in original). Two comments can be made here. One is that this new potential benefit can be achieved through tariffs. Another is that it is possible to compensate losers to make them better off.

5 Stolper–Samuelson 1941 Paper

Currently, many people are concerned that free trade is lowering real wages in the United States to the extent that it has wiped out the net benefit to wages from free trade in the United States. In 2004, Samuelson used numerical data to hypothesize trading conditions between China and the United States that could make the United States worse off (see Samuelson 2004 [2011]). We have organized his data in the following Table 1.

Table 1 has two sections representing trade between the United States and China under autarky vs. specialization and trade. The given data relates to the labor force and productivity. The average of productivity is in favor of the United States with a ratio of 10:1. Under autarky, the labor force is split 50:50 between the production of two goods, yielding 125 units of output for each country. In the Ricardian vein, one can now assess the opportunity cost (O.C. in the table) to each country. It favors goods 1 (q1) for the United States and goods 2 (q2) for China.

After the countries specialize, output increases by 60% for each of them. We come to a point of a metric to measure gains. Ricardo's example indicates that specialization and trade saves labor. Samuelson's teacher, Jacob Viner, liked to use this cost-saving approach while John Stuart Mill would consider a utility function. For Millian demand, Samuelson took the sum-product of the square root of output. In his wider research on linear programming, he and his colleagues vied for the maximization of national product subject to production possibilities. All these methods are covered in an early piece by Kuhn (1968: 61, 64, 68). Samuelson also used another metric, the geometric mean of productivity.

The demonstration in Table 1 underscores several predictions of his model:

1. If China's population decreases relative to the US population, then China's real per capita income will go up at the expense of lowering US gains from free trade.
2. If China's productivity is quadrupled in its export sector, from 2/10 to 8/10, then China's output will increase from 200 to 800, increasing total world output.

Table 1 Samuelson numerical data for modern global trade

I. Autarky								
Givens:		US	China	US/China		Comments		
Laborforce (LF):		100	1000 LF	0.1 to 1		China LF is 10:1		
Q/LF	Q1/LF =	2	0.05 = q1/LF	40 > 10:1		Productivity is better than 10:1		
	Q2/LF =	0.5	0.2 = q2/LF	2.5 >.1:1		Not as bad as .1 :1		
Productivity	Average	1.25	0.125	10 to 1				
The split of the laborforce going to Goods 1 =					0.5			
		Work Hours devoted to Goods 1 and 2						
Analysis for US		**Good 1**	**Good 2**	**Sum hrs.**	**Units**	Matrix of Productivity x Hours		
U. S.		50	50	100	Hours	(50,50) x	(2, .5)Tram	
Output		100	25	125	Goods	O.C. US	Q1/Q2 :	4 to 1
Mills:Cons. Income:		10	5	50		Sumproduct of the square root of outputs.		
Percapita Real Income: Income/Lf in US				0.5				
Alternative Measure of Real Income via the real wage rate and not the actual goods produced.								
This measure is 1/2 times the sqrt(productivity for goods1 x productivity of good 2):								
Alternative Measure for US:				0.50				
Do the same analysis for China								
Analysis for China		500	500	1000	Hours	(500, 500) x (0.05,0.2)^T		
Output		25	100	125	Goods	O.C. Ch.	q1:q2	0.25 to 1
Mills:Cons. Income:		5.00	10.00	50		Sumproduct of the square root of outputs.		
Percapita Real Income: income/LF in China				0.05				
Alternative Measure for China				0.05				
II. Specialization and Trade								
Using the O.C estimates in Autarky, US will do only Q1, and China will do q2								
Repeat Givens:		**US**	**China**	**US/China**				
Laborforce (LF)		100	1000 LF	0.1 to 1		China LF is 10:1		
Q/LF:	**Q1/LF =**	2	**0.05 = q1/LF**	40 > 10:1		Productivity is better than 10:1		
	Q2/LF =	0.5	**0.2 = q2/LF**	2.5 >.1:1		Not as bad as .1 :1		
Productivity Average		1.25	0.125	10 to 1				
US uses all its 100 LF in Goods 1:								
The split of the laborforce going to Goods 1 =					1			
		Work Hours devoted to Gooda 1 and 2						
		Good 1	Good 2	Sum hrs.		Matrix of Prod x Hrs		
U. S.		100	0	100	Hours	(100, 0) x (2, (2, .5)^T		
Output		200	0	200	Goods	O.C. US	Q1/Q2	
Mills:Cons. Income:		14.14	0	3.76		The square root of output measure consumption.		
Percapita Real Income: Income/Lf in US				0.04				
Alternative Measure of Real Income via the real wage rate and not the actual goods produced.								
This measure is 1/2 times the sqrt(productivity for goods1 x productivity of good 2):								
Alternative Measure for US:				0.50				
Trade increase Output over autarky by:				**Trade**	**Autarky**	**Pct. Change**		
				200	125	60		
China:		0	1000	1000	hrs	(0, 1000) x (.05, .02)^T		
Output		0	200	200	goods	O.C. Ch.	q1:q2	0 to 1
Mills Geo. Mean		0	14.14	3.76		The square root of output measure consumption.		
Percapita Real Income: income.LF China				0.00				
Alternative Measure for China				0.05				
Trade increase Output over autarky by:				**Trade**	**Autarky**	**Pct. Change**		
				200	125	60		

Source The authors

3. If China's productivity in good 1 increases from 2/10 to 8/10, then China's labor productivity will beat that of US productivity, but China will be poorer in autarky with a lower average real wage. Each country will have a ratio of productivity of 4, so that they can do as well in a new autarky as in free trade. Samuelson concludes that one needs only to compare "the United States' post-invention autarky geometric mean with it pre-invention free trade geometric mean, ignoring Ricardo and Mill" (Samuelson 2004 [2011]: 822).
4. Some other concerns of Samuelson on free trade.

Avinash Dixit and Gene Grossman gleaned two ideas from the logic of Samuelson's new position. Assume that the United States has a free trade policy. Situation 1 is that China's productivity is low in the sector that the United States is specializing in. Situation 2 is that China has high productivity in the same sector. They reasoned that "the US terms of trade are worse and the aggregate US economic welfare is lower in situation 2 than in situation 1" (Dixit and Grossman 2005 [2011]: 839). Samuelson included their comments in his *Collected Scientific Papers*. However, while they do not question that Samuelson's logic is a possibility, they do not see any policy implications to take China back to its low productivity levels.

The older version of these discussions harks back to the Stolper–Samuelson theorem. This theorem has reached the textbook level for training business graduates. One popular text carries it as "The Samuelson Critique" (Hill and Hult 2018: 165). This book cites studies that pinpoint the problem to certain regions of the United States and to government subsidies accounting for around two-thirds of the gains from trade with China. They see most of the gain in productivity as upgrades in skill level, which is subject to diminishing returns, although statistics show, for example, that Asian countries continue to award more than 10 times the engineering degrees than the United States (ibid.: 167).

The rest of this section presents the original Stolper–Samuelson model. It is said that Samuelson had delayed the publication of the paper because of his commitment to free trade. After all, the "argument seems to have relevance to the American discussion of protection versus free trade … Labor is the relatively scarce factor in the American economy. It would appear that trade would necessarily lower the relative position of the laboring class as compared to owners of other factors of production" (Samuelson 1941 [1966]: 832).

The purpose of the 1941 paper is to show "a special relationship between commodity and factor prices, namely, that an increase in the price of a commodity will bring about a more than proportionate increase in the price of the corresponding 'intensive' factor" (Chipman 1969: 399). Usually, commodity prices are determined in the world market, and factor prices determined locally; but the theory applies also to when factors are traded internationally and goods are not. In the main, this mapping relates prices determined in the world market to prices determined locally (see Leamer and Levinsohn 1995: 1,348).

The assumptions of the Stolper–Samuelson model are perfect competition, two countries, two homogenous goods, namely wheat (A), and watches (B), relative prices, P_a/P_b, two fixed factors, i.e., labor (L) and capital (C), fully employed with perfect factor mobility and the same production function (Stolper and Samuelson 1941 [1966]: 835). Four additional assumptions—two relating to the Heckscher–Ohlin model and two for case studies—are assumed. These assumptions are: (a) Capital is abundant and labor is scarce; and (b). Capital is more important in the production of wheat (A) than in the production of watches (B). Also, (1) Capital is relatively more important in wheat (A) as the wage-good; and (2) Capital is relatively more important in watches (B) as the wage-good (ibid.: 838). The equations provided are:

$$L_a + L_b = L \tag{2}$$

$$C_a + C_b = C \tag{3}$$

$$C_a + C_b = C \tag{4}$$

$$B = B(L_b.C_b) \tag{5}$$

where the subscripts of the factors indicate the amount of the factor required to produce wheat (A) or watches (B).

5.1 Predictions of the Stolper–Samuelson Model

The main points of this model include:

1. Central theorem: "International trade necessarily lowers the real wage of the scarce factor expressed in terms of any good."
2. "The introduction of trade lowers the proportion of capital to labor in each line [of production] and the prohibition of trade, as by a tariff, necessarily raises the proportion of capital to labor in each industry" (ibid.: 841). These address the two aspects of Point 1, namely, (a) Trade will lower the real wages of the scarce factors of production, and (b) Protection will increase the real wages of the scarce factors of production.
3. Bhagwati summarizes the literature under a third assumption, namely that the factor intensity of imports also matters, this due to the works of Metzler, Lancaster, Heckscher–Ohlin, and Leontief (see Bhagwati 1959 [1983]: 151). Under these models, Stolper–Samuelson will be true in its predictions if "the elasticity of foreign demand is greater than the marginal propensity to consume exportable goods ($n_x > c$)" (ibid.: 156). Extracts from Bhagwati's diagrammatic exposition show that the Stolper–Samuelson model might not hold under, (1) Lancaster: if tariffs are non-prohibitive, (2) Heckscher–Ohlin: First, if production functions are different, second, if production functions are identical but factor intensity is reversible, and third, if production functions are identical, factor intensity is non-reversible, and tariffs are non-prohibitive, and (3) Leontief: First, if production functions are different, second, if production functions are identical but factor intensity is reversible, third, if production functions are identical, factor intensity is non-reversible but tastes are different, and fourth, if production functions are identical, factor intensity is non-reversible, tastes are identical, and tariffs are non-prohibitive. Bhagwati makes the understanding of all of this easy for the reader by providing a diagram (ibid.: 158).
4. A review by Deardorff highlighted propositions (a) and (b) as forming the essential Stolper–Samuelson proposition (see Deardorff 1994: 12). Chipman is credited with a "weak version" that is concerned with only factors that gain from a price increase, and a "strong version"

> that is concerned not only with factors that gain but with those that lose consequent to a price increase. Another characterization comes under the "friends and enemies version," where "every good is a friend to some factor and an enemy to some other factor" (ibid.: 16). Yet another characterization is a "correlated version," which correlates a vector of goods prices, a vector of factor prices, and a matrix of factor requirements (ibid.: 18).

To determine the predictions of the model, we need to solve a consistent set of equations for their unknowns. Given the production functions above, equilibrium conditions require that the factor prices must equal their marginal productivities. Since we assumed that the production functions for the two goods are the same, instead of writing two equations for labor, i.e., a wage rate equation for wheat and a wage rate equation for watches, we can write one wage rate equation for labor and one for capital:

$$w = \frac{P_a \partial A}{\partial L_a} \tag{6}$$

$$w = \frac{P_b \partial A}{\partial L_b} \tag{7}$$

$$r = \frac{P_a \partial A}{\partial C_a} \tag{8}$$

$$r = \frac{P_b \partial A}{\partial C_b} \tag{9}$$

Along with the four equations above, we now have eight equations for the production side of the economy. Equations are required on the demand side to close the system to have a solution. We can add at least two more equations, one representing the demand for wheat and the other representing the demand for watches. With ten equations at hand, one is redundant according to Walras' law, leaving nine independent equations to solve for nine variables, two for quantities of labor in each industry, two quantities for capital used in each industry, total amount of watches and wheat, the real wage rates, the real returns on capital, and the relative prices of the two goods (see Burmeister and Dobell 1970: Chapter 4; Takayama (1972: 47)).

Samuelson next examined the system through the Edgeworth-Bowley box, with the height of the box representing Eq. (2), the width representing Eq. (3), and isoquants that are derived from Eqs. (4) and (5). We will follow a more general equilibrium approach to the diagram. Figures 1a and c are Edgeworth representations. In Fig. 1c, the subscripted origins (0) and isoquant curves (I) refer to the countries I and II, respectively. x_2 represents labor on the vertical axis and x_1 represents capital on the horizontal axis. The tangency of the isoquant along the line PO gives Pareto optimal outcomes, and the segment AB represents the core. The tangent of the two unlabeled indifferent curves in the core represents the Walrasian ratio of equilibrium prices, namely, (p_1/p_2) for wages to interest, indicated by the double arrow lines normal to the budget line (north-east pointing arrow) through the tangent point. This line marks the separation point of the two I's.

In Fig. 1c, the south-west corner of the box represents the production of wheat, *A* and the north-east corner represents the production of watches, *B*. The contract curve joining these two corners can be derived from the Lagrange function constraining the production of wheat, *A*, by given amounts of watches, *B*.

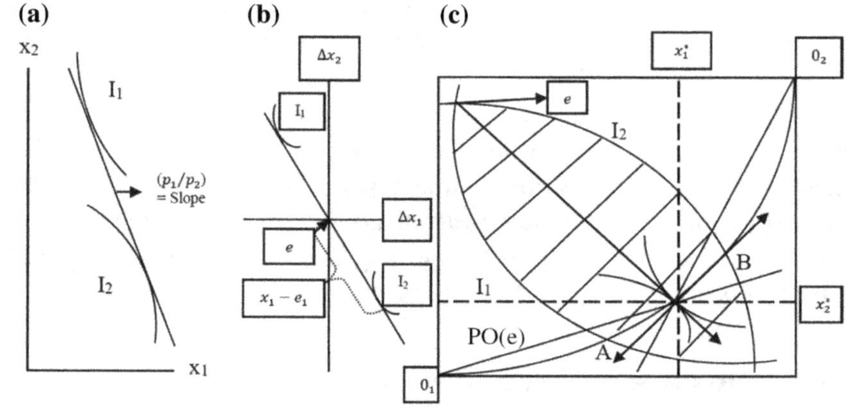

Fig. 1 Three general equilibrium views of trade, relative price change (**a**), net trade (**b**), edgeworth box (**c**) (*Source* The authors)

The letter $y = e_1 + e_2$ represents the endowment point on the budget line. Once the endowment for one trader is given, the endowment for the other trader is the residual. If one were to tear the diagram through the endowment point and arrange the two parts as in Fig. 1b, one gets a net trade diagram that can generalize the Edgeworth box to a large economy (see Ellickson 1997: 22).

Trading without prices can take place with the concept of an unblocked coalition in the sense that player one (or type one players if there is a coalition) can trade by moving their I_1 curve freely in a north-easterly direction, and player two can trade by moving their I_2 curve freely in a south-westerly direction. In a Walrasian auction, we are interested in trading where prices are given (see Takayama 1972: 213).

Figure 1a shows a situation where there is a change in relative prices, such as where p_1 is high, and p_2 is low, thus steepening the slope. One can imagine also a situation where p_1 is low and p_2 is high, thus flattening the slope and switching around the I curves. The main point is that as the slope steepens or flattens, it will pass through the equilibrium prices in Fig. 1a, which would represent the fixed point solution of Walrasian prices in the core (see Tatsuro 1997: Chapter 4).

Samuelson, however, did not use the fixed-point theorem. However, we can show how general the analysis can be. Traditionally, one would use calculus, employing the Lagrange multiplier to maximize the function: $L = A(L_a, C_a) + \gamma\left[B(\bar{L} - L_a, \bar{C} - C_a\right) - \bar{B}$, where γ is the Lagrange multiplier (see Ferguson 1962: 100). Given the way that the Edgeworth Box is constructed, production wheat, A is assumed to be more capital-intensive than the production of watches, B, therefore, the curve bellies below the south-west and north-east diagonal. The points where the two straight lines from the origins to the tangency of the isoquants, say M, indicate a position of no trade.

5.2 The Case of Trade to No Trade

A higher point than M on the contract curve, say N, higher up on the PO curve from 0_1, would represent trade. Movement from trade N to no trade M is done through protections such as tariffs. It would make wheat

(A) and watches (B) use more capital to labor, as the angle of the straight line with respect to the horizontal would be larger in Fig. 1a. More capital implies increased productivity for labor, the scarce factor. This means that the real wage to the worker will increase in terms of either the wage-good wheat, or the wage-good watches, or a combination of both (see Lancaster 1957: 201).

However, the theory argues that the real wage rate for the scarce factor should fall. By assumption (a) of the model, a country is capital-abundant. In conjunction with assumption (1), which lets wheat (A) be the capital-intensive industry, there will be a tendency to expand the output of wheat (A) and contract the output of watches (B). This is achieved by transferring capital and labor from watches (B) production to wheat (A) production. The key point is that not enough of capital will be transferred to employ all the labor released in the watch (B) industry because wheat production is more capital-intensive than watch production. For full employment of all the labor in the economy, therefore, the real wage of the scarce factor has to decline (see Stolper and Samuelson 1941 [1966]: 838).

A restriction of the argument is that as more capital-intensive output of wheat will be produced, some will be exported. Similarly, as fewer watches will be produced, so some will be imported. Workers are paid with a wage-good by assumptions (1) and (2). If wheat (A) is the wage-good, then workers receive wheat as payment, or if given watches (B), they will exchange them for wheat as payment. When wheat is the wage-good, net wheat imports = (labor force) × (marginal product of labor in wheat) – (production of wheat) or $NWI_a = L.MPL_a - A$. When watches are the wage-good, only the capitalists will demand watches, so the net wheat import has to be rewritten as $NWI_b = L.MPL_b - B$. These two import constraints set break-even points for which the Stolper–Samuelson theorem holds. Using these two definitions of imports, Lancaster reached the conclusion that "*protection will raise the real wages of labor if, and only if, the country imports the labor intensive good*" (Lancaster 1957: 209; italics in original).

What is visible through the use of Edgeworth Box analysis corresponds with the algebra. Samuelson equates the overall $C/L = \bar{K}_b$ to a weighted average of the $C_a/L_a = k_a$ for the wheat industry and $C_b/L_b = k_b$ for the watch industry. The weights are the labor shares for the wheat and watch industries, i.e., $L_a/(L_a + L_b) = \lambda_a$ and $L_b/(L_a + L_b) = \lambda_b$, respectively. One can then write a line combination of the capital-labor ratios as follows:

$$\lambda_a k_a + \lambda_b k_b = k_b \tag{10}$$

Since the weights in Eq. (10) sum to one, we can now consider specialization in goods A as λ_a approaches one and specialization in goods B as λ_b approaches one. The various profiles were summarized by Takayama in the following lemmas (see Takayama 1972: 47–52):

Lemma 1 *If* $k_a \gtreqless k_b then \lambda_a \lesseqgtr \lambda_b$. *This relationship predicts that if the capital-labor ratio in A is greater than in B, then the labor share in A is less than in B, and* vice versa.

Lemma 2 $\frac{d(p_a/p_b)}{p_a/p_b} = [\lambda_a - \lambda_a].\left[d\left(\frac{w}{r}\right)/(w.r)\right]$. *This predicts that the percentage change in the ratio of the factor prices will affect the percentage change in the relative price of commodities through the differences of their labor share.*

Lemma 3 *The marginal product of capital increases in each industry as capital becomes more expensive than labor. This lemma is expressed as follows:*

$$\frac{\mathrm{d}(r/p_a)}{(r/p_a)} = -\lambda_a\left[\frac{\mathrm{d}(w.r)/(w/r)}{(w/r)}\right], \text{ and}$$

$$\frac{\mathrm{d}(r/p_b)}{(r/p_b)} = -\lambda_b\left[\frac{\mathrm{d}(w.r)/(w/r)}{(w/r)}\right]$$

Lemma 4 *The factor price ratio,* w/r, *increases monotonically with the factor intensity,* k_a *and* k_b.

Although Takayama developed a fifth lemma that would help to solve the Stolper–Samuelson theorem, he resorted to the Edgeworth-Bowley box to illustrate this particular proof (see Takayama 1972: 94–96). We pick the story up from the notion that a movement from trade to protection will use more capital in each industry. This translates to the argument that both k_a

and k_b will rise for the two industries, with total capital and labor for the economy, $\bar{k}$, fixed. By Lemma 4, the w/r will increase monotonically as k_a and k_b intensify. Now three critical phases of the proof are important in the two goods and two-factor (2×2) cases. First, protection on imported goods will increase the ratio of import to export prices at home. This is a juncture where several counteracting tendencies for prices to increase may occur, such as foreign retaliation to the protection. Second, the imported goods use the scarce factor intensively. Third, a rise in the price of the imported goods will increase the return to the scarce factor. For the 2×2, Samuelson argued that either the share of labor in the scarce factor industry, λ_a, or the share of labor in the abundant factor industry, λ_b, must be lowered. As not enough capital will be transferred to the capital-intensive wheat industry, the scarce factor share λ_a would be lowered (see Stolper and Samuelson 1941 [1966]: 838). This will not, however, hold in general, as we shall endeavor to show in the next section.

6 Samuelson's 1948, 1949, 1953, and 1967 Papers

In 1948, Samuelson took up the topic of factor price equalization (FPE). The purpose of the 1948 paper was to probe the proof of Ohlin's partial equalization theorem that "(1) *free mobility of commodities in international trade can serve as a partial substitute for factor mobility* and (2) *will lead to a partial equalization of relative (and absolute) factor prices*" (Samuelson 1948 [1966]: 847; italics in original). Samuelson enunciated four propositions, of which the first two are proved, and the latter two are derived. The two main propositions are:

1. Given partial specialization and each country producing some of the two goods, factor prices will be equalized, absolutely and relatively, by free trade.
2. If factor endowments are not too unequal, commodity mobility will always substitute perfectly for factor mobility (ibid.: 853).

In his 1949 paper, Samuelson admitted that his 1948 article, in which he argued that "free commodity trade will, under specified conditions, inevitably lead to complete factor-price equalization" (ibid.: 869) appears to be in need of further amplification. In the 1948 paper, he postulated a relationship between wage-rent to the labor-land ratio that was tied to Europe and the US (ibid.: 847). In 1949, he added a wage-rent to commodity price ratio and used a more integrated model, treating the world as a country (see Samuelson 1949 [1966]: 876).

According to Ronald Findlay, although the factor price model is also credited to Abba Lerner, it was Samuelson who first introduced it to the economics profession (see Findlay 1995: 7). Findlay quoted a rare citation of Samuelson stating that it also pointed out another of Samuelson's novel contributions in regard to the Heckscher–Ohlin model as well, which is worth quoting in full:

> Already in 1924 Ohlin has melded Heckscher and Walras. But neither then, nor in 1933 and 1967, did Ohlin descend from full generality to strong and manageable cases—such as two factors of production and two or more goods. What a pity. Not only did Ohlin leave to my generation these easy pickings, but in addition he would for the first time have really understood his own system had he played with graphable versions. (Samuelson quoted in ibid.)

Intuitively, John Hicks gave the essence of the FPE model in simple general equilibrium algebraic terms. Assume the same number of factors is needed to make a unit of output in each country for goods 1 and 2. Call the labor coefficients l_1 and l_2, and capital coefficients c_1 and c_2, respectively. Let $w, w' and r, r'$ be the prices of labor and capital respectively for the two countries. In equilibrium, we will have two equations for the two products:

$$l_1 w + c_1 r = l_1 w' + c_1 r' \;\ldots\ldots\ldots\ldots \text{(good 1)}$$

$$l_2 w + c_2 r = l_2 w' + c_2 r' \;\ldots\ldots\ldots\ldots \text{(good 2)}$$

Solving the equations simultaneously yields: $r' - r = \left(\frac{l_1}{c_1}\right)(w - w') = \left(\frac{l_2}{c_2}\right)(w - w')$, where the ratios indicate capital intensities.

Since capital intensities can differ, they can differ only if $w - w'$ is the same, and therefore, $r = r'$ (see Hicks 1983: 226). Hicks concluded that "the analysis which emerges does not sound to be so unrealistic. It sounds to me like ringing true" (ibid.: 233).

We have provided an extensive discussion elsewhere of the papers by Samuelson that have been referred to so far in this section (Ramrattan and Szenberg 2010). We will only give a precis of the results here. Samuelson summarized his 1949 paper with the finding that:

> *Within any country:* (a) *an increase in the ratio of wages to rents will cause a defined decrease in the proportion of labor to land in both industries;* (b) *to each determinate state of factor proportion in the two industries there will correspond one, and only one, commodity price ratio and a unique configuration of wages and rent*; and (c) *the change in factor proportions incident to an increase in wage/rents must be followed by a one-directional increase in clothing prices relative to food prices.* (Samuelson 1949 [1966]: 875; italics in original)

In support of this argument, he started by postulating two production functions. Food and clothing are made homogenous functions of the inputs, namely, labor and land, $F = T_f f(L_f/T_f)$ and $C = T_c f(L_c/T_c)$. Partial derivatives for the marginal physical products for (1) labor in food, (2) land in food, (3) labor in clothing, and (4) land in clothing are taken. These marginal productivities are converted into values by multiplying by their respective prices. The values of labor in food and clothing industries are equated to form one equation. The values of land in both industries are then equated to form a second equation. We now have two equations with three variables, namely $L_c/T_c, L_f/T_f, and P_f/P_c$. Given prices, we can then solve for the other two variables. Samuelson looked for conditions on the determinants of the Jacobian which must not vanish. The following equation indicates the Jacobian and its determinant for Samuelson's 2 × 2 case:

$$\Delta = \begin{vmatrix} \frac{P_f}{P_c} f'' & -c'' \\ -\frac{P_f}{P_c} \frac{L_f}{T_f} f'' & +\frac{L_c}{T_c} c'' \end{vmatrix} = \frac{P_f}{P_c} f'' c'' \left[\frac{L_c}{T_c} - \frac{L_f}{T_f} \right] \qquad (11)$$

where f'' and c'' are the second derivatives of the food and clothing production functions, respectively, which will be negative because of diminishing returns. Prices and quantities are positive and clothing is more labor-intensive, which makes the square bracket items positive. As the Jacobian determinant did not vanish, Samuelson therefore concludes that the "equilibrium is unique" (ibid.: 880).

In his 1953 article, Samuelson began to address more general cases beyond the 2 × 2 trade model. This means that he had to look for global conditions for a unique solution of relationships between commodity and factor prices. He started to relate these prices with equations of the following form (Samuelson 1953 [1966]: 903):

$$p_i = A^i(w_1, \ldots, w_r), and[\partial p_i/\partial w_j] = [a_{ij}] \qquad (12)$$

where p is commodity price with $i = 1 \ldots n \gtreqless r$, a_{ij} representing the required amount of input, j, to produce a unit of the good, i (ibid.: 889–890).

Case (i): *Equal goods and factors* $(n = r)$: This case deals with the situation where the number of factors and goods are equal, the $n \times n$ case. The conclusion is that

> if two countries have the same production functions, and if they do produce in common as many different goods as there are factors, and if the goods differ in their 'factor intensities,' and if there are no barriers to trade to produce commodity price differentials, then the absolute returns of every factor must be fully equalized. (ibid.: 893)

Case (ii): *More Goods than Factors* $(n > r)$: In this case, the number of factors is less than the number of goods. We have more commodity equations than factors to be determined. This may be called an overdetermined system. Samuelson argued that if prices are arbitrarily fixed, then certain industries will shut down, reducing Case (ii) to Case (i). If the market determines prices, however, r factor prices will adjust to the market price, and the n-r prices will require factor endowment to be determined.

Case (ii) can be looked at from the point of view of least-square problems in regression analysis where the number of observations is greater than the coefficients to be determined. In such a case, we get the best solution. As in this statistical overdetermined system, we project the observation onto a line. Similarly, we can imagine projecting the factor price spaces into the commodity price space. We can think of the price spaces as the four walls of a room, and the factor space as just one wall. The projection is therefore a projection of the w-space to a subspace of the p-space. This projection restricts the commodity space from its n dimension, to be compatible with the r-dimension of the factor space.

Case (iii): *More Factors than Goods* ($n < r$): This is an underdetermined system characterized by fewer equations than unknowns to be solved. Samuelson proposed an additional equation for endowments to enable a solution.

Solution for case (i) where the number of commodity and goods prices are equal ($n = r$):

Essentially, Eq. (11) is a mapping between commodity prices and factor prices, namely:

$$f : p \rightarrow W \quad \text{or} \quad p_i = f_i(w) \tag{13}$$

In 1953, Samuelson refocused his attention on the Jacobian of the a_{ij} of Eq. (12) to satisfy the inverse requirements of Eq. (13). He wrote: "Fortunately, the economics of the situation was clearer than my mathematical analysis; because all the elements of the Jacobian represented inputs, or $a's$, they were essentially one-signed; and this condition combined with the non-vanishing determinant, turns out to be sufficient to guarantee uniqueness in the large" (ibid.: 903). This was met with much resistance in the literature, as summarized in Ramrattan and Szenberg (2010).

In 1967, Samuelson summarized the FPE literature. He also perused the development of the use of factor endowment to bring about a solution. The model was now converted to a maximization problem using Lagrange multipliers (see Samuelson 1967 [1972]: 351). It did not answer all the objections in the literature, but the Hessian matrix formed for the partials of the Lagrange equations accommodated the maximum (see ibid.).

7 The Transfer Problem

In an interview with economist William Barnett, Samuelson stated that he is responsible for "resolving the age-old 'transfer problem' relating terms of trade and capital flows" (Samuelson 2011: 555). Essentially, the problem deals with how transfers of income from one country to another affect the terms of trade of the transferer. This problem runs through the classical economic schools of thought and is most significant when large transfers have to be made, such as after the world wars.

In 1952, Samuelson used the traditional Edgeworth box to illustrate the problem. In Fig. 1c, let us measure European trade from 0_1, and American trade from 0_2. Clothing is on the x-axis, and food is on the y-axis. On the contract curve, PO, the line passing through the two tangent indifference curves, measures the terms of trade at equilibrium. Now, suppose Europe makes a unilateral transfer, such as for reparations, to America, then the tangent indifferent curves will move down the PO line toward 0_1. The question now is will the slope of the new terms of trade be steeper or flatter? "If the slope becomes flatter, Europe's unilateral payments causes its terms of trade to deteriorate as in the orthodox view; but if the slope remains the same or becomes steeper, the Ohlin view is vindicated" (Samuelson 1952 [1966]: 990–991).

The slope of the terms of trade line after a transfer will depend on the marginal propensities to consume (MPC) the two goods in both Europe and America. Europe's terms of trade will deteriorate if the following ratio holds (ibid.: 993):

$$\frac{MPC_{(\text{Europe, Clothing})}}{MPC_{(\text{Europe, Food})}} > \frac{MPC_{(\text{America, Clothing})}}{MPC_{(\text{America,Food})}}$$

The ratio is set this way because Europe is exporting clothing for America's food, and we are showing that its ratio of MPC for the export product is greater at home relative to that of America. The reason for this is that "each dollar of income loss [goes] more largely to its own product than each dollar of income received by the foreigners" (ibid.). This will cause a decrease in world demand at the original price for the donor country product, leading to a deterioration in its terms of trade. Diagrammatically, one needs to pass two income consumption Engel curves through the original equilibrium curve to see this point (ibid.: 884). In the rest of his analysis, Samuelson doubted that the conclusion representing the orthodox view can be reached. He looked into the cases of no transportation costs and no impediments to trade or market imperfections and dropped the fixed proportion assumption. The result is that the orthodox position fails (ibid.: 1005–1006).

The transfer problem of Samuelson is also an active research program. Bhagwati and others have built a classical system of 13 equations to investigate the problems of welfare impact and immiserizing transfers (see Bhagwati et al. 1998: 248–253). In another study, a three-country case was examined. It discussed Gale's three-agent transfer problem where both the donor and recipient can be enriched. One finding was that "the welfare of a country not involved in the transfer improves if and only if the price of its export good goes up as a result of the transfer" (Bhagwati et al. 1983: 609). The analysis of Samuelson's transfer problem can get very technical. For example, Balasko has used the mathematics for a regular economy to show that "Samuelson's conjecture that there is no transfer problem at tatonnement stable equilibria is therefore true for any number of goods" (Balasko 2014: 435).

8 Conclusion

In conclusion, Samuelson has improved and expanded the core of international trade theories and made them operational in modern economies. This is in line with his development of marginal productivity theory as a solid foundation of neoclassical economics. His contributions to international theory have served as an active research program for researchers in the past, present, and possibly into the future. Samuelson's writings of more than half a century ago are still being used to predict current trends in modern global trade. Some of his contributions may be easy pickings left by the classical economists, but some contributions are certainly the work of a genius. In the case of transfer pricing, Samuelson seemed to bring the debate to a close. His ideas are at work in modern concerns about the convergence of global factor prices and in spotlighting issues on protectionism versus free trade. Finally, one cannot neglect to mention that Samuelson enhanced his theories by his efforts to state them in the language of mathematics and science.

References

Backhouse, R.E. (2017) *Founder of Modern Economics: Paul A. Samuelson, Volume 1*. Oxford, Oxford University Press.

Balasko, Y. (2014) "The Transfer Problem: A Complete Characterization," *Theoretical Economics*, 9: 435–444.

Baldwin, R.E. (1948) "Equilibrium in International Trade: A Diagrammatic Analysis," *Quarterly Journal of Economics*, 62: 748–762.

Bhagwati, J.N. (1959 [1983]) "Protection, Real Wages and Real Incomes," in R.C. Feenstra (ed.) *Essays in International Economic Theory: The Theory of Commercial Policy, Volume 1*. Cambridge, MA, The MIT Press: 151–166.

Bhagwati, J.N., R.A. Brecher and T. Hatta (1983) "The Generalized Theory of Transfers and Welfare Bilateral Transfers in a Multilateral World," *American Economic Review*, 73: 606–618.

Bhagwati, J.N., A. Panagariya and T.N. Srinivasan (1998) *Lectures on International Trade*. Second edition. Cambridge, MA, The MIT Press.

Burmeister, E. and A.R. Dobell (1970) *Mathematical Theories of Economic Growth*. New York, Macmillan.

Chipman, J.S. (1969) "Factors Price Equalization and the Stolper–Samuelson Theorem," *International Economic Review*, 10: 399–409.

Corden, W.M. (1984) "Normative Theory of International Trade," in P.B. Kenen and R.W. Jones (eds.) *Handbook of International Economics: International Trade, Volume 1*. Amsterdam, North-Holland: 65–130.

Deardorff, A.V. (1994) "Overview of the Stolper–Samuelson Theorem," in A.V. Deardorff and R.N. Stern (eds.) *The Stolper–Samuelson Theorem: A Golden Jubilee*. Michigan, IL, University of Michigan Press: 7–34.

De Marchi, N. (1976) "Anomaly and the Development of Economics," in S. Latsis (ed.) *Method and Appraisal in Economics*. Cambridge, Cambridge University Press: 109–128.

Dixit, A. and G.M. Grossman (2005 [2011]) "Comment," in J. Murray (ed.) *The Collected Scientific Papers of Paul A. Samuelson, Volume 6*. Cambridge, MA, The MIT Press: 839–840.

Ellickson, B. (1997) *Competitive Equilibrium: Theory and Applications.* Cambridge, Cambridge University Press.

Ferguson, C.E. (1962) "Transformation Curve in Production Theory: A Pedagogical Note," *Southern Economic Journal,* 29: 96–102.

Findlay, R. (1995) *Factor Proportions, Trade, and Growth.* Cambridge, MA, The MIT Press.

Hicks, J. (1983) "The Factor Price Equalization Theorem," in J. Hicks (ed.) *Classics and Moderns: Collected Essays on Economic Theory, Volume III.* Cambridge, MA, Harvard University Press: 224–233.

Hill, C.W.L. and G.T.M. Hult (2018) *Global Business Today.* Tenth edition. New York, McGraw-Hill.

Jones, R.W. and J.P. Neary (1984). "The Positive Theory of International Trade," in P.B. Kenen and R.W. Jones (eds.) *Handbook of International Economics: International Trade, Volume 1.* Amsterdam, North-Holland: 1 62.

Krugman, P. (1995) "Increasing Returns, Imperfect Competition and the Positive Theory of International Trade," in G.M. Grossman and K. Rogoff (eds.) *Handbook of International Economics: International Trade, Volume 3.* Amsterdam, North-Holland: 1243–1277.

Kuhn, H.W. (1968) "Lectures on Mathematical Economics," in J.E. George, B. Danzig and A.F. Veinott (eds.) *Mathematics of the Decision Sciences.* Providence, RI, American Mathematical Society: 49–84.

Lancaster, K. (1957) "Protection and Real Wages: A Restatement," *Economic Journal,* 67: 199–200.

Leamer, E. and J. Levinsohn (1995) "International Trade: Theory, Strategies, and Evidence," in G.M. Grossman and K. Rogoff (eds.) *Handbook of International Economics: International Trade, Volume 3.* Amsterdam, North-Holland: 1339–1394.

Letiche, J.M. (1982) "The Development of Gains from Trade: Classical and Modern Literature," in J.M. Letiche (ed.) *International Economic Policies and Their Theoretical Foundation: A Source Book.* New York, Academic Press: 119–149.

Ramrattan, L. and M. Szenberg. (2010) "Memorializing Paul A. Samuelson: A Review of His Major Works: 1915–2009," *The American Economist,* 55: 67–82.

Samuelson, P.A. (1938 [1966]) "Welfare Economics and International Trade," in J.E. Stiglitz (ed.) *The Collected Scientific Papers of Paul A. Samuelson, Volume 2.* Cambridge, MA, The MIT Press: 775–780.

Samuelson, P.A. (1939 [1966]) "The Gains from International Trade," in J.E. Stiglitz (ed.) *The Collected Scientific Papers of Paul A. Samuelson, Volume 2.* Cambridge, MA, The MIT Press: 781–791.

Samuelson, P.A. (1947 [1974]) *Foundations of Economic Analysis.* New York, Atheneum.

Samuelson, P.A. (1948 [1966]) "International Trade and the Equalization of Factor Prices," in J.E. Stiglitz (ed.) *The Collected Scientific Papers of Paul A. Samuelson, Volume 2.* Cambridge, MA, The MIT Press: 847–868.

Samuelson, P.A. (1949 [1966]) "International Factor-Price Equalisation Once Again," in J.E. Stiglitz (ed.) *The Collected Scientific Papers of Paul A. Samuelson, Volume 2.* Cambridge, MA, The MIT Press: 869–885.

Samuelson, P.A. (1952 [1966]) "The Transfer Problem and Transport Costs: The Terms of Trade When Impediments are Absent," in J.E. Stiglitz (ed.) *The Collected Scientific Papers of Paul A. Samuelson, Volume 2.* Cambridge, MA, The MIT Press: 985–1011.

Samuelson, P.A. (1953 [1966]) "Prices of Factors and Goods in General Equilibrium," in J.E. Stiglitz (ed.) *The Collected Scientific Papers of Paul A. Samuelson, Volume 2.* Cambridge, MA, The MIT Press: 888–908.

Samuelson, P.A. (1958 [1966]) "Review of *Theoretical Welfare Economics* by J. de V. Graaff," in J.E. Stiglitz (ed.) *The Collected Scientific Papers of Paul A. Samuelson, Volume 2.* Cambridge, MA, The MIT Press: 1099–1100.

Samuelson, P.A. (1962 [1966]) "The Gains from International Trade Once Again," in J.E. Stiglitz (ed.) *The Collected Scientific Papers of Paul A. Samuelson, Volume 2.* Cambridge, MA, The MIT Press: 792–801.

Samuelson, P.A. (1967 [1972]) "Summary of Factor-Price Equalization," In R.C. Merton (ed.) *The Collected Scientific Papers of Paul A. Samuelson, Volume 3.* Cambridge, MA, The MIT Press: 346–355.

Samuelson, P.A. (1986) "Bergsonian Welfare Economics," in K. Crowley (ed.) *The Collected Scientific Papers of Paul A. Samuelson, Volume 5.* Cambridge, MA, The MIT Press: 3–46.

Samuelson, P.A. (1990 [2011]) "Trimming Consumers' Surplus Down to Size," in J. Murray (ed.) *The Collected Scientific Papers of Paul A. Samuelson, Volume 6.* Cambridge, MA, The MIT Press: 931–967.

Samuelson, P.A. (2004 [2011]) "Where Ricardo and Mill Rebut and Confirm Arguments of Mainstream Economists Supporting Globalization," in J. Murray (ed.) *The Collected Scientific Papers of Paul A. Samuelson, Volume 6.* Cambridge, MA, The MIT Press: 816–834.

Samuelson, P.A. (2011) "An Interview with Paul A. Samuelson," in J. Murray (ed.) *The Collected Scientific Papers of Paul A. Samuelson, Volume 6.* Cambridge, MA, The MIT Press: 553–574.

Stolper, W.F. and P.A. Samuelson (1941 [1966]) "Protection and Real Wages," in J.E. Stiglitz (ed.) *The Collected Scientific Papers of Paul A. Samuelson, Volume 2*. Cambridge, MA, The MIT Press: 831–846.

Takayama, A. (1972) *International Trade: An Approach to the Theory*. New York, Hold, Rinehart and Winston.

Tatsuro, I. (1997) *Microeconomic Theory*. Oxford, Blackwell.

19

Samuelson's Contributions to Population Theory and Overlapping Generations in Economics

Ronald Lee

1 Introduction

Paul Samuelson's death in 2009 was followed by an explosion of biographical articles extolling his numerous seminal contributions. Many of these articles mention that Samuelson was "born" as an economist when, as an undergraduate at the University of Chicago, he attended a lecture about Thomas Malthus. Malthus, of course, propounded a seminal theory of how population and the economy interacted. But I was disappointed to find that none of the many articles I read made any other mention of population in relation to Samuelson's work, except for Dixit (2012). This strikes me as odd, because as an economic demographer myself, I view Samuelson's contributions to demography and its interface with economics as deep and important.

R. Lee (✉)
Departments of Demography and Economics, University of California, Berkeley, CA, USA
e-mail: rlee@demog.berkeley.edu

R. A. Cord et al. (eds.), *Paul Samuelson*, Remaking Economics: Eminent Post-War Economists, https://doi.org/10.1057/978-1-137-56812-0_19

The work that might be claimed for economic demography, such as his famous paper on the consumption-loan economy with overlapping generations, is very well known and enormously influential. But his other work on population, some of it also related to biological evolution, is barely known or remembered at all, to the detriment of the field. Who now knows that Samuelson published two papers on the two-sex problem in demography? Or two papers on predator–prey models? A paper on the reversibility of time in population processes? Five papers generalizing and critiquing Fisher's concept of reproductive value, a concept that plays a key role in evolutionary theory? Analyses of evolutionary theories of altruism and kin selection? I think this work has remained largely overlooked because he very rarely published in population journals (I know of only one instance). Samuelson's published work on population is scattered among biological and general science journals for the most part. His demographic work has never been collected in a single volume targeted at a demographic readership. So far as I know, Samuelson never went to population meetings or sought to publicize this work in the demographic community. Furthermore, the analysis in his papers is highly mathematical, and much is too difficult for most demographers, even those who, like myself, think of themselves as mathematical types. It is clear from comments in his papers that he often discussed his work with the leading mathematical demographer Nathan Keyfitz. In the 1970s, when he did much of this work, Samuelson had a grant from the National Institute of Child Health and Development (NICHD) to pursue these issues. To attempt to draw together some of these various lines of Samuelson's work here is an opportunity, a challenge, an education, and a pleasure.

2 Population Dynamics, Cycles, and Sex

Much of Samuelson's work in population was about population dynamics, that is, change over time. He particularly focused on the constraints on change that were often omitted in analyses by demographers, such as natural resource limits. For example, in his *Foundations of Economic Analysis*, he develops a formalization of the basic Malthusian model of population growth and equilibrium, noting that the equilibrium was stable under

Malthus's assumptions. He also develops a simple model of the optimal size for a population that first experiences increasing returns and then decreasing returns to labor. Samuelson makes the useful point that the optimal population size could not be maintained as the equilibrium in a Malthusian-type system, or we might now say under population homeostasis. The reason is that the equilibrium is only stable on the upside; on the downside, it is unstable. A positive shock to population size would reduce per capita income so population would shrink back toward the optimum size. But a negative shock would also reduce per capita income, so the population would shrink further and further reduce per capita income and population size in this region of increasing returns to labor, rather than converging back up to the optimum size and income.

When population age distribution is integrated into the theory, the dynamic issues become more complicated, and this also interested Samuelson. Most of his work on population occurred in the 1970s and early 1980s when the "New Home Economics" approach to household behavior, and particularly fertility, was prominent through the work of Becker (1960, 1981, Becker and Lewis (1973), and Willis (1973) among others. Samuelson was not a fan of this line of work, which he contrasted unfavorably to the more socio-economic-demographic approach of Richard Easterlin (1968):

> The Easterlin theory is all the more valuable for its scarcity among economic theories, standing out in welcome relief from the rather sterile verbalizations by which economists have tended to describe fertility decisions in terms of the jargon of indifference curves, thereby tending to intimidate non-economists who have not misspent their youth in mastering the intricacies of modern utility theory. (Samuelson 1976a: 244)

Samuelson's demographic work took a rather macro-approach, as opposed to the microeconomic theories he described as sterile. This is also true of Easterlin's theory, which emphasized aggregate-level economic feedbacks within the context of a fertility theory in which the income of each generation relative to that of its parents drove the generation's marriage, fertility, and labor force participation. Malthus and other Classical economists claimed that the long-run supply of labor was infinite at a wage equal to the subsistence level, while suggesting that this subsistence level depended on workers' changing notions of what consumption was necessary. Samuelson (1985) viewed this approach as vacuous, while Easterlin's idea of relative income was well-defined and operationalized by comparing income levels of children and parents.

Easterlin noted that the small generations born during the Great Depression of the 1930s in the USA grew up to experience high wages and easy labor market entry as young adults, marrying early and having high fertility in the 1950s and 1960s. This small generation of parents produced a large generation of children, giving rise to the Baby Boom. Easterlin predicted that as this large generation aged, it would experience relatively lower wages, slower promotion, later marriage, and lower fertility—all of which came to pass in the Baby Bust years of the 1970s. Samuelson (1976a: 244) says: "Thus the Easterlin hypothesis can explain fertility waves not unlike those actually experienced in the United States during the last 40 years." Samuelson proceeds to develop a simple model of the Easterlin theory and analyzes its dynamic behavior, showing that depending on sensitivities, it may have an unstable equilibrium, away from which it moves to a self-generating limit cycle with oscillations every other generation, much as Easterlin described (Easterlin 1968).[1]

A different kind of constraint arises in the so-called two-sex problem in demography. Most demographic models and analyses are based on a single-sex population. For example, population projections are virtually always done for the female population, based on measured and projected female fertility and mortality rates. Once the female population has been projected, including future female births, then the sex ratio at birth is used to derive the future numbers of male births from the female ones. Then future male mortality can be used to complete the projection of the male population by age. This is called a "female dominant" projection. Just as actual real-world projections almost always ignore the possibility that natural resource constraints will affect future population growth, they also ignore constraints arising from the requirement that male and female fertilities and growth rates are interlinked in a nonlinear way. This is a

[1] I myself had published a very similar analysis in Lee (1974), which Samuelson generously acknowledged but learned about too late to take into account in his own analysis, for the most part.

classical problem in mathematical demography, and the contributions to it by Yellin and Samuelson (1974, 1977) draw on that earlier work. Pollak (1986, 1990) subsequently made seminal contributions to this problem. Yellin and Samuelson (1977) proved a theorem for the general case of an age-structured population with asymmetric birth functions (e.g., young females have births with both younger and older men, but younger men are unlikely to have births with older women) and non-diagonal birth functions (so males and females of different ages have births). They show that for arbitrary initial age distributions for each sex, the female dominant and male dominant single-sex growth rates need not bracket the true non-linearly generated rate, but they also show that it is always possible to find initial age distributions sufficiently close to the stable case such that the true rate is bracketed by the single-sex rates. Well, this is good to know. However, the demographer in me is disappointed that they did not discuss whether all this matters from a practical point of view. I would have liked to see some realistic simulations over a 50- to 100-year time horizon to learn whether the two-sex nonlinearity is a practical problem for projections.

Samuelson also did valuable work on the time symmetry and asymmetry of forward and backward dynamics in population (Samuelson 1976b). It is well established that going forward in time, populations tend to forget their past, in the sense that from different initial age distributions they will converge to the same final age distribution if subjected to the same trajectories of fertility and mortality. But this feature also makes the attempt to infer earlier age distributions by going backward (reversing the projection dynamics) impossible or exceedingly data-demanding, and this difficulty is compounded by the problem of choosing how many old people to move into and out of the open oldest age interval as we go backward. This may sound like an obscure academic point, but it is actually of practical importance in attempts to reconstruct the demographic past, and it has sometimes led to confusion and controversy. An example is a method called "inverse projection" in which, going forward from a given initial population, series of births and deaths (derived from records of baptisms and burials) are used to estimate future population sizes and age distributions, while a method called "back projection" sought (unsuccessfully, in my view) to perform a similar procedure backward in time, from a given more recent population age distribution and again using series of births and deaths (Lee 1985, 1993; Vaupel et al. 2004; Wrigley &Schofield 1981). Samuelson (1976b) made the point that, mathematically, this has nothing to do with ergodicity of population age structures, since convergence is never complete and if one has an exact stable population age distribution at some time then, with constant rates in the past, it must have always been stable. Instead, the problem comes from the singularity of the Leslie Matrix, derived from the problem of the open age interval at the top. But I should add here that, practically, given the limits to accuracy of demographic data, particularly historical data, the problem of age distribution convergence is indeed key in this context, and unknown levels of net migration during the study period add a further layer of uncertainty.

3 Biodemography: Reproductive Value, Predator–Prey Models, and Evolution of Altruism

Samuelson continued on this path of careful mathematical analysis of central issues in population theory in greater generality, in particular in the presence of two-sex dynamics and environmental constraints, with five papers between 1977 and 1980 on Fisher's "reproductive value." This concept, formalized by Fisher in 1930, quantifies the expected number of female descendants of a given female at a given age, discounted at the steady-state population growth rate. It is therefore closely related to success in achieving the transmission of genes into future generations, which drives evolution by natural selection. As explained in a recent article in *Genetics*: "In the long term, alleles that increase the reproductive value will be the ones that increase, and traits will evolve that tend to maximize an individual's reproductive value" (Barton and Etheridge 2011). Samuelson's first two papers on this topic (Samuelson 1977a, b) considered reproductive value in populations that were sufficiently sparse that natural resource constraints would not limit their growth in the medium term, so linear models of population growth could be used, and birth functions (depending on numbers of both males and females) are linear homogeneous: Doubling the numbers of males and females would double the numbers of births. For this case, he then analyzed biparental reproduction, drawing on his earlier work with Yellin on the two-sex problem. He was able to show that important properties of Fisher's reproductive value remained valid in this case of sparse population relative to natural resources. However, he also found that in the more realistic case of a population constrained by the carrying capacity of its environment, the reproductive value would be zero for females at every age, because varying the size of age elements of the initial population would have no effect on long-run equilibrium population, which is determined only by environmental carrying capacity. In Samuelson (1978a), he shows that finding the reproductive values in the two-sex case would involve an infinite number of calculations, meaning that the concept can no longer be used as Fisher (1930: 25) had hoped, in relation to his Fundamental Theorem of Natural Selection. In his next paper on this topic, Samuelson (1978b) considers how the situation might be at least partially saved by considering approximations. First, he suggests that even if the long-run population dynamics are constrained by the environment, nonetheless at very low population sizes the dynamics will be close to linear, and the reproductive value calculation can be of some use for demography and genetics. Second, he suggests that a somewhat modified calculation can provide useful information in the neighborhood of the equilibrium size determined by the carrying capacity.

Samuelson did additional work at the interface of biology and demography. One topic, the Lotka–Volterra predator–prey model, is analyzed in two articles. In the predator prey model, the growth rate of predators is positively related to the abundance of prey and negatively related to the number of predators, while the growth rate of prey is negatively related to the abundance of predators. Samuelson sometimes interprets predators as capitalists and laborers as prey. This model generates periodic cycles in the sizes of both populations. In 1971, he generalizes the math of the original model to many interacting species and to other functional forms. Samuelson then goes on to develop more realistic models in which there are environmental resource constraints via diminishing returns. "Ecological equilibrium without the law of diminishing returns is like Hamlet without the Prince" (Samuelson 1971: 982). In these models, cycles are no longer self-exciting, instead spiraling down to equilibrium. But cycles can be sustained by continuing external shocks, such as weather. An article in 1974 further generalizes and simplifies the mathematics.

In 1983, Samuelson took on a new problem: the evolution of altruism through kin selection, a centrally important topic in evolutionary theory since the second half of the twentieth century, with seminal contributions by Hamilton on altruism and kin selection, by Wilson on sociobiology, and by Trivers on other applications of kin selection. Samuelson, in his famous 1958 essay, wrote:

> The economics of collusion provides an important field of study for the theorist. Such collusions can be important elements of strength in the struggle for existence. … But culture in which altruism abounds – because men do not think to behave like atomistic competitors or because men have by custom and law entered into binding social contracts – may have great survival and expansion powers. (ibid.: 481)

It is a small step from acknowledging these powers to asking why they might not evolve through some sort of natural selection, and that is the topic of Samuelson's 1983 paper. I think it is fair to say that on this topic, Samuelson introduced more powerful, comprehensive, and general mathematical treatments of the earlier theories and cleared up some points and controversies, but did not fundamentally advance the topic in the way he did so many others.

The work discussed up to this point should be of great interest to demographers and evolutionary biologists, but now it is time to turn to Samuelson's research at the interface of demography and economics. This seminal work originates at an earlier date, with his famous consumption-loan paper published in 1958, and then continues in the 1970s with papers on optimal population growth rates (Samuelson 1975a) and optimal social security programs (Samuelson 1975b) and with comments and rejoinders to this work. Doubtless there are other relevant contributions by Samuelson, but I will focus on these issues and papers.

4 Consumption-Loan Model with Overlapping Generations

Robinson Crusoe was on his own as he moved through his life cycle. Most people, though, live in populations that include individuals at every age and every stage of the economic life cycle. Such individuals interact through economic markets, but they also give and receive support through social relationships such as parent–child, elder and adult offspring, taxpayer and public beneficiary, and giver/receiver of bequests, which I will refer to as "transfers." One reason to use "overlapping" generations models to analyze general equilibrium outcomes is to take into account the relative numbers of actors at different ages/stages of their life cycles. As relative numbers of people at different ages change, this will affect their interactions through markets and through social relations and cause adjustments in prices (e.g., wages and interest rates), social transfers (e.g., spending per child, public pensions, taxes), and life cycle behavior (e.g., saving, age at retirement). Crusoe could save, accumulate capital, and dissave and in these ways reallocate his income to some degree across his life cycle, for example, by building a dwelling that yielded services over the long run or storing food for later consumption. Most people, however, have a much richer menu of ways to shift income across their life cycles. Like Crusoe, they can save, invest, and dissave. But in addition, they can borrow and lend to others, and they can give and receive public and private transfers.

Samuelson (1958) set up his analysis to rule out all durable goods, including capital. This meant that on the one hand, accumulation of consumption goods could not be used to shift income to later in the life cycle, and on the other, construction of productive assets like a home or machine was not possible. This leaves two ways to reallocate income across the life cycle: transfers (either public or private) or credit markets. Credit markets could be used only for "consumption loans," not to fund capital investment, since capital does not exist.

Samuelson (ibid.: 468) develops his model with three adult ages—two ages of workers and one of retirees. "Let us assume that men enter the labor market at about the age of twenty. They work for forty-five years or so and then live for fifteen years in retirement. (As children they are part of their parents' consumptions, and we take no note of them.)" He later comments (ibid.: 475): "By introducing overlap between workers of different ages, the three-period model is essentially equivalent to a general n-period model or to the continuous-time model of real life." The model with three age groups is amenable to analytic solutions and is quite intuitive, and since children do not make their own consumption decisions, it can make sense to view them as a part of their parents' consumption. Nonetheless, it may be of interest both theoretically and empirically to consider the "continuous-time model of real life" with realistic demography in which people can be any age, are constantly at risk of death, and live part of their lives as children (Lee 1994; Bommier and Lee 2003). We can give them more realistic economic life cycles in which productivity and labor effort vary across age, and even children and the elderly work to some extent, albeit less productively. Children do not participate in credit markets, but they do consume by virtue of receiving transfers from their parents or the public sector.

Consider a world with no capital, output is produced solely from labor, and there are no durable goods—Samuelson's consumption-loan world. People produce an amount $y(x)$ at age x, which will be taken as given. They choose a lifetime consumption trajectory $c(x)$, presumably by seeking to maximize lifetime utility, but the details of the origin of $c(x)$ need not concern us here. However, given the earnings age schedule, consumption is constrained by the life cycle budget constraint, which, for interest rate r, is given by:

$$\int_0^{\omega} e^{-rx} p(x)\left[y(x) - c(x)\right]dx = 0 \quad (1)$$

In addition, there is a social budget constraint that must be satisfied, and it also limits the consumption possibilities. Since there are no durable goods, and therefore, it is impossible to borrow or loan from Nature (in Samuelson's words), total consumption in each period must be no more than total output; since it would be inefficient to leave excess output unconsumed, output and consumption must be equal in any efficient program. The social budget constraint depends in part on the population age distribution, and we will assume it is in steady state, or what demographers call "stable." Let $p(x)$ be the probability of surviving from birth to age x, and let $p(x)$ be 0 for $x \geq \omega$. The age-specific birth rates, together with the survival schedule, will generate a stable growth rate n and a corresponding population age distribution. In the stable population, the number of births grows exponentially at rate n, $B(t) = B(0)e^{nt}$, so at time t, the number of people aged x will be $B(0)e^{n(t-x)}p(x)$. The total population in year t, $P(t)$, is the integral of this over x, and $B(t)$ divided by $P(t)$ is the crude birth rate, b. From this, it follows that the proportion of the population at age x is just $be^{-n(t-x)}p(x)$, and these proportions will, of course, integrate to 1.0.

The social budget constraint is then:

$$b \int_0^{\omega} e^{-nx} p(x)\left[y(x) - c(x)\right]dx = 0 \tag{2}$$

We can immediately note that a rate of interest equal to the population growth rate, $r = n$, satisfies both the individual and the social budget constraints. This is Samuelson's biological interest rate result.

If the $c(x)$ consumption path has been chosen to maximize lifetime expected utility given interest rate r, then we can also note that the biological interest rate program is optimal, in the sense that it maximizes steady-state utility subject to the social budget constraint. It is therefore Pareto optimal, as in Samuelson's model with three age groups.

The question now arises: Is the Pareto optimal outcome with $r = n$ attainable as a competitive equilibrium? To address this question, we begin by noting that there is one additional constraint which holds for credit markets in the aggregate. If the economy is closed and there is no government debt or credit, then for every dollar of credit in the economy there must also be a corresponding dollar of debt, so that the aggregate net credit balance is identically 0. We can calculate this credit balance as follows. Consider an individual at age x. Looking to the future, and taking into account the probability of surviving from x to each future age a, this individual's net credit balance—the amount of credit the individual would need to hold at age x in order to balance the future budget, given future earnings and mortality—is the present value at age x of all future differences between what is consumed and what is earned, which Samuelson called "net" or "excess demands," negative excess demands, or negative "net saving" (Samuelson 1958: 470).

$$\int_x^{\omega} e^{-r(a-x)}\left[\frac{p(a)}{p(x)}\right]\left[c(a) - y(a)\right]da \tag{3}$$

The aggregate credit balance is found by integrating this across all ages, weighting by the number of people at each age, and dividing by the total population to get a per capita value (or just weighting by the proportional age distribution derived above):

$$W = b\int_0^{\omega} e^{-nx}\int_x^{\omega} e^{-r(a-x)}p(a)\left[y(a) - c(a)\right]da\,dx \tag{4}$$

Now consider the special case of the biological interest rate at which the optimal life cycle consumption occurs, $r = n$. After some manipulation as described in Bommier and Lee (2003) and Lee (1994), building on Gale (1973) and Willis (1988), we find the elegant result (due to ibid.):

$$W = c\left(A_c - A_y\right) \tag{5}$$

In this expression, c is aggregate per capita consumption, A_c is the average age of consuming in the population (the age at which the average dollar of consumption takes place in the population), and A_y is the average age of earning in the population. This tells us that if the average age of consuming is greater than the average age of earning, then the population as a whole will have to hold a positive amount of wealth W, because the average unit of output will be held for $A_c - A_y$ years before it is consumed. Here is the definition of the average age of consuming, for example:

$$A_c = \frac{\int_0^{\omega} x e^{-nx} p(x)c(x)dx}{\int_0^{\omega} e^{-nx} p(x)c(x)dx} \tag{6}$$

Evidently, this average age depends both on the shape of consumption across the life cycle, $c(x)$, and on the age distribution of the population by which it is weighted.

Returning to our question of whether credit markets can support the biological interest rate, note that in a closed economy, for every dollar of debt there is a corresponding dollar of credit, so W, aggregate credit, must be identically equal to zero. While individuals can smooth consumption across age by borrowing and lending, for society as a whole this is not an option. The credit market can support only reallocations of income that are symmetric with age. Therefore, it cannot support the optimal age pattern of consumption that corresponds to the biological interest rate n, except in the probability zero case where the corresponding average ages happen to be equal. In particular, it could not support the age patterns that Samuelson assumes, with work when young and retirement when old, which is highly asymmetric. Indeed, in Samuelson's example, in a stationary population with equal consumption by young workers, old workers, and the retired and equal earning by the two worker groups, if ages are 1, 2, and 3 then the average age of consuming is 2 and of working is 1.5, so the difference is .5 time units, or ten years in Samuelson's example of 20-year age groups (Samuelson 1958: 473).

In fact, as Samuelson (ibid.: 478) reports, the credit market outcome for his three-age group model with a logarithmic utility function would be a negative interest rate of .70 per 20-year period or about −2% per year. At this negative interest rate, young workers choose to borrow from older workers rather than lend, and then they repay these older workers once they retire. The result is a very unappealing pattern of life cycle consumption, with very high consumption when young and very low when old, yielding much lower lifetime utility than the optimal pattern under the biological interest rate of zero for a stationary population. Samuelson (ibid.: 479) comments: "If each man insists on a quid pro quo, we apparently continue until the end of time, with each worse off than in the social optimum, biological interest case." He reaches this conclusion by starting with Adam at the beginning of time and making sure that every borrowing is offset by a loan, although the argument above based on the aggregate credit balance seems simpler. (If Samuelson were here, he might demolish the argument in one withering sentence, however.)

How, then, can the biological interest rate outcome be achieved? Samuelson (ibid.: 479–480) continues:

> Yet how easy it is by a simple change in the rules of the game to get to the optimum. Let mankind enter into a Hobbes-Rousseau social contract in which the young are assured of their retirement subsistence if they will today support the aged, such support to be guaranteed by a draft on the yet-unborn. Then the social optimum can be achieved within one lifetime.

In other words, nonmarket social transfers can get us to the optimum. Here is how. Let the gap between consumption and earnings at any age be filled by a transfer $\tau^+(x)$ received from other ages at which earnings exceed consumption and which make an average transfer $\tau^-(x)$, with the net transfer received at each age given by $\tau(x) = \tau^+(x) - \tau^-(x)$. Then the aggregate transfer balance, T, can be calculated in the same way as the aggregate credit balance:

$$T = \tau^+(A_{\tau^+} - A_{\tau^-}) \tag{7}$$

Like borrowing and lending, the flow of transfers given and received must exactly cancel at any moment. But unlike credit, the aggregate transfer balance, which we might call "transfer wealth," can take any value, positive or negative. For example, in a public pension system, workers pay taxes and retirees receive benefits, and the transfer flow is solely from young to old and highly asymmetric, with a large positive value for T. By contrast, in a society where the elderly continue to work and all transfers go to children, T would have a large negative value, as is true in hunter-gatherer societies. The point is that such nonmarket transfers, whether public or private, can support the optimal age pattern of consumption, through the "social contract" that Samuelson referred to above. They do this through the device of committing those not yet alive, the unborn but to-be-born, either to make transfers in the future or in some cases to receive them. In addition, the "social contrivance of money," as Samuelson puts it, can bring about the same pattern of intergenerational transfers through induced inflation, in the way he describes in his paper—but in practice, I find this is an unappealing interpretation of his results.

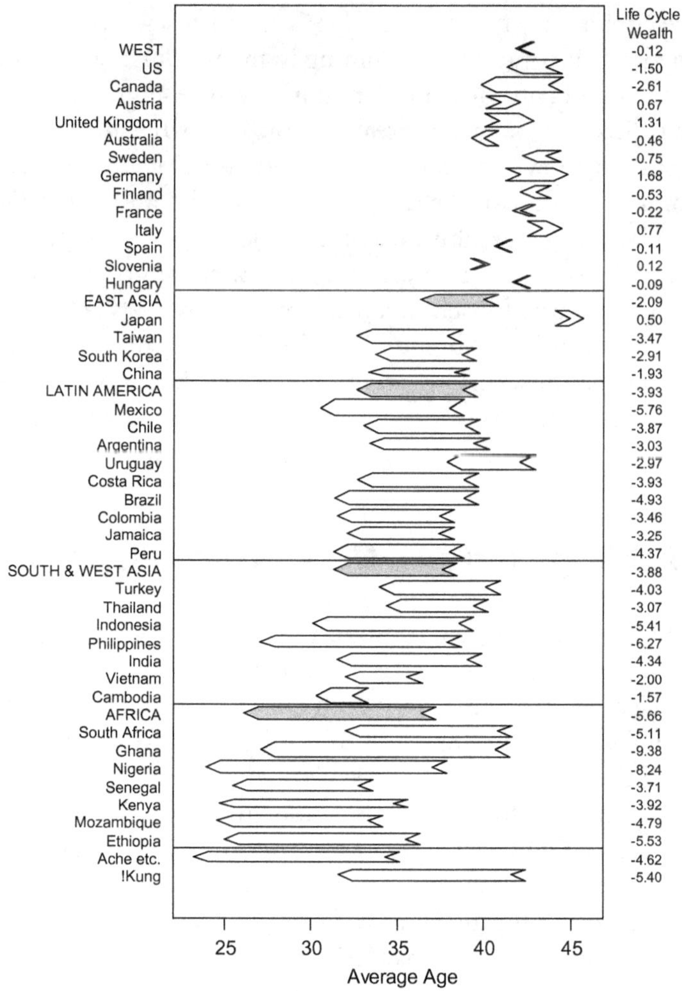

Fig. 1 Arrows showing the average age of earning labor income (at the tail) and the average age of consuming (at the head) weighted by actual population age distributions, for 39 countries around the world in a recent year and for two contemporary hunter-gatherer/forager groups (*Source* For countries of the world, the data come from the National Transfer Accounts project [NTA] at ntaccounts.org. The hunter-gatherer data come from Kaplan [1994] for the Ache and Howell [2010] for the !Kung)

To give all this empirical context, Fig. 1 uses arrows to plot average ages of earning labor income and consuming in many countries all around the world[2] and also in two contemporary hunter-gatherer groups. We see that the actual direction of income reallocation is downward, from older to younger, in most low- and middle-income countries, but has reversed in a half dozen rich industrial nations. These patterns are partly due to the older population age distributions of most rich industrial nations and the younger age distributions in most non-rich other countries, but that is far from the whole story. In rich nations, labor supply ends at younger ages, facilitated or incentivized by public and private pension systems, and in many of these nations, consumption at older ages has grown more rapidly than at younger adult ages, tilting the consumption age profile upward, due to the rising costs of publicly provided health care.

5 Adding Capital—Now What Is Optimal?

Samuelson developed his consumption-loan model the way he did, with no capital and no durable goods, because he wanted to show that these were not necessary underpinnings of the interest rate and therefore not its fundamental source. But durable goods and productive capital can readily be added to the model, as Diamond (1965) did. In the Solow model, for a given saving rate, the slower the population growth the better, because that leads to more capital per worker and higher productivity and per capita income. But in the consumption-loan model, *faster* population growth is beneficial because it means more workers per retiree, so everyone can be better off. As Samuelson (1975a: 531) put it:

---

[2]These data come from the National Transfer Accounts project (Lee and Mason et al. 2011), which was inspired in part by Samuelson (1958). Using a mathematical framework much like that presented in this chapter, the project estimates age profiles of consumption, labor income, saving, asset income, and public and private transfers by age for about 80 countries. There are research teams in 55 countries in Europe, Asia, Africa, Latin America, North America, and Oceania making these estimates according to a strict methodology set out in a manual published by the United Nations Population Division (2013). The project Web site, where much of this data can be found, is www.ntaccounts.org.

> In the usual version of that growth model, the slower the rate of exponential growth the higher can be the level of steady-state consumption; on the other hand, in a life cycle pure-consumption model of the 1958 Samuelson type, which permits no trades with nature, the faster the population growth the better, since more children means better support for retired parents.

It seems plausible that there would be an intermediate level of the population growth rate at which the trade-off between capital dilution and dependency ratio maximizes economic well-being, at least in this rarefied world in which natural resource constraints are ignored. This was the argument and analysis in Samuelson's (1975a) paper on "The Optimum Growth Rate for Population."

For a given population growth rate n, we can calculate the optimal steady-state saving rate, s^*, per capita consumption c^* and capital-labor ratio, k^*. Now we can ask how the optimal level of consumption, c^*, is affected by the population growth rate n. Samuelson gives the answer:

$$\frac{dc}{dn} = -k* \tag{8}$$

If δ is the rate of depreciation, then $n = -\delta$ is the most rapid rate of population decline consistent with a steady state, so that is the optimal rate of population growth that maximizes steady-state consumption.

Samuelson then derives the "two-part golden rule," similar to the standard one for the Solow model, but with workers and retirees who arrange life cycle consumption as guided by the biological interest rate of g. Now Samuelson can ask: What is the goldenest golden rule which gives maximum lifetime utility when we vary both saving rates and the population growth rate? He provides an answer (ibid.: 534). Samuelson then proves his famous "serendipity theorem." He notes that in general, for a given population growth rate n, the private saving induced by life cycle saving will not correspond to the rate needed to achieve the golden rule. To achieve the golden rule would require intervention. For example, a pay-as-you-go (PAYG) public pension system would substitute for some private saving, which would move the economy toward the golden rule if the capital-labor ratio were inefficiently high. Similarly, if the capital-labor ratio were too low, he suggests that a funded compulsory public pension system in which contributions were invested in capital could raise the saving rate, moving the system toward the golden rule. His Serendipity Theorem states that at the goldenest golden rule rate of population growth, private saving would be exactly right to achieve the golden rule, with no public intervention needed.

Unfortunately, Samuelson had not checked the second-order conditions for an optimum, and Deardorff pointed this out in a 1976 article to which Samuelson issued a gracious mea culpa and noted: "Professor Deardorff has shown that it can well be the case that the only root to my extremum condition corresponds to a minimum rather than a maximum of well-being" (Samuelson 1976c: 516). His "Agreement and Evaluations" response to Deardorff is a valuable contribution in itself, dealing with the role of the ignored natural resource constraints, declining fertility, and other important issues.

A quite different comment by Arthur and McNicoll (1978) is extremely interesting. This brief and compact comment has been fundamentally important in pointing the way to combining rich and realistic demography and descriptive empirics of economic behavior over the life cycle with neoclassical growth theory. Rather than seeking the optimal population growth rate or birth rate, in this comment Arthur and McNicoll (1978: 242) set out to "evaluate the implications of a change in population growth assuming that production and consumption are spread realistically over a continuous-age life cycle and that people are treated as individuals from birth, with a welfare criterion that reflects their expected lifetime utility of consumption." They are concerned with assessing the real-world consequences of high versus low fertility. It turns out that this was also what Samuelson had in mind. Samuelson (1976c: 519) tells us that "the original purpose of the 1975 exercises was to shed possible light on the vital public policy questions involved in social security, Modigliani life cycle saving-investing patterns, apparent declining patterns of demographic fertility, and normative discussions of family planning." Later, he refers specifically to the consequences of the decline in US fertility following the Baby Boom.

Arthur and McNicoll compare the life cycle utility achieved for different population growth rates across golden rule steady states, assuming that a social planner makes the kinds of adjustments described above by

Samuelson to keep the economy on a golden rule path. The set-up presented earlier in this chapter was derived in part from this Arthur and McNicoll comment, and using the earlier notation, I will summarize a result that is closely related to their main result:

$$\frac{dC(n)/\,dn}{C(n)} = A_c - A_{yl} - \frac{k}{c}. \tag{9}$$

where C is lifetime survival-weighted consumption of an individual at birth and k is capital per capita (rather than the capital-labor ratio). An increase in the population growth rate requires that more output be saved to provide capital for the more rapidly growing labor force, as reflected in the last term on the right. But an increased population growth rate also alters the relative numbers of people at different ages, changing the relative numbers of supporters and dependents, as in the consumption-loan model. These changes require many adjustments throughout the economy, including in the amount consumed at each age. Whatever the age pattern of changes in consumption, the left-hand side of the equation tells us the proportional change in the present value of lifetime consumption that results from a change in n, and the right-hand side tells us that there is an intergenerational transfer effect given by the difference in the average ages and a capital dilution effect, and these are additive. As Arthur and McNicoll tell us, once we include the consumption of children in the story, it is no longer necessary that the effect of more rapid growth on dependency, as expressed in the difference in average ages, will be beneficial. It may well be that more rapid population growth, leading to higher proportions of children in the population and lower proportions of elderly, is itself costly.

From Fig. 1, we know that the difference in average ages is negative in low- and middle-income countries, so that the intergenerational transfer effect reinforces rather than offsets the capital dilution effect. In rich countries, however, it may be either positive or negative with a difference in the range of plus or minus five years, at most.

Lee and Mason et al. (2014) examined the effect of fertility on the steady-state levels of consumption under the golden rule given the empirically observed age profiles in 40 countries (based on Eq. 9) and concluded that, in most cases, lower fertility would be beneficial. The exceptions were countries with fertility below 1.5 births per woman (total fertility rate). In general, the effects of fertility variation in rich industrial nations were small since actual fertility is typically fairly close to the maximizing level. As Samuelson put it (1976c: 519), "Paradoxically, Deardorff's minimizing g^t is as encouraging as Samuelson's maximizing g^* to reduce the fears that declining population growth makes old-age security more difficult. In the neighborhood of an extremum, whether it is a minimum or a maximum, a function does not change much."

The takeaway message here is that although low fertility does raise the costs per worker of old-age dependency and in rich countries raises total dependency even when the dependency costs of children are taken into account, these rising dependency costs are largely offset by reduced need for saving to provide capital for a growing labor force, so the net effect on lifetime consumption is quite small.

6 Wealth, Social Security, and Capital

In 1975, when Samuelson published his (flawed) paper on the optimal rate of population growth, he also published a paper on the optimum social security program. In his analysis, the reason for social security is not to compensate for people's inability to save for their retirement. Samuelson assumes people save rationally for retirement. In his analysis, social security is a policy instrument whereby the government can adjust the national saving rate and capital stock to reach the golden rule steady-state growth path. He already showed, with his Serendipity Theorem, that if the population growth rate happens to be at its optimal level, say n^*, then private life cycle saving will also be exactly right to achieve the golden rule capital intensity, and no government intervention is required. However, if population growth n^1 is more rapid than n^* then he finds that the saving rate will be too low to achieve the corresponding golden rule path for n^1. In this case, Samuelson suggests that a more than fully funded mandatory social security program can move the economy to the golden rule path, raising life cycle consumption. Alternatively, if fertility is very low and the population growth rate n^2 drops below its optimum, then the saving rate and capital intensity may be too high, and the rate of interest may drop below n^2. This economy is on an inefficient growth path with too much capital. Now a PAYG social security program can substitute for some of private saving, reducing the national saving rate and moving the economy to the golden rule path with less capital and higher interest rates.

We hear similar ideas today in discussions of "secular stagnation" with interest rates dropping to zero or below, while investors still do not borrow out of fear that slow population growth will reduce future demand for their products. Secular stagnation is said to be caused in part by declining rates of technological progress, but also by slowing population growth rates and population aging. One of the proposed policy interventions is to raise PAYG public transfers to the elderly, thereby reducing the motivation for private saving, reducing capital intensity, and raising interest rates, much as Samuelson suggested.

These ideas can be addressed using the accounting machinery introduced earlier. Recall that the aggregate demand for wealth, *W*, is the amount of wealth that the whole population would have to hold in order for each generation to achieve its future consumption plans given its future expected labor earnings. Since debt and credit must exactly cancel in a closed economy, net credit must be zero and cannot be a store of aggregate wealth. As we saw earlier, socially constructed transfer patterns, public or private, can be a store either of aggregate wealth or of its negative, aggregate debt, with transfer wealth denoted *T*. The other possible store of aggregate wealth is capital *K*: houses, machines, roads, and so on. So aggregate wealth, *W*, can be held either as capital or as transfer wealth (Willis 1988; Lee 1994):

$$W = K + T \tag{10}$$

Here, government policy can manipulate *T*, for example, by expanding or reducing the generosity of a PAYG social security program. This then leads to a change in *K*, which will alter interest rates, wages, and *W*, leading to a series of changes before arriving at a different equilibrium that could be closer to the golden rule.

We also have (Eqs. 5, 7, and 9). Combining these, we arrive at the striking result across golden rule steady states:

$$\text{d In}\ \frac{C(n)}{dn} = \frac{T}{c} \tag{11}$$

This tells us that the proportional effect of a slight increase in the population growth rate on lifetime consumption equals aggregate transfer wealth relative to per capita consumption. If transfer wealth is positive, which is the case when the net direction of transfers is from younger to older ages as in modern welfare states with the strong net transfers to the elderly for pensions and health care, then an increase in the population growth rate can raise lifetime consumption. When the net direction of transfers is downwards, as in most lower- and middle-income countries, more rapid population growth is costly. But note also that when transfer wealth is zero, a small variation in the population growth rate has no effect on lifetime consumption, indicating that the growth rate is there at the optimal level and that the golden rule has been achieved without the sorts of government intervention that Samuelson discusses. This result is closely related to the Serendipity Theorem.

7 Conclusion

In his work on population, as elsewhere, Samuelson stripped problems to their essential elements and went straight to the heart of the matter both through his models and through his interpretations of the results. At the same time, he was wary of analyses that oversimplified so that results depended on the omission of a key constraint, as with natural resources in relation to both population growth and economic growth. Although the work reviewed here is very abstract and mathematical, according to Samuelson himself it was motivated by a desire to address issues of compelling policy importance. This was true of his work on fertility cycles in relation to the Baby Boom and Bust and also in relation to the fertility decline and population aging in industrial nations and their consequences for economic growth, dependency, and lifetime consumption. No other mainline economist in the twentieth century contributed so broadly and deeply to population theory for humans, for other species, for evolution, and for the significance of age-structured life cycles in economic equilibrium and growth.

References

Arthur, B.W. and G. McNicoll (1978) "Samuelson, Population and Intergenerational Transfers," *International Economic Review*, 19: 241–246.

Barton, N.H. and A.M. Etheridge (2011) "The Relation Between Reproductive Value and Genetic Contribution," *Genetics*, 188: 953–973.

Becker, G.S. (1960) "An Economic Analysis of Fertility," Demographic and Economic Change in Developed Countries. Princeton, National Bureau of Economic Research: 209–231.

Becker, G.S. (1981) *A Treatise on the Family*. Cambridge, MA, Harvard University Press.

Becker, G.S. and H. Gregg Lewis (1973) "On the Interaction Between the Quantity and Quality of Children," *Journal of Political Economy*, 81: S279–S288.

Bommier, A. and R. Lee (2003) "Overlapping Generations Models with Realistic Demography," *Journal of Population Economics*, 16: 135–160.

Deardorff, A.V. (1976) "The Optimum Growth Rate for Population: Comment," *International Economic Review*, 17: 510–515.

Diamond, P.A. (1965) "National Debt in a Neoclassical Growth Model," *American Economic Review*, 55: 1126–1150.

Dixit, A. (2012) "Paul Samuelson's Legacy," *Annual Reviews of Economics*, 4: 1–31.

Easterlin, R.A. (1968) *Population, Labor Force, and Long Swings in Economic Growth: The American Experience*. New York, Columbia University Press.

Fisher, R.A. (1930) *The Genetical Theory of Natural Selection*. Oxford, Clarendon Press.

Gale, D. (1973) "Pure Exchange Equilibrium of Dynamic Economic Models," *Journal of Economic Theory*, 6: 12–36.

Howell, N. (2010) *Life Histories of the Dobe !Kung*. Berkeley, University of California Press.

Kaplan, H. (1994) "Evolutionary and Wealth Flows Theories of Fertility: Empirical Tests and New Models," *Population and Development Review*, 20: 753–791.

Lee, R. (1974) "The Formal Dynamics of Controlled Populations and the Echo, the Boom and the Bust," *Demography*, 11: 563–585.

Lee, R. (1985) "Inverse Projection and Back Projection: Comparative Results and Sensitivity Tests for England," *Population Studies*, 39: 233–248.

Lee, R. (1993) "Inverse Projection and Demographic Fluctuations: A Critical Assessment of New Methods," in D. Reher and R. Schofield (eds.) *Old and New Methods in Historical Demography*. Oxford, Oxford University Press: 7–28.

Lee, R. (1994) "The Formal Demography of Population Aging, Transfers, and the Economic Life Cycle," in L. Martin and S. Preston (eds.) *The Demography of Aging*. Washington, DC, National Academies Press: 8–49.

Lee, R. and A. Mason et al. (2011) *Population Aging and the Generational Economy: A Global Perspective*. Cheltenham, UK and Northampton, MA, USA, Edward Elgar.

Lee, R. and A. Mason, et al. (2014) "Is Low Fertility Really a Problem? Population Aging, Dependency, and Consumption," *Science*, 346: 229–234.

Pollak, R.A. (1986) "A Reformulation of the Two-Sex Problem," *Demography*, 23: 247–259.

Pollak, R.A. (1990) "Two-Sex Demographic Models," *Journal of Political Economy*, 98: 399–420.

Samuelson, P.A. (1947) *Foundations of Economic Analysis*. Cambridge, MA, Harvard University Press.

Samuelson, P.A. (1958) "An Exact Consumption-Loan Model of Interest with or Without the Social Contrivance of Money," *Journal of Political Economy*, 66: 467–482.

Samuelson, P.A. (1971) "Generalized Predator-Prey Oscillations in Ecological and Economic Equilibrium," *Proceedings of the National Academy of Sciences USA*, 68: 980–983.

Samuelson, P.A. (1974) "Generalizing Fisher's "Reproductive Value": Nonlinear, Homogeneous, Biparental Systems," *Proceedings of the National Academy of Sciences USA*, 74: 5772–5775.

Samuelson, P.A. (1975a) "The Optimum Growth Rate for Population," *International Economic Review*, 16: 531–538.

Samuelson, P.A. (1975b) "Optimum Social Security in a Life-Cycle Growth Model," *International Economic Review*, 16: 539–544.

Samuelson, P.A. (1976a) "An Economist's Non-linear Model of Self-Generated Fertility Waves," *Population Studies*, 30: 243–247.

Samuelson, P.A. (1976b) "Time Symmetry and Asymmetry in Population and Deterministic Dynamic Systems," *Theoretical Population Biology*, 9: 82–122.

Samuelson, P.A. (1976c) "The Optimum Growth Rate for Population: Agreement and Evaluations," *International Economic Review*, 17: 516–525.

Samuelson, P.A. (1977a) "Generalizing Fisher's 'Reproductive Value': Linear Differential and Difference Equations of 'Dilute' Biological Systems," *Proceedings of the National Academy of Sciences USA*, 74: 5189–5192.

Samuelson, P.A. (1977b) "Generalizing Fisher's 'Reproductive Value': Nonlinear, Homogeneous, Biparental Systems," *Proceedings of the National Academy of Sciences USA*, 74: 5772–5775.

Samuelson, P.A. (1978a) "Generalizing Fisher's 'Reproductive Value': Incipient and Penultimate Reproductive Value Functions when Environment Limits Growth; Linear Approximants for Nonlinear Mendelian Mating Models," *Proceedings of the National Academy of Sciences USA*, 75: 6327–6331.

Samuelson, P.A. (1978b) "Generalizing Fisher's 'Reproductive Value': Overlapping and Nonoverlapping Generations with Competing Genotypes," *Proceedings of the National Academy of Sciences USA*,75: 4062–4066.

Samuelson, P.A. (1980) "Fisher's 'Reproductive Value' as an Economic Specimen in Merton's Zoo," *Transactions of the New York Academy of Sciences*, 39: 126–142.

Samuelson, P.A. (1985) "Modes of Thought in Economics and Biology," *American Economic Review*, 75: 166–172.

United Nations Population Division (2013) *National Transfer Accounts Manual: Measuring and Analyzing the Generational Economy*. New York, United Nations.

Vaupel, J., E. Barbi, S. Bertino, and E. Sonnio (eds.) (2004) *Inverse Projection Techniques: Old and New Approaches*. Berlin, Springer-Verlag.

Willis, R. (1973) "A New Approach to the Economic Theory of Fertility Behavior," *Journal of Political Economy*, 81: S14–S64.

Willis, R. (1988) "Life Cycles, Institutions and Population Growth: A Theory of the Equilibrium Interest Rate in an Overlapping-Generations Model," in R. Lee, W.B. Arthur and G. Rodgers (eds.) *Economics of Changing Age Distributions in Developed Countries*. Oxford, Oxford University Press: 106–138.

Wrigley, E.A. and R. Schofield (1981) *The Population History of England 1541–1871: A Reconstruction*. London, Edward Arnold.

Yellin, J. and P.A. Samuelson (1974) "A Dynamical Model for Human Population," *Proceedings of the National Academy of Sciences USA*, 71: 2813–2817.

Yellin, J. and P.A. Samuelson (1977) "Comparison of Linear and Nonlinear Models for Human Population Dynamics," *Theoretical Population*, 11: 105–126.

20

Paul Samuelson's Contributions to Public Economics

Michael J. Boskin

1 Introduction

Paul Samuelson's contributions to economics are so fundamental, the scope so broad, the continuing impact so pervasive, that an essay on their impact on public/fiscal economics must roam far beyond his surprisingly few direct contributions to the field. Researchers, teachers and practitioners of what might be broadly labeled public sector economics or economics relevant to public sector issues are deeply in his debt for foundational methods and tools, for clarifying conditions under which problems can be clearly stated, testable implications derived, relevant empirical parameters identified and evidence-based policies debated and implemented.

This chapter is divided into five parts. Following this introduction, Sect. 2 briefly discusses the importance of the influence of Samuelson's microeconomic methodological contributions. Three in particular stand

M. J. Boskin (✉)
Hoover Institution and Economics Department,
Stanford University, Stanford, CA, USA
e-mail: boskin@stanford.edu

R. A. Cord et al. (eds.), *Paul Samuelson*, Remaking Economics:
Eminent Post-War Economists, https://doi.org/10.1057/978-1-137-56812-0_20

out to me. First is the formulation of models of constrained optimization that became the backbone of modern economic models. Second is revealed preference theory, which explicitly or implicitly lies behind the application of modern welfare economics to public economics issues. Third is his formulation of the overlapping generations (OLG) model, with its many implications for thinking about long-run positive and normative issues. Indeed, his OLG model and its descendants are one of the two workhorses (along with the infinite-horizon Ramsey model) in many subfields in public economics, examples of which are discussed.

Section 3 discusses Samuelson's primary contribution to public economics, namely the theory of public goods. Ask any public finance economist to name Samuelson's most important contribution to the field and virtually all will immediately respond: public goods theory. Samuelson's contribution has had such a profound influence on generations of teaching in public economics, and on thinking about the appropriate role of the public sector in mixed capitalist democracies, as to deserve special attention. In particular, many issues raised or implied by Samuelson's analysis have led to extensions, modifications and caveats to his conclusions. The section also briefly discusses Samuelson's main contribution to tax theory—the proof that true economic depreciation is neutral with respect to types of investment.

Section 4 briefly discusses Samuelson's intellectual contributions to the macroeconomics of fiscal policy for countercyclical stabilization, with brief comments on the evolution of macroeconomics since Samuelson's highly successful, indeed market dominant, textbook popularized Keynesian economics among students, teachers and policy makers. I focus on issues that have gained widespread importance in recent decades in the evaluation of fiscal policy: the roles of time horizons, expectations and incentives in the analysis of the effects of taxes, spending, deficits and public debt. In addition, I briefly discuss the influence of Samuelson's textbook, public intellectual writing, including his *Newsweek* column, and advising policy makers. Section 5 concludes with my evaluation of his place in the history of economic thought.

Much has happened since Samuelson made his most important contributions to public economics: in the economy, economic policy and in the now numerous subfields of public economics itself. In a short chapter on contributions to fiscal economics, I cannot even pretend to embark on a comprehensive history of modern public economics or macroeconomic thought. But I present what will hopefully be a useful impressionistic personal account based on decades of teaching graduates and undergraduates and of helping to formulate public policy. I emphasize that this essay reflects my discussions of, and has been influenced strongly by, the views of numerous academics and policy makers, especially my students (some now leaders in the field) and the terrific economists with whom I had the privilege of sharing the teaching of public economics at Stanford: John Shoven, Doug Bernheim, Antonio Rangel, Joe Stiglitz and David Starrett.

2 Microeconomic Methodological Contributions

While Samuelson's contributions to economic theory influenced virtually all fields of economics and his methodological tool development is still useful in many, I mention here a few that are particularly relevant to public economics. First, in his 1947 *Foundations of Economic Analysis*, which was based on his 1941 doctoral dissertation, Samuelson presented a consistent, coherent theoretical framework based on the principle of constrained maximization. While aspects of this treatment existed in varying degrees of mathematical sophistication prior to Samuelson, he is widely credited with "pulling it all together" and certainly was the most important voice in popularizing and disseminating this approach (only Hicks [1939] comes close). In short, Samuelson made it acceptable then, and necessary subsequently, to use mathematics to increase the clarity and precision of economic analysis. Every economics student who has solved the consumer's utility maximization subject to a budget constraint problem who came to understand Lagrangian multipliers as shadow prices and the like, knowingly or not is a student of Samuelson. While Samuelson's derivation of the Slutsky conditions and more has long since given way to duality theory in teaching and operationalizing theory to derive and utilize demand and supply curves, his legacy is profound and is incorporated, often subconsciously, into most economists' way of thinking about problems.

I would add next in importance, from my own perspective, Samuelson's revealed preference theory (Samuelson 1938). It demonstrated how preferences could be accurately inferred by observing consumption bundles at different prices and incomes. It provides an important foundation for much economics, from chained price indexes to applying traditional welfare economics to a wide variety of public economics and industrial organization problems and policies (see Blundell 2005).

Third in my brief impressionistic survey is Samuelson's OLG model. It provides a foundational analytical structure for dealing with some of the most important long-run public economics issues, especially the analysis of public debt and pay-as-you-go-social insurance systems. Samuelson developed his OLG model at a time when the US national debt was shrinking rapidly relative to GDP from its the Second World War peak of over 100%. Dwight Eisenhower was president at the time and often argued that budget deficits and the national debt were a burden to our children and grandchildren. Samuelson (1958) challenged that conclusion (under some conditions). His analysis revealed many gems: the possibility of multiple equilibria; the biological determinants of interest rates; and that decentralized competitive economies can be dynamically inefficient. This framework has been used in some of the most influential papers in public economics. For example, Peter Diamond's (1965) analysis of public debt (among other things) emphasizes the substitution of government bonds for tangible capital in people's portfolios. Since external, as opposed to internal, debt has that substitution in foreigners' portfolios, the external holding supports domestic investment and higher wages. Robert Barro (1974) used the OLG framework, combined with assumptions about intrafamily bequests, to derive the Ricardian equivalence result. Also, Larry Kotlikoff with a series of coauthors, especially Alan Auerbach (1987), used OLG to develop empirically tractable dynamic general equilibrium models of fiscal policy effects via generational accounts for many dozens of age cohorts. To be sure, the OLG model and its primary competitor, the infinite-horizon Ramsey dynastic model, can yield different conclusions. In the latter, for example, the long-run supply of capital is perfectly elastic.

3 The Samuelsonian Public Goods Revolution

In just three insightful pages, Paul Samuelson launched a revolution in thinking about what he called "collective goods," what we now call "public goods." It is helpful to remember that the classic paper (Samuelson 1954) was published less than a decade after the Second World War and the year after the Korean War armistice was signed. In those days, not only did wartime result in 80–90% of (expanded) federal government spending going to defense, but even after the peace, almost 80% of federal spending was on purchases of goods and services and very little on transfer payments to people. Of course, in all advanced democracies, most central government spending is now on transfer payments to the poor, to the old, to the ill and to many others in less apparent need. Back then, the memory of the failure of democracies to maintain a strong military—recall Winston Churchill's prescient, unheeded interwar warning to Great Britain—would quite naturally lend support to the types of conclusions that Samuelson derived. Although I know of no acknowledgment that did or did not play a role in his thinking—he claims to have thought of it as mainly an application of mathematical economics—it may well have played a role in the very rapid dissemination of his conclusion that public goods like national defense would be insufficiently provided.

Around the same time, Harvard economist John Kenneth Galbraith published *The Affluent Society*, which argued that the poverty of America's public sector stood in stark contrast to the wealthy private sector. These two works laid the intellectual foundation and the public policy impetus, respectively, for the dramatic expansion of the public sector that ensued. Millions of Americans learned about "public" goods in their introductory economics classes, many from successive editions of Samuelson's own textbook. While his rigorous analysis of what turns out to be a polar case was often expanded by others beyond his original meaning, it serves as a reminder to this day of a remarkable fact: The very characteristics of some goods and services make it virtually impossible for private markets to produce them. Their very nature requires public financing, if not public production. Remarkably, in those three pages Samuelson not only laid the foundations—non-rival consumption, the preference revelation free rider problem, inability of a decentralized price system to achieve efficiency, the social welfare function choosing the best among the infinity of Pareto-optimal points and simultaneous determination of income distribution and public goods provision—but even presaged the political economy needed for a more complete story.

This section continues with a discussion of the theory of public goods by going through a series of questions that form the basis of teaching of public goods theory, including some important extensions, limitations and caveats to Samuelson's original analysis. What is a public good? Why will private markets undersupply these goods? What is the free rider problem? What determines an efficient supply of a pure public good? Is it affected by income distribution and/or distortionary taxes?

Define two properties:

i. *Rival consumption* refers to the fact that when something is used by one person, it is not available to another. For example, nobody else gets the orange juice I had for breakfast; to get another person orange juice, we need to produce more of it, which implies using more resources. *Non-rival consumption*, in contrast, occurs when one person's consumption does not detract from others' consumption (e.g., national defense protects all simultaneously; an additional baby born or immigrant does not require additional defense spending).
ii. *Non-excludable consumption* asks whether it is possible, at least avoiding great cost, to exclude someone from reaping the benefits of a good. For private goods, the price system does the exclusion. Pay and you get the good; do not pay and you are excluded. Historically, the classic ship passing the lighthouse case is a non-excludable example. If the light is on for the lighthouse company's boats or customers, nonpaying ships can see it too (modern technology now enables firms to filter signals).

Thus, *private goods* are defined by the core properties of rival consumption and excludability, whereas pure *public goods* are defined by non-rival consumption and are impossible to exclude.

Market failures with public goods: Start by separating rivalry and excludability. Suppose consumption is non-rival, but exclusion is possible, e.g., watching a TV show like *The Voice*, the marginal cost = 0 and the number of times I watch the show does not decrease the number of times you can watch it. But exclusion is possible (if costly), e.g., with signal scramblers for cable or satellite TV. If exclusion is possible, when a good is non-rival, it is not efficient to exclude. Charging a price would exclude some people, but their consumption has no marginal (social) cost. So, charging would lead to too little consumption. If exclusion is possible, even if consumption is non-rival, governments often charge user fees to those who benefit from a publicly provided good or service, e.g., for non-congested toll roads. Worse yet, if there is no charge for a non-rival good, there will be no incentive to supply the good because firms would go broke doing so, and thus there would be too little supply, perhaps none in a private market.

The free rider problem: Some of the most important publicly provided goods—national defense and public health—seem to have the non-excludability property, which makes rationing (exclusion) by price unfeasible. For example, the international smallpox vaccination program wiped out the disease (almost), benefiting everyone, whether they paid or not. National defense, likewise, is non-excludable and has zero marginal cost of adding another consumer. Some goods have high exclusion costs, but have non-trivial marginal cost, e.g., congested roads.

Revelation of preferences—the free rider: As a result of non-excludability, we all have an incentive to under-report our truthful preferences for public goods. Why? We might get away with paying less and what we say will have little or no effect on the amount of the public good given a large population. Clarke (1971) and Groves and Ledyard (1977) discovered potential solutions to the free rider problems, at least for some specifications of preferences (quasi-linear utility), but, of course, they face practical difficulties.

Is private provision of pure public goods possible? The firm would have to charge for services, but since everyone knows they will get the benefits of the services whether they contribute or not, no one has an incentive to pay voluntarily, e.g., for defense. They have an incentive to be a "free rider" on other people's payments. The only way to finance provision is to require everyone to pay, e.g., via taxation. In some limited cases, non-excludable public goods may be provided privately despite the free rider problem, e.g., historically, big shipping companies built lighthouses, but then only their private value is considered in the decisions on how many lighthouses to build and where. The results are a tendency toward undersupply.

Many goods are not pure public goods but have one or the other property (non-rivalrousness or non-excludability) to some extent.[1] Take fire protection as an example. Exclusion is easy. Indeed, in Hong Kong before 1976, the firefighters would arrive and demand payment before turning on the water. As the marginal costs of covering an additional person is low, exclusion increases the risk of fires spreading to those who pay from fires in buildings whose owners do not pay. Vaccination is another, and increasingly controversial, policy issue. There is a marginal cost to vaccinating more people, but we cannot exclude people from the benefit of a vaccinated populace, and the risks from those refusing vaccination rises with their number.

There are also publicly provided private goods, goods for which there is a non-trivial marginal cost of supplying more people (unlike pure public goods). Education, one of society's most important services, is usually provided publicly, but is not a pure Samuelsonian public good. Its marginal cost is greater than zero. If we double the number of students, we roughly double costs. Likewise, water has a positive marginal cost, in droughts quite high, including purification and delivery costs. If these goods are provided free, private decisions drive the marginal value of their consumption to zero, below the marginal cost, causing a welfare (deadweight) loss. In this case, demand is likely to be very inelastic, so the deadweight loss is small. For others, e.g., elective medical services, however, demand is likely more elastic, and the deadweight losses or inefficiency costs are higher.

When publicly provided goods are free, too much is consumed. Thus, governments sometimes try to limit consumption. Any method of restricting consumption is a rationing system. The most commonly used, of course, is the price system. Since demand curves slope down, a price greater than zero reduces the quantity demanded. Sometimes government provides everyone the same (or roughly the same) level of a good or service, e.g., free public education. In these cases, of course, there is often a social purpose not completely congruent with purely private motives. However, public provision does not as readily adapt to individuals' needs as would a

[1] Samuelson discusses these deviations from his pure case in his later writing.

private market (an exception is noted below when goods are provided by many competing governments and people are free to migrate in or out).

In addition to user charges and uniform provision, another method of rationing is queuing. People pay costs in waiting time, e.g., for publicly provided health services. Queuing is also used in many private and quasi-private authorities—lines at airports, waiting for access to supercomputers and waiting in doctors' offices. But queuing replaces willingness to pay, the basis of the efficiency of the market, of Adam Smith's invisible hand, with willingness to wait. Some argue it is unfair that money is the basis on which medical services are rationed. However, queuing may also be unfair as well as inefficient, e.g., a low-wage single working mother going to night school may not be able to afford to wait either; a wealthy retiree might easily afford both. The cost of waiting is real, i.e., the value of people's time, approximated by the after-tax wage rate.

Efficient supply and consumption of public goods: How much of a public good should be supplied? How do we determine the demand for a public good? For private goods, where consumption is rivalrous, markets equilibrate at a price and quantity where supply equals demand that automatically equates the marginal cost of production (the marginal rate of transformation in production) to the marginal value of consumption (the marginal rate of substitution) and both to the equilibrium price. However, for public goods, consumption is non-rivalrous. The provision of one more unit has a marginal cost, but the marginal value is the *sum*[2] of what each of us is willing to pay: $MRS_1 + MRS_2 = MC(= MRT)$, where MRS is how much of private goods persons are willing to give up to get one more unit of a public good and the MRT is how much of private goods must be foregone to free up resources to produce one more unit of the public good.

Demand for public goods: Generally, public goods are provided by governments, not directly purchased by individuals. However, we can ask how much would they demand if they had to pay a given amount for extra units of public goods, just like demand for private goods. For the government to provide more of a public good, it must raise revenue to pay for it, either from taxes or borrowing (which is much the same as future taxes). Think

[2]Samuelson acknowledges the prior contribution of Bowen (1948) on this point.

of this extra payment as a tax price faced by an individual and ask: How does demand vary as the tax price changes?

Let p = *tax price*, with the price of consumption goods set equal to one as numeraire. Then, the consumer's budget constraint is:

$C + pG = Y$, where C = consumption of private goods, G = total amount of public good provided and Y = income, then

$$C = Y - pG.$$

We can also derive a societal demand curve. Total market demand for private goods is found by summing (horizontally, at each price) the demand for each individual. We must also sum individual demands to get societal demand for public goods. However, in this case of public goods, we must sum vertically at each quantity to get the aggregate willingness to pay for each quantity! This is perhaps the most enduring (graphical) representation of Samuelson's theory of public goods, etched in the minds of millions of economics students. Vertical summation is necessary because the same (non-rival) quantity is provided to every person. Since the demand curve, by construction, is a marginal willingness to pay curve, at each point on each individual's demand curve the (tax) price is equal to the marginal rate of substitution, what he or she is willing to give up in terms of private goods consumption to consume one more unit of the public good.

Efficiency: The supply curve for a public good, just like the supply curve of a private good, represents the marginal cost of producing each additional unit. So, when $S = D$ (the vertical sum of what each individual is willing to pay and the societal willingness to pay), *marginal cost* would and should be set equal to demand to determine output, the standard efficiency result. However, note one huge difference between public and private goods: For private goods (under the usual assumptions), supply equals demand, marginal value equals marginal cost equals price, or $S = D \Rightarrow MV = MC$ is a characterization of the equilibrium of the decentralized market economy. For public goods, supply decisions are made by government officials through political processes that may be, perhaps likely are, at least sometimes, far removed from these efficiency considerations.

Income distribution: Samuelson notes extensively—indeed, a careful reading of those famous three pages suggests that this is his *main* point, but it tends to receive less attention than the efficiency conditions—that there are many points on the utility-possibility frontier, each corresponding to a different initial distribution of income. The market equilibrium in a decentralized price system corresponds to one such point. Suppose government transfers incomes via taxes, welfare, etc. from urban to rural, or rich to poor, or middle-aged to old (generally rural citizens are poorer than urban and middle-aged richer than old). We would expect the demand for pubic goods by recipients of transfers to rise and demand for public goods by those paying higher taxes to fall. These changes will generally not exactly cancel each other out. Also, by providing the set of public goods, the marginal valuation of these equally consumed goods will generally differ among individuals. Even if income elasticities were constant across the population, the percentage change in real income from the public goods will be higher for lower income people. In addition, as we shall see shortly, the tax prices they pay will also differ. So, the societal demand (the vertical sum of the changed individual demand curves) will be changed, and therefore, the optimum level of public goods provision *depends* upon the distribution of income. Changes in the distribution of income will be reflected (as in demand for private goods) in changed demand for public goods. In practice, of course, this is only a major issue if there are large changes in taxes, transfers and/or public goods provision. So, in principle, the optimal supply of public goods must be determined simultaneously with the distribution of income to achieve the "social optimum point" among all the Pareto-optimal points. Samuelson, at this point, invokes Bergsonian social welfare functions to do that job (see Samuelson 1947: Chapter 8; Bergson 1938).

Distortionary taxes: To collect revenue to finance the provision of public goods, governments levy taxes, e.g., income taxes. These distort some decisions, e.g., how much to save, how long to work, when to retire, etc. These distortions involve welfare efficiency costs. They also entail administrative costs to the government and compliance costs to taxpayers. These are extra costs, above and beyond the resources necessary to produce the goods. Thus, the amount of private goods that must be given up to raise revenue to provide one more unit of a public good is higher than if the government could raise revenue in a non-distortionary manner, via the hypothetical construct of lump-sum taxes and transfers.

We must therefore amend the *MRT* in production (which was given by technology) to include these distortionary, administrative and compliance costs. What we obtain is a marginal economic rate of transformation, call it *MERT*, which lies below the physical technology-determined production-possibility curve, relating the maximum amount of private goods that society can produce for each amount of the public good. In general, the more public goods that are provided, the higher the necessary taxes and the distortionary costs, which, from basic demand theory, rise with the square of tax rates.[3] It costs more than $1 for the government to raise $1 (or pound, euro, yen, etc.). The estimates for the USA run at about $1.30–$1.40. Thus, the efficient level of public goods provision is lower than if these added costs are ignored. This is one important limitation of, and qualification to, Samuelson's original analysis, especially as interpreted and employed in arguments for more public spending.

Effective, efficient and transparent government may also be considered a public good; we all benefit from responsible government and it is approximately non-rival. It is difficult and undesirable to exclude anyone from the benefit of such a government (non-excludable). The converse is true for an inefficient, overly bureaucratic or corrupt government. Of course, rent-seeking, regulatory capture and the like mean that most governments fall well short of the ideal.

Revelation of preferences: In markets for private goods, prices play two crucial roles: information and incentives. They provide: (1) Incentives for firms to produce what consumers want and to allocate goods among consumers (rationing), and (2) prices also convey information: from consumers to producers about the value of commodities and between producers and consumers about the costs of production and scarcity. If demand increases, prices increase and firms produce more.

However, no such automatic mechanism exists for public goods. So, public resource allocation is very different. In democracies, individuals vote for elected representatives. The representatives (in Congress, on school boards, etc.) vote for a public budget; administrative agencies do the actual spending. Given this, how can we determine what people want and how to aggregate different wishes into a social decision? While Samuelson

[3] See Dahlby (2008).

ends his paper with a note on this score, by referencing recent landmark works by Black (1948) and Arrow (1951) as early pioneers in serious political economy, he leaves it to others to explore further. I elaborate with a simple classroom example.

Taxes and the demand for public goods: The reasons why demand for public goods differs among individuals are analogous to those for private goods: tastes, income and prices in the form of taxes. Higher incomes generally imply consumers want more private and public goods. The tax price is the additional amount an individual must pay when government spending increases by $1. The tax payment is tax price × government spending. The tax price is related to income via the tax system. Suppose there are N people and government spends G to provide public goods.

With uniform taxation everyone pays the same amount of taxes, so, the tax price = $1/N$ and the tax payment = tax price × public goods spending $= G \times 1/N = G/N$.

With proportional taxation, everyone pays the same percentage of income:

If Y_i = individual i's income
and $\hat{Y}$ = average income,
then $N\hat{Y}$ = total income.

At tax rate t, total government revenue $= tN\hat{Y}$, which equals government spending

$$G = tN\hat{Y},$$

or $t = G/N\hat{Y}$.

For individual i, with income Y_i, the tax payment is: $tY_i = GY_i/N\hat{Y}$, i.e., government per person spending × his/her share of total income. If *G increases $1*, the additional payment, or tax price is just $Y_i/N\hat{Y}$. Those with above-average income ($Y > \hat{Y}$) face a higher, and those with below-average income a lower, tax price per dollar of G. For example, to raise $20,000 from two people where Y_1=$10,000, Y_2=$90,000, $N\hat{Y}$ = $100,000 (2 × $50,000), *then if* $t = 20\%$, tY_1 = $2,000, tY_2 = $18,000 *i.e., person 2 pays 9 times more.*

With a progressive tax system, tax payments increase more than proportionally with income; with a regressive tax system, tax payments increase less than proportionally with income. So, high-income people have higher tax prices under a progressive tax system, and low-income people lower, than under proportional taxation, and conversely under regressive tax systems. As with private goods, income and prices affect the quantity demanded of the public goods. For example, with proportional taxation, poorer individuals face lower tax prices than higher income people; even though they pay the same proportion of their income, the absolute dollar amount will be lower. (Recall that for a pure public good, everyone gets the same quantity, whether or not they value it the same, more or less, or even negatively.) Thus, the preferred level of public goods would be higher at the same income; but as they are poorer, their lower income leads them to demand less. Hence, whether they demand more or less depends upon the strength of the income and substitution effects.

However, if the income distribution is skewed to higher incomes, the median will be less than the mean and the decisive median voter under majority voting might well lead to too much spending. The median voter faces a low tax price and gets the same consumption; if valued at the mean, and if the price elasticity of demand is large enough to more than offset the lower demand due to modest income, there will be too much public goods provision under majority voting. This illustrates the need to tie the spending to the tax side of the budget, a point Samuelson tends to downplay—his remarkable ability to model parsimoniously helped focus attention, but here as elsewhere, left lots for others to elaborate. Nevertheless, it is appropriately featured in Musgrave (1959, 1980), drawing on the voluntary exchange approach of Continental writers in the late nineteenth and early twentieth centuries and of fiscal sociology.

One such solution was proposed by the Swedish economist Eric Lindahl (1958), following work by his great fellow countryman Knut Wicksell (1958), a vague remembrance of which Samuelson recognizes through Musgrave (1939). The solution to efficient public goods provision was to set tax shares based on preferences and require unanimity in voting for the amount of the public good.

Lindahl Solution:

s_i = share of cost of person *i*, with two people,

$s_1 \neq s_2$.

The tax shares act as prices but *personalized* prices and so are not the same price for everyone.

Lindahl Prices:

$$\mathrm{p}_1 = G * s_1 \ (\text{e.g., } s_1 = 75\%)$$

$$\mathrm{p}_2 = G * s_2 \ (\text{e.g., } s_2 \, 25\%).$$

The sum of the tax shares equals 100% and thus covers the cost of the good. Wicksell appears to have been the first to derive the fact that if a social project—a dam, for example—has total social benefits greater than total social costs, there must be an assignment of the costs to each individual (via taxes, fees, etc.) such that for all of them, their benefits would exceed (or at least equal) their costs. So, all would vote in favor of the project. Thus, a unanimity requirement could be used to discover or force such a financing scheme and efficient public goods provision. There are, of course, practical problems with unanimity, such as strategic voting and difficulty in making redistribution policy, so qualified supermajorities were recommended. Why not simple majority rule? Again, the median voter, assuming a skewed distribution of income toward the upper tail, has both lower income and tax price than the average and may tend to vote for too much (or too little) public goods provision. Samuelson, while crediting the Swedes, was insistent that their solution could not find the optimum optimorum; for that, only a social welfare function would suffice.

Local public goods: Perhaps the most important of many extensions and qualifications of Samuelson's public goods theory and its implications was Charles Tiebout's (1956) analysis of "local public goods," in a model of people sorting among communities competing in their bundles of public goods and taxes. In markets for private goods, firms do not have to balance different interests of potential customers. Anyone willing to pay the market price is someone the firm is willing to sell to. Decisions are made on an individual basis. In the public sector, decisions are made collectively. Elected officials vote on expenditures; they do not pay for them personally. Votes generally are thought to represent constituents, whose opinions are likely to differ. Some want more welfare, some less; some want more military spending, some less, etc.

For one class of public goods, those provided locally, there is another force that tends toward efficiency. Tiebout pointed out that goods provided locally by many competing jurisdictions will tend toward efficient allocation (under some strong assumptions). Empirical support for efficiency induced by Tiebout-sorting includes Caroline Hoxby's analysis of K-12 education (Hoxby 2000). So, here is another example of the practical policy relevance of ideas that Samuelson helped launch with his trenchant analysis. The efficiency of public goods provision must often engage the question, if public goods must be provided or financed by government, at what level of government should that be done?

Surprisingly, Samuelson made few direct contributions to the theory of taxation (although many of his students, especially Peter Diamond (Diamond and Mirrlees 1971a, b), Joe Stiglitz (Atkinson and Stiglitz 1976) and Bob Hall (Hall and Rabushka 1985) were highly influential). The two most relevant for our purposes (Samuelson 1964, 1986) are concerned with efficiency. The latter paper builds on the canonical Ramsey optimal commodity taxation theorem. The former, again remarkably in just three pages, established the fundamental theorem of tax rate invariance. To wit, "If, and only if, true loss of economic value is permitted as a tax deductible depreciation expense will the present discounted value of a cash-receipt stream be independent of the rate of tax" (Samuelson 1964: 604). He did this by considering Irving Fisher's (1930) formula for the valuation of a stream of net cash receipts as a function of time over a finite period with a person being able to borrow or lend at the market rate of interest in unlimited amounts.

Typically, Samuelson generates a series of important results: First, that the only neutral tax treatment of alternative investments is that which allows true economic depreciation; second, that in a perfect capital market the only effect on the saving/consumption decision caused by uniform income tax is what a lower interest rate would have; third, that if the tax rate varies with time, a proper system of carryforwards and carrybacks which makes the tax rate average out to a constant can preserve tax neutrality; and fourth, that the only "sensible definition of depreciation relevant to measurement of *true money income* is putative decline in economic value" (ibid.: 606; italics in original).

Samuelson expresses concern that accelerated depreciation for tax purposes does not accurately account for economic obsolescence. That may or may not be true (see Hulten and Wykoff 1981). However, he does admit that it may obviate the bias against capital formation when income rather than consumption is taxed. Moving closer to consumption taxation has often been the goal of many American tax reforms and, of course, many countries have relied increasingly on value-added taxes to limit the damaging effects of capital income taxes (see Harberger 1980). I use a football field analogy to describe these issues. A neutral income tax would be level sideline to sideline; a pure consumption, or consumed income, tax would also be neutral end zone to end zone, goal to goal as well. Both are important, the latter more so, because the tax distortion in the saving decision grows exponentially with the time horizon of saving decisions, e.g., to retirement.

4 Fiscal Policy and Countercyclical Stabilization

Samuelson made several contributions to the analysis of fiscal policy for stabilization purposes. While his interaction of the multiplier and accelerator model (Samuelson 1939) was important for some time, it has faded in influence (although Jorgenson's (1971) flexible (via user cost) accelerator model of investment remains influential to this day). Far more important was Samuelson's role as the teacher of Keynesian economics to: (1) millions of students through his textbook; (2) presidents (especially President Kennedy), central bankers and finance ministers through his personal advice and public intellectual writing; and (3) through the teaching and advising of his many graduate students that went on to become influential macroeconomists and policy makers. In the same sense, though he never had a formal policy role in government, at the Council of Economic Advisers, the Treasury or the Fed, Samuelson's imprint on stabilization policy was profound.

While known primarily as a microeconomic theorist, Samuelson's textbook emphasized a "neoclassical synthesis," an early attempt to integrate neoclassical microeconomic theory with Keynesian macroeconomics. While many of these issues are discussed elsewhere in this volume, and it has become common for the public economics field to cede fiscal policy for stabilization to macroeconomics, the economics profession benefited from the intellectual and policy clashes between Samuelson and Milton Friedman. From debates about Keynesian multipliers and the stability of the velocity of money, to specific real-time disagreements over inflation and its causes to the ability of fiscal policy to permanently reduce unemployment below a certain level, Samuelson and Friedman dueled in alternating columns in *Newsweek*, for a while the second most widely read weekly magazine and one of a handful of setters of national debate.

Friedman consistently argued for the superiority of rules over discretion. He called for a simple money supply growth rule (although that has given way, with the Fed's dual mandate, to the Taylor (1993) or similar rule as a guide to policy). Samuelson preferred (well-chosen) discretion for policy makers. The debate occurred amid the backdrop of the development of large-scale macroeconometric models promising to deliver real-time policy prescriptions for dealing with inflation and recession. The inflation of the 1970s and the failure of the simplest Phillips curve models to correctly predict economic performance led to a dramatic reevaluation. An immense macroeconomics literature has developed since then, with new tools for analyzing and calibrating dynamic stochastic general equilibrium (DSGE) models, and both the quantity theory of Friedman and the old Keynesian macroeconomics of Samuelson have been replaced by second- and third-generation models of the macroeconomy.

These models can be broadly classified as emphasizing one or more of three previously underdeveloped issues in Keynesian economics: time horizons, expectations and incentives. Time horizons have played an increasingly important role, tracing back to Fisher (1930), Modigliani (Modigliani and Brumberg 1954), and Friedman (1957) himself. Importantly, these analyses indicate that longer-term forces can have important influences on current economic decisions. The rational expectations revolution (see Lucas 1976) built expectations of future economic conditions and policy into decisions. Finally, empirical analyses of saving, investment and the several dimensions of labor supply also began to influence economists' thinking (see Boskin 1978; Feldstein 1978; Lucas 1990), as part of what is now called supply-side economics.

A combination of these three approaches would suggest, for example, that expectations about future tax rates could affect decisions now and that tax and budget policy now affects expectations of future taxes and spending. These various strains of thought are incorporated in some new schools of macroeconomic modeling. New Keynesian models incorporating the sticky wages that Keynes invoked as one reason why unemployment would not automatically be self-correcting leave potential room for discretionary fiscal policy of the type Samuelson favored to increase output and decrease unemployment when the Fed is at the zero lower bound.

However, by incorporating the microeconomic foundation of forward-looking consumers, the expectation of higher future government spending beyond the zero lower bound period can dramatically dampen this effect or even turn it negative (see Woodford 2011). The zero lower bound is potentially relevant in most advanced economies today and central bankers are rethinking how to conduct monetary policy when it is not an extremely rare situation. Adding supply-side considerations can also be quite important. For example, the disincentive problems caused by the high implicit marginal tax rates in the phaseout ranges of the new and expanded government transfer payments that were part of the fiscal response to the financial crisis/Great Recession demonstratively reduced its potential beneficial impact (see Mulligan 2012).

My view is that none of these macroeconomic schools of thought—New Keynesian, supply side, rational expectations, real business cycle theory, monetarism—is sufficient by itself to describe the performance of the economy or to guide or evaluate economic policy. They each contain important seeds of truth, more relevant in some scenarios than others, and an eclectic blending is beneficial if not easy. Fortunately, many macromodels now include supply-side incentives, for example, and virtually all include, to some extent, forward-looking consumers.

The most overarching legacy of Samuelson's own teaching and writing on these developments, in addition to his direct theoretical contributions, is surely his emphasis on synthesizing macro- and microeconomics. While he apparently disapproved of some of these modern developments—particularly those that are most clearly lineal descendants of Friedman's thinking—he surely approved of exploring the microfoundations of macroeconomics, the hallmark of modern research.

5 Conclusion

The great Nobel Laureate University of Chicago microeconomist George Stigler, himself like Samuelson imbued with a passion for the history of economic thought, was fond of saying that every interesting piece of research raises more questions than it answers. In that sense, Paul Samuelson opened many doors and many eyes with his theoretical contributions. His fundamental insights often produced or implied so many fruitful nuggets for future research that virtually all practicing economists can trace some of what they do, some of how they think or approach problems, to one or even several of Samuelson's works. For that inspiration, he stands, along with Kenneth Arrow and Milton Friedman, at the very pinnacle of great mid-twentieth-century economists, who must be added to the likes of Adam Smith, David Ricardo, Alfred Marshall, Léon Walras and John Maynard Keynes in any serious history of economic thought. Such an accolade would certainly have delighted him no end.

References

Arrow, K.J. (1951) *Social Choice and Individual Values.* New York, Wiley.

Atkinson, A.B. and J.E. Stiglitz. (1976) "The Design of Tax Structure: Direct versus Indirect Taxes," *Journal of Public Economics*, 6: 55–75.

Auerbach, A.J. and L.J. Kotlikoff. (1987) *Dynamic Fiscal Policy.* Cambridge, UK, Cambridge University Press.

Barro, R.J. (1974) "Are Government Bonds Net Wealth?" *Journal of Political Economy*, 82: 1095–1117.

Bergson, A. (1938) "A Reformulation of Certain Aspects of Welfare Economics," *Quarterly Journal of Economics*, 52: 310–334.

Black, D. (1948) "On the Rationale of Group Decision-Making," *Journal of Political Economy*, 56: 23–34.

Blundell, R. (2005) "Presidential Address: How Revealing is Revealed Preference?" *Journal of the European Economic Association*, 3: 211–235.

Boskin, M.J. (1978) "Taxation, Saving and the Rate of Interest," *Journal of Political Economy*, 86: S3–S27.

Bowen, H.R. (1948) *Toward Social Economy*. New York, Rinehart.

Clarke, E.H. (1971) "Multipart Pricing of Public Goods," *Public Choice*, 11: 17–33.

Dahlby, B. (2008) *The Marginal Cost of Public Funds*. Cambridge, MA, The MIT Press.

Diamond, P.A. (1965) "National Debt in a Neoclassical Growth Model," *American Economic Review*, 55: 1126–1150.

Diamond, P.A. and J.A. Mirrlees. (1971a) "Optimal Taxation and Public Production I: Production Efficiency," *American Economic Review*, 61: 8–27.

Diamond, P.A. and J.A. Mirrlees (1971b) "Optimal Taxation and Public Production II: Tax Rules," *American Economic Review*, 61: 261–278.

Feldstein, M. (1978) "The Welfare Cost of Capital Income Taxation," *Journal of Political Economy*, 86: S29–S51.

Fisher, I. (1930) *The Theory of Interest*. New York, Macmillan.

Friedman, M. (1957) *A Theory of the Consumption Function*. Princeton, NJ, Princeton University Press.

Groves, T. and J. Ledyard. (1977) "Optimal Allocation of Public Goods: A Solution to the 'Free Rider' Problem," *Econometrica*, 45: 783–809.

Hall, R.E. and A. Rabushka. (1985) *The Flat Tax*. Stanford, Hoover Institution Press.

Harberger, A. (1980) "Tax Neutrality in Investment Incentives," in H. Aaron and M. Boskin (eds.) *The Economics of Taxation*. Washington, DC, Brookings Institution Press: 299–313.

Hicks, J.R. (1939) *Value and Capital: An Inquiry into Some Fundamental Propositions of Economy Theory*. New York, Oxford University Press.

Hoxby, C. (2000) "Does Competition Among Public Schools Benefit Students and Taxpayers?" *American Economic Review*, 90: 1209–1238.

Hulten, C.R. and F.C. Wykoff. (1981) "The Estimation of Economic Depreciation Using Vintage Asset Prices: An Application of the Box-Cox Power Transformation," *Journal of Econometrics*, 15: 367–396.

Jorgenson, D.W. (1971) "Econometric Studies of Investment Behavior: A Survey," *Journal of Economic Literature*, 9: 1111–1147.

Lindahl, E. (1958) "Just Taxation—A Positive Solution," in R.A. Musgrave and A.T. Peacock (eds.) *Classics in the Theory of Public Finance*. London, Macmillan: 168–176.
Lucas, R.E., Jr. (1976) "Econometric Policy Evaluation: A Critique," in K. Brunner and A.H. Meltzer (eds.) *The Phillips Curve and Labor Markets*. Carnegie-Rochester Conference Series on Public Policy. Amsterdam, North-Holland Publishing Company: 19–46.
Lucas, R.E., Jr. (1990) "Supply-Side Economics: An Analytical Review," *Oxford Economic Papers*, 42: 293–316.
Modigliani, F. and R.H. Brumberg. (1954) "Utility Analysis and the Consumption Function: An Interpretation of Cross-Section Data," in K.K. Kurihara (ed.) *Post-Keynesian Economics*. New Brunswick, N.J., Rutgers University Press: 388–436.
Mulligan, C.B. (2012) *The Redistribution Recession: How Labor Market Distortions Contracted the Economy*. New York, Oxford University Press.
Musgrave, R.A. (1939) "The Voluntary Exchange Theory of Public Economy," *Quarterly Journal of Economics*, 53: 213–237.
Musgrave, R.A. (1959) *The Theory of Public Finance*. New York, McGraw-Hill.
Musgrave, R.A. (1980) "Theories of Fiscal Crisis: An Essay in Fiscal Sociology," in H. Aaron and M. Boskin (eds.) *The Economics of Taxation*. Washington, DC, Brookings Institution Press: 361–390.
Samuelson, P.A. (1938) "A Note on the Pure Theory of Consumer's Preference," *Economica*, New Series, 5: 61–71.
Samuelson, P.A. (1939) "A Synthesis of the Principle of Acceleration and the Multiplier," *Journal of Political Economy*, 47: 786–797.
Samuelson, P.A. (1947) *Foundations of Economic Analysis*. Cambridge, MA, Harvard University Press.
Samuelson, P.A. (1954) "The Pure Theory of Public Expenditure," *Review of Economics and Statistics*, 36: 387–389.
Samuelson, P.A. (1958) "An Exact Consumption-Loan Model of Interest with or Without the Social Contrivance of Money," *Journal of Political Economy*, 66: 467–482.
Samuelson, P.A. (1964) "Tax Deductibility of Economic Depreciation to Insure Invariant Valuations," *Journal of Political Economy*, 72: 604–606.
Samuelson, P.A. (1986) "Theory of Optimal Taxation," *Journal of Public Economics*, 30: 137–143.
Taylor, J.B. (1993) "Discretion versus Policy Rules in Practice," *Carnegie-Rochester Conference Series on Public Policy*, 39: 195–214.

Tiebout, C.M. (1956) "A Pure Theory of Local Expenditures," *Journal of Political Economy*, 64: 416–424.

Wicksell, K. (1958) "A New Principle of Just Taxation," in R.A. Musgrave and A.T. Peacock (eds.) *Classics in the Theory of Public Finance*. London, Macmillan: 72–118.

Woodford, M. (2011) "Simple Analytics of the Government Expenditure Multiplier," *American Economic Journal: Macroeconomics*, 3: 1–35.

21

Samuelson on Ricardo and on Technical Change

Arnold Heertje

1 Introduction

David Ricardo's chapter on machinery in the third edition of his *Principles* (1821) is a concise and well-balanced picture of the level of technology in his lifetime and its impact on the factors of production, in particular labour. In a remarkable analysis, Paul Samuelson devoted two articles to Ricardo's change of mind concerning machinery. The first article was entitled "Mathematical Vindication of Ricardo on Machinery", which appeared in 1988 in the *Journal of Political Economy*, and the second was "Ricardo was Right!" in the *Scandinavian Journal of Economics* in 1989. Both articles are fully fledged mathematical analyses. They bear a formal and methodological character, as a rational reconstruction of a specific, historical situation, wholly described by Ricardo in verbal terms. In both articles, the analysis is carried out in terms of relationships between quantities—like production—and prices, and a quantitative relationship like

A. Heertje (✉)
University of Amsterdam, Amsterdam, The Netherlands
e-mail: joab@heertje.nl

R. A. Cord et al. (eds.), *Paul Samuelson*, Remaking Economics: Eminent Post-War Economists, https://doi.org/10.1057/978-1-137-56812-0_21

the production function. The solution of the formal system of Samuelson's equations allows the conclusion that Ricardo was right with respect to the negative effects of machinery both on demand for labour and on the level of workers' wages.

2 Ricardo

After a chapter (number 30) of only four pages on the influence of demand and supply on prices in the first and second editions of *On the Principles of Political Economy, and Taxation*, David Ricardo in 1821 published the third edition of his classic book with a completely new chapter, number 31, of eleven pages long, "On Machinery". This chapter is a more in-depth treatment of "the influence of machinery on the interests of the different classes of society" (Ricardo 1821: 466). This, Ricardo wrote, was "a subject of great importance, and one which appears never to have been investigated in a manner to lead to any certain satisfactory results" (ibid.). This wording reflects a direct link between technical change, exemplified by machinery as a powerful force on the one hand, and the economic and social roles of landlords, capitalists and labourers in the social process of production and distribution of consumer goods, capital goods and services on the other. Ricardo here clearly appears as a forerunner of Karl Marx. In his consideration of the dynamics of capitalism, Ricardo makes clear that the application of machinery with the effect of saving labour was, in his terms, a "general fund" for landlords; provided they had the same money rents, the latter would benefit from the reduction in prices of commodities that would occur as a consequence of the employment of machinery and on which those rents were spent. The capitalist benefits in the same manner, either as the inventor of a machine or as being the first to apply the invention in practice. This may be seen as an example of Ricardo refining the economic analysis of technical change.

Ricardo argues that workers would benefit as well, because they would be able to buy more commodities with the same money wages. It was Ricardo's view that no reduction in wages would take place, because the capitalist would have the power of demanding and using the same quantity of labour as before. The demand for labour would be as before, but wages would be no lower. The labouring class would be in the same position as the two other classes, the landowners and the capitalists. They all benefit from the lower price of commodities that is a consequence of the greater use of machinery. However, Ricardo was to change his mind on this issue, realizing that he had made a mistake. The error was his assumption (in the first edition of the *Principles*) that a rise in the income of society as a whole, the sum of rent and profit, would accompany a rise in gross income, namely net income plus profits. His revised view (which appeared in the third edition of the *Principles* (1817)) was that the fund from which landlords and capitalists receive their revenue may increase, while the size of the other, the wage fund, may decrease. The same factor that may increase the net revenue of a country may render more of the population redundant and lower the standard of living for labour by reducing demand for it, in turn cutting wages and gross income.

It is time to devote a few words to the economic analysis of technical change in general. There is a lot of confusion around this issue, including with respect to inventions and innovations, technical change as the development of new technology and its application, and the diffusion of new technical insights and of new technical applications. Ricardo was mostly concerned with the price-reducing effect of labour-saving machines, which he found compatible with rising wages, the introduction of machines being the consequence of labour becoming more expensive. The longer the useful life of machines, the lower the prices of consumer goods would drop. It is important to note that Ricardo's view that mechanization would benefit the whole community refers to the accumulation of capital over time, the ratio between fixed capital and circulating capital being determined by the relation between the wage rate and the return on capital. Often, the process of accumulation of capital over the course of time is the stand-in for a pure invention or new application of technology. Ricardo's well-known observation that machinery and labour are in constant competition is a statement about the substitution of capital for labour caused by price changes with a given production function. This observation does not exclude the possibility of a technical change *caused* by wage increases and appearing in the application of inventions embodied in better machines. In this case, it is important to distinguish this type of technical change from the introduction of an improved machine that reduces the prices of consumer goods and makes some of the labour force redundant. On balance, a careful wording of technological problems and related issues is needed.

3 Ricardo's Revised Views

To understand Ricardo correctly, it should be noted that we are not dealing with mechanization at a given state of technology, but with the technical change embodied in new machines. Originally, in his first and second editions, Ricardo's starting point was that, like other social groups, labourers would profit from mechanization because of a fall in the price of goods. However, in the third edition of the *Principles* he comes to the conclusion that the replacement of labour by machines is "often very injurious to the interest of the class of labourers" (Ricardo 1821: 468). Ricardo adds that his previous mistake came from thinking that an increase in total profits would be accompanied by an increase in wages.

Ricardo's argument can best be illustrated by examining the example he himself gives (ibid.: 469): "A capitalist has a capital of £20,000, of which £7,000 is fixed capital (buildings, implements, etc.) and…the remaining is employed as 'circulating capital,' in support of labour". A little later, Ricardo uses the formulation that this circulating capital—an amount of £13,000—represents the food and other necessities that the capitalist possesses, which he sells to his workmen every year as well as paying them the same amount in wages. At the end of each year, the workers deliver to the capitalist £15,000 of food and necessities, £2000 of which the capitalist may spend on himself or in any other way he wishes. The capitalist's annual profit is £2000.

Let us assume that one year he instructs half his labour force to build a machine while the other half carries on producing consumer goods. His wage fund is again £13,000. In this year, his factory produces £7500 worth of consumer goods and a machine also worth £7500. His profit again is £2000. The capitalist now dismisses the workers who built the machine and puts the machine into operation. His wage fund for the next year has dropped from £13,000 to £7500. The machine and the remaining labour force now only need to produce goods worth £7500 to cover wages and profit. This example is illustrated in Fig. 1.

At this point, the following question may arise: what advantage does Ricardo's capitalist derive from making and using a machine, since his profit is still the same, i.e. £2000 per annum, and his total capital is still only £20,000? The answer lies in Ricardo's basic assumption that mechanization lowers the prices of consumer goods. This implies that the useful life of the machine is more than a single year. The increase in total net income also applies to the real income of the capitalist while the drop in the wage fund reflects the dismissal of half his labour force. The purchasing power of the workers who are still employed by him has increased. It appears from this case that Ricardo assumes a constant money wage. If the capitalist halved wages, he could re-employ the other half of

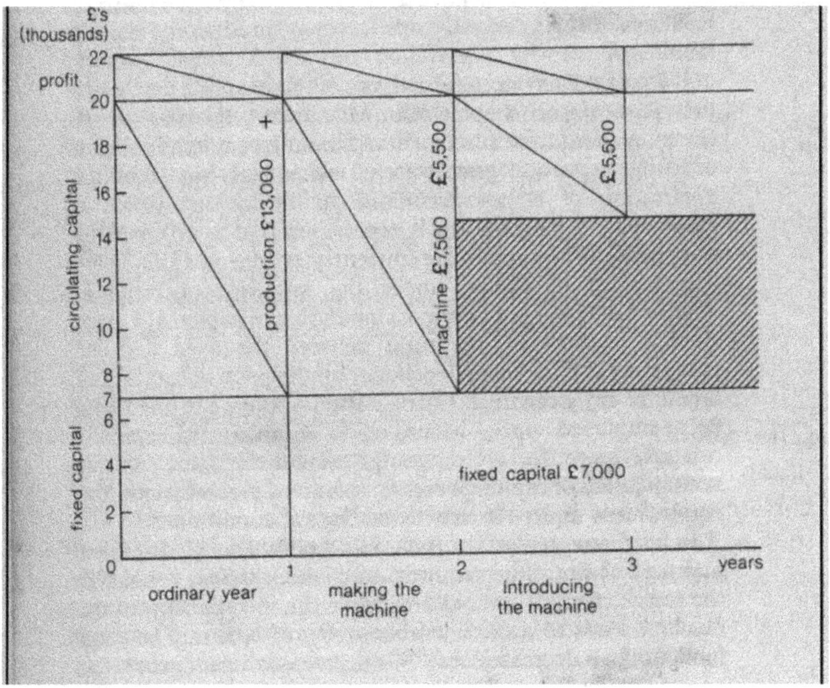

Fig. 1 Ricardo on the long-run influence of changes in technology on the labour market (*Source* Heertje [1977: 15])

his labour force. Finally, an important assumption underlying Ricardo's argument is that the quantity of the original fixed capital remains the same. The extent of the capitalist's premises and buildings remains the same, though the labour force has been halved. The introduction of the new machine seemingly results in a saving in only one factor of production, that is labour.

From a careful analysis of this example, it emerges that, in the first part of his chapter "On Machinery", Ricardo does not think of the replacement of labour by capital as a result of rising wages at a given state of technology, but of the application of a new technology which is embodied in a machine and is expected to lead to a drop in the price of consumer goods. He concentrates here on a shift in the composition of capital under the influence of technical development, and not on the accumulation of capital at a given state of technology, the ratio between the fixed and the circulating capital being dependent on the price of capital and labour at any given time. The dismissed workers can eventually be re-employed, since—according to Ricardo—the capitalist can save more, for his outgoings remain the same. As this accumulation of capital proceeds, more and more workers find employment under the new technological conditions.

Ricardo separates the discussion of the change in the composition of capital from the rest of the "On Machinery" chapter. In the second part, he starts with the following: "Independently of the consideration of the discovery and use of machinery, to which our attention has been just directed, the labouring class has no small interest in the manner in which the income of the country is expended" (Ricardo 1821: 475). This second part also deals with the accumulation of capital in the course of time, with the effect of rising wages on the composition of total capital and with the resulting demand, due to population growth, for more production. This discussion, therefore, does not touch on technical change, a topic that is central to the argument in the first part of the chapter. Since Ricardo places these two parts together in one chapter, it is not surprising that his analyses of them have subsequently been lumped together. Ricardo remarks:

> The statements which I have made will not, I hope, lead to the inference that machinery should not be encouraged. To elucidate the principle, I have been supposing that improved machinery is suddenly discovered, and

> extensively used; but the truth is, that these discoveries are gradual, and rather operate in determining the employment of the capital which is saved and accumulated, than in diverting capital from its actual employment. (ibid.: 478)

This passage shows that Ricardo distinguishes not only between technical change and mechanization, but also between (a) a sudden change in the composition of a given total capital and (b) the distribution of the new capital between fixed and circulating capital. The following quotation shows that no connection should be sought between Ricardo's revised thoughts on mechanization and his famous statement about the constant competition between labour and capital; this statement fits in with his theories of the accumulation of capital, propounded earlier:

> With every increase of capital and population, food will generally rise, on account of its being more difficult to produce. The consequence of a rise of food will be a rise of wages, and every rise of wages will have a tendency to determine the saved capital in a greater proportion than before to the employment of machinery. Machinery and labour are in constant competition, and the former can frequently not be employed until labour rises. (ibid.: 478–479)

Ricardo is thinking here of the substitution of capital for labour under the influence of price changes at a given state of technology—the connection between mechanization and wage increases, which is now known as the "Ricardo effect". What Ricardo says is that the demand for labour increases with increasing capital, but not in proportion with the latter.

Apart from pointing out that improvements in machines are usually a gradual process, Ricardo also maintains that if the government curbed mechanization, then capital would migrate elsewhere and that "this must be a much more serious discouragement to the demand for labour than the most extensive employment of machinery" (ibid.: 481). When part of the capital is invested in "improved machinery there will be a diminution in the progressive demand for labour; by exporting it to another country, the demand will be wholly annihilated" (ibid.). The use of more efficient machines can lower production costs, and the goods produced can be sold abroad at a lower price; conversely, if mechanization is discouraged while it is encouraged in other countries, one is forced to "export your money, in exchange for foreign goods" (ibid.)—with an unfavourable effect on the balance of trade.

The new discussion of mechanization that first appeared in the third edition of the *Principles* cannot be compared with Ricardo's typical approach to theoretical issues as he did not work out the long-term effects of the case that he examined. This then leaves some unanswered questions about the lifespan of new machines and about the hypothesis that the real profit of the capitalist remains unaffected by the introduction of machines. The main point for Ricardo is that when labour-saving machines are installed, workers are withdrawn from consumer goods production, so that the wage fund, i.e. the circulating capital, decreases. With a given total capital, the fixed capital increases, so that the demand for labour, which depends on the amount of the wage fund, is reduced, as wages remain the same.

Ricardo's views on the change in the ratio between fixed and circulating capital appear in a completely different light within the context of the history of economic thought if we replace the words "fixed" and "circulating" with Marx's terms "constant" and "variable". The accumulation of capital consists in converting the surplus value into human labour and inanimate means of production, the value of which Marx calls "value" and "constant capital". Surplus value only comes from constant capital. The instrument of labour, when it takes the form of a machine, immediately becomes a competitor of the workman himself. The self-expansion of capital by means of machinery is henceforth directly proportional to the number of workers whose livelihoods have been destroyed by that machinery. With each improvement in the machinery, fewer people will find employment. The ratio between constant and the variable capital—insofar as it is determined by the technical composition of capital—is called the organic composition of capital. As capital is being accumulated, the variable component decreases, while the constant component increases: "The labouring population therefore produces, along with the accumulation of capital produced by it, the means by which it itself is made relatively superfluous…to an always increasing extent" (ibid.: 582).

These quotes show that Marx's theory about the increasing share of constant capital in the organic composition of capital (and about its effect on the demand for labour) can be regarded as a dynamic and "absolutized" version of Ricardo's treatment of technical change.

4 Say's Law and Technical Change, a Bridge

Both excessively fast and excessively slow technical change will undermine the equality between expenditure and production postulated by Say's law. Mechanization that is too rapid can lead to a supply of consumer goods that demand cannot quickly absorb. This happens when the employees who have become redundant cannot be immediately re-employed, for example because of insufficient complementary capital goods. On the other hand, technical change that is too slow can lead to a situation in which selling in certain sectors becomes sluggish, owing to relatively high prices. Jean-Baptiste Say mentions this possibility in a chapter in volume II of his *Cours Complet d'Economie Politique* (Say 1828) that deals with the "limits of production" (ibid.: 299). Here, he speaks about a stage in production where output ceases to increase and the price of the goods exceeds their utility, partly because production techniques are not sufficiently advanced to permit production at a low cost. Furthermore, this lag in technical development undermines Say's law in the strict sense.

Unemployment resulting from the introduction of machines had already been mentioned by Say in the first edition of his *Traité d'Économie Politique*, where he says that, when workers lose their jobs as machines are installed, their position is "truly deplorable" (Say 1803: 46), unless there are some additional capital goods ensuring their re-employment. The disadvantages are temporary and incidental when the new machines are invented in a society where capital formation is taking place. It is interesting that Say points out that new machines do not only save labour, but also change the nature of goods, i.e. the psychological, subjective character and quality of goods in the eyes of the consumer.

So far, the gist of Say's argument is that if technical change is so fast that capital formation cannot keep pace and because of this cannot generate new jobs for dismissed workers, unemployment may arise. Say's law then ceases to hold, with expenditure lagging behind rising production. To

Say, however, it does not seem likely that this situation in fact will occur, partly because mechanization is usually a relatively slow process and partly because the higher the degree of mechanization, the more difficult it is to invent new machines. If unemployment still occurs, forces re-establish the original situation. This is described in the second edition of the *Traité*: "Mechanization in a certain sector creates such a large supply of goods that prices fall; this brings the goods within reach of more people, and this increased demand creates new jobs" (Say 1814: 54). It can thus be seen that Say recognizes compensating factors both on the demand and on the supply side so that, while technical change that is too slow or too fast disturbs the equilibrium and jeopardizes the validity of his law, such a disequilibrium is not very likely to come about in practice. If it does, the compensating factors that provide work for the displaced labour come into operation, and expenditure can again keep up with rising production.

A further question is how far technological unemployment can be reconciled with Say's law. Ricardo assumes that (a) a new machine is made by workers who have been taken out of the production of consumer goods, and (b) it brings about a considerable saving of labour. This change on the supply side does not invalidate Say's law, according to which expenditure is always equal to the value of production. In Ricardo's view, both the wage fund and the level of production contract—profits remaining the same—so that the reduced expenditure is equal to the reduced value of production.

Malthus maintained that mechanization invalidated Say's law if it adds so much to the gross produce of a country that the commodities produced cannot be consumed. In contrast, Ricardo contended that the introduction of new machines diminishes the quantity of gross produce, and although the propensity to consume is unlimited, demand will decrease, due to a lack of purchasing power.

5 Paul Samuelson and David Ricardo on Technical Change

The analytical question is whether Ricardo was right in his view that viable inventions can reduce the total of real output after competitive prices adjust to clear all markets. In other words, that the invention of a viable machine may reduce the short- and long-run demand for labour, reduce wages and reduce net national income, the latter defined as rent plus profit plus wages. For that matter, and as Samuelson points out, the three effects can all result from a mere accumulation of capital.

In order to better understand what, from the point of view of economics, lies behind the formal structure of the set of equations and the numerical solution of the system set up by Samuelson, I would like to make the following observations. In both articles, Samuelson uses the word "invention" for machinery, sometimes combined with the word "viable". In view of the literature on technical change, this may be a source of confusion. "Invention" is normally used to describe either a new technical possibility for which, in most cases, new knowledge is needed or, in the case of a new product, a new method of production.

When it comes to applications of new technical insights, it is common practice to use the term "innovation". Samuelson causes confusion by not adhering to the well-known custom of distinguishing between "invention" and "innovation". My concern here is part of the general question of the role of technical change in Samuelson's two articles, as well as that of the character of technical change that we are envisaging, i.e. either embodied in capital goods or not, either endogenous or not, either capital-saving or not. This brings me to my second observation. The main question in the 1989 article is: "Is Ricardo right that viable invention can reduce the total of real output after all competitive prices adjust to clear all markets?" (Samuelson 1989: 48). How are we going to interpret the numerical answers to this question if we have no clear picture of "technical change" in general and of a "viable invention" in particular? The answer to this question is relevant because, as Samuelson points out, "The invention need not necessarily involve 'machinery'" (ibid.: 47). If that were so, what else can we think of? The question is striking as Samuelson observes that "three effects can all result from *mere* capital accumulation" (ibid.; italics added). We can have "*mere* capital accumulation", however, without any change in the technology of production.

In Samuelson's (1989) article, the mathematical appendix starts with a production function dependent on a technological improvement parameter α. The appendix presents a thorough discussion of several numerical relations and inequalities, but nothing at all with respect to the possible economic assumptions regarding the character of technical change. There is, indeed, a discussion of marginal-product distributive shares and of real factor prices—along the lines of traditional economics. On the other hand, Samuelson followed Ricardo's analysis, but added a number of quantitative relationships without looking for the content of the technical change involved.

We are confronted, on the one hand, with Samuelson's mathematical description of Ricardo's chapter on machinery in the third edition of his *Principles* and on the other with the overwhelming presence of technology in our modern world, i.e. a blackboard full of equations and, on the other hand, to give but one example, the reality of medical technology used by mankind. The field of technology has its own laws, its own development and is full of miracles. Part of the behind-the-scenes knowledge belongs to the economic analysis of technical change. It is here that Samuelson and technology come to face to face: formalism versus the empirical world of the economics of technical change.

Concepts like capital-saving and endogenous technical change are necessary to describe the technical character of a market economy and its impact on the allocation of scarce resources. Today, capital-saving as a feature of technology is arguably far more important in the world economy than labour-saving was in the day of, say, Karl Marx. Investment in research and development as a vehicle for endogenous technical change is a powerful force for new technology, innovations and possible solutions to the problem of climate change.

6 By Way of Conclusion

The essential hypothesis is that technical change in production has a purely labour-saving character on all labour markets of the economy. It is the main building block for Ricardo's opinion that

> the discovery and use of machinery may be attended with a diminution of gross produce; and whenever that is the case, it will be injurious for the labouring class as some of their number will be thrown out of employment, and population will be redundant compared with the funds which are to employ it. (Ricardo 1821: 472)

Ricardo's view is consistent and sensitive to the assumption of the labour-saving aspect of machinery. Without labour-saving being connected to changes in technology, the capitalists do no harm to labourers. It may be that a substantial reduction in gross product will cause a lack of financing for the employment of labourers, but that is a less compelling factor than a change in technology. Under normal conditions of the relevant factors, Ricardo is right. If capital-saving enters the scene, the fate of labourers is less injurious.

Let us now assume that we live in a world with a different technological background. New machinery is not labour-saving, but capital-saving, with far-reaching consequences for the position of labour and of capital in society. With endogenous technical change, new capital is the fruit of investment in research and not only the outcome of the savings behaviour of capitalists. Even if there is a certain amount of labour-saving, the technological dynamics of the formation of capital play a highly positive role on the labour market. This is why I pointed out that whether Samuelson was right about Ricardo depends on technical change being only labour-saving, in which case Samuelson is right about Ricardo, or is only capital-saving, with a substantial positive effect on the demand for labour, the wage rate and total real output, in which case Samuelson is not right about Ricardo.

Samuelson neglected an important feature of modern technology. Capitalism is no longer the natural enemy of labourers, but their friend, in getting decent jobs and wages. Another aspect of this is the relationship with government, as the private sector is often better equipped when it comes to carrying out public works. If companies like Google, Facebook, Apple, Amazon and Microsoft continue to grow, a handful of huge firms are going to run the world, based on the increasing advancement of non-labour-saving technology. These firms are the nodes of a worldwide data-processing system that justifies the leadership and moral authority of Big Data and algorithms of all sizes and complexities that operate as the cornerstone of permanent new technical developments, based on the interaction of endless flows of data, information and knowledge.

Acknowledgements The author is grateful to Professor Donald Walker for encouraging him to write this chapter and for his comments on earlier versions of the text.

References

Heertje, A. (1977) *Economics and Technical Change*. New York, Wiley.

Ricardo, D. (1817) *On the Principles of Political Economy, and Taxation*. First edition. London, John Murray.

Ricardo, D. (1821) *On the Principles of Political Economy, and Taxation*. Third edition. London, John Murray.

Samuelson, P.A. (1988) "Mathematical Vindication of Ricardo on Machinery," *Journal Political Economy*, 96: 274–282.

Samuelson, P.A. (1989) "Ricardo was Right!" *Scandinavian Journal of Economics*, 91: 47–62.

Say, J.-B. (1803) *Traité d'Économie Politique*. First edition. Paris, Crapelet.

Say, J.-B. (1814) *Traité d'Économie Politique*. Second edition. Paris, Antoine-Augustin Renouard.

Say, J.-B. (1828) *Cours Complet d'Économie Politique Pratique, Volume II*. Paris, Chez Rapilly.

22

Divergence and Convergence: Paul Samuelson on Economic Development

Mauro Boianovsky

1 Two Worlds?

Paul A. Samuelson (1986: 62) was proud of his position as the "last generalist" in economics. "My finger has been in every pie," he claimed, with a very broad range encompassing significant contributions to virtually every field in economics—"in talking about modern economics I am talking about me." William Baumol (2007) called him the "Generalists' Generalisimo" and suggested that his hugely successful textbook *Economics: An Introductory Analysis*—published for the first time in 1948 and regularly revised until 1980, with new editions with co-author William Nordhaus from 1985 to 2010—was a "revolutionary" work that only a "very capable generalist" could have carried out alone. However, development economics was an exception to Samuelson's claim. He acknowledged its relevance in the face of the problem of underdeveloped economies, "one of the most challenging problems of the next quarter century" (Samuelson 1961: 775),

M. Boianovsky (✉)
University of Brasília, Brasília, Brazil
e-mail: boianovs@unb.br

R. A. Cord et al. (eds.), *Paul Samuelson*, Remaking Economics: Eminent Post-War Economists, https://doi.org/10.1057/978-1-137-56812-0_22

but would regret that "precisely because the theory of economic development has been so hard to perfect, this is a field that will appeal to the venturesome" (Samuelson 1978: 8). It was the inherent complexity of the phenomena that lay behind economic development that rendered them not "tractable" (ibid.) and beyond the limits of economic science as a modeling endeavor (see also Boianovsky 2019a).

Nevertheless, that did not prevent Samuelson from paying close attention to the economic features of underdeveloped economies and to debates about development theory and policy, especially throughout the several editions of his *Economics*. In the third edition, Samuelson (1955) introduced a new Chapter 36 on "Problems of Economic Growth and Development," as part of the new part 6 on "Current Economic Problems." As he put it in the Introduction, "the new chapter on underdeveloped countries...provides important applications of economic tools (preliminary experience suggests that students will find it among the most interesting of all chapters)" (ibid.: vi). On the same page, Samuelson famously announced his new concept of the "neoclassical synthesis," which argued that the "classical" theory of the efficient allocation of resources would come into its own once modern (mostly Keynesian) aggregate demand management eliminated involuntary unemployment and inflation. The neoclassical synthesis was relevant for industrialized developed economies like the United States, but not for underdeveloped countries, with their own problems of poverty and "disguised" unemployment which could not be alleviated by macroeconomic stabilization policies. The "paradox of thrift," for instance, a main feature of *Economics* since its first edition, did not apply to underdeveloped economies:

> Until we learned how to prevent mass unemployment, many economists worried about *oversaving* in *advanced* countries. But for *underdeveloped* countries the problem is often the classical one of *undersaving*: more precisely, the problem is underinvestment in productive instruments capable of increasing the nation's rate of economic progress ... The Prime Minister [of an underdeveloped country] sometimes gets a little impatient with students who have studied depression economics abroad and do not seem alert to the different set of realities at home – in particular to the crucial need for *more* personal saving. (Samuelson 1961: 785, 794; italics in original)

The relevance of the neoclassical synthesis for underdeveloped countries came from the notion that the ability to control domestic purchasing power had made obsolete the neo-Marxian view, that full employment and growth in industrialized countries is impossible without imperialist exploitation of colonial nations through international trade (ibid.: 781; 1971 [1972]: 706).

Samuelson's remarks about the limits of Keynesian economics in dealing with economic development echoed similar claims by prominent development economists such as Arthur Lewis (1954). The 1955 new chapter in *Economics* appeared when the economic development of less-developed countries was turning into a major focus of economic policy and theory, partly because of the political backdrop of the Cold War. The 1950s was the time when a set of ideas put forward by a relatively small group of economists—including Lewis, Rosenstein-Rodan, Myrdal, Prebisch, Rostow, Gerschenkron, Nurkse, Balogh, Schultz, Hirschman, Singer, Bauer, Furtado, among others—established development economics as a new field (see Alacevich and Boianovsky 2018). Those were the years of "high development theory," as put by Krugman (1993). In his 1949 Inaugural Address, President Truman announced his "Point Four," a turning point in international economic development policy, hailed by Samuelson (1951: 689–690) as a "bold new program" for making the benefits of American "scientific advances and industrial progress" available to underdeveloped areas. As Samuelson (1961: 775) argued, "for conscience's sake, we are impelled to help," not just through foreign aid but also by applying the tools of economic theory to the study of the determinants of and obstacles to economic development. Moreover, "history teaches that men do not always starve quietly" (ibid.).

The postwar period was also the time when growth economics—in the sense of the investigation of the formal properties of dynamic steady states and the long-term performance of industrialized economies—attracted significant attention from model builders (including Harrod, Domar, von Neumann (originally from 1937), Solow, Swan, Robinson, Kaldor, and many others). Samuelson, sometimes in collaborative work with Robert Solow, further elaborated von Neumann's (1937 [1945–1946]) model in order to examine balanced growth paths and derive the well-known turnpike theorems about optimal growth trajectories (Samuelson and Solow

1953; see also Chapter 12 of Dorfman et al. 1958; Samuelson 1965 and Niehans 1990: 438–439 and the references cited therein). This became influential in the application of optimal control theory to development planning (see, for example, Chakravarty 1969). Even if somewhat indirectly and unexpectedly, the turnpike theorems (discussed further below) represented a significant contribution to a particular branch of development economics—this being to Samuelson's (1969a) satisfaction. Clearly, they were the work of a growth theorist, not a development economist.

It was only in the sixth edition of *Economics* that Samuelson (1964: Chapter 35) introduced a chapter on the "Theory of Growth." By then, Solow and Samuelson had turned the Department of Economics at the Massachusetts Institute of Technology (MIT) into the foremost center of research on economic growth. Moreover, since 1951, MIT had been home to the Center for International Studies (CENIS), which gathered together influential development economists such as Rostow, Rosenstein-Rodan, and Eckaus. Methodological differences between growth and development economists at MIT and elsewhere made co-existence sometimes problematic (see Boianovsky and Hoover 2014). Samuelson (1964: vi; italics in original) announced the "new chapter on the *theory* of growth." While acknowledging that "development problems are all the rage these days among economists," he stressed the need to "bring economic analysis to bear" instead of boring students with "dated anecdotes and statistics" about different countries.

Samuelson's (1964) new Chapter 35 provided one of the first textbook discussions ever of growth theory, covering the classical "magnificent dynamics" of Malthus and Ricardo, Solow's neoclassical model (the focus of the chapter), and, in an appendix, topics such as Schumpeterian innovation, the Harrod–Domar Keynesian growth model, the von Neumann general equilibrium growth model, and the Cambridge approach of Kaldor and Robinson. Sometimes he used the words "growth" and "development" interchangeably, but the context made the meaning clear. Chapter 35 provided the "*principles* of economic theory to the process of growth and development," in preparation for the next chapter's "application" of those ideas to underdeveloped economies (ibid.: 721). Development economics was perceived as essentially an applied field, not a distinct part of economic theory, despite efforts by development economists to give it a proper identity. While development economists "have developed no unified theory that differs from the basic growth model introduced in the last chapter, they have added to that some special features" (ibid.: 760).

The distinctive elements of development economics, as compared to neoclassical growth theory, were Rosenstein-Rodan's (1943, 1961) emphasis on external economies and increasing returns and Lewis's (1954) concept of perfectly elastic labor supply and its associated notion of disguised unemployment in economies with a surplus of labor. From Samuelson's neoclassical perspective, these were the features that could bring some analytical distinctiveness to development economics (see Arrow 1988 for a similar take on the theory of economic development). However, whether the assumption of labor surplus (under the double influence of von Neumann and Lewis) would be formally incorporated into growth and development planning models, as attempted at MIT in the 1960s (see, for example, Chakravarty 1969), increasing returns proved to be more difficult to tackle. It was only in the late 1980s and early 1990s, with the development of endogenous models of technical progress in New Growth Theory by Paul Romer and others, that increasing returns became integrated into growth and development modeling (see Samuelson 2001; Krugman 1993).

Samuelson did not go as far as John Hicks (1965: 3), who claimed that there was no real connection between growth theory and the economics of underdevelopment. But he came close. Hicks regarded development economics as a "vastly important subject," but denied that it was a "formal or theoretical subject." According to Hicks (ibid.), it was a "practical subject which must expect to call upon any branch of theory...which has any relevance to it. If there is any branch of economic theory which is especially relevant to it, it is the Theory of International Trade." Samuelson, the generalist, liked trade theory better than any other topic in economics: "Our subject puts its best foot forward when it speaks out on international trade" (Samuelson 1969b: 9). His main contribution to trade theory—the seminal factor price equalization (FPE) theorem—had vast implications for the study of economic divergence and convergence in the international economy (see Samuelson 1948a, 1949). That formal proposition (further discussed below) appeared around the same time as the first edition of *Economics* and the emergence of development economics as a new field.

It was no coincidence, argued Albert Hirschman (1977 [1981]: 60), that development economics emerged in the same period as Samuelson's pivotal articles on the pure theory of international trade. According to Hirschman, Samuelson's FPE theorem was constructed just as awareness of the persistent and increasing international income divergence was becoming sharp in the postwar period. From that perspective, maintained Hirschman (ibid.), the contrast between observed facts and Samuelson's (1948a, 1949) theoretical findings "acted as a devastating boomerang for the traditional theory and its claim in explaining the problems of the real world." Hirschman ascribed the relative success of Prebisch and Singer (and other development economists who focused on trade issues) to the fact that they took international inequality seriously and "because of the self-inflicted wound" from which neoclassical trade theory was then enduring due to the FPE theorem.

Nevertheless, as discussed further below, Samuelson did acknowledge the evidence about international divergence, which raised issues concerning the proper interpretation of his theorem. In a section entitled "Two Worlds?"—added to the 1958 edition of *Economics* and kept ever since—Samuelson (1961: 116–118) contrasted the economic growth of the United States and other industrialized countries since the end of the nineteenth century on one side and the prevailing poverty in most of Asia and Africa on the other. The goal of that section was to indicate how "fortunate" Americans were. As one might expect, an American perspective on economic matters pervaded Samuelson's textbook, especially in its first few editions. In the Preface to the first edition, Samuelson (1948b: v) announced that the book aimed at an understanding of the "economic institutions and problems of American civilization in the middle of the twentieth century." He removed that passage from the third edition, when the new chapter on development was introduced.

The international success of *Economics*, including massive sales in India, Latin America, the Middle East and other underdeveloped areas, signaled to Samuelson that its economic principles applied beyond the American economy. In the Preface to the fourth edition, Samuelson (1958: vi) celebrated the book's wide use abroad and its translation into many foreign languages as a "reflection of the fact that there do exist certain objective principles of economics which are relevant to societies of quite different institutional development." Some development economists disagreed, however. Dudley Seers (1963: 88–89) contended that Samuelson's "brilliant" textbook illustrated the dominant approach of most American and European economists of focusing on the economics of rich industrialized countries as if it was the rule, when it was really the economics of the "special case." Developed industrial economies were not typical, but rare cases, historically and geographically. Development economics was deemed more general, with its study of economies with a diverse range of structures. Seers (ibid.) referred in passing to Samuelson's chapter on development, but, apart from appearing only in the final part of the book, the chapter was criticized for lacking a discussion of the growth patterns revealed by contemporary research. Seers, however, did not engage with the actual arguments contained in the chapter.

Although Samuelson never explicitly contributed to the theory of economic development—which he found wanting—he remained an acute observer of the economic performance and policies of developing countries from the mid-twentieth century to early twenty-first century. He was particularly impressed by the economic transformations undergone by Japan, a country he would visit a couple of times: "The most remarkable phenomenon of economic development in this last century and in this last decade has undoubtedly been the Japanese" (Samuelson 1964: 759). In that same sixth edition, Samuelson added a front-leaf chart displaying the evolution of income per capita in the United States, Great Britain, the Soviet Union and Japan since 1870 and in India (since the mid-1950s), kept and updated until the eleventh (1980) edition with the inclusion of West Germany. It showed the prominence that growth and development topics gradually acquired in the book. Data confirmed the convergence of incomes for the set of industrialized countries, including the Soviet Union, whereas poorer countries, represented by India, lagged behind. Samuelson's (1964: 806–808) forecast that, in some scenarios, the Soviet economy would eventually overtake the US economy proved to be more controversial (see Skousen 1997: 148).

In the 1980s, Samuelson became attracted to the case of Argentina, a potentially rich country beset by poor economic performance since the 1950s. Referring to his Harvard Professor Joseph Schumpeter (1942),

Samuelson ascribed Argentina's problems to political factors that undermined the working of capitalism in general and feared that a similar process could take place in the United States. The economic development of the so-called Asian Tigers and China was another major event that caught Samuelson's attention in several editions of *Economics* after 1985 and in a 2004 article in the *Journal of Economic Perspectives*, which vindicated his FPE theorem in the context of international technology transfer à la Gerschenkron.

By the last (posthumous) edition of *Economics*, Samuelson and Nordhaus (2010: Chapter 26), in contrast with the first editions, referred to "decades of experience" and "learning" by development economists in the field, leading to a summary view of economic development policy largely based on market forces with an outward orientation instead of the import-substitution industrialization strategy that prevailed in the 1950s and 1960s. The "practical" or "applied" dimension of the subject, present from its inception, became even more prominent, although Samuelson and Nordhaus (ibid.: 531) warned against development policies based on "simple, holistic explanations" and "oversimplified approaches to a complex process." By the early twenty-first century, Samuelson was less pessimistic about the status of development economics, but only slightly so.

2 Widening Differentials

Samuelson's (1947) *Foundations of Economic Analysis*—which launched the idea that mathematical modeling was essential to the formulation of operational theorems in economics—was based on his Harvard Ph.D. thesis written mostly in the late 1930s. Apart from a passing remark on Gustav Cassel's concept (advanced around 1918) of uniform growth and a discussion of Malthusian and optimum population theories (Samuelson 1947: 312, fn. 6 and 296–298), there is close to nothing about economic growth and development in that book, despite a whole Chapter 11 on "Some Fundamentals of Dynamic Theory." In the last paragraph of *Foundations*, Samuelson (ibid.: 355) hoped for further progress in economic theory along the lines of comparative dynamics, especially in tackling the "majestic problems of economic development." Samuelson (1948c) was his first foray into growth economics, with special attention to the Harrod–Domar model put forward in articles and books by Roy Harrod and Evsey Domar between 1939 and 1948. Development planners often adapted the so-called Harrod–Domar formula, interpreted as the proposition that the rate of economic growth is determined by the quotient of the savings rate and the capital-output ratio. It was regarded as the theoretical cornerstone of the so-called capital fundamentalism, that is, the notion that physical capital accumulation is the primary determinant of growth and development (see Boianovsky 2018). However, as Samuelson (1964: 743–746) explained, the relation between the natural, warranted and actual rates of growth in Harrod's model is complex, with cyclical oscillations of and around the warranted rate. In particular, an increase in the savings rate may, under certain conditions, bring about a reduction in the actual growth rate.

Harrod (1948) denied that his model should be applied to problems of economic development. Whereas he assumed away in his dynamic economics the classical law of diminishing returns from land and Malthus's population doctrine, he also suggested that the "old classical analysis" applied better to vast "poverty-stricken areas of the world today," where population is "pressuring upon the means of subsistence" (ibid.: 19, 114). Samuelson largely shared Harrod's neo-Malthusian perspective on development. From the first edition of *Economics*, demography was regarded as one of the foundations of the study of any economic system. Malthusian population theory was deemed relevant for understanding the economic underdevelopment of India, China, and other areas where the balance between the size of the population and the food supply was a vital factor (see Samuelson 1948b: 25–26). In fact, it was a lecture on Malthus that got Samuelson started as a student of economics back in 1932 (see Barnett 2004: 528) and ignited his long-term interest in demography.

Samuelson (1964: 724–730) discussed classical "magnificent dynamics" (a term coined by Baumol) at the outset of his growth chapter. As a result of technological innovation and a reduction in fertility rates, developed economies had surpassed Thomas Carlyle's description of economics as a "dismal science." But Carlyle's term still applied to poor underdeveloped countries. Samuelson's (1973: figure 38-2, p. 769) diagram of the divergence between advanced and less-developed countries in the period 1960–1972 indicated that the rate of growth of total output was on average higher for less-developed countries. However, such growth was "frittered away in burgeoning population growth," resulting in "widening differentials" between the two groups of countries, as illustrated by a Lorenz curve showing unequal world income distribution—the poorest half of nations received 8% of total world income (ibid.: 768). This was one of the first applications of the Lorenz curve for that purpose. While visiting Japan in 1971, Samuelson, as part of a paper on "Economic Growth," observed that, "When science introduces medical improvements that increase life expectancies in the developing nations, birth rates drop only after a lag, with the result that rapidly growing population again brings into play the classical law of diminishing returns. Among the developing nations economics remains what Carlyle called 'the dismal science'" (Samuelson 1971 [1972]: 708).

The notion of the demographic transition—of the kind experienced by developed countries in the nineteenth and twentieth centuries—as a "precondition" for economic development (Samuelson 1964: 761, 765) became especially prominent after the 1985 edition co-authored with Nordhaus. The chapter on development opened with a section on "Population Growth and Development," including subsections on "Malthus and the Dismal Science" and "Neo-Malthusianism," followed by a discussion of the "Population Explosion: The Legacy of Malthus" (see Samuelson and Nordhaus 2010: Chapter 26). Some developing countries (e.g., Mexico, South Korea, and Taiwan) had gone through demographic transitions, but not Sub-Saharan Africa and other parts of the world, such as India (ibid.: 526).

Like the Harrod–Domar model, Solow's (1956) neoclassical growth model assumed away classical diminishing returns to land and Malthusian population dynamics (although it did feature a poverty trap caused by multiple equilibria when the rate of population growth depends on per capita income; see Boianovsky and Hoover 2014: 204). As Samuelson asserted (1964: Chapter 35), the neoclassical growth model explained well the basic observed trends ("stylized facts") of economic growth in developed countries (as did Harrod–Domar). However, those models could not easily account for the divergence between developed and underdeveloped economies. Growth models applied to both groups of nations, but, as Samuelson (ibid.) pointed out at the end of Chapter 35, "for the poor countries in particular, there must be added the important additional concepts of 'external economies', 'social overhead capital or infrastructure', and 'increasing returns' – as is done in the next chapter" (ibid.: 752).

Increasing returns were not a feature of growth models at the time; it would take a couple of decades for that to happen. Development economists of the postwar period, however, made extensive, if informal, use of the concept, especially Rosenstein-Rodan, Samuelson's colleague at MIT and author of an article often regarded as a founding work in the field of development economics (see Rosenstein-Rodan 1943). Rostow (1960) was another MIT economist who used increasing returns as part of his broad and influential concept of economic "take-off" (see Samuelson 1964: 761). Market failures associated with external economies and increasing returns were supposed to bring about a low-level inertial equilibrium trap in poor countries.

External economies played an important role in Samuelson's (1954) path-breaking theory of public goods as joint consumption. He referred to Rosenstein-Rodan for the first time in the fourth edition of *Economics* (Samuelson 1958: 769)—when he ascribed to Rosenstein-Rodan the concept of "social overhead capital," in the sense of indivisible public utilities—shortly after the release of Rosenstein-Rodan's 1957 MIT working paper on the "Big Push," eventually published in 1961. Whereas Samuelson's (1964) growth chapter assumed a neoclassical production function according to the "conventional principle of diminishing returns" and constant returns to scale, "in dynamic economic development, the phenomenon of 'increasing returns' is to be expected" (ibid.: 761). This assumption had been understood since Adam Smith's study of the advantages of large-scale division of labor in the *Wealth of Nations*, Samuelson observed.

The phenomenon of increasing returns "can make it possible for dramatic spurts and accelerations to occur in economic development" (ibid.: 762), which went a long way in explaining income divergences between countries (assuming they had undergone their "demographic transitions" already). External economies did not necessarily involve increasing returns (and vice versa); the same applied to social overhead capital. Nevertheless, the close connection between these three concepts warranted lumping them together, Samuelson claimed. From that perspective, economic underdevelopment resulted from a "vicious circle" or trap: "poverty creates want, want destroys thrift, absence of capital formation prevents improvement, limitation of mass production makes poverty – and so the vicious circle goes" (Samuelson 1955: 722). Productivity affected output, but the size of output also affected productivity—as also pointed out by Myrdal, Kaldor, and others in connection with the principle of "cumulative causation" and the so-called Verdoorn's law of economic growth.

The very interconnectedness of different sectors and firms provided a way out, since, once the economy makes a breakthrough on any front, there tend to be "favorable repercussions throughout the length and breadth of the economy. These 'external economies'…can break the vicious circle and lead to accelerating spirals of development" (ibid.). This was close to Hirschman's (1958) later notion of unbalanced growth through the promotion of certain sectors of the economy with strong linkage effects. Indeed, Samuelson (1964: 762–763) criticized Rosenstein-Rodan's (1943) "fascination" with "balanced growth," for both theoretical and historical reasons that some sectors develop before others, especially in open economies: "The phenomena of increasing returns, externalities, and social overhead capital provide some substance to notions of take-offs, spurts and big pushes. They suggest a scope for supplementation of competitive market forces. But they do not lead unequivocally to any simple concept of 'balanced growth'" (Samuelson 1964: 773).

Samuelson (1948b: 49) had put forward a preliminary version of the "vicious circle of poverty" while contrasting the high capital-intensity and productivity of the American economy and the "plight of those backward nations that cannot get their heads above water because their production is so low that they can spare nothing for capital formation by which their standard of living could be raised." Samuelson's remark raised criticism from Peter Bauer (1958a, b), presented at the ninth meeting of the Mont Pelerin Society held in Princeton in September 1958. Bauer regarded Samuelson's 1948 passage as a "typical formulation" of the vicious circle notion that dominated what he called the "new orthodoxy of economic development." The "orthodox" view, from which Bauer dissented, ascribed the stagnation of underdeveloped countries to "the failure of the traditional forces of economic progress, such as development of production for the market ... This vicious circle can only be broken by drastic national and international action" (Bauer 1958b: 2; see also Plehwe 2009 and Bauer 1971: Chapter 9). Bauer—like Jacob Viner and Gottfried Haberler—rejected the then emergent mainstream view of development economics and argued instead for the role of market incentives in the development process, as elaborated in his joint 1957 textbook with Basil Yamey (see Tribe 2018).

Bauer's early criticism would be repeated and expanded in Jane Shaw's (1999) overview of how Samuelson addressed economic development issues through a sample of editions of *Economics* from 1951 to 1995. According to Shaw (ibid.: 135), Samuelson "merely reported" what the emerging dominant view was saying, instead of challenging the conventional wisdom based on "Keynesian growth theories." In particular, she charged Samuelson with disregarding problems associated with government intervention in the economies of poor countries (e.g., corruption and other cases of "government failure") and the role of institutions in shaping the development process. Samuelson (1964: 759) did mention corruption and institutions, but those factors would only come to the fore with the development of Neo-Institutional economics by Douglass North and others in the 1980s and 1990s, when Samuelson increased his awareness of institutional elements (see, for example, Samuelson and Nordhaus 2010: 529–530). Samuelson (1995) criticized the Coase Theorem proposition that market economic agents are able to cope with market failures (see also Skousen 1997: 145). He doubted the issue of allocation of property rights addressed by the Theorem could be understood mainly in terms of "transaction costs."

Bauer was correct in putting Samuelson's *Economics* together with works by Rosenstein-Rodan, Nurkse, Myrdal, Lewis, Prebisch, Hirschman, and other 1950s development economists who stressed market failures and supported development planning. Samuelson (1958: 761, fn. 1) noted Bauer's argument that no matter how poor some groups are, they do save, especially immigrants, but held to his original view and removed that note after the 1964 edition. By the eleventh edition, Samuelson (1980: 717, fn. 2) acknowledged

Bauer and Yamey's (1957) "reasoned defense of the market as the main instrument for economic development." Yet, he remained unconvinced. As fashions changed and the neoclassical liberal counterrevolution took hold of significant parts of development economics (see Toye 2018), Samuelson and Nordhaus paid increasing attention, through several editions of *Economics*, to the so-called East Asian miracle, but pointed out that "the secret to success was not a doctrinaire laissez-faire policy," as East Asian governments had in fact practiced selective planning and intervention. Rather, the openness and outward orientation "allowed the countries to reap economies of scale and the benefits of international specialization" (Samuelson and Nordhaus 2010: 532–533).

In fact, instead of smothering the traditional "vicious circle of poverty" idea, Samuelson and Nordhaus (2010: 530–531), along the lines of new approaches to economic development modeling built on ideas originally advanced in the 1950s (see Ray 2008), reinterpreted it as a poverty trap caused by multiple equilibria, which could be avoided by a "big push" of coordinated investments helped by lower population growth. The new development models of the 1980s and 1990s were able to tackle analytical problems, notably increasing returns and external economies, that had remained unsolved in the 1950s and 1960s. These issues, and his inability to solve them, had bothered Samuelson since the 1940s, as showed by the following revealing recollection:

> Constant returns to scale, sans chance, change, externalities, and information uncertainties, is pretty much a finished book in economic theory … Lively scholars…periodically stress deviations from this chaste model. In particular, increasing returns to scale received notice from Smith's division of labor…in connection with international trade by Bertil Ohlin…in vague connection with developmental growth in Allyn Young … Always a bridesmaid but never a bride, so to speak. The trouble with increasing returns to scale is that after you have said the first things about it, it is deucedly hard to find second and third themes to develop … My conscience was long bothered by our guild's neglect of a subject on the ground that it is so hard to tackle. (Samuelson 2001: 498–499)

Regardless of the solution to the analytical issues involved, the view that poverty and underdevelopment are closely related to market failures—a perspective that can also be found, in another guise, in Samuelson's approach to Keynesian economics in his *Economics* and elsewhere (see Skousen 1997; Backhouse 2015)—is conspicuous in his discussions of those topics. This is well illustrated by Samuelson's (1979 [1983]) positive reaction to the World Bank's *World Development Report 1978* (the first of a series of annual reports), with a Foreword by Robert McNamara, Bank president from 1968 to 1981. Samuelson had welcomed McNamara's strategy of "War on Poverty" carried out since the early 1970s (see Samuelson 1973: 710). In his *Newsweek* column, Samuelson (1979 [1983]: 71) supported McNamara's recognition of "poverty as the enemy to be fought." The Bank, under McNamara and his predecessors, had successfully promoted economic development in poor nations, "encouraging the use of market incentives and profitability tests to do so." More than that, as put by Samuelson (ibid.), "I take off my hat to Robert McNamara for what has been his unique vision – his recognition that successful market forces alone can't be relied on to mitigate flagrant inequality and abject poverty."

One of the main elements of postwar development economics was the emphasis on underemployment—often called "disguised unemployment"—as an essential feature of underdevelopment. Disguised unemployment was generally associated with near zero-marginal productivity of labor caused by low capital accumulation in economies with excess supply of labor. It was not the same as Keynesian unemployment caused by insufficient effective demand. Joan Robinson (1937) had introduced the notion of disguised unemployment in another context, but it gained prominence after Lewis (1954, 1955) turned it into a main ingredient of his model of development in dual economies (see Boianovsky 2019b). Samuelson's new chapter on development included a paragraph about "disguised unemployment." In "poor countries, particularly rural ones," asserted Samuelson,

> there often exists a large part of the manpower pool that does almost nothing because there is nothing for it to do ... When a boom or a development plan comes along sweeping them into productive city jobs, there is almost no reduction in the product back in the farm. (Samuelson 1961: 783)

That was very close to Lewis's (1954, 1955) framework. The theoretical concept and the empirical relevance of disguised unemployment were contentious issues in the 1950s, drawing criticism from Viner, Haberler, and Schultz. Samuelson (1961: 783, fn. 1) acknowledged Haberler's and Schultz's misgivings, but removed that note after the 1964 edition.

A similar phenomenon could be found in developed countries, both in the subsistence farms regions and in the city streets, "where men eke out a bare existence doing door to door selling whenever productive jobs are unavailable" (Samuelson 1961: 783), as Robinson (1937) had pointed out. Indeed, in a joint paper with R.A. Nixon (his former Harvard colleague), Samuelson discussed in some detail the complications introduced by Robinson's disguised unemployment in the measurement of unemployment and the connections between cyclical changes in output and employment in the American economy (see Nixon and Samuelson 1940). Moreover, while discussing "poverty in agriculture" in the United States, Samuelson (1961: 490) noticed that most family farms do not share in the "nation's economic progress" and that a "hidden surplus of population exists in the form of low-productivity marginal farms residents," just as in underdeveloped economies à la Lewis. Again, in his new Chapter 39 on the economics of racial and sexual discrimination, Samuelson (1973: 783) claimed that the tools of development economics should be applied to foster understanding of the problems of American ghettos, which he regarded as underdeveloped areas contiguous with and in competition with the most developed economy in the world. Samuelson's interest in economic divergence and underdevelopment at the international level reflected, to some extent, his original concern with income distribution, inequality, and poverty in the American economy and society—a distinguishing feature of early editions and drafts of his *Economics* as compared with previous textbooks, kept and enlarged in later editions (see Giraud 2014: 138; see also Samuelson 1948b: Chapter 4 on "Individual and Family Income").

von Neumann's (1937) famous general equilibrium linear growth model, translated in 1945–1946, attracted Samuelson's attention from the day von Neumann presented it at a Harvard seminar in 1945 (see Samuelson 1972: 260). In von Neumann's model, wage goods are fed back into the productive process as inputs, the supply of which determines the size of labor supply. Like Lewis's (1954) later, non-mathematical, formulation, it was a "closed" model (see Boianovsky 2019b). Samuelson (1964: 748–749) provided a rare, for then, discussion of von Neumann's model—"in which everything could be produced out of everything"—in an introductory textbook (see also Samuelson and Nordhaus 1985: appendix to Chapter 36, section on "The Expanding Universe"). In von Neumann's model, there is a maximal rate of balanced growth, which is equal to the rate of interest. The model was not just an impressive theoretical construction; it was deemed relevant for the interpretation of the actual economic development process:

> Because development theory, for countries like India and the United States, is preoccupied with the concept of "balanced growth," the Neumann model is of considerable interest. It is particularly relevant to the case where an industrial sector in a poor country finds it can get an unlimited supply of laborers from the rural sector at the same wage cost in terms of subsistence; needing little land, the industrial sector can "take off" and grow at a constant Neumann percentage rate per year, provided it can produce the capital goods needed to match the new labor. (Samuelson 1964: 748)

That was not the same as "balanced growth" in Rosenstein-Rodan's sense as discussed above. Rather, it was related to the proof of existence and stability of a balanced growth path in a multi-sector growth model, first advanced by Samuelson and Solow (1953) in their extension of von Neumann's (1937 [1945–1946]) linear model to smooth linear homogenous production functions. As noted by Samuelson (1964: 749, fn. 2), the interpretation of the expansion of an industrial sector through the utilization of an unlimited supply of rural labor was mainly associated with Lewis (1954). Japan's economic development from 1890 to the First World War could be understood in Neumann/Lewis terms, as real wages remained relatively stable because of rural migration—the Japanese economy at the time "grew like a colony of yeast, with human labor being as necessary an input-output as cotton or fodder" (Samuelson 1964: 749).

Other Lewisian themes recognizable in Samuelson's (ibid.: Chapter 36) development chapter are the positive link between income inequality and saving (ibid.: 761, 764) and the unproductive use of the economic surplus in underdeveloped countries (ibid.: 768). However, Lewis's accumulation mechanism—based on the difference between the average productivities of workers in the capitalist and traditional sectors—is not spelled out. In later editions, Samuelson (1973: 776) mentioned yet another aspect of labor surplus economies, that is, the argument that planners should apply "shadow prices" of factors (zero in the case of abundant labor) in order to maximize growth, an idea he associated with development planner and econometrician Jan Tinbergen.

Development planning benefited from Samuelson's turnpike theorem as a dynamic generalization of von Neumann's closed system, in the sense that whatever composition of consumption and capital goods the planner would like to achieve, one obtains the most of all goods if the (efficient) growth path is close to the von Neumann path for most of the time (see Niehans 1990: 438–439; for a comprehensive survey of the literature see Turnovsky 1970). In his Foreword to a book by Indian economist Sukhamoy Chakravarty (1969)—who was a visitor at MIT in the 1960s—Samuelson (1969a: ix; italics in original) asked: "What makes for a beautiful problem in science?" It was the combination of "logical beauty" and, above all, "*useful* knowledge." Chakravarty's application of optimal control to development planning, through the use of turnpike theorems and other analytical instruments, passed the test, since "India, and indeed much of the world, has a desperate need to develop economically. Bringing the beautiful tools of optimal control theory to bear upon this vital problem thus cannot help but add to their luster." That applied to both production-terminal and consumption-terminal turnpike theorems. Samuelson was clearly pleased by the fact that his turnpike theorems proved to be helpful in the development planning literature, despite the fact that this did not happen by design.

3 Learning by Watching Others Doing

Although divergence was the dominant theme in Samuelson's writings on development, he occasionally discussed episodes of international convergence throughout several editions of *Economics* and elsewhere. "Imitation of technology" was one of the main explanations of convergence, as illustrated by the economic growth of Japan, Germany, and Russia, especially after the end of the nineteenth century. As put by Samuelson (1961: 789–790): "Here the underdeveloped countries have one possible advantage. They can hope to benefit by copying the more advanced technology of the developed nations." Although he did not refer to Alexander Gerschenkron (1952) in that connection, he very likely had in mind the Harvard economic historian's concept of "advantage of backwardness," as the two men were close friends in Cambridge. He referred instead to Veblen's (1915) study of German industrialization and catching up with Britain. Samuelson (1961: 778) did mention Gerschenkron (1952) but in connection with the Russian Revolution of 1917 as the result of Russia's backwardness and its neglect by advanced countries.

Gerschenkron's "advantage of backwardness" would be listed as one of the main approaches to economic development from the twelfth edition on (Samuelson and Nordhaus 1985: Chapter 37), when the convergence debate became prominent among growth economists (see Jones 2002: Chapter 3). Samuelson (1961: 791) used the Veblen/Gerschenkron framework to interpret early twentieth-century American technological development, perceived as the result of the ingenuous application of inventions mostly originating abroad. Deploying one of his favorite expressions, Samuelson (ibid.) asserted that "'Yankee ingenuity' is a phrase that explains nothing; but it does refer to a real phenomenon."

Unlike the case of the countries listed at the start of this section, nations that were economically successful from the 1950s to the 1970s were usually perceived as the outcome of economic planning—which is related to another aspect of Gerschenkron's thesis, that is, backwards countries' search for "substitutes for prerequisites" for the productive factors, internal demand, or institutions that they lacked. Samuelson (1973: 81, fn. 3) pointed to "some success stories" of countries that had made "remarkable sprints of progress." Planning, he noted, had become fashionable and widespread in the underdeveloped world—and of course (although in another guise) in socialist countries such as the Soviet Union—sometimes with the use of input–output techniques of general equilibrium and of linear and nonlinear programming. Planners, however, often made mistakes, which was part of the learning process. In fact, "a cynic can find in the annals of the 1950s and 1960s countless examples of governmental and private bungling." But an optimist, "looking at 'miracles' of development in Thailand, Taiwan, Korea, Puerto Rico, Brazil, Mexico, Israel and El Salvador, can face the 1970s and 1980s with some confidence in the ability of nations to accelerate their own economic development" (ibid.: 784–785). Samuelson's overall positive view of planning reflected as well his own experience as a planner at the National Resources Planning Board during the Second World War (see Backhouse 2017: Chapter 19).

Brazilian economic growth between 1950 and 1980, when it doubled its fraction of US income per capita, was seen as a "notable and all too rare phenomenon" in less-developed countries (see Samuelson 1984 [1986]: 499). Brazil's rate of output growth was particularly intense in the period 1967–1973, when it reached as high as 10% a year and turned the country into "the veritable Japan of Latin America" (Samuelson 1973: 871). This "economic miracle" took place, as Samuelson pointed out, while the country was run by a military authoritarian regime, described as "fascist." As the 1970s advanced, Samuelson suggested that the unfortunate positive association between economic growth and authoritarianism was also apparent in other successful developing countries at the time, including the Asian Tigers of Taiwan, South Korea, and Singapore.

After the 1973 military coup d'état in Chile and the country's economic reforms based on a free-market approach imported from Chicago, Samuelson (1980: 815–816) coined the term "capitalist fascism" to describe the new pattern of alliance between efficient free markets and dictatorial or repressive political orders. The lack of a clear connection between business freedoms and personal freedoms—against the views of Friedrich von Hayek and Milton Friedman—had been a matter of concern for Samuelson since the 1930s (see Samuelson 1983a: 6–7). In the absence of a democratic welfare state, there tends to be a significant increase in income inequality, as happened in Brazil at the time (see Samuelson 1980: 816; 1983a: 7). Given the historical record, Samuelson (1980: 816) did not expect capitalist fascism in developing countries to last, since its business freedoms were *imposed* on the "populistic voters."

The influence of political and institutional variables made clear that Samuelson's (1964: 764–772) approach to economic development through changes in production functions—as determined by skilled and unskilled labor supply, capital accumulation, natural resources, and technical progress—was not enough. While discussing Japanese economic development in the early 1970s, he still believed, along the lines of growth accounting exercises by Solow, Angus Maddison, and others, that "there can be no substitute for an economic theory of growth based upon the determinants of production" (Samuelson 1971 [1972]: 709). However, he would change his mind about the ability of the production function to explain different growth paths across countries. As he put it: "I erroneously hypothesized that a function F (unskilled labor; simply and poorly allocated capital; scientific knowledge, however acquired) might succeed in achieving respectable progress for approximate *Q/L* estimates of a society" (Samuelson 2001: 495). Likewise, Samuelson and Nordhaus (2010: 531) pointed out that the view that countries must combine productive factors and technology to grow rapidly is "no real formula," as it is the equivalent of saying that an Olympic sprinter must "run like the wind." The issue was why "Do some countries succeed in running faster than others?"

Samuelson (1964: 759–760) had eschewed explanations based on non-economic factors—such as Max Weber's emphasis on the "Protestant work ethic"—for posing new unsolved problems. However, the publication of Mancur Olson's (1982) analysis of how the struggle between interests groups in democracies may end up in deadweight loss, prompted Samuelson to go back to Schumpeter's (1942) discussion of the problems faced by capitalism and the reasons for nations' economic and political failures. Samuelson (1983b) was attracted to his old Harvard Professor's argument that the competition for political leadership in democracies would lead to the use of power relations by self-interested voters and elites to form collusions and depart from laissez-faire Pareto-optimum equilibrium. He believed Schumpeter's perspective could illuminate what he saw as one of the great puzzles of economic development in the postwar era: the failure of Argentina to catch up with the United States and other developed economies (on Argentina as a classic example of "growth disaster," see, for example, Jones 2002: 149–150). If asked in 1945 what part of the world would experience the most dramatic growth takeoff in the next decades, Samuelson's answer would have been Argentina, because of its temperate climate, favorable natural resources, homogenous population formed by migrants from Western Europe—as opposed to Brazil's racial heterogeneity and tropical climate (here Samuelson gives some credit to the role of racial and climatic factors he had denied in his *Economics*, for example, Samuelson 1964: 759)—and for being in an intermediate stage of development poised for rapid growth (see Samuelson 1983b: 69):

> How wrong would I have been … The reasons do not seem to be narrowly economic. We cannot explain what has happened by appeal to Malthus's law of diminishing returns. There has been no exogenous shift in world demand peculiarly unfavorable to that region of the world. [Argentina's] sickness, Schumpeter would claim, is political and sociological rather than economic. It has to do with the breakdown of social consensus. It has to do with the workings out of the logic of populist democracy. (ibid.: 70)

The same argument applied to other southern countries of South America (Chile and Uruguay), with similar conditions and also beset by a lack of social cohesion and ensuing growth failures until the early 1980s. Samuelson thought Argentina and, to a lesser extent, Chile and Uruguay represented a paradigmatic confirmation of Schumpeter's forecast of "capitalism in the oxygen tent," which had not been confirmed (yet) for the United States and other industrialized economies, but, in view of widespread stagflation, had turned into a likely possibility. The "Argentinian sickness" of economic stagnation and chronic inflation—caused by a social system more concerned with the division of the social pie through wage and price policies (started by Colonel Perón's populism in the 1950s) than its total size and growth—haunted the American economy and brought about the risk of a "fascist solution," according to Samuelson (ibid.).

As the 1980s advanced and the average growth rate of Latin American countries (including Mexico and Brazil) declined, the contrast with the economic success of the Asian Tigers (and China later) became conspicuous. Samuelson (1980: 720; 1984 [1986]: 498–499) mentioned studies indicating the superior performance of the Asian export promotion strategy over Latin American import-substitution industrialization policies adopted since the 1950s under the intellectual leadership of the Argentinian economist Raul Prebisch, executive secretary of the United Nations Economic Commission for Latin America (CEPAL). Samuelson (ibid.) at first remained skeptical and argued against drawing sweeping conclusions from "controlled experiments" that were not in fact controlled.

Samuelson (1955: 682–683) had given qualified support to protectionist industrialization policies based on Prebisch's (and Hans Singer's) influential (if controversial) thesis of falling terms of trade against agricultural goods exported by Latin American countries. According to Samuelson (ibid.; italics in original), Prebisch's point was "really an argument about what will be the *future* comparative advantage of the countries in question. To the degree that governments are smarter than private investors in discerning trends threatening to the terms of trade, a valid case can be made for their interfering with free market forces." Even before Prebisch's argument appeared, Samuelson (1948a: 183–184) had asserted, in his famous paper about FPE, the existence of a "historical drift" in terms of trade of primary producers to decline (see also Toye and Toye 2003: 439). Moreover, (limited and temporary) protectionism was justified on the basis of the traditional infant-industry argument of "standard international trade theory" (Samuelson 1961: 795).

By the early 2000s, the "fundamental issue" of a country's policy toward international trade had been settled in development theory and practice (see Samuelson and Nordhaus 2010: 533–355). Outward-orientated policies, as in East Asia, had won the day, if not in the laissez-faire shape some had imagined but in the form of a "managed-market approach" combining strong government oversight with effective market forces. The matter was relevant also from the point of view of American international trade performance and policy, particularly in connection with outsourcing, international competition and their effects on employment and real wages. In a controversial article, Samuelson (2004) argued, using a Ricardian trade model, that if China or South Korea made technical progress (probably through imitation) in producing a good in which the United States previously had a comparative advantage, this would cause a permanent decline in real wages in the United States, especially of unskilled workers. The result would be the same if mass immigration to the United States of similar workers was allowed, accompanied by a substantial increase in income of the new immigrants as compared to their previous income before immigration.

The apparent ability of Samuelson's (ibid.) theoretical result to explain observed facts in the early twenty-first century, he claimed, vindicated his seminal FPE theorem advanced in 1948/1949. That theorem went beyond

Ohlin by arguing that trade brings about actual and complete FPE, not just a partial tendency (the theorem had been proved by Abba Lerner in 1933 as a student paper written at the London School of Economics and unknown to Samuelson until the mid-1950s):

> Therefore, as a result of my 1948–1949 revival and perfecting of the 1919–1933 Heckscher–Ohlin argumentation of *factor price quasi-equalization by trade in goods alone*, one could have foreseen the following at World War II's end. Historically US workers used to have a de facto monopoly access to superlative capitals and know-hows…of the United States … However, after the Second World War, this US capital and know-how begun to spread faster away from the United States. That meant that in a real sense foreign educable masses—first in Western Europe, then throughout the Pacific Rim—could and did genuinely provide the same kind of competitive pressures on US lower-middle-class wage earnings that mass migration would have threatened to do. (ibid.: 144; italics in original)

The narrowing of the gap, separating the rest of the world from American affluent productivity, was the "leitmotif" of the half-century from 1950 to 2000, in Samuelson's (2001: 500) view. It was not so much "learning by doing" as "learning by watching others doing" (ibid.). Imitation was apparently easy, but it did not operate in vast areas of Asia and Africa, which showed no signs of income convergence. International FPE—a concept close to, although not exactly the same as, income convergence—could only happen if technology transfer à la Gerschenkron took place, as implied by Samuelson (2004). In fact, one of the key assumptions of Samuelson's (1948a) mathematical demonstration that factor prices are equalized through international trade was that countries have identical production functions, as in the Heckscher–Ohlin factor proportions trade model. He further assumed constant returns to scale and no specialization by any country in one product only (see also Niehans 1990: 428–430). Moreover, as was common in general equilibrium models of the kind used by Samuelson, the supply of productive factors was given and constant.

Upon deriving his theorem, Samuelson (1948a: 178) acknowledged that historically, even in periods when free trade was nearly achieved as from the late 1800s to the early 1900s, international differences in wages and other factor prices persisted. He ascribed the discrepancy between theory and facts to the unrealistic character of some of the theoretical assumptions. Nevertheless, Samuelson (1964: 737) kept claiming that a "strong polar case" like the one established by his theorem could shed light on reality, by referring to his suggested "policy implication" (Samuelson 1948a: 183–184) that moving goods by trade should have nearly the same effect on British living standards as moving British migrants to Australia—the same inference of his 2004 article concerning East Asian workers. Likewise, the empirical refutation of the Heckscher–Ohlin–Samuelson factor proportions model implied by the "Leontief paradox," enunciated in the early 1950s, was not enough to challenge the positive heuristics of Samuelson's theoretical investigation of international trade as part of the general competitive equilibrium research program (see de Marchi 1976).

As pointed out by Hirschman (1977 [1981]: 60), Samuelson's (1948a, 1949) FPE theorem raised strong reactions from the then burgeoning field of development economics, though not exactly from Prebisch and Singer, the names mentioned by Hirschman in this connection. Moreover, against Hirschman's reading of the textual evidence, not all reactions by development economists were negative. In the following, responses by three prominent development economists (Thomas Balogh, Gunnar Myrdal and Paul Rosenstein-Rodan) are briefly considered (see also Boianovsky 2019c).

Oxford economist Thomas Balogh (1949) provided the first and, in some respects, most detailed critical assessment of Samuelson's 1948 theorem by a development economist. The problem was not so much the contrafactual implications of Samuelson's proposition—although Balogh (ibid.: 193) did notice that such implications do not "seem so strange to him as they do to other people"—but the overall static nature of the Heckscher–Ohlin–Samuelson trade model. Balogh's main piece of criticism was Samuelson's assumption of linear homogeneity, which ruled out indivisibilities and increasing returns, deemed essential in treating international trade as the interaction between societies on different levels of development. As discussed above, Samuelson regarded increasing returns as hard to tackle in growth and trade models alike. Balogh (ibid.: 198) concluded that the role played by "Professor Samuelson's brilliant mathematical feat" was to clarify the static basis of "modern" pure trade theory and, by that, open the way to a new dynamic approach to an essentially dynamic problem.

Gunnar Myrdal (1957) addressed the issue of the incompatibility between trade theory and the international inequality problem in Chapter 11 of his well-known book. A Swedish economist himself, Myrdal was well acquainted with and critical of the Heckscher–Ohlin trade model, and of its extension by Samuelson. The main problem with the pure theory of international trade (which was also true of the classical Ricardian version) was its inability to explain international income divergence. It was in this context that Myrdal (ibid.: 149, fn. 1) referred to Samuelson's (1948a, 1949) discussion of the problem of FPE as a result of trade:

> We thus see the strange thing that in recent decades, while international economic inequalities have been growing...the theory of international trade has developed in the direction of stressing more and more the idea that trade initiates a tendency toward gradual equalization of factor prices and incomes as between different countries.

The main problem with trade theory, as developed by Samuelson, was its prevailing assumption of stable equilibrium, instead of the more realistic assumption that economic processes are cumulative because of "circular causation." The latter (Myrdal's) approach would make clear the role of trade in increasing inequalities between developed and underdeveloped countries, Myrdal (ibid.: 152) claimed.

Paul Rosenstein-Rodan's (1961: 65) interpretation of Samuelson's theorem differed from both Balogh and Myrdal. He referred to Samuelson (1948a, 1949) while discussing the argument that international trade would reduce the indivisibility of demand and therefore the size of the "big push" necessary to break the vicious circle of poverty, or even eliminate the need of a push altogether. Rosenstein-Rodan pointed out that the expansion of trade in the nineteenth century had led neither to equalization nor even a reduction of inequality of factor prices. The theoretical reasons for that, he argued, should be found precisely in Samuelson's discussion of the *obstacles* to FPE: transportation costs, complete specialization, and different production functions across countries. Indeed, this view—that Samuelson's theorem was not really about the equalization of factor prices, but about bringing out the circumstances that may prevent even a tendency to equalization—could be found in surveys of trade theory (see, for example, Corden 1965: 31).

The fact that Rosenstein-Rodan and Samuelson were colleagues at MIT increases the likelihood that they discussed economic development issues, as also indicated by Samuelson's references to Rosenstein-Rodan in *Economics* after 1955. Rosenstein-Rodan's influential 1961 paper had circulated at MIT as a CENIS working paper since 1957. The main explanation for increasing international inequality in factor rewards, according to Rosenstein-Rodan (1961), was the heterogeneity of production functions. He quoted Samuelson to that effect. Although the "laws of nature" may be the same everywhere, the economic laws relating inputs and outputs differed due to the influence of "knowledge":

> Effective knowledge ('know-how') is probably as important a variable in understanding economic history and geography as is specific factor endowment ... It would be artificial in the extreme to explain any such empirical case by saying that 'knowledge' is 'scarce'...in the one place relative to the other ... Knowledge is *not* an input such that the more you use of it, the less there is left. (Samuelson 1948a: 181–182; italics in original)

The matter, Rosenstein-Rodan suggested, was at the core of the explanation of increasing returns in economic development. Indeed, Samuelson's brief remarks about the character of knowledge as a non-rival good pointed the way to New Growth Theory that would be established by Paul Romer and others 40 years later.

A main difference between Samuelson's (1948a, 1949) general equilibrium international trade models and trade models put forward by development economists was the assumption about labor supply and wage determination. Lewis's (1954) extension of his path-breaking model of development, based on surplus labor, to an open economy provided new insights on the Prebisch-Singer hypothesis of deteriorating terms of trade between the "periphery" and the "center" (see also Boianovsky 2019b). The matter was further elaborated by Arghiri Emmanuel (1969 [1972]) from the perspective of the Marxian labor theory of value, which attracted Samuelson's (1976) critical attention. Emmanuel's argument, constructed by means of involved arithmetical examples, did not make for easy reading. He criticized the theory of comparative advantage (in both its Ricardian and Heckscher–Ohlin–Samuelson vintages) by maintaining that a country with labor surplus and a given low wage is exploited by a country with a given high wage when they trade and capital is mobile between countries. Samuelson (ibid.) counterattacked what he understood as Emmanuel's denial of the gains from international trade and investment. Upon his restatement of the validity of the theory of comparative advantage under Emmanuel's assumptions, Samuelson (ibid.: 107) concluded that "no new light has been thrown on the reason why poor countries are poor and rich countries are rich." Samuelson's criticism induced a response from Emmanuel, followed by a reply by Samuelson, without ever reaching an agreement. This was Samuelson's only engagement in debate with a development economist; unsurprisingly, the topic was international trade, his favorite one.

However, as Negishi (1985: 137–139; 1991) pointed out, Samuelson missed the point that Emmanuel was not refuting the existence of gains from trade as such, but arguing about the deterioration of terms of trade of the lower wage country in comparison with the situation when there is no wage differential. As put by Bacha (1978: 319) in his restatement of unequal exchange in a Ricardian model of international trade with surplus labor and specialization, trade under these conditions is unequal to poor countries in the normative sense that "its terms of trade are lower then they would be under a Pareto-efficient trade arrangement allowing for perfect international labor mobility." Samuelson (1981) would eventually acknowledge the effects of low wages on the terms of trade and unequal economic development. As part of an exercise in the forecasting of economic development trends, he stated that, only after underdeveloped countries experienced their "industrial revolutions" and demographic transitions,

> Only then will the affluent nations stand to lose some of the historic consumer surplus that they have enjoyed from international trade – trade that has historically involved imports of fiber, food, and ores produced in the

> tropics by low-wage populations ... If that happy day comes when Southeast Asia, Africa and Latin America afford a comfortable middle class standard of living to their stabilized populations, we should be content to depend upon mechanized mines and farms for our needed raw materials, uncomplainingly paying the necessary costs for the goods we need. (ibid.: 412)

This differed from Samuelson's FPE theoretical framework. If development economics was a field that appealed to the "venturesome" only (see Samuelson 1978), he was on occasion willing to take a chance.

4 Conclusion

Paul Samuelson paid close attention to economic development and international economic heterogeneity, especially, but not only, throughout the several editions of his *Economics.* This reflected in part his overall interest in the inequality of income distribution at the domestic and global levels, as well as the impact of widespread theoretical and political debates about international development. He was aware of the specific analytical issues raised by development economists, such as the roles of increasing returns and labor surplus in economic growth. At the same time, he acknowledged the theoretical hurdles posed by them, especially poverty traps caused by market failures prompted by increasing returns and externalities. Moreover, Samuelson deployed the Malthusian approach to population dynamics as a key tool for discussing underdevelopment. Productions functions were seen as important but insufficient to explain distinct development paths, particularly under conditions of political instability, as in South America. Samuelson was generally positive about planning as a development strategy; indeed, development planners made use of the optimal control and turnpike theorems he had advanced in pure theory. On the other hand, his FPE theorem of international trade proved to be very controversial among development economists.

Acknowledgements I would like to thanks G.C. Harcourt for his helpful comments. Research support from CNPq is gratefully acknowledged.

References

Alacevich, M. and M. Boianovsky (eds.) (2018) *The Political Economy of Development Economics: A Historical Perspective.* Annual supplement to *History of Political Economy,* 50. Durham, Duke University Press.

Arrow, K.J. (1988) "Presidential Address: General Economic Theory and the Emergence of Theories of Economic Development," in K.J. Arrow (ed.) *The Balance Between Industry and Agriculture in Economic Development.* Proceedings of the Eighth World Congress of the International Economic Association. London, Macmillan: 22–32.

Bacha, E.L. (1978) "An Interpretation of Unequal Exchange from Prebisch-Singer to Emmanuel," *Journal of Development Economics,* 5: 319–330.

Backhouse, R.E. (2015) "Samuelson, Keynes and the Search for a General Theory of Economics," *Italian Economic Journal,* 1: 139–153.

Backhouse, R.E. (2017) *Founder of Modern Economics: Paul A. Samuelson, Volume 1: Becoming Samuelson, 1915–1948.* New York, Oxford University Press.

Balogh, T. (1949) "Static Models and Current Problems in International Economics," *Oxford Economic Papers,* 1: 191–198.

Barnett, W.A. (2004) "An Interview with Paul Samuelson," *Macroeconomic Dynamics,* 8: 519–542.

Bauer, P.T. (1958a) "Economic Growth and the New Orthodoxy," *Fortune,* May: 142–143, 194, 196, 198.

Bauer, P.T. (1958b) "The New Orthodoxy of Economic Development." Presented to the 9th Meeting of the Mont Pelerin Society, Princeton.

Bauer, P.T. (1971) *Dissent on Development.* Cambridge, MA, Harvard University Press.

Bauer, P.T. and B. Yamey (1957) *The Economics of Under-Developed Countries.* London, Nisbet.

Baumol, W.J. (2007) "Generalists' Generalisimo," *The American Economist,* 51: 22–24.

Boianovsky, M. (2018) "Beyond Capital Fundamentalism: Harrod, Domar and the History of Development Economics," *Cambridge Journal of Economics,* 42: 477–504.

Boianovsky, M. (2019a) "'Voluminous and Somewhat Repetitive'—Samuelson on Development Economics." Unpublished typescript.

Boianovsky, M. (2019b) "Arthur Lewis and the Classical Foundations of Development Economics," in L. Fiorito, S. Scheall and C.E. Suprinyak (eds.) *Research in the History of Economic Thought and Methodology*, 37A. Bingley, UK, Emerald Publishing: 103–143.

Boianovsky, M. (2019c) "Reacting to Samuelson: Early Development Economics and the Factor Price Equalization Theorem." Unpublished typescript.

Boianovsky, M. and K.D. Hoover (2014) "In the Kingdom of Solovia: The Rise of Growth Economics at MIT, 1956–1970," in E.R. Weintraub (ed.) *MIT and the Transformation of American Economics*. Annual supplement to *History of Political Economy*, 46. Durham, Duke University Press: 198–228.

Chakravarty, S. (1969) *Capital and Development Planning*. Cambridge, MA, The MIT Press.

Corden, W.M. (1965) *Recent Developments in the Theory of International Trade*. Princeton, NJ, Princeton University, International Finance Section.

de Marchi, N. (1976) "Anomaly and the Development of Economics: The Case of the Leontief Paradox," in S.J. Latsis (ed.) *Method and Appraisal in Economics*. Cambridge, Cambridge University Press: 109–127.

Dorfman, R., P.A. Samuelson and R.M. Solow (1958) *Linear Programming and Economic Analysis*. New York, McGraw-Hill.

Emmanuel, A. (1969) [1972] *Unequal Exchange: A Study of Imperialism of Trade*. Translated by B. Pearce. New York, Monthly Review Press.

Gerschenkron, A. (1952) "Economic Backwardness in Historical Perspective," in B. Hoselitz (ed.) *The Progress of Underdeveloped Areas*. Chicago, University of Chicago Press: 3–29.

Giraud, Y. (2014) "Negotiating the 'Middle-of-the-Road' Position: Paul Samuelson, MIT, and the Politics of Textbook Writing, 1945–55," in E.R. Weintraub (ed.) *MIT and the Transformation of American Economics*. Annual supplement to *History of Political Economy*, 46. Durham, Duke University Press: 134–152.

Harrod, R.F. (1948) *Towards a Dynamic Economics*. London, Macmillan.

Hicks, J.R. (1965) *Capital and Growth*. New York, Oxford University Press.

Hirschman, A.O. (1958) *The Strategy of Economic Development*. New Haven, Yale University Press.

Hirschman, A.O. (1977) [1981] "A Generalized Linkage Approach to Development, with Special Reference to Staples," in *Essays in Trespassing: Economics to Politics and Beyond*. Cambridge, Cambridge University Press: 59–97.

Jones, C.I. (2002) *Introduction to Economic Growth*. Second edition. New York, Norton.

Krugman, P. (1993) "Toward a Counter-Revolution in Development Theory." Proceedings of the World Bank Annual Conference on Development Economics, 1992. Supplement to the *World Bank Economic Review*. Washington, DC, World Bank: 15–38.

Lewis, W.A. (1954) "Economic Development with Unlimited Supplies of Labor," *Manchester School*, 22: 139–191.

Lewis, W.A. (1955) *The Theory of Economic Growth*. London, Allen & Unwin.

Myrdal, G. (1957) *Economic Theory and Underdeveloped Regions*. London, G. Duckworth.

Negishi, T. (1985) *Economic Theories in a Non-Walrasian Tradition*. Cambridge, Cambridge University Press.

Negishi, T. (1991) "Samuelson, Saigal and Emmanuel's Theory of International Unequal Exchange," in S. Dahiya (ed.) *Theoretical Foundations of Development Planning: Sectoral and Regional Planning*. New Delhi, Concept Publishing: 37–49.

Neumann, J. von. (1937) [1945–1946] "A Model of General Economic Equilibrium," *Review of Economic Studies*, 13: 1–9.

Niehans, J. (1990) *A History of Economic Theory*. Baltimore, Johns Hopkins University Press.

Nixon, R.A. and P.A. Samuelson (1940) "Estimates of Unemployment in the United States," *Review of Economics and Statistics*, 22: 101–111.

Olson, M. (1982) *The Rise and Decline of Nations*. New Haven, CT, Yale University Press.

Plehwe, D. (2009) "The Origins of the Neoliberal Economic Development Discourse," in P. Mirowski and D. Plehwe (eds.) *The Road from Mont Pelerin*. Cambridge, MA, Harvard University Press: 238–279.

Ray, D. (2008) "Development Economics," in S.N. Durlauf and L.E. Blume (eds.) *The New Palgrave Dictionary of Economics, Volume 2*. Second edition. Houndmills, Basingstoke, and Hampshire, Palgrave Macmillan: 468–483.

Robinson, J.V. (1937) *Essays in the Theory of Employment*. London, Macmillan.

Rosenstein-Rodan, P. (1943) "Problems of Industrialization of Eastern and South-Eastern Europe," *Economic Journal*, 53: 202–211.

Rosenstein-Rodan, P. (1961) "Notes on the Theory of the 'Big Push'," in H. Ellis and H. Wallich (eds.) *Economic Development for Latin America*. London, Macmillan: 57–67.

Rostow, W.W. (1960) *The Stages of Economic Growth*. Cambridge, Cambridge University Press.

Samuelson, P.A. (1947) *Foundations of Economic Analysis*. Cambridge, MA, Harvard University Press.

Samuelson, P.A. (1948a) "International Trade and Equalization of Factor Prices," *Economic Journal*, 58: 163–184.

Samuelson, P.A. (1948b) *Economics: An Introductory Analysis*. New York, McGraw-Hill.

Samuelson, P.A. (1948c) "Dynamic Process Analysis," in H.S. Ellis (ed.) *A Survey of Contemporary Economics, Volume 1*. Homewood, IL, Richard D. Irwin: 352–378.

Samuelson, P.A. (1949) "International Factor-Price Equalization Once Again," *Economic Journal*, 59: 181–197.

Samuelson, P.A. (1951) *Economics: An Introductory Analysis*. Second edition. New York, McGraw-Hill.

Samuelson, P.A. (1954) "The Pure Theory of Public Expenditure," *Review of Economics and Statistics*, 36: 387–389.

Samuelson, P.A. (1955) *Economics: An Introductory Analysis*. Third edition. New York, McGraw-Hill.

Samuelson, P.A. (1958) *Economics: An Introductory Analysis*. Fourth edition. New York, McGraw-Hill.

Samuelson, P.A. (1961) *Economics: An Introductory Analysis*. Fifth edition. New York, McGraw-Hill.

Samuelson, P.A. (1964) *Economics: An Introductory Analysis*. Sixth edition. New York, McGraw-Hill.

Samuelson, P.A. (1965) "A Catenary Turnpike Theorem Involving Consumption and the Golden Rule," *American Economic Review*, 55: 486–496.

Samuelson, P.A. (1969a) "Foreword," in S. Chakravarty (ed.) *Capital and Development Planning*. Cambridge, MA, The MIT Press: ix–xv.

Samuelson, P.A. (1969b) "Presidential Address: The Way of an Economist," in P.A. Samuelson (ed.) *International Economic Relations*. Proceedings of the Third Congress of the International Economic Association. London, Macmillan: 1–11.

Samuelson, P.A. (1971) [1972] "Economic Growth," *Gendaisekai Hyakka Daijiten, Volume I*. Tokyo, Kodansha. Reprinted in *The Collected Scientific Papers of Paul A. Samuelson, Volume 3*. Edited by R.C. Merton. Cambridge, MA, The MIT Press: 704–709.

Samuelson, P.A. (1972) "Maximum Principles in Analytical Economics," *American Economic Review*, 62: 249–262.

Samuelson, P.A. (1973) *Economics*. Ninth edition. New York, McGraw-Hill.

Samuelson, P.A. (1976) "Illogic of Neo-Marxian Doctrine of Unequal Exchange," in D. Belsley, E. Kane, P.A. Samuelson and R.M. Solow (eds.) *Inflation, Trade and Taxes*. Columbus, Ohio State University Press: 96–107.

Samuelson, P.A. (1978) "Economic Development Looked at From the Standpoint of a Theorist." Unpublished typescript. Paul A. Samuelson Papers, Economists' Papers Archive, David M. Rubenstein Rare Book & Manuscript Library, Duke University.

Samuelson, P.A. (1979) [1983] "Good News on Development," *Newsweek*, 23 July 1979. Reprinted in *Economics from the Heart: A Samuelson Sampler*, by P.A. Samuelson (1983). New York, Harcourt Brace Jovanovich: 68–71.

Samuelson, P.A. (1980) *Economics*. Eleventh edition. New York, McGraw-Hill.

Samuelson, P.A. (1981) "To Protect Manufacturing?" *Journal of Institutional and Theoretical Economics*, 137: 407–414.

Samuelson, P.A. (1983a) "My Life Philosophy," *The American Economist*, 27: 5–12.

Samuelson, P.A. (1983b) "The World's Economy at Century's End," in S. Tsuru (ed.) *Human Resources, Employment and Development, Volume I*. London: Macmillan: 58–77.

Samuelson, P.A. (1984) [1986] "Japan and the World Economy at the Century's End," *NEXT Magazine*, August 1984: 4–15. Reprinted in *The Collected Scientific Papers of Paul A. Samuelson, Volume 5*. Edited by K. Crowley. Cambridge, MA, The MIT Press: 496–509.

Samuelson, P.A. (1986) "Economics in My Time," in W. Breit and R. Spencer (eds.) *Lives of the Laureates*. Cambridge, MA, The MIT Press: 59–76.

Samuelson, P.A. (1995) "Some Uneasiness with the Coase Theorem," *Japan and the World Economy*, 7: 1–7.

Samuelson, P.A. (2001) "Sparks and Grit from the Anvil of Growth," in G. Meier and J. Stiglitz (eds.) *Frontiers of Development Economics*. New York, Oxford University Press: 492–505.

Samuelson, P.A. (2004) "Where Ricardo and Mill Rebut and Confirm Arguments of Mainstream Economists Supporting Globalization," *Journal of Economic Perspectives*, 18: 134–146.

Samuelson, P.A. and W.D. Nordhaus (1985) *Economics*. Twelfth edition. New York, McGraw-Hill.

Samuelson, P.A. and W.D. Nordhaus (2010) *Economics*. Nineteenth edition. New York, McGraw-Hill.

Samuelson, P.A. and R.M. Solow (1953) "Balanced Growth Under Constant Returns to Scale," *Econometrica*, 21: 412–424.

Schumpeter, J.A. (1942) *Capitalism, Socialism and Democracy*. New York, Harper & Brothers.

Seers, D. (1963) "The Limitations of the Special Case," *Oxford Bulletin of Economics and Statistics*, 25: 79–98.

Shaw, J.S. (1999) "Paul Samuelson and Development Economics: A Missed Opportunity," *Journal of Private Enterprise*, 15: 18–35.

Skousen, M. (1997) "The Perseverance of Paul Samuelson's *Economics*," *Journal of Economic Perspectives*, 11: 137–152.

Solow, R.M. (1956) "A Contribution to the Theory of Economic Growth," *Quarterly Journal of Economics*, 70: 65–94.

Toye, J. (2018) "The Counterrevolution in Development Economics," in M. Alacevich and M. Boianovsky (eds.) *The Political Economy of Development Economics: A Historical Perspective.* Annual supplement to *History of Political Economy*, 50. Durham, Duke University Press: 269–285.

Toye, J. and R. Toye (2003) "The Origins and Interpretation of the Prebisch-Singer Thesis," *History of Political Economy*, 35: 437–467.

Tribe, K. (2018) "The Colonial Office and British Development Economics, 1940–60," in M. Alacevich and M. Boianovsky (eds.) *The Political Economy of Development Economics: A Historical Perspective.* Annual supplement to *History of Political Economy*, 50. Durham, Duke University Press: 97–113.

Turnovsky, S.J. (1970) "Turnpike Theorems and Efficient Economic Growth," in E. Burmeister and A.R. Dobell (eds.) *Mathematical Theories of Economic Growth.* London, Macmillan: 311–351.

Veblen, T. (1915) *Imperial Germany and the Industrial Revolution.* Akron, OH, Macmillan.

World Bank (1978) *World Development Report 1978.* Washington, DC, World Bank.

Index

Note: Page number followed by 'f' and 't' represents figure and table.

R. A. Cord et al. (eds.), *Paul Samuelson*, Remaking Economics: Eminent Post-War Economists, https://doi.org/10.1057/978-1-137-56812-0

B

Q

R

S

U

CPSIA information can be obtained
at www.ICGtesting.com
Printed in the USA
LVHW080931130421
684343LV00002B/90

9 781137 568113